ST
MA
CHANNEL
MANAGEMENT

McGraw-Hill Series in Marketing

Allen, Spohn, and Wilson: Selling Dynamics
Anderson, Hair, and Bush: Professional Sales Management
Baier: Direct Marketing
Bennett: Marketing
Berkman and Gilson: Advertising
Bovee and Thill: Marketing
Bowersox and Cooper: Strategic Marketing Channel Management
Britt, Boyd, Davis, and Larreche: Marketing Management and Administrative Action
Buell: Marketing Management: A Strategic Planning Approach
Buskirk and Buskirk: Selling: Principles and Practices
Corey, Lovelock, and Ward: Problems in Marketing
Dobler, Burt, and Lee: Purchasing and Materials Management: Text and Cases
Guiltinan and Paul: Cases in Marketing Management
Guiltinan and Paul: Marketing Management: Strategies and Programs
Guiltinan and Paul: Readings in Marketing Strategies and Programs
Johnson, Kurtz, and Scheuing: Sales Management: Concepts, Practices, and Cases
Kinnear and Taylor: Marketing Research: An Applied Approach
Loudon and Della Bitta: Consumer Behavior: Concepts and Applications
Lovelock and Weinberg: Marketing Challenges: Cases and Exercises
Monroe: Pricing: Making Profitable Decisions
Rossiter and Percy: Advertising and Promotion Management
Shapiro: Sales Program Management: Formulation and Implementation
Stanton, Etzel, and Walker: Fundamentals of Marketing

STRATEGIC MARKETING CHANNEL MANAGEMENT

Donald J. Bowersox
Michigan State University

M. Bixby Cooper
Michigan State University

McGRAW-HILL, INC.

New York St. Louis San Francisco Auckland Bogotá
Caracas Lisbon London Madrid Mexico Milan Montreal
New Delhi Paris San Juan Singapore Sydney Tokyo Toronto

STRATEGIC MARKETING CHANNEL MANAGEMENT

International Edition 1992.

Exclusive rights by McGraw-Hill Book Co-Singapore for manufacture and export. This book cannot be re-exported from the country to which it is consigned by McGraw-Hill Book Co.

4 5 6 7 8 9 0 KKP SW 9 6

ISBN 0-07-006757-0

Library of Congress Cataloging-in-Publication
Data is available: LC Card 91-35022.
This book was set in Times Roman by Arcata Graphics/Kingsport.
The editors were Bonnie K. Binkert and Mimi Melek;
the production supervisor was Leroy A. Young.
The cover was designed by John Hite.
Project supervision was done by the Total Book.

When ordering this title, use ISBN 0-07-112916-2

Printed in Singapore

ABOUT THE AUTHORS

Donald J. Bowersox is The John H. McConnell University Professor of Business Administration at Michigan State University. He has been a consultant or speaker for over 175 Fortune 500 corporations and numerous government agencies. He has lectured internationally in 15 nations. He serves as a member of the editorial review board of the *Journal of Business Logistics* and the *Annals of the Society of Logistics Engineers* and is associate editor of the *International Marketing Review.*

Dr. Bowersox has authored over 100 articles on marketing, transportation, and logistics. He is author or co-author of nine books, including *Logistical Management, A Managerial Introduction to Marketing, Introduction to Transportation, Physical Distribution Management, Dynamic Simulation of Physical Distribution Systems, Simulated Product Sales Forecasting,* and *Readings in Physical Distribution Management.* Since 1986 he has directed comprehensive research concerning North American logistics practices. The results were initially published in *Leading Edge Logistics: Competitive Positioning for the 1990's* by the Council of Logistics Management. A second book, *Logistical Excellence,* examines the managerial implications of the research and was published by Digital Press in November 1991.

A founding member and the second president of the Council of Logistics Management, Dr. Bowersox is a recipient of the council's Distinguished Service Award. He was the recipient of the Michigan State University Distinguished Faculty Award. He also received the Harry E. Salzberg Honorary Medallion presented by Syracuse University.

M. Bixby Cooper is an associate professor in the Eli Broad College of Business at Michigan State University. He received his B.S. from the University of North Carolina, his M.B.A. from the University of Virginia, and Ph.D. from the University of Alabama. His articles on marketing, customer service, and distribution have appeared in such journals as the *Journal of the Academy of Marketing Science, Industrial Marketing Management, Business Journal of Consumer Satisfaction/ Dissatisfaction and Complaining Behavior,* and *The Akron Business and Economic Review.* He is a frequent speaker at educational and professional conferences dealing with the subjects of distribution and customer service. Professor Cooper is a member of the American Marketing Association, the Council of Logistics Management, and the International Customer Service Association. He also served for 4 years on the executive board of the International Customer Service Association as Chairman of Education and Research.

The book is dedicated to Susan I. Bowersox and Ann R. Cooper. Ultimately the authors' families pay the dearest price— time, encouragement and patience.

CONTENTS

PREFACE   xvii

PART 1   THE SCOPE OF MARKETING AND DISTRIBUTION CHANNELS

1   Marketing Channels   3

REALITIES AND CONTRADICTIONS   4
    Awareness   6
    Visibility   9
    Multiple Engagements   10
    Involvement   11
    Acceptance   13
    Cooperation and Conflict   14
WHY BUSINESSES SEEK CHANNEL ARRANGEMENTS   14
    Functional Performance   15
    Reduced Complexity   18
    Specialization   20
ORDER OF PRESENTATION   22
    Channel Planning   23
    Implementation   25
QUESTIONS   26

2   Primary Participants   28

MANUFACTURING   29
    Manufacturing Structure   30
    Key Management Issues   33
    Emerging Manufacturing Strategies   37
    Conclusion: Manufacturing   39
WHOLESALING   40
    Wholesale Structure   40

Key Management Issues   44
Emerging Wholesale Strategies   44
Conclusion: Wholesaling   45
RETAILING   46
Retail Structure   46
Key Management Issues   46
Emerging Retail Strategies   49
Conclusion: Retailing   52
SUMMARY   52
QUESTIONS   53

3 Specialized Participants   55

CHANGING NATURE OF SPECIALIZED SERVICE PROVIDERS   56
Economic Justification   57
Risk Involvement   58
Concentration and Alliances   59
Service Specialist Leadership   60
Conclusion: Specialized Service Providers   62
CLASSIFICATION OF SPECIALIZED SERVICE PROVIDERS   62
Functional Specialist   62
Support Specialist   63
FUNCTIONAL SERVICE PROVIDERS   63
Transportation   63
Warehousing   68
Assembly   69
Fulfillment   70
Sequencing   71
Merchandising   72
Conclusion: Functional Service Providers   73
SUPPORT SERVICE PROVIDERS   74
Financial   74
Information   75
Advertising   76
Insurance   76
Advisory/Research   76
Arrangers   77
Conclusion: Support Service Providers   79
EXTENSION OF CHANNEL PARTICIPANTS   79
Integrated Service Providers   79
Consumers as Channel Participants   80
SUMMARY   82
QUESTIONS   83

4 Channel Structure   **85**

EMERGENCE OF DISTRIBUTION CHANNELS   87
    Direct Distribution   87
    Direct Distribution versus Central Marketplace   87
    Multistage Distribution   89
A THEORY OF DISTRIBUTION PROCESSES   90
    Sorting   90
    Spatial Closure   92
    Temporal Closure   95
COMPLEX DISTRIBUTION ARRANGEMENTS   96
    Structural Separation   96
    Postponement   99
STRUCTURAL CLASSIFICATION   102
    Single-Transaction Channels   102
    Conventional Channels   103
    Vertical Marketing Systems   104
    Conclusion: Channel Classification   107
SUMMARY   107
QUESTIONS   108

Cases for Part 1

1-1 GILLETTE SENSOR—AN INTERNATIONAL LAUNCH   110
1-2 A TALE OF TWO WHOLESALERS   118
1-3 RUNDEL'S DEPARTMENT STORE   124
1-4 CSX—A CHANNEL PARTNER IN TROUBLE   129
1-5 SIMPLESSE—GOING TO MARKET WITH A FAT SUBSTITUTE   135

PART 2 CHANNEL STRATEGY AND DESIGN

5 Enterprise Positioning   **143**

CORPORATE STRATEGY   145
    Strategic Alternatives   145
    Mission Statement   147
    Objectives   148
CUSTOMER ANALYSIS   148
    Defining The Market   148
    Market Segmentation   150
COMPETITIVE ANALYSIS   150
    Industry Structure   150
    Identification and Assessment of Competitors   152

INTERNAL ANALYSIS   152
    Performance Analysis   153
    Functional Strengths and Weaknesses   153
ENVIRONMENTAL ANALYSIS   153
    Sociocultural Environment   154
    Technological Environment   155
    Economic Environment   155
    Legal Environment   156
CHANNEL OBJECTIVES   165
    Market Coverage and Distribution Intensity   165
    Channel Control   166
    Flexibility   166
SUMMARY   167
QUESTIONS   167

6   Marketing Design   **169**

CUSTOMER ANALYSIS   170
    Market Segmentation   170
    Customers' Buying Behavior   172
PRODUCT IMPACT ON MARKETING CHANNEL DESIGN   176
    Product Attributes   177
    New-Product Development   178
    Product Life Cycle   179
    Brand Strategies   180
PROMOTION IMPACT ON MARKETING DESIGN   181
    Push versus Pull Strategy   182
    Advertising   182
    Sales Promotions   184
    Personal Selling   186
PRICE IMPACT ON MARKETING DESIGN   187
    List Price   187
    Discounts   188
    Transportation Charges   190
    Price Changes   191
SUMMARY   191
QUESTIONS   192

7   Logistics Design   **194**

THE LOGISTICS MANAGEMENT PROCESS   195
    Value-Adding Process   198
    Boundary Spanning   201
ESTABLISHING SERVICE GOALS   203
    Basic Customer-Service Measurements   204

Zero Defects   209
Selective Service Segmentation   211
INTEGRATED LOGISTICS PERFORMANCE   212
Total-Cost Analysis   212
Cost-Service Sensitivity Analysis   218
SUMMARY   221
QUESTIONS   222

8 Planning and Analysis Framework   **224**

TRANSACTION COST ANALYSIS   225
Human Factors   227
Environmental Factors   227
Conclusion: Transaction Cost Analysis   229
ANALYTICAL TOOLS FOR EVALUATING ALTERNATIVE STRUCTURES   230
Key-Factor Scoring   230
Profitability Analysis   233
Mathematical and Simulation Techniques   237
EVALUATION OF CHANNEL MEMBERS   239
Manufacturer's Evaluation of Intermediaries   239
Supplier Evaluation by Intermediaries   240
CHANNEL MODIFICATION   242
Stimulus for Modification   242
Modification Strategies   243
MULTIPLE CHANNELS   244
SUMMARY   244
QUESTIONS   245

Cases for Part 2   **247**

2–1 W-G-P CHEMICAL COMPANY   247
2–2 SEARS: A GIANT IN TRANSITION   252
2–3 BASKIN-ROBBINS 31 FLAVORS—MANAGING
     "COOPERATIVE" ADVERTISING   265
2–4 HAPPY GROVE DAIRY   271
2–5 WILLIAMS INSTITUTIONAL FOOD COMPANY   276

PART 3   CHANNEL DEVELOPMENT AND MANAGEMENT

9 Negotiation   **285**

NEGOTIATION IN MARKETING   286
Negotiation Process   287
Negotiation Framework   287
Conclusion: Negotiation in Marketing   290

NEGOTIATION STRATEGY   290
    Scope of Channel Negotiation   290
    Prerequisites for Negotiation   291
POWER IN NEGOTIATION   292
    Power-Dependence Relationships   292
    Sources of Power   294
    Conclusion: Channel Power   297
CHANNEL NEGOTIATION PROCESS   298
    Transaction Negotiation   298
    Operational Negotiation   301
    Conclusion: Negotiation Process   303
SUMMARY   303
QUESTIONS   304

10   Channel Management   **305**

LEADERSHIP   306
    Tolerance to Follow   306
    The Leadership Process   307
    Example of Channel Leadership   308
VERTICAL MARKETING SYSTEM   308
    The Business Rational for VMS   309
    VMS Principles   311
    Creating a Successful VMS   313
    Reasons Why VMS Arrangements Fail   316
    Integrating a VMS Arrangement: Electronic Linkage   321
CONFLICT   323
    Types of Conflict   324
    Conflict Defined   325
    Causes of Conflict   326
    Results of Conflict   330
    Conflict Resolution   332
SUMMARY   336
QUESTIONS   337

11   Performance Measurement   **339**

A MACRO PERSPECTIVE OF CHANNEL PERFORMANCE   340
    Macro Objectives   340
    Macro Efficiency   341
MEASURING FINANCIAL PERFORMANCE   342
    Segment Definition   343
    Revenue and Cost Analysis   344
    Strategic Profit Model   350

MEASURING CUSTOMER SATISFACTION 355
Satisfaction and Service Quality 356
Methodology 359
SUMMARY 362
QUESTIONS 362

Cases for Part 3 **364**
3–1 P&G MEETS WAL-MART 364
3–2 OAKVILLE MALL 370
3–3 SOUTH BOTTLING COMPANY 374
3–4 ACE BROKERAGE COMPANY 378
3–5 THE FORMATION OF A STRATEGIC ALLIANCE 382

PART 4   EXPANDED CHANNEL PERSPECTIVES

12   **Channel Dynamics** **389**

DAWNING OF THE INFORMATION AGE 390
Information Technology 390
Competing in Time 393
Organizational Structure Impact 394
CHANNEL CHANGE 397
The Economics of Differentiation 397
Explanations of Channel Change 398
Channel Change Model Limitations 402
MANAGEMENT OF CHANNEL CHANGE 404
Institutionalizing Process 404
Role of the Change Agent 405
Characteristics of Successful Change Agents 405
SUMMARY 407
QUESTIONS 408

13   **International and Service Channels** **409**

INTERNATIONAL DISTRIBUTION CHANNELS 410
Export 410
Export Documentation 414
Channels of Distribution within Foreign Countries 415
International Logistics 417
Evaluation of International Channel Alternatives 418
Countertrade 419
CHANNELS OF DISTRIBUTION FOR SERVICES 420
Characteristics of Services 420
Classification of Services 421

SUMMARY 426
QUESTIONS 426

14 **Future Distribution Arrangements** **428**

CHANNEL MANAGEMENT—A SYNTHESIS 429
    Universal Foundation of Channel Systems 429
THE NEED FOR DISTRIBUTION INNOVATION 432
    Invention versus Innovation 433
    The Productivity Gap 433
INNOVATIVE DISTRIBUTION IDEAS: FACT OR FICTION? 433
    Speeding Autos to Market 433
    Home Delivery of Food 435
    Applianceless Dealers 436
    Purchasing Corporations 437
CONCLUDING STATEMENT 438

Cases for Part 4

4–1 IKEA NORTH AMERICA—THE VIKINGS REDISCOVER AMERICA 439
4–2 1–800–PIRATES 448
4–3 THE RECALL OF PERRIER BRAND BOTTLED WATER 452
4–4 THIRD WORLD INSTITUTION BUILDING: THE CALI EXPERIMENT 460
4–5 HERSHEY GOES HOME 467

INDEX 477

PREFACE

Business executives and academicians increasingly acknowledge the important role distribution relationships play in marketing strategy. The development and management of efficient relationships among organizations is a critical factor in gaining and maintaining competitive success. The frequent use of the terms "partnerships" and "strategic alliances" in the business media reflects the increasing importance of these complex relationships in the business world. This book is devoted to helping the reader better understand the role of distribution channels in a firm's strategy and throughout the global economy.

The introductory chapters of the text lay a solid foundation of channel management, including a comprehensive discussion of the structures and participants. Following the introductory chapters, *Strategic Marketing Channel Management* covers three main topics: the process of designing and developing marketing and logistical channel arrangements; the management of these relationships in a competitive market; and the application of channel management principles to nontraditional situations. The text presents a comprehensive treatment of distribution channel concepts and practices and provides a strategic framework for managing the process of planning and implementing marketing channel arrangements.

Strategic Marketing Channel Management distinguishes itself from other channel texts by offering the following features:

- First, the text presents a comprehensive treatment of all participants in marketing channels including manufacturers, wholesalers, retailers, and a full range of service providers.
- Second, marketing channels are covered from a managerial or executive perspective in the text.
- Third, to facilitate skill development each part of the text is supported with five cases that focus on essentials of channels management discussed in the corresponding parts. These cases followed by thought-provoking questions, have been developed to address the challenges of applying concepts to practical situations. In fact, they are much more than a chronology of a firm's problems; rather, they are designed to act as workshop settings in which the student can apply channel concepts.

• Fourth, the text addresses several aspects of channel management that are often neglected. Topics such as logistics, performance measurement, negotiation, international and service industries, are covered comprehensively.

• Fifth, the text explores various aspects of developing and managing strategic alliances among firms engaged in interorganizational arrangements.

• Finally, even though theory is essential to developing an in-depth understanding of any profession, we have departed from the traditional method of presenting theoretical developments. Concepts such as power, leadership, performance measurement, conflict resolution, and change management are treated in an integrated framework for managerial planning and decision making throughout the text. Selected environmental aspects of channel management such as legal and regulatory discussions are also integrated throughout the text.

A complete Instructor's Manual is available as an aid for course preparation. It contains lecture outlines, answers to all end-of-chapter questions, case summaries, answers to all case questions, a complete test bank with objective true/false, multiple-choice and essay questions that test text concepts, and transparency masters that highlight lectures.

A major feature of this text is its positioning as a part of a new technology of publishing. *Strategic Marketing Channel Management* is linked to McGraw-Hill's PRIMIS database that serves to tailor college textbooks to fit specific teaching requirements. Since channels course presentations range from introductory undergraduate to capstone MBA, a wide range of supplemental cases and readings are provided to accommodate such required diversity in presentation. The text material, cases, and *Business Week* readings are keyed into the PRIMIS database and can be selected and arranged to fit any channels course. Instructors can, in essence, custom design their course materials to reflect their unique managerial perspectives at any level of sophistication. Of course, the option of PRIMIS is an individual choice. The standard text, cases, and teaching support materials offer a comprehensive package as is.

Countless individuals have contributed to the development of this book. Dean Richard J. Lewis of the Eli Broad Graduate School of Management and Chairperson Robert W. Nason of the Department of Marketing and Transportation Administration and Michigan State University foster an environment that encourages scholarly research and writing. All of our colleagues in the Department of Marketing and Transportation Administration provided support and encouragement for our efforts. In particular, we wish to thank Donald A. Taylor, Professor Emeritus, for his continued support and encouragement. Don, even in retirement, remains a professor's "professor."

Special appreciation is also due to the reviewers who made extensive comments and suggestions for improvement on the manuscript: John R. Grabner, The Ohio State University; Jan B. Heide, Case Western Reserve University; Michael J. Houston, University of Minnesota; Charles A. Ingene, University of Washington; James M. Kenderdine, The University of Oklahoma; and Lynne D. Richardson, The University of Alabama at Birmingham.

Bonnie Binkert, Mimi Melek, and the McGraw-Hill staff are appreciated for their encouragement and guidance throughout the painful process of bringing the book from concept to finished product. Numerous students and hundreds of business executives have all, in their own way, made important contributions to *Strategic Marketing Channel Management*. Particular appreciation is due to David J. Frayer, research assistant, for the hundreds of hours he spent helping us with all aspects of development of both the text and the associated instructor's manual; and to Pamela Kingsbury for her tireless work in manuscript preparation.

In the final analysis, even with so much assistance, we bear sole responsibility for any shortcomings that appear.

Donald J. Bowersox
M. Bixby Cooper

STRATEGIC
MARKETING
CHANNEL
MANAGEMENT

PART ONE

THE SCOPE OF MARKETING AND DISTRIBUTION CHANNELS

MARKETING CHANNELS

CHAPTER OUTLINE

REALITIES AND CONTRADICTIONS
    Awareness
    Visibility
    Multiple Engagements
    Involvement
    Acceptance
    Cooperation and Conflict
WHY BUSINESSES SEEK CHANNEL ARRANGEMENTS
    Functional Performance
    Reduce Complexity
    Specialization
ORDER OF PRESENTATION
    Channel Planning
    Implementation

One marvel of a free-market system is the complex process by which products and services are matched with customers' wants and preferences. Business, as the dominant economic force in an advanced industrial society, coordinates the talents and resources of many different organizations to achieve effective distribution. As a result, the consuming public enjoys a quality of life characterized by broad assortments of products and services available at times, in places, and in quantities desired. The distribution process offers customers freedom to choose products and services at affordable prices. This book examines the process by which choices of products and services become everyday realities. In particular, attention is directed to how managers make strategic decisions related to channels.

The arena for competition in a free-market system is the marketing channel. It is in the marketing channel that the process and dynamics of competition take place and the success or failure of enterprises and individual initiatives is determined. Marketing channels do not have uniform dimensions, and they often defy simple description. Some channels are very direct, linking manufacturers or growers of a product or originators of a service directly to consumers; there is no (or little) intervention by other business establishments. For example, a consumer's purchase of sweet corn at a farmer's roadside market represents a simple and direct channel. Other channels contain many intermediate and unique activities that occur as products or services flow from origin to consumption. During the distribution process, ownership may transfer many times. In terms of elapsed time, the distribution process may require from a few hours, to days, weeks, or months. Likewise, the channel may function at one geographic location or around the globe—even involve outer space. Garments manufactured in Asia can be presented for sale throughout United States department stores within hours of when they were produced as a result of using fast air distribution. More likely than not, the entire garment distribution process, given today's technology, will be coordinated by a satellite-based information and communication network. The fact that channel structures can be uniquely designed to gain competitive advantage is at the heart of *Strategic Marketing Channel Management*.

The players in the distribution game are analogous to an athletic team. Each channel member performs a specified role. Marketing channel players ''wear the jerseys'' of manufacturers, retailers, wholesalers, plus a wide variety of other types of specialized businesses that perform activities vital to successful distribution. The channel that results from such collaboration is defined as *a system of relationships existing among businesses that participate in the process of buying and selling products and services.*

To facilitate understanding of the unique roles that specific businesses perform in the overall distribution process, let's separate channel players or participants into two groups—primary and specialized. A primary channel member is a business that takes inventory ownership and thereby shoulders substantial risk. A specialized channel member, in contrast, performs services vital to the overall distribution process but does not participate in inventory ownership risk. The important point is that a wide variety of unique businesses and specialized service providers form a relationship identified as a distribution channel, one that competes with other channels for customer patronage. The activities of channel management involve designing and selecting appropriate structures, negotiating agreements, and administering ongoing relationships. However, what results is an overall situation that is difficult to fully comprehend. To start the careful examination of channel management, let's review some of the many inconsistencies found in commonly observed business arrangements.

REALITIES AND CONTRADICTIONS

Historically, marketing channels have been described as neatly arranged alignments of independent businesses. The primary channel participants are retailers, wholesalers,

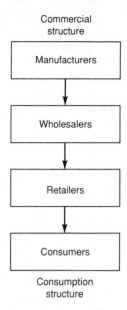

FIGURE 1-1   Traditional representation of marketing channel.

and manufacturers. Marketing students are typically exposed early in their studies to a review of the traditional role these three basic institutions perform during the distribution process. In fact, the typical introductory marketing textbook describes traditional channel structural alignment among firms as in Figure 1-1.

Manufacturers are enterprises primarily concerned with creating products. As the creators of brand products, manufacturers are highly visible and typically considered to be channel originators. As such, manufacturers that initiate the distribution process automatically become the focal point for channel discussions. In fact, highly successful manufacturers such as General Electric, General Motors, Kellogg, Sony, and Phillips are significant forces in their respective distribution channels. Such highly visible business firms operate on a global basis and have a proprietary position regarding brands and products. It is correct to assume that manufacturers are prime-time players in the process of channel creation and management. However, comprehensive channel study must offer more than a typical manufacturer's perspective. Many manufacturers engaged in industrial marketing have limited or no direct visibility to customers. Firms that produce services, such as travel or hospitality marketers, face unique channel requirements. Firms engaged in business-to-business marketing also require unique channel arrangements to facilitate successful exchange. Not all such manufacturing or service providers are the most dominant or visible members in their respective channels.

In direct contrast to manufacturers are retailers that, typically, function near the terminal point of the distribution process. Retailers offer consumers assortments of products from many manufacturers which are presented in a variety of different shopping environments. While the scope of retailing is vast, the dynamic role retailers can play in creating and managing channel arrangements is not adequately communicated in illustrations such as Figure 1-1. In many channel situations, retailers are powerful and dominant in determining how the overall distribution process will be organized and what the management practices will be. Retailers such as Sears, Wal-Mart, J. C. Penney, K mart, Kroger, and Macy's have a great deal at stake in successful channel performance. Consequently, they can be expected to take an active role in the orchestration of channel affairs. It would be a gross error to position retailers as passive channel members. In fact, as will be elaborated later, the rapid development of information technology has served to shift the relative power in the channel in favor of retailers.

The role wholesalers perform in distribution channels is less visible and more difficult to describe than either that of manufacturers or retailers. The traditional mission of wholesalers has been to provide retailers with assortments of products from many manufacturers. Because the need to generate merchandise assortment has been so fundamental to economic development, wholesalers have been the power centers of early channel development. They have served to unite the activities of many small retailers and manufacturers by designing and developing channel arrangements. In recent years, many retailers and manufacturers have expanded operations through vertical integration to perform functions typically considered the responsibility of wholesalers. Such vertical integration has raised doubts concerning the long-term vitality of wholesaling. In fact, wholesalers and selected other types of businesses that generate profits by operating between manufacturers and retailers are often viewed as nonessential or parasitic to the distribution process. The reality is that wholesalers are far from being eliminated from most distribution processes. While firms such as Burgen Brunswig, McKesson, Genuine Parts, Spartan Stores, Super Value, Gordon Food Service, and ACE Hardware are hardly household names, they and many other wholesalers dominate their respective channels of distribution. It is clear that rumors concerning the death of wholesalers in at least one advanced industrial economy, the United States, are greatly exaggerated!

Because of the wide variety of channel arrangements that exist, it is difficult to generalize the structure or alignment of channels across all industries. Figure 1-2 illustrates a variety of different channel alignments that are currently employed in the distribution of food products. In Figure 1-3 the array of channel arrangements utilized by J. R. Simplot, a highly diversified firm, is illustrated. A brief review of some fundamental contradictions about channels and participants offers a realistic feel for the complexity of distribution arrangements. The realities and contradictions involve members' awareness, degree of visibility, multiple engagements, intensity of involvement, degree of acceptance, and level of cooperation and conflict.

Awareness

The distribution channel performs the process of ownership and physical transfer of commodities, products, and services. In the marketing of any group of items or services, a wide variety of different enterprises is typically involved. Many individual businesses, that, in fact, participate in a channel may not be aware of their involve-

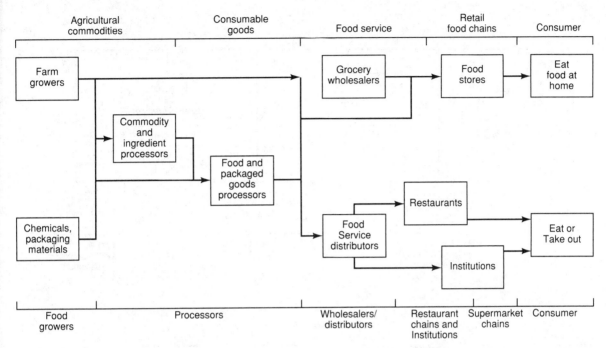

Range of channels in packaged-food distribution. (*Source:* Digital Equipment Corporation. Reproduced by permission.)

ment. Awareness means that a firm acknowledges that it is a member of a channel and that it acts to facilitate overall performance of the arrangements. Many distribution channel members are not aware of the many other organizations or individuals who are also involved in the overall distribution process. Smaller enterprises are often only aware of the face-to-face buying or selling in which they participate. Many institutions involved in marketing goods or services may not acknowledge or identify themselves, or be aware of or remotely think of themselves as channel members.

In almost every community retailers exist that sell merchandise ranging from flowers to rugs, paintings, or watches at discounted prices. This form of specialty discount retailer may operate from a truck, a tent on a street corner, or a low-rent facility such as an abandoned gas station. The products they sell are typically obtained from a variety of supply sources such as import distributors, closeout liquidators, and bankruptcy administrators. Merchandise purchased from such supply sources often represents a one-time buy. Neither party to the transaction anticipates repeat business. After sale, support such as warranties or guarantees is nonexistent. It is extremely doubtful that such a retail proprietor feels any identification with or loyalty to a channel organization. As channel participants, these firms and individuals come and go based on short-term needs. They have low relative financial risk and no interest in long-term survival of the channel. In short, they have no loyalty to the channel to which they

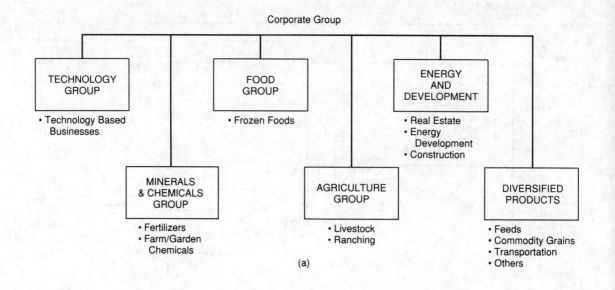

(a)

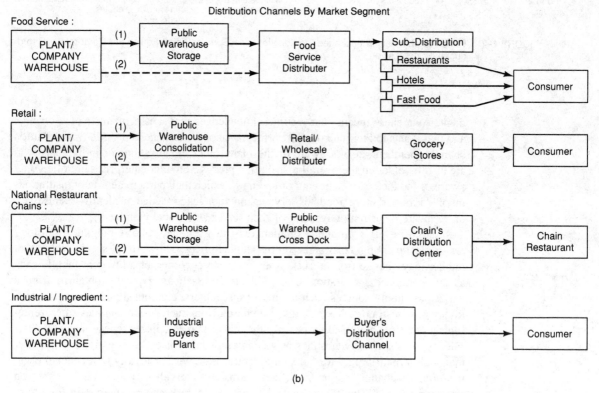

(b)

FIGURE 1-3   Channel alignment of one manufacturer. (*Source:* J.R. Simplot Company, Logistics Group. Reproduced with permission).

are a part because they have no awareness that such an arrangement even exists. Because they are not aware of the role they play in the channel, it follows that they will not be receptive to efforts by more-aware members to provide overall leadership.

In stark contrast to the low-end discounter is Sam's Club, a division of Wal-Mart Stores, Inc. At Sam's, a limited assortment of national brand merchandise is offered for sale to club members in special multiple-item packs. For example, Crest toothpaste may only be sold as multiple tubes packaged together as a single retail sales unit. To facilitate this form of retailing, close coordination is required between the product supply division of Proctor & Gamble, maker of Crest, and Sam's merchandise buyers. Proctor & Gamble negotiates with Sam's concerning the size and price of the exclusive product package. It is safe to conclude that managers involved in the planning and negotiation required to develop a strong relationship, such as that between Proctor & Gamble and Sam's, feel a deep involvement with and identify themselves as distribution channel members.

The above examples serve to illustrate the extremes among channel members; from complete independence to acknowledged involvement. Because many members have little or no awareness or loyalty, they come and go from channel arrangements as they individually seek to improve competitive position. Such realignment renders channel structure very dynamic. The result is that channel arrangements range from very loose to very tight, with various degrees of stability. Concern over the channel's direction of change and overall well-being is only important to managers who acknowledge a commitment to an ongoing channel organization.

Visibility

Another way to view channel arrangements is in terms of the visibility or identification of participating members. Many loose channel arrangements have limited visibility because they are organized around intermittent or infrequent buy-and-sell transactions. In extreme contrast to loose channels are highly visible arrangements organized around and identified with established marketers such as Ethen Allen, ACE Hardware, Ford, Holiday Inn, or Burger King. These highly visible firms offer channel partners identity as well as an enduring sense of stability. Such channels are typically legitimatized by the dominant organization that provides leadership and direction for the coordination of activities and practices of all participants.

Individual channel member visibility can vary significantly within the same arrangement. For example, an independent business that obtains a McDonald's franchise assumes a highly visible position in the fast-food industry. The owner of such a franchised restaurant must adopt standardized operations and enforce procedures and guidelines provided by the McDonald's organization. The details of such a franchise agreement typically cover operational aspects such as business hours, menu offerings, prices, and agreements to purchase specific supplies and ingredients. As a result, the franchised restaurant is highly visible as a McDonald's affiliate. In contrast, relatively few people are aware that Martin Brower, a food-service supply specialist, is also an integral part of the McDonald's distribution arrangement. Martin Brower provides logistics support for a wide variety of standardized ingredients for individual restaurants under terms and conditions orchestrated by the McDonald's organization. While having substantially different visibility in the eyes of the consuming public, both the independent restaurant owner and Martin Brower are deeply committed members of the McDonald's distribution channel.

As one might expect, highly visible channels typically have longer-term stability or endurance than those more loosely structured. However, the degree of stability between loose and dominated channels is relative. While the dominant organization in a highly visible channel may enjoy stability, a close examination of channel associates in such arrangements often reveals considerable instability, unrest, and desire for change.

Multiple Engagements

A further complication to understanding marketing channels is the fact that many individual businesses are simultaneously involved in multiple-channel arrangements. For some, involvement in multiple channels is a direct reflection of their marketing strategy that focuses around product offerings and unique customer segments. For others, involvement in multiple channels is more accidental than strategic.

From the viewpoint of a manufacturer, a key aspect of a marketing strategy is to determine how best to go to market. Major corporations selling national brand merchandise, such as ready-to-eat cereal industry leaders Kellogg, General Mills, Kraft General Foods, Ralston Purina, and Quaker Oats, often need to have a wide distribution network, to establish market share. Cereal manufacturers engage with different types of food retailers and institutional food service providers and compete in a $7 billion-a-year market—in the United States alone! Such broad-based manufacturing organizations must establish and maintain channel relationships with most prominent wholesalers and retailers in a large market. Smaller manufacturers, in contrast, may sell their entire output to a single retail chain or cooperative. Private-label manufacturers of ready-to-eat cereals, for example, may be contracted to sell exclusively to A&P or Spartan Stores.

Wholesale establishments most often focus operations in a specific industry or class of trade. While this focus reduces the scope of channel engagements, the wholesaler must develop business relationships with a variety of manufacturers and retailers that are all, more or less, direct competitors. Thus, wholesalers must adopt techniques for surviving the competition between manufacturers and retailers.

The practice of *scrambled merchandising* in retailing has created some strange channel relationships. Retail locations at which specific merchandise has traditionally been sold have been supplemented with a wide variety of other outlets selling identical products. Historically, products were available only at traditional outlets. For example, selected products such as garden rakes were expected by consumers to be found at specialty garden supply or hardware stores. In today's retailing environment, garden rakes are also sold at a variety of outlets wherever consumers are willing to purchase, such as mass merchandisers, food stores, gasoline stations, and convenience stores. Scrambled merchandising results, because the competitive nature of retail trade dictates that products be sold at any legitimate outlet that will attract consumers' patronage. A neat configuration or structure of channel arrangements is difficult to visualize in such scrambled situations.

From the manufacturer's channel strategy perspective, considerable choice exists regarding alternative ways to reach customers. A marketing strategy of *dual distribution* implies that a manufacturer has selected to simultaneously cultivate alternative channels for the same basic products. One example is a manufacturer's decision to market competitive products under separate labels or brands within the same retail store. For example, national brand and private-label food products processed by the same packer are frequently offered for sale side by side on the same retailer's store shelf.

Dual-distribution strategies are also common in industrial and service marketing arrangements. For example, Johnson & Johnson Hospital Supply Company, a wholly owned subsidiary of Johnson & Johnson (J&J), was established to provide a full assortment of products manufactured and marketed by separate J&J companies to hospitals. The basic strategy of J&J Hospital Supply is to offer hospitals all J&J products on a single order with the convenience of one delivery and invoice. Despite such steps to facilitate hospital buyers' ways of purchasing, J&J's individual business units continue to sell through drug wholesalers and hospital supply firms. For example, J&J products are also sold to hospitals by Baxter International. As a consequence, one of J&J's largest single customers, Baxter International, is also one of their largest competitors in the hospital class of trade.

To support highly segmented marketing strategies, manufacturers may seek to channel different variations of their products into distinct selling outlets. A classic example has been Whirlpool's strategy to market variations of its appliances under the Kenmore brand exclusively in Sears retail stores while selling Whirlpool brand products via a network of independent dealers. Sears recent *brand-central* strategy that features competitive brand merchandise such as GE appliances for sale in their stores is evidence that selective distribution arrangements typically confront considerable competitive pressure.

The reality of multiple engagements renders it difficult to envision clean or clearcut channel arrangements. Separate channels may be needed when buyers' requirements are sufficiently unique to justify use of special marketing arrangements. However, in complex contemporary channels, routine patterns of conducting business emerge among certain firms, those that feel that stabilized relations with trading partners will yield beneficial results. Any given firm may be simultaneously engaged in multiple-channel arrangements.

Involvement

A substantial amount of business is conducted among businesses that fully accept and encourage regular involvement with specific trading partners. Business managers in these firms acknowledge that their best long-term interest is to work out interorganizational relationships or alliances that go beyond traditional buying and selling. These managers realize that they will be better off in the long run by cultivating a close working relationship with major trading partners. Therefore, they are receptive to modifying the way they normally conduct day-to-day business operations so that they can facilitate a closer working relationship and, one hopes, cement a long-term association.

To illustrate intensity of channel involvement, let's consider the business relationship that has developed between independent drug wholesalers and local pharmacists. Both traditional wholesalers and individual or independent retail pharmacies were placed at serious competitive disadvantage during the 1970s, at which time the vertically integrated retail drug chains grew rapidly. Chains such as Walgreen's, Eckerds, Rite-Aid, Osco, and Revco captured significant market share as they offered consumers national brand merchandise at discount prices. By vertically absorbing responsibility for wholesale distribution, such chain operations were able to exploit purchasing and logistic efficiency associated with economy of scale. For a while it appeared that independent drug wholesalers and many local pharmacies would be forced out of businesses. In fact, many were!

A few wholesalers rallied for survival by totally revamping their way of doing business and the basic relationship with pharmacy customers. They forged a technology-based interorganizational alliance that matched the purchasing and logistic efficiency of the vertically integrated chains while retaining the entrepreneurial initiative of the owner-operated pharmacy. The result has concentrated independent wholesale drug volume in five firms that, in combination, enjoy over 70 percent of nationwide sales. Their customers are pharmacies that openly acknowledge involvement as associates in the wholesaler distribution network of such firms as Bergen Brunswig, Alco Health Services, and McKesson. As a result of intensive channel involvement, both the wholesaler and retailer are jointly positioned to compete with the vertically integrated drug chains.

A fact of channel structure is that business volume throughout industry is becoming more concentrated. In 1990, less than 10 percent of all retailers did 50 percent of total United States retail sales. During that year, the top ten retailers accounted for roughly 8.5 percent of all retail sales. The top ten food retailers had combined sales of $102 billion. This represented 41.4 percent of total retail food sales.[1] Among mass merchandisers, market share is also highly concentrated. In combination Sears, K mart, Wal-Mart, J. C. Penney, and Dayton-Hudson account for over $110 billion in retail sales. Similar increased concentration has occurred in hardware, food service, auto parts, and hospital services.

One result of concentration is a well-identified path for firms to follow as they develop channel arrangements in their respective industries. Thus, while individual firms continue to proliferate in numbers and multiple engagements remain typical across many industries, the paradox is that volume of transactions continues to concentrate into fewer channel arrangements. As the overall economy grows, a disproportionate amount of new volume or market share tends to be captured by the fastest-growing enterprises at all levels of the trading channel. These fast-growing enterprises

---

[1] These data were constructed from *United States Industrial Outlook: 1990*, p. 40–1, *Chain Store Age*, **67**:2, February 1991, p. 96, and *WARDS Business Directories—1990*.

and the reaction of their direct competitors facilitates intensive involvement in well-defined channel arrangements.

Acceptance

Firms participating in channels exhibit significantly different levels of acceptance concerning membership roles and associated responsibilities. *Acceptance* refers to the degree to which a firm is willing to identify with and integrate individual operations with those of the overall channel. Different levels of acceptance are illustrated by two transportation carriers that participate with 3M in the distribution of industrial tapes and fasteners. Keep in mind that transportation carriers are typically involved in distribution arrangements as specialized or support channel members. However, even as specialized channel participants, their prescribed roles and acceptance of channel operating rules can be vastly different. Schneider National participates as a primary carrier deeply involved in developing unique ways to service 3M's core customer base. In fact, during one period of time Schneider actually provided information systems services and support to help 3M introduce new operating procedures for all carriers. Schneider's perception of their functional role and associated responsibility is substantially different from the other carrier's, in which channel involvement is limited to providing point-to-point transportation service.

Each firm has the right of self-resolution when it comes to participation in channel engagements. *Self-resolution* means the right to select or reject participation in a specific channel arrangement. The degree of acceptance that a channel member exhibits is directly related to that firm's managerial perceptions concerning the risk or benefit to be gained from channel membership. The more positive the perception of potential long-term benefit from channel alignment, the more overt and direct will be a firm's acknowledgment or acceptance of channel membership.

Firms that openly accept and acknowledge continued membership in a channel can be expected to take a high degree of interest in resolving problems. Those that acknowledge membership perceive that a great deal of benefit is associated with overall channel success. Therefore, they will be open to developing new or unique solutions to improve the overall competitive vitality of the channel system. In most channel situations, codes of conduct or rules of the game emerge that members acknowledge and are willing to comply with. Within the framework of these codes of conduct, each participant accepts a role to perform, containing well-understood responsibility. The codes of conduct typically extend far beyond legal regulations and requirements. In the previous example, Schneider National, as a transportation carrier, had no legal obligation to provide 3M with information management services to help facilitate overall coordination of all their carriers. Many of these other carriers were direct competitors of Schneider National.

In part, organization of channel affairs results from the culture and social setting of the specific nation in which the channel operates. However, in international situations, channels function across national borders and are able to retain their structure and functional ordering. Most firms have some degree of either direct or indirect involvement in global commerce. The more intense the degree of international involvement, the greater the need to accommodate constraints associated with doing business in a variety of different sociopolitical settings. Thus, participation in channel membership across different nations accentuates a firm's requirement to simultaneously play different roles and accommodate a variety of formal and informal rule structures. The prevailing relationships among institutions that constitute a channel are both formal and informal with respect to rules and expectations regarding conduct.

Cooperation and Conflict

There is an abundance of literature concerning the various types and intensities of conflict that inevitably arise among channel participants. Without doubt, the development and resolution of conflict is important to the maintenance of channel solidarity. Conflict does arise. Most often it is resolved on a mutually satisfactory basis before it becomes dysfunctional or destructive to the channel. In fact, a level of conflict can facilitate overall channel performance.

A channel member may, at any time, aspire to goals that are incongruent with those of the overall distribution arrangement. To a degree, such differences can result in conflict. Many channel organizations establish dealer councils and advisory boards to provide feedback. These formal devices serve to resolve conflict before it becomes dysfunctional.

The resolution of conflict is important. In extreme cases it can result in a channel being dissolved. A classic confrontation took place between Computerland and Apple over the introduction of IBM PCs in Computerland's franchise outlets. Apple felt that Computerland's decision to add IBM products violated their working agreements, and they therefore refused to continue dealing with Computerland.

Once parties in a channel confrontation take steps to dissolve their working relationships it is difficult to reestablish a healthy channel arrangement. In some situations conflict is so dysfunctional that it causes irreparable damage. However, examples of reconstruction are available. In the Apple–Computerland conflict, individual franchises felt at a competitive disadvantage without Apple products. Therefore, they began to deal directly with alternative sources willing to provide Apple products. The end result was that Computerland agreed, in the interest of maintaining franchise solidarity, to reestablish business arrangements with Apple.

Describing the nature of conflict is far more intriguing than carefully delineating how cooperation develops in a channel arrangement. Despite this fact, the *prevailing state of affairs within channels is cooperative.*

WHY BUSINESSES SEEK CHANNEL ARRANGEMENTS

The previous discussion illustrated the complexity of channel arrangements and highlighted the many realities and contradictions that can easily be observed. One way to initiate the study of management in marketing channels is to identify reasons or motivations that cause businesses to seek establishment of distribution arrangements. This section presents a discussion of three important motivations that cause individual businesses to formalize marketing channels: (1) functional performance, (2) reduced complexity, and (3) specialization. Naturally, motivations to enter into channels tend to overlap, with an element of each present in most arrangements. In combination, these motivations serve as cohesive forces to maintain channel structure over time.

Functional Performance

Those who study marketing have long acknowledged that a number of specific acts or activities are essential to the successful completion of the overall distribution process. Although there are many different ways to classify and list marketing functions, the traditional list includes selling, buying, transportation, storage, financing, standardization, risk taking, and market information.[2]

Selling and *buying* are complementary to each other and are often referred to as the functions of exchange. The selling effort seeks to cultivate product demand through the development of products that satisfy market needs and through various techniques of demand stimulation, such as advertising and personal selling. *Buying,* on the other hand, consists of activities required to arrange an assortment of goods at an appropriate time and place. Buying involves planning and assembly of assortments so that proper quantities and qualities of desired goods are available.

Transportation and *storage* are concerned with the process of supplying physical goods. In most modern treatments, the terms *logistics* and *physical distribution* are used to describe the physical movement and storage aspects of channels. Because the location from which a product is supplied rarely is the same as where it is consumed, products must be transported as part of ownership transfer. Storage is also essential in marketing because of differences in times of production and consumption. Goods produced seasonally, such as fruits and vegetables, must be maintained as inventory until demanded. Goods produced continuously but demanded seasonally, such as toys or lawn furniture, must also be stored to accommodate the time gap. The strategic location of inventory coupled with a firm's ability to rapidly respond to customer requirements can be critical in selection between alternative suppliers and channel arrangements. Firms that possess superior logistic competency may be positioned to offer customers efficiency coupled with an overall ease of doing business, which can make them a preferred supplier. Logistics is directly related to the solution of a channel's spatial and temporal requirements.

The other four functions—financing, standardization, risk taking, and market information—are often collectively referred to as *facilitating* because their performance is necessary to complete exchange and logistic activities. Since marketing involves vast resources of machines, materials, land, and labor, capital must be supplied to finance the smooth functioning of the process. *Financing* is needed to maintain inventories throughout the channel and to support requirements of customer credit. *Standardization* refers to development of high-quality uniform products and services. Standard-

---

[2] For a traditional review of functional classification, see Rayburn D. Tousley, Eugene Clark, and Fred E. Clark, *Principles of Marketing,* New York: Macmillan, 1962, pp. 14–20, and Edmund D. McGarry, ''Some Functions of Marketing Reconsidered,'' in *Theory In Marketing,* ed. Reavis Cox and Wroe Alderson, Homewood, IL: Irwin, 1950, pp. 269–273.

ization is the process by which products are sorted into desired quantities for consumption. *Risk taking* is inherent in the marketing process. The nature of risk ranges from potential physical losses, such as fire or theft, to misjudging of consumer demand. One or more firms within the channel system must assume the burden of such risks. Collection, interpretation, and communication of *market information* are all critical to the effective operation of a channel system. Because business decisions are based on information concerning market size, preferences, and supply availability, accurate data is essential to the marketing decision maker.

One way to better understand a marketing channel is in terms of the integrated flow of activities or functions required to complete ownership transfer. The general idea is that channels are created to facilitate or coordinate functional flow from product creation to consumption. Channel specialists are businesses whose positions and functions in the flow between production and consumption can be justified because they increase overall efficiency and facilitate ownership transfer. Viewing channels from the perspective of flows places emphasis on the critical need to integrate the overall process.[3]

From a manager's viewpoint, functions and flows represent alternative ways of looking at the essential ingredients of ownership transfer. Each function is essential to the ownership transfer process. From a managerial perspective, trading partners and distribution specialists are incorporated into channel structure because they offer the potential to increase the efficiency or effectiveness of the process. The functions that channel members perform are essential to the process and cannot be eliminated. However, a specific business can be eliminated, and the alternative ways available to accomplish a specific functional requirement are often numerous.

For example, a manufacturer may face a need to transport finished products to a specific wholesaler. The range of practical alternative methods of transportation may include truck, standard rail, piggyback (TOFC), or double-stack containers. The manager involved must first select an appropriate transportation method that can satisfy the time and service requirements for the specific movement. Then, a specific transportation firm or carrier must be selected to perform the service. Thus, the process consists of first monitoring the field (searching) and then selecting a specific carrier to perform the move (specialized channel member selection).

It is clear that a manager arranging for performance of transportation has a variety of options concerning type of service as well as the specific firm or supplier to perform the service. The manager does not have a choice concerning the fundamental need to perform the required transportation. Thus, one can substitute ways and means of performing a function but one cannot eliminate the need.

The ability to select ways and means for performing all functions essential to the process of ownership transfer is the essence of channel management. To satisfy all channel requirements, the managers involved must select these ways and means. The result is an arrangement of businesses linked as a channel. As noted earlier, participating institutions can be classified as primary or specialized on the basis of their degree of risk assumption. Once the selection process is completed, the initial structure

---

[3] R. S. Vaile, E. F. Grether, and Reavis Cox, *Marketing in the American Economy,* New York: Ronald Press, 1952.

FIGURE 1-4 UNIVERSAL MARKETING
FACTORS PERFORMED
BY CHANNEL ARRANGEMENTS

Group	Function
Exchange	Selling
	Buying
Logistics	Transportation
	Storage
Facilitating	Financing
	Standardization
	Risk
	Market information

of the channel is determined. This selection process is typically referred to as the *channel structure design.* Once the channel structure is designed, the act of assuring that the goals of all the involved enterprises are achieved is undertaken; this is referred to as *channel leadership.* The combined process of channel structure design and leadership is referred to as *channel management.* Figure 1-4 presents a classification of marketing functions.

The discussion of functions establishes the basis for introducing two important concepts related to channel management: *functional spin-off* and *absorption.* Both spin-off and absorption represent ways to transfer a function from one channel member to another. As the names imply, functions are either spun off or absorbed, depending upon who initiates the action. However, in terms of channel management the differences and their implications are not subtle. Individual firms are engaged in a constant process of functional spin-off or absorption, depending upon relative economics and power balance.

Functional spin-off occurs when one firm transfers a function to another firm. The spin-off may or may not be desired by the receiving firm. Functional spin-off usually happens when a dominant channel member finds it economically advantageous to subcontract or delegate specific functions to specialist firms.[4] Two common examples of spin-off are the use of for-hire transportation or public warehousing in logistics operations and a manufacturer subcontracting product packaging to another firm. The basic theory is that the firm accepting the spun-off function can perform the requirements at a lower operating cost. The firm initiating the spin-off expects to benefit from sharing the resultant efficiency. In reality, however, many firms receiving a spun-off function take on the added work only because they fear repercussion if they do not cooperate. Thus, a manufacturer may agree to extend credit terms or perform customized packaging for a retailer only because it fears losing business if it does not cooperate.

[4] For expanded discussion, see Louis P. Bucklin, "Postponement, Speculation, and the Structure of Distribution Channels," *Journal of Marketing Research,* **2**:5, February 1965, pp. 26–31; and Bruce Mallen, "Functional Spin-off: A Key to Anticipating Change in Distribution Structure," *Journal of Marketing,* **37**:3, July 1973, pp. 18–25.

In a conceptual sense, functional absorption is the opposite of spin-off. It is true that one firm must absorb a function for another firm to spin it off. However, situations may develop wherein one firm may desire to absorb a function when the firm currently performing it does not want to change the existing situation. The firm wishing to absorb a function may enjoy lower average cost or may be seeking greater control over the marketing channel. A prime example of functional absorption was one major manufacturer's decision to ship appliances directly to dealers from assembly plants. The traditional logistic channel arrangement had been from manufacturer to distributor to dealer. In the revised flow, appliances were shipped directly to the dealer and the distributor was bypassed. As a result of the functional absorption, the distributor no longer performed logistic services. The incentive for establishing direct factory-to-dealer delivery was a reduced per-unit logistic cost resulting from elimination of duplicate transportation and warehousing. The resulting savings were shared among all channel participants, including the distributor. However, the scope of distributor participation and control in the channel was reduced, despite the fact that the total channel became more efficient.

With sensitivity to functional performance, considerable insight into the dynamics of channel management can be gained. Functions are essential to the process of ownership transfer, and how, where, and by whom they are performed is a key concern in channel management. Businesses enter into channel arrangements because they expect that their overall objectives can best be achieved by participating in such relationships. The alternative to participating in a channel arrangement is to actually own and operate facilities capable of performing all necessary functions. The ownership of consecutive stages of distribution and the performance of multiple functions in the distribution process is referred to as *vertical integration*. While primary participants in a specific channel arrangement may be more or less vertically integrated, the fact remains that no firm commands sufficient resources to be totally self-sufficient.

In business history there are two well-documented examples of firms that attempted to implement a strategy of controlling as many functions as possible in the distribution chain. Henry Ford had a vision that he could best facilitate the process of automotive creation and marketing if he owned all stages of the process from the raw-material extraction to finished auto showrooms. In the 1950s, the Great Atlantic and Pacific Tea Company (A&P) had a similar vision. Their objective—to offer consumers high-quality food at the lowest possible price—appeared most attainable to management if they owned and operated all stages of production and distribution of private-brand merchandise. Thus, in tuna, for example, they owned and operated all facilities and processes required to complete distribution, from fishing fleets to retail stores. While Ford and A&P had channel strategies primarily based in vertically integrated ownership, both organizations still required the support of thousands of outside businesses to help achieve their vision.

Reduced Complexity

A major motivation for firms seeking channel arrangements is to decrease the overall complexity involved in transferring ownership. The varied aspects of complexity have been carefully developed by channel scholars who have sought to explain the reasons behind channel origin.[5] Two aspects of the reduction in complexity are critical to the understanding of why businesses seek channel arrangements: (1) routinization, and (2) sorting.

Routinization Routinization deals with the need to reduce the range of alternatives in channel design to a manageable size. The complexity of channel management is reduced by the extent to which the search for alternatives is limited based on past experience. In other words, it would be neither efficient nor practical to review all alternatives each and every time a new supplier or outlet was required. Channel arrangements reduce the complexity of doing business by building a history of relationships; these serve to reduce search time when new arrangements are required and provide experience regarding how to conduct operations.

Routinization relates to the rules and procedures used to guide functional performance in a channel. For each channel participant, routinization reflects its unique business goals, expectations, and preferences regarding the channel arrangement. For a group of businesses linked together in a channel, routinization is the foundation for creating transactional efficiency. Because business relationships build upon a performance track record, which reduces the need to search out new participants and creates a routine way of conducting business, channels perpetuate themselves.

Sorting A vital contribution of a channel arrangement is the reduction in managerial problems related to geographic location and timing. Products are produced and consumed throughout the world, resulting in a significant flow of goods among nations. The process of providing the desired assortment of products and services when and where needed requires substantial coordination. The process is referred to as *adjustment.*

A typical supermarket offer consumers an in-store selection of over 25,000 items. Some mail-order merchandise firms offer customers product assortments, sizes, and colors that exceed 100,000 items. While such expansive offerings are impressive, even more astonishing is the fact that each of these institutions is in fact offering its customers a relatively small assortment of all available products.

Sorting is a broad label applied to the process that channel members collectively perform to efficiently develop unique product assortments. In terms of consumer markets, the final assortment is often expansive. In industrial marketing situations, where businesses are selling to other businesses, the range of products may be less than in consumer marketing, but the need for reduced complexity and precise performance is critical.

The sorting process requires that a channel generate a never-ending array of products into desired assortments positioned throughout the channel in a timely manner.[6]

[5] For example, see Louis P. Bucklin, *A Theory of Distribution Channel Structure,* Berkeley: University of California Institute of Business and Economic Research, 1967; and George E. Stigler, "The Division of Labor Is Limited by the Extent of the Market," *Journal of Political Economy,* **59**:3, June 1951, pp. 185–193.

[6] The sorting concept is fully developed in Wroe Alderson, *Marketing Behavior and Executive Action,* Homewood, IL: Irwin, 1957, Chapter 7. This concept is developed in greater detail in Chapter 4, pp. 90–92.

It is incomprehensible to imagine all requirements for developing assortments being performed by a single firm. Channels emerge to resolve the discrepancy of quantity and assortment problems by developing efficient adjustment alternatives. The process of efficient adjustment is facilitated by specialization.

Specialization

The demand for functional performance coupled with complexity leads to a high degree of *specialization* in marketing channel arrangements. Specialization and its related benefits represent the third motivation for the formation of channel arrangements. Specialization is fundamental in advanced industrial societies. Products in the United States are produced and distributed by approximately 2.3 million business establishments. These establishments represent a source of supply and demand to each other as well as to over 92,830,000 households. Figure 1-5 illustrates numerically the 1990 demand and supply structure of the United States economy.

Specialists can perform specified activities or functions for users at a lower cost per unit by virtue of economy of scale, which is a notion having long standing in economic and business literature.[7] The specialist firm develops a market niche in terms of its uniqueness. For example, almost one-third of the ready-to-eat cereals is targeted to the youngster segment. Such items as Teenage Mutant Ninja Turtles, Batman, Ghost Busters, Nintendo Cereal Systems, and Breakfast With Barbie cereals were the rage of the 1990 summer selling season. Ralston Purina produced approximately 90 percent of all "licensed character" cereals for youngsters.[8] To exploit this marketing niche, Ralston needed to perfect rapid manufacturing accommodation and quick-to-the-market logistic capabilities while maintaining essential product quality. Such specialized performance gave Ralston Purina effective dominance in this highly volatile segment of the ready-to-eat cereal market.

In recent years fulfillment companies—specialized organizations that support merchandising used in marketing promotions—have gained prominence. When manufacturers offer products or other incentives to consumers in return for box tops or coupons, often a fulfillment company actually handles redemption and delivery. Likewise, many point-of-sale merchandise displays are assembled by firms that specialize in constructing and logistically positioning such units in retail stores.

Specialization, as a form of advanced economic activity, extends far beyond institutions that perform services within the marketing channel. In fact, most manufacturing firms are specialists. The vast arena of industrial marketing, wherein the product of one enterprise serves as an input or component for another firm, is reflective of this extensive specialization. In the production of a television set, several hundred component parts manufactured by different firms throughout the world may be involved, all of which have to be assembled into the final retail product. Beyond assembly, the services of specialists are required for packaging and all aspects of logistics. In terms of marketing channel structure, such specialists serve to combine the output of varied manufacturers into an assortment for sale at the retail or industrial market level. In

---

[7] Stigler, op. cit.
[8] "Ah, How Sweet It Is!" *Time,* May 28, 1990, p. 79.

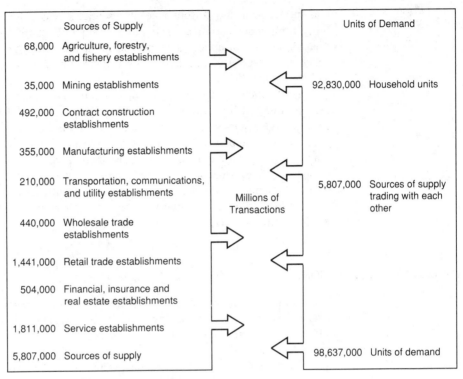

FIGURE 1-5   Exchange—matching demand and supply in the United States economy. (*Source: 1990 Statistical Abstract of the United States,* U.S. Department of Commerce, p. 528.)

fact, use of wholesalers can be economically justified by their capability of efficiently offering a product assortment for sale at prices that reflect the economies of scale inherent in large-volume operations.

The economic justification for using a specialist is challenged when an individual firm's requirements result in sufficient volume to consider performing the activity internally. In other words, when a user enjoys sufficient volume of trade and technical capability to internally enjoy maximum economy of scale, it may bring the process inside. At the point of potential vertical integration, the specialist stands in jeopardy of either being absorbed into the buyer organization or being eliminated. However, the fear of specialists being absorbed has significantly declined as a result of firms generally focusing more attention toward their core business competency. Whereas vertical integration to reduce cost has always been a viable alternative, an increasing number of firms have begun to send more activities to outside sources. This is done in an effort to reduce asset deployment and increase specialization in areas essential to their core business.[9] Such "outsourcing" has led to a proliferation of businesses

[9] Russell Johnson and Paul R. Lawrence, "Beyond Vertical Integration—The Rise of the Value-Adding Partnership," *Harvard Business Review,* **66:**4, July–August 1988, pp. 94–101.

that specialize in the performance of essential services. For example, in 1990 over thirty firms announced their entry into multiple-function logistic services business. These broad-based service companies positioned themselves as logistic specialists who stand ready to offer unique services on a contract basis to manufacturers, wholesalers, and retailers.[10]

Specialization creates economic opportunity. The small-scale specialists are to a degree protected by antitrust policy that seeks to prevent their absorption into gargantuan organizations. However, specialists' only real protection from being absorbed is remaining competitively attractive to large organizations – adding an element of efficiency and flexibility to the overall distribution process. The continued proliferation of specialized organizations serves as proof that their talents are in demand in the operation of marketing channels. The result is a sufficiently large and varied assortment of institutions performing in distribution arrangements. Specialization is a universal feature of marketing channel management.

ORDER OF PRESENTATION

The overall presentation of material is divided into four parts. Part One is concerned with a broad scoping of marketing channels. Following this introductory chapter, three additional chapters establish the foundations for developing marketing channel strategy. Chapters 2 and 3 discuss the wide range of business establishments that participate in typical channel arrangements. Chapter 2 is devoted to primary channel participants. Chapter 3 provides a survey of the most common types of specialized firms that are available to provide essential services as channel members. Chapter 4 is a pivotal chapter in the overall presentation. The chapter serves to integrate the materials of Part One around the topic of channel structure.

The development of channel strategy represents only one part of the overall marketing concerns of an enterprise. However, channel decisions are fundamental because they provide institutional structure through which the overall marketing strategy is orchestrated. The overall process of channel planning assumes that firms will seek to implement distribution arrangements they perceive to most likely result in achievement of their individual business objectives. Thus, channel design is integral to overall business strategy. For some firms, channel arrangements represent the pivotal feature or focus of their competitive strategy. For other firms, channel considerations represent a critical part of a balanced business strategy. For all firms, channel decisions are critical to success.

From a managerial viewpoint, the formulation and implementation of a channel strategy is viewed as a six-step process. The process is illustrated in Figure 1-6. Channel planning and implementation is neverending. Modifications and adjustments should be constantly implemented to perfect strategies and respond to competitive initiatives.

---

[10] See Chapter 3, Table 3–7, for a list of new multiple-function logistics service businesses.

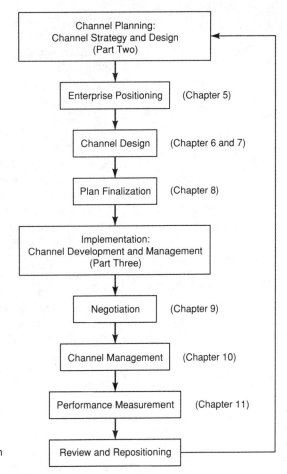

FIGURE 1-6 Channel planning and implementation framework.

Channel Planning

The first three steps involved in developing a channel strategy relate to various aspects of planning. They are: (1) enterprise positioning, (2) channel design, and (3) plan finalization.

Enterprise Positioning   The most macro dimension of channel planning involves relating channel requirements to enterprise strategy. The starting point in enterprise positioning is the establishment of specific requirements that the channel must satisfy. Items of concern are a careful delineation of the basic mission and goals of the enterprise. The enterprise strategy must be molded in terms of customers' requirements, competitive initiatives, and the unique competencies of the firm involved. A broad range of environmental issues must be evaluated in terms of their potential impact upon initiatives that a firm may deem desirable. Such assessment must consider, but is not necessarily limited to, an examination of the socio/cultural, economic, and legal environments within which a firm's distribution network must function.

Early in the process of channel planning it is necessary for the managment of a firm to evaluate the enterprise's power position with respect to compatibility and conflict with potential channel members. All channel arrangements require some degree of negotiated effort. In a simple channel, negotiation may be limited to price, guarantees, terms of delivery, and payment. In a more formalized channel arrangement, negotiations extend beyond transactional considerations to include performance expectations and identification of who will perform specific functions. Negotiated channel relationships typical of those found in advanced channel systems are extensive and to a significant degree the by-product of relative power. The bedrock of formulating a channel strategy from among the wide range of alternatives is a comprehensive, up-front assessment of the enterprise's relative negotiating position. Chapter 5 is devoted to the dual concerns of establishing distribution objectives and making a realistic assessment of relative negotiating power.

Channel Design The second step in the design process is identifying and evaluating a specific channel structure. Fundamental to channel strategy planning is the identification of desired channel commitments. It is also necessary to isolate a process by which feasible structural choices capable of satisfying objectives can be identified and evaluated. A given channel strategy may involve two sets of design specifications that are logically separated. One dimension of channel design is primarily concerned with generation of transactions. The other design dimension focuses on required logistics support. The two design aspects may or may not, in the final analysis, operate with quasiautonomous structures.[11]

Marketing channel design is concerned with satisfying customers' needs in a manner that will stimulate sales and achieve business objectives. As such, marketing channel design must reconcile and coordinate the simultaneous impact of product, promotion, and price aspects of the marketing mix upon sales revenue. In essence, the marketing channel design represents the translation of overall business strategy into an implementation plan. Marketing channel design is the topic of Chapter 6.

The aspect of the overall channel concerned with the physical movement of products is logistics. The logistics aspects of channel operations are unique in comparison to transaction-stimulating activities. In an overall sense, logistics exists to service and complement efforts of the marketing channel. Such support may be passive in the sense that logistics operations are primarily viewed as needing to efficiently meet requirements established during sales negotiations. Logistics support may also be positioned as a primary focus of the overall business strategy. Thus, depending upon how it is positioned in a firm's overall strategy, logistics may be either reactive or proactive. Logistics channel design is unique because a specialized group of intermediaries is available to provide functional services. Whereas the domain of most primary partic-

---

[11] The formal name for specialized channel structure to accommodate marketing transaction and logistics support is *channel separation*. Channel separation is more fully developed in Chapter 4, pp. 96 to 99.

ipants spans all aspects of demand cultivation, few, if any, firms are self-sufficient when it comes to logistics. Logistics design is the focus of Chapter 7.

Plan Finalization   The third step in the development of a distribution arrangement is plan finalization. Plan finalization involves the development of a framework to help analyze and select the most desirable channel structure arrangement. Design finalization requires comparative evaluation of alternative structures to isolate specific channel partners with whom negotiation will be initiated. Chapter 8, Planning and Analysis Framework, introduces a range of tools available to assist managers in the finalization of a channel plan. The completion of the plan results in a blueprint of desired action.

Implementation

The final three steps involved in developing an effective channel strategy relate to various aspects of implementation. They are: (1) negotiation, (2) channel management, and (3) performance measurement. Implementation is the topic of Part Three.

Negotiation   The establishment of a channel is typically the product of negotiation between potential participants. In many situations the parties to a negotiation are a combination of primary and specialized participants. The general thesis is that all channel arrangements, regardless of formal structure, require some level of negotiation in order for operational ground rules to be established. Ground rules are essential to even the most loose channel arrangement. The more complex the relationship and the longer its planned duration, the more comprehensive the negotiation process required to establish channel structure. Channel negotiation is a unique form or subset of the broad spectrum of bargaining. A basic feature of marketing negotiation is that it tends to focus on problem solving as contrasted to share bargaining. The more relational the proposed channel arrangement, the greater the attention devoted to problem solving during the negotiation process. Channel negotiation is the topic of Chapter 9.

Channel Management   Channels, similar to firms, require continuous management. Because channel arrangements span the legal boundaries of individual businesses, the normal practices of management must be augmented with interorganizational techniques. The extent to which a channel is, in fact, managed will be directly related to how clear-cut the member's perceptions are concerning interorganizational dependency and leadership. If the leadership role is well established, member firms are likely to respond to coordination initiatives. Keep in mind that the prevailing state of relationships that exist in a long-surviving channel is cooperation.

As in all forms of organizations, behavior problems can be expected to arise in even the most stable channel situations. While most day-to-day operational problems are resolved without open conflict, from time to time serious differences of opinion and fact can be expected to arise. Understanding the most common causes of conflict and developing methods of resolution are critical aspects of channel management. Extended enterprise management is the topic of Chapter 10.

Performance Measurement A final aspect of distribution strategy is accurate channel performance measurement. Performance assessment requires both financial and physical measurement of the contribution of individual participants as well as success of the overall channel. Effective performance assessment must start with an accurate calibration of customer satisfaction. In fact, little else the channel members do or plan has any real relevancy if the final customer is dissatisfied. Thus, during assessment the critical dimension of performance is the effectiveness of the channel. All channel members have a major and joint concern regarding customer satisfaction.

There are many quantitative measures that assist managers in the financial measurement of a channel's efficiency. Measurement of channel efficiency is directly related to each member's performance of roles in actual practice. Thus, efficiency measures are relative to each individual channel member as well as to the overall channel. Measurement of channelwide or combined productivity and financial performance is critical to the continuous evaluation of a channel arrangement.

The six-step channel planning and implementation process is appropriately viewed as neverending. Few, if any, channels are designed from a ground-zero level. Most channel structures evolve from members' participation over a number of years. The degree to which such evolution gives way to planned change is directly related to innovative behavior on the part of one or more channel members. Thus, one anticipated result of performance assessment is the identification of ways to improve existing distribution arrangements. The need to change structure from time to time renders channel planning and implementing a dynamic change-management process. Performance assessment is the topic of Chapter 11. Chapter 11 concludes Part Three.

Part Four discusses the general application of channel structure and strategy concepts in less traditional situations. Chapter 12 develops the increasing importance of information technology on practices of channel management and reviews processes of institutional change and the role of change agents in channel dynamics. Chapter 13 illustrates less traditional applications of channel concepts, techniques, and management practice by showing international, third-world, and service channel arrangements. The coverage concludes in Chapter 14 with a speculative look at the future composition of channel systems.

At the conclusion of each chapter, discussion questions are presented to help focus attention on the main concepts developed. Cases are presented at the conclusion of each part. Cases serve to illustrate key channel concepts in a practical setting. The typical channel case touches on a variety of issues and topics that span the materials presented in various chapters. These case studies serve to integrate topical material.

QUESTIONS

1 Discuss: "The actual process of competition in a free-market system is between alignments of independent organizations in the form of marketing channels." How does this differ in an economy that does not have a free-market system?

2 How can you distinguish between primary and specialized channel participants?

3 Why is awareness an important concept in understanding channel arrangements?

4 Why are manufacturers highly visible as channel members?

5 Why do relatively simple products such as packaged foods (Figure 1-2) require such complex channel arrangements to reach consumers?

6 Provide examples of the realities and contradictions that reflect the complexity of distribution arrangements. Why do these realities and contradictions prohibit generalization?

7 What is meant by complexity as common feature of marketing systems?

8 How do specialization and routinization lead to dependence in marketing channels?

9 Explain and illustrate functional spin-off and absorption. How do the two concepts differ?

10 What is the adjustment process and how does it relate to channel structure?

11 Discuss the relationship between specialization and vertical integration.

12 Contrast channel design and leadership. How do they relate to the overall process of channel management?

CHAPTER 2

PRIMARY PARTICIPANTS

CHAPTER OUTLINE

MANUFACTURING
  Manufacturing Structure
  Key Management Issues
  Emerging Manufacturing Strategies
  Conclusion: Manufacturing
WHOLESALING
  Wholesale Structure
  Key Management Issues
  Emerging Wholesale Strategies
  Conclusion: Wholesaling
RETAILING
  Retail Structure
  Key Management Issues
  Emerging Retail Strategies
  Conclusion: Retailing
SUMMARY

In Chapter 1, primary channel participants were defined as businesses that acknowledge their dependence upon one another in a channel arrangement and assume risk during the value-adding distribution process. In this chapter, the primary participants discussed are manufacturers, wholesalers, and retailers. The section devoted to each one reviews the basic nature of that business type and presents data describing quantitatively their structure. The purpose is to illustrate the extent, size, and complexity of potential distribution arrangements in an economy encompassing over 359,000 manufacturers, 450,000 wholesalers, and 1.5 million retailers. Individual sections also review key management issues confronting each type of business. The presentation of issues is designed to offer a basic understanding of significant changes and how they relate to channel decisions. Each section concludes with a review of new strategies emerging as primary channel participants seek innovative solutions in response to competitive pressures.

MANUFACTURING

The process by which materials and components are joined into products is typically called *manufacturing,* or *production.* Manufacturing firms represent significant and highly visible channel participants because they create products that become the primary concern of the overall distribution process. Manufacturing establishments create *form* utility. Manufacturing in combination with agriculture and mining serves to generate a flow of products, services, commodities, and materials that ultimately become the focal concern of marketing channels. Attention in this section is directed to manufacturing because it is the link in the value-adding chain that converts most agricultural commodities and extracted materials into products for industrial or consumer use.

The balance of the distribution process serves to provide assortments of many different manufacturer's products for wholesalers, retailers, and customers. Manufacturing firms take on significant risk with the creation of products. For example, Procter & Gamble, Lever Brothers, and Colgate-Palmolive invested hundreds of millions of dollars in developing, market testing and launching superconcentrated or compact powder detergents such as Ultra Tide, Wisk Power Scoop, and Fab Ultra. Reputable manufacturers assume full responsibility for the quality of products they produce and for their ultimate acceptance by customers. This responsibility is typified by widespread manufacturers' warranties and money-back guarantees for customers who are not fully satisfied. While the extent of manufacturers' risk in the overall distribution process is significant, it is focused or limited to the specific products produced, which typically represent a small proportion of those handled in the overall marketing channel.

The most visible manufacturers are firms that produce consumer products such as automobiles, appliances, food, clothing, pharmaceuticals, and beauty aids. Businesses that manufacture products for mass consumption often have highly publicized brands that are better known than the firm itself. Few consumers realize that such diverse consumer brands as Luvs, Oil of Olay, Duncan Hines cake mixes, Pert Plus, and Pringles are but a few of the many products manufactured and distributed by Procter & Gamble. In reality, firms that produce highly visible consumer brand products represent a small percentage of all establishments engaged in manufacturing. The majority of manufacturing establishments produce components, subassemblies, or ingredients that are sold to other business firms. Such business-to-business or industrial marketing is critical to the overall performance of final-product manufacturing. A manufacturer such as Ford is reported to regularly conduct business with thousands of vendors despite an aggressive program to reduce the number through supplier certification programs. Each of Ford's vendors, in turn, has a network of suppliers, resulting in a significant proliferation of firms. The vast majority of manufacturing firms are relatively small and not highly visible to the consuming public.

Manufacturing Structure

In 1987, nearly 360,000 United States businesses were engaged in some form of manufacturing. From a statistical viewpoint, the structure of manufacturing can be viewed in terms of the primary products produced. The Standard Industrial Classification (SIC) format groups manufacturing based on products produced. Table 2-1 presents the number of establishments and the value of shipments for twenty categories of manufacturing for 1982 and 1987. The sheer size of manufacturing increased in terms of both number of businesses and value of shipments over the five-year period.

Because of the rapid increase in the service sector of the United States economy, there is a general belief that manufacturing has been declining. This belief is in part created by the deficit in balance of foreign trade and the high visibility of durable consumer products imported from Asia and Europe. In fact, a structure shift has occurred in the composition of manufacturing away from heavy, or so called smokestack, industries to such value-added areas as electronics, chemicals, printing, and lumber. Despite a significant trade deficit, the United States remains the second largest exporting nation, with 1988 foreign shipments of $322.3 billion.[1]

A useful way to view manufacturing structure is in terms of the basic production process and the degree to which products are produced in anticipation of future sale. Both process and anticipation have a direct impact upon a manufacturer's channel requirements. Buffa and Miller structured production inventory systems using a two-dimensional classification scheme.[2] In terms of manufacturing process technology they classified firms as continuous or intermittent. Firms are also grouped based on relative inventory risk. Manufacturing performed in response to specific customer orders typically confronts less risk than one that produces in anticipation of future orders. Where a firm falls with respect to this two-dimensional classification scheme has a direct impact upon its channel requirements. For example, firms that build to inventory typically require a far more complex channel arrangement involving many more trading partners than those who build to customer orders. Figure 2-1 illustrates the four main classes or production inventory systems.

In terms of process technology, firms engaged in continuous manufacturing are forced to place a great deal of attention upon rationalizing the production process. Because of the high cost of production-line changeover and the need to focus manufacturing efforts to achieve maximum economy of scale, continuous-process firms require a highly reliable supply vendor network, one capable of flowing materials and component parts as required to support production requirements. Because the nature

[1] *1990 Statistical Abstract of the United States,* U.S. Department of Commerce.
[2] Elwood S. Buffa and Jeffrey G. Miller, *Production Inventory Systems,* Homewood, IL: Irwin, 1979, p. 9.

TABLE 2-1   MANUFACTURERS—SUMMARY BY INDUSTRY GROUP: 1982 AND 1987

SIC	Industry group	1982		1987	
		Establishments (number)	Value of shipments (million $)	Establishments (number)	Value of shipments (million $)
20	Food and kindred products	22,130	280,529.3	20,624	330,115.0
21	Tobacco products	163	16,061.4	138	20,761.0
22	Textile mill products	6,630	47,515.4	6,412	63,508.2
23	Apparel and other textile products	24,391	53,387.9	22,872	65,765.4
24	Lumber and wood products	32,984	42,934.9	33,982	69,607.9
25	Furniture and fixtures	10,003	24,128.6	11,613	37,137.5
26	Paper and allied products	(NA)*	(NA)	6,342	108,249.7
27	Printing and publishing	53,406	85,796.9	61,774	134,901.5
28	Chemicals and allied products	11,901	170,736.9	12,109	230,089.8
29	Petroleum and coal products	2,322	208,918.6	2,254	130,683.5
30	Rubber and miscellaneous plastics products	13,449	55,415.8	14,515	36,273.3
31	Leather and leather products	2,735	9,719.2	2,193	8,908.5
32	Stone, clay, and glass products	16,545	45,180.6	16,166	60,918.0
33	Primary metal industries	7,061	104,666.3	6,771	120,169.9
34	Fabricated metal products	35,560	119,444.0	36,105	148,263.2
35	Industrial machinery and equipment	52,912	187,895.7	52,135	220,097.5
36	Electronic and other electric equipment	(NA)	(NA)	15,962	172,136.7
37	Transportation equipment	9,443	201,346.1	10,500	332,470.3
38	Instruments and related products	(NA)	(NA)	10,326	108,269.9
39	Miscellaneous manufacturing industries	15,871	26,891.4	16,544	31,909.6
(X)	All manufacturing establishments, including central administrative offices	348,385	1,960,205.8	359,328	2,480,236.2

* Not available.
Source: U.S. Bureau of the Census. *Census of Manufactures, 1987 Preliminary Summary,* MC87-SUM-1(P).

of this process is so dependent upon vendor performance, many continuous-process manufacturers seek to maintain control by vertical integration or very formalized strategic alliances with key vendors.

Firms engaged in intermittent manufacturing place a high premium on vendor flexibility. Because their production schedule is rapidly changing or switching from one product to another, vendors must be able to rapidly change to accommodate volatile supply specifications. A supplier base capable of supporting quick changeovers is

FIGURE 2-1 PRODUCTION INVENTORY SYSTEM CLASSIFICATION, FOUR MAIN CLASSES

	Positioning policy: To stock	Positioning policy: To order
Process technology	*Continuous/to stock systems* Office copiers Agricultural chemicals TV sets Vacuum cleaners Calculators Wholesalers Distributors	*Continuous/to order systems* Construction equipment Buses, trucks Some chemicals Some wood and pulp products Wire and cable Textiles Some polyethylene resins Electronic components
	Intermittent/to stock systems Medical instruments Testing equipment Some steel products Electronic components Molded plastic products Spare parts	*Intermittent/to order systems* Machine tools Tools, dies Industrial equipment Nuclear pressure vessels Electronic components Military aircraft, ships Gemini project Construction projects

Reprinted with permission: Elwood S. Buffa and Jeffrey G. Miller, *Production-Inventory Systems,* Homewood, IL: Irwin, 1979, p. 9.

required for the support of intermittent manufacturing. The capability to accommodate eliminates the need for the manufacturer to stock large raw-material and component inventories.

Independent of the type of basic manufacturing technology utilized, a firm may build to inventory or to customer order. When customer orders are available before manufacturing has begun, most of the uncertainty associated with production and distribution is eliminated. Firms that produce to order can effectively exploit information-based planning systems to coordinate or time-phase the flow of inbound materials and components without fear that the planned production schedule will be disrupted by sudden variations in end-market consumption. Firms that produce to customer order are prime users of direct-distribution channel arrangements because of the high degree of certainty concerning required time and place of delivery.

In sharp contrast are firms that build to inventory by completing manufacturing in anticipation of future demand. These firms typically manufacture to forecast. The master production schedule serves to quantify a best estimate of future distribution requirements. Ideally, projected distribution requirements will be based on currently available inventory, forecast, promotional plans, and the details of any available specific customer orders.[3] However, when all is said and done, the manufacturing is

[3] For details concerning the development of a statement of distribution requirements, see Donald J. Bowersox, David J. Closs, and Omar K. Helferich, *Logistical Management,* 3d ed., New York: Macmillan, 1986, pp. 48–53.

performed to fulfill a vision of future requirements that is rarely accurate. The anticipatory nature of build-to-stock operations typically requires use of channel intermediaries as well as the support of many different specialized channel participants such as warehouse and transportation service firms. Because production and consumption are seldom perfectly matched, the elapsed time of distribution in a build-to-stock channel arrangement may span several months.

This brief introduction to manufacturing structure serves to highlight the complex nature of the overall production process that initiates or drives many channel arrangements. The specific nature of manufacturing has a great deal of impact upon the choice of which channel arrangement to use. Factors leading to the adoption of specific channel strategies are treated in Part Two. At this point the objective is to gain an appreciation of the unique issues faced by a firm that participates in a channel arrangement primarily as a product manufacturer.

Key Management Issues

While manufacturing firms face an agenda of issues related to finance, marketing, and industrial relations, attention is focused on selected topics of manufacturing that directly impact marketing channel arrangements. Two key manufacturing issues are discussed: (1) product proliferation and dynamics and (2) total-quality initiatives. Although not a comprehensive list of all channel manufacturer–related issues, these two issues are significant drivers for a typical firm in determining how channel requirements will be delineated.

Product Proliferation and Dynamics A major concern throughout industry is the rapid expansion that firms are experiencing in the number of stock-keeping units (SKUs) that they maintain in their product list. The traditional concept of new-product development is that an idea is generated and tested by marketing research in response to identification of a basic customer need. Fully understanding basic customer needs is viewed as a key to a successful new-product launch. Although this idea is sound in concept, the reality is that few firms have a highly successful new-product track record. A large number of new products fail, resulting in conflict within the distribution process and the need to remove obsolete inventory.

The product-line issue is intensified by a trend toward acceleration of product life cycles. The product life cycle is a concept that tracks a new item from introduction to obsolescence. The life-cycle model, which is useful for planning marketing and distribution strategies, is discussed in Chapter 6. The important point in terms of key manufacturing issues is the fact that average elapsed time from product inception to termination is accelerating. Because of the competitive dynamics of most industries, few products command long-term marketplace longevity. Most new ideas and product features are rapidly neutralized by competition.

Numerous examples are available from the food industry to illustrate the product-proliferation dilemma. The industry is characterized by a constant effort on the part of manufacturers to introduce new products into distribution. Many supermarkets offer the public over 10,000 different food items, which represent approximately 20 percent of those available in the channel of distribution. Retailers and wholesalers faced with a continuous deluge of new products have increasingly resorted to requiring manufacturers to sign performance agreements in which they agree to buy all unsold inventory back at the retail price if a product fails. Independent of the fairness of such agreements, the fact remains that the inventory mistakes must be cleansed from the channel.

Many critics of marketing cite the high incidence of minor package changes and slight product modifications that manufacturers institute in an effort to regenerate existing-product sales. For example, disposable-diaper manufacturers recently introduced specific products designed to accommodate basic anatomy differences of boys and girls. Without questioning the real differences or the value added by such proliferation, we still note the fact that the channel of distribution was forced to accommodate a significant expansion in overall SKUs. Nabisco Foods has been criticized for its proliferation of cookie and cracker packages that appear to offer little new in terms of product choice to the consuming public. However, to offset the critics, Nabisco can point to such product successes as Whole Wheat Triskets and Teddy Grahams, which represent highly successful new versions of old products.

The scope of proliferation is not limited to off-the-shelf consumer products. An increasing number of new-product ideas are being launched as a result of basic research and development. Whereas a few years ago only two products were available to combat high blood pressure, today dozens of alternatives are available from which prescribing physicians may select. In many situations, vendor-based research and development is driving features that ultimately become part of new products. In the automotive industry such items as nonheadlight nighttime illumination, elimination of all engine belts required to drive accessories, materials that have form and shape memory that resists denting, and environmentally toxic-free air conditioning are a few examples of technology-based development.

From the manufacturer's level in the distribution arrangement new-product frenzy is launched. Because the rate of new-product introduction is competitively driven, many manufacturers have reduced or eliminated the time traditionally devoted to market testing. Instead, they move directly into launch if the product appears to have the attributes of success. Since all new-product ideas have their champions, it is easy to see how the failure and recall rates could multiply as a result of the "throw it at the market and hope it sticks" philosophy. The sorting out of new-product mistakes is a costly channel management responsibility.

Total-Quality Initiatives   Manufacturing the right way the first time has become a key issue throughout United States industry. Once considered the world's vanguard, United States firms failed to adopt leading-edge manufacturing processes and concepts during the decade of the 1970s, during which time they relinquished leadership to such nations as West Germany and Japan. The decade of the 1980s was a period of closing the gap by bringing plant, work practices, and process up to competitive standards. Total-quality initiatives represented the primary focus of the revitalization drive.

The concept of total quality is elusively simple—do it right the first time. Embodied in this hard-to-dispute theorem are a host of practical and philosophical issues. The general concept of total quality is to focus managerial attention to three key concepts of manufacturing: people, process, and design.

Human Resources In Manufacturing The concerns of human resources essentially are the same faced through all aspects of channel management, namely, how to attract high-quality individuals to a process that has traditionally been viewed as unskilled, low-status work. The manufacturing human resource issue is captured in the following perspective of the situation:

> Somehow during the post-war years plants and the people who run them came to be regarded as second-class. A caste system grew up, separating engineering, where things are designed, from production, where things are made. Engineers kept their distance from operations people, and factories often became dead ends for people who weren't too bright.[4]

The challenge for manufacturing management is to seek ways to involve workers in the process of manufacturing to the extent that they begin to take ownership or responsibility for the outcome of the effort. Such empowerment means that the work force must be positioned to share in the risk and the rewards related to overall success of basic manufacturing strategies. Realization that meaningful involvement of people would ultimately result in producing products quicker and better was an essential step toward quality attainment.

Manufacturing Process The processes of manufacturing have changed radically to help achieve total quality. Four related process-oriented notions tend to dominate the manufacturing environment: (1) group technology, (2) statistical process control, (3) zero defects, and (4) continuous improvement. While these four concepts do not fully convey the effort to upgrade manufacturing, they are reflective of the key points of managerial emphasis.

The basic idea of *group technology* is to design overall manufacturing work flow in a manner that minimizes material handling distances, eliminates unnecessary or unproductive movement, sequences production steps to reduce required handlings, and focuses responsibility concerning who performs selected tasks in the overall process. So that group technology can be fully implemented, traditional first-line supervision is eliminated in favor of group or team leadership. Thus, process design to focus group responsibility reflects the integration of equipment layout, material handling, and procedures, and has pinpointed responsibility for high-quality performance to the level of the individual worker.

Statistical process control (SPC) is a technique used to identify and resolve potential or developing product-quality problems. It is based on measurement of trends in manufacturing variance. The implementation of SPC permits the elimination of output quality inspection. With the application of SPC comes continued monitoring of manufacturing variance to assume that each step of the process remains within tolerance. When variances begin to track toward tolerance limits, corrective action is taken and verified as part of the basic manufacturing process. As a result of continuous monitoring and correction, the cost and quality of the manufacturing process become highly predictable.

---

[4] Jeremy Main, "Manufacturing the Right Way," *Fortune,* May 21, 1990, p. 55.

The concept of *zero defects* means that there is only one acceptable way of man-ufacturing—the correct way. The correct way in modern manufacturing is to assume that all aspects of the process will be in tolerance and that total quality is essential. The managerial mind-set required to implement a zero-defect program is significantly different from one that assumes that goals will not be achieved a given percentage of the time. A program designed to do 100 percent of the time what is expected will require a far different style of management than one designed to achieve 98 percent compliance. Implementation of a successful zero-defect process means that the tra-ditional quality department can be eliminated.

Continuous improvement initiatives represent one logical conclusion of the total-quality initiative. The idea is to introduce a program to seek out and implement ways to achieve zero defects more efficiently. Manufacturing firms are reporting continuous improvement in productivity and controllable plant costs up to 40 percent per year.[5] The key to continuous improvement is to identify and implement innovative work concepts to manage productivity breakthroughs. The traditional perspective of the United States manufacturing firm has been to place two-thirds of its overall effort into product development and one-third into design of the manufacturing process. The typical Japanese and German firms reverse these ratios.[6] The traditional allocation of effort among United States firms is now being revised to assure that continuously higher levels of productivity are achieved.

Manufacturing Design   The final aspect of total quality deals with the actual design of products. The traditional product-design approach has been to follow a sequential path or development track. Each group of specialists, such as engineering or marketing, has been expected to perform specific tasks in sequence with the overall design process, progressing through steps required to ultimately bring the product into production. Thus, marketing's responsibility has been to hand off the ideal design specifications to engineering, which completes the blueprints, which are turned over to packaging, which designs the container, and so forth. Finally the product plan is given to the manufacturing people who are expected to figure out if and how the collage of ideas can be designed into a workable product. At the end of manufacturing, the completed product is turned over to the logistics group which then must begin planning for specific transportation and storage requirements. The inherent fallacy of the sequential-design approach is at least twofold.

First, sequential design is time consuming, often taking as many as three to five years to complete. For many progressive firms, time from initial idea to market has been collapsed from years to months. For example, Hewlett-Packard recently devel-oped their DeskJet printer in twenty-two months. Similar development used to require nearly four years. AT&T used to require two years to design a new phone. Their development cycle is now one year.[7] The concept of sequential or stepwise design has been replaced by a simultaneous process wherein all involved groups work

---

[5] Brian Dumaine, "Who Needs a Boss," *Fortune,* May 7, 1990, pp. 52–60.

[6] Main, op. cit., p. 56.

[7] Brian Dumaine, "How Managers Can Succeed through Speed," *Fortune,* February 13, 1989, pp. 54–59.

together to concurrently engineer a product. The ability to manage concurrent design teams has been greatly facilitated by advancements in information technology. Since information technology has radically changed many different aspects of distribution management, in-depth discussion is reserved for Chapter 12.[8]

The second problem inherent in sequential design is the vulnerability to suboptimization. If ten different groups of specialists work on parts of a design assignment individually and sequentially, with each doing their job to perfection, no guarantee exists that the combined end-product design will meet performance specifications. In fact, a specific aspect of the design, while optimal in terms of its own construction, may create operational barriers or obstacles to other critical aspects or product components. In contrast, a product designed as a result of concurrent involvement by a crossfunctional team which may include potential buyers has a far greater likelihood of satisfying all performance specifications. Finally, the end product of a simultaneous-design process tends to be simpler and better positioned for future incremental improvement.

Emerging Manufacturing Strategies

The revitalization of manufacturing has resulted in management attention being directed toward the implementation of one of two significantly different, or polar, strategies: (1) flexible and (2) focused. Each of these strategies requires a different type of channel management support. Few firms fully commit manufacturing resources to either extreme. The manufacturing strategy of most firms reflects a synthesis of the two concepts, as firms seek to align manufacturing capacity utilization with basic business objectives.

Flexible Manufacturing   With flexible manufacturing, sometimes called market-paced manufacturing, a premium is placed on being able to respond as rapidly as possible to market demand. The ideal flexible manufacturing vision is to postpone all manufacturing and purchasing until a customer or replenishment order is received. What flexible manufacturing is trying to accomplish is the elimination of producing to stock by the development of an overall system, one that is sufficiently responsive so that products can be built during normal order-cycle lead time. The result is a job-shop environment for products that have traditionally been produced in large batches into inventory. If such ideal responsiveness could be realized, the anticipatory nature of manufacturing could be reduced or even eliminated in what have traditionally been build-to-stock situations. While ideal flexibility is difficult to realize, firms committed to flexible manufacturing have made significant advances in reducing manufacturing lead time while maintaining essential economics of scale.

Significant advancements have been made in techniques of production or assembly-line changeover. Technologies and procedures have been perfected that reduce setup times for machines to minutes as contrasted to previous requirements for hours. In many situations, modular assembly or painting units can be rapidly installed in the manufacturing line to replace units scheduled for cleaning, retooling, or preventive

[8] See Chapter 12, pp. 390–392.

maintenance. These essential tasks are performed off-line, thereby significantly reducing downtime.

A second aspect of flexible manufacturing is reduced production-run length. Short runs or small lot sizes mean that manufacturing processes need to achieve lowest-cost-per-unit status more quickly and on less volume than traditional manufacturing. In some situations, the absolute lowest cost per unit of potential manufacturing must be sacrificed so that the desired flexibility can be achieved. In such situations that support higher-cost manufacturers, the trade-off is between the cost per unit of production and the expense and risk associated with maintaining large inventories. A basic concept of flexible manufacturing is that the benefits of responsiveness and reduced inventory risk gained from small production-lot sizes increase operational agility.

In summary, the goal of flexible manufacturing is to increase responsiveness. Having the capability to manufacture what is needed reduces the amount of inventory that must be committed in anticipation of future demand, increases the likelihood of having the exact items requested by customers, and can significantly reduce obsolescence. Carried to its extreme, flexible manufacturing has the potential to transform a traditional built-to-stock situation into a made-to-order one. The operational trick is to develop flexible capabilities without losing critical economy of scale while maintaining total-quality control.

Focused Manufacturing   Contrasted with the flexible vision is the concept of focused manufacturing. Whereas flexible manufacturing tends to favor small-scale decentralized or market-positioned manufacturing and assembly, focused manufacturing has as its goal the highest possible level of capacity utilization. So that a focused factory strategy can be fully implemented, manufacturing is typically concentrated into a limited number of production facilities or even a single one. For example, all feminine hygiene products produced by Kimberly-Clark are concentrated in one multiple-line state-of-the-art manufacturing facility. While such concentration increases risk of damage from natural disasters and requires significant logistic support to service an entire market area from a single location, the compensating benefits are twofold.

First, focused manufacturing allows adoption of the most advanced manufacturing technology. Because of concentration of volume into a limited number of manufacturing plants, the most advanced technology can be adopted and continuously updated. The benefits of concentration extend to having the critical mass to adopt the most sophisticated support equipment such as automated process-control technology. The vision of the focused factory is to create the potential for a firm to be a low-cost producer in its industry.

The second benefit of focused manufacturing is capacity utilization. With concentration of all requirements into limited facilities, the goal of the maximum level of rated output can be achieved. The typical focused factory operates seven days per week around the clock. Prior to development of the focused manufacturing concept, such high-intensity capacity utilization was only considered feasible in continuous-process industries such as chemical and paper manufacturing and metal processing. Traditional continuous processing required long setup times and substantial volume throughput for the realization of lowest unit production cost. Newer concepts of focused manufacturing seek to achieve absolute low cost per unit and zero-defect quality of output in situations that have not traditionally been continuous-process.

In summary, the goal of focused manufacturing is lowest possible per-unit cost and fail-safe quality. The basic idea is to adopt leading-edge manufacturing technology and utilize it to maximum capacity. In the situation of focused manufacturing the trade-off is to build inventory as necessary in order to achieve maximum manufacturing efficiency. In situations where demand for a product varies seasonally or for some other reason, focused manufacturing will require building significant inventories in anticipation of future sales. The operational trick is to plan manufacturing schedules to keep anticipatory inventories balanced to market demand.

Conclusion: Manufacturing

The manufacturing sector of the United States economy underwent radical change during the 1980s. Such change is projected to continue into the 1990s as United States firms seek to establish a manufacturing capability that is competitive in the world economy. Because manufacturers are key participants in channel arrangements, it is logical that the significant change they are undergoing will transcend the entire value-added chain impacting wholesalers, retailers, and specialized-service companies.

In summary, basic manufacturing is changing in two fundamental ways. First, the basic culture of manufacturing is being radically altered to more effectively align resources to meet rapidly changing requirements of customers. Table 2-2 provides a summary of the basic changes in traditional manufacturing philosophy that firms are

TABLE 2-2   TWO WAYS OF MAKING THINGS

The lean system	The rigid system
Can be profitable making small batches of products	Profitable only when making large batches.
The product and the process for making it are designed concurrently.	The process is designed after the product has been designed.
The lean inventory turns over fast.	The fat inventory turns over slowly.
Suppliers are helped, informed, and kept close.	Suppliers are kept at arm's length.
Engineers search widely for ideas and technology.	Engineers are insular, don't welcome outside ideas.
Employees learn several skills, work well in teams.	Employees are compartmentalized.
The company stresses continuous small improvements.	The company looks for the big breakthroughs.
The customers' orders pull the products through the factor.	The system pushes products through to the customers.

Source: Modified and adopted from Jeremy Main, "Manufacturing The Right Way," *Fortune,* May 21, 1990, p. 60. Copyright © 1990 The Time Inc. Magazine Company. All rights reserved.

undergoing. It is logical that such fundamental change will significantly modify a firm's traditional posture with respect to channel alliances.

Second, there is a basic change in how a firm approaches the task of building things. Modern concepts of manufacturing seek to involve employees at all levels of the organization to effect process improvement and to take initiatives related to customer service. Manufacturers, because of the nature of their brand products, are typically held responsible for performance of the entire marketing channel. Both consumers and channel trading partners expect manufacturers to maintain high-quality standards. Manufacturers have responded by radical changes in how they go about the process of manufacturing in an effort to gain and maintain total-quality status.

It is clear that with emerging manufacturing strategies a premium is placed on gaining and maintaining customers' satisfaction through speed and quality. These strategies are designed so that technologies to achieve greater efficiency can be sought at the same time that total cost can be lowered in an effort to improve value. What is not fully clear is how these rapidly changing manufacturing strategies will ultimately impact the design and operations of final-product channels; nor is it clear how they will impact the process by which materials and components required in the manufacturing processes are supplied.

WHOLESALING

Wholesale trade is defined by the Bureau of the Census as "all establishments or places of business primarily engaged in selling merchandise to retailers; to industrial, commercial, institutional, or professional users; or to other wholesalers; or acting as agents in buying merchandise for or selling merchandise to such persons or companies."[9]

Wholesale Structure

In 1987, total sales by wholesalers in the United States exceeded $2.5 trillion and involved 466,000 separate establishments employing over 5.5 million people. Table 2-3 presents comparative wholesale statistics for 1982 and 1987, categorized by major product sold. It is important to understand that there are many different types of wholesalers, all of which differ in product categories handled as well as in specific marketing functions performed. Generally, three basic types of wholesale establishments can be identified: merchant wholesalers, merchandise agents, and establishments owned and operated by manufacturers. Within these three categories there are also important subcategories. Table 2-3 illustrates sales achieved by merchant wholesalers and by other types of wholesale establishment.

Merchant Wholesalers   Merchant wholesalers are the backbone of the wholesale structure. They are the primary institutions that buy and sell merchandise among

[9] *Wholesaling in Marketing Organization,* David A. Revzan, Wiley, 1961, pp. 16–17.

TABLE 2-3 WHOLESALE TRADE—BY TYPE OF OPERATION AND KIND OF BUSINESS: 1982 AND 1987

Type of operation and kind of business	Establishments (1000)		Sales (mil. $)	
	1982	1987	1982	1987
Wholesale trade	435.1	466.7	1,997,895	2,523,688
Merchant wholesalers	353.1	388.1	1,159,334	1,477,132
Other operating types	82.1	78.6	838,561	1,046,557
Durable goods	267.4	292.8	881,212	1,258,483
Motor vehicles, automotive equipment	41.1	43.0	187,607	(NA)
Furniture, home furnishings	13.1	14.5	32,452	48,123
Lumber, construction materials	17.9	19.1	50,694	79,946
Sporting, recreational, photographic goods	7.6	8.9	26,980	40,965
Metals and minerals, except petroleum	10.6	11.1	102,690	114,528
Electrical goods	30.4	35.3	120,062	(NA)
Hardware, plumbing, heating equipment	21.6	23.1	43,529	57,126
Machinery, equipment, supplies	103.4	114.4	263,309	336,976
Miscellaneous	21.7	23.4	53,889	75,506
Nondurable goods	167.8	173.9	1,116,683	1,265,205
Paper, paper products	14.5	16.8	53,493	83,173
Drugs, drug proprietaries	4.0	4.9	33,987	64,280
Apparel, piece goods, notions	15.0	16.9	55,897	81,476
Groceries and related products	40.4	42.1	288,659	380,945
Farm-product raw materials	14.4	12.6	153,419	117,606
Chemicals, allied products	11.2	12.7	76,103	94,620
Petroleum, petroleum products	20.3	16.7	296,995	234,874
Beer, wines, distilled alcoholic beverages	6.7	5.8	42,122	49,433
Miscellaneous	41.2	45.3	116,008	158,800

Source: U.S. Bureau of the Census, *Census of Wholesale Trade, 1982*, Geographic Area Series, WC82-A-52, and *1987*, Geographic Area Series WC87-A-52.

manufacturers and retailers. The distinguishing feature of merchant wholesalers is that they take ownership and associated risk related to the goods in which they trade. Merchant wholesalers accounted for over 80 percent of all wholesale firms in 1987 and were responsible for about 58 percent of sales volume (Table 2-3). The percentage of wholesale volume that moves through merchant wholesalers has been steadily increasing for over forty years.

The most common type of merchant wholesaler is the *full-function* or *full-service* merchant. This type of wholesaler is also often referred to as a distributor or jobber. As the name implies, full-function wholesalers typically perform a broad range of marketing functions in the value-added distribution process of the channel in which they operate as intermediaries. They assume risk as a result of purchasing inventory, and they typically provide storage and transportation, maintain a sales force to service retail or industrial accounts, provide financing through the extension of customer credit, and disseminate market information to both manufacturers whose products they sell and retailers whom they service.

In addition to the full-function merchant wholesaler, there are also numerous specialized firms that perform a unique combination of services. The following paragraphs review some of the more significant "limited-function" or "limited-service" merchant wholesalers.

Rack merchandisers specialize in handling all aspects of distribution, from the manufacturer to placement of merchandise on display racks or shelves, which they provide to retail customers. Frequently, rack merchandisers sell on a consignment basis to retailers, only charging for items the retailers sell to customers. This form of specialized wholesaler is frequently used by grocery stores and convenience markets for nonfood items such as pet products, housewares, toys, games, books, and magazines.

Cash-and-carry wholesalers, as the name implies, typically do not provide customer credit or delivery. Once thought to be a vanishing form of wholesaling, growth has been restimulated through the establishment of such firms as Costco, Price Club, Office Max, and Sam's Club. Although the primary customers who patronize these companies are individual consumers, over 50 percent of the company's sales are made to small businesses for resale or to businesses purchasing office and operating supplies.

Wagon, or truck, distributors, are firms that sell an assortment of merchandise from stock carried on board vehicles. This form of wholesaler combines the functions of sales and delivery using a driver representative. Generally, truck distributors offer a limited assortment of well-known, fast-moving items. Among the better known truck distributors in industrial markets is Snap-On Tools, which provides service stations, garages, and other similar locations with high-quality work tools for mechanics.

Drop shippers typically sell bulky commodities such as lumber and building materials. They arrange for direct shipment from manufacturers to retailers, thereby avoiding the need for physical possession and intermediate storage. This type of wholesaler typically takes ownership of the merchandise, thereby becoming at risk during the distribution process.

Mail-order wholesalers typically perform the full range of merchant wholesaler marketing functions except personal selling. Catalogs featuring the wholesaler's product lines are provided for industrial or retail customers who typically place orders by telephone or mail. While a relatively small portion of wholesale firms are purely mail order, many full-function merchant wholesalers provide some sort of mail-order service for smaller customers.

Terminal grain elevators are establishments that purchase grain or other agricultural products from farm assemblers, which they store and resell to such commercial firms as flour millers, distillers, brewers, and exporters. Frequently, terminal wholesalers perform other services such as grading, mixing, and drying during storage. While small in number, these firms are among the largest of all merchant wholesalers.

Merchandise Agents   Merchandise agents are wholesalers who perform selected marketing functions while buying and selling for other firms. They typically negotiate sales as representatives of other firms and do not take title to merchandise. In actual practice, there is considerable vagueness and overlapping of terminology, so that it is often difficult to distinguish one type of merchandise agent from another. This category of wholesaler is extremely important to channel operations. In total, over 42,000 firms function as merchandise wholesale agents. Traditional definitions are provided below.

Manufacturers' agents function as the sales force for manufacturers whose products they represent. The typical manufacturer's agent operates in a limited geographic territory and represents several complementary but noncompeting product lines. Although manufacturers' agents sometimes maintain warehouses in which manufacturers consign products, they typically serve as the intermediaries who obtain customers' orders that are passed to manufacturers for processing and delivery.

Selling agents are similar to manufacturers' agents, but they generally assume more responsibility and perform a broader range of functions for their clients. Selling agents often serve as their clients' entire marketing department. The typical manufacturer contracts to sell all or the majority of planned production through one selling agent; that agent, in turn, is positioned to exercise considerable authority over price and terms of sale. In some industries, such as industrial equipment and raw materials, the relationship between the agent and supplier is long-term and continuous. In other industries, such as fashion, the relationship is generally limited to one year or may even be restricted to a single selling season.

Brokers are wholesalers whose primary activity is to establish contacts between buyers and sellers. They negotiate and facilitate sales and are compensated by a fee or commission. They do not take title or possession of merchandise.

Commission merchants receive products on consignment and negotiate sales in their own names. They typically operate on an autonomous basis. They frequently also offer credit and may provide value-added services such as specialized packaging. Commission merchants are most often used in distribution channels for farm produce, textiles, and lumber products, where the manufacturers' identity is relatively unimportant to buyers.

Commercial auction companies operate facilities for exchange of such products as livestock and used automobiles. Their participation in a channel is typically limited to facilitating an ownership transfer.

Export-import agents facilitate international exchange by either buying or selling products for their clients and providing advice on shipping, tariffs, customs, and financing. Their role is more fully explored in Chapter 13.[10]

Purchasing agents are firms that specialize in representing buyers, generally for a limited number of clients for a limited set of products. Typically, they are specialists in particular industries that can offer the firms they represent a quality of expertise that could not be maintained in-house.

Manufacturers' Sales Branches and Sales Offices Functioning like a merchant wholesaler, a sales branch intermediary is distinguished by the fact that it is owned by a manufacturer and maintained separately from the producing plant to sell and market its products. The sales branch includes a warehouse with inventory, whereas

---

[10] See Chapter 13, pp. 413–414.

sales offices do not. Manufacturers' branch stores selling to consumers and individual users are classified within retail trade.

Key Management Issues

Each wholesaler has to determine a unique business strategy that defines the niche it wants to fill in the overall channel process. One of the most fundamental decisions concerns the wholesale role it intends to perform. This role will identify the product assortment and functional service that it will offer participating manufacturers and retailers. As far as product assortment is concerned, the decision can range from complete specialization (carrying only nuts and bolts) to a broad general line within a product group (carrying a complete line of hardware). The strategy could be to cut across commodity groupings in an unorthodox manner. Similarly, decisions can range from complete performance of all functions and their component elements to highly streamlined or specialized functional arrangements.

Building on basic functional and product-assortment decisions, each wholesaler must seek to arrange operational capabilities in a manner that will position it as the preferred supplier. The service package offered by a wholesaler is the main way it gains a differential competitive advantage. Other key management issues include a wholesaler's geographic decisions with respect to the extent of the market to serve (national, regional, state, etc.) and the choice of location.

The range of differences in wholesale strategy is illustrated by review of two food wholesalers.[11] Super Value stores distribute food and general merchandise through both corporate-owned and independent retail stores. Super Value carries both private-label and manufacturer's-label products, which are sold to over 3000 stores in thirty-three states. With twenty warehouse facilities throughout the country, Super Value has a total sales volume of over $10 billion.

First World Cheese markets and distributes brand cheese and specialty foods to the delicatessen section of supermarkets. Cheeses are purchased from independent manufacturers and marketed under the company's proprietary trademark. The company also produces private-label cheese for retailers located in the western United States. Additionally, the company purchases and distributes a line of cheeses to the food-service industry on a nationwide basis. Sales volume for 1988 was $72 million.

The two firms, both of them wholesalers in the food business, have established different strategies for product assortments chosen, functions performed, and geographic locations covered. Nevertheless, each has combined a unique set of managerial decisions, which has resulted in highly profitable operations.

Emerging Wholesale Strategies

To remain viable in an increasingly competitive environment, wholesalers have come up with several strategies for continued success. Some of the more important of these are discussed.[12]

---

[11] This discussion is adapted from Bert C. McCammon, Jr., *Wholesaling in Transition: An Executive Chartbook,* 1990, University of Oklahoma, Norman, OK: Distribution Research Program, pp. 20–25.
[12] Ibid.

Proprietary Brands Virtually all successful wholesalers have developed strong proprietary brand products as one aspect of gaining and maintaining a sustained competitive advantage. W.W. Grainger, which distributes electrical equipment and tools to commercial and industrial markets, achieves over 50 percent of total sales from proprietary brands. Inmac Corporation, which sells computer supplies and accessories to businesses, enjoys over 90 percent of its sales from Inmac brand products.

International Expansion Wholesalers, like other organizations, are becoming more aggressive about expanding operations into international markets. Snap-On Tools distributes more than 12,000 different hand tools, electronic products, and tool storage units to professional mechanics throughout the world. Foreign operations account for almost 18 percent of Snap-On's $850 million in revenue. All indications are that international expansion will continue as leading wholesalers enter joint ventures and marketing alliances to penetrate foreign markets.

Value-Added Services Wholesalers are constantly striving to find value-added services to expand margins and strengthen relationships with key customers. For example, United Stationery is the largest distributor of office equipment and supplies in the United States. It has developed specialized pricing and merchandising programs for office supply dealers to support aggressive competition against office supply superstores and warehouse membership stores. Bergen Brunswig, in the drug wholesale industry, has developed value-added services for independent pharmacies which include modular merchandising programs and computerized information systems. Bergen Brunswig's value-added service strategies are described in detail in the case at the end of this part entitled "A Tale of Two Wholesalers."

Niche Marketing Some wholesalers are enjoying substantial success by perusing niche marketing strategies that specialize in limited or unique product categories. Richardson Electronics, for example, is a specialized distributor of electron tubes and semiconductors which describes itself as being on the "trailing edge of technology." Specifically, the firm stocks and distributes replacement parts for technologically obsolete equipment that is still being used by a wide range of manufacturing firms.

New Technology New technology in wholesale distribution involves the development of online order-entry systems, advanced inventory management systems, mechanization and automation of warehouses, and other computer device applications, which streamlines operations and strengthens relations with both customers and suppliers. Computer-to-computer linkages with both sides of the distribution channel are increasingly common as application of new technology becomes a prerequisite for success in wholesale trade.

Conclusion: Wholesaling

Similar to manufacturing, the wholesale sector of the United States economy underwent radical change in the 1980s. Wholesalers do not have a great deal of visibility in the eyes of the consuming public, because they operate as intermediaries between manufacturers and retailers. The sales of wholesalers are large, accounting for over $2.5 trillion in 1987. This activity far exceeds the level of retail sales because many products are sold a number of times from the time they were first manufactured until they are finally sold to retailers or end users. To expand their role in the distribution process, wholesalers are actively pursuing strategies of broader assortments of proprietary brands, expansion into international markets, a broader range of value-added services, increased focus on niche markets, and the adoption of new technology. All evidence suggests that the *new-breed* wholesaler of the 1980s will continue to be a prime-time player in the distribution arrangements of the 1990s and beyond.

RETAILING

In simplest terms, retailing is the business of selling goods and services to the consuming public for their own use and benefit. Because of this relationship to the consuming public, there are many similarities among all types of retailers. The range of functions performed by retailers combine to satisfy five basic consumer rights: having the right merchandise, at the right place, at the right time, at the right price, and in the right quantities. However, it is misleading to think of all retailers as the same. The retail structure of the United States is actually a composite of many diverse types of businesses. Following an examination of retail structure, we will focus attention on key management issues of retailing. The section concludes with a discussion of emerging retail strategies that have important implications for distribution channel management.

Retail Structure

In 1987, the 1.5 million retail establishments in the United States had sales approaching $1.5 trillion. Table 2-4 provides sales data by store type. This specific retail classification is used because it is the most common format utilized by the U.S. Bureau of the Census and other organizations that specialize in collecting and analyzing retailing data. One shortcoming of the broad grouping of stores is that the data tends to obscure many important retail classifications. The Bureau of the Census classifies a store on the basis of the major merchandise category sold. However, included in the sales volume of that store may be many other nonrelated or loosely related merchandise groups. For example, there are few supermarkets in the United States today that limit their product assortment to food. The typical food store also sells health and beauty aids, women's hosiery, and housewares, and may even offer for sale such items as hardware, clothing, and toys. The process of scrambled merchandising, whereby retailers in a particular store type and different and unrelated merchandise groups, may make it difficult to classify sales data for any particular store category.

Key Management Issues

Retail management involves the translation of the business mission objectives and strategies into a specific operating profile. The retailing mix consists of all of those

TABLE 2-4   RETAIL TRADE BY NUMBER AND SALES: 1982 AND 1987

1972 SIC code	Kind of Business	Establish-ments (1000)		Sales (mil. $)	
		1982	1987	1982	1987
	Total retail trade	1,425	1,506	123,619	177,708
52	Building materials and garden supplies stores	70	74	49,939	81,487
53	General merchandise stores	36	35	124,066	181,147
54	Food stores	190	191	240,520	301,847
55	Automotive dealers	221	218	284,396	435,417
56	Apparel and accessory stores	141	149	54,622	77,391
57	Furniture and home furnishings stores	100	110	45,314	74,783
58	Eating and drinking places	352	391	101,723	148,776
59	Miscellaneous retail stores	316	338	138,449	193,264

Source: U.S. Bureau of the Census, *1987 Census of Retail Trade*, RC87-A-52.

variables that are directly under the control of the manager. Managers must make logical decisions with respect to each component of the retail mix so that they fit together to create a consistent and desirable image in the minds of target consumers. Each retail firm develops its own strategic profile by mixing these elements to create a unique method of presenting products to target consumers.

Merchandise   The component of the retail mix that is most obvious to consumers is the merchandise variety. The investment in merchandise and the resulting inventory risk assumed by retailers is substantial. In fact, investigation of a typical retailer's balance sheet will reveal that over 50 percent of all asset investment is represented by inventory. The types or varieties of merchandise carried by a store serve to limit the kinds of consumer needs and wants that a store seeks to satisfy. Closely related to variety are decisions concerning assortment. For any one product line, the retailer must decide how many brands, colors, styles, sizes, and so on, to carry. Likewise, decisions are required concerning how many units of each item to stock. Merchandising decisions are not limited to only product varieties and assortments. Choices also must be made concerning the quality, fashion, and supply sources. Finally, the retailer must develop a negotiation strategy to follow in dealing with suppliers to ensure favorable terms.

Price   The second critical element of the retail mix is price. Decisions concerning price are closely related to those concerning merchandise assortments and related services. For the facilitation of successful retailing, decisions are required regarding the various price lines to be carried and overall markdown or sale policies. Some retailers, such as New York Carpet World, follow a strategy on continuous price promotion. Other retailers follow a more traditional practice of limiting sales to specific times of the year.

Store Atmosphere   The internal environment of a store has a major impact on customers and the overall efficiency of operations. Some of the decisions concerning internal atmosphere are related to space utilization. Decisions regarding selling versus nonselling (offices and storage) space must be reached as well as the amount of space devoted to aisles and open areas. Space must also be allocated to various products and departments. General layout designs must be evaluated. Display equipment must be chosen. There are, however, some more artistic considerations in the creation of store atmosphere. For example, lighting, different colors, floor and wall coverings, and methods of merchandise presentation have a direct impact on the mood and behavior of customers while in the store.

Communication   In a broad sense, all retail decisions ultimately communicate something about the store to its customers. In a specific context, communication involves traditional marketing tools such as advertising, personal selling, promotion, and public relations. Communication strategies must be planned, objectives established, and budgets determined and allocated to communication formats, media, and merchandise categories. The use of personal selling or self-service approaches to dealing with consumers must be evaluated. A wide range of promotional devices are available to stimulate specific purchase patterns by consumers.

Services   To support retail operations there are an infinite number of services that can be offered to potential customers, depending upon their appeal and the desired retailer image. One major service is retail credit. The decision to offer credit requires a range of additional policy decisions such as Who should it be offered to? and Should it be offered in the form of a proprietary or an independent charge plan? Other important services to be considered are delivery, alterations, guarantees, and check cashing, which are ancillary to the main purpose of the retail store.

Logistics   Logistic operations are not highly visible to retail customers. However, the smooth functioning of a retail store is dependent upon the physical flow of products from manufacturers and wholesalers. Many retailers operate their own distribution centers to ensure continuous efficient supply. As such, ultimate-customer satisfaction is largely determined by the logistic competency of retail operations. Decisions are required concerning distribution centers, inventory, transportation, and materials handling. As noted above, retailing logistics may extend to consumer delivery as a key service.

Location   No single decision in the retail mix is more critical than the choice of location. Once sites are selected and operations are committed, it is extremely difficult to relocate a store. Retail management must choose the trade area or areas in which stores will be located. Such decisions often establish the fundamental direction that a firm will ultimately follow. For example, Wal-Mart's rapid growth has centered around a strategy of building in medium-size communities that are not the primary trading centers of their market areas. In a broader sense, decisions are required concerning the type of location and whether it should be downtown, in a shopping center, or free standing.

Emerging Retail Strategies

Because it is difficult to categorize retailers solely by one type of merchandise they carry, it is useful to view store types in terms of their basic strategy mix. Table 2-5 presents two extreme polar strategic alternatives: low-end and high-end. Within any merchandise category, it is generally possible to identify specific firms that pursue the two extremes. There are usually an assortment of firms that attempt to operate between the two extremes. For example, in general-merchandise retailing, department stores such as Macy's or Dayton Hudson feature merchandise having moderately to extremely good quality. They also provide significant sales assistance, credit, delivery, and other services in a store atmosphere that is spacious and visually appealing. Most full-line discounters such as K mart or Target offer similar merchandise categories but they typically have popular brands of average quality, fewer support services, lower prices, and a less sophisticated store atmosphere.

Supermarkets provide a further example of a differential retail strategy. The Bureau of the Census identifies six different supermarket store categories. A *conventional* supermarket is a departmentalized store offering a wide variety of food and food-related products. Sales of general merchandise is quite limited in a conventional store.

TABLE 2-5 RETAIL STRATEGY MIX ALTERNATIVES

Low-end strategy	High-end strategy
Low rental location, side street	High rental shopping center or central business district location

No services or services charged at additional fee (or service may be limited to credit and returns)	Elaborate services available included in price, such as:
	  alterations decorating
	  credit gift-wrapping
	  delivery layaways

Spartan fixtures and displays	Elaborate fixtures and displays
Simple retail personnel organization	Elaborate retail personnel organization
Price emphasis in promotion	No price emphasis in promotion
Self-service or high sales per store personnel ratio	Product demonstrations, low sales per store personnel ratio
Crowded store interior	Spacious store interior
Most merchandise visible	Most merchandise in back room

Source: Barry Berman and Joel R. Evans, *Retail Management: A Strategic Approach*, p. 95. Reprinted with permission of Macmillan Publishing Company. Copyright © 1989 by Macmillan Publishing Company.

A *superstore* offers a wider variety of products than a conventional supermarket and devotes considerable space to nonfood or general merchandise. *Warehouse* stores typically offer limited product variety and few, if any, services. Products are generally displayed in manufacturers' cases in a no-frills setting. *Combination* stores combine two forms of conventional retailing such as supermarkets and drugstores within one facility. A *superwarehouse* is simply an expanded warehouse store that includes meat, delicatessen, and/or seafood departments and greater product variety. *Hypermarkets* are extremely large stores that offer a wide assortment of general merchandise in addition to the full-line grocery departments.

Although the number of retail outlets in the United States has not changed dramatically over the past several decades, there have been major shifts in type of operations within the overall retail structure, as the data presented in Table 2-6 clearly illustrates. Some outlets, such as conventional supermarkets, have declined dramatically while other types, such as superstores, have increased in significance. Retailers are constantly searching for a new retail-mix combination that they can package as innovative strategies to gain greater consumer acceptance and competitive advantage. Some of the more prevalent of these innovative strategies are discussed in the following sections.

Superspecialty Strategy   Superspecialty stores are generally small in size and very narrow in merchandise-line offering. Their strategy revolves around meeting customers' needs in one of two ways: (1) offering a broad, deep selection within a very limited product category, or (2) catering to very narrowly defined market segments.

The Sock Shop and Home Depot are two examples of companies that have chosen a superspecialist strategy based on a limited product category. The Sock Shop, for

TABLE 2-6   SUPERMARKETS—NUMBER AND SALES BY TYPE: 1980 TO 1988

Supermarket format	Number				Sales (bil. $)			
	1980	1984	1986	1988	1980	1984	1986	1988
Supermarkets, total	26,321	26,947	27,005	26,300	157.0	192.8	210.5	230.9
Conventional	21,009	17,644	17,169	15,590	114.7	95.8	99.8	98.8
Superstore	3,150	4,608	4,994	5,600	27.8	54.6	57.9	69.5
Warehouse	1,670	3,584	3,332	3,375	6.6	22.9	25.9	28.8
Combination food and drug	475	943	1,133	1,250	6.3	15.4	16.8	19.9
Super-warehouse	7	108	297	375	1.6	3.3	6.7	3.9
Hypermarket	10	60	80	110	(NA)*	.8	3.4	5.0

* Not available

Source: U.S. Department of Agriculture, Economic Research Service, *Food Marketing Review*, annual.

example, stocks several thousand different types of socks and hosiery, emphasizing new styles and designs in very small outlets. In contrast, Home Depot specifically targets the do-it-yourself market with a broad range of products. According to the chain's founder,

> In some cases we have 25,000 to 30,000 people walking through a store in a week, 50 percent of whom are women. We could sell them anything. If we wanted to put pantyhose up at the front register, we'd sell a fortune in pantyhose. But we don't. We don't want the customer to think we're a discounter, a food store, a toy store, or anything else. The perception of customers always has to be, when they think of a do-it-yourself project, they think of Home Depot.[13]

Mass Merchandising   While some retailers will follow a "superspecialist" strategy, others select the opposite approach. As consumers continue to place high value on convenience and time saving in shopping, very large stores that combine apparel, household items, electronics, hard goods, and, in some cases, food continue to grow. Wal-Mart, K mart, and Meijer are three examples of firms successfully pursuing this strategy.

Discounting Strategies   While not new, discounting as a strategy continues to grow, often in combination with other retail strategies. For example, warehouse stores such as Price Club and Sam's Club are staking powerful claims to a significant share of the retail market. These stores feature many merchandise categories but restrict assortments within a category. Because of high average transactions, such discounters achieve high rates of return as a result of high inventory turnover velocity and asset utilization.

In fact, at least two distinct approaches to discounting have emerged. One approach features frequent promotions and reduced-price "sales" in the store. Another approach, known as the "everyday low price" approach, features a consistent day in, day out low price but few promotions or "sale" events. Wal-Mart has been the modern-day pioneer of the latter approach and has caused other retailers to rethink their traditional pricing practices.

Focused Service   Driving the success of a number of retailers is an increased emphasis on customer service. The key to this strategy is defining service in terms that are meaningful to a particular group of customers. Nordstrom's, a high-quality department store, is widely known for its outstanding sales staff that offers personalized shopping. To satisfy customers, Nordstrom's staff has been known to deliver products to customers in their personal cars. L.L. Bean, a national mail-order retailer, is renowned for its product quality, rapid delivery, and money-back guarantees. The specific services offered may differ by retailing format, but the service focus strategy

---

[13] Susan Campiniti, "The New Champs of Retailing," *Fortune,* September 24, 1990, pp. 86–90.

has been successful for many firms that have determined characteristics leading to customer satisfaction and have provided them consistently.

Direct Retailing   Direct retailing includes the traditional mail-order business as well as telephone shopping, vending, and the more recent electronic formats such as television's *Home Shopping Network*. The consumer's increasing desire for convenience is at the root of the success of direct retailing. Direct retailing is, in fact, the most rapidly growing segment of all retail forms. Such companies as L.L. Bean, Land's End, Eddie Bauer, and Horchow have experienced rapid growth by offering guarantees and excellent service, which were neglected by many of the initial direct-retail firms.

Increased Emphasis on Supplier Relationships   Underlying all of the above strategies is a major change in the manner in which successful retailers manage their relationships with suppliers. There are increasing examples of closer communications with suppliers through computer-to-computer linkages, partnershipping to develop operating efficiencies and improve inventory flow, and rationalization of product assortments through such techniques as direct product profitability (DPP) analysis. J.C. Penney, for example, is pushing supply-based technology into their retail stores. Direct satellite transmission allows trends in retail sales to be rapidly communicated to buyers who, in turn, may be directly hooked into suppliers via an electronic ordering system. At Dillard department stores, electronic systems allow stores to be restocked within a week, as opposed to the several weeks experienced by most other stores.

Conclusion: Retailing

Retailing, like wholesaling and manufacturing, is constantly changing as individual firms seek to exploit new and different ways to appeal to consumers. The retailer represents the final link in the distribution channel in which merchandise is sold to consumers. In total, over 1.5 million retail establishments in the United States have combined annual sales in excess of $1.5 trillion. Most visible retailing is conducted from stores that offer consumers instant access to inventory. However, one of the fastest-growing forms of retailing is direct selling, which typically is conducted without the support of traditional stores. The most visible forms of retail strategies are superspecialty stores, mass merchandising, new forms of discounting, focused service, and direct retailing. Each of these strategies builds upon a unique retail mix to gain customer appeal and support.

SUMMARY

Primary channel participants are those institutions that acknowledge their dependence upon one another and assume risk in the value-added process. Typically classified as manufacturers, wholesalers, or retailers, the primary channel participants face many issues; the emerging strategies for dealing with these issues have been the focus of this chapter.

Over 359,000 firms in the United States are engaged in manufacturing. Manufacturing structure can be viewed in terms of basic production processes and the degree to which firms produce products in anticipation of sales. Each of these characteristics has a direct impact on channel requirements. Production processes can be classified as continuous or intermittent. Additionally, some firms produce after a customer's commitment has been obtained, while others produce in anticipation or to stock. Key issues in manufacturing management include product proliferation, total-quality initiatives, and emerging strategies of flexible versus focused manufacturing. Resolution of these issues is resulting in new strategies that place a premium on achieving customer satisfaction through speed and quality.

Wholesaling is accomplished by over 466,000 firms in the United States, each of which can be categorized according to its participation in marketing functions. Merchant wholesalers take title to the goods they distribute, whereas agent wholesalers perform their services without owning inventory. Manufacturers' branches represent a third basic form of wholesaling. While there are many subcategories of wholesale activity, the key management issues focus on the product responsibilities and functional services provided. Important new strategies in wholesaling include proprietary brands, international expansion, value-added services, niche marketing, and adoption of new technologies.

Retail structure in the United States involves over 1.5 million retail establishments. Retail managers make decisions regarding merchandise assortments, pricing, store atmosphere, communications, services, logistics, and location in an effort to achieve a differential strategy appealing to specific target markets. Among the more pervasive strategies being employed in the 1980s and 1990s are superspecialization, mass merchandising, discounting, increased service emphasis, direct retailing, and emphasis on supplier relationships. Attention is next directed to a review of specialized service suppliers.

QUESTIONS

1 Who are the major manufacturers in your local area? What types of products do they produce? Classify their processes as continuous or intermittent. Do they produce for stock or do they produce to order? How do these processes impact the channels needed to complete distribution of these products to end users or consumers?

2 Discuss reasons why manufacturers are highly visible members of the trading channel. Why are some not so visible?

3 How does the risk related to inventory compare among manufacturers, wholesalers, and retailers in a typical channel?

4 Discuss the role of a manufacturer's supplier base in terms of supporting quick changeover requirements.

5 Is the concept of total quality primarily a manufacturing concern? How can the concept be translated into wholesaling and retailing terms?

6 Contact two local wholesalers. How do they differ in terms of functions performed and

product assortments? Is there evidence that they are adopting any of the "emerging strategies" mentioned in the chapter?

7 Illustrate and discuss value-added services that can be provided by wholesalers.

8 Proprietary branding is important in both wholesaling and retailing. What are the risks associated in extensive private labeling?

9 Why do wholesale sales far exceed retail sales during any time period?

10 Research the food outlets in your local area and classify them as conventional supermarkets, superstores, or warehouse stores. What specific differences in merchandise assortments, space utilization, pricing, and other retail-mix variables can you identify?

11 What products have you purchased from direct retailers? In your class, take a survey of direct-retail purchases during the past year. What merchandise categories have been most frequently purchased? How would you explain this situation?

12 In a retail sense, discuss the strategy of focused service.

CHAPTER 3

SPECIALIZED PARTICIPANTS

CHAPTER OUTLINE

CHANGING NATURE OF SPECIALIZED SERVICE PROVIDERS
Economic Justification
Risk Involvement
Concentration and Alliances
Service Specialist Leadership
Conclusions: Specialized Service Providers
CLASSIFICATION OF SPECIALIZED SERVICE PROVIDERS
Functional Specialist
Support Specialist
FUNCTIONAL SERVICE PROVIDERS
Transportation
Warehousing
Assembly
Fulfillment
Sequencing
Merchandising
Conclusion: Functional Service Providers
SUPPORT SERVICE PROVIDERS
Financial
Information
Advertising
Insurance
Advisory/Research
Arrangers
Conclusion: Support Service Providers
EXTENSION OF CHANNEL PARTICIPANTS
Integrated Service Providers
Consumers as Channel Participants
SUMMARY

In Chapter 2 primary channel participants were discussed in detail. Primary channel participants were identified by their role in the typical distribution channel arrangement. Manufacturers, wholesalers, and retailers were introduced as the primary institutions participating in product-ownership transfer. The primary institutions, in their varied forms, are positioned as the prime risk takers in the channel. Most of the risk traditionally associated with primary channel participation results from inventory ownership.

Less visible in the conduct of channel affairs are a wide variety of businesses that provide essential services to primary channel members. Support businesses that assist primary channel members have traditionally been referred to as *facilitators*. The typical channel facilitator is positioned in the channel in a role somewhat analogous to that of a subcontractor in the construction industry. The facilitator is a specialized firm that performs vital tasks and services important to the overall distribution process. However, similar to a construction subcontractor, the facilitator has typically not been viewed as a channel member because it typically does not make key decisions or assume risk. In the discussion that follows, examples will be presented to illustrate the significant role that specialized service providers are playing in many contemporary channel arrangements. Some service providers have assumed extremely risky positions in the formation and operation of innovative channel arrangements. Others are playing more active leadership roles in planning channel arrangements, generating information, and in day-to-day decision making. Therefore, the importance of these service providers justifies their classification as *specialized participants* who in some situations may function as dominant institutions in specific channel arrangements.

This chapter begins with an examination of the role of specialized participants in the design and operation of channel arrangements. Specialized participants are examined from the viewpoint of justification, risk involvement, consolidation and alliances, and leadership potential. The second section presents a classification scheme that groups specialized channel participants on the basis of the services they provide. Specialists are categorized as functional or support service suppliers. Naturally, many specialized channel participants provide a combination of both services. The next two sections discuss the range of businesses that specialize in each type of service. The final section discusses the emergence of large-scale service organizations that have begun to offer a range of integrated specialized services. In total, the chapter presents in-depth coverage of the important role that specialists play in the managerial and operational affairs of channels.

CHANGING NATURE OF SPECIALIZED SERVICE PROVIDERS

The role that specialized members play in channel operations has been undergoing significant change over the past decade. The traditional notion of a support member providing a passive service designed to facilitate operations of primary channel members has gradually given way to an image of a more dynamic participation in channel affairs. To better understand the changing role of specialized channel members, four aspects of their participation are examined: (1) economic justification, (2) risk involvement, (3) concentration and alliances, and (4) potential leadership. The section concludes with a classification of specialized channel members in terms of their involvement as providers of functional or support services.

Economic Justification

The historic justification for including specialized businesses as channel members is economically based. The fundamental importance of specialization to the formation and functioning of channels was discussed in Chapter 1.[1] Widespread realization that specialists can often perform a specific activity for primary channel members at a lower cost as a result of specialization and division of labor is a long-standing economic principle.[2] Based on a combination of experience, focused performance, business relationships, and economy of scale, the specialized organization can often provide a service more efficiently and/or effectively than can a primary channel member internally. While economic foundations remain the bedrock of the specialist organization, at least three additional trends have encouraged the more active involvement of specialized businesses in overall channel affairs.

First, changing managerial attitudes and philosophies of primary channel members has made them more willing to outsource the performance of essential services.[3] For a considerable period of time the option of vertical integration of operations was widely accepted among primary channel members. Vertical integration of channel functions by virtue of ownership was appealing both for economic and control reasons. A belief that absorption of functions could reduce channel cost and increase direct control led to the establishment of internally owned and managed services such as warehouses, transportation, research, and advertising. During the 1980s the attitude of ''do it yourself'' came under serious challenge. Perhaps the most persuasive force encouraging the return to favor of the specialist organizations was a growing awareness that primary channel members needed to refocus their managerial talents and resources on the core requirements of their basic business. The business of retailing, for example, is to operate well-managed, attractive stores that appeal to the consuming public. Managers began to fully understand that the minimal potential gains in operating efficiency that resulted from such operations as warehousing and transportation were insignificant in comparison to the potential dilution in primary business focus that could result from preoccupation with such operations. The overall appeal of getting back to the basics of the primary business reestablished a positive attitude concerning using outside specialists.

A second force that justifies increased use of specialists is resource driven. Whereas the variable expense of performing a specific function may not be significantly different among internal performers or external service specialists, the resources required to support the service are often significantly different. The use of a specialized service

---

[1] See Chapter 1, p. 20.

[2] George E. Stigler, ''The Division of Labor Is Limited by the Extent of the Market,'' *Journal of Political Economy,* **59:**3, June 1951, pp. 185–193.

[3] See Donald J. Bowersox, ''Logistical Partnerships''; and John Gardner and Martha Cooper, ''Elements of Strategic Partnership'' in *Partnerships: A Natural Evolution in Logistics,* ed. Joseph E. McKeon, Cleveland: Logistics Resource, 1988.

firm means that a primary channel member need not devote scarce human and financial resources to performing the service. Widespread problems related to maintaining a work force to perform front-line service tasks such as warehouse order selection and truck driving make the use of a specialized service firm appealing. Likewise, the ability to leverage the financial assets of a service firm has great appeal. The cost of a single heavy-duty over-the-road truck and trailer can easily exceed $100,000. If a primary channel member can avoid the purchase or not use credit lines to lease such equipment, greater financial resources can be employed in the basic business. The use of specialized service suppliers amounts to off-balance-sheet leveraging.

A final force stimulating use of outside specialists is the increased confidence among primary channel members that their information technology is adequate to maintain control over outsourced services. Recent research into the practices of outsourcing logistic services confirms that control confidence is not a major concern among firms fully committed to using service specialists. The capability to network and coordinate the combined use of external and internal resources is part of a larger transformation taking place as the full impact of information technology upon business organization structure and management practice unfolds.[4] The increased use of specialized service providers is consistent with the drive to flatten organization structures, increase overall response time, and enhance operating flexibility.[5]

In summary, the basic justification for using a specialist organization is economic. The recent increased utilization of high-performance service organizations has resulted from three trends: (1) a shift in managerial attitudes in which attention is now focused on core business requirements, (2) the opportunity of primary channel members to leverage the human and financial resources of service suppliers, and (3) increased confidence concerning the primary channel members' internal ability to coordinate the performance of service suppliers in the channel value-added process.

Risk Involvement

The trend toward increased use of external service providers has, in part, resulted from increased willingness on the part of specialists to assume more active participation in risks associated with channel performance. Naturally, the willingness to assume greater risk has its reward structure. To fully understand this change in traditional posture, it is necessary to explore the changing nature of services being provided. Examples are drawn from the public warehouse industry as an illustration.

The initial concept of public warehousing was to provide temporary storage of products. In a passive sense, the public warehouse specialist concentrated on providing high-quality storage and material handling for a fee. The risk of the warehouse operator was limited to providing safe, damage-free storage. In today's environment, many public warehouse firms contract and operate dedicated facilities that are leased to customers on a long-term basis. Such contract warehousing typically involves management, staffing, material handling equipment, and the provision of specified infor-

---

[4] *Management in the 1990s Research Program,* Boston: Massachusetts Institute of Technology, 1989.
[5] For further development of these concepts, see Chapter 12, pp. 393–396.

mation services. It is also common practice for warehousing firms to perform dedicated transportation services. Many warehousing firms contract to perform customized value-added services such as product sequencing, labeling, and various forms of light assembly and manufacturing. Thus, public warehousing as it exists today is significantly different from the original concept. The firm specializing in warehousing has significant assets at risk and offers an array of value-added services focused to the needs of specific customers.

The trend toward greater specialization and dedicated facilities is not limited to warehousing. Similar trends more or less exist in almost all forms of support services. An area of extensive specialization is in the design and operation of customized transportation services. Because the providers of customized services have a great deal at risk with a single user or buyer, new and innovative ways of pricing and sharing or spreading liability have evolved. One example is an upside-downside contract.[6] What the contract amounts to is a sharing of productivity benefits between supplier and user. When the service is conducted at near-optimum upside performance levels, users share in productivity benefits. Likewise, when volume drops below a preagreed performance level necessary to cover fixed cost, the financial burden is shared on a preagreed basis by the service user. Other examples of risk sharing are performance-related incentives and penalties, agreements to purchase assets in contract termination situations, and arrangements to suspend or reduce service contract payments if the primary channel business fails to achieve a predetermined percentage of forecast.

A wide variety of performance agreements exist among suppliers and buyers of specialized services. While the specifics of such agreements vary significantly, their objective does not. The primary motivation behind such customized agreements is a basic recognition of the risk that many specialized service providers have in overall channel performance. As one industry executive explained, "We're not willing to bet the company on the performance of each channel we participate in."[7]

Concentration and Alliances

The concentration of specialized services has followed trends similar to those of most other industries. For example, in 1988 the for-hire ICC-authorized carrier-truck transport sector consisted of over 39,000 companies that participated in $72 billion freight revenue. In the less-than-truckload sector of for-hire trucking, which had total sales of $18 billion, the top twenty firms had combined revenues of over $10.5 billion, or 58 percent of the total.[8] In the public warehouse industry, less than 20 percent of all service suppliers operate over 65 percent of all available space.

Large-scale multiple-facility warehouse operations that offer a range of integrated services are growing rapidly. Small-scale single-facility public warehouse operators are rapidly being absorbed. Itel Distribution Systems was formed in 1988 by the

---

[6] William G. Sheehan, "Contract Warehousing: The Evolution of an Industry," *Journal of Business Logistics,* **10:**1, 1989, pp. 31–49.

[7] Interview with William G. Sheehan, Distribution Centers Inc., *Distribution Issues Forum VII,* February 21, 1990.

[8] James Arron Cooke, "The Shakeout Intensifies," *Traffic Management,* May 1990, pp. 39–43.

purchase of Leaseway Warehousing. Within two years Itel further expanded system-wide capacity by the acquisition of two regional warehouse operations, the Dornbush group and Paul-Jeffrey. A similar collection of individual service businesses is being orchestrated by Exel Logistics, a subsidiary of the United Kingdom–based conglomerate NFC. By early 1990, Excel had acquired Dauphin Distribution Services Company, Distribution Centers Inc., Allied Van Lines, Merchant's Delivery, and Yankee Express as the nucleus of a nationwide logistics-based service.

Supply-side concentration means that fewer specialists are more deeply involved in the business affairs of primary channel participants. Most firms that use outside services have reduced the number of different suppliers they regularly utilize. Whereas the popular purchasing strategy of the recent past was to spread service requirements across many suppliers, relying on competition to assure lowest price, the trend today is to develop a closer working relationship with a few key service providers. The essence of supplier alliances is to generate a cooperative forum for continuous productivity improvement.[9] In fact, some organizations have gone so far as to source service requirements with a single supplier. For example, the core-carrier concept of transportation is to use a single for-hire specialist to provide all service requirements. The basic core-carrier idea is that focusing all transportation requirements with a single service supplier creates an optimum balance of economic and operational concentration. Needless to say, such concentration has inherent risk that must be offset or contrasted by detailed working and terminating agreements.[10]

It is clear that both the composition of specialized service industries and the procurement practices followed by primary channel participants have significantly changed over the past few years. These structural changes have significantly altered the relative involvement of specialized service firms in the planning and execution of overall channel affairs. While specialized participants may not have the same level of risk as primary channel members, service industry concentration and the growth of service alliances has intensified their participation in the channel management process. As specialized service firms become more involved in integrated channel arrangements, they become more dependent upon the success of the primary business members.

Service Specialist Leadership

It is generally recognized that most channel situations that are engaged in continuous or repeat business formally or informally require leadership. The structural circumstances that encourage and facilitate leadership are explored in Chapter 4.[11] The nature of the leadership process in extended enterprise management is the focus of Chapter 10.[12] At this point it is appropriate to briefly note the channel leadership potential for service specialists.

---

[9] Donald J. Bowersox, "Logistical Partnerships," op. cit.
[10] Ibid.
[11] See Chapter 4, p. 102.
[12] See Chapter 10.

A few years ago it would have been unrealistic to illustrate a situation wherein a service specialist could emerge as the overall channel leader. Each of the factors discussed above—namely, expanded justification, increased risk involvement, and service industry concentration and growth of alliances—serves to make the advent of service specialist–led channels more realistic. Two additional events of the 1980s serve to further increase the potential of such leadership.

The rash of leveraged buyouts and business acquisitions of the 1980s have resulted in some strange business relationships. To illustrate, the sequence of events that led to the control of RJR Nabisco and Beatrice Foods by Kravis, Kohlberg and Roberts has been well documented.[13] The fact of the matter is that after all the smoke settled, management control of Nabisco, for example, was in the hands of a financial service supplier that was positioned to control the commitment of the giant food and tobacco firm to its primary channel arrangements and overall supplier base. The widespread consolidation of primary participants, manufacturers, wholesalers, and retailers throughout industry has served to elevate the relative power of stockbrokers and insurance companies that are involved in the financial structure of such business deals. It is clear that selected service-support firms of the 1990s such as financial institutions are more powerful and better positioned to take a leadership role in primary channel arrangements than in the past.

The second potential for primary channel leadership by service providers is emerging out of the power of information technology. For example, a comprehensive new service firm, Global Logistics Venture, a joint venture of AMR, the holding company that controls American Airlines and CSX, a broad-based transportation services company, is building service alliances using a unique marketing strategy. Global Logistics is providing primary channel members with information technology to coordinate the purchase of essential services from a number of specialized providers. Thus, Global is positioned as a potential intermediary between the user and the provider of special logistical services. A similar information-based strategy is followed by C. H. Robinson, which is a major provider of coordinated logistic services. Information may be among the most powerful forces to effectively lead management practices of primary channel members.

Beyond financial and information-based service specialists, the potential also exists for firms that actually perform logistic services such as transportation or warehousing to exercise channel leadership. A logistic service firm is typically a neutral participant that provides essential services for primary channel members at a negotiated fee. The potential does exist for such service providers to exploit power sources available to them from day-to-day operations. A transportation carrier, for example, is ideally positioned to reward shippers in the form of rate reductions and the introduction of cost-reducing technologies such as automatic tracing. Carriers also represent a source of expert knowledge concerning all forms of transportation management. Because of access to critical business information such as customers' locations and purchase patterns, carriers are ideally positioned to have a channelwide perspective concerning business operations. As carriers provide these services and engage in routine opera-

---

[13] "The Best and Worst Deals of the 80s," *Business Week,* January 15, 1990, pp. 52–62.

tions, they are ideally positioned to gain dependency of primary channel participants and even to resolve potential conflicts.

American President Companies (APC), a double-stack rail container service that links vendors to Ford Motor Company's auto assembly plant in Hermosillo, Mexico, is a prime example of a carrier quarterbacking a channel arrangement. APC coordinates all information, truck and rail transportation, customs clearance, and inventory handling necessary to collect parts and components from vendors and sequence-load them into containers for delivery on a just-in-time basis to Ford's Hermosillo assembly plant. APC also coordinates the return to the United States of containers carrying components produced by vendors located in the Maquiladora region. It is clear that APC's role in the above logistic service arrangement is far more extensive than simply providing double-stack container service. While service specialists are not typically considered to be prime candidates for leadership of channel arrangements, their unique positioning and the power base associated with their activities does not prohibit such a role.

Conclusion: Specialized Service Providers

The point of the previous discussion is that specialized service providers and the role they play in the distribution process are rapidly changing. The perspective that service providers only serve to facilitate the performance of primary channel participants does not fully capture the dynamic contribution they are capable of making to overall channel performance. Firms that provide essential services have a great deal at stake regarding successful channel performance. To view support service providers as passive members of the channel structure does not properly position their critical contribution to channel success. The complexity of today's channel arrangements necessitates a clear understanding of the contribution such service providers can make to the decision and negotiating processes that guide channel performance. The term *specialized service provider* is adopted to highlight the important role that such firms play in channel management.

CLASSIFICATION OF SPECIALIZED SERVICE PROVIDERS

Specialized channel participants are classified as *functional* or *support,* based on the type of services they provide.

Functional Specialist

A *functional specialist* is a service provider that is engaged in the basic process of moving, modifying, or otherwise physically handling a product during the distribution process or that is directly involved in the selling process. In other words, a functional service provider is actively engaged in the day-to-day performance of the channel. The range of services performed by such functional specialists is broader than pure logistics. Many firms specialize in performing services related to physical sequencing of products to meet customers' requirements. In some situations specialists may modify a product to a customer's specification while it is passing through the distribution channel. Others are engaged in performing special merchandising services related to their customers' marketing operations.

The wide variety of specialized functional services available to primary channel members are: (1) transportation, (2) warehousing, (3) assembly, (4) fulfillment, (5) sequencing, and (6) merchandising. Firms that perform multiple functional services are referred to as *integrated service providers.* In the physical or functional provision of specialized services there is a clear trend toward proliferation of integrated service providers. This trend is discussed in greater depth in the last section of this chapter.

Support Specialist

A *support specialist* is a firm that facilitates overall channel performance by providing an essential ingredient or service. Unlike the functional specialist, a support firm does not engage in actual selling or the logistics processes of the channel. In most situations, the service provided is truly support in the sense that proximity in time and place to the products being distributed is not necessary. Many support services are not readily apparent in the physical path a product follows to market. However, they are essential to satisfactory completion of the overall distribution process.

The variety of specialized support services available to primary channel participants are: (1) financial, (2) information, (3) advertising, (4) insurance, (5) advisory/research, and (6) arrangement. Given the technical nature of support services, most firms that provide such assistance tend to focus on performing a single service.

Table 3-1 provides a summary and brief definition to each significant type of specialized support service provider. The final two sections of this chapter examine the twelve specialized service providers in greater detail.

FUNCTIONAL SERVICE PROVIDERS

Functional specialists are actively involved in getting products to the right place at the correct time to support the marketing strategies of primary channel participants. The range of services required to support the physical flow of products can include a variety of value-added efforts. Choice exists concerning which business will provide a function and when it will be performed. No choice exists concerning whether the function will be performed during the distribution process. Each of the six types of functional services listed in Table 3-1 is discussed in greater detail.

Transportation

The most visible functional service performed by specialists for primary channel members is freight transportation. Total expenditure for freight movement in the United States in 1989 was $377 billion. The composition of freight expenditures by type or mode of transportation is presented in Table 3-2.

Two aspects of the data are particularly noteworthy. First, the vast majority of dollars expended for freight go for the purchase or performance of truck transportation.

TABLE 3-1   SPECIALIZED SERVICE PROVIDERS

Type	Typical activity
Functional specialization:	
Transportation	Moving products between geographic locations.
Warehousing	Store and sort merchandise.
Assembly	Modify products to customers' specifications.
Fulfillment	Take customers' orders and provide specialized product shipment as a value-added service.
Sequencing	Arrange products in specialized ways as a value-added service.
Merchandising	Work at point of sale to increase appeal of product assortment.
Support specialization	
Financial	Provide funding for inventory, account receivables, and factoring as well as basic assets.
Information	Provide communication services to link channel operations.
Advertising	Assist in planning and executing promotional efforts.
Insurance	Protecting against loss risk due to unexpected events.
Advisory/research	Provide basic data and expert information to facilitate channel planning and operations.
Arrangers	Create special situations and incentive to facilitate product movement or sale in other than primary business operation methods.

The $256 billion expended on trucking in 1989 represents 78.2 percent of the total freight bill. The cost of performing necessary trucking was $156 billion for intercity hauling and $100 billion more for local freight and delivery services. It is clear that trucking represents the primary source of transportation used to support channel performance.

The second relationship that stands out in Table 3-2 is the significant amount of trucking that is performed by manufacturers, wholesalers, and retailers for themselves. Private-industry intercity hauling represented $84 billion, which is 32.8 percent of all truck expenditures. In fact, private trucking was larger in total cost than the combined expenditures for rail, water, pipeline, and air services. Table 3-3 provides a breakdown of the 1989 $72 billion for-hire transportation services purchased by primary channel members.

Table 3-4 describes the relative cost structure of each type or mode of transportation. Each mode can be viewed from the perspective of fixed and variable cost as well as the composition of typical freight hauled. The reason that trucking represents the backbone of the transportation infrastructure is the versatility it offers in comparison to other modes. The relative operating characteristics of the five modes is pre-

TABLE 3-2 COMPOSITION OF FREIGHT EXPENDITURE BY MODE 1989 (IN BILLIONS)

Truck		
Intercity for-hire hauling	$ 72	
Private	84	
Local freight services	100	
Total truck		256
Other		
Rail	30	
Water	21	
Oil Pipeline	9	
Air	11	
Total other		71
Total freight expenditure		$327

Source: Robert Delaney, "Trends in Logistics and Our World Competitiveness," *State of Logistics Annual Report,* Cass Logistics, Inc.

sented in Table 3-5. While trucking only ranks first in terms of one operational attribute, availability, it is near the top regarding overall operating characteristics. The composite score of trucking across the five attributes is 10, which is significantly lower than any of the other modes.

Another useful way to view transportation services is in terms of revenue and intercity ton-miles. Table 3-6 provides a comparison of these two vital statistics. Because of the nature of traffic transported and the versatility of the service provided, trucking handles the vast majority of shipments and generates by far the largest revenue. In terms of ton-miles, the primary hauler is the railroad industry, which

TABLE 3-3 1989 FOR-HIRE TRANSPORTATION EXPENDITURE BY CATEGORY

Category	Cost (in billions)	Percent of total
Truckload general	24	33.3
LTL	18	25.0
Parcel	11	15.3
Bulk commodities	5	6.9
Household goods	5	6.9
Auto haul	3	4.2
Refrigerated frozen	3	4.2
Building materials	2	2.8
Heavy machinery	1	2.4
Total	$72	100

Source: Robert Delaney, "Trends in Logistics and Our World Competitiveness," *State of Logistics Annual Report,* Cass Logistics, Inc.

TABLE 3-4   MODAL COST STRUCTURE AND TYPICAL FREIGHT COMPOSITION

Mode	Cost Structure	Typical freight composition
Rail	High fixed–low variable	Extracting industries Heavy manufacturing Autos and agricultural commodities
Truck	Low fixed–medium variable	Medium and light manufacturing Distribution between wholesaler and retailers All consumer distribution
Water	Medium fixed–low variable	Mining and bulk commodities Chemicals Cement Some agricultural products
Oil Pipeline	Highest fixed–lowest variable	Petroleum
Air	Medium fixed–high variable	All freight handled on an emergency basis Regular freight that is extremely perishable or high value

Adapted from: Donald J. Bowersox, David J. Closs, and Omar K. Helferich, *Logistical Management*, 3d ed., New York: Macmillan, 1986, p. 165. Adapted with permission of Macmillan Publishing Company. Copyright © 1986 by Macmillan Publishing Company.

has significant capability for hauling a wide variety of different commodities and products.

Since 1980, the transportation industry in the United States has been undergoing significant deregulation. The original purpose of transportation regulation was to scrutinize the activities of for-hire carriers for the public interest. Beginning in the late 1970s a number of efforts were made to reduce the extent of regulatory control. In 1980, the Motor-Carrier Regulatory Reform and Modernization Act of 1980 (MCA-80) and The Staggers Rail Act[14] were enacted. These baseline laws launched a decade of regulatory relaxation that, for all extensive purposes, has made interstate transpor-

TABLE 3-5   RELATIVE OPERATING CHARACTERISTICS BY TRANSPORTATION MODES
(Lowest Rank Is Best)

Operating characteristic	Rail	Truck	Water	Pipeline	Air
Speed	3	2	4	5	1
Availability	2	1	4	5	3
Dependability	3	2	4	1	5
Capability	2	3	1	5	4
Frequency	4	2	5	1	3
Composite score	14	10	18	17	16

Source: Donald J. Bowersox, David J. Closs, and Omar K. Helferich, *Logistical Management*, 3rd ed., New York: Macmillan, 1986, p. 166. Reprinted with permission of Macmillan Publishing Company. Copyright © 1986 by Macmillan Publishing Company.

[14] Public Law 96–296 and Public Law 96–488, respectively.

TABLE 3-6   FOR-HIRE REVENUES AND TON-MILES BY MODE, 1987

Mode	Percentage of revenue	Percentage of intercity ton-miles	Percent revenue Percentage of ton-miles
Rail	9.8	31.1	.03
Highway	77.8	21.1	3.65
Water	6.6	28.6	.23
Oil pipeline	2.7	18.8	.14
Air	3.0	.3	10.0

Source: National Transportation Strategic Planning Study, Department of Transportation, March 1990, p. 5–25.

tation a free market. In contrast, intrastate transportation is still regulated in forty-three states.

The overall result of deregulation has been a significant change in the composition of for-hire transportation services. Among the most significant changes have been the following:

1 The expansion of ICC-authorized motor carriers to nearly 40,000.
2 The consolidation of less-than-truckload (LTL) carriers that specialize in shipments weighing 10,000 pounds or less into significantly fewer large carriers. Thirteen of the top twenty LTL carriers existing in 1979 have merged or gone out of business.[15] Three, Yellow Freight Systems, Consolidated Freightways, and Roadway Express, ranked as the top three LTL carriers, have combined revenues exceeding $5 billion.
3 The development of a strong small-package and parcel service dominated by United Parcel Service, with revenues over $13 billion, and Federal Air Express, which in 1989 had revenues of nearly $4 billion. The package and parcel services offer a combination of next-day premium transportation and a dependable assortment of two- to three-day basic service packages.
4 The consolidation of market share by fourteen independent railroads that together account for over 90 percent of total rail revenues. Railroad services have focused on bulk and commodity hauling with their market share expanding in coal and chemicals.
5 The emergence of multimodal transportation companies involving joint ownership of railroad, trucking, and water operations. Examples are CSX's acquisition of SeaLand Corporation in 1987 and Union Pacific Corporation's 1987 acquisition of Overnite Transportation Company. The expansion of multimodal operations has also followed two other growth patterns. Many railroads have received ICC permission to establish trucking subsidiaries. Alliances have also been estab-

[15] Cooke, op. cit., p. 41.

lished between railroads and trucking companies to bolster their competitive positioning. An example is the recently announced Quantum service that links the resources of the Santa Fe Railway and J. B. Hunt Transport Services.

6 The expansion of integrated intermodal transport beyond traditional trailer-on-flatcar (TOFC) and container-on-flatcar (COFC) services. As a result, there has been the establishment of scheduled trains dedicated to intermodal movement and, in 1984, the introduction of double-stack container service. The intermodal sector of the transport industry is growing at an annual rate exceeding 3 percent. In 1990, over 50 percent of all rail shipments were in some form of intermodal service.

It is clear that the transportation industry offers manufacturers, wholesalers, and retailers a wide variety of key services. Primary channel members continue to perform a great deal of their own trucking. However, such propitiatory transportation is most often supplemented by services provided by for-hire specialists.

Warehousing

The use of for-hire warehousing by primary channel participants represents a growing segment of functionally specialized services. In 1988, the public warehouse industry and associated terminal services represented a $7 billion industry. Various forms of public-type warehousing represented 11.6 percent of the estimated $60 billion expended for this specialized service. The balance of $53 billion (88.3 percent) were performed as an internal or propitiatory service. While it is clear that primary channels are far less dependent upon warehouse specialists than upon for-hire transportation specialists, the use of for-hire warehouse services is growing. The reason for this growth can be traced to the changing nature of the warehousing industry.

The traditional concept of *public warehousing* was one of providing temporary storage space for raw materials, work-in-process, and finished goods inventory. The economic justification for public warehousing was that it provided the flexibility of temporary space to satisfy short-term storage requirements. The *overflow* nature of these warehouse services resulted in a traditional fee structure based upon short-term occupancy time supplemented by a charge for in and out material handling. Dominated by the convenience factor, original public warehouse fees typically covered thirty-day usage. The level of such short-term rates was not cost-competitive with longer-term propitiatory warehouse alternatives. The availability of short-term storage arrangements solved operating problems for manufacturers, wholesalers, and retailers when confronted with a need for seasonal or unexpected short-term storage. They also served to stopgap permanent requirements by providing facilities until private warehouses could be constructed. The availability of such public warehousing also offset the need for investment in private facilities that would be underutilized year round.

During the past two decades the composition of for-hire warehouse services have changed in four significant ways:

1 Warehouse operators have expanded their basic services to more fully accommodate customers' distribution requirements. The expanded services have

included supplying an assortment of buildings, providing flexible storage to support marketing efforts, mixing together into integrated shipments products being distributed by different channel members, and providing various forms of manufacturing support services. With the proliferation of such services public facilities have been established as viable economic and service alternatives to proprietary warehouse operations.

2 The shift from pure storage to full-line warehouse services has resulted in significant revision in the way that public warehouse firms conduct their business operations. The traditional pricing structure of public warehousing is being supplemented by longer-term contractual arrangements that facilitate the development of customized turnkey distribution facilities. Such contracts offer users a service solution that combines the flexibility of public warehousing with the stability of proprietary arrangements.

3 During the past few years a number of warehouse groups have been consolidated as a result of acquisitions, mergers, and the establishment of operating alliances. The result of these collaborations is an increasing capability to present potential users a broad-based, nationwide warehouse service system.

4 The warehouse industry is expanding their traditional services to include a wide range of special value-added and terminal services. The nature of these services will be developed in the following discussion of assembly, fulfillment, sequencing, and merchandising because they are not exclusively provided by warehousing firms. However, since for-hire warehouses are involved in the physical handling of materials and products, they are ideally positioned to perform such specialized services.

Assembly

The providers of *assembly* services modify products while they are being processed in the distribution channel. The economic justification for conducting final-product assembly within the distribution channel is based on the potential benefits of form postponement. This principle is fully developed in Chapter 4.[16] The basic idea of form postponement is to eliminate the inherent risks associated with anticipating demand by delaying the final form of products until as late as possible in the transaction process, allowing greater product customization.

Examples of *in-channel assembly* are numerous. In one public warehouse, packaging machines are operated to customize spark plugs into an assortment of consumer and trade packs designed to meet the demand requirements of different markets. In another situation a trucking concern inserts specialized circuit boards into computers to accommodate specific requirements of customers. One of the more innovative assembly services is a service performed by Southern Bonded Warehousing. Southern Bonded repackages bubble gum and soccer balls into a combined, point-of-sale promotion package. The total process requires five assembly tasks. The end result is a unique inventory item assembled at the warehouse for a lower-cost-per-unit expen-

---

[16] See Chapter 4, pp. 99–102.

diture than the manufacturer is able to achieve.[17] These few examples illustrate a broad range of assembly tasks that can be performed by specialists. Other commonly performed tasks are labeling, painting, and mixing, but virtually any other activity is capable of anticipatory commitments in the channel.

Assembly operations can be performed by a wide variety of different types of service businesses. Transportation and warehouse firms are ideally positioned to perform assembly because they can provide such value-added services as a supplement to hauling or storing the associated freight.

Fulfillment

A special form of value-added service that can be performed by functional specialists is *fulfillment*. Fulfillment is a relatively new label applied to a specialized form of handling and arranging for shipment of promotional or point-of-sale advertising materials. The fulfillment firm is contracted to process and ship particular types of merchandise or supplies on behalf of a manufacturer, wholesaler, or retailer. The typical arrangement is for the fulfillment company to physically maintain but *not* own the associated inventory. This discussion concerning inventory ownership is the essential factor that contrasts a fulfillment company from a merchant wholesaler. Manufacturers, wholesalers, and retailers engage the services of a fulfillment firm because of its expertise in handling small customized orders.

A classical example of a fulfillment service is Procter & Gamble's arrangement for the distribution of disposable diapers for premature babies. Confronted with the desire to retain the patronage of mothers of premature babies for future diaper purchases and in light of the low volume of such items in terms of retailer shelf-space management, P&G worked out an arrangement with a specialized company to fulfill distribution requirements. Mothers were provided an 800 number at the time of hospital release that they could call for placement of diaper orders. The fulfillment company received and processed the order, prepared the shipment, and arranged for home delivery of the diapers by United Parcel Service. The result was effective distribution that represented profitable business for the specialized fulfillment business while offering a distribution solution that was cost effective for P&G and the retailer, and, most importantly, one that was convenient for the mother.

Fulfillment services are common in the distribution of sales promotion, catalog, sales force, and point-of-sale advertising and support materials. Many primary channel members feel that distribution of such materials by a specialist that operates outside of their normal product distribution system represents the best way to maintain control. Many mail-order-type businesses use fulfillment companies to handle customer merchandise shipments. For example, products are often purchased by consumers based on inserts placed in credit-card billing statements by companies such as Shell Oil and American Express. These products are distributed by specialized fulfillment companies.

---

[17] For expanded discussion of assembly examples, see Donald J. Bowersox et al., *Leading Edge Logistics: Competitive Positioning for the 1990s,* Oakbrook, IL: Council of Logistics Management, 1989, Chapters 7 and 9.

It is difficult to fully describe the range of businesses that specialize in fulfillment. A great many operations are small-scale cottage industry efforts. Others are specialized units imbedded within the structure of a large business which were created to provide value-added services. The feature that all fulfillment firms have in common is the ability to perform specialized distribution of small-quantity orders in a flexible manner and at a cost difficult for large-scale primary channel members to duplicate.

Sequencing

Sequencing consists of sorting merchandise into a unique configuration to satisfy a particular customer's requirements. Since most customers have unique requirements, sequencing is, by definition, customized. Three examples illustrate the widespread range of sequencing services.

In the retail garment industry the product of contract manufacturers needs to be size-sorted and style- and color-sequenced to satisfy retail market requirements. American President Companies (APC) offers retailers a service that links procurement with Pacific Rim garment manufacturers. The service offers containerized delivery of garments, on hangers, that are size- and color-sequenced to the retailer's specifications prior to loading. The service is capable of providing direct-to-store (retail) delivery of a customized garment sequence. Federal Express Logistics offers a similar service through their Memphis-based distribution facility in which air shipment of garments is used. With this premium transportation system, garments produced in France can be in United States retail stores within forty-eight hours. Of course, many primary channel participants provide their own sequencing. For example, The Limited performs store-level sequencing and distribution of garments flown in from Asia using internal systems, facilities, and transport capabilities.

A second example of sequencing is typically found in industries in which one public warehouse is the distribution facility for a number of different manufacturers that sell to the same retailer. Dauphin Distribution Services, a warehouse specialist, is capable of providing multiple-vendor consolidated inbound delivery for Shaw's Supermarkets. Rather than receiving truckload shipments of each supplier's products, Shaw's can accelerate inventory velocity by frequently receiving a mixed trailer containing products purchased from a combination of suppliers. Perhaps even more important than the mixing is the ability to sequence load trailers to facilitate receiving. Continental Freezers of Illinois offers an inbound staging, assorting, and sequencing of frozen foods that allows direct delivery to Jewel Food retail stores. Such sequencing bypasses handling by frozen-food distributors as well as by the Jewel warehouse, thereby reducing total cost and incorporating the efficiency of direct-to-store distribution.

A popular form of sequencing is related to the support of manufacturing operations. A vital aspect of just-in-time manufacturing support is to sequence parts shipments into the order in which they will be used in assembly. Such sequencing may involve a combination of parts purchased from one or multiple vendors to support scheduled assembly of products. Manufacturing sequencing is typically provided by transportation or warehouse firms that, in numerous situations, operate specialized equipment or facilities to perform the value-added service. For example, the development of curtain-sided transportation trailers was a response to a need to simultaneously unload a number of different parts. By having access to the full side of a trailer as well as to the end, it is possible to sequence-load a number of different parts on the same trailer.

Many sequencing operations can be performed without the benefit of warehouse facilities. A popular form of sequencing is to use specially designed terminals. Such terminals allow trailer contents to be sequenced to the specifications of customers without the need to actually place merchandise into a warehouse facility. In most situations, terminal or cross-dock sequencing allows products from multiple sources to be coordinated and comingled as desired. Terminal-based sequencing is typically facilitated by the use of material handling equipment and bar-code technology. Examples of terminal-based sequencing are Buick City in Flint, which is operated for General Motors by Pilot Distribution. In the retail distribution environment, multiple-vendor cross-dock sequencing, facilitating direct-store delivery, is utilized by Sam's Club and Meijer Thrifty Acres.

Similar to other specialized services, sequencing can be performed on an internal or a for-hire basis. Because of the high degree of coordination required to properly sequence, a recent trend has been to exploit the flexibility of firms that specialize in such services. Because of the highly customized nature of sequencing, many such services are integral to the basic business of the primary channel members. Therefore, it is difficult to isolate the aggregate cost of providing sequencing and to identify all specialized firms that provide such value-added services.

Merchandising

A significant amount of functional specialization is undertaken during the distribution process to support merchandising initiatives. Merchandising-based or value-added services may require physical handling and modification of products. However, the primary purpose behind such arrangements is to facilitate sales and marketing initiatives.

The most visible form of merchandising support provided by specialized firms is the assembly and distribution of specialized point-of-sale display units. For example, end-of-aisle display units widely used to sell consumer food products typically need to be customized to accommodate specific retail-store requirements. Such display units typically need to be delivered direct to retail stores because their unique configuration prohibits efficient handling through a warehouse distribution system. During specific selling seasons, retailers may opt to feature joint promotions of two or more manufacturers' products. Such joint promotions typically require unique point-of-sale displays to be assembled and positioned in retail outlets.

Many merchandising strategies call for unique retail sale units. The most common type of value-added service required to promote special consumer offerings is the special pack. A special pack is a retail sales unit that is assembled for a promotion or exclusively for sale by a given retailer or wholesaler. A special promotional pack typically groups multiple units of a product's regular consumer packages into a combined single unit for retail sale. With use of some form of an outer- or overwrap, information and prices related to the deal pack can be affixed to a combination of regular consumer cartons. Using special packs, manufacturers avoid restricted labeling and are able to use normal rotation merchandise to support promotional dealing. A pack developed exclusively for a given retailer or wholesaler facilitates offering consumers a unique quantity-price combination of an otherwise standard product. For example, Target stores may offer five tubes of Colgate toothpaste in a bag at a promoted price per ounce. Many deep-discount retailers only stock national brand merchandise if it is available in customized or exclusive combination packs. Because each brand product assortment is unique to a specific retailer's merchandising requirements, most manufacturers elect to accommodate special packaging outside of normal processing or manufacturing. The provision of such special promotional packaging is an ideal service to be provided by specialized firms.

Two additional services related to merchandising offer significant opportunities for specialized service providers. Many industries extensively use manufacturers' coupons to stimulate retail sales. A group of specialized firms provide coupon sorting and accounting to assist firms in the administration burden associated with such promotional devices. Other firms provide merchandising assistance in the form of retail shelf stocking and product presentation. *Detailers,* a name given to merchandising specialists who visit food, drug, and general-merchandise retail outlets, assist both the manufacturer and the retailer in the performance of in-store shelf merchandising. Many manufacturers use their sales force to provide detail merchandising. Other firms, such as Nabisco Foods Biscuit Division and Frito-Lay, use a special group of employees to deliver and detail at the retail level. Many other companies use firms that specialize in detail merchandising.

The significant thing about special merchandising services is the reason they are performed. Unlike other functional specialized service providers, firms that perform merchandising support are not enlisted to improve the efficiency or effectiveness of logistic performance. Merchandise services exist to increase sales and marketing impact. The use of outside specialists is often the best way to accommodate unique merchandising requirements and poses the least risk in terms of potential disruption of primary channel member normal operations.

Conclusion: Functional Service Providers

Functional service providers are specialized firms that get intimately involved in the basic process of distribution. Functional services provided by firms range from very comprehensive services for the total channel to the performance of customized value-added services for specific channel members. The nature of functional services is such that they can be internally performed by primary channel participants. In fact, a significant portion of transportation and a majority of warehousing requirements are performed on a proprietary basis. The unique composition of selected services, the requirement for absolute flexibility, the benefit of specialization, and the possession of specific expertise are among the most important reasons why primary channel participants cultivate the use of specialized service providers. Attention is now directed to service providers that perform essential activities for primary channel members but do not necessarily come into direct contact with products being distributed.

SUPPORT SERVICE PROVIDERS

Support specialists are active channel participants that provide services essential to the overall distribution process. Unlike the functional service counterparts, the typical support firm does not engage in actual day-to-day channel operations. To understand the role of support service providers one's appropriate perspective must be that their channel involvement is essential, even critical, at the time and for the duration they are required. Many support services are not very apparent, in contrast to the highly visible operations of primary and functional specialized channel members. The support specialist has one additional distinction in comparison to a functional specialist. Whereas a significant portion of the services performed by functional specialists is capable of being completed internally, few firms are able to provide support services internally. Thus, when a channel alignment requires critical support services, the critical issue is to identify the most attractive source. Few do-it-yourself options are available. Each of the six types of support specialists listed in Table 3-1 is discussed in greater detail.

Financial

The provision of adequate and attractively priced financial support is crucial to most business endeavors. A significant aspect of financing is to provide capital for the inventories and accounts receivables that are required at each level within the distribution channel. A wide range of financial institutions, such as commercial banks, brokerage houses, savings and loans, insurance companies, investment bankers, and finance companies, are available to provide primary channel members with sophisticated advice and essential operating capital. Because most firms use debt to finance fixed assets, they require credit lines to facilitate operations. To the extent that a firm depends upon credit to facilitate operations, its relationship with financial institutions is extremely important.

During the past decade considerable restructuring has taken place in the financial services industry. The result, similar to the outcome of transportation deregulation, has been a general blurring of historic differences between institutions. While traditionally the role of financial institutions has not been readily apparent to the marketing channel structure, several have recently become very active as a result of their involvement in acquisitions and takeovers. The result is that some financial firms such as Kravis, Kohlberg and Roberts have become very active managerially in the firms they have acquired.

Public corporations can generate cash from stock sales, retained earnings, and debt. Private firms must rely upon owner equity, earning, and debt for cash generation. Because of a critical need to fund expansion, research and development, capital improvements, and new business opportunities, the support provided by specialized financial institutions is essential to channel members. Few firms can sustain operations without the assistance of external financial partners.

Information

A large number of firms provide information services to primary channel members. A variety of specialized firms have proliferated as a result of the rapid expansion of information hardware and software technology.

The most fundamental type of information specialists participating in channel operations are firms that provide basic communication services and equipment such as telephones, computers, leased lines, and facsimile machines. Basic communication services and technical assistance are essential to the maintenance of sales and logistics continuity throughout the marketing channel.

With the advent of satellite technology a variety of new types of service specialists have emerged. Specialists such as Hughes Network Systems, Quick Response Service, Inc., IBM Information Network, and GE Information Services provide channel members with a variety of coordinated services. The rapid growth of such service businesses is linked to varied aspects of Electronic Data Interchange (EDI). Specialized firms, such as value-added networks (VANs), standards associations, consultants and coordination groups, communication protocol translators, UPC electronic catalogs, and various other highly focused technical services, have become regular channel participants.

While such technical service providers have not been around long, they can be expected to become more significant as future channel arrangements emerge. In an increasing number of channels, suppliers are receiving what is called the *EDI mandate*. Leaders in many industries, such as automotive and retailing, are committed to expanding EDI arrangements and expect channel partners to become actively involved. Some firms such as GE require potential suppliers to certify EDI capabilities as a prerequisite to further consideration as vendors.[18] In 1988, there were approximately 5000 firms in the United States using EDI. The projection is for the number of EDI-active firms to double annually during the immediate future. By 1995, experts anticipate that close to 70 percent of United States firms will have gained some degree of EDI literacy.[19] Similar EDI adoption rates are projected throughout the world. The variety and number of information services and technical support firms that will ultimately emerge to facilitate information-technology adoption throughout the channel are difficult to estimate. The overall subject of information technology is more fully developed in Chapter 12.[20]

[18] Anne E. Skagen, "Nurturing Relationships, Enhancing Quality with Electronic Data Interchange," *Management Review,* **78**:2, February 1988, pp. 28–32.

[19] Kathleen Hinge, *EDI: From Understanding to Implementation,* New York: American Management Association, 1988.

[20] See Chapter 12, p. 00.

Advertising

It has long been acknowledged that advertising agencies often play a significant role in assisting manufacturers, wholesalers, and retailers in planning and implementing marketing strategies. Most firms employ independent agencies to help generate innovative promotional ideas and themes. In order to offer knowledgeable support, successful advertising agencies maintain highly qualified and well-informed research staffs. Many such advertising and communication professionals are acknowledged experts in specific industries. To support their programs and expand overall understanding of business requirements, successful agencies also undertake active marketing research efforts.

Advertising agencies provide technical assistance to channel members in the establishment of budgets, media selection, promotional themes and content, and timing of campaigns. To be fully effective, members of a channel must coordinate promotional strategies. The technical and managerial expertise of advertising agency personnel often serves as the catalyst for channelwide promotional coordination.

Insurance

To some degree, risk related to channel operations can be offset by insurance. The range of potential insurance requirements in a channel is significant. At the most fundamental level, capital assets, facilities, and inventory must be protected against casualty loss. Firms also have a social obligation to provide employees with health care programs and to help protect them against unexpected sickness or death. Beyond these basic requirements, some firms feel that particular assets that are critical to their success must be protected with respect to continued performance. Firms such as Lloyds of London are often engaged to help insure very critical assets. Finally, as noted earlier, many insurance companies also represent primary sources of finance. Loans from insurance companies and retirement pension funds are particularly attractive sources for funding capital expenditures for office and plant construction. Groups such as the Teachers' Insurance and Annuity Association (TIAA) are the owners of prime real estate such as New York City's Seagram's building.

While it is generally acknowledged that insurance companies are typically passive channel members, their role is important in terms of risk coverage and expert advice. The complex nature of channel arrangements can result in the creation of joint risk. Highly coordinated channel operations create a need for insurance coverage that embraces joint operations. Many financial institutions require a specified level of insurance protection as a prerequisite for funding. The participation of insurance expertise and coverage is an essential, growing part of channel management.

Advisory/Research

Firms engaged in channel arrangements may decide to call upon consultants and independent research firms to help them develop a better understanding and evaluation of options. The use of marketing and behavioral research specialists has long been an important part of strategic planning. Advisory and research groups can provide expert information to assist in the planning of channel strategy.

In terms of channel formation and management advisory and research, specialists firms can make at least three very important contributions. First, they can provide a neutral assessment or benchmark of how a particular channel arrangement measures in comparison to competition. Assessing comparative performance has become an important part of strategy planning.[21]

A second role that advisory and research firms often perform is to provide information and training, both of which facilitate planning and adoption of new management procedures and practices. The adoption of unique practices by channel members that challenge long-standing paradigms can be a difficult process, one that may require substantial assistance. It is a very common practice for a channel leader to undertake and sponsor extensive training and management development for primary and support channel members.

The third role that can be performed from an advisory/research perspective is the direct facilitation of alliances between channel members. The *outside expert* can often resolve what appear to be major obstacles blocking the formation of a new channel arrangement. Some firms report using respected consultants as neutral members of negotiating teams that are forging out channel agreements. Union Pacific Logistics has used outside facilitators to help build joint trust during the evaluation and negotiation of an alliance. They use an independent facilitator acceptable to all parties to maintain a neutral and fair focal point during bargaining.[22]

A vast range of expertise is available to assist firms involved in developing channel arrangements. Such assistance ranges from legal advisors to educational experts who possess knowledge and contacts that can help facilitate attainment of channel objectives. Most firms opt not to maintain large internal staffs to provide these essential services. The use of outside assistance, when and where needed, reduces a firm's fixed expense and helps it to maintain its objectivity.

Arrangers

The term *arranger* is used to describe a type of specialized firm that provides facilitation services. In many situations, the service is unique to a few specialized users. In other situations, the service may be specific to an industry. Three typical examples of the broad variety of potential arrangers are: (1) specialized agents and brokers, (2) liquidators, and (3) diverters.

In Chapter 2, merchant agents and brokers were presented as a specialized type of wholesaler that engages in selling or buying goods for others.[23] Agents and brokers do not typically take either ownership or physical possession of the products for which they arrange transactions. Beyond the more typical brokers that deal in merchandise

---

[21] Robert C. Camp, *Benchmarking,* Milwaukee: ASQC Quality Press, 1989.
[22] Donald J. Bowersox, "The Strategic Benefits of Logistics Alliances," *Harvard Business Review,* **68:**4, July–August 1990, pp. 44.
[23] See Chapter 2, pp. 40–46.

transactions, there are numerous very *specialized agents* and *brokers* who function in the service industries. Among the most visible are agents who represent sports and entertainment celebrities. Examples are Peter Johnson, who represents quarterback Joe Montana, and Michael Ovitz, chairman of Creative Artists Agency, Inc., who packaged promotional arrangements for such clients as Earvin (Magic) Johnson, Dustin Hoffman, and Tom Cruise. Specialized agents are also common in the travel industry, real estate, stock market, investment banking, trucking, international custom facilitation, and speaking tour engagements for current and former public figures. Because the services performed by these specialized agents and brokers range so widely from situation to situation, it is difficult to offer a profile of a typical agent. While closely related to their counterparts in the merchandise wholesale structure, agents and brokers who specialize in arranging are active participants in service marketing channels.

A *liquidator* is a special type of channel participant who arranges disposition of overstocked or closeout merchandise. For example, when Johnson & Johnson decided to discontinue manufacturing and marketing infant disposable diapers in the United States, they arranged for a liquidator to dispose of their existing inventory in Central and South America. One unique liquidation arrangement is promoted by its sponsor as *marketing insurance*.[24] The liquidator arranges disposition of merchandise overstocks in exchange for advertising media time and space. This exchange permits firms to divert planned expenditures for promotional media time to offset the cost of inventory markdowns. The nature of the liquidator's function makes its activities very user-specific. Liquidators are common in the general-merchandise, paper, heavy-machinery, farm implement, and transportation equipment industries. While many liquidators specialize in facilitating bankruptcies, others regularly operate to help balance channel inventory.

The *diverter* is a long-standing type of arranger that has recently become a very active participant in the consumer food, health and beauty aids, and general-merchandise marketing channels. The diverter flourishes in a marketing environment characterized by very active promotional dealing. To stimulate volume, many firms resort to promotions during which they offer products at very attractive prices. The typical promotion runs for an announced period of time, during which involved customers can purchase at *deal* prices. Because the typical promotion price is significantly lower than the regular price, customers are tempted to *forward buy* merchandise. The diverter stands ready to arrange resale of the forward-buy merchandise if the retail or wholesale firms gets overcommitted. (Forward buy is a practice by which firms purchase a larger quantity than their normal needs in order to take advantage of a specially priced deal.) Since most promotions are regional in nature, a potential buyer can typically be found that does not currently qualify for the promotion. In fact, many diverters will seek out customers who need a specific product and then locate a firm that is eligible to buy at the promotional price. They will then arrange for the eligible manufacturer to purchase products for resale to the diverter's customers. The impact of a diverter on an industry can be significant. In effect, diverters serve to neutralize the impact of price promotional deals. Whereas they take some of the risk out of forward buy for

---

[24] Advertising of Tradewell International, New York.

retailers, they cause manufacturers' promotional strategies to become very distorted. In some situations, diversion of merchandise that was forward-purchased earlier to take advantage of deep discounts can result in a product with limited remaining shelf life being forced into distribution. Many retailers feel that regional promotions put them at a disadvantage in terms of remaining price competitive and that the margin earned by the diverter is rightfully theirs. Some, such as Winn-Dixie, will only buy from a supplier that guarantees they are being offered the merchandise at the lowest deal price being promoted anyplace throughout the nation. From a manufacturer's viewpoint, diverters are viewed as being slightly better than child molesters. Many manufacturers would probably like to find ways to take revenge on retailers who sell to diverters. Thus, this form of arranger introduces conflict into channel relationships. Despite attempts to eliminate their impact, diverters continue to thrive by matching need and opportunity in the marketing channel.

Conclusion: Support Service Providers

This discussion has reviewed a representative sample of highly specialized businesses that are regular marketing channel participants. Because of the wide variety of specialized support service providers, no attempt has been made to catalog or document the full population. The essential feature of support services is that they most often do not directly engage in participation in day-to-day channel operations. In many ways, channel support services are not readily apparent. The fact that an essential service is available when needed, such as insurance or a line of credit, is sufficient for that to be considered a contribution to channel performance. Unlike functional service providers, support firms offer assistance that is difficult for primary channel members to provide themselves. Most firms can undertake basic functional services using proprietary facilities, but they most often lack the resources, expertise, or adequate contacts to internally perform essential support services.

EXTENSION OF CHANNEL PARTICIPANTS

Before we conclude the overall treatment of specialized channel participants, two unique and difficult-to-classify developments should be mentioned: (1) proliferation of integrated service providers, and (2) role of consumers as formal channel participants.

Integrated Service Providers

During the past decade, a number of firms have begun to offer primary channel members very comprehensive, or ''total service,'' packages. While no provider of integrated services has developed or promoted a package that embraces all functional and support services reviewed in this chapter, many are offering unique combinations. For example, numerous logistic service firms are introducing a wide range of integrated functional services augmented by a selected assortment of support activities. Because each firm has a unique service assortment, it is difficult to generalize the extent of its

TABLE 3-7 INTEGRATED SERVICE PROVIDERS

ADS Distribution	NYNEX Material Enterprises Co.*
Allied	NYK (Nippon Yusen KK)
American Airlines	Ogden
American President Companies	Roadway Logistics
Caterpillar Logistics Services	C.H. Robinson, Inc.
Consolidated Freightways	Ryder Distribution
CSL Logistics (CSX)	Sears Logistics Services
CSX/ARM Logistics Information Services	Skyway Systems
CTI, Inc.	Sony Logistics*
Excel Logistics	TLC Group
Federal Express (Business Logistics Services)	TNT North America
Grace Distribution Services	Trammel Crow Distribution Corp.
Intral (Gillette)	TRW
ITEL Distribution, Inc.	Union Pacific Logistics*
KLS Logistics	Unit Distribution, Inc.
LogiCorp (division of Rockwell, Inc.)	USCO (Uniroyal—Goodrich)

* No longer providing services to customers outside the parent corporation.

true integration. Primary channel participants should be fully aware of both the benefits and risks of designing channel arrangements utilizing comprehensive service providers.

Table 3-7 provides a partial list of integrated firms that perform a combination of functional and support services. Most of these firms are willing to custom-design their service offering to satisfy specific requirements of customers. As one president of a progressive service company explained, "Our firm will perform any legal service for our clients, providing we can make a profit doing it.[25] The statement conveys the customer-oriented spirit behind the integrated service business. The dynamics of the specialized service business and its increasing popularity is underscored by the fact that all of the business units listed in Table 3-7 were established in the 1980s. While a parent company may have existed prior to the 1980s, the business unit providing integrated services did not.

Consumers as Channel Participants

A final point concerning channel participants is the role that consumers may or may not play. A debate of long standing is the relative merit of including consumers as channel members, basing inclusion upon their participation in selected risk taking and performance of the final product delivery from point of sale to point of consumption.[26]

[25] Bowersox, *Leading Edge Logistics: Competitive Positioning for the 1990s*, p. 233.
[26] Louis W. Stern, Adel I. El-Ansary, and James R. Brown, *Management in Marketing Channels*, Englewood Cliffs, NJ: Prentice-Hall, 1989, pp. 16–17; and Stanley C. Hollander, "Who Does the Work of Retailing? *Journal of Marketing*, **28**:7, July 1964, pp. 18–22.

Since channel functions and activities can be shifted among organizations, it is logical that some primary participants will seek to enlist or encourage consumers to perform selected duties. For example, AMOCO (Standard Oil Company of America) and ARCO (Atlantic Richfield Oil Company) both revised long-standing practices of providing free consumer credit financing. Under revised programs, consumers were offered their choice of either paying higher prices per gallon and retaining the convenience of free credit or purchasing gasoline at lower prices.

It would appear that the logical criteria to judge if consumers should or should not be treated as channel participants are the functions they perform and the degrees of risk they assume. In selected situations, where major commitments are made in advance and consumers assume considerable risk, consumers should be treated as active channel participants. Being active participants means that consumers or their representatives acknowledge channel dependency and engage in the performance of specific roles.

Consumers' engagement solely in purchase behavior is not viewed as risk absorption sufficient to qualify them as channel participants. Thus, choosing to pay higher prices to receive the convenience of limited free credit for gasoline purchase is no more risk absorbing than a decision to shop at a full-service department store rather than a cash-and-carry discounter. Each purchase decision involves choosing between different price and service combinations. When involvement is limited to low-risk shopping, no justification exists to include consumers as channel members.

An illustration of a shopping situation in which consumers assume greater risk is when they join discount groups or clubs. When consumers shop at club stores such as Sam's Club or Price Club, they clearly agree to buy greater-than-normal quantities of product which they plan to inventory until needed for consumption to take advantage of lower prices. Club members typically agree to restrict choices to narrow product-line assortments to facilitate efficiency in the retailer's operation. As a result of consumers' commitment to perform selected functions, assume risk, and hold inventory, they are participating as channel members. Many wholesale clubs seek feedback from members on advisory committees concerning such items as stock assortment, hours of operation, and supplemental services. Participation by way of membership may also have supplemental benefits such as purchase discounts at associated noncompetitive retailers, travel agencies, and even restaurants.

At the extreme of a dependence-risk relationship is the *consumer cooperative*. This special type of cooperative is owned by its participating members. The cooperative serves as a buying organization for its members who seek out selected types of merchandise at the lowest available purchase prices. However, even consumer cooperatives fall short of locking their members into the full responsibility associated with active channel participation. Unless a member assumes specific risk such as future purchasing guarantees, the actual day-to-day involvement as a cooperative member may not be much different than purchasing from any other retailer. Once again, risk absorption is the key determinant for channel membership.

In summary, the idea that consumers should be treated as channel members is loaded with intrinsic appeal. Indeed, consumers do take limited risks associated with shopping and traditionally perform final-product transportation and limited storage.

Several difficult dependence-risk relationships exist between primary channel participants and consumers. While some channel-consumer arrangements are more formalized than others, most fall short of committing the consumer to the same degree of risk as a typical firm engaged as a primary or service support member. Most consumers maintain their freedom of choice to shop at competitive retail locations when they can improve their overall purchase performance. Little evidence exists to equate shopping loyalty to channel membership. In most situations, consumers, rather than being treated as channel members, are more appropriately viewed as the prime customers of the overall distribution process.

SUMMARY

This chapter provided an in-depth look at the variety of firms that participate in the distribution process by assisting primary channel members. These service firms have traditionally been viewed as facilitators because of their passive involvement in the mainstream affairs of the channel. Evidence suggests that the degree of channel involvement by firms that supply essential services is rapidly changing. The forces changing in the role of service members are: (1) expanded economic justification, (2) greater risk involvement in channel performance, (3) increased concentration of services in fewer provider firms that are developing stronger alliances with primary channel members, and (4) increased evidence that some service firms are capable of providing channel leadership. The notion of a passive or facilitating channel member does not fully capture the dynamic nature of service providers and the role they are capable of playing in complex channel arrangements. Therefore, service firms have been positioned as *specialized participants* that, to varying degrees, increasingly play an important role in channel success. Specialized channel service providers are classified into two groups: (1) functional specialists, and (2) support specialists.

The functional specialist is most often directly involved in the mainstream of channel affairs. The services of the functional specialist range from assisting in merchandising to providing the channel's logistic services. The functional specialist's primary involvement is in the performance of hands-on channel activities. In most situations, manufacturers, wholesalers, and retailers have the choice of internally performing services otherwise provided by functional specialists. The attractiveness of using outside functional specialists as contrasted to proprietary operations is grounded in the principle of specialization. Six types of commonly found functional specialists are: (1) transportation, (2) warehousing, (3) assembly, (4) fulfillment, (5) sequencing, and (6) merchandising.

The support specialist is a channel participant that provides critical services. However, unlike a functional specialist, the support participant does not actively get involved in the selling or physical handling processes of the channel. While services provided by the support specialists are essential to channel performance, their importance is often not readily apparent to those in the overall distribution process. In some situations, provision of the services appears to be totally divorced from the main channel. Often, support services are performed at separate locations. Difficulty in fully understanding the role of support specialists is increased by the fact that some services, such as a line of financial credit, may never be actually used. The service may be critical and its contribution to a channel's success may simply be that it is available if and when needed. The dynamic nature of marketing channel arrangements has increased the overall importance of support specialists. The six types of support specialists are: (1) financial, (2) information, (3) advertising, (4) insurance, (5) advisory/research, and (6) arrangers.

To complete the treatment of specialized service providers, two additional types of participants have been discussed: (1) integrated service providers and (2) consumers. During the late 1980s, a number of firms began to offer primary channel participants a variety of integrated services. The key to comprehensive service packages is the attractiveness of what could be referred to as "one-stop shopping." Many of these firms offer an integrated combination of functional and support services. While the integrated service firm is a relatively new channel player, evidence suggests that its importance will grow in the future.

Consumers represent the final stop, or terminal point, of the distribution process. Because some consumers perform selected channel activities and assume a degree of risk, it has been suggested they should be viewed as active channel participants. The determination if consumers should be treated as channel members rests in their relative degree of acknowledged dependency and risk acceptance. While some consumers are far more involved in channel affairs than others, most fall short of total commitment. The ideal perspective to have toward consumers is to view them as the main benefactors of channel performance. Consumers, by virtue of purchase behavior, have the ultimate veto over the acceptability of all channel arrangements.

The stage has now been set for an in-depth look at how primary and specialized channel members align their efforts into a working arrangement—*channel structure.*

QUESTIONS

1 What are the basic reasons why specialized service suppliers are playing a more active role in overall channel affairs?

2 Contact a local public warehouse and interview its management. What functions does the warehouse perform? What special services have been added in recent years? Why does the management believe they can perform these functions and services more economically than manufacturers could?

3 Select two trucking companies for research. How do they differ in size, geographic coverage, and types of merchandise carried? Have they entered into specialized arrangements with any firms whose products they transport?

4 What is the purpose of performance agreements between primary channel members and specialized service providers?

5 Is it practical for a service specialist to function in the capacity of channel leader? Provide a specific example.

6 Discuss and provide examples of assembly, fulfillment, and sequencing services provided by a functional specialist.

7 What is the most fundamental difference between a functional specialist and a support specialist?

8 What is an integrated service provider? What events or forces have stimulated the growth of such specialized service providers?

9 Why can't primary channel members perform many support services on a proprietary basis?

10 How important is private trucking in terms of overall transportation requirements?

11 What potential roles can insurance companies play in a channel arrangement? Do situations develop requiring insurance on an interorganizational basis?

12 Discuss the pros and cons of considering consumers as channel members. Why would one want to treat a consumer as a channel member? Provide specific examples of channel functions performed by consumers.

CHAPTER 4

CHANNEL STRUCTURE

CHAPTER OUTLINE

EMERGENCE OF DISTRIBUTION CHANNELS
    Direct Distribution
    Direct Distribution versus Central Marketplace
    Multistage Distribution
A THEORY OF DISTRIBUTION PROCESSES
    Sorting
    Spatial Closure
    Temporal Closure
COMPLEX DISTRIBUTION ARRANGEMENTS
    Structural Separation
    Postponement
STRUCTURAL CLASSIFICATION
    Single-Transaction Channels
    Conventional Channels
    Vertical Marketing Systems
    Conclusion: Channel Classification
SUMMARY

The practices of individual businesses and their working relations with one another combine to form *channel structure*. Channel structure is a by-product of negotiation and the accumulated result of past business practice. When firms carefully evaluate alternative channel arrangements and then negotiate alignments with specified trading partners, they, in effect, *design* their channel structure. Such design effort is often the result of joint planning among businesses that desire to participate in a specific channel arrangement. In contrast to carefully designed channels, many distribution arrangements have evolved without the benefit of analysis or deliberation. Businesses are often loosely aligned in distribution arrangements based on their perception that continued work together is in their individual best interest. Channel alignments can grow out of interactions such as participation in trade shows or routine sales-force prospecting. Based upon mutually perceived success, firms may continue their business relationship indefinitely. Thus, a channel may be created with successful experience as contrasted with careful deliberation, analysis, and negotiation. Most channels are typically the result of both successful experience and planning. The result is a channel structure that often endures for a long time.

A basic premise of *Strategic Marketing Channel Management* is that channel structure arrangements represent a fundamental way to gain and maintain competitive superiority. A carefully planned channel strategy may enable a firm to position itself in a way that is difficult for competitors to duplicate. The potential to gain competitive advantage as a result of channel alignment is why the process of designing and implementing channel arrangements represents a fundamental part of overall marketing strategy.[1]

This chapter begins with an examination of channel structure from the vantage point of relative directness. Complex channels emerge as individual participants increase their degree of specialization. The forces that lead to multistage distribution are discussed.

The second section reviews theory that explains how and why complex channels emerge. Intermediaries serve to improve overall channel efficiency by resolving three fundamental distribution problems. Each of these three fundamental aspects of the distribution process is examined and illustrated.

The result of firms seeking to satisfy and strategically exploit distribution requirements is a series of complex channel structures. To facilitate efficiency, firms reviewing channel design often find it advantageous to implement separate and unique structures to achieve basic marketing and logistic requirements. A channel notion of long standing, *structural separation,* has become increasingly practical and easier to implement, given the improved control capabilities resulting from advanced information technology. A second concept of importance in designing channels is postponement. Postponement offers a way to reduce risk in a complex channel arrangement. The nature of complex channel structure and the concepts of separation and postponement are reviewed in the third section.

The variety of basic channel relationships that can be observed in contemporary business are described and clarified in the final section of the chapter. The classification is based upon the intensity of acknowledged dependency among channel participants.

In total, Chapter 4 serves to integrate many of the ideas initially presented in Chapters 1, 2, and 3. The integrated treatment of structural considerations provides

[1] Robert Bartels, *The History of Marketing Thought,* 3d ed., Columbus: Publishing Horizons, 1988, pp. 215–218.

the foundation for implementing the managerial planning and implementation process (Figure 1-6), which provides the structure used to present Parts Two and Three.

EMERGENCE OF DISTRIBUTION CHANNELS

The most fundamental distinction among distribution arrangements is the inherent degree of *directness* that alternative channel structures provide. Directness in marketing channels refers to the lack of intermediary stages in the sales or product flow from point of origin to consumption destination. Indirect channels, which include intermediary stages of product handling, emerge as the most effective way to execute exchange in a highly developed society. In this section, direct and multistage channel arrangements are contrasted.

Direct Distribution

Channels that involve manufacturers' sales direct to end users offer the simplest and least-restricted distribution arrangements. Direct-marketing arrangements such as vending, telephone solicitation, mail-order and door-to-door sales, and television home shopping have emerged as forms of nonstore retailing. The high percentage of affluent double-wage-earning households and the widespread availability of instant financing have served to increase the attractiveness of nonstore retailing for busy consumers. Many firms such as L. L. Bean, Eddie Bauer, Lillian Vernon, Hammacher Schlemmer, and Cabelas have created unique and uptempo markets for specialized merchandise by offering quality products, rapid delivery, and extensive satisfaction guarantees. Other direct-marketing organizations have developed assortments of merchandise that appeal to the lower-end market.

Business-to-business sales have always been relatively more direct than marketing to consumers.[2] The industrial buying process is specification driven and generally committed to total-quality performance. As a result, intermediaries only emerge in business-to-business marketing channel structures when they offer unique advantages to either the buyer or the seller. The most fundamental departure from direct distribution is the establishment of a central marketplace.

Direct Distribution versus Central Marketplace

Figure 4-1 illustrates three alternative exchange structures for a hypothetical economy having five households. Each household produces a product desired by other households. In a direct-distribution structure, each household must conduct business with all other households in order to procure a product assortment. To complete the exchange process, the direct-distribution structure requires ten transactions. The number of transactions are expressed by $[n(n-1)]/2$, where n represents the number of households. Direct distribution would be impractical in a complex society. However,

---

[2] Michael D. Hunt and Thomas W. Speh, *Industrial Marketing Management,* 2d ed., New York: Dryden, 1984, Chap. 13.

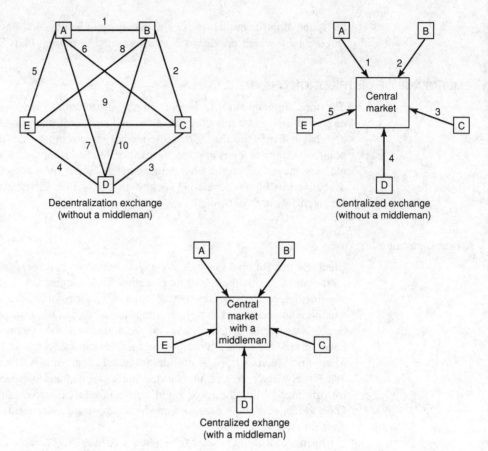

FIGURE 4-1   Alternative exchange patterns.

in developing nations direct distribution often represents the dominant method of conducting business.

So that efficiency is promoted, direct distribution typically evolves toward a central-market structure. A central marketplace emerges when the trading households decide to meet at a central location to conduct business. Trading at a central location offers a distinct advantage over direct distribution. The number of overall contacts is reduced from ten to five, resulting in a saving of time and lower transportation cost. However, when each household performs its own buying and selling, ten transactions still have to be undertaken.

In most developing countries, a significant portion of such products as food, household utensils, textiles, and clothing are distributed through an elementary central-market system. Such central-market structures are typically owned and operated by local government.

A channel arrangement emerges when an independent business sees an opportunity to function as a specialist in the central marketplace. The specialist provides each household with a source to sell or barter its products by the willingness to assume risk of inventory ownership. Because timing and location of each household's production is different, surpluses will exist. The advent of surplus creates a functional opportunity for the specialist to maintain inventory. The establishment of inventory reduces the transactions required to satisfy demand from ten to five. Hence, retailing is born.

Such elementary channels are inefficient in comparison to modern distribution arrangements. The distribution structure in a developing nation typically involves high variable costs and does not facilitate economy of scale. Nevertheless, central markets offer distinct advantages in comparison to direct distribution. First, products move in large quantities to the central market, which introduces transportation efficiency. Second, the required number of transactions are reduced. Finally, doing business at a central market with a specialized intermediary is convenient. The cost associated with establishing a distribution specialist will depend upon the range of services and risk assumed.

A vestige of the central-market system exists in farmers' markets, in which produce is sold in a central location, usually a city's downtown. A more elaborate variation are the furniture marts that operate in many cities. In High Point, North Carolina, for example, several large buildings have been constructed. Many manufacturers lease space in these buildings so that buyers for furniture stores and department stores from across the country can visit displays of products from many manufacturers at one time. Other variations of the central-market system are trade fairs such as the Machine Tool Trade Fair and the World Trade Centers located throughout the globe. In these fairs and centers, producers exhibit merchandise for the buyers' examination and potential purchase. These modern variations of the central marketplace are efficient for selected types of trading. However, the dominant means of modern distribution is the multistage exchange structure.

Multistage Distribution

The limited operating scope of a central market is typically replaced by intermediate specialization. Hence, wholesaling is born. Wholesalers accumulate and sell assortments of goods to retailers. In many developing countries, independent businesses that operate out of their trucks perform the wholesale function. Unlike typical transportation companies in the United States, these independent truckers actually purchase the goods and therefore assume a significant element of risk.

As producers have supported establishment of wholesalers to facilitate distribution, retailers have perceived an opportunity to improve customer service by locating stores in places convenient to customers. As more and more wholesale and retail entrepreneurs have entered the distribution process, multistage structures have evolved.

Modern marketing channels are dominated by a wide variety of distribution specialists.[3] Most manufacturers depend upon the services of specialists for effective

---

[3] See Chapter 3 for a discussion of distribution specialists, pp. 62–63.

distribution. Dependence on the central marketplace has been replaced by a vast network of wholesalers, retailers, and specialized intermediaries.

A THEORY OF DISTRIBUTION PROCESSES

Three basic problems of exchange must be resolved by the overall distribution processes. The first is a basic need to match specialized production with specific demand. This matching process resolves discrepancy of quantity, assortment, and search during the distribution process. The second problem is one of spatial discrepancy, which involves the transportation of goods from location of production to location of consumption. The third problem is to reconcile supply with demand when they occur at different times.

These basic exchange problems are resolved by the overall distribution process. The manner by which distribution arrangements resolve these inherent problems represents the core of channel theory. In this section, the key processes of sorting, spatial closure, and temporal closure are reviewed. Each process is fundamental to high-level distribution.

Sorting

Specialization and competition for differential advantage creates a wide range of products and services. Manufacturers and producers supply large quantities of unique products that are demanded by other producers, intermediary businesses, and consumers in combination. Each buying unit seeks a unique assortment of goods. The process of reconciling discrepancies in quantity and assortment is *sorting* The quantity of an individual product demanded for a specific assortment is typically much less than the quantity manufactured. Furthermore, specialized production tends to be geographically concentrated. In contrast, demand is typically scattered in time and location.

Sorting is the distribution process used to overcome discrepancy of assortments and reduce required searching. The sorting process was first described by Hovde and more fully developed by Alderson.[4] Sorting consists of four basic activities: (1) standardization, (2) accumulation, (3) allocation, and (4) assortment.

Standardization Standardization is the task of collecting uniform products from alternative suppliers. The idea of standardization evolved from agriculture, where grains and fruits needed to be sorted by quality grade. In an industrial context, standardization consists of grading manufactured goods. Businesses specializing in standardization typically concentrate in specific products. Thus, they often function as the standardization specialists for a specific industry.

---

[4] The concept of sorting was first developed by Hovde in Howard T. Hovde, special ed., "Wholesaling in our American Economy," *Journal of Marketing,* supplementary issue **14:**2, September 1949, pp. 84–107. It was later articulated by Alderson in Wroe Alderson, *Marketing Behavior and Executive Action,* Homewood, IL: Irwin, 1957, Chapter 7.

Accumulation   Because of the vast geography of many producing areas and the dispersion of buying units, it is necessary to match supply and demand. From a practical viewpoint, no individual business can control the entire supply of any product. Accumulation consists of assembling standard products into large quantities. Accumulation is typically performed geographically closer to demand than is standardization. For example, standardization of the state of Washington's apples will typically occur near the orchards, while accumulation will usually be performed in major markets by product and fruit wholesalers. One purpose of accumulation is to reduce transportation cost. The transportation cost reduction results from moving quantities in truckloads to the accumulating business rather than shipping many small amounts long distances directly to retailers.

Allocation   Allocation is the development of adequate supplies to satisfy the demand of numerous customers. Allocation results in a broad choice of individual goods that have similar or related end use. For example, tools, housewares, and building materials may be purchased from the same wholesaler. Similarly, carpets, drapes, and furniture can often be purchased from a single source. Allocation represents the general wholesale stage of the distribution process.

Assortment   The last stage in sorting activity is the assembly of specific goods into a customized order. A department store, for example, must offer a product assortment that appeals to a specific clientele. Department store buyers must arrange an overall merchandise assortment consisting of men's and women's clothing, appliances, hardware, furniture, and so forth. With assorting, a retailer achieves a customized selection of merchandise designed to satisfy its specific customers.

Illustration of Sorting   Figure 4-2 uses furniture to illustrate the sorting process. Sorting starts with a number of manufacturing firms specializing in such items as carpets, drapery textiles, and furniture. During standardization, production of two suppliers is graded from among all carpet suppliers. During accumulation, standard carpet is assembled to meet expected demand in a specific market. At the same time, a similar standardization and accumulation process is occurring for drapery textiles and furniture. During allocation stage, the carpets, drapery textiles, and furniture are combined into a selection of household furnishings. At the assortment stage, the unique requirements of specific buyers are accommodated.

Sorting resolves the product-discrepancy problem created by specialization. A major distinction between a developing and a highly industrialized economy is the degree to which the distribution infrastructure is capable of performing sophisticated sorting. Sorting efficiency is essential in an advanced economy.

Related to sorting is the search aspect of distribution. In an economy characterized by freedom of consumption and production, a great deal of uncertainty exists concerning what is going on. Manufacturers are not certain which products consumers will buy. On the other hand, buyers are not certain that products they desire will be available. Businesses engaged in sorting are required to anticipate or forecast customers' product preferences. A great deal of sorting efficiency depends upon the ability

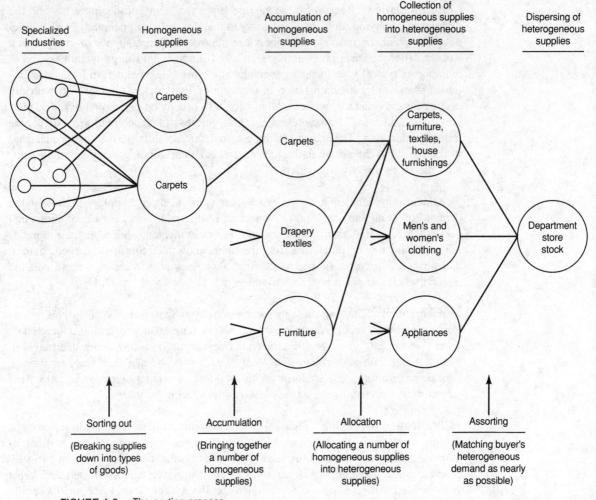

FIGURE 4-2 The sorting process.

to assemble products that match demand requirements reasonably well. This process of reconciliation is referred to as *searching*. Intermediaries in the marketing channel facilitate the search process. In a free-market system, sorting and search are both driven by market demand.

Spatial Closure

The discussion of sorting highlights the basic need for the distribution process to overcome geographic problems. Direct-market, central-market, and multistage systems are examined from the viewpoint of space closure.

As a multistage exchange system develops, additional complexity enters the dis-

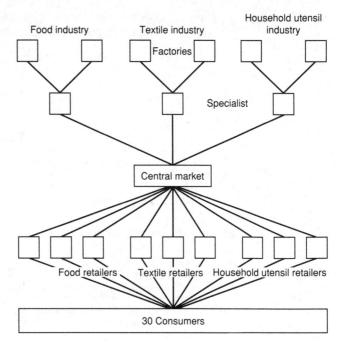

FIGURE 4-3   A multistage distribution system.

tribution process. The multistage distribution system characteristic of more advanced societies is illustrated in Figure 4-3. Assume that there are six manufacturers, two each in food, textiles, and household utensils. A distribution specialist concentrates on each of the three product lines. To understand the process, assume that the channel structure consists of a central market—nine retailers and thirty consumers. The three specialists must make two transactions with each manufacturer, for a total of six transactions. Each specialist also requires a transaction with the central market, for a total of nine transactions. The nine retailers will each require a transaction to obtain goods from the central market. Thus, the total system requires twenty-four transactions for spatial closure to be completed to the retail level. For the completion of retailer-to-consumer linkage, a total of 270 additional transactions (9 × 30) may be necessary should each consumer find it necessary to visit each retail outlet.

Table 4-1 provides an example of costs associated with direct-market, central-market, and multistage systems. At the top, five participants in a direct system are illustrated as requiring ten transactions to match supply and demand. Because of the small quantities demanded by each, the total cost per shipment is high. As an illustration, let's assume that each shipment costs $5 and each transaction $1 in a direct-distribution system. The total transportation cost is $50 and the transaction cost $10. The total cost of direct distribution is $60. With a central market, let's assume transport from production to market is in large quantities at $6 per shipment. Transportation

TABLE 4-1   TOTAL COST OF THE DIRECT-, CENTRAL-MARKET, AND
MULTISTAGE DISTRIBUTION STRUCTURES

Direct distribution		
Transactions		
Ten transactions at $1.00	=	$10.00
Movements		
Ten movements at $5.00	=	50.00
Total cost		$60.00

Central-market distribution		
Transactions		
Ten Transactions at $1.00	=	$10.00
Movements		
Producer to central market		
Five movements at $6.00	=	30.00
Central market to buyer		
Ten movements at $1.00	=	10.00
Total cost		$50.00

Multistage distribution		
Transactions		
Producer-specialist, central market		
Nine transactions at $1.00	=	$ 9.00
Central-market retailer		
Nine transactions at $1.00	=	9.00
Retailers-buyers		
270 transactions at $.50	=	135.00
		$153.00
Movements		
Producer-specialist, central market		
Six movements at $4.00	=	$ 24.00
Central-market retailer		
Nine movements at $2.00	=	18.00
		42.00
Total cost		$195.00

from the central market to the buyer is $1. The inbound per-shipment cost is higher, but the unit cost is less because only five shipments are required. The transaction cost is still $1 per transaction. Total inbound transportation cost is $30. Total transaction cost remains at $10. Outbound distribution cost is $10, for a total of $50 using a central market. The central market has a $10 efficiency advantage over direct distribution. With the emergence of a specialized intermediary, cost is further reduced to $45 because fewer transactions are required. To evaluate the multistage exchange, assume an intermediate transaction cost of $1 and of $.50 between consumers and retailers. Assume that the transportation cost from the manufacturer through the specialist to the central market is $4. All other shipments have a transportation cost of $2. Table 4-1 presents comparative total cost of the direct-market, central-market, and multistage distribution structures. The least cost or most efficient distribution results from transaction minimization offered by the multistage approach.

The basic concept that facilitates spatial closure is referred to as the *principle of minimum total transactions.*[5] It illustrates the basic justification for using a multistage exchange distribution structure. The introduction of specialists serves to reduce total transactions. It also facilitates the transport of products in larger quantities over a long distance, thereby reducing transportation cost.

At least one nagging question remains concerning channel structure. Is it possible to proliferate intermediaries to the point that a multistage system will increase total cost? An unjustified proliferation of intermediaries could result in increased transactions and consequently increased distribution cost. The concern of potential overdevelopment and potential misuse of intermediaries is the basic reason for continuous reexamination of the structural arrangement that a firm employs to achieve effective and efficient distribution.

In terms of cost-benefit balance, intermediaries may be added for reasons other than distribution economy. Each distribution system has what Bucklin has termed *service outputs.*[6] These outputs include: (1) *lot size,* or the ability to procure small quantities; (2) *waiting time,* or the length of time it takes following purchase to obtain actual possession of goods; (3) *market decentralization,* or the proximity of goods to the buyer and associated convenience; and (4) *product variety,* or combinations of products that most closely match desired assortments. As value-added service benefits increase, more intermediaries are likely to be involved and distribution costs can be expected to increase independently of the economics of realizing minimum total transactions.

Temporal Closure

An additional demand that must be satisfied during the distribution process is related to time limitations. Temporal closure refers to the fact that there is a difference between the time when products are produced and the time when products are demanded. This time difference must be overcome. Since manufacturing often does not occur at the same time as products are demanded, warehousing is required. A second aspect of temporal closure is concerned with the flow of products throughout the distribution system in a timely manner, one likely to ensure acceptable customer satisfaction. Both aspects of temporal closure require product storage. Thus, the economics of maintaining inventory becomes an important concern.

At first glance it may appear that establishing a multistage distribution structure will automatically increase channel inventory. On the contrary, inventory may be lower in a multistage distribution arrangement. Without the specialization of multistage distribution, each channel participant is required to maintain a large inventory

---

[5] Margaret Hall, *Distributive Trading,* London: Hutchinson's University Library, 1951, p. 80.
[6] Louis P. Bucklin. *A Theory of Distribution Structure,* Berkeley: IBER Special Publications, 1966.

to reduce inconvenience and cost of uneconomical transportation. In undeveloped societies, consumers are required to stockpile inventory. Since there are many more consumers than distribution specialists and producers, the total inventory in a direct-distribution economy would be large. In a multistage system, the flow of goods can be planned to satisfy demand with minimum inventory. The key to efficient temporal closure is inventory velocity that results in rapid turnover. This relationship of temporal closure to inventory requirements is known as the *principle of massed reserves*.[7] In addition to keeping overall inventory and associated storage costs down, multistage distribution serves to increase the buyers' convenience.

This brief look at channel theory serves to highlight the universal relationships upon which channels are built. It also serves as a foundation for applying channel concepts to a variety of situations that involve distribution process, which will expand understanding.

COMPLEX DISTRIBUTION ARRANGEMENTS

Channel structures become complicated as firms seek arrangements for the resolution of three distribution problems associated with sorting, spatial closure, and temporal closure. Unless all three problems are simultaneously resolved, the aggregate distribution infrastructure will fail. The 1990 consumer crisis of the Soviet economy is a prime example of an aggregate infrastructure failing to resolve the three basic exchange requirements for effective distribution.[8] The primary reasons that specialized intermediaries exist is that they facilitate resolution of the exchange process.

From the simple notion of direct marketing, the introduction of specialized intermediaries results in a complex channel structure. Figure 4-4 illustrates the variety of channels used to distribute household furniture. These variations in distributive arrangements result from the dynamic process of seeking better ways to resolve the inherent exchange requirements. The concept of channel separation provides a way to resolve some aspects of the inherent exchange problems through increased specialization.

Two concepts are fundamental to the development of complex or specialized channel arrangements. They are channel separation and postponement. Channel separation provides a way to resolve some aspects of the inherent exchange problems through increased specialization. Postponement offers a way to reduce risk associated with exchange. All of these concepts are more fully developed because they are fundamental to channel design, which is discussed in Part Two.

Structural Separation

The separation of channel focus into two activities—demand creation and supply—offers a way to view overall requirements that may facilitate specialization.[9] Although

---

[7] Hall, op. cit., p. 81.

[8] ''Soviet Economic Reform: 500 Days—Does It Stand A Chance?'' *Business Week,* October 1, 1990, pp. 138–148.

[9] See Bowersox, *Logistical Management,* op. cit., pp. 89–92.

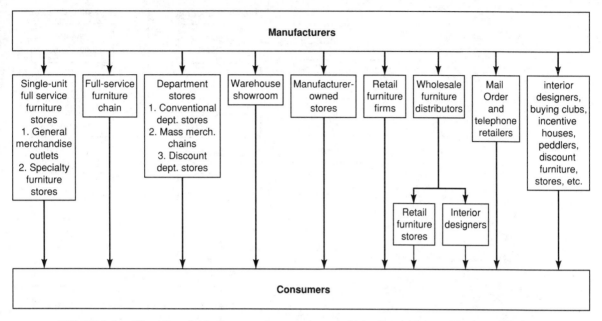

FIGURE 4-4   Alternative distribution arrangements household furniture. (*Source: Furniture Marketing,* p. 191. Courtesy of Fairchild Books, Division of Fairchild Group.)

both physical and legal exchange of ownership must take place for a distribution channel to achieve its mission, there is no requirement that the work efforts must be performed simultaneously or by the same network of intermediaries. A product may change ownership one or more times without physically moving. Alternatively, a product may be transported across the nation without changing ownership.

The Logic of Separation   Activities involved in logistics are not directly related to transaction-creating efforts such as advertising, pricing, credit, and personal selling. This basic independence can be exploited to increase functional specialization. In fact, the most effective network for facilitating profitable sales may not be the most efficient logistics arrangement.

The marketing channel consists of primary and specialized intermediaries such as manufacturing agents, sales personnel, jobbers, wholesalers, and retailers, all of whom are engaged in negotiating, contacting, and administrating sales on a continuing basis. The logistics channel contains a network of intermediaries engaged in the functions of physical movement. Participants are logistics specialists concerned with achieving product transfer. The logistics channel provides time and place utility at a cost consistent with marketing objectives.

Examples of Channel Separation   Figure 4-5 illustrates potential separation of the overall distribution channel for color televisions. The only time the marketing and physical distribution channels formally merge is at the manufacturer's factory and the

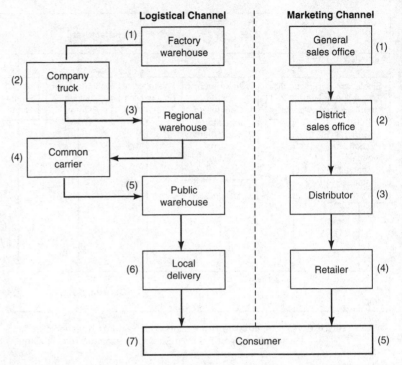

FIGURE 4-5   Example of marketing channel separation for color televisions. (*Source:* Donald J. Bowersox, David J. Closs, and Omar K. Helferich, *Logistical Management,* 3d ed., New York: Macmillan, 1986, p. 91. Reprinted with permission of Macmillan Publishing Company. Copyright © 1986 by Macmillan Publishing Company.)

consumer's home. Two groups of intermediaries are deployed within the overall channel to maximize specialization. Three specialists are employed in the physical distribution channel: a common transportation carrier, a public warehouse, and a specialized local-delivery firm. In addition, three levels of logistics operations are performed by the manufacturer. Television sets are initially stored in the company's factory warehouse, transported in proprietary trucks, and then stored in a regional warehouse facility before specialized intermediaries begin to participate in the logistics channel.

The distributor has legal title to the television sets from the time they are shipped from the manufacturer's regional warehouse. Retailers are served from the public warehouse. During the logistics process, the distributor never physically stores, handles, or transports the television sets. When the retailer sells a set, delivery is made to the consumer's home from the distributor's stock being held in the public warehouse. The retailer maintains limited stock for point-of-sale display. Sales are negotiated between the retailer and consumer, including a commitment to deliver a specified television set model and color directly to the consumer's residence. Direct-to-home customer shipment is completed from a strategically located public warehouse which may be many miles from the point-of-sale transaction and product-delivery destination.

Another example of channel separation is a factory branch sales office that does not carry inventory. Such branches exist exclusively to facilitate ownership transfer transactions. The ultimate logistics transfer between buyer and seller is based on such factors as value, size, weight, and perishability of the shipment. The network of branch offices is planned to provide the manufacturer the greatest market impact for purposes of stimulating sales. The logistics process is designed so that specified customer-service performance levels can be achieved as efficiently as possible.

The concept of separation should not be interpreted to mean that either the transaction or the logistics channel can stand alone. Such a conclusion could be drawn from the emphasis placed on the transaction channel and the neglect of consideration of logistics in recent marketing literature. Both channels must function for a profitable sale to be realized. Both aspects of channel performance are essential to the overall marketing process.

Separation should be encouraged to the extent that it results in improved performance as a result of functional specialization or spin-off. Separation does not necessitate separate legal entities. The same intermediary may be capable of performing both transactional and logistics requirements. Successful wholesalers typically combine the performance of both basic requirements.

Postponement

The concept of postponement has received considerable attention in the marketing literature over the years.[10] However, a considerable gap has existed between the theory and practice of postponement. This gap has rapidly begun to close as a result of the impact of information technology. Over the past few years, channel structures have begun to reflect wider managerial implementation of postponement strategies.

In traditional channel arrangements, emphasis has been placed on forward positioning of products in anticipation of future transactions. Anticipatory effort is characteristic of most manufacturing, wholesaling, and retail methods of distribution. The typical arrangement is for products to be manufactured, transported, stored, handled, bought, and sold numerous times before they arrive at a location ready for sale to an industrial user or consumer. The risk associated with anticipatory distribution has traditionally been viewed as being inherent to the value-added process.

Postponement is a risk-reducing concept.[11] The basic idea is to seek structural arrangements or agreements that postpone final-product configuration or geographical positioning until a final customer commitment or order is received. In other words, postponement strategies do not seek to finalize products or move them to forward markets until they are sold. To the degree that advanced commitment from customers

---

[10] For example, see Wroe Alderson, "Marketing Efficiency and the Principle of Postponement," *Cost and Profit Outlook, 3, September 1950;* Wroe Alderson, *Marketing Behavior and Executive Action,* Homewood, IL: Irwin, 1950, p. 424; Louis P. Bucklin, "Postponement, Speculation, and the Structure of Distribution Channels," *Journal of Marketing Research,* **2,** February 1965, pp. 26–32; and Donald J. Bowersox, David J. Closs, and Omar K. Helferich, *Logistical Management,* 3d ed., New York: Macmillan, 1986, pp. 57–58.

[11] Alderson, *Marketing Behavior and Executive Action,* op. cit.

can be obtained, anticipatory effort is reduced, resulting in little or no risk of manufacturing or distribution error.

The ultimate in postponement is manufacturing to order. If a customer is willing to wait for a product to be built to specification and delivered at some future date, the ideal of postponement is captured. While some capital goods such as mainframe computers, heavy machinery, and transportation equipment have traditionally enjoyed made-to-order lead time, few consumer products are produced and distributed under such time-delayed arrangements. However, the speed of response using advanced information technology makes it increasingly possible to build postponement strategies into some channel arrangements without sacrificing customers' satisfaction.

The benefits of postponement can be incorporated into a channel system around *form* or *time*. Each is described and illustrated.

Form Postponement   Form postponement consists of delaying final manufacturing, assembly, or packaging until the customer's preference is established. From an operational viewpoint, the product is customized to the customers' specification during the order cycle and delivered without time delay as promised. From an ideal perspective, the postponement of final form is completed without the knowledge of the customer. The channel arrangement in which a postponement strategy is implemented typically has an overall response time to orders that is equal to that of competitors who follow traditional anticipatory distribution practices.

The classic example of form postponement is mixing paint to customers' specifications in retail stores. Many consumers may not remember, but the original paint distribution process consisted of a wide variety of colors and sizes of paint being factory mixed and then distributed to dealers in anticipation of future sale. The result was an inventory-intense distribution channel that was prone to excessive out-of-stocks. There was always the risk of inventory being poorly distributed as a result of the inability to accurately forecast forced-color assortments, alternative paint varieties, and a limited number of sizes. The perfection of in-retail-store mixing literally changed paint distribution overnight. As a result of form postponement, product lines offering consumers wider choice proliferated, and out-of-stocks of specific sizes or colors became virtually nonexistent.

Numerous examples of form postponement, many of which involve final manufacturing, exist in today's information-intensive channel arrangements. One of the earliest examples of form postponement involved consumers being provided with a range of appliance panels for home installation. General Electric and Whirlpool dishwashers and trash compactors were sold with a kit consisting of a variety of front panels in different colors that could be installed by consumers. Providing the kit served to reduce the color assortment of appliances that needed to be manufactured and stocked to accommodate customers' color preferences. The kit feature allowed a standard appliance capable of accommodating a wide variety of colors to be manufactured and distributed.

Information technology has also introduced form postponement flexibility into assembly and packaging. For example, products such as aseptic juice drinks can be configured into multi-packs of different quantities and flavors during warehouse order processing. Point-of-sale product-assortment displays designed to fit specific retail stores' merchandising space can be assembled to specification during order assembly. Benetton has perfected the process of dying sweaters specific colors that are in popular demand at their retail stores as part of normal retail inventory replenishment.[12] Many producers of private-label merchandise delay affixing labels to what are referred to as *bright* cans until specific customer orders are received.

The above examples represent a few of the many unique ways that form postponement is being structured into channel arrangements. Information technology is increasingly making it possible to postpone performance of selected tasks until orders are being processed. Such arrangements typically require the cooperation of downstream channel members such as dealers or distributors for the performance of final-product configuration. Such functional transfer serves to reduce overall channel risk while at the same time dramatically improving customer-service capabilities. The end result is being at the competitive edge of highly customized manufacturing while retaining the benefits of mass-production economy of scale.

Time Postponement In many ways, time postponement operates in a manner directly opposite to that of form delay strategies. The basic idea of time postponement is to delay product location or positioning until receipt of the customers' orders. Once the exact order requirements are identified, then shipment directly to customers is performed as expeditiously as required to satisfy promised customer-service performance.

Time postponement exploits a basic principle of inventory management.[13] To the extent that inventories can be consolidated into one or a few stocking locations, the total quantity required to provide a specified level of availability to customers can be reduced. The idea behind time postponement is to complete manufacturing in the most economical manner but to avoid the risk of poor distribution by maintaining inventory in a few centralized stockpiles. Thus, a full assortment of products can be maintained at the central stocking location. The centralization of inventory increases the capability to completely fill orders because the risk associated by anticipatory forward distribution to field-stocking locations has been postponed.

The Parts Bank warehouse that Federal Express operates as part of its Business Logistics Services (BLS) is a prime example of time postponement. The Parts Bank distribution system operates twenty-four hours a day and is capable of receiving customer orders as late as 7 P.M. for nationwide delivery before noon the next day. The Parts Bank integrated distribution program combines advanced information technology and premium transportation capacity to operationalize time postponement. The benefits of time postponement are very appealing to firms that confront extreme demand variation or that distribute high-valued products. The Parts Bank services are used by over forty medical supply companies, which has resulted in the facility being labeled the "Bionic Boulevard."[14]

---

[12] "Benetton's Colorful Franchises," *Marketing Communications*, **11**:5, May 1986, p. 27.
[13] See Bowersox, *Logistical Management,* op. cit., pp. 281–288.
[14] Charles Von Simson, "America's Warehouse," *Information Week*, May 16, 1988, pp. 20–32.

While time and form postponement initiate from different starting points, their objectives are similar—reduce anticipatory distribution risk. To avoid anticipatory distribution, both types of postponement exploit advanced information technology. Form postponement delays final-product configuration until as late as possible in the distribution process. To operationalize form postponement, channel arrangements must be negotiated that can accomplish decentralized final-product assembly in a high-quality manner. Time postponement relies upon rapid distribution for the satisfaction of customers' requirements. High levels of product availability result from the strategy of centralized stocking. Naturally, with many channel designs structural arrangements are sought that will enable some degree of both time and form postponement to be achieved simultaneously. The available range of channel structure alternatives continues to expand as a result of advancements in information technology.

STRUCTURAL CLASSIFICATION

A formal classification of channel arrangements is now presented, based upon the overall presentation of Part One. Channel structures are classified on the basis of acknowledged dependence of participants. Three channel classifications are specified, ranging from least- to most-open acknowledgment of dependence: (1) single-transaction channels, (2) conventional channels, and (3) vertical marketing systems. Figure 4-6 provides a graphic illustration of channel arrangement based on relative acknowledged dependence.

Single-Transaction Channels

A great deal of marketing activity results from transactions negotiated with the expectation that the business relationship will not be repetitive. Business negotiated on the expectation of a single transaction usually follows a search on the part of both the buyer and seller to locate suitable sources. Prime examples of single-transaction chan-

FIGURE 4-6   Classification of channel relationships based on acknowledged dependency.

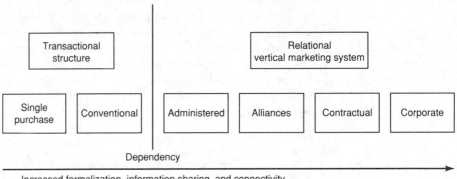

nels are real estate sales, stock and bond ownership transfers, and the sale of selected forms of durable industrial equipment. For example, the sale of an asphalt-mixing plant that has an extended useful economic life is likely to result from a single-transaction negotiation.

In a technical sense, no channel arrangement of lasting duration exists to facilitate ownership transfer in a single-transaction channel. At the time of the actual transaction negotiation, a channel capability is required to meet and fully execute the specified transaction terms. Once all requirements agreed to by parties to the transaction are completed, mutual obligation ceases. To the extent that warranties and guarantees are specified as part of the ownership transfer, they must be fulfilled. However, even if the transaction proceeds without a hitch and all parties are fully satisfied, the likelihood for repetitive transactions is minimal.

Single-transaction channels are common in international trading. Using the services of an import or export agent, two firms may undertake a large-scale purchase or may even exchange goods through a barter or arbitrage arrangement with no expectation of future involvement. However, if the experience is positive, the initial transaction may potentially result in repeat transactions and ultimately evolve into a conventional channel arrangement.

Conventional Channels

Channels classified as conventional are also often referred to as free-flow. The free-flow notion is descriptive because it clearly captures the basic nature of this type of channel arrangement. Firms engaged in conventional channels do not perceive extensive dependence. They do, however, acknowledge the benefits of specialization and focus their performance to a specific area of the overall channel. Enterprises that participate in conventional channels seek benefits of specialization whenever and however possible. Thus, whereas participants in conventional channels seek improved marketing efficiency, they do so without becoming fully committed as members of a behavioral marketing system.

It follows that, over time, conventional marketing channels will exhibit less stability than expected in more dependent systems. The primary force for solidarity in a conventional system is the continued perception by two or more firms that they are benefiting from a satisfactory arrangement. The channel arrangement can be terminated rapidly by either party if and when the business relationship loses its appeal.

Three points regarding conventional channels are important. First, the loose arrangement or affiliation of firms in a conventional channel structure requires a minimal degree of dependency. However, business negotiations are typically adversely based, and the prime element of channel solidarity is transaction price. This relationship is described as conventional since it is by far the most common channel arrangement.

Second, a great many enterprises that function on a conventional basis conduct regular business with one or more vertical marketing systems. However, because of their failure to acknowledge dependence or formalize arrangements, the free-flow firms do not become full participating members of the behavioral channel system.

Third, the term "conventional" is not meant to include all channel participants that perform a service. For example, a common-carrier transportation company would not necessarily qualify as a channel member by providing a transportation service to a single manufacturing firm. However, the combination of a buyer, seller, and carrier would constitute a three-party channel. Thus, the conventional classification is restricted to primary channel participants.

Vertical Marketing Systems

The essential feature of a vertical marketing system is that the primary participants both acknowledge and desire interdependence. As such, they consider their long-term interest and benefits to be best achieved by participating in what is described as a *vertical marketing system* (VMS). Participation in a VMS is a behavioral relationship because of acknowledged dependence.

In order to participate in a behavioral channel system, each channel member must be willing to accept a role. The assumption is that the mutual relationship will be something greater than a non-zero-sum game and that all parties will enjoy the synergistic benefits of the arrangement. In other words, the participants feel as a result of active channel involvement that their combined organizations will be better off than they would be in a conventional channel arrangement. In this sense, the relevant competitive unit becomes the channel system.

For the channel to function as a VMS, typically one of the member firms emerges and is generally acknowledged as the leader. The leader is most often the dominant firm in terms of size and is typically committed to significant risk related to channel success. The leader usually has the greatest relative power within the channel.

While dependence is the cohesive force in VMS arrangements, it also serves as a source for potential conflict. The fundamental perception is that all who enter into a formal channel organization desire to benefit from cooperative behavior. However, conflicts evolve occasionally and must be resolved if the channel structure is to survive. One of the primary roles of channel leadership is to resolve conflict and thereby maintain stability. Another important role is to plan and implement channel change. The importance of leaders providing direction and planned change is second only to leaders providing stability.

Many behavioral channel systems are classified as VMS because they function as integrated combinations of two or more independent enterprises. Vertical marketing systems are further classified as corporate, contractual, and alliance. They are also sometimes administered on the basis of formal cohesive devices over and above acknowledged dependence.

Corporate   The corporate VMS is operated as a single business by virtue of ownership. Corporate VMS arrangements, in a pure sense, are rare because few firms can command the resources to perform all activities required at all levels of a marketing channel. Perhaps the closest example to a fully integrated channel of distribution was achieved by Ford Motor Company during the early 1930s. Firms that approach this type of channel in today's competitive environment are Singer, Otis

Elevator, and Thom McAn shoes. For practical purposes, the corporate vertical marketing system is defined as an arrangement wherein a single firm owns and operates two or more consecutive levels of a distribution channel.

Contractual   A contractual VMS is one in which dependence is defined in a formal contract. The most common form of contractual arrangements are franchises, exclusive dealerships, joint ventures, and agreements between cooperative and voluntary groups. The essential difference between a corporate and contractual arrangement is the absence of single ownership of two or more consecutive levels in the channel. In many cases, the operating expectations under a contractual VMS are more clearly specified than within a corporate system. Prime examples of contractual channels are found in the automotive industry. However, all voluntary chains such as Tru-Value, Spartan Stores, and IGA are classified in this channel category. Likewise, alignments in the fast-food industry such as Taco Bell, Pizza Hut, and most of the burger-oriented franchises represent contractual channel arrangements.

Alliances   Alliances are a voluntary form of extended organizations typically not formalized by contractual arrangements. When two or more firms agree to develop a close working relationship, the resulting alliance can exhibit many different degrees of acknowledged dependence. At the most elementary level, the alliance and resulting working relationship is classified as a partnership. In a partnership arrangement, all participants feel and exhibit a sense of loyalty to other businesses in the arrangement. However, their commitment typically falls short of a willingness to modify fundamental ways of doing business to accommodate their partners. While a desire exists to facilitate the value-added process for the good of the overall channel, a sense of individuality often causes firms to fall short of full commitment to the alliance.

In more advanced alliances, participating members are likely to modify their basic ways of doing business in an effort to gain mutual benefits as a result of their acknowledged dependence.[15] These alliances are often described as strategic because the participants are willing to alter basic business practices to more effectively synchronize operations. Strategic alliances may be either vertical or horizontal in structural alignment. An example of a vertical strategic alliance is the four-tier arrangement between Du Pont, Milliken, Leslie Fay, and Dillard Department Stores. An example of a horizontal strategic alliance is the corporate alliance that includes Abbott Laboratories, 3M, Standard Register, IBM, Kimberly Clark, and C. R. Bard. Alliances are common between primary and support participants that develop close working relationships. In selected situations, the support channel participant may serve as the catalyst in formation of the working relationship. Figure 4-7 provides an example of a vertical and horizontal strategic alliance.[16]

The key features of alliances are the open acknowledgment of dependency and the

---

[15] Donald J. Bowersox, "Logistical Partnership," in *Partnerships: A Natural Evolution in Logistics,* ed. Joseph E. McKeon, Cleveland: Logistics Resources, 1988, pp. 1–12.

[16] Donald J. Bowersox, "The Strategic Benefits of Logistics Alliances," *Harvard Business Review,* **90:**4, July–August 1990, pp. 36–45.

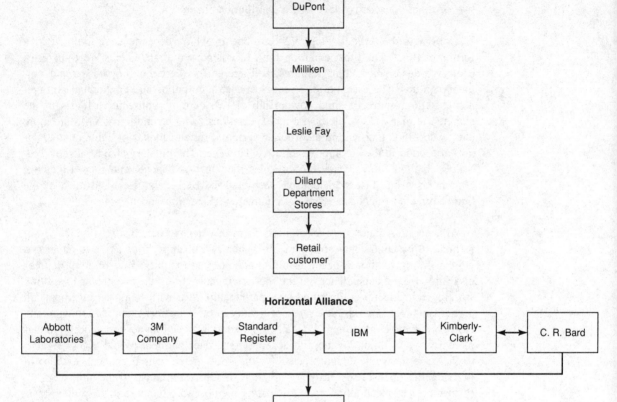

FIGURE 4-7   Vertical and horizontal strategic alliances. (*Source:* Adapted from Donald J. Bowersox, "The Strategic Benefits of Logistics Alliances," *Harvard Business Review,* **68:**4, July–August 1990, p. 38.)

potential for synergy. The alliance is a mutually acknowledged way for channel members to leverage their relationship to gain competitive advantage.

Administered   The administered vertical marketing system typically does not have the mutually acknowledged dependence typical of an alliance, nor the formalized arrangement of a contractual system, nor the clarity of power characteristic of the corporate system. The member firms acknowledge the dependence and adhere to dominant-firm leadership. However, dependence is based on the realization by participating channel members that it is necessary to *follow the leader* if they desire continued participation in the administered arrangement. With this type of vertical marketing system, operational stability based upon sharing rewards is capable of being maintained over an extended period of time. The dominant firms exist and operate from any level of the channel. However, large retail organizations such as Wal-Mart, Sears, K mart, and J. C. Penney and their supplier relationships are prime examples of administered vertical marketing systems. A situation that illustrates the power of mutual recognition without formal contractual arrangement is the Sears–Whirlpool channel. Although the two firms do not have a formal contract, their active business relationship spans more than thirty years, during which Whirlpool has been a prime supplier of Sears-brand appliances.

Conclusion: Channel Classification

Classification of channel structural arrangements as behavioral relationships is based on an acknowledged level of mutual dependence. Existence of dependence and willingness to participate on a more or less formal basis as a member of a behavioral system are the main features that result in vertical marketing systems. Figure 4-6 provides a classification of channel relationships based on acknowledged dependence. The four types of vertical marketing relationships vary significantly with respect to degree of shared dependence. In an administered system, the clear dominance of one party and its consequential leadership tends to shape the dependent relationship. When the vertical marketing system results from ownership of consecutive stages of the channel or the granting of a contractual right such as a franchise, clear lines of dependence result. The alliance is unique in that dependence appears to flow from mutual acknowledgment of the potential synergism of the alignment. Alliances in the form of partnerships and strategic arrangements are becoming increasingly popular forms of vertical marketing systems. While the concept of alliances is not new, advancements in information technology have greatly facilitated their development.

The size and relative volume of business conducted by vertical marketing systems render them important channel structures. In fact, the process of designing a channel arrangement implies that a behavioral relationship can be developed that results in some form of a vertical marketing system. However, it is incorrect to assume that the majority of business transactions are dominated by vertical marketing systems. Channels classified as conventional and single-transaction constitute major segments of marketing activity that cannot be ignored when alternative channel strategies are evaluated. The relative advantages and efficiencies of the transactional-based channels must be evaluated in comparison with various vertical marketing arrangements when a channel strategy is being formulated.

SUMMARY

Channel structure refers to the working relations among firms involved in a distribution arrangement. Such structural arrangements include all primary and support members that participate in the overall ownership transfer process. While channel arrangements are often loose affiliations that evolve over time, many firms carefully plan their channels in an effort to gain competitive advantage.

Distribution arrangements emerge for the facilitation of specialization. Three typical channel structures evolve: (1) direct systems, (2) central marketplaces, and (3) multistage distribution channels. In a direct structure, there are no middlemen. Each producer or user must visit or be directly contacted by all others with whom specialized output has been exchanged. The number of transactions is high. In a central-market structure without intermediaries, each producer assembles output in a central location from which selling or trading is conducted. Both the number of trips required to complete a central-market exchange and transportation costs are reduced. In a formal central-market structure, specialists enter to buy and sell products. The specialists assume inventory ownership risk, and the number of transactions is reduced over a decentralized structure. The central-market structure offers a savings in transportation cost since inbound products can be shipped in large quantities. Also, there is a convenience of location for buyers and producers. In a multistage structure, a wide range of specialists are introduced into the process and serve to create broader product assortments.

All exchange channels must perform three basic activities: sorting and search, spatial closure, and temporal closure. The constructs within which these activities are accomplished represent basic channel theory. Sorting involves standardization, accumulation, allocation, and assortment. The overall sorting activity requires considerable search on the part of channel participants. The spatial activity involves the use of structure to achieve movement at minimal transport cost. The temporal activity involves flow of goods through time and minimization of inventory and associated cost.

To facilitate specialization, channel structure may be logically separated on the basis of marketing and logistics requirements. Separation affords the potential for a firm to benefit from a variety of different support channel participants.

So that distribution arrangements can be better understood, a classification scheme that differentiates among channel members by perceived dependence is used. In a broad sense, channel structures are classified, ranging from least to most open acknowledgement of dependence, as: (1) single-transaction, (2) conventional, and (3) vertical marketing systems. Vertical marketing systems are further classified as corporate, contractual, alliances, or administrative, based on the existence of formal cohesive devices over and above acknowledged dependence.

QUESTIONS

1 It has been said that "the exchange system is designed to achieve spatial and temporal closure in the economic sector." Explain what is meant by this statement.
2 What is the difference between a decentralized and a centralized marketplace system?
3 How does sorting overcome the problems inherent in heterogenous supply and demand?
4 Is sorting a function designed to cope with the discrepancy of quantity, assortment, and search activities? Explain.
5 Given the principle of minimum total transactions, is it possible to have too many intermediaries? Explain.
6 Why do various forms of indirect or complex distribution arrangements emerge in advanced industrial economies?

7 What is the primary logic behind potential separation of transaction and logistics channel structure?

8 What is the essential difference between time and form postponement? How do the two forms of postponement relate to anticipatory distribution?

9 Why are single-transaction and conventional channel arrangements important channel-design alternatives?

10 What role does channel-participant dependence play in the different types of vertical marketing system arrangements?

11 Which types of vertical marketing system arrangements are currently most prevalent? Which are growing in prevalence and importance?

12 What is the importance of channel structure in making managerial decisions?

CASES FOR PART ONE

CASE 1-1: Gillette Sensor—An International Launch*

In April 1990, Gillette was faced with a serious dilemma. Earlier in the year, the company had launched its first major product innovation in several years, the Sensor Shaving System.

Since the launch, the razor had been a tremendous success; in fact, consumers cleared the shelves. Gillette had not expected such immediate success. Demand exceeded the company's most ambitious forecasts due to the attention the product received prior to its launch. Production was running at capacity, but orders from wholesalers and retailers could still not be filled. Gillette shipped 4.5 million razors to United States retailers through January, and by March it estimated that two million of those were already in consumers' bathrooms. Gillette knew that the cartridges for the razor would be very hard to find on store shelves until manufacturing caught up with demand, which was not expected until midyear. The shortage was most severe among high-volume drugstore chains in the United States.

COMPANY BACKGROUND

The Gillette Company is an international consumer products firm that manufactures and distributes a wide variety of products for personal care or use. The major product lines include razors and blades, toiletries and grooming aids, writing instruments, toothbrushes, small appliances, and Braun electric shavers. Exhibit 1 provides sales data from the product groups. Gillette operates sixty-two plants in twenty-eight countries and distributes products (via wholesalers) in over 200 countries and territories. Gillette employs over 30,000 people worldwide, three-quarters of which are in the United States.

Gillette's primary goal is sustained profitable growth. To achieve this goal, they place emphasis on strong technical and marketing efforts to assure vitality in existing lines; selective diversification, both internally and through acquisition; elimination of product and business areas with low growth or limited profit potential; and strict control over product costs, overhead expenses, and working capital. Income has been steadily increasing for the past ten years (Exhibit 2). In 1989, Gillette's net profit

* *Gillette Sensor—An International Launch* was initially written by Robert S. Bradley.

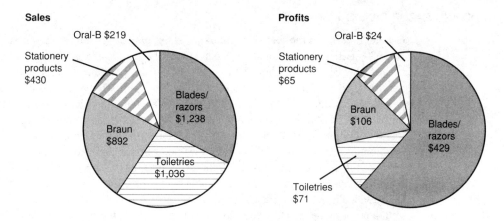

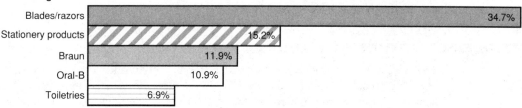

EXHIBIT 1 Gillette sales and income by product. (*Source:* A Radical New Style for Stodgy Old Gillette," *The New York Times,* February 25, 1990, p. F5. Copyright © 1990 by the New York Times Company. Reprinted by permission.)

climbed an estimated 6 percent, to $285 million, on sales of $3.8 billion. Sixty-five percent of operating profits and 32 percent of revenues came from razors and blades. Of their 1989 sales and earnings, more than half came from foreign operations.

THE GILLETTE COMPANY SELECTED FINANCIAL DATA (in millions)

Year	Net sales	Profit from operations	Income before taxes	Net income
1989	3,819	664	474	285
1988	3,581	614	449	269
1987	3,167	523	392	230
1986	2,818	229	58	16
1985	2,400	371	272	160
1984	2,289	347	259	159
1983	2,183	319	239	146
1982	2,239	319	225	135
1981	2,334	312	217	124

In 1986, special charges for restructuring expense reduced profit from operations by $179 million and, along with tender offer response costs and a change in accounting for oil and gas investments, reduced income before taxes by $243 million, net income by $165 million and net income per common share by $1.30.

THE BLADE AND RAZOR DIVISION

Gillette dominates the wet shave market for permanent systems and disposable razors. In 1989, Gillette maintained 21.4 percent of the disposable market. Its closest competitor, the Bic Corporation, had 9 percent. In the permanent razor market, Gillette controls 32.4 percent while Schick, *its closest competition,* has 8.8 percent. In double-edged blades and injector cartridges, Gillette accounts for nearly 62 percent (dollar market share) of the world market and 50 percent of the domestic blade and razor market. Gillette's Atra and Trac II system razors combined hold the number-one position, and their disposable Good News razor line is the leading disposable product.

As a result of continuous innovation, Gillette has been a dominating force in the razor and blade market. In 1971, Gillette introduced the Trac II razor, the first razor with twin blades. Six years later, the Gillette Atra was introduced as the first razor with a pivoting head. This led to the Atra Plus in 1985, the first razor with a lubricating strip. In 1990, the company introduced Gillette Sensor, the first razor with twin blades independently mounted on springs.

THE GILLETTE SENSOR RAZOR SYSTEM

The Sensor is the product of 157 raw materials, 39 finished components, and 34 assembly processes. In all, there are 230 discrete items to manage and virtually all of them are different from Gillette's other razor lines. "The only common thing is the raw steel for the blade," said Herbert Bomengen, division manager of materials management at Gillette's Shaving Division.[1] The razor has more than twenty patents and there are thirty-four steps in the assembly process. Assembly involves thirteen moving parts. The razor has platinum-hardened chromium blades that are welded by lasers. For ten years Gillette's R&D struggled with all of the Sensor's moving parts and finally developed lasers which would place thirteen welds onto each blade at a rate of two cartridges per second. These lasers bond the millimeterwide blades to steel supports that suspend the blades over plastic springs.

Gillette made a $125 million capital investment ($75 million in R&D to design and manufacture this revolutionary shaving system. Gillette believes that the three most important attributes of a razor are closeness, comfort, and safety. According to Peter Hoffman, Gillette's marketing vice president, "Sensor is the *only* razor that combines all three."[2] Sensor has a suggested retail price of $3.75 for the razor and three blades, but the razors have generally been selling for $2.50 to $3.00 and as low as $1.99. Gillette also suggests that a five-pack of blades retail for $3.59 to $3.79, and a ten-blade pack for $6.50 to $6.70. It is estimated that the Gillette Sensor system will cost the average shaver approximately $20 per year to use.

Gillette hoped to sell 15 million razors the first year and snare 15 percent of the $770 million United States wet shaver market. Gillette predicted that by year end (1990) Gillette Sensor would have a 6 percent market share instead of 4 percent as the company had originally forecast. Furthermore, the Gillette Sensor is particularly

[1] *Computerworld,* November 27, 1989, p. 113.
[2] *The Wall Street Journal,* February 21, 1990, p. C2.

important for Gillette's profitability. Because Sensor is priced higher, Gillette will still stand to make modest profits on those users who switch from Atra or Trac II. But the real boost in profits will come from shavers who switch from Gillette's disposable razor or from other brands.

The idea for Sensor was first conceptualized in 1977 by John Francis, one of the forty engineers, metallurgists, and physicists at Gillette's Research facility in Reading, England. Francis had considered the idea of setting thinner razor blades on springs so that they would follow the contours of a man's face. Thus, he built a simple prototype. The model proved its merit and resulted in the central concept of the Sensor razor.

Computer technology made a major improvement in the engineering of the Gillette Sensor razor. Without the use of computer-aided design (CAD) workstations and a completely new production line running on Management Science America, Inc.'s AMAPS software, the product probably would not have met the January 1, 1990, deadline. With the help of three-dimensional CAD, Gillette's ten product designers went to work on the design of the new razor and cartridge, some fifty others using CAD to design all of the new factory floor machines that produce the Sensor. Peter Valorz said that without the use of three-dimensional CAD, the time from the concept to finished design would have been three years as opposed to eighteen months for Gillette.[3]

Gillette's marketing strategy for the Sensor razor relied on an international advertising and sales promotion campaign. Gillette planned to spend more than $100 million in 1990 to advertise the new razor in the United States, Canada, and Europe. This compares to the $80 million spent in 1989 and $43 million spent in 1988 for its Atra and other blade products. In the United States alone, Gillette planned to spend $55 million for advertising in 1990. Just to recoup the advertising budget, Sensor must add about 4 percentage points to Gillette's current market share. This is a very difficult task, especially at a time when competitors are introducing new products of their own—both systems and disposables.

Advertising began in January 1990 and ran in sixteen countries. Peter Hoffman, vice president of marketing of Gillette North Atlantic Shaving Group said, ''We are blessed with a product category we're able to market (shaving systems) across multinational boundaries as if they were one country.''[4] Although Sensor is the first Gillette product to be launched simultaneously across Western Europe and North America using one brand name, global ad campaigns had been used previously for other products.

To kick off the new product in the United States, Gillette spent $57 million for advertising and promotion for Sensor during the 1990 Super Bowl period and used teaser ads in early January to lead up to the Super Bowl blitz. The commercial that broke during the Super Bowl proclaimed, ''Gillette announces a razor so revolutionary that it can sense the individual needs of your face.'' This catchy line was intended to attract the younger shavers. European TV spots were launched in early February. Coinciding with the TV introduction, full-page newspaper ads were displayed in all

---

[3] *Computerworld,* November 27, 1989, p. 113.
[4] *Advertising Age,* October 16, 1989, p. 34.

major markets in North America and three-page gatefolds were carried in the February 1990 issues of male-related magazines. Gillette is using a "one-campaign-fits-all" strategy for its advertising crusade.

Although Gillette executives believe the ads to be universal, some people tend to disagree. Regarding the ads, one Swiss journalist who previewed the ads noted that few of this country's men surf or play football. He added, "I think it's a very, very American commercial, and with me it didn't go down well."[5] Hoffman said that Gillette did alter their commercials by replacing some of the predominantly American Sports such as football with European sports such as soccer.[6] Following their own extensive market research, Gillette believed that its marketing messages could focus on the similarities among men rather than the differences. Gillette's message that good grooming helps a man be his best in all of his relationships—father, son, husband, lover, athlete—is a universal message which transcends national boundaries. Mr. Hoffman also said that Sensor advertising will increase in 1991 and again in 1992. The goal would be to spend $200 million a year on Gillette *megabrand advertising*. These ads will focus on Sensor but will also feature other Gillette products. The majority of their advertising dollars will be directed at shaving systems rather than disposables. This represents a major change, because as recently as 1987 the North Atlantic Group spent nearly 70 percent of its advertising budget on disposable razors.

TAKEOVER ATTEMPTS AND DIVESTITURES

In December of 1989, Gillette made plans to sell some of its European toiletry units and reorganize its United States operations. Gillette's plan to reorganize and consolidate its United States shaving and personal-care product businesses into one group resulted in the elimination of 750 employees, one-third of them in North America. Furthermore, Gillette announced that it would sell its Antica Eroboristeria line of herbal toiletries in Italy and its La Toja bath products in Spain.

In November, 1986, Ronald D. Perelman's Revlon Group initiated a tender offer for all outstanding shares of Gillette common stock at a price of $16.25. Revlon had accumulated some 14 percent of Gillette's shares prior to the offer. Revlon withdrew its offer and signed a standstill agreement in which it agreed not to buy Gillette stock or attempt to influence the operations of Gillette for 10 years. Gillette purchased the shares held by Revlon at a profit to Revlon of $34 million. In the summer of 1987, contrary to the agreement, Revlon made two more offers to buy the company which were rejected. The importance of these defensive activities for the company is that they reportedly prompted hundreds of layoffs, delays of new products, and the disposal of smaller divisions.

In February of 1988 the Coniston Group, an investment firm whose goal was to put Gillette up for sale, mounted a proxy fight but narrowly lost. Coniston owned a 5.9 percent stake in Gillette. Gillette bought back the shares of all shareholders who were willing to sell. This saddled the company with nearly $1.7 billion in debt.

---

[5] *The Wall Street Journal*, October 4, 1989, p. B4.
[6] *Advertising Age*, October 16, 1989, p. 34.

The takeover talk boosted Gillette's stock substantially. From June 1986 to March 31, 1988, total return to shareholders was 39.3 percent, compared to the S&P 500 return of 4.9 percent. Stemming from these takeover attempts, Gillette counteracted further attempts by selling several of its smaller businesses and laying off 2400 workers. Cost cutting yielded striking improvements in their Stationary Products Group, which makes Paper Mate pens, Waterman writing instruments, and Liquid Paper correction fluid. However, that unit accounts for only 9 percent of total profits. As a result, analysts expected 1990 profits to increase 28 percent to nearly $365 million, despite a modest 6 percent sales advance to $4.1 billion.

Gillette's chairman, Colman M. Mockler, Jr., spent considerable time and effort to keep Gillette independent. He needed to convince doubters that the Gillette Sensor could be a major breakthrough. Some industry observers believe that the Gillette Sensor was a strategic weapon in the fending off of other takeover attempts, and convinced skeptical shareholders to speculate on the prosperity of the razor.

INTERNATIONAL EXPANSION

During the next decade the United States domestic shaving market is expected to remain flat. Therefore, Gillette's management is committed to expanding its distribution, marketing, and labor resources internationally. Gillette proposed a $50 million razor-blade manufacturing facility in the Soviet Union which would have the capability to produce 800 million blades a year, or roughly 80 percent of the total amount exported annually to the Soviet Union. This plan is a joint venture with Leninets, a Soviet government group. The proposed plant location is in Leningrad and would be Gillette's third-largest overseas facility. Currently, Gillette's largest facilities outside of the U.S. are a Brazilian plant with a capacity of 1 billion blades per year and a West German plant with a 1.3 billion capacity. The Soviet factory will make double-edged blades of the type popular in the United States years ago. The factory also would produce twin-blade razors similar to the Gillette Atra and disposable razors similar to the Gillette Good News brand. The Soviet government is the only domestic producer of blades in that country, but Warner-Lambert and Wilkinson Sword both have a major presence in the country. Gillette has some apprehension about the venture because the Soviet ruble is not hard currency and using the barter system is the usual way to repatriate earnings from the Soviet Union.

GILLETTE'S CORPORATE STRATEGY

With Gillette's new Sensor razor, the company is hoping to regain some of the market share for disposable razors and shift sales to the more profitable shaving systems. Gillette is still the leader in both types of razors but makes only $.08 to $.10 gross profit on each disposable razor. This compares to $.25 to $.30 profit per cartridge refill for its system shavers. Gillette suggests that Sensor will provide men with the "ultimate" in shaving and will help to convert ardent disposable-razor users to system users.

Disposable razors were introduced in the mid-1970s and since that time their sales have grown considerably, from 16.8 percent of the world shaving market in 1979 to 49.6 in 1989. In 1989, disposable razors accounted for 56 percent of the unit sales of blades in the United States and are particularly popular among women of all ages and men ages eighteen to twenty-four.

Manufacturers favor system razors because the disposable razors usually receive low profit margins and are relatively expensive to produce. System razors receive favorable profit margins and are less expensive to produce. Some retailers are backing Gillette's strategy. One buyer for a drugstore chain said, "We would love to ring up five dollars instead of ninety-nine cents at our registers."[7] Retailers make more money on system refills than on disposables, and system refills do not take up as much shelf space as disposables. Other retailers are more apt to promote the disposables because they claim they bring more customers through their doors. These retailers are usually very sensitive to any actions that may disrupt their business. In Gillette's favor, some studies have supported the superiority of systems razors over disposables. *Consumer Reports* concurs that shaving systems provide a better shave than disposables. In its May 1989 issue, 500 men rated Gillette's Trac II the best of twenty-four products. Atra was ranked third. The top disposable razor, Gillette's Good News, ranked number 10. Gillette also believes that as the population ages, men will tend to prefer the more expensive permanent razors, which are popular with men over thirty.

Sensor is Gillette's only razor not sold in both metal and disposable plastic versions. Sensor can only be purchased as a system razor. This is a major shift away from Gillette's traditional two-tiered approach of selling metal and plastic handles. If Sensor is to succeed, analysts say, Gillette must convince about 10 percent of disposable-razor loyalists to use the sleek new product. But while Gillette concentrates on Sensor, competitors such as Bic, Schick, and Wilkinson-Sword will have a golden opportunity to obtain some of Gillette's 40 percent of the disposable market. Also, makers of blades compatible with Gillette's Trac II and Atra systems may stand to benefit. Furthermore, if Gillette neglects to improve the products released in the 1970s and 1980s, competition may. For example, Wilkinson-Sword, with 5 percent of the market, is now the only company offering improvements (blade improvements) to the Atra and Trac II systems.

CURRENT PROBLEM

Gillette now faces quite a dilemma. The company had expected to ship 3.5 million razors by March 31, but now has orders for 6 million. Obviously, Gillette did not foresee Sensor's huge success so rapidly. Sensor is selling so well that current demand is straining manufacturing capacity. Empty display racks in stores attest to this. Gillette did an excellent job promoting its "super" razor but made an unfortunate miscalculation in terms of demand. Leon Cohen, senior vice president of the Duane Reade drugstore chain, says he received only 12 percent of the 24,000 razors he needed. Priced at about $3 each, "they didn't last three hours" he adds.[8] Gillette contends that retailers miscalculated when estimating the number of razors to purchase as retail-

---

[7] *Business Week,* May 29, 1989, p. 58.
[8] *Business Week,* March 5, 1990, p. 30.

ers did not anticipate huge consumer demand. Many retailers say that Gillette sales-people have attributed the shortages to problems at the company's South Boston plant, but Gillette denies any assembly problems. Because of the high demand and the lack of product, Gillette has diverted production in South Boston, some of which has been earmarked for European markets, to fill orders from United States retailers. This will delay the Sensor's launch in Italy, Spain, and Portugal for several months. Gillette is even pushing up its plans 8 months for the installation of Sensor manufacturing lines in its German factory because of the strain on manufacturing. Sensor is off to a fast start, but will sales continue? Andrew Shore, an analyst at Shearson Lehman Hutton, comments, "Sensor is selling well, but the real test will be repeat purchases, and we won't know that for several months."[9]

QUESTIONS

1 What are the advantages for simultaneous international launch of a new product such as the Gillette Sensor shaving system? What are the complexities of this approach?
2 Many of the problems faced by Gillette are apparently the result of an underforecast of demand. Trace the implications of this underforecast throughout the channel, beginning at the retail level and extending backwards through production and purchase of raw materials.
3 What alternative does Gillette have? Discuss the impact of each alternative on distribution channel relationships.
4 Why is success of the Sensor so vital to Gillette? What steps should Gillette take to ensure its success?

REFERENCES

1988 Gillette Company Annual Report.
1989 Gillette Company Annual Report.
"At Gillette, Disposable Is a Dirty Word," *Business Week,* May 29, 1989, pp. 54, 58.
"Gillette to Buy Stake in Wilkinson Sword," *The New York Times,* December 21, 1989, p. D4.
"Gillette Challenge to the Disposables," *The New York Times,* October 4, 1989, pp. D4, D19.
"Gillette Inches Closer to the Razor's Edge," *Business Week,* February 29, 1988, p. 36.
"Gillette Is Hoping Sensor Razor Will Give It the Edge," *The Wall Street Journal,* October 4, 1989, p. B4.
"Gillette Is Planning to Open a Plant in the Soviet Union," *The New York Times,* February 2, 1990, pp. D1–D2.
"Gillette Job Cuts Set as Part of Overhaul," *The New York Times,* December 16, 1989, p. 37L.
"Gillette May Be Setting Closer to the Blade," *Business Week,* April 25, 1988, pp. 84–85.
"Gillette's New Razor Is Sharp Item but Stock Barely Budges on Worry Success May Fizzle," *The Wall Street Journal,* February 21, 1990, p. 2C.
"Gillette's Rivals Predict a Razor War," *Adweek's Marketing Week,* October 16, 1989, p. 3.
"How A $4 Razor Ends Up Costing $300 Million," *Business Week,* January 29, 1990, pp. 62–63.
"International Ad Effort to Back Gillette Sensor," *Advertising Age,* October 16, 1989, p. 34.
"Investor Jacobs to Turn to Proxy Fight in Bid to Put Gillette into Takeover Play," *The Wall Street Journal,* September 14, 1987, p. 24.

[9] *The Wall Street Journal,* February 21, 1990, p. C2.

"It's One Sharp Ad Campaign, but Where's The Blade?" *Business Week,* March 5, 1990, p. 30.

"A New Razor for Gillette," *The New York Times,* September 30, 1989, p. 33.

"A Radical New Style for Stodgy Old Gillette," *The New York Times,* February 25, 1990, p. F5.

"Systems Give Gillette the Razor's Edge," *Computerworld,* November 27, 1989, pp. 1, 113.

"A $200 Million Close Shave," *U.S. News & World Report,* October 16, 1989, p. 24.

"A $200 Million Shave," *Time,* October 16, 1989, p. 60.

CASE 1–2: A Tale of Two Wholesalers*

In 1966, the Bergen Drug Company was just ten years old, having been incorporated as the Essex Drug Company, and changing its name to reflect the acquisition of another firm. Bergen Drug was a wholesaler of ethical drugs, medicines, toiletries, and personal health products. Bergen's 1966 sales were $24.3 million, and its sales activity was limited to the northeastern United States, operating from distribution facilities in New Jersey and Connecticut.

In the same year, Belknap Hardware and Manufacturing Company celebrated 126 years of business. Its sales were $57.3 million, concentrated in the south-central states, served from a single massive warehouse in Louisville, Kentucky.

Both of these wholesalers were healthy, profitable companies. Each of the companies appeared to have a bright future, though changing market conditions for wholesalers called for changes in strategic direction to maintain their growth and profitability.

By 1983, Bergen Drug had sales of $1.4 billion, some sixty times its 1966 sales. Bergen had become a major national player in the wholesale drug industry. Belknap Hardware had tripled its sales to $170 million, and remained a regional wholesaler.

In 1990, Bergen-Brunswig was the second largest drug wholesaler in the United States, with 1989 sales of $3.9 billion. Meanwhile, Belknap Hardware was but a memory to the residents of Louisville. Its former corporate offices and principal distribution center were being redeveloped as office and retail space along the banks of the Ohio River. Belknap filed a Chapter 11 bankruptcy on December 4, 1985, and closed for good on February 4, 1986.

How could two firms, in such similar circumstances in 1966 have taken such divergent paths? That's the *Tale of Two Wholesalers.*

THE 1966 SITUATION

Wholesalers of all types were the dominant form of intermediaries in many industries. Goods moved from manufacturer to the retail market through the hands of wholesalers, many of whom were regional firms that exerted a significant amount of influence on both their suppliers and their customers. The wholesalers performed many traditional middleman functions—sorting, assorting, and breaking bulk—whatever was required

* *A Tale of Two Wholesalers* was written by Daniel L. Wardlow.

to transform manufactured lot quantities into acceptable retail formats. Retailers typically dealt with only one or two full-line wholesalers. Most retailers' merchandise assortment was selected from the goods offered by its principle wholesaler-supplier, with a second wholesaler as a ''backup'' source for stockout situations.

In the 1960s, hardware retailing was dominated by the independent hardware store. Similarly, retailing for prescription drugs and health and beauty aids was dominated by the independent drugstore. While there were national, or in some case, regional chain-store operations in each line of business, the one-store independent dominated.

Discount stores were a relatively new phenomenon in the United States in 1966. The first systematic development of discounting as mass merchandiser on the national level was undertaken by the S. S. Kresge Company in 1962 with the opening of the first K mart store in Garden City, Michigan. By dealing in substantial volume, discounters purchased goods directly from the manufacturer, and performed the traditional wholesaling functions themselves. For the most part, discounters avoided dealing with wholesalers whenever possible, preferring backward vertical integration to gain economies of scale. By 1966, discounting was a high-growth industry but not yet the dominant form of mass merchandising that it is today. Independent hardware stores and drugstores still existed in large numbers, and they were profitable businesses for their proprietors.

As the influence of these new mass merchandisers began to grow, many independent hardware and drug retailers began to band together to face the competition. ''Cooperative'' chains formed, where individual retailers created an umbrella organization to group together purchasing power. These new ''chains'' (such as ACE Hardware) consisted of independently owned retailers who used a common buying and distribution source that they collectively owned. In a sense, they created their own middleman to deal with manufacturers, and they surrendered a portion of their individual control of merchandising to group decision making. Such buying cooperatives took sales away from the traditional full-line wholesalers. Similar developments were taking place simultaneously in the drug industry.

In short, the market environment for traditional full-line wholesalers in both the drug and hardware industries was changing quickly and dramatically. Crucial decisions defining the strategic directions of wholesaling had to be made. Bergen Drug and Belknap Hardware took different paths in their response to the changing business environment.

BERGEN DRUG COMPANY

In 1966, the Martini brothers headed a firm that employed 500 people. Emil was president and Robert was vice-president. The company had a little over 100,000 square feet of distribution space under its control, following recent mergers and acquisitions among small local wholesalers. Bergen's trading area was the northeastern United States.

The initial response of Bergen's management to the rapid development of the discounters and cooperatives was opportunistic. Many formerly viable drug wholesalers began to fail, opening market opportunities for Bergen to fill the competitive void. It was obvious that tremendous consolidation was taking place among drug wholesalers. Small local and regional firms simply did not have the substantial "critical mass" to compete with the growing discounters. The easiest way to develop the needed mass was through the acquisition of market areas (and customers) from other wholesalers.

In April 1968, Bergen Drug began a period of intensive expansion through merger and acquisition. The Martini brothers, armed with cash from their profitable business base and offers of stock in the growing Bergen Drug began an aggressive expansion. In April, they traded stock for the New Jersey Wholesale Drug Company, a competitor of Bergen's. In August, they purchased the assets of the Kny-Scheerer Company. In October, they traded stock for Reinhold-Schumann Corporation and Crown Surgical Manufacturing Corporation of Brooklyn, New York.

On March 26, 1969, the Martinis engineered a merger with the Brunswig Drug Company of Los Angeles which left the Bergen management team in control of the new Bergen-Brunswig Corporation. This major strategic move instantly created a national distribution network for the new company. In August Bergen-Brunswig acquired Allied Churgin Labs of Newark, New Jersey. In November, they purchased Mediservice, Inc. for cash.

March 1970 marked the trade of Bergen-Brunswig stock for Gem State Wholesale Drug Company (Boise, Idaho), Sadkin Laboratories (Irvington, New Jersey), and Irwin C. Unger Dental Technicians Inc. (New York City). In May, Bergen-Brunswig acquired Cooperative Dental laboratories. In 1970, the company also acquired the W. A. Kyle Company of Houston, Rocky Mountain Surgical Supply of Denver, Valley Medical Supply and San Joaquin Surgical Company of Sacramento, Norton Chemical and Tannehill Pharmaceutical (Los Angeles), Temkin Standard Dental Lab of Rochester, New York, and Custom Cast Company of Maplewood, New Jersey.

By the mid-1970s, the Bergen-Brunswig Corporation had over 2400 employees in twenty-one states. Its market area included most major metropolitan areas of the United States. Emil Martini was the chairman of the new firm, and Robert Martini the president.

Bergen-Brunswig also broadened its product line and customer base through this series of acquisitions. In addition to the firm's original strength in the distribution of pharmaceuticals and personal-care products to drugstores, Bergen-Brunswig became an important distributor of medical, surgical, and scientific supplies to hospitals, laboratories, and clinics, thus expanding its business base away from the volatile retail drug market.

In addition to broadening its customer base and product lines, Bergen-Brunswig began to think beyond the traditional wholesaling functions. The firm began to offer value-added services to its retail-store customers. Such services as retail inventory management, shelf labeling, pricing, coupon redemption, advertising allowances, management reports, point-of-sale equipment with customized software, and direct electronic data interchange with retail locations went far beyond the traditional functions performed by wholesalers. Essentially, Bergen-Brunswig recognized the potential of the cooperatives and mass merchandisers, and created bundles of services for its customers which equaled or surpassed those offered by competitors. Independent druggists continued to exist in the competitive arena because Bergen-Brunswig responded to market changes proactively.

One example of the way Bergen-Brunswig met the challenge of the cooperatives was the creation of the "Good Neighbor Pharmacy" voluntary organization. Bergen-Brunswig offered a voluntary membership group for customer pharmacies to join. The Good Neighbor Pharmacy program offers its members group identification, advertising support, in-store promotional programs, professional image-builders, product exclusives, and other benefits. Members are actively involved through member advisory panels. In 1989, there were some 800 thriving community pharmacies who had joined the Good Neighbor Pharmacy organizations.

The guiding force behind Bergen-Brunswig's strategy was the firm's core beliefs: (1) to provide quality products and services, (2) to create viable working partnerships, (3) to generate continuous improvement in all areas, (4) to operate with respect and integrity, and (5) to acknowledge success. The shakeout among drug wholesalers reduced the industry to a "Big Five," with Bergen-Brunswig as the number-two firm. The Big Five controlled over 70 percent of the wholesale market; some 85 remaining small wholesalers had the other 30 percent.

THE BELKNAP HARDWARE AND MANUFACTURING COMPANY

Belknap Hardware was a tradition-minded organization. Founded in 1840, the firm had long been a successful wholesaler, and attributed its success to "sticking to the knitting." Ways of doing business were long established, and maintained by a long history of conservative management that was promoted from within the organization. Viewed from outside as a Louisville rock of corporate stability, Belknap employed some 1500 workers in Louisville at its peak. Many of its workers had been there a long time; in fact, finding thirty- and thirty-five-year employees was not at all uncommon. Many of its employees were the spouses, sons, daughters, and grandchildren of other employees. The conservative managerial bent of the firm seemed to indicate security and stability.

Within the organization, change came slowly and only with great reluctance. It was not until 1964 that Belknap held an annual convention meeting for its customers in an attempt to rally them around the firm and discourage them from joining the developing cooperatives. Belknap was one of the last hardware wholesalers to join a merchandising group (1980), and then only through the acquisition of a smaller wholesaler which was already a PRO Hardware member organization. Belknap was in an unfortunate position: its sales were steadily rising, but its profits were being squeezed. In 1973, the firm had $85 million in sales, and reported pretax profits of $2 million. By 1983, sales rose to $170 million, but profits had remained at $2 million.

Throughout the 1970s, Belknap continued with its traditional management and service policies. While most hardware wholesalers had begun to carefully examine their merchandise assortment to help in controlling inventory, Belknap continued to offer its retailers some 50,000 SKUs—more than double that of its competition. Even such products as guitar strings could be ordered from Belknap during this time of increasingly specialized retailing and mass merchandising. As the 1970s progressed, Belknap was plagued by high operating costs from antiquated facilities, low profit margins, and a steady decline in market share as its retail customers succumbed to the mass merchandisers or defected to the new cooperative groups.

The unexpected death of the president, Charles Brewer, in 1979 represented a time of potential change. Brewer and his managers, all promoted from within the Belknap organization after beginning as salespeople, represented the old guard. Belknap's board of directors, however, realized that the firm's decade of poor performance had left the firm undervalued and in substantial danger of failure. The board took the bold step of appointing an outsider as president of Belknap—Jerry Barton, the former president of a small Atlanta hardware wholesaler. Barton began an immediate evaluation and reorganization of the company. Barton found a stagnant organization that needed revitalization. He recognized Belknap's strengths and developed a plan to put the firm back on track.

In 1980, Belknap began a cautious expansion through the acquisition of small, regional hardware wholesalers. Arriving late to the consolidation game, Belknap chose to stay in the southeastern United States and attempt to become a strong regional player. Barton trimmed overhead costs by eliminating head-office positions, tightened inventory controls, and planned a new Louisville distribution facility to replace the old, inefficient Main Street warehouse. Through 1983, growth was constant, and the firm retained a low-debt position by paying for its acquisitions with internally generated funds.

When Jerry Barton first arrived at Belknap, he was greeted with enthusiasm by the company's managers and sales force. The field staff had begun to clamor for change within the firm. It was felt that Barton, coming from within the hardware wholesaling industry, would be a progressive leader who would rescue the firm with a savvy approach to marketing. Indeed, Barton established the first "marketing department" in Belknap's history in 1980. But soon, Barton came to be known as a bit too "radical" for Belknap. His expansion plans and belt-tightening were not seen as consistent with the conservative foundations of the firm. Within the company, anti-Barton employees characterized him as extravagant, focusing on his purchase of a corporate airplane. Whether the plan was essential to Barton's expansion plans was not the issue; rather, erosion of confidence in the Barton management team had become evident.

Through Barton's expansion-through-acquisition plan, Belknap's retail customers had expressed increasing satisfaction with the firm's performance. Belknap had achieved a 92 percent stock fill rate, while turning its inventory some 3.6 times per year. For a wholesaler, these were not outstanding performance figures, but they did represent a substantial improvement over the 1970s-era Belknap. From the customer's point of view, things seemed to have turned around at Belknap with the improvements in service and the addition of new merchandising programs for retailers. The sales force had been retrained as problem-solvers from order-takers, with a renewed emphasis on customer service. Belknap had begun to focus on supplying its largest customers with fast-turning goods.

Due to Belknap's undervalued position, the firm was seen as a likely takeover candidate. Structurally, Belknap was considered a reasonably managed firm that was undervalued due to its poor performance history in the 1970s. During 1983, the board of directors received three serious offers to purchase all the outstanding stock of Belknap. One of the groups was headed by Jerry Barton, attempting a managers' leveraged buyout with the help of an investor group. A raider-investor from Chicago made a second offer after acquiring a substantial position in Belknap stock on the open market. The third prospective buyer was David Jones, the founder and chairman of Louisville-based Humana, Inc., a large contract operator of hospitals. Jones intended to acquire Belknap and operate it as a distinct entity from Humana.

Barton and his buyout group had begun to lose support on the corporate board. Internal dissension damaged Barton's chances at grabbing control of Belknap. When Jones entered the fray, he simply outbid the Barton group and acquired control of Belknap for $35 million.

Jones, as the new owner, ordered a study of the organization by the management consulting firm of Rogers, Lambert and Company. This consulting firm had worked previously with Jones on Humana projects, though they admittedly had little knowledge of the hardware wholesaling industry. Predictably, Barton was fired in July of 1984 and was replaced as president by Frank Lambert, the namesake of the consulting firm.

Lambert quickly purged the corporate management of Barton lieutenants, and installed managers hired from outside the firm and indeed from outside the hardware industry. Lambert himself came from a background as a professional football player, school teacher, salesperson for IBM, and management consultant. He had no direct experience in wholesaling or retailing of any kind. Lambert's management style has been characterized by ex-Belknap employees as cold, impulsive, and intolerant of dissenting views.

Within weeks of his installation as president of Belknap, Lambert announced an aggressive expansion program to turn Belknap into a nationwide $500 million company by 1990. Lambert planned extensive expansion through acquisition, cost cutting, and improved customer service. The essentials of the plan were those of the Barton plan, simply larger in scope and more rapid in implementation. The Belknap organization, encouraged by Jones' deep pockets, launched on a course of development from which it would not return.

Lambert ordered a reduction in the number of items sold by Belknap, from 50,000 to 30,000 SKUs. At the same time as trimming the inventory selection, the number of vendors was to be cut from 1700 to 700. In 1984, Belknap operated three distribution centers: Kentucky, Florida, and Alabama. In a 6-month period in early 1985, the firm brought online three new distribution centers: Charlotte, Dallas, and a new facility just outside Louisville. The new Louisville warehouse replaced the outdated eleven-story warehouse that Belknap had operated from the turn of the century. The inventory required to support these new distribution centers increased from $27 million to $60 million.

Aside from the great difficulty management had in allocating resources and expertise to these new ventures, Belknap expanded into new territories. In 1983, Belknap supported about $8 million in sales in Texas and Oklahoma from its distribution center in Alabama. In 1985, Belknap had the same sales volume in those two states, supported from the new Dallas warehouse. But the Dallas warehouse required approximately $8 million in inventory investment. Sales didn't increase appreciably, but the investment required to support those sales had increased dramatically.

Belknap also attempted to change its merchandising strategy to include more name brands and fewer of its highly successful "Blue Grass" house brands. In a rush to add name brands, Belknap ignored the competitive forces of the cooperatives and mass merchandisers. In one notorious incident, Belknap retail customers were offered a name-brand paint at a wholesale cost that was $2 per gallon higher than the selling price at competing retailers. Belknap stocked some $1 million worth of this paint at its distribution centers; only $60,000 was sold to its retail customers.

As the firm strayed farther afield from its traditional approach to business, many Belknap employees became disenchanted and left the firm. Morale deteriorated further with the layoffs of some 300 employees in 1985. Customers started to defect in droves. Belknap's service and fill-rate levels declined precipitously, causing a further estrangement of the firm from its customers. Death knells began to sound when Belknap's suppliers began to demand advance payment from the firm before shipping orders to the distribution centers or drop-ship direct to Belknap retailers. The firm's trade credit was exhausted, and the firm acknowledged that it was running as much as two months behind in its payables. Lambert directed a massive inventory reduction, and in late 1985 closed three of the firm's distribution centers—two of which had been open just six months.

On February 4, 1986, Belknap filed for bankruptcy. A last-ditch effort by Lambert to rescue the firm involved the rehiring of fired Belknap executives to turn the organization around. It was too little effort and far too late to save the firm. Some 390 remaining Belknap employees were furloughed. While not a dramatic economic blow to Louisville, it was a blow to morale that the city would not soon forget. Many Belknap staffers were long-time employees, and many were prominent in civic activities. The closure of the firm left a visible dent in Louisville's pride, and to this day it has left a bitter aftermath.

QUESTIONS

1 What were the key strategic decisions made by the Bergen-Brunswig management in establishing, managing, and maintaining a strong channel position?

2 What were the key strategic decisions made by Belknap Hardware management which led to the firm's demise?

3 Sketch out parallel timelines for the two firms. What challenges were faced by each at different stages? How were the two firms similar? How were they different? What do you think was the most critical decision made by each of the firms?

4 Take the vantage point of a retail customer of each of these two firms. What would your reaction have been to the critical decisions identified above?

5 Consider the different channel environments faced by the two firms. What critical steps did Bergen-Brunswig take to consolidate its position? What steps could Belknap have taken?

CASE 1–3: Rundel's Department Store

On February 2, 1990, Gordon Franklin, buyer of men's slacks for Rundel's Department Store, was reflecting on his previous day's meeting with Sue Anderson. As field representative for Davis Manufacturing Company, Ms. Anderson had been trying for some time to increase Davis's volume with Rundel's. In the meeting, Franklin had agreed to take on Davis as a major supplier if Davis would agree to several major points in a vendor program Franklin had prepared. Franklin felt confident that Ms. Anderson would meet with Davis executives who would ultimately agree to the program.

COMPANY BACKGROUND

Rundel's Department Store is located in a medium-sized midwestern city with a population of 385,000. With sales in excess of $156 million from its downtown and four suburban branch stores, Rundel's is the dominant department store in the market (see Table 1 for Rundel's financial data). There is only one other department store in the market, Youngston's. Since Youngston's is a privately owned company, exact sales data are not known. It is generally assumed, however, that the company's revenue is about half that of Rundel's. The two firms are located about one block apart in the downtown area. Youngston's also has outlets in the same four suburban shopping centers as Rundel's. Youngston's branch outlets, however, average 86,000 square feet, whereas Rundel's branches average 121,000 square feet.

Rundel's is a division of Urban Stores, Incorporated, a major department store ownership group. With sixteen operating divisions in addition to Rundel's, Urban has outlets in most of the major market areas in the United States. In fact, 62 percent of the population of the United States lives within 10 miles of an outlet owned by one of the Urban divisions. Each division is operated autonomously due to variations in local market conditions, but there is a tendency for buyers of similar merchandise to correspond regularly. Although Rundel's is one of the smaller stores in the ownership group, buyers in other divisions tend to look to Rundel's for information concerning new products. In fact, because of its relatively small size, Rundel's management is encouraged by Urban to be a leader in trying new concepts. Urban feels that trends can be identified more quickly in the smaller division and, in the event of a mistake, losses can be minimized.

TABLE 1   RUNDEL'S DEPARTMENT STORES CONDENSED INCOME STATEMENTS

	1989	1988	1987
Net sales (including leased departments)	$156,400,000	$136,200,000	$116,200,000
Cost of sales (including occupancy and buying costs)	116,200,000	100,200,000	95,200,000
Selling, publicity, delivery, and administrative expense	26,400,000	23,000,000	19,800,000
Provision for bad debts	500,000	440,000	400,000
Interest	640,000	580,000	540,000
Income before taxes	12,660,000	11,980,000	10,260,000
Income taxes	6,260,000	7,800,000	5,020,000
Net income	$ 6,400,000	$ 4,180,000	$ 5,240,000

MEN'S SLACKS DEPARTMENT

As buyer of men's slacks, Gordon Franklin has responsibility for a department that currently contributes about 2.8 percent of all sales to Rundel's. The department has experienced impressive growth in the three years that Franklin has been buyer. In 1987 sales for the department were only $1,510,000, which represented 1.3 percent of total store sales. Much of the growth had occurred because of the addition of new products to the department and the tremendous expansion in the demand for men's clothes.

Franklin had added one major product line to the department since he became buyer. He decided that men's jeans should be represented in his department, and in three years this line became a major contributor to the department sales. Franklin has used three resources for men's jeans: Levi, Farah, and a lower-priced supplier of unbranded jeans. The jeans sold in his department are specifically designed for the over-thirty male who, in Franklin's terms, "has lost that youthful trimness but still wants to wear comfortable pants." Thus, these men's jeans are made with a fuller waist and seat, unlike boys' or young men's jeans. They are, however, available with contemporary styling.

Franklin's department also carries a full line of regular men's pants. Although suppliers vary from season to season, he typically has had slacks from Levi, Farah, Spotwood, and at least two other suppliers, including Davis Manufacturing. However, the bulk of this business has been done with the first three resources. "Off brands," he commented, "are all right for special sales or the 'Charlie Six-Pack' customer, but most of our business is in regular price, quality merchandise." He explained that "Charlie Six-Pack" is a term used to describe male customers who have the money to buy clothes in quality outlets but lack the clothes consciousness to do so effectively. "You can easily recognize Charlie since he likes to wear Hawaiian print shirts with plaid slacks," he added.

Franklin feels that his major competition comes from Youngston's and the numerous men's specialty shops in the area. A consultant recently conducted research that revealed that 22 percent of all men's slacks in the local market are purchased in department stores (see Table 2). Since his department is much larger than his counterpart's at Youngston's and since no specialty store has more than two outlets in the area, he is quite satisfied that his is the primary outlet for men's slacks in the area.

TABLE 2 CONSULTANT'S REPORT CONCERNING MEN'S PURCHASING PATTERNS IN RUNDEL'S MARKET AREA

	Market shares (percent)	
Store type	Men's slacks	Men's jeans
Department	22	15
Specialty	43	40
Discount	22	30
Chain	13	15
	100	100

TABLE 3   DAVIS MANUFACTURING COMPANY CONSOLIDATED INCOME STATEMENTS

	1989	1988	1987
Net sales	$91,000,000	$96,000,000	$112,000,000
Cost of sales	73,100,000	75,200,000	84,400,000
Selling and administrative	19,300,000	20,200,000	21,100,000
Interest	1,500,000	1,200,000	800,000
Income before taxes	$(3,200,000)	$ (600,000)	$ 5,700,000
Income taxes	cr 1,600,000	cr 300,000	2,800,000
Net income (Loss)	$(1,600,000)	$ (300,000)	$ 2,900,000

DAVIS MANUFACTURING COMPANY

Davis Manufacturing Company is a large manufacturer of a broad line of men's clothing. The firm has a nationally known brand name and ranks among the top five manufacturers of men's apparel. Recent years, however, have not been as successful. See Table 3 for financial data concerning Davis Manufacturing Company. Gordon Franklin explained Davis's problems:

> Rundel's carries Davis products. Three or four years ago we deemphasized them, though, because they simply failed to keep pace with trends in the industry. Whereas our market became much more fashion conscious, demanding new colors and styles, Davis continued to make your basic pants for good ol' Charlie Six-Pack. Their line was fine for discount stores which wanted a well-known name, but most major department stores, including all of Urban stores, deemphasized them. We just didn't want to deal too heavily in that kind of merchandise.

Table 4 presents Davis's performance data in Rundel's Department Store.

Although Franklin's perceptions generally reflect those of other department store buyers, Sue Anderson asserted that Davis was now making a concerted effort to recapture its quality image and regain a considerable share of department store distribution. New designers had been hired and an entire new designer line of slacks, jeans, and coordinates developed. Davis executives and representatives were very excited about the prospects for this line. She said that Davis had made a commitment to men's fashion apparel and, given anticipated growth of the market, was determined

TABLE 4   DAVIS MANUFACTURING COMPANY'S PERFORMANCE IN RUNDEL'S DEPARTMENT STORE

	1989	1988	1987	1986
Retail volume (in thousands)	68.0	75.8	114.0	188.2
Cost (in thousands)	42.6	47.2	85.8	112.0
Markup (percent)	37.3	39.7	40.4	40.5
Markdowns (in thousands)	23.0	24.0	28.2	30.0
Turnover	2.9	2.8	3.2	3.1
Cooperative advertising (in thousands)	.6	3.0	5.2	6.8
Source rank (in sales volume)	Sixth	Fifth	Fourth	Second

to establish itself as a major factor in the market. Since Davis wanted to regain department store distribution, Anderson had targeted Rundel's as a key account.

THE VENDOR PROGRAM

Sue Anderson and Davis Manufacturing Company executives did not hide their desire to become a major resource for Rundel's. Franklin was somewhat reluctant to develop a third major resource in addition to Levi and Farah, but decided that if Davis would agree to several points, it would be worth his while to do so. Thus, he outlined the following program to Anderson:

Business needs of Rundel's from Davis:

1 Davis agrees to maintain continuity of supply of the regular stock by being able to fill orders on a 2-week basis.
2 The ability to maintain markup of 48 percent on basic stock.
3 A guaranteed turnover rate of 3.5 in 1990, 4.0 thereafter.
4 Markdown rates on regular in-line merchandise are not to exceed 10 percent, including vendor participation during sale events.
5 Davis cooperative advertising is to include 60 percent of all newspaper linage costs, plus full cost of color, to a maximum of 10 percent of Rundel's purchases from Davis.

Rundel's support for Davis:

1 Departmental feature and display of regular running key items.
2 Commitment to develop Davis as a major department vendor, including directions toward new product areas to expand commodity base.

RETAIL VOLUME GOAL

	Spring	Fall	Total
1990	12.0	82.0	94.0
1991	90.0	105.0	195.0
1992	115.0	125.0	240.0
1993	130.0	180.0	270.0

Anderson was very excited about the proposed program. She knew that some of Franklin's requests asked for more than was offered by either Levi or Farah. For example, no other firm could guarantee fill-in or small orders on a two-week basis. To do so would almost certainly require that either United Parcel Service or air freight be used for these orders. The guaranteed markup on the basic stock was also something that other manufacturers didn't offer. The requested markdown participation on sales events, and cooperative advertising levels were somewhat higher than normal for the trade. On the other hand, she felt that such concessions should be granted by Davis if the firm ever hoped to reestablish its position in major department stores. "Perhaps later," she thought, "we can bring our vendor support more in line with the industry. Until then, however, we should offer more than our competitors so we can regain strong distribution.''

QUESTIONS

1 From the information provided in the case, describe the retail mix of Rundel's Department Store.
2 If you were an executive of Davis Manufacturing Co., would you agree to the program as outlined by Gordon Franklin? Why or why not?
3 In terms of retail structure, do you believe the metropolitan area for Rundel's Department Store is unique in the United States? Why or why not?
4 How would you prepare for the next meeting if you were Sue Anderson? Gordon Franklin?

CASE 1–4: CSX—A Channel Partner in Trouble*

INTRODUCTION

As the rain gently fell against the window of his office, Robert L. Kirk sat at his desk, deep in thought. It had been only three weeks since he assumed the reigns as president and chief executive officer of CSX Transportation, the railroad unit of Virginia-based CSX Corporation. Mr. Kirk, a nonrailroader with a mechanical engineering background, had been recruited from the aerospace industry to lead the 36,000 employees of CSX's three rail units, marketing, equipment maintenance, and operations. It had been widely speculated that Mr. Kirk was prepared to address the shortcomings of CSX's rail management system. Prior to his arrival, a number of serious rail accidents had placed the safety record of CSX Transportation under the scrutiny of federal regulators and a number of citizens' groups. In the morning, Mr. Kirk was scheduled to address these varied concerns in a public meeting of the company's Board of Directors.

Fortunately, he had been forewarned by John W. Smith, his immediate predecessor and current president of CSX Corporation, that representatives of a Michigan-based organization, Citizens Against Toxic Trains, planned to attend the meeting. Since he was convinced this group would raise serious questions about CSX Transportation's role in a particularly bad derailment in Freeland, Michigan, during the previous year, Mr. Kirk had researched the incident completely. While he felt that CSX was not the primary source of blame in the accident, he needed to establish an acceptable level of responsibility for his firm.

THE ACCIDENT

On Saturday, July 22, 1989, at about 11:30 A.M., fourteen rail cars from a thirty-two-car Chessie System Railroad (CSX) train derailed in Freeland, Michigan. The accident occurred on a heavily traveled stretch of track owned by the Central Michigan Railway

* *CSX—A Channel Partner in Trouble* was written by David J. Frayer.

Company, about 10 miles northwest of Saginaw, Michigan, in Tittabawassee Township. According to eyewitness accounts, as the train approached a street crossing, the engineer sounded his horn. Shortly thereafter, train cars began to careen from the tracks. Smoke appeared from within the tangled wreckage, and heat from the fire engulfed the area.

Back in the town of Freeland, residents were jolted by the force of the explosion. A huge black cloud appeared in the vicinity of the accident and fire fighters rushed to the area. By the time emergency crews arrived at the scene, the fire had engulfed a nearby house. According to Saginaw County sheriff's deputies, fire fighters were unable to approach the wreckage due to the intense heat. Unsure of the exact contents of the burning rail cars, officials began to evacuate a 25-mile area within Saginaw and Midland counties. Initially, this evacuation affected 400 people, including some in the extreme southeastern corner of the 40,000-population city of Midland. Twenty-six people, including at least one state trooper and three sheriff's deputies, were sent to area hospitals for respiratory irritation caused by fumes.

While the intensity of the flames began to decline around 8 P.M., the fire continued to burn in several rail cars throughout Saturday night. The hazardous nature of toxic chemicals resulted in almost 3000 people being evacuated from their homes by late Sunday night. By the following morning, the fire in one tank car had burned itself out. However, the other car, which carried mixed chlorosilenes, continued to burn. On Monday, officials decided that the area was safe enough to reduce the evacuation zone from 25 square miles to 4 square miles. Many of the 3000 evacuees returned to their homes Monday after spending two nights in hotels, public buildings, or cars. It was not until 9 P.M. on Saturday, July 29, 1989, that the remaining 800 people who lived within 4 miles of the accident site were permitted to return home.

SPECULATION AND THE INVESTIGATION

The train which derailed in Freeland, Michigan, on July 22, 1989, was on a regularly scheduled run from Port Huron to Midland carrying chemicals for Chevron, Du Pont, Dow Corning, and Dow Chemical. According to Al Crown, a CSX spokesperson in Detroit, the train included thirty-two cars, of which seventeen were full and fifteen were empty. The three-member crew reported the train was traveling at approximately 35 miles per hour (mph) (in a 40-mph speed zone) around a slight curve when they looked back to ensure that the train passed smoothly over a switch. Moments later, they felt the emergency air brakes go on. When they turned back around, they observed two cars lying on the side of the track.

A spokesperson for Dow Chemical indicated that the derailment occurred when the engine became separated from the car immediately behind it. CSX was unable to confirm this report, but Kevin Beeson of the Midland County Sheriff's Department blamed the mishap on the oversize load of equipment on the car behind the locomotive. "It looks like it was either too big or too wide for the tracks and the tracks just couldn't hold it," Beeson said.[1]

---

[1] *Detroit Free Press*, July 24, 1989, p. A12.

The wide-load, flatbed car, owned by the Santa Fe Railroad, carried a 278-ton boiler for installation at a "cogeneration" project between Dow Chemical and Consumers Power Company in Midland. It was added to the train in Flint. According to National Transportation and Safety Board (NTSB) reports, the heavy-duty flatcar had been involved in two other Michigan derailments earlier in the year. The flatcar derailed on April 1, 1989, in Flint and again on April 7 in Midland. In addition, five of the flatcar's sixteen brake shoes were found to be worn and were replaced in Chicago two days before the accident. However, NTSB board member James Burnett said the car's recent history of problems was "noteworthy" but not necessarily the cause of the accident.[2] R. Lindsay Leckie, a CSX spokesperson, called the news "highly suspicious" but also declined to speculate on the cause of the derailment.[3]

The derailed train cars, which belonged to Dow Corning and Dow Chemical Company, carried chlorosilene, acrylic acid, petroleum naphtha, and acrylonitrile. These are substances used in production of plastics, silicon products, cleaning solutions, and paint thinners. According to a spokesperson for Dow Chemical, the fire should turn the chlorosilene into hydrochloric acid, a dangerous corrosive. The acid then should rise into the air and dissipate at about 10,000 feet. The acrylic acid and petroleum naphtha, on the other hand, convert into relatively harmless carbon monoxide and water. The Dow Chemical spokesperson expected natural dissipation to rid the area of the chemicals. Leckie of CSX agreed that the chances of long-term environmental damage were minimal. In a related matter, Tittabawassee Township Deputy Fire Chief Patrick Haley clarified that a drain near the derailment site posed no health hazard since the water there was stagnant.

Meanwhile, a Michigan State University specialist on hazardous-waste disposal said that chemicals produced by the prolonged burning of the tanker full of chlorosilene may be more dangerous than the chlorosilene itself. In accidental burnings such as this one, the temperatures are not controlled at all and, potentially, other by-products may result due to incomplete combustion.

Claire Austin, director of public affairs for the Federal Railroad Administration (FRA), called the Freeland derailment a "major" accident because of the fires.[4] She indicated that representatives of the National Transportation and Safety Board, as well as local law-enforcement agencies, would be completing full investigations.

On Sunday, it was determined that a natural-gas line that ran alongside the tracks was similar to one that ruptured and exploded following a train derailment in San Bernardino, California, on May 26, 1989. The accident killed three people. To prevent an explosion, Consumers Power Company on Tuesday cut off the flow of natural gas through the 10-inch-high pressure pipeline buried 4 feet from the tracks.

While financial estimates of the damage were not immediately available, it was believed that the value of the fourteen derailed tankers could reach several hundred thousand dollars. The American Red Cross supplied financial assistance and medication for those residents who required alternative lodging, and CSX claim adjusters

[2] *The Detroit News,* July 26, 1989, p. B2.
[3] Ibid.
[4] *The Detroit News,* July 24, 1989, p. A1.

took inventories of residents' and business owners' losses as a result of the accident. CSX estimated that the cost of damage to the train, tracks, and signals was $460,000. This figure did not include destroyed cargo, expenses of displaced residents, and losses to local businesses forced to shut down for several days. CSX agreed to help clean and test houses to make sure they were safe. CSX also promised to pay hotel bills of displaced residents. Final calculations indicate that the accident cost CSX at least $1.5 million to repair equipment damage and for other related expenses.

The three-member train crew, as required by federal law, submitted blood and urine samples for mandatory testing on Saturday after the accident. Unfortunately, results were not available for two weeks and once completed, were not made public. Investigators found no evidence of drugs or drug paraphernalia in the front locomotive following the accident. On Monday, July 24, the CSX brake operator voluntarily admitted himself to an alcohol detoxification unit. However, railroad and federal officials insisted that they did not believe human error was the cause of the derailment. Claire Austin called this development "a freak thing, something to complicate the story."[5] While she admitted the possibility that the brake operator might have done or failed to do something that caused or contributed to the accident, her "gut feeling" was that human error was not a factor.[6] Reports from the scene indicated that the brake operator was alert following the derailment and even helped notify and evacuate local residents. Leckie reaffirmed that up to that point, there had been no reason to assume human error caused the accident and he did not foresee a change in that situation.

In another surprising development, the train's engineer told a union representative that he had weighted down the engine's "dead man's pedal" with an air hose in violation of federal regulations. Regulations call for an engineer to keep one foot on the "dead man's pedal." This would automatically trigger emergency brakes if something happened to the engineer, causing the pressure to be released. The engineer, whose name was not released under the union's and company's privacy rules, could have been disciplined by CSX or criminally prosecuted. However, CSX did not believe that the weighting of the pedal or any other human error by the three-member crew caused the derailment.

None of the train's seven derailed chemical tanker cars were equipped with head shields, which are recommended but not required for chemical cargoes that would call for evacuation of at least a half-mile area in the event of a spill. Investigators did not know whether the shields would have provided more protection.

A CSX spokesperson noted that regular inspections of the train tracks and cars indicated that they were in good working order. In fact, the track between Saginaw and Midland where the train derailed had been jointly inspected by railroad and federal officials only days before the accident, and no problems were detected.

THE PUBLIC RESPONSE

Immediately after the accident, a Michigan group called Citizens Against Toxic Trains called on Governor James J. Blanchard to impose a twenty-five mile per hour speed

[5] *The Detroit News,* July 25, 1989, p. A4.
[6] Ibid.

limit on all trains hauling hazardous materials in Michigan. At a press conference in suburban Detroit, a spokesman for Citizen Action, a Washington-based national public interest group, further claimed that CSX reported 410 major train accidents and 58 accidents involving hazardous materials in 1987, the highest numbers for any rail carrier in America. CSX's Leckie defended the railroad, saying the figures cited by the citizen's group could have been manipulated to make CSX's record look bad. "We do not have the worst record," he said. "In fact, we're slightly above average in accident rates. It all depends on how you look at the numbers and I would say they're using some 'cooked figures.' "[7]

CSX had three train derailments in Michigan in a five month period. Ten cars of a CSX freight train derailed in Brighton on March 12, 1989. On April 25, ten cars of a Dow Chemical train pulled by CSX derailed near Midland. In a related incident, a CSX train derailed in Chatham, Ontario requiring the evacuation of hundreds of residents.

In the wake of the accident, four Michigan congressmen asked U.S. Transportation Secretary Samuel K. Skinner for a special safety audit of CSX. They urged the Federal Railroad Administration to conduct unscheduled inspections of the railroad. In April 1989, a U.S. General Accounting Office (GAO) report showed CSX underreported accidents by 43 percent. Again, Leckie denied the charge, stating: "It's all in how you look at the numbers. We do not underreport accidents, because that would be counterproductive."[8]

Following the accident, U.S. Republican Representative Bill Schuette of Michigan announced that he would introduce legislation requiring all trains to be equipped with "black box" recorders, similar to those used on airplanes. Schuette believed an on-board recorder would have provided information as to the throttle position, amperage, and brake manipulation on the train, making it easier for investigators to determine the cause of the wreck.

The Natural Resources and Environmental Affairs Committee of the Michigan Senate planned to hold a special hearing on the safety of transporting hazardous materials in Michigan. According to John D. Cherry, the top-ranking Democrat on the committee, they needed to examine the safety of rail transport of hazardous materials, the cause of recent derailments, the adequacy of emergency response planning, and federal regulation.

Public Citizen increased its lobbying efforts against pending bills that would reduce a railroad's liability for damages resulting from spills. While industry leaders have promised to boost investment in safety devices if the liability provisions are eased, many citizen's groups argue that such legislation would in effect remove the incentive for further investment.

Michigan State Police Lieutenant Art Nash said the incident confirmed the need for a state hazardous materials training facility. Local fire departments remain undertrained or ill-equipped to handle accidents involving the toxic materials that move regularly through their communities. A planned Hazardous Materials Training Center in Lansing would provide necessary training for fire fighters, police officers, and

---

[7] *The Detroit News,* July 28, 1989, p. B3.
[8] *The Detroit News,* July 28, 1989, p. B3.

chemical industry workers to prepare them for such an event. A coalition of Michigan industries is working within the state to construct the $300,000 training complex, which was scheduled to open early in 1990.

A number of displaced residents complained of the uncertainty surrounding the accident. Many did not understand the dangerous conditions that resulted from burning chemicals. As CSX spokesperson, Leckie indicated that since this was the company's first fire involving the chemical chlorosilene, it was hard to predict how long the evacuation would last. "Nobody's ever had to deal with a fire like this," he said. "We're writing the book."[9]

And yet the feelings of many area residents were summarized by Karl Watt, a retired grocer who lives next to the tracks in Freeland. He had often worried about the passing chemical trains, but remained silent.

> Dow has done a lot for the people around here, and you don't like to bite the hand that feeds you.[10]

CONCLUSION

As Mr. Kirk perused documents that showed CSX to have spent $238 million in 1989 to maintain its cars and locomotives and an additional $150 million to upgrade traffic signals and communications networks, he wondered what else could be done. In 1988, 3051 railroad accidents occurred in the United States, and forty-four of these involved hazardous materials. Total United States train accidents were up by over 400 from the previous year. On a more localized scale, Michigan ranked third highest among states with ten or more rail accidents per 1000 miles of track where hazardous materials were present. Unfortunately, CSX was involved in several of these incidents.

Still, the fact remained that CSX was the first railroad in the nation to implement a limited employee-testing program for substance abuse in 1987. They had adopted a proactive stance toward railroad safety, but the accidents continued to happen. Some industry analysts felt that feuding between the NTSB and FRA had compromised rail safety. While the NTSB investigates accidents and makes safety recommendations, the FRA holds the authority to order those improvements. Most of the time, though, the FRA chooses not to force such changes.

As the rain began to pound against his window, Mr. Kirk attempted to reconcile these divergent opinions and derive a consistent statement of responsibility for the accident. He needed to determine whether CSX's accident reporting policies might have contributed to the firm's recent safety problems, including the Freeland derailment. It was going to be a long night.

QUESTIONS

1 Discuss the role, responsibility, and potential liability of the following direct- and indirect-channel participants mentioned in the case. Be sure to discuss who, if anyone, should accept responsibility for the accident. Also, discuss who is responsible for future health risks.

---

[9] *The Detroit News,* July 30, 1989, p. A10.
[10] *The Detroit News,* July 23, 1989, p. A14.

        a CSX Transportation
        b Santa Fe Railroad
        c Central Michigan Railway Company
        d Dow Chemical
        e Dow Corning
        f Consumers Power Company
        g Federal government (Congress, NTSB, FRA)
        h State of Michigan
        i Local governments
        j Train engineer
        k Brake operator

2 Could this situation have been handled differently? Would a joint response have been appropriate?

3 Who should have assumed leadership of public response to the accident? Were appropriate roles actually assumed by individual channel participants?

4 What are the implications of this (and other similar incidents) on relationships between primary and specialized channel participants?

REFERENCES

"Brakeman Seeks Alcohol Treatment after Wreck," *The Detroit News,* July 25, 1989, p. A1.

"CSX Names Kirk, a Non-Railroader, to Head Rail Unit," *The Wall Street Journal,* February 26, 1990, p. B5.

"CSX Safety Record Criticized," *The Detroit News,* July 28, 1989, p. B3.

"Derailment Fire Keeps Hundreds from Homes," *Detroit Free Press,* July 24, 1989, p. A1.

"Derailments 'a Growing Problem'," *The Detroit News,* July 27, 1989, p. B3.

"Freeland Derailment Triggers Action," *The Detroit News,* August 6, 1989, p. L1.

"Freeland Evacuees Go Home to 'Lives . . . Put on Hold'," *The Detroit News,* July 31, 1989, p. A1.

"Home Burns as Tank Cars Explode in Saginaw County," *The Detroit News,* July 23, 1989, p. A1.

"Last of Derailed Cars Hauled Away; Evacuation Ends," *The Detroit News,* July 30, 1989, p. A1.

"Many in Freeland Fear What They'll Find Back Home," *The Detroit News,* July 30, 1989, p. A1.

"State 10th in Rail Spills, Report Says," *The Detroit News,* September 14, 1989, p. B1.

"Third Wreck for Train Flatcar," *The Detroit News,* July 26, 1989, p. B1.

"Train Wreck Fumes Keep Thousands from Homes," *The Detroit News,* July 24, 1989, p. A1.

CASE 1–5: Simplesse—Going to Market with a Fat Substitute*

INTRODUCTION

Robert B. Shapiro, chairman and chief executive officer of The NutraSweet Company of Deerfield, Illinois, was delighted. He had just been informed that the U.S. Food

* *Simplesse—Going to Market with a Fat Substitute* was written by G. Peter Dapiran.

and Drug Administration (FDA) had approved Simplesse, a fat substitute, as generally recognized as safe (GRAS) for use in frozen desserts. He immediately set February 22, 1990, as the date of the news conference that would announce the FDA decision and the launch of Simple Pleasures, the first product to contain Simplesse. It may not have been on his mind at that very exciting moment, but the question could still be posed: "Was the manufacture of a frozen desert the best way to capitalize on this approval?"

PHONY FOODS AND DIET CONTROL

The Surgeon General's warnings on the dangers of high salt and cholesterol levels in diets and the growing general awareness by the United States consumer of health and fitness issues ensured that shoppers were ready to accept a range of product offerings. The market for low-calorie products, and products with reduced sugar, natural ingredients, and/or low levels of preservatives and artificial ingredients was constantly growing. Additionally, research now suggested that fat consumption was related to obesity and heart disease, and was also related to some forms of cancer. It was advisable that the average diet contain a reduced fat content. A fat substitute with its associated reduced caloric intake would seem to be a highly marketable development.

Research by the Calorie Control Council, a trade association of diet-product manufacturers, found in 1986 that 65 million adult Americans dieted (see Exhibit 1). The diet-control and weight-loss industry was estimated to be around $30 billion in 1986. This included such areas as exercise clubs, weight-control programs, and diet-control foodstuffs.

SERENDIPITY AND THE NUTRASWEET COMPANY

Aspartame, the ingredient of the leading sweetening agent, NutraSweet, was discovered in 1965 by James Schlatter. During work on protein compounds, he licked his finger to turn the page of his research notes and tasted a pleasant sweet taste. This was the birth of NutraSweet.

The artificial sweeteners of the time, saccharin and cyclamates, had limited acceptance because of their association with cancer in experimental animals and their bitter aftertaste. Aspartame had a more acceptable taste, was synthesized from protein components, and was metabolized by the body into components found in many natural foods.

After exhaustive testing, aspartame was approved for use by the FDA in July 1981. Since that time aspartame, under the brand name NutraSweet, has been used in more than 1700 products in twenty-seven broad food-product categories and has gained the widespread acceptance of health and medical organizations.

The Monsanto Company, a diversified chemicals organization based in St. Louis, acquired NutraSweet when in 1985 it bought G. D. Searle & Co., a long-established pharmaceutical manufacturer. It subsequently established The NutraSweet Company as a separate division of Monsanto.

NutraSweet became a marketing success. It was decided that the best strategy was to sell the sweetener to food manufacturers as an ingredient. In a unique marketing

EXHIBIT 1   AMERICAN DIETING DEMOGRAPHICS

Number of dieters

43 million women (47 percent of American women)
22 million men (25 percent of American men)

Age of dieters

Most dieters are between 25 and 49.
The 35 to 49 age group is 20 percent more likely to be dieting than the average American.

Proportion of overweight persons in the population (based on weight-to-height ratios)

24 percent of men
27 percent of women

Source: "The Demographics of Dieting," by Jeremy Schlosberg, *American Demographics,* July 1987, p. 35. Reprinted with permission © *American Demographics,* July 1987.

move, the company succeeded in establishing a brand ingredient by getting these manufacturers to carry the NutraSweet name and logo on all their products.

In spite of the undoubted success (see Exhibit 2) of The NutraSweet Company, it was negatively labeled as a "one-product" company. Patent protection of aspartame had expired in a number of countries and would lapse in 1992 in the United States. This would leave the door open to a rash of competitors in this lucrative market and would result in a certain impact on prices and market share. New product lines had to be developed quickly.

SIMPLESSE—THE LAUNCH

The search for suitable products resulted in a fat substitute called Simplesse, which was revealed in a fanfare news conference on January 27, 1988, in New York. The NutraSweet Company announced that it expected to have products containing Simplesse on the market within twelve to eighteen months.

The high-visibility product launch was made without obtaining product approval of the FDA. The role of the FDA is to review new food products and to ensure their

EXHIBIT 2   THE NUTRASWEET COMPANY FINANCIAL RESULTS, 1985–1989
(in millions of dollars)

	1985	1986	1987	1988	1989
Net sales	317	711	722	736	869
Operating income	58	142	145	154	180
Research and development	11	25	31	35	39
Total assets	1,862	1,883	1,724	1,484	1,344
Capital expenditures	4	39	31	36	49
Depreciation and amortization	73	205	206	209	215
(1) For five-month period, August to December 1985.					

Source: Monsanto Annual Reports.

safety for human consumption. To this end, it examines data provided by applicants regarding their products, their manufacturing processes, and the proposed uses and the effects on people's diets of the new foods or ingredients. The FDA can also request additional data from the applicant during the review process.

NutraSweet had not sought approval for Simplesse because it thought that such approval was not needed, given the natural protein source of the new product. It was also anxious to get into the market quickly, ahead of the already formidable competition, and to have a new product well underway before expiration of the sweetener patents in 1992.

On January 28, 1988, the FDA informed NutraSweet that any Simplesse products would be seized if they were released without approval. NutraSweet acquiesced to the FDA requests and petitioned the FDA for approval of Simplesse.

SIMPLESSE—THE PRODUCT

Simplesse was discovered by Norman Singer in 1979 while he was looking at alternative uses of cheese by-products for John Labatt, Limited, the Canadian brewing and food manufacturer. In 1985 the process was sold to NutraSweet, where it was refined and the product was adapted to be used in about twenty different foodstuffs.

Simplesse is made from egg white and/or milk protein, the actual choice depending on the application and the price and availability of the source raw materials. The manufacturing process, termed "microparticulation," involves coagulating the protein and emulsifying the result to form tiny beads (50 billion to a teaspoon). The size and shape of these beads creates the sensation of creaminess and fools the mouth into tasting the richness one gets from fat in food.

Simplesse seems to offer some considerable benefits: it is cholesterol-free, is digested like the original natural protein ingredients, and most importantly, it can be substituted for all the fat in some products without loss of flavor and texture but with only 15 percent of the calories of fat.

Its main drawbacks are that it cannot be used in cooked products because prolonged heating will destroy the structure that causes the tongue to perceive smoothness. However, hot foods can be used in conjunction with Simplesse such as hot fudge on Simplesse-based ice cream or cooked meats with a Simplesse-based sauce.

Although approval had only been granted for frozen desserts, NutraSweet considered that Simplesse was suitable for a range of product categories, including salad dressings, mayonnaise, margarine spreads, butter spreads, cheeses and cheese spreads, sour cream, cream cheese, yogurt, dips, and, of course, ice cream.

A major marketing drawback is that it was not the first fat substitute on the market. However, it is unique in its ability to replace all the natural fat content of certain products. An early release in the market has been essential so that market penetration can be gained and competitive entry forestalled.

THE COMPETITION AND THE MARKET

CPC International Inc., already had a low-calorie fat substitute made from emulsified starch, which was used in their Hellmann's Light mayonnaise. This emulsified-starch product also simulated the feel of fat in the mouth. However, it could not substitute all the required fat in mayonnaise and so the caloric content was only half of the regular product. Starch-based products had limited applications, and so CPC was continuing research into other fat substitutes.

Procter & Gamble had petitioned the FDA for approval of a product called olestra whose main benefit was that it could be used in cooked products. Olestra was a synthesized chemical. It passed through the body undigested and hence was a real zero-calorie fat substitute. However, there was some concern about the health implications if the product were eaten in large amounts, and therefore extensive testing was required. Unilever and Frito-Lay were also developing olestra-type and emulsified-protein or starch-fat substitutes.

The prize for the best fat substitute is high. Potential sales of fat substitutes in the dairy, cheese, and salad dressing markets has been estimated to be worth $15 billion. The mayonnaise segment alone was worth $660 million in 1990. Hellmann's Mayonnaise, made by CPC, held a 53 percent share of this market, compared with Kraft General Foods's 23 percent. Kraft, in a move to protect any further erosion, had signed a supply agreement with NutraSweet in 1989 before the FDA had granted approval for Simplesse.

SIMPLE DECISIONS

The choice of channel for marketing Simplesse could well determine its ultimate success. A marketing strategy like that developed for NutraSweet did not seem appropriate. Simplesse did not appear to be the universal product that NutraSweet had become. Also, NutraSweet had been introduced into a market already familiar with sugar substitutes. Perhaps there was also some merit in drawing the distinction between low-calorie and fat-free.

Like all protein-based products, Simplesse carries the flavor notes of the parent protein source, so the choice of product, especially for the launch of Simplesse, is important to achieve rapid market acceptance.

The NutraSweet Company decided that it wanted more control over the application of Simplesse. There was also the consideration that entry into manufacture might deliver higher margins than a simple licensing of the product as it had done with NutraSweet. It therefore decided to form the Simplesse Company to market Simplesse and manage the manufacture and marketing of its first range of products, a frozen dessert line called Simple Pleasures. This was an ice cream substitute that could not be called "ice cream" because food-labeling laws tied the name to a product with a given butterfat content.

Simple Pleasures, in a variety of six initial flavors, was positioned against super-premium ice creams like Haagen Dazs, with the main marketing thrust stressing the fact that the products had the taste and richness of premium ice cream but a much lower calorie content (see Exhibit 3).

The frozen dessert was distributed nationally by Dreyer's Grand Ice Cream, a California-based company that had its own line of ice cream and frozen yogurt and was also the sole New York distributor for Ben & Jerry's ice cream. It had also recently introduced its own line of fat-free frozen desserts. Dreyer's sales had grown from $136 million in 1986 to $227 million in 1989.

EXHIBIT 3   CALORIE COMPARISON—SIMPLESSE PROTOTYPES VS. TRADITIONAL PRODUCTS (per serving)

	Traditional	Simplesse	Calories Saved
Superpremium ice cream (4 fluid ounces)	283	130	153
Yogurt (8 ounces)	139	100	39
Salad dressing (1 tablespoon)	87	21	66
Mayonnaise (1 tablespoon)	99	30	69
Butter/margarine (1 tablespoon)	36	8	28
Processed cheese spread (1 ounce)	82	36	46
Cream cheese (1 ounce)	99	45	54
Sour cream (1 tablespoon)	26	10	16

Source: The NutraSweet Company reported in *Food Processing,* April 1988, p. 22. Reprinted with permission of *Food Processing* Magazine, Putman Publishing Company, Chicago, Illinois, USA.

Simple Pleasures was not the first fat-free ice cream on the market. Kraft's Sealtest brand, manufactured without Simplesse, was already available to the consumer and labeled "ice cream" in spite of its low butterfat content. Blue Bell Creameries, Inc. (Texas), also had a no-fat ice cream in regional supermarkets, and Dean Foods Company was close behind in the marketing race to have no-fat ice cream on the shelves by the summer. No-fat frozen yogurt, with which consumers might also compare Simple Pleasures, was also well represented on the supermarket shelves by companies such as General Mills and Dannon Company.

The eve of February 22, 1990, during the press conference, was not the time to contemplate the wisdom of the decision to go into ice cream making. But soon someone had to assess the success of the move, review the alternatives that had been available (and whether these options were still open), and plan the next moves for Simplesse.

QUESTIONS

1 What market-entry options were available to The NutraSweet Company in launching Simplesse? What were the advantages and disadvantages of each?
2 Having decided to release Simplesse in a frozen dessert, discuss the advantages/disadvantages of the channel options available to NutraSweet.
3 What key logistics decisions needed to be made by NutraSweet in its launch of Simple Pleasures? What impact did the product characteristics have on the logistics and channel decisions?
4 Can Simplesse now be marketed as a brand ingredient the way NutraSweet was? Or has The NutraSweet Company cut off this option because of its own entry into finished goods?

REFERENCES

"Fat Substitute Yields 'Rich-Tasting' Foods with Less Calories," *Food Processing,* April 1988.
"Kraft Is Looking for Fat Growth from Fat-Free Foods," *Business Week,* March 26, 1990.
"NutraSweet Sets Out for Fat-Substitute City," *Business Week,* February 15, 1988.
The New York Times, February 23, 1990, pp. A1, A16; and February 25, 1990, p. F15.
The Wall Street Journal, August 2, 1989, p. B6.

PART **TWO**

CHANNEL STRATEGY AND DESIGN

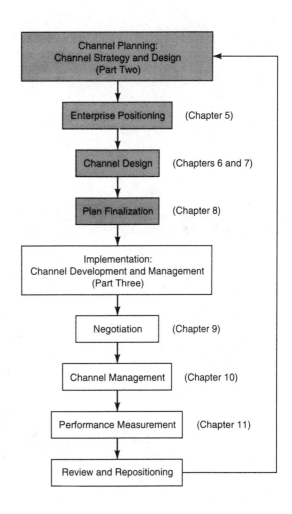

The first three steps involved in developing a channel strategy relate to various aspects of planning. They are: (1) Enterprise Positioning; (2) Channel Design; and (3) Plan Finalization.

ENTERPRISE POSITIONING

The most macro dimension of channel planning involves relating channel requirements to enterprise strategy. Chapter Five is devoted to the dual concerns of establishing corporate strategy and distribution objectives.

CHANNEL DESIGN

The second step in the design process is concerned with identifying specific channel structures. Marketing channel design is concerned with satisfying customer needs in a manner that will stimulate sales and achieve business objectives and is the topic of Chapter Six. The aspect of the overall channel concerned with product physical movement is logistics. Logistics design is the focus of Chapter Seven.

PLAN FINALIZATION

Step three in development of a distribution arrangement consists of plan finalization. Plan finalization involves the development of an analysis framework to help evaluate and select the most desirable channel structure arrangement. Chapter Eight, Planning and Analysis Framework, introduces a range of tools available to assist managers in the finalization of a channel plan. The completion of the plan results in a blueprint of desired action.

CHAPTER 5

ENTERPRISE POSITIONING

CHAPTER OUTLINE

CORPORATE STRATEGY
  Strategic Alternatives
  Strategic Alternatives: Conclusion
  Mission Statement
  Objectives
CUSTOMER ANALYSIS
  Defining the Market
  Market Segmentation
COMPETITIVE ANALYSIS
  Industry Structure
  Identification and Assessment of Competitors
INTERNAL ANALYSIS
  Performance Analysis
  Functional Strengths And Weaknesses
ENVIRONMENTAL ANALYSIS
  Sociocultural Environment
  Technological Environment
  Economic Environment
  Legal Environment
CHANNEL OBJECTIVES
  Market Coverage and Distribution Intensity
  Channel Control
  Flexibility
SUMMARY

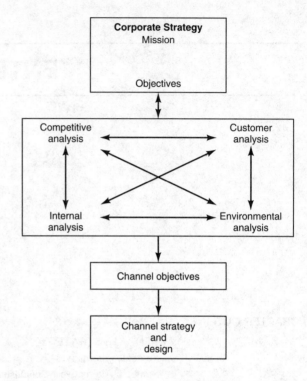

FIGURE 5-1   The business strategy and positioning process.

A fundamental responsibility of corporate management is to continuously position the enterprise to exploit the changing market environment. Management must monitor and assess the marketplace, competitive activity, economic conditions, laws and regulations, consumers and customers, and other significant factors impacting the firm's strategic position. As general strategies are developed to cope with environmental opportunities and threats, distribution channel strategies must be formed to effectively link the firm with its markets.

This chapter begins with a discussion of the broad strategic alternatives that face management in the contemporary competitive environment. As depicted in Figure 5-1, the discussion proceeds with the importance of defining a clear corporate mission and a set of goals and objectives to guide the formulation of strategy. Attention is then focused on the analytic requirements for development of strategy. Analysis of customers, competition, internal operations, and the environment are each discussed, with emphasis placed on how these analytic processes influence strategic options available to an organization. The chapter concludes with a discussion of channel objectives, which are derived from an organization's general strategic posture. These objectives guide specific marketing and logistics channel strategies, which are the subject of Chapters 6 and 7. The purpose of the chapter is to establish the foundation for channel management within the context of the firm's corporate strategy.

CORPORATE STRATEGY

While there are numerous frameworks for corporate strategy planning, Andrews, a well-known expert in corporate strategy, offers the following basic description: "Corporate strategy defines the businesses in which a company will compete, preferably in a way that focuses resources to convert distinctive competence into competitive advantage."[1] Thus, a clear definition of what constitutes the core business serves to focus a firm's unique position in the competitive marketplace. Firms must develop a process that results in a strategy to gain differential advantage in a significant segment of the market. The elements of a strategic management process are described in this section.

Strategic Alternatives

Michael Porter has articulated three basic strategies a firm may follow to develop industry position and generate superior profitability: cost leadership, differentiation, and focus.[2] Each broad strategy places different requirements upon marketing performance and necessitates differences in channel structure. Each generic strategy is discussed in terms of channel requirements.

Cost Leadership   A cost-leadership strategy involves producing and distributing products at the very lowest per-unit cost possible for price-sensitive customer segments. The primary competitive advantage achieved by cost leadership is a per-unit cost structure that yields high market share and above-average profitability. The strategy is to insulate the firm from competition by having it achieve higher profit margins than current or potential competitors.

A cost-leadership strategy is frequently associated with low-cost production, technological improvements in processes, and continued capital investment.[3] However, when distribution costs in an industry are high, creative channel strategies can also lead to a low-cost position within an industry. In the computer industry, for example, mail-order firms have thrived. These firms appeal to customers who have little need for the extra services offered by computer retailers or who choose to fulfill their need for these services in an alternative manner. The low-cost structure of nonstore retailing offers significant cost advantages over full-service retailers.

Differentiation   A differentiation strategy emphasizes product or service uniqueness in a manner that is meaningful to non-price-sensitive customers. The uniqueness can be achieved through design, performance, quality, or meaningfully differentiated distribution networks and service offerings. A firm attempts to protect itself from competition by developing high brand or customer loyalty through differentiation.

[1] K. R. Andrews, *The Concept of Corporate Strategy,* Homewood, IL: Irwin, 1987, p. 13.

[2] Michael Porter, *Competitive Advantage,* New York: Free Press, 1985, p. 5.

[3] Roger A. Kerin, Vijay Mahajan, and P. Rajan Varadarajan, *Contemporary Perspectives on Strategic Market Planning,* Boston: Allyn and Bacon, 1990, p. 302.

The classic example of differentiation achieved through distribution occurred when Hanes introduced the L'eggs brand of hosiery. At a time when competitors utilized conventional channels such as department stores and women's clothing stores, L'eggs were being positioned in supermarkets and drugstores, thanks to a new, unique package design that facilitated distribution. Within a few years, the brand commanded leading market share in the industry.

Focus   A focus strategy involves concentration on a particular market segment in an industry. Whereas cost leadership and differentiation are typically aimed at an entire industry, focused strategies are designed to appeal to unique market segments. The focused competitor attempts to insulate itself from competition by serving a narrow market more efficiently or effectively than firms that are competing for the bulk of the market.

A firm employing a focus strategy may also seek advantage through differentiation or cost leadership, or a combination of the two strategies. The key to the focus strategy is presenting the product-service offering in a manner that is very appealing to a unique segment of buyers. Snap-on Tools successfully focuses on a narrow market of professional mechanics. Snap-on offers a line of very high quality tools that are distributed directly to mechanics by a nationwide network of delivery vans. Although Snap-on products are higher-priced than competing tools, the company has developed a successful position by concentrating on the needs of its market for quality and rapid service.

Strategic Alternatives: Conclusion   It is important to realize that in a given industry, competing firms may simultaneously attempt to gain advantage by employing any one of the three aforementioned generic strategies. A typical example is in consumer television. General Electric follows essentially a cost-leadership strategy. It manufactures a broad line of low-priced televisions that are distributed nationally through multiple distribution channels. GE televisions are sold in a wide variety of retail electronics outlets ranging from traditional dealers to mass-merchandise stores such as K mart, Sears and Wal-Mart, and even in selected supermarkets and drugstores.

Sony, on the other hand, employs a differentiation strategy. It is well known for quality televisions, broadly advertised, which are available primarily through specialty television and electronics outlets or upscale department stores.

Curtis Mathes has employed a focus strategy aimed at risk-averse consumers; it emphasizes very high quality products backed by six-year product guarantees. Curtis Mathes televisions are distributed through a limited network of franchised dealers that sell only Curtis Mathes electronics.

This example illustrates how three successful firms in the same industry can differentiate strategically. While employing diverse strategies that require various products and different distribution channels, each can achieve significant profitability and return on investment. The next section explores the process by which a firm determines an appropriate competitive posture within an industry.

Mission Statement

Every business organization is established for some intended purpose. For a typical business firm, the fundamental purpose is usually expressed in the mission statement. The mission is a general statement of the markets that the firm plans to serve which includes some indication of how the firm intends to position itself. A mission statement can also describe opportunities that the firm's management perceives as being available in the market and detail how resources will be deployed to reach specific goals. The process of developing a mission statement is not as simple as it may seem. A mission statement too narrowly defined may result in management overlooking many exciting opportunities upon which the enterprise could capitalize. On the other hand, a mission statement too broadly defined could fail to provide clear direction to the employees and managers who must seek to reach specific goals.

Most business organizations begin operations with a clear and focused mission. However, over time, due to operational problems, continued growth, and unexpected opportunities, the original mission may lose its clarity and fail to reflect what a firm is really all about. Thus, management must continuously evaluate opportunities in terms of resources and capabilities, and ask itself such vital questions as: What really is our purpose? Who are our customers? What values do we provide to our customers? What should our business be in the future? The answers to these questions should lead to continuous revision and reconfirmation of the mission statement. Management also has a responsibility to both incorporate ideas into the mission statement and communicate any revisions to all personnel within the organization. The mission statement provides personnel with a sense of responsibility, a sense of direction, and a greater understanding of their role in the firm.

Consider the following example of a mission statement elaborated by Sears management in the mid-1970s:

> "Sears is a family store for middle class, home-owning America. We are the premiere distributor of durable goods for these families, their homes and their automobiles. We are the premiere distributor of non-durable goods that have their acceptance base in function rather than fashion. . . . We are valued by middle class America for our integrity, our reputation for fair dealing, and our guarantee. . . . We are not a fashion store. We are not a store for the whimsical nor the affluent. We are not a discounter nor an avant-guarde department store. We are not, by the standards of the trade press or any other group of bored observers, an exciting store. We are not a store that anticipates. We reflect the world of middle America and all of its desires and concerns and problems and faults and we must all look on what we are and pronounce it good, and seek to extend it, and not be swayed from it by the attraction of other markets no matter how enticing they might be."[4]

While recent events have resulted in a significant reorientation of Sears' basic mission, it is clear that the target market of the 1970s consisted of middle-class, home-owning Americans. It was also clearly defined how Sears planned to service this market segment with goods and services that were based in function rather than in fashion. The mission statement also specified management's perception of Sears'

[4] "Sears New Five Year Plan: To Serve Middle America," *Advertising Age,* December 4, 1975, p. 3. Reprinted with permission of Advertising Age, December 4, 1975 © Crain Communications, Inc. 1975.

major strengths: integrity, reputation, and guarantee. It provided a sense of direction by clearly defining the merchandise assortment to be sold. However, in the 1980s Sears seemed to lose sight of that mission and move into fashion merchandise, new product lines, and soft goods. The resulting impact on the firm was deterioration in profitability, the loss of clear direction, and finally a need to refocus.[5]

Objectives

The mission statement offers a broad vision of what an enterprise seeks to achieve and its general code of conduct. The next step in the strategic management process is to develop more specific objectives. This actually may be thought of as a process of developing a hierarchy of objectives, gradually refining the objectives into more specific statements of expected accomplishments. In general, each enterprise has two types of objectives: financial and market. Management has traditionally focused primarily on profit as the financial objective. However, over time there has become an increasing awareness that profit, in and of itself, is not a meaningful measurement. Of much more importance is the firm's return on investment: the relationship between net profit and the investment that is needed to produce that profit. Much more will be said about financial performance in Chapter 11.

There are many different types of market objectives. They may be specific statements delineating target markets consistent with the mission statement. Or they may be figures relating to sales volume or market share to be achieved in each target market. While it may be appealing to state market and financial objectives independently, they cannot be separated in practice. It is by the fulfillment of market objectives that financial results are realized.

The process of developing and implementing corporate mission and objectives involves careful analysis of customers, competition, internal capabilities, and the forces at work in the external environment.

CUSTOMER ANALYSIS

Because businesses exist to serve customers, the beginning point in developing competitive strategy is customer analysis. To establish a strategic edge over its competition, the firm must define the broad market it intends to serve, segment the market, and identify specific segment(s) it intends to concentrate upon. In this section, the steps in customer analysis that are essential for the development of a competitive strategy are reviewed.

Defining the Market

Proper market definition is critical to strategic success. It is a difficult task, however, since markets can be defined in a wide variety of ways. Frequently, markets are

[5] See the case Sears—a Giant in Transition on pp. 252–264.

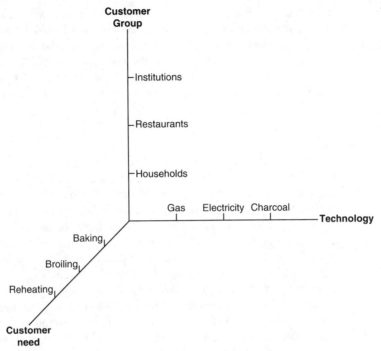

defined in terms of products or product classes. For example, it is common to hear people speak of "the automobile market" or "the soft-drink market." Such market descriptions imply that buyers of products are relatively homogeneous in needs and can therefore be defined in terms of those products. In fact, the underlying delineating factor in market definition should be customer need. An effective strategy develops a way to satisfy customer needs better than competitors. A second factor useful for defining a market is the type of basic technology that is utilized. In some situations, such as home entertainment, several different technologies may be employed to satisfy a particular customer need. For example, stereos, phonographs, tape players, or compact disc players represent different technologies for music reproduction. The third factor in defining a market is the customer group(s) served. Each customer group typically has a preference for a somewhat different product or service. To establish an effective market definition, the range of alternative customer segment(s) must be considered.

Figure 5-2 illustrates the three-dimensional approach to market definition. In the example, three alternative customer needs are identified, each of which can be satisfied with different technologies, and may be required by three different customer segments.

A specific firm may choose to define its market narrowly (baking in household with gas appliances) or quite broadly (all cooking needs and technologies). The decision in terms of market definition is critical to the analysis of competition and the development of specific strategy. From the standpoint of distribution, for example, quite different channels would be necessary for the distribution of charcoal broilers to restaurants than for the marketing of natural-gas ovens to households.

Market Segmentation

Even given the definition of customers illustrated in Figure 5-2, each ''group'' could be further subdivided into finer segments. Since different buyer segments tend to seek different benefits, not only in terms of product features, but also in terms of purchasing convenience, product availability, and servicing, channel strategy must be responsive to heterogeneous demands. Clearly, for example, household users of cooking appliances differ in their needs for specific features, their preferences for where to shop, the amounts they want to cook, the prices they want to spend, and a multitude of other factors. The various bases for specific market segmentation are discussed in Chapter 6, where their direct relevance to design of specific distribution channels is discussed. The broad market definition developed at this stage of analysis provides the parameters for determining certain critical information: market size and growth rates, sales patterns and cycles, and overall attractiveness of an industry. This information can be used as a guide for the evaluation of strategic opportunities. It also provides the necessary foundation for identifying the competitive arena in which the firm will operate and the specific competitors. Broad market segments must be identified for the purpose of developing a strategic position, but more specific segment identification and analysis is necessary to implement distribution channel strategy.

COMPETITIVE ANALYSIS

The second major analytic process in developing a *strategic position* is competitive analysis. The fundamental purpose of strategy is to beat competition. Competitive analysis begins with an examination of the structure of an industry. This structural overview provides insight into the attractiveness of an industry and the competitive rivalry. Competitors must be identified and their strengths and weaknesses assessed to understand how different firms in the market are likely to perform with and respond to a new competitor entering the marketplace.

Industry Structure

Michael Porter's five-factor model of industry structure is reproduced in Figure 5-3. The model focuses on the causes of competitive intensity within an industry. Each of Porter's five forces are directly related to distribution channel structure.

Competitive rivalry is a function of the number of competitors and their relative sizes, similarities in strategies, asset and cost structures, and exit barriers. Generally,

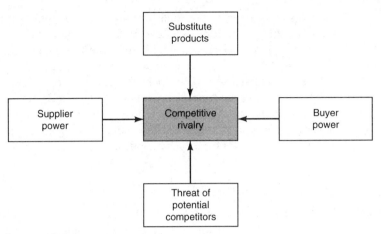

FIGURE 5-3   Porter's industry structure analysis.

in industries dominated by a few large firms competition is less intense than in industries in which all competitors are relatively the same size. Industries with high fixed costs tend to have high levels of competitive intensity due to companies' desire to fully utilize assets. If competitors have highly differentiated strategies, there is less competitive intensity and price cutting. Finally, exit barriers such as specialized assets or contracts and commitments to customers may serve to increase rivalry.

New players that enter an industry are likely to increase competitive rivalry. If there are significant barriers to entry, however, this threat is reduced. Barriers to entry may be cost related, such as the need for significant capital investment, the existence of large economies of scale, or distribution arrangements that are difficult to duplicate. Barriers to entry may result from new firms having difficulty in gaining access to distribution channels necessary for success or from the existence of high levels of customer loyalty to the existing firms in an industry.

Substitute products affect industry competition by providing a ceiling on prices in the industry and a benchmark for product performance. Substitutes are products that provide the same function or the same benefit for customers but have different features. For example, soft drinks were originally packaged only in glass bottles. Development of cans (and, later, plastic bottles) as substitute products had major implications for producers of glass bottles.

Substitutes that have similar price and performance attributes and for which the customer's cost of switching is low are of particular importance. For example, as double-stack containers improved delivery performance of railroads, significant pressure was placed on long-haul trucking firms to improve price and performance offerings.

The main factor influencing suppliers' power is their ability to supply material, products, and services that affect the prices and strategies of their customers. Suppliers' power is also directly related to the number of suppliers and their concentration, the costs to customers of switching to alternative suppliers, the availability of substitutes, and the potential of suppliers for forward integration.

Buyers' power refers to the ability of customers in an industry to keep prices low and demand more services. The factors influencing buyers' power are similar to those influencing suppliers' power. When the number of customers is limited, when a customer's purchases are a large proportion of the seller's output, or when there is high potential for backward integration, buyers can significantly affect profitability in an industry by keeping prices low and/or demanding higher levels of service performance. A full discussion of power, power sources, and leadership is presented in Chapter 9.

Identification and Assessment of Competitors

While examination of an industry's structure is an important first step in competitive analysis, more specific information concerning individual competitors and their capabilities is required when a strategic position is being developed. In many instances, the primary competitors are quite visible and easily identified. John Deere competes in the lawn tractor business with such brands as Toro, Lawn Boy, Murray, Roper, and Cub. It is frequently useful, however, to look more closely to related competitors that fulfill the same generic customer need. Thus, John Deere could also define its lawn tractor competitors as all lawn mowers or even lawn maintenance services.

Once the competitive set is identified, there are four basic questions that must be answered about all competitive firms:

1 What are the competitors' major objectives?
2 What is the current strategy being employed by the competitors to achieve their objectives?
3 What are the capabilities of the competitors' to implement their strategies?
4 What are likely future strategies for the competitors?[6]

The methodologies employed to answer these questions are beyond the scope of this text. However, the answers themselves are critical to a firm in the development of its own strategic position and channel strategy.

INTERNAL ANALYSIS

Customer and competitive analysis are key steps in strategic positioning. Just as important is a clear, unbiased evaluation of a firm's own capabilities. A critical assessment of a company's strengths and weaknesses can be a painful process for management. It forces managers to identify things they have done well and can continue to do well and requires them to identify weaknesses and limitations. Without a factual assessment, however, it will not be possible to objectively develop a firm's strategy. Internal analysis begins with an examination of the firm's performance. The second step is an

---

[6] Donald R. Lehman and Russell S. Winer, *Analysis for Marketing Planning,* Homewood, IL: BPI/Irwin, 1988, p. 61.

assessment of strengths and weaknesses in each functional operation. To be effective, an internal analysis can not ignore any significant aspect of a firm's overall performance.

Performance Analysis

Evaluation of past performance is invaluable since it provides insight into the firm's strategy and success. This evaluation must consider performance in terms of financial performance as well as market standing. Chapter 11 provides a comprehensive framework for performance analysis, with specific attention paid to the measurement of distribution channel strategy performance.

Functional Strengths and Weaknesses

Table 5-1 provides a checklist of the areas for analysis of strengths and weaknesses. The first area of concern is production. Even nonmanufacturing firms should consider production capabilities in the sense of their cost structure, flexibility of operations, capacity, and similar concerns. These aspects of operations determine the ability of a firm to adapt to different strategic options.

The second area is finance and whether the firm has or can acquire needed funds. The firm's balance sheet condition, liquidity, and overall financial "health" influence its ability to implement its strategy. Consider, for example, the ability of Wal-Mart as opposed to a small local retailer to develop and implement an expansion strategy.

Marketing is a third area of concern. A firm's product-quality reputation, name recognition, customer loyalty, distribution channels, and the like may be strengths or weaknesses that will affect its strategic position.

The fourth general area is management itself. The capabilities, quality, and even the depth of management talent are important factors in determining a firm's ability to develop and implement strategy. For example, a major reason for Coleman's divestiture of the popular Hobie Cat line of sailboats was the lack of management expertise and experience in the distribution channels for that product category. In fact, several studies of business performance in the past decade have indicated that the most successful firms "stick close to the knitting," limiting themselves to the areas in which management has its experience and expertise.[7]

ENVIRONMENTAL ANALYSIS

Environmental analysis is concerned with identifying trends, opportunities, threats, and limitations that will affect and influence a firm's strategic position. In this section, the sociocultural, technological, economic, and legal environments that strategic planners must accommodate are discussed. Particular attention is given to the legal envi-

---

[7] Thomas J. Peters and Robert H. Waterman, Jr., *In Search of Excellence: Lessons from America's Best Run Companies,* New York: Harper & Row, 1982; and Carol J. Loomis, "Secrets of the Superstars," *Fortune,* April 24, 1989, pp. 50–62.

TABLE 5-1   CHECKLIST FOR INTERNAL ASSESSMENT

Production

Cost structure
Flexibility
Equipment
Capacity
Work force

Finance

Balance sheet condition
Profitability
Working capital
Ability to attract capital

Marketing

Quality
Differentiation
Customer loyalty
Name recognition
Product line
Sales force
Advertising/promotion skills
Distribution capabilities
Channel relationships
Segmentation

Management

Experience
Depth
Expertise
Culture
Creativity
Organization

ronment, not because it is more important than the others, but because culture, economics, and technology and their affect on specific decisions in channel design and strategy are discussed throughout the text.

Sociocultural Environment

The sociocultural environment, perhaps more than any other, is directly involved with shaping the nature of consumers' needs and preferences. Such factors as changing cultural values or social norms have a major impact on individual preferences for products and the way in which those products are distributed. Consider, for example, the trend toward consumer demand for convenience in satisfying hunger. This trend has had a major impact on all levels of the food distribution channel. An increasing share of the consumer's food dollar has shifted to away-from-home eating establishments. Restaurants and fast-food outlets have significantly increased their share of the food dollar. Food manufacturers and processors have responded by focusing more attention on the distribution channels required to reach those outlets. Simultaneously, grocery stores and supermarkets have responded to this competition by introducing more convenience for consumers through such devices as in-store salad bars and deli-prepared food sections.

A second example of sociocultural impact is visible in increased concern for health and physical well-being. This concern, coupled with increasing cost of traditional means of health care, has led to the development of new forms of distribution for health care services. Hospital satellite clinics and visiting nurse programs are two manifestations of these changes.

These are only two examples of the impact of culture on distribution channels. Other cultural trends such as the desire for immediate gratification, increased numbers of females in the workplace, concern for physical fitness, and changes in family structure all have their implications for strategy development in general, and distribution channels in particular.

Technological Environment

The technological explosion of the post–World War II period seems in no danger of ending. New technology means new products as well as new ways of conducting business. Within the realm of new products, one need only consider that just a few years ago the idea of in-home computers seemed far-fetched. Today, in-home computers are a reality. Within the realm of business operations, the development and adoption of new technology has had a tremendous impact on the efficiency and effectiveness of organizations and has considerable potential for increasing productivity. For example, increased automation and new applications of information processing equipment are just two ways in which companies have attempted to increase the efficiency of their operations.

Technology has had an impact on distribution that extends far beyond simple automation and increased efficiency of existing channels. New technological developments have, in fact, transformed distribution networks and created new channels. Consider, for example, the development of cable television and satellite shopping networks as new forms of retail distribution, and the use of information technology (as discussed in Chapter 12) in forging new relationships among distribution channel partners. It can only be expected that these and other technological advancements will continue to find increasing application. Perhaps the major problem is that technological change may occur more rapidly than people are prepared to adapt.

Economic Environment

The economic environment shapes the consumer's ability to pay for goods and services. While there are enumerable forces within the economic environment that are of great importance to strategic planning, a few of the more important ones include unemployment, inflation, recession, and disposable income. The strategic planner must constantly be aware of changes within these forces that may ultimately result in changes in consumer's ability to pay for goods and services offered by a firm. For example, a rise in consumers' disposable income or a change in the distribution of disposable income among the population may open new market segments or bring new consumers into existing market segments for the firm's products or services. On the other hand, increasing unemployment rates may change the nature of demand for specific products, services, or stores. When unemployment rates increase, consumers may delay certain purchases, choose to trade down in the types of products they purchase, or look for lower-cost distribution outlets. Regardless, changes in economic conditions have significant impact on consumer markets with resulting consequences for corporate strategy and distribution alternatives.

Legal Environment

The legal framework that regulates business is a complex and constantly evolving phenomenon. Federal, state, and local governments all have the power to impose restrictions through legislative, administrative, and judicial processes.

Major Legislation   The following federal statutes, all of which affect channel relationships, are reviewed: the Sherman Antitrust Act, The Clayton Antitrust Act, the Federal Trade Commission Act, the Robinson-Patman Act, and the Celler-Kefauver Act. Other statutes affecting business are more concerned with regulation of enterprises than with relationships between enterprises. A review of the major provisions of each act follows.

The Sherman Antitrust Act, 1890   Often referred to as the ''antitrust law,'' this act is aimed at protecting the public from monopoly. It is grounded in the belief that competition is the only form of economic activity that can stimulate growth through innovation, lead to efficiency in operation, and result in low prices to the consumer. Section 1 of the Sherman Act prohibits contracts, combinations, and conspiracies in restraint of trade or commerce. A contract or a conspiracy is either a written instrument or an implied agreement that may be legal in itself but which may be illegal under the Sherman Act if the effect is to restrain commerce or trade. Section 2 attempts to prevent any action that results in the monopolization of any part of interstate or foreign commerce. Whenever an excessive concentration of market power appears to be vested in a single firm, the courts may order dissolution and divestiture.

The Sherman Act was intended to cover all restraints of commerce, but it soon became apparent that clarification was necessary if all possible abuses were to be covered.

The Clayton Antitrust Act, 1914   This act was designed to prevent situations that *tend* to lessen competition or create a monopoly. The Sherman Antitrust Act was not fully adequate to such cases. Under the Clayton Act, proof of violation is easier since it prohibits those situations which *tend* to lessen competition or create a monopoly. Under the Sherman Act it was necessary to prove that the action actually *did* lessen competition or create a monopoly. The Clayton Act prohibits interlocking directorates (individuals serving on the board of directors of two or more competing firms), price discrimination, tying contracts, and exclusive dealing. At the same time that the Clayton Act was passed, the Federal Trade Commission (FTC) was established to enforce the Clayton Act and related laws.

The Federal Trade Commission Act, 1914   In addition to creating the FTC, this act specified that all "unfair methods of competition" were unlawful. Congress did not specify which unfair methods it meant, but it left the determination to the FTC. The law was passed in an attempt to stop those acts that were not illegal under the Sherman Act or the Clayton Act. As we shall see later, an act by a business may fall short of violation in a judicial proceeding but can be stopped by a "cease and desist" order from the FTC.

The Robinson-Patman Act, 1936   The Clayton Antitrust Act, although designed to prohibit price discrimination, was inadequate since it allowed for discrimination in price "on account of difference in the grade, quality, or quantity of the commodity sold, or that make only due allowance for difference in the cost of selling or transportation." This provision allowed many large retailers to use their buying power to negotiate for discriminatory prices. The Robinson-Patman Act was passed as an amendment to the Clayton Act in an effort to specify illegal price discrimination.

Major provisions of the Robinson-Patman Act are as follows. Section 2(a) defines an illegal price discrimination. An illegal price discrimination exists when different prices are charged for goods of "like grade and quality . . . where the effect of such discrimination may be substantially to lessen competition or tend to create a monopoly in any line of commerce, or to injure, destroy, or prevent competition with any person who either grants or knowingly receives the benefit of such discrimination, or with customers of either of them." The section then grants two important exclusions: (1) "differentials which make only due allowance for differences in cost of manufacture, sale or delivery resulting from the differing methods or quantities . . . sold or delivered," and, (2) differentials "in response to changing conditions affecting the market . . . such as . . . actual or imminent deterioration of perishable goods, obsolescence or seasonal goods, distress sale under court process or sales in good faith in discontinuance of business in the goods concerned." Section 2(a) provides three defenses to charges of price discrimination. First, a cost-savings defense is implied in the act, but the courts have not been willing to accept a standard for measuring cost. Second, sale of goods is legal under changing conditions such as deterioration, obsolescence, or seasonal goods, or distress sale under court order, or discontinuance of the goods. Finally, price discrimination is legal when there is no injury to competition.

Section 2(b) states that "the burden of rebutting the prima facie case of discrimination thus made by showing justification shall be upon the person charged. . . ." Thus, the burden of proof in price-discrimination cases is "showing that the lower price or the furnishing of service or facilities to any purchaser or purchasers was made in good faith to meet an equally low price of a competitor, or the services of facilities furnished by a competitor."

In the 1920s and early 1930s, large retailers were able to extract lower prices by billing the seller for brokerage services provided by a brokerage subsidiary of the buyer. The payments by the seller amounted to a reduction in the sale price and were interpreted as price discrimination. Therefore, Section 2(c) of the Robinson-Patman Act attempts to prevent price discriminations arising through payment of unearned brokerage fees to a buyer. It states that "it shall be unlawful for any person engaged in commerce . . . to pay or grant, or to receive or accept, anything of value as a commission, brokerage or other compensation, or any allowance or discount in lieu thereof . . . either to the other party to such transaction or to an agent, representative or other intermediary . . . where such intermediary is acting in fact for or in behalf, or is subject to the direct or indirect control, of any party to such transaction other than the person by whom such compensation is so granted or paid."

Another common practice was for larger buyers to extract promotional allowances from sellers for cooperative advertising. To the extent that these allowances were not offered to all buyers or were never used for promoting, they were a way of granting a discriminating price. Section 2(d) was inserted to prevent discrimination in price arising from payment of such promotional allowances by the seller to some customers. It states "that it shall be unlawful . . . to pay or contract for the payment of anything of value . . . in connection with the processing, handling, sale or offering for sale . . . unless such payment . . . is available in proportionately equal terms to all other customers competing in the distribution of such products or commodities."

Rather than offering promotional allowances, a seller may have made the services of a demonstrator available to a retailer. Such arrangements were common in the cosmetics industry. The demonstrator acted as a salesperson and, in effect, provided a service at no cost to the buyer. Since the buyer did not incur the cost of providing this service, it amounted to a discrimination in price. Section 2(e) makes this practice illegal if offered "upon terms not accorded to all purchasers on proportionately equal terms."

The activities described in Sections 2(d) and 2(e) of the Robinson-Patman Act were considered legal if they were made in "proportionately equal terms" to all customers. However, the Federal Trade Commission and the courts have had a difficult time interpreting "proportionately equal terms." For example, a manufacturer's offer of a 5 percent cooperative advertising allowance may be meaningful for a large retailer who often advertises but meaningless to a small retailer who rarely uses advertising.

Section 2(f) makes it illegal "knowingly to induce or receive a discrimination in price which is prohibited by this section." Thus, a buyer who receives the benefit of price discrimination may be subject to the same penalties as the supplier who grants the price differentials. Enforcement of the Robinson-Patman Act was delegated to the Federal Trade Commission. The enforcement procedure is described in the section dealing with administrative law.

The Celler-Kefauver Act, 1950   Section 7 of the Clayton Antitrust Act, which prohibits acquisitions or mergers tending to lessen competition or to create a monopoly, was inadequate for the scrutinizing of the large number of acquisitions occurring in the 1940s and 1950s. That act required proof that the acquisition of stock had a reasonable probability of lessening competition. The Celler-Kefauver Act of 1950 was passed as an amendment to Section 7 of the Clayton Antitrust Act to slow the tide of acquisitions and mergers. It prohibits acquisition of stock or assets if the result is a tendency to lessen competition or create a monopoly. It further changed the wording of the Clayton Antitrust Act, which originally stated that there must be a tendency to lessen competition between the corporation whose stock is being acquired and the acquiring corporation. This wording implied that horizontal mergers were prohibited but vertical mergers were not. The Celler-Kefauver amendment simply states ''where the effect may be to lessen competition substantially in any line of commerce in any section of the country.''

Figure 5-2 contains the major legislative acts applicable to interorganizational relationships found in a channel of distribution. Other acts, such as the Lanham Act (trademarks), the Consumer Product Safety Act, the Hazardous Substances Act, the National Environmental Policy Act, and the Cooperative Research and Development Act, can be relevant since they regulate institutions in the channel, but they influence channel relationships only incidentally.

Administrative Law   The increasing complexity of our society—the result of new technology and rapid growth, changing social goals, and conflicting objectives—has placed a heavy burden on the legislative, executive, and judicial branches of government. Legislators do not have time to legislate all facets of our lives; the judicial branch is inundated with an enormous backlog of cases. Furthermore, neither legislator nor judge can be an expert in all areas needing regulation. To ease the burden, the legislature has delegated part of the task to federal agencies and has conferred on them a quasi-judicial capacity. Some of these agencies at the federal level are the Justice Department, the National Labor Relations Board, the Occupational Safety and Health Administration, the Consumer Product Safety Commission, the Food and Drug Administration, the Department of Transportation, the Interstate Commerce Commission, the Securities and Exchange Commission, and, as we have already seen, the Federal Trade Commission.[8]

Enabling legislation is passed by Congress to create both the agency and the legislation it is to oversee. As other legislation is passed, it is sometimes delegated to an existing agency for administration.

Judicial Processes   Judicial law in the United States has its roots in English common law. Under common law the courts ''make the law'' as they decide controversies brought before them. The doctrine of *stare decisis,* whereby prior decisions provide precedents for subsequent cases involving similar legal questions, has been adopted in this country. If no similar case has been adjudicated, the court renders its decision and a precedent is established for future cases. Common law is thus used to interpret legislation and to create legislation when none exists.

In preparing for court under judicial law, an attorney spends a great deal of time reviewing past cases, searching for legal precedents that the court will follow in rendering a decision. A single court decision is usually not sufficient to establish a rule of law. Rather, a precedent is established when a rule of law is cited by the courts over years in many different cases.

[8] Robert Corley, Robert Black, and O. Lee Reed, *The Legal Environment of Business,* 7th ed., New York, McGraw-Hill, 1987, p. 277.

TABLE 5-2   APPLICABLE FEDERAL LEGISLATION AFFECTING CHANNEL RELATIONSHIPS

Act	Year	Provisions	Applicable defenses	Maximum penalty	
				Individual	Corporate
Sherman Antitrust Act	1890	1 Prohibits contracts, combinations, and conspiracies on restraint of trade or commerce 2 Prohibits any action that results in monopolizing any part of interstate or foreign commerce	1 Prove the action did not lessen competition or create a monopoly	Up to $100,000 and/or up to three years in prison: a felony	Up to $1,000,000, injunction, divestiture, triple damages to injured party
Clayton Antitrust Act	1914	1 If the result is to tend to lessen competition or create a monopoly. It prohibits: a Interlocking directorates b Price discrimination c Tying contracts d Exclusive dealing	1 Prove the action would not tend to lessen competition or create a monopoly	Criminal sanction for directors or agents; $5000 and/or one year	Injunction, triple damages to injured party, time, civil penalty
Federal Trade Commission Act	1914	1 In enforcing the Clayton Antitrust Act and enforcing other acts. It prohibits: a All unfair methods of competition	1 Prove the action would not tend to lessen competition or create a monopoly	Restitution, injunction, fine up to $5000 or up to three years	Restitution, injunction, divestiture. $10,000/day for violation of rules or orders; for each violation—a civil penalty
Robinson-Patman Act	1936	1 Prohibits price discrimination where the effect may be to substantially lessen competition or tend to create a monopoly, such as: a Unearned brokerage fees b Promotional allowances under some circumstances c Promotional services under some circumstances	1 Prove no injury to competition 2 Cost/savings to justify discrimination 3 Sale under changing market conditions 4 Discrimination made in good faith to meet the equally low price or service or facilities furnished by a competitor 5 Promotional allowances made on proportionately equal terms for all buyers 6 Promotional services made on proportionately equal terms to all customers	Same as Clayton Antitrust Act	Same as Clayton Antitrust Act

TABLE 5-2   (Continued)

Act	Year	Provisions	Applicable defenses	Maximum penalty	
				Individual	Corporate
Celler-Kefauver Act (amendment to Clayton Antitrust Act)	1950	1 Prohibits both horizontal and vertical acquisitions or mergers through purchase of stock or assets if the effect is to tend to lessen competition or create a monopoly	1 Prove the action would not tend to lessen competition or create a monopoly	Same as Clayton Antitrust Act	Same as Clayton Antitrust Act

Judicial law attempts to provide an element of certainty. It is *retrospective* in that it looks to the past for a solution to disagreements among litigants. However, the sheer number of judicial decisions in federal courts coupled with an equally large number in state courts renders judicial law anything but certain. Any decision ultimately depends upon which set of legal precedents put forth by the plaintiff and the defendant is determined applicable by the judge.

Major Recurring Legal Issues   Although the legislative, judicial, and administrative processes discussed above provide a foundation for the understanding of the legal environment, a number of specific issues continue to reoccur in distribution arrangements. Although there are many such issues, the major ones involve exclusive territories and exclusive-dealing, tying agreements, discounts and allowances, collusion, price maintenance, and mergers.

Exclusive Territories and Exclusive Dealing   Exclusive territorial arrangements and exclusive dealing often occur together within a distribution channel. In utilizing exclusive territories for distributors, a supplier will either agree to sell to only one distributor within a given geographic region or will require that distributors restrict their selling activities to one specific region. Such arrangements may be desirable for manufacturers of certain types of goods that require strong reseller support, as the purpose of the policy is to encourage resellers to develop their regions without fear of being raided by another reseller of the same brand. Exclusive territories have been used in the soft-drink industry, where high capital investment and strong effort by local bottlers are necessary to ensure effective market penetration for a brand. Fear of competition by another bottler offering the same brand might discourage such efforts.

The legality of exclusive territorial agreements has been an on-again, off-again situation. In 1967, the U.S. Supreme Court determined that exclusive territorial arrangements are per se violations of Section 1 of the Sherman Antitrust Act if legal title to the goods has passed from seller to buyer. In that decision concerning the Arnold Schwinn Company, the court reasoned that such arrangements are, in effect, nothing more than attempts to divide the market and, therefore, represent contracts that restrict competition. The court determined that they were violations of the law. However, in a 1977 case involving GTE Sylvania, the same court overturned the *Schwinn* decision and determined that territorial restrictions may be legal, and the "rule of reason" should be utilized in determining the legality of such arrangements. The court ruled that, since exclusive territorial agreements can have positive benefits such as promoting interbrand competition, inducing retailers to be more aggressive, helping smaller retailers to compete against larger ones, and encouraging marketing efficiency, the extent to which intrabrand competition is restricted should be balanced against the extent to which potential interbrand competition is enhanced.[9] The net result of these decisions is that the ability of a supplier to restrict dealers to specific geographic territories, or to reward dealers with a geographic monopoly, has been severely limited.

An important distinction made by the courts is whether an agreement on exclusive territories is vertical or horizontal. A horizontal agreement is one among firms at the same level of the distribution channel to divide the market geographically. Such agreements have been judged to be illegal. Vertical agreements between a supplier and its customers or dealers are subject to the rule-of-reason analysis.[10]

In an exclusive-dealing agreement, a buyer agrees to handle the products of only one seller. Although exclusive dealing can exist without territorial restrictions, the two arrangements are closely related, as originally manufacturers offered exclusive territories in return for the reseller's promise not to deal in a competitor's goods. Under the Clayton Antitrust Act, exclusive dealing is illegal if it results in substantial lessening of competition or encourages a tendency toward monopoly. The major issue in the determination of the legality of a particular exclusive-dealing agreement is the extent of competitive harm. In order to establish that substantial competitive harm has occurred, the courts must attempt to determine both the total size of the relevant market and the portion of that market from which the exclusive-dealing arrangement excludes competition. Two classic court cases demonstrate the nature of this problem. In the first case, the Standard Fashion Company, a producer of dress patterns, prohibited its retailers from selling competitors' patterns. Since the firm had a 40 percent share of the market for dress patterns, the court determined that exclusive dealing would lead to further concentration in the industry and result in substantial lessening of competition.[11] However, in another case involving J.I. Case Company, a manufacturer of farm implements, the court determined that exclusive dealing was not illegal because other manufacturers were able to find dealers to distribute their products and that many manufacturers were represented in most geographic regions.[12] Thus, for J.I. Case, there was no substantial reduction in competition nor any tendency toward monopoly.

Tying In a tying arrangement, a seller refuses to sell one product unless the potential buyer agrees to purchase other products. Since such arrangements often result in the buyer's inability to deal with other suppliers, the effect of tying may be exclusive dealing. Tie-in agreements are not necessarily illegal but will usually be judged

[9] For a discussion of the Schwinn and GTE Sylvania cases, see *Journal of Marketing,* **42**:1, January 1978, pp. 106–107.
[10] For a discussion, see "Arnold Pontiac vs. General Motors," in *Journal of Marketing,* **53**:4, October 1989, pp. 85–86.
[11] Marshall C. Howard, *Legal Aspects of Marketing,* New York: McGraw-Hill, 1964, p. 97.
[12] Ibid, p. 98.

so if the supplier is large enough to force a restraint of trade. For tying to be determined illegal, five conditions must be met: (1) two distinct products or services must be present; (2) there must be actual coercion by the seller, forcing the buyer to purchase the tied product; (3) the seller must have sufficient market power to force purchase of the tied product; (4) there must be anticompetitive effects in the tied market; and (5) a "not insubstantial" amount of interstate commerce must be in the tied market.[13]

The growth of franchising as a means of conducting business has spawned considerable litigation because franchisees are often required or strongly encouraged to purchase numerous products and/or services from the franchisor. The fear exists that the franchisor may charge exorbitant prices for supplies and that other suppliers will be excluded from the market. On the other hand, franchisors claim that such practices are necessary to protect the image and quality of the franchise. In a decision concerning Kentucky Fried Chicken, the opinion of the courts was that if a gain in quality resulting from such tie-ins is greater than the detriment to competition, such arrangements are legal.[14]

A special form of illegal tie-in arrangement is known as full-line forcing. A manufacturer that attempts to utilize this practice refuses to sell one item to a middleman unless that party agrees to handle the manufacturer's full line of merchandise. A farm equipment manufacturer required its retailers to buy and display each of its products. Like other forms of tying, full-line forcing is also subject to rule-of-reason analysis. If the manufacturer does not prohibit the dealer from carrying competing lines, line forcing may actually increase competition by making these other products (models of tractors, for example) available to consumers when they might not otherwise be stocked by the dealers.[15]

Discounts and Allowances   Although the Robinson-Patman Act and its provision had supposedly clarified price discrimination, suppliers continue to seek ways to use various promotional, quantity, and functional discounts in channel strategy. Most quantity and promotional allowances can be justified under the provisions of the act. Recently, however, functional discounts have come under attack in a case involving gasoline distribution. Historically, the Robinson-Patman Act was interpreted to allow suppliers to give wholesale functional discounts to customers at different levels in the distribution chain as long as the same discounts were available to all buyers at a given level in the channel. Lower courts have ruled in a Texas case that the size of discount given by Texaco to wholesale distributors cannot be justified by the functions the distributors perform. This is the first instance in which the courts have attempted to analyze the relationship between the size of a discount and the functions provided. There is considerable interest in the case, which has not yet been resolved in higher courts,[16] and in its implications for channel strategy.

---

[13] "Legal Developments in Marketing," *Journal of Marketing,* **54**:3, July 1990, pp. 92–98.

[14] "Marketing Abstracts," *Journal of Marketing,* **39**:3, July 1975, pp. 93–113.

[15] See "Smith Machinery Co., Inc vs. Hesston Corp.," *Journal of Marketing,* **54**:2, April 1990, pp. 96–97.

[16] For an excellent discussion see "Texaco, Inc. vs. Hasbrouck," *Journal of Marketing,* **54**:3, July 1990, p. 97.

Collusion and Price Maintenance The ways in which collusion can be practiced by businesses are almost limitless. In general, the Sherman and Clayton Antitrust Acts can be invoked against any collusion involving an attempt by several people or firms to restrain trade. Perhaps the most important form of prohibited collusion is price fixing. Under no circumstances may competitors form any agreement concerning prices to be charged for products. In addition, since April 1976 a manufacturer is no longer able to agree with retailers on "fair trade" prices, nor is it able to require all other retailers within a given territory to abide by those prices. Such agreements, allowed under the Miller-Tydings and McGuire Acts in states that had established fair-trade laws, are now illegal.

However, price maintenance that is not the result of collusion appears to be acceptable to the courts. Under the Colgate Doctrine a manufacturer can announce its resale prices in advance and refuse to sell to anyone who refuses to comply.[17] The important distinction is that the manufacturer's decision must be unilateral and not the result of collusion with a group of resellers. In fact, suppliers may legally refuse to sell to selected customers for a variety of other reasons as long as the decision is reached unilaterally and is not used as a threat to force compliance with manufacturer's policies. In 1991, *Nintendo* was charged with illegal price-fixing due to its policy of threatening slowdown of shipments to retailers who discounted its system consoles. Without admitting guilt, Nintendo agreed to settle state and federal charges by providing discount coupons worth up to $25 million to consumers and to pay $4.75 million in damages and legal costs.[18]

Mergers When two or more business firms agree to merge (a form of cooperation), the potential impact upon competition is typically evaluated. Regardless of whether the agreed-upon merger occurs through acquisition of stock or of assets, possible violations of either the Clayton or Celler-Kefauver Acts and their provisions concerning anticompetitive mergers exist.

When mergers occur among firms at the same level of competition, many factors must be considered to determine the potential impact on competition. These factors include the relevant geographic market, the number of sellers in the market, the size of the companies and their relative market positions, the economies of scale in the industry, and the products being sold and the degree to which they can be substituted.[19] Thus, Lever Brothers' acquisition of All detergent was judged to be legal when the relevant market was defined by the court as "low-sudsing heavy-duty detergents" in which the firm had no product offering at the time of the acquisition. The case might have been determined differently had the court determined the market to be "detergents" in which Lever had several products. On the other hand, Procter & Gamble was forced to divest itself of the Clorox Chemical Company, even though acquisition of that firm represented Procter & Gamble's first entrance into the bleach market. The court ruled that Procter & Gamble was so large and had such vast resources that it should have developed its own brand of bleach rather than acquire an existing brand.[20]

[17] Marshall C. Howard, op. cit., p. 41.
[18] Paul M. Barrett, "Nintendo's Latest Novelty Is a Price-Fixing Settlement," *Wall Street Journal,* April 11, 1991, p. B1.
[19] Ibid., p. 79.
[20] Ibid., pp. 82–83.

If a merger involves vertical integration, competitors may be foreclosed from the opportunity to do business with the acquired buyer. If the industry is highly concentrated, such mergers may be illegal. In a recent case, Work Wear Corporation, a major manufacturer of work clothes and uniforms, was determined to be in violation of antimerger statutes with its acquisition of eleven laundry leasing companies. The government argued that the acquired firms provided a captive market for Work Wear's clothing production. It also reasoned that the amount of business foreclosed to other uniform producers was substantial enough to require that the firm divest itself of the laundry leasing facilities.[21]

CHANNEL OBJECTIVES

The fundamental objective of distribution channels is to enable an enterprise to meet strategic objectives. The framework described above consisting of customer, competitive, internal, and environmental analyses allows management to develop general strategies and to set the parameters for appropriate distribution channel objectives within those strategies.

A distribution channel is, ultimately, an economic entity that is orchestrated by its participants to achieve their desired profitability and return on investment. While channel objectives must be specified concerning traditional financial performance measures such as volume, market share, profitability, and return on investment, operational channel objectives should also be developed in terms of market coverage and distribution intensity, channel control, and flexibility.

Market Coverage and Distribution Intensity

The strategic-positioning process guides the firm in determining the appropriate levels of market coverage and distribution intensity. Three levels of market coverage may be chosen.

Intensive Distribution   Intensive distribution involves the placement of products in as many locations as possible. It is generally an appropriate objective when a cost-leadership strategy is employed as the firm's basic position and the emphasis of the target market segments is on low price and convenience in purchasing. In the example discussed earlier in this chapter, GE television sets are intensively distributed through a broad range of outlets in order to reduce per-unit costs and appeal to a mass market.

Selective Distribution   Selective distribution involves placement of products in a more limited number of locations. It may be an appropriate objective when a differentiation strategy is employed. Sony selectively places its televisions in outlets that will enhance its quality image and provide a higher level of commitment and support to the brand than would occur if an intensive objective were chosen.

[21] "Work Wear Tries to Be No. 1 Again," *Business Week,* November 7, 1977, p. 84.

Exclusive Distribution An exclusive-distribution objective limits availability of a product to a very small number of locations. It is usually an appropriate objective when a firm employs a focus strategy. It is frequently employed when a firm desires to enhance a product's image or when considerable reseller support is desired. Of course, as discussed in the legal environment, there are also limitations to this approach.

While certain products may seem to fit a particular market coverage objective, generalizations can be quite misleading. For example, conventional wisdom would dictate that intensive market coverage would be a desirable objective for a candy manufacturer. However, Godiva Chocolates has chosen a differentiated, highly focused strategy that dictates an exclusive-distribution objective. The key factor in developing market coverage objectives is indeed the strategic position desired by the firm in the marketplace.

Market coverage objectives are guided to a major extent by careful consideration of buyers' behavior within selected target markets. Chapter 6 explores more fully the impact of buyers' behavior on the decision as to whether to distribute intensively, selectively, or exclusively. At this point it is important to note that the coverage objective has a significant impact on channel structure, as the number and types of channel partners needed is closely related to the extent of market coverage desired by a firm.

Channel Control

Channel control refers to the need or desire of the firm to maintain control over the full range of distribution activities. Manufacturers frequently desire control over intermediaries in order to gain greater selling effort or quality of after-sale support. Intermediaries may desire greater control over manufacturers to ensure continuous supply, product-quality improvement, or lower prices. Again, the degree of control desired is a function of the firm's chosen strategic position.

Decisions regarding market coverage and channel-control objectives are frequently interrelated. For example, intensive distribution is frequently inconsistent with a channel-control objective. In fact, a manufacturer may have an overriding objective of control that may require exclusive distribution to be the only logical means of controlling intermediaries' activities.

Flexibility

Development of a distribution channel normally involves a degree of commitment among channel participants. While this commitment is typically desirable from the standpoint of ensuring performance, it may inhibit the ability of participants to adapt to changing market, competitive, or environmental conditions. Because of the dynamic nature of these forces, flexibility may become an overriding objective in certain channel situations.

Flexibility may be particularly critical in new-product industries. Recent experiences in personal computers provide an excellent example. In the late 1970s and early 1980s there was considerable uncertainty about the optimal distribution channels for personal computers. Were business firms or households the most appropriate market segments? Should manufacturers utilize their own sales forces, mass-merchant retailers, and specialty computer stores, or should they open their own retail outlets? The uncertainty involved in answering such questions placed a premium on maintaining flexibility in distribution channels. Today's survivors in the industry are those firms that have maintained the ability to adapt quickly as the answers have become clearer.

SUMMARY

This chapter has presented the framework by which a firm develops a strategy to position itself in the marketplace. There are three broad categories of strategies that a firm might employ to fulfill its mission. A cost-leadership strategy involves producing and distributing low-cost products for price-sensitive customers. A differentiation strategy emphasizes uniqueness that is meaningful to customers. A focus strategy involves concentrating on the needs of a limited market segment. Each strategy has significant impact in terms of distribution channel requirements. The process begins with the development of a mission for the firm and specific overall corporate objectives.

The choice of strategy can be made only after careful analysis of customers, competition, internal capabilities, and external environments. Customer analysis involves market identification and segmental analysis. Competitive analysis includes an assessment of an industry's characteristics and assessment of specific competitive firms. Internal analysis is concerned with the performance of a firm and with capabilities in operations, finance, marketing, and management.

Environmental analysis seeks to uncover trends, opportunities, threats, and limitations in the external environment. While the sociocultural, economic, and technological environments are all critical, this chapter has focused on the legal environment of distribution channels. Major federal legislation includes the Sherman Antitrust Act, Clayton Antitrust Act, Federal Trade Commission Act, Robinson-Patman Act, and the Celler-Kefauver Act. Judicial decisions and administrative agencies also add to the legal complexity faced by business firms. A number of specific issues such as exclusive territories and exclusive dealing, tying agreements, discounts and allowances, collusion, price maintenance, and mergers constantly reoccur in the legal process.

Channel objectives and strategies for implementing them must be developed so that the firm can maintain or improve its strategic position in the distribution channel. Intensive, selective, and exclusive distribution represent alternative market coverage objectives. Decisions must also be made concerning the level of channel control necessary for strategic success. Due to the dynamic nature of market conditions, competition, and external environments, flexibility is a third channel objective to be considered.

QUESTIONS

1 What are the differences among cost, differentiation, and focus strategies? Select an industry and provide examples of three firms, each of which follows one of the three generic strategies. Pay particular attention to the distribution strategies of the firms.

2 What is the relevance of a mission statement? Find examples of mission statements that you believe demonstrate this relevance.

3 Describe the three-dimensional approach to market definition. Why is market definition such a difficult process in actual practice?

4 How does industry structure affect competition in Porter's model? Choose an industry, such as breakfast cereal, and describe that industry in terms of Porter's model.

5 Is it possible for a firm's management, when assessing internal strengths and weaknesses, to be objective? Should this analysis be conducted by an outside party?

6 Describe three current social trends and how you think they may influence distribution channels for food products. How may they influence distribution for fashion clothing?

7 Radio frequency (RF) technology is being applied by many firms in their logistics operations to increase speed and efficiency. Conduct research in your library or by contacting local firms to determine how this technology is being applied in distribution.

8 How might changes in the economic environment, such as rapid inflation, affect distribution strategy?

9 What is the difference between exclusive territorial arrangements and exclusive dealing? What is the importance of interbrand versus intrabrand competition in exclusive dealing?

10 When might a tying agreement be illegal? Do you believe that the "rule of reason" is a proper way to judge such arrangements?

11 Why would a manufacturer want resellers to maintain suggested resale prices? How can this desire be legally enforced?

12 Describe intensive, selective, and exclusive distribution. Give examples of firms in each of the following industries that exhibit one of these objectives: cosmetics, golf clubs, cookware.

CHAPTER 6

MARKETING DESIGN

CHAPTER OUTLINE

CUSTOMER ANALYSIS
  Market Segmentation
  Customers' Buying Behavior
PRODUCT IMPACT ON MARKETING CHANNEL DESIGN
  Product Attributes
  New Product Development
  Product Life Cycle
  Brand Strategies
PROMOTION IMPACT ON MARKETING
  Push Versus Pull Strategy
  Advertising
  Sales Promotions
  Personal Selling
PRICE IMPACT ON MARKETING DESIGN
  List Price
  Discounts
  Transportation Charges
  Price Changes
SUMMARY

The previous chapter dealt with the development of an overall corporate strategy, corporate positioning, and channel objectives. The distribution channel is the mechanism by which the firm implements its strategy and positions itself in the marketplace.

The design of channels encompasses two phases: marketing design and logistics design.

In this chapter, decisions related to marketing channel design are discussed. The theme of customer analysis and market segmentation is continued from Chapter 5, with emphasis on the role of segmentation in developing the functional channel strategy. The customers' buying behavior is discussed as the driving force underlying marketing channel design. From this beginning, each element of the marketing mix is then presented with a focus on the interrelationship between product, promotional, and pricing strategies on the design and implementation of marketing channels. Chapter 7 focuses on logistics channel decisions.

CUSTOMER ANALYSIS

Marketing channel design, as with all marketing strategy decisions, must focus first on analysis of customers. Just as a macro-level approach to customer analysis is fundamental to development of corporate strategy, as discussed in Chapter 5, a micro-level approach is necessary to development of specific channel design strategies. This analysis must incorporate two interrelated stages: (1) identification and selection of target market segments, and (2) analysis of customers' buying behavior.

Market Segmentation

It is a well-recognized fact that there is no single market for any given product or service. All markets are made up of different segments, each of which has somewhat different needs, or at least different wants, relative to that product or service. Effective market segmentation requires, then, that the marketer clearly identify the groups or segments to which products may be offered and choose the group (or groups) that the firm will attempt to serve.

There are obviously many ways in which markets can be segmented, and a comprehensive treatment of the subject is beyond the scope of this text. The discussion here is intended to highlight the importance of this process in the design of marketing channels, since channel design cannot be initiated without a clear understanding of the intended segments and their behavior.

A typical first approach to segmentation is to divide markets into either consumer markets, individuals purchasing to satisfy personal needs, or "industrial" markets, where the intended purchaser-user is an organization. Most products can, in fact, be targeted toward either ultimate consumers or ultimate organizations. Many firms, in fact, target both types of segments. Pillsbury and General Mills, for example, target households as well as restaurants and institutions for their flour, cake mixes, and related products. The distribution channels utilized to reach these two segments are, however, quite different. Even resellers such as Sam's Club and Price Club may target both industrial and consumer markets. While many consumers purchase products in these outlets for their own use, many small businesses also purchase products for resale or for operating supplies.

Such broad segment definition, however, is generally not useful in further analysis

**TABLE 6-1 SEGMENTATION VARIABLES
IN CONSUMER MARKETS**

Demographic variables	
Age	Education
Sex	Family size
Race	Family life cycle
Occupation	Social class
Income	Religion

Geographic variables	
Region	Urban, suburban, rural
City size	Climate

Psychographic variables	
Personality	Attitudes
Motives	Lifestyle

Behavior patterns	
Brand loyalty	Volume usage
Benefits expected	Price sensitivity

or development of marketing channels. More clearly defined groupings must be developed. Consumer markets may be further defined by such variables as demographics, geography, psychographics, or behavior patterns. Table 6-1 provides selected examples of each type of segmentation variable. Industrial markets can be similarly segmented on such bases as geography, the type of organization (manufacturer, wholesaler, retailer, government, etc.), customer size, and use of the product.

Even when segments are relatively narrowly defined by one or a combination of the above variables, it should be recognized that no two individuals or organizations are exactly alike in terms of their needs or wants. The ultimate-market segment is the individual consumer or organization. Few firms, however, are able to implement a segmentation system that so precisely defines their targets. Marketers typically depend upon aggregations of customers who are similar enough in their needs so that they can be satisfied economically. The ultimate test of the viability of a target market segment is that it must have the following characteristics:

1 Adequate customer potential
2 A recognized need
3 Economic ability to purchase
4 Efficiently reached[1]

[1] Dik Warren Twedt, "The Concept of Market Segmentation," in *Handbook of Modern Marketing,* ed. Victor P. Buell, New York: McGraw-Hill, 1986, p. 8-11.

Customer's Buying Behavior

Effective design of marketing channels does not end with identification of target market segments. It is also critical to understand the buying behavior of the customers in the target market segment(s), for this behavior is the driving force behind proper channel design. Of particular importance to marketing channel design are answers to the questions of where customers buy the product, when they buy it, and how they buy it. The answers to these questions dictate the necessary market coverage objective as well as customers' requirements for lot size, information, and financing.

Consumer Behavior A very popular framework for considering differences in consumer segments and answers to the above questions has been suggested by Louis Bucklin and is presented in Table 6-2. The implications for marketing channel design are also indicated.

It must be emphasized once again that not all consumers are alike. In fact, differences in buyer behavior, if they can be identified, represent an excellent opportunity for market segmentation and development of unique channel strategies. For example, as shown in Bucklin's framework in Table 6-2, one firm may choose those buyers whose behavior is best described as "convenience store–convenience good" while another firm may target "specialty store–specialty good" buyers for the same product category. Consider, for example, the differences in behavior among those consumers who choose Revlon brand lipstick at a supermarket or general-merchandise store versus those who are willing to seek out Merle Norman lipstick at an exclusive Merle Norman store. Another example can be found in Sears's attempt to market appliances as a "specialty good–specialty store" situation, which it did for many years. The Kenmore line of appliances was available only at Sears, and no other brand was available. In 1989, however, Sears abandoned that strategy and recognized that a large segment of consumers treat appliances as "shopping good–shopping store" purchases. Sears opened "Brand Central" departments in its stores, competing with other appliance retailers with such brands as GE, Whirlpool, and Maytag. This seemingly simple change in focus on customer segments and the buying behavior of the segments had enormous implications for Sears' marketing channels. Relationships had to be established with many new suppliers, and the capability to warehouse, transport, display, sell, and service these added product lines had to be developed.

Industrial Buyer's Behavior While there are several competing models of an industrial buyer's behavior, a particularly interesting and useful approach has been offered by Barbara Bund Jackson.[2] In simplest terms, she suggests that there are two basic categories of behavior by industrial buyers: "always-a-share" and "lost-for-good." As a practical matter, these two actually represent the extremes of a behavioral spectrum with many intermediate types of behavior.

Always-a-Share The first type of buyer behavior is best illustrated by the cus-

---

[2] This section is based on Barbara Bund Jackson, "Build Customer Relationships That Last," *Harvard Business Review,* **63**:6, November–December 1985, pp. 120–128; and *Winning and Keeping Industrial Customers: The Dynamics of Customer Relationships,* Lexington MA: Lexington Books, 1985.

TABLE 6-2   CLASSIFICATION OF STORE AND PRODUCT TYPE

Classification	Behavior	Required distribution coverage
Convenience store–convenience good	Consumer buys most readily available brand at most accessible outlet	Intensive
Convenience store–shopping good	Consumer compares and chooses among brands at most accessible outlet	Intensive
Convenience storage–specialty good	Consumer purchases favored brand from most accessible outlet carrying that brand	Selective/exclusive
Shopping store–convenience good	Consumer is indifferent to brand but compares outlets based on price and service	Intensive/selective
Shopping store–shopping good	Consumer compares both brands and outlets	Selective/exclusive
Shopping store–specialty good	Consumer purchases most preferred brand but compares outlets carrying the brand on basis of price and service	Selective/exclusive
Specialty store–convenience good	Consumer is loyal to specific store but is indifferent to brand	Selective/exclusive
Specialty store–shopping good	Consumer is loyal to specific store but compares the brands available	Selective/exclusive
Specialty store–specialty good	Consumer is loyal to specific store and specific brand	Selective/exclusive

Source: Adapted from Louis P. Bucklin, "Retail Strategy and the Classification of Consumer Goods," *Journal of Marketing,* January 1963, pp. 53–54, published by the American Marketing Association.

tomer that prefers to maintain multiple sources of supply and therefore, over time, spreads purchases of a given product category among several vendors. This type of buyer switches from supplier to supplier frequently. In some cases, this buyer may even parcel out its purchase of a large quantity of product at one time to several different vendors. For example, an apartment complex needing 1000 refrigerators could buy 500 from one vendor and the remainder from another vendor. Admittedly, this particular form of behavior is rare, but it does describe the behavior of the United States government and state government agencies in some situations. More commonly, buyers will make a purchase from one supplier, but the next time they are faced with a need for the same product they may purchase it from a different supplier. The essence of this purchasing behavior is that the customer maintains multiple sources of supply and gives a share of its purchases to several different vendors. Thus, Jackson terms these "always-a-share" buyers.

Lost-for-Good   A contrasting type of behavior is demonstrated by the buyer that is committed to one vendor and makes all of its purchases of a product over time from that vendor. The buyer remains committed to that vendor as long as its needs are satisfied. If, however, the supplier does lose that customer, the customer will form a relationship with a new vendor and is "lost for good" to the original vendor.

Determinants of Behavior   The basic determinant of industrial buying behavior is the cost, to the customer, of switching suppliers. The two major categories of cost are investment and risk. Each cost category must be considered. Industrial customers actually "invest" in many ways when they choose suppliers. Obviously, they pay for their purchases, but they also invest in people, assets, and business procedures. People are hired and trained, some specifically to deal with a supplier or the supplier's products. Changing suppliers may necessitate changing personnel or at least retraining. The same is true for investments in assets (equipment, for example) and business procedures that may have to be changed if supplies are switched. To some extent, such changes are always necessary when suppliers are changed. The actual amount varies, as does each firm's sensitivity to these costs and awareness of their size.

Risk is a less tangible, but nevertheless real, cost of change. Buyers incur risk in any relationship with a supplier, whether it be short- or long-run. Performance risk from the buyer's viewpoint concerns whether the seller will continuously offer satisfactory products and *service*. Increasing experience with a vendor may serve to increase or decrease the buyer's perception of that risk. Personal risk also is involved for the individual within the buyer's firm who is responsible for selection of vendors.

Table 6-3 summarizes the typical characteristics of customers at the extreme points of the behavior spectrum.

Marketing Implications   Two benefits can be derived from analyzing industrial buyers in terms of nvestment and risk. First, companies can select strategies most appropriate to the type of customer they are serving. Short-term tactics can be applied to short-term (always-a-share) customers; lost-for-good customers must be met with long-term tactics.

TABLE 6-3   CHARACTERISTICS OF LOST-FOR-GOOD AND ALWAYS-A-SHARE CUSTOMERS

Lost-for-good	Always-a-share
Buyer perceives high switching costs	Buyer perceives low switching costs
Substantial investment, especially in procedures and assets	Small investments
High perceived risks	Low perceived risks
Focus on vendor	Focus on product
Long-term horizon	Short-term horizon

Low-cost pricing is generally the shortest-term tactic, with use of sales promotions and advertising also relatively short-run. Improvements in sales force, distribution, and product quality are examples of long-range tactics. To address the needs of the lost-for-good segments, the entire vendor organization must be coordinated to meet those customers' expectations. An interesting anomaly is that long-term customers are more sensitive to any failure from their vendors than are always-a-share buyers. They are aware of their vulnerability and thus tend to perceive risk developing at any sign of lack of coordination or other failure by a vendor. Always-a-share customers expect to purchase from many vendors and are influenced primarily by price and other short-term approaches.

The second benefit of this approach is that actions may be taken to change customers' behavior and their positions along the spectrum. This is not to suggest that all customers can be changed, or that drastic change is possible. However, certain actions may be taken that change customers' switching costs and/or their perception of risk. If the vendor can offer *substantial real benefits* to convince the short-term customer to invest in assets or procedures, stronger relationships may be forged. It may be argued, in fact, that the best channel relationships exist when channel partners perceive that they are economically better off in the existing channel than in any alternative relationship.

As one example, in the distribution of drugs and drug-related products to independent drugstores, Bergen Brunswig has developed systems that many stores have implemented for the purpose of more efficient ordering, delivery, and inventory control (for a full description, see the case in Part I entitled "A Tale of Two Wholesalers"). Many store owners have invested time and effort, if not money, in learning to use these systems, and their stores have become dependent on them. They also perceive that the systems reduce their overall total cost of store operation, Thus, many of these stores now realize that costs would increase substantially if suppliers were changed. As a result, many stores that once were always-a-share buyers, purchasing from several wholesalers, now concentrate their purchases and deal exclusively with Bergen Brunswig.

While the above discussion was originally developed by Jackson to describe industrial purchasing behavior, it has very important implications for firms in consumer products distribution. Many manufacturers of consumer products have historically developed marketing strategies oriented toward generating ultimate-consumer demand for their brand to "pull" the product through the distribution channel. Retailers faced with consumers' loyalty toward specific manufacturer's brands would be required by the strength of that loyalty to include those brands in their product assortment. There is growing evidence, however, that consumers' brand loyalty is not as strong as was once assumed.[3] Table 6-4 shows results of consumer research that indicate that brand loyalty is actually relatively low.

One explanation of these results is that most consumers may have a weak preference for a particular brand but generally find any one of several competing brands to be acceptable. Alternatively, consumers may feel little psychological "involvement"

[3] "Glitzy Brands Make Small Impressions," *The Wall Street Journal,* December 15, 1989, p. B1.

TABLE 6-4 PERCENTAGE OF USERS LOYAL TO
ONE BRAND

Product	Percent loyal
Cigarettes	71%
Toothpaste	61%
Coffee	58%
Bath soap	53%
Beer	48%
Automobiles	47%
Pet food	45%
Gasoline	39%
Televisions	35%
Blue jeans	33%
Athletic shoes	27%

Source: Wall Street Journal, October 19, 1989, p. B1. Reprinted by permission of Wall Street Journal, © 1990 Dow Jones & Company, Inc. All rights reserved worldwide.

with these product categories and therefore delay making purchase decisions until they are in a retail store. For example, consumers may find Tylenol, Datril, Excedrin, and Bayer aspirin all to be acceptable pain relievers. Essentially, the implication is that a great deal of consumer purchasing may be closely approximated by the convenience, shopping, or specialty store–convenience good categories of Bucklin's framework. If this is true, the impact on distribution channel design and strategy cannot be over-emphasized. For resellers such as retailers, it means increased flexibility in product-assortment decisions. They may be able to eliminate suppliers of marginally performing products, reducing the number of brands made available to consumers without reducing sales. In fact, the resellers' purchasing behavior may come closer to the lost-for-good model as they choose to develop relationships with a smaller set of vendors that more effectively meet their needs and/or help reduce their total cost of operation. Such an eventuality does not seem to be speculative when one considers the efforts of many retailers during the 1980s to reduce the number of their suppliers. Later in this text, direct product profitability is discussed as a tool used by wholesalers and retailers to evaluate the total cost of distribution and choose products and suppliers with whom to develop channel relationships.[4]

PRODUCT IMPACT ON MARKETING CHANNEL DESIGN

Marketing channel design must be closely correlated and integrated with all other aspects of a firm's marketing strategy. Decisions about and strategies for dealing with products have a particularly critical role in shaping the design and structure of channels. Product attributes, new-product development, product life cycles, and brand strategies are discussed below, with an emphasis being placed on their influence on channel design.

[4] See Chapters 8 and 11 for a discussion of direct product profitability.

Product Attributes

A product is actually a bundle of attributes, all of which have important implications for channel design. Attributes such as unit value, perishability, handling characteristics, technical complexity, and standardization are key determinants of appropriate channel structure.

Unit Value Products that have a low unit value generally move through several distribution levels, resulting in longer marketing channels. The rationale for this is that these products generally do not generate sufficient gross margin dollars to allow manufacturers to absorb the high cost of more-direct forms of distribution. Thus consumer products such as processed foods, health and beauty aids, and hardware tend to involve several intermediaries. Similarly, industrial goods such as office supplies or maintenance and repair items generally move through industrial distributors to the end user. Conversely, items with high unit value usually generate sufficient gross margins to allow more-direct distribution channels. In such cases, the cost of distribution may be a low percentage of the total product value, allowing one channel member to easily absorb that cost.

Unit value also tends to correlate with the intensity of distribution coverage, although there are clearly many exceptions. As a general rule, low-unit-value items tend to be considered convenience items by customers; thus they require intensive distribution. Higher-unit-value products tend to be treated as shopping or specialty items, allowing more flexibility in decisions concerning selective or exclusive distribution.

Perishability Perishability is another product attribute that affects channel design. Highly perishable products such as fresh produce and seafood usually require direct channels so that delays in movement and handling, which would increase the danger of product spoilage, are avoided. Perishability is not limited to physical deterioration. It may involve products whose commercial life is limited because of short-lived customer demand, as in the case of high-fashion apparel; these products are usually directly distributed.

Handling Characteristics Products that are heavy, bulky, fragile, or otherwise difficult to handle generally require direct forms of distribution. Because of the difficulty in handling such products, each turnover results in significantly increased cost. Handling also increases the likelihood of damage to more-fragile items. So that costs associated with handling are reduced, the number of times a product is physically exchanged is minimized in direct channels.

Technical Complexity Technically complex products frequently require exacting service, or at least highly trained personnel for product demonstration. For these reasons, such products frequently involve direct-distribution channels. Most industrial products as well as many consumer goods fit this category. For example, one problem encountered by manufacturers of personal computers in the early 1980s was the lack of technically competent retail sales personnel. For this reason, some manufacturers opened their own computer stores or used very selective policies in choosing stores that could provide adequate service and training for customers.

Standardization   Product standardization is frequently related to technical complexity, with highly nonstandard products generally requiring greater technical knowledge or skills in the distribution channel. To the extent that each customer has a unique need and products must be customized to fit those needs, direct channels are required. Thus, industrial buyers' needs for customized facilities and equipment or consumers' demand for custom homes or clothing require direct contact between producer and buyer. More standardized items that do not require such customization may move through more indirect channels.

New-Product Development

New-product development activity can be undertaken by any channel member and may have significant impact on the structure and relationship of channel members. While the term "new product" can have several meanings, generally it is applied to a new product that a given firm has not marketed before. In the following pages, new-product development efforts by manufacturers and middlemen and the interrelationship of these efforts with marketing channel design are discussed.

Manufacturers   Each year manufacturers develop thousands of new products. In the grocery industry alone, it is estimated that over 10,000 new products are introduced each year. These new-product introductions have a significant impact on distribution channels, and distribution channels have a significant impact on the success of manufacturers' efforts. For many manufacturers, existing distribution channels are a major determinant of which new products will even be considered. A product concept that requires a new distribution structure may be dropped early in the development process. Thus, BIC requires all new products under consideration to meet the same distribution requirements as its existing lines of disposable lighters and ballpoint pens.

Failure to consider distribution channels in product development can have disastrous consequences. This is true even when the new product is closely related to an existing product. A new size, color, or slight variation of an existing model or a close copy, a "me-too" variation, of a competitor's product may meet with strong channel resistance. In the grocery industry, for example, retailers now require that some manufacturers pay a special fee, called a "slotting allowance," just for the right to have a new product displayed on store shelves. Additionally, some retailers require that for every new product displayed, an existing product must be removed from the store's shelves.

When new-product development requires modified or new distribution channels, most manufacturers move cautiously. As noted earlier in this text, many firms restrict their efforts to expand products and to diversify because they lack expertise in unfamiliar distribution channels.

Intermediaries Wholesalers and retailers also have new-product development decisions. Any choice to extend the width or depth of their product assortments may require new channel arrangements. Sources of supply must be found, new relationships developed, and existing products in the assortment either deleted or at least somewhat restricted. There may also be incompatible desires between manufacturers and intermediaries regarding product development. Where a specific manufacturer may want its products added and featured, wholesalers and retailers may be more concerned with their portfolio of products across several suppliers.

Intermediaries may also frequently be the source of new-product development ideas for manufacturers. Because of their proximity to customers in the distribution channel, they frequently receive considerable feedback and market intelligence, which they pass back to suppliers.

Product Life Cycle

The product life cycle is a model that illustrates the stages through which a typical product passes over time. It tracks the sales and profitability of a product as it moves from introduction, through growth and maturity, to decline. It is also a well-accepted framework for structuring marketing channel design related to each life-cycle stage. The product life cycle is discussed in detail below.

Introduction In introductory stages, new products generally meet with some resistance in distribution channels. Manufacturers that desire intensive market coverage may be unable to accomplish that objective, as middlemen resist additions to their product assortments. Additionally many manufacturers move cautiously during this period, restricting their coverage to limited geographic areas. This is due to the uncertainty of demand and the reluctance of manufacturers to invest in production capacity in the face of that uncertain demand. While caution may be necessary, it may also disrupt channels when demand turns out to be high. As presented in the Gillette Sensor case[5] when Gillette introduced its new Sensor razor and blades, consumer acceptance was extremely rapid and much greater than had been forecast. Since the product required new production facilities, Gillette had limited its initial production in preparation for the introduction. Strong consumer acceptance meant that retailers quickly sold their initial stock. Gillette was unable to fill all orders for resupply and was forced to allocate available production. Because of these problems, channel relationships were severely damaged and some retailers even decided to drop the product.

Growth Assuming that a new-product introduction is a success, rapid market growth follows, competitors enter the field, and overall market demand increases. Distribution structure may be broadened to new geographic markets and intensity increased in an attempt to foreclose the market to competition. Because the market expands rapidly in this stage, the key distribution tasks are to maintain product availability (to avoid problems experienced by Gillette) and to obtain greater market pen-

[5] See *Gillette Sensor: An International Launch* on pp. 110–118.

etration. As market growth slows and approaches maturity, increased competition may require some price or promotional concessions to be made to middlemen as the various competitors fight one another for distribution outlets.

Maturity   As sales stabilize, reseller margins erode and the established distribution structures begin to pressure for reduced prices, increased margins, and other similar concessions. A key objective is maintaining the distribution intensity at the appropriate level by satisfying the requirements of the participants in the channel.

It is also in this stage when many firms begin to seek new markets or new users for the product in an attempt to revitalize growth. These efforts generally require altered or even new distribution channels. The effort may be as simple as expansion to international markets—bringing new channel participants into the structure—or as complex as changing the existing structure to appeal to different market segments. Many firms have revitalized growth in stable markets through such channel redesign. Hanes revolutionized the market for hosiery with its distribution of L'eggs through supermarkets, as did Avon through its direct-to-home distribution for cosmetics.

Decline   As demand for a product declines, the ability to maintain distribution intensity becomes increasingly difficult (and frequently undesirable). Some channel participants drop the product, as their strategy necessitates dealing with high-volume products. Others may desire to continue the product, but their volume may be too low to justify continuance of existing distribution practices. All channel members face a decision regarding the appropriate strategy to employ. Low-cost channel arrangements become increasingly important as price competition frequently intensifies as channel members attempt to forestall declining demand. Some intermediaries may drop the product from their assortment; others continue it as competition is reduced for remaining consumers. Simultaneously, some producers may delete the product while others delete marginal intermediaries, cut expenses, and perhaps add some intermediaries who were eliminated by their competitors. The end result is typically a reduced level of competition at all channel levels and new channel arrangements among those who choose to maintain the product.

Brand Strategies

A third critical area of product impact on distribution channels is the brand policies and strategies of channel participants. Specifically, decisions must be made by all participants relative to manufacturers' brands or private-distributor brands. A manufacturer's brand is developed and owned by the producer of the item. Private-distributor brands are developed and owned by resellers (wholesalers or retailers).

For manufacturers, the advantages of manufacturers' brands are numerous. Through promotional efforts and quality control, consumer loyalty may be built. Intermediaries may feel it desirable to handle the products since the manufacturer carries the burden of primary marketing effort. An image may develop for the manufacturer which extends to other products and enhance the likelihood of successful new-product introductions. Kellogg's, Nabisco, and Gillette are just three examples of well-known, successful manufacturer brands.

Intermediaries typically find manufacturers' brands to be desirable. The product is generally presold to some target customers, and intermediaries have some assurance of product-quality standards. If quality declines, the manufacturer is legally at fault and customers may be shifted to other brands. Of course, consumers may also be dissatisfied with the intermediary in such instances. Thus, retailers and wholesalers do have a stake in manufacturers' quality standards.

Private-distributor brands have been effectively utilized by many intermediaries. Wholesalers such as IGA and SuperValu in the food industry and Tru-Value in the hardware industry have successfully utilized private-distributor brands. Sears with its Craftsman line of tools and Kenmore appliances, Kroger's with its Cost Cutter brand, and J.C. Penney with its Penncraft brand are just a few examples of retailers utilizing successful private brands.

The advantages to the intermediary of private brands are numerous. They build customer loyalty to the outlets carrying them, as these brands are not available elsewhere. Typically, intermediaries pay lower prices to suppliers for private-brand merchandise than they would for manufacturers' brands because the supplier does not have to include in its price any promotional expense for the private brand. Thus, intermediaries typically earn higher margins on private brands and still maintain lower selling prices than they would for a manufacturer's brand.

Although some manufacturers refuse to produce products for distributor brands, it is difficult to ignore the opportunity to do so. Usually, if one manufacturer refuses, a competing manufacturer will get the business. Also, the production of a private brand utilizes excess capacity, the cost of which otherwise would have to be absorbed by the manufacturer's own brands.

In recent years, the competition between manufacturers' and private-distributor brands has intensified. This "battle of the brands" has frequently resulted in altered distribution channel relationships as some manufacturers refuse to produce private distributor brands and some intermediaries reduce the number of manufacturers' brands carried. At the very least, these brand strategy decisions on the part of all distribution channel participants frequently increase the stress and conflict within the marketing channel.

PROMOTION IMPACT ON MARKETING DESIGN

Promotional activities and strategies play a crucial role in marketing channels. These activities consist of advertising, sales promotions, and personal selling efforts of firms engaged in the distribution channel. Much of an individual channel member's promotional efforts is directed toward influencing the behavior of other firms within the channel. For example, a substantial portion of a manufacturer's promotions may be aimed at encouraging wholesalers and retailers to participate in the manufacturer's marketing efforts. Additionally, considerable promotional effort consists of joint activities by all channel members to stimulate consumer or end-user purchases. In this section, the fundamental strategy decision of using a ''push'' versus a ''pull'' promotional strategy is discussed. Attention is then focused on advertising, sales promotion, and personal selling efforts of channel members as these efforts relate to channel strategy.

Push versus Pull Strategy

There are two basic promotional strategy alternatives available to manufacturers. Most promotional activities within the distribution channel hinge upon this strategic choice. A *pull* strategy attempts to stimulate buyers' or consumers' demand for a product by promotional efforts aimed at the ultimate consumer or industrial user. The goal is to build demand at that level so that retailers, wholesalers, or distributors feel compelled to stock that product in their respective assortments. Ultimately, the product is ''pulled'' through the distribution channel by the end-user demand created. Advertising and consumer promotions are the most commonly used elements of a pull strategy.

By contrast, a *push* strategy focuses the manufacturer's promotional efforts on the members of the distribution channel itself, rather than the final user. Trade advertising and allowances, trade promotions, and personal selling are designed to influence middlemen to stock the manufacturer's products and promote them to the final consumer.

Very few manufacturers employ ''pure'' pull or push strategies. An effective promotional effort generally makes use of both. For example, Procter & Gamble spends over $1 billion per year on advertising aimed at ultimate consumers in an attempt to generate consumer pull for its products. As part of its pull strategy, P&G promotes continuously with coupons in newspapers and through direct mail. Nevertheless, P&G also employs thousands of sales representatives who call on wholesalers and retailers to convince those channel members to stock and support P&G products. In addition to this personal selling effort, P&G employs extensive trade promotions and allowances tied to their consumer advertising for channel members who agree to support those products and programs.

Advertising

Advertising can, of course, be employed by any member of the distribution channel and may be directed toward end users or other distribution channel members. Of particular interest in this text are trade advertising and cooperative advertising.

Trade Advertising   Trade advertising is designed to communicate with members of the distribution channel. Most firms with products nationally advertised to consumers also depend upon trade papers and magazines to reach their channel members. Such publications as *Chain Store Age* and *Supermarket News* are frequently read by manufacturers, wholesalers, and retailers and provide excellent vehicles for promotion within the channel.

Trade advertising is generally more informative and detailed than consumer advertising. The appeals used are typically more rational than emotional. Manufacturers frequently employ such advertising to describe products, suggest methods for handling or presentation, or point out the advantages to wholesalers and retailers of stocking

TABLE 6-5   PROCTER & GAMBLE TRADE ADVERTISEMENT FOR RETAILERS

PROCTER & GAMBLE
NOTICE TO OUR CUSTOMERS

ATTENTION: STORE MANAGER OWNER

We offer annual funded Marketing Agreements to all retailers in the U.S.A. Payments are made for performance under the applicable plan: FMA plan—purchase, distribute, or reduce price; CMF plan—purchase and/or distribute cases for print/electronic media featuring and/or display and/or price reduction and/or in-store sampling/couponing and/or selling/consumer shows. Other programs involve distribution by agencies of product coupons and samples in stores, in various markets at various times. Also, we offer display material, newspaper proofs, etc., to assist you in merchandising our brands.

Details are set forth in specific agreements. These offers are practical and usable by all retailers regardless of size. You may now be performing under an agreement, and payments are being made to you or your headquarters or wholesaler on your behalf. In some instances, wholesalers commingle these funds for the benefit of all their retail customers.

If you are not receiving benefit of these offers either directly or through your wholesale supplier and would like to do so, send your name, address and telephone number to Procter & Gamble, Box 162, Cincinnati, Ohio 45201 and we will contact you. Please specify the Company product line.

Beauty Care Sector
Health Care Sector
Food/Beverage Sector
Paper Sector
Soap Sector

Source: Reprinted by permission of *Supermarket Business,* September 1990, p. 138.

those products. It may also be employed to explain new marketing programs or to build goodwill with the trade. Table 6-5 provides one example of a trade advertisement placed by Procter & Gamble to explain its discounts for retailers.

Cooperative Advertising   A significant form of advertising in distribution channel arrangements is cooperative advertising, a joint promotional effort between retailers and their suppliers. While the details of cooperative advertising arrangements vary, the essence of such programs is that the supplier furnishes the retailer with materials and financial support in return for the retailer's advertising of the supplier's product. For example, Du Pont provides carpet dealers with advertising formats and logos for Stainmaster carpets. The local dealer need only insert the outlet's name and location. After the ad is run in the local newspaper, the dealer is required to submit a copy of the ad and the invoice from the newspaper. Du Pont then reimburses the dealer for a portion of the cost of placing the ad.

Cooperative advertising is common in almost every consumer product industry. Clothing, household goods, food, hardware, electronics, and virtually all other industries employ these joint promotional activities. The advantages to retailers are numerous. They receive the benefit of professionally designed advertisements without the expense of developing them. In addition, their own advertising budgets are supplemented considerably. The major disadvantages for retailers are that the ads frequently have a national rather than local orientation and they generally stress the manufacturer's brand name rather than patronage at a particular store.

Manufacturers and wholesalers receive benefits from increased advertising and promotion of their products at a local level, at a reduced cost. However, there are disadvantages to cooperative advertising for suppliers. Retailers frequently group products into one ad, thus reducing effectiveness from the supplier's viewpoint. Suppliers, in fact, have little control over the exact content of these ads. The cost of developing and administering these programs may also be quite large. Finally, there are also legal implications of such programs.

Despite these disadvantages, cooperative advertising continues to grow as a practice in distribution channels. In many industries, a manufacturer that failed to incorporate cooperative advertising allowances into the promotional strategy would have little chance of success, as many retailers would refuse even to stock that supplier's products.

Sales Promotions

Sales promotion has become a common element of the marketing strategy of all channel members. While the exact dollar figure for expenditures on sales promotion efforts is unknown, there is considerable evidence that the financial commitment is larger than that for advertising.[6] While there are numerous specific forms of sales promotion, those considered below have the greatest impact on distribution channels. For the sake of convenience, these are divided into categories of consumer-oriented promotion and trade-oriented promotion.

Consumer Promotion When used by manufacturers, consumer promotions are an integral part of an overall "pull" strategy. The intent is to stimulate immediately the consumers' interest in the manufacturer's product. The most common (but certainly not the only) forms of consumer promotions are coupons, bonus packs, and tie-in arrangements.

Coupons In 1989, package-goods manufacturers alone distributed over 221 billion coupons to consumers.[7] These coupons were distributed by mass media and direct mail, or on packages. These figures do not even include coupons distributed by retailers themselves. Coupons generally provide consumers with a price discount when redeemed at the time of purchase. The retailer is then reimbursed by the supplier for the amount of the discount plus an agreed-to handling charge. The objective is generally to stimulate immediate sales by attracting new users, brand switchers, and price-sensitive consumers, or by increasing repeat purchase rates. Frequently, such coupons also provide incentive for wholesalers and retailers to add the couponed item to their assortment.

While coupons have an important role in pull strategies, they also have implications

[6] Robert C. Blattberg and Scott A. Neslin, *Sales Promotion Concepts, Methods, and Strategies,* Englewood Cliffs, NJ: Prentice-Hall, 1990, p. 13.
[7] Ibid.

for channel design and coordination. A mechanism must be developed to provide for reimbursement for the retailer. As discussed in Chapter 3, special institutions have evolved specifically to facilitate this process. Also, couponing activities must be coordinated with channel members. A frequent retailer's complaint is that manufacturers distribute coupons without providing notice to the retailer. Consumers bring these coupons to the store for redemption and consequently the retailer may run out of the featured product. The result is that other consumers are not able to redeem their coupons. This generates considerable ill will throughout the channel. With notification in advance, the retailer could have built stock levels in anticipation of the manufacturer's coupon distribution.

A second administrative problem associated with coupons is potential misredemption and counterfeiting, the costs of which can be quite high. Situations in which thousands of coupons are clipped by an individual or an organized group and then submitted (to the manufacturer or the clearing house) for payment have been documented. Manufacturers must be careful to assure that each redeemed coupon in fact corresponds to an actual sale of a product.

Bonus Packs and Tie-Ins   Another common consumer-oriented promotion involves the development of special packaging to create a particular value for consumers, or a tie-in package of two separate products. For example, Ralston-Purina may develop a special package of its Dog Chow in which 30 pounds of chow are sold rather than the normal 25 pounds. The intent is to give the consumer 5 pounds "free" as a bonus for purchasing. These special bonus packs frequently cause problems in the distribution channel because wholesalers and retailers must handle the new package as if it were a new or unique product, stock it, track it, and then dispose of it when the promotion ends. Some wholesalers and retailers frequently refuse to participate in such promotions because of the extra expense involved with handling the item for a short time period. Similarly, some intermediaries are reluctant to handle tie-in promotions where two separate products are combined into one package. This reluctance may defeat the best-intentioned promotional strategy of the manufacturer.

Trade Promotion   Trade promotions represent a supplier's attempt to induce wholesalers or retailers to purchase, promote, discount, and/or display a particular product. Most trade promotions actually involve some sort of price discount for the retailer as an inducement. The discount may be allowed as an off-invoice deduction or may be billed back to the supplier by the retailer based on the number of items purchased during the promotional period. Trade promotions generally have a set time period during which the deal is in effect and frequently require specific behavior on the part of the retailer. For example, the retailer may be required to purchase a minimum quantity, provide special display or promotion of the product, or pass through part of the discount to the consumer. Such promotions have become so common as a competitive device in some consumer-goods industries that some manufacturers sell 90 to 95 percent of all their production "on deal."

The primary reason for this phenomenon has been the growth of a distribution practice called "forward buying." Wholesalers and retailers have found that it is frequently possible not only to purchase the quantity needed during the promotional period but also to place large orders during the promotion to reduce the future cost of goods. The size of the promotional discount offered by the supplier is traded off against the increased cost of storage and inventory carrying cost of the large purchase to determine the appropriate amount to order. When the promotional discount is high and storage and carrying costs are relatively low, forward buying is likely to occur. The result is that manufacturers have high levels of activity during promotional periods and little activity when products are not being promoted to the trade.

Another problem created by trade dealing is diversion. Because different deals are frequently offered in different regions of the country, a wholesaler or retailer in one region may purchase a product on promotion in one area and resell to another whole-saler or retailer in a different region where the promotion is not available. Chapter 3 described the emergence of "diverters" that specialize in this practice. At any given time, it may be possible for a retailer to purchase a manufacturer's product from a diverter at a lower price than that product could be purchased from the manufacturer itself.

The clear result of many trade promotions is that they have significantly altered marketing channel design and relationships. This does not suggest that the consequences of trade promotions are always negative. They can be very effective when properly planned and implemented. However, the consequences of such promotions on marketing channels should be carefully evaluated.[8]

Personal Selling

It would be difficult to find a firm that does not utilize some form of personal selling effort. Even those manufacturers that employ selling agents to contact wholesalers and retailers must initially "sell" their products to those agents. At the retail level, even "self-service" retailers have clerks who can provide information or assistance to consumers. The question is not whether personal selling exists, but the role that it will play in the marketing channel.

The channels for industrial products generally place a heavier burden on the personal-selling component of promotion. More technically complex products generally require considerable personal selling at each level of the distribution channel. Clearly, the more oriented a manufacturer is to a push strategy, the greater the role of personal selling to obtain intermediary commitment and support, to convince or persuade wholesalers and retailers, and to provide those channel partners with information and assistance in marketing that manufacturer's products. Sales training programs and missionary selling are two promotional strategies frequently employed.

Training Programs   Wholesalers and retailers frequently require considerable assistance from their manufacturers in many areas of operation, particularly in the training of their own salespeople. Such training programs should focus on the wholesalers' and retailers' needs for both product-related and sales-related training. Inter-

[8] Lloyd M. Rhinehart, M. Bixby Cooper, and George D. Wagenheim, "Furthering the Integration of Marketing and Logistics through Customer Service in the Channel," *Journal of the Academy of Marketing Science,* **17**:1, Winter 1989, p. 66.

estingly, many manufactures overlook the basic fact that wholesale and retail salespeople are most likely to favor those items about which they are most knowledgeable and with which they feel most comfortable.

Missionary Selling Missionary selling is a form of personal selling designed to influence decisions rather than "get the order" and to help move products through the distribution channel. It is frequently used by manufacturers in both industrial- and consumer-goods industries to aid the personal-selling efforts of wholesalers and distributors. Missionary salespeople may have responsibility for much of the training of wholesalers and may even make sales calls on the wholesaler's customers, either with or without the wholesaler's representative present. The purpose of such activity is generally to supplement the wholesaler's effort and gain orders for the wholesaler.

Extreme care must be exercised in the use of missionary salespeople. Frequently, wholesaler's sales personnel resent missionary salespeople calling on their accounts. Such activities may also be viewed as the first step toward elimination of the wholesaler from the distribution channel. It is also generally an expensive tool to utilize.[9]

The development of sales training programs and use of missionary selling is clearly dependent upon the focus of the overall promotional effort in marketing channel design. The types of intermediaries in the channel and their specific roles may dictate whether these personal-selling techniques are even desirable. A strong retailer of computers, with technically capable salespeople, may desire little in the way of training from computer suppliers. Conversely, many retailers may be quite anxious to receive such training. The point is that the personal selling capabilities of specific firms at each level in the distribution channel may dictate the appropriate channel structure and the relationships that evolve in the structure.

PRICE IMPACT ON MARKETING DESIGN

Price is most properly viewed as the value placed on the combination of product, communication, and distribution functions that each firm performs in channel arrangement. It is also the mechanism by which profits are divided in the channel. Price levels are initiated by the manufacturer with consideration of the value of the product to the consumer or end user, the competitive price levels, and the margins needed or demanded by intermediaries to induce them to participate in the channel structure and perform their functions properly. In the section below, the concepts of list price, various discounts and terms of sale, and the special problems created by transportation and price changes in distribution channels are discussed.

List Price

Most products have a "list," or base, price. Frequently, this price is quoted by the manufacturer in terms of the price to be paid by the final consumer or end user. When

[9] Allen B. Huellmantel and Noel B. Zabriskie, "The Use of Missionary and Detail Salespersons," in *Handbook of Modern Marketing,* ed. Victor P. Buell, New York: McGraw-Hill, 1986, p. 76–1.

this practice is employed, resellers are not required to actually sell at that price (as was discussed in Chapter 5), but the list price is used as a basis for negotiating prices within the distribution channel.

More commonly, list price is quoted by the manufacturer as the price to be paid by the ultimate customer under normal selling conditions. While the development of list prices is a complex topic beyond the scope of this text, it is important to note here that when "list price" is being determined one thing must be considered— margins necessary to compensate resellers for the functions they are expected to perform under normal circumstances. In many industries, conventional normal margins have developed that wholesalers and retailers regard as a "fair" compensation for their efforts. For example, retailers of expensive jewelry generally expect a retail margin of at least 50 percent. There are also certain specific prices at the retail level to which consumers have become accustomed for some products. Chewing gum at $.40 per pack provides one example. In such situations, the manufacturer generally must establish a list price that allows the conventional margins to be maintained.

Finally, it must be recognized that these conventional prices may vary in any given channel relationship. The negotiating capability of the supplier and the customer ultimately determines the transfer price. Within the parameters established by the Robinson-Patman Act, there is some flexibility to negotiate variations on the list price based on quantities purchased, functions performed, and other extenuating circumstances.

Discounts

As suggested above, discounts from list price are common in the negotiations between buyers and sellers. The most common forms of discount are quantity, functional, seasonal, and cash discounts.

Quantity Discounts Many firms offer discounts to customers who place large orders. This order size may be computed in terms of the actual dollar volume or in terms of the number of units ordered. Typically, it costs the seller less per unit to sell and deliver a large order than a small one. There is less paperwork and time involved, and transportation expense per unit is reduced. In general, it is easy to visualize that it is less expensive to deal with one order for 10,000 units of an item than ten orders of 1000 units each.

Quantity discounts can be cumulative or noncumulative. A cumulative discount is computed by totaling the buyer's purchases during a period of time. For example, an automobile dealer receives a percentage rebate each year from the manufacturers which is based on the number and total value of the automobiles that dealer sold during the year. Generally, cumulative discounts are offered to encourage the customer to continue to purchase from the same supplier during a time period in order to qualify for larger discounts.

Noncumulative discounts are based on the size of an individual order. While such discounts do not encourage repeat purchases, they do encourage buyers to purchase more at one time, thus reducing the seller's expense.

Quantity discounts may be structured by manufacturers to encourage retailers to purchase from wholesalers rather than directly from manufacturers. The wholesaler may purchase a volume sufficiently large to earn a discount for which few retailers could qualify. Retailers then are encouraged to continue buying from wholesalers rather than directly from manufacturers. Of course, this discount structuring also helps explain the rise of retailer cooperatives, whereby small retailers pool their purchases in order to qualify for such discounts. This example clearly demonstrates the impact of discount strategies on marketing channel design.

Functional Discounts In some cases, when a manufacturer quotes a retail list price, it is also common to express discounts from that price which are to be taken by channel members, based on the functions performed. A discount structure might read as a series of percentages to be deducted. For example, a manufacturer might quote a list price of $1000 less 30% − 10%. The $1000 is the suggested retail selling price. The retailer deducts 30 percent from $1000, paying $700. Wholesalers, in turn, deduct 10 percent from $700 (not from $1000) and pay $630 to the manufacturer.

While functional discounts are theoretically based on functions performed by various channel members, the complicated nature of distribution networks often makes it difficult to determine whether or not a particular firm should receive a discount. As discussed in Chapter 5, there are legal implications in actual implementation of functional discount structures.

Seasonal Discounts A seasonal discount may be offered to channel members to encourage purchases of merchandise out of season. These discounts allow manufacturers to continue production year-round with assurance that the product will be sold. Products such as bathing suits and lawn and garden equipment may be discounted in the fall and winter, whereas winter clothing or snowblowers are discounted in the spring. Frequently, firms also offer warehousing allowances to customers who take early delivery of product.

Cash Discounts In theory, a cash discount is offered to customers who pay in cash rather than take advantage of seller's credit terms of sale. In practice, few channel members actually pay in cash. (In fact, few sellers within the distribution channel desire to be paid in cash due to the risk of handling.) Cash discounts and terms of sale may therefore be offered to encourage prompt payment. For example, a typical cash discount and terms of sale agreement might read "invoice, less 2/10, net 30." If the buyer pays within 10 days, 2 percent can be deducted from the invoice amount. Otherwise, the buyer must pay the full invoice amount within 30 days.

The amount of the cash discount, the timing allowed, and the time the counting of days begins vary from industry to industry and even from firm to firm within an industry. These terms may be intensely negotiated in distribution channels, again within the parameters established by the Robinson-Patman Act.

Transportation Charges

An important issue in pricing for distribution channel structure is the assignment of transportation charges. The cost of freight can have significant impact on the total cost of products within a channel (see Chapter 7). Several different pricing alternatives may be used to assign this cost.

F.O.B. Pricing   Free-on-board (F.O.B.) pricing is a common method of treating transportation charges. F.O.B. *origin* means that the seller places the product aboard a transportation carrier and at that time title and risk transfer to the buyer. The buyer also assumes responsibility for paying the transportation charges. While this is seemingly a simple and fair approach because it treats all buyers equally, F.O.B. origin pricing presents a marketing problem for sellers. Since transportation rates generally increase with distance, buyers located far from the seller's point of origin pay a higher total cost for their order than do buyers who are located closer. Thus, the seller is less competitive when buyers are located close to other sellers and when transportation is a significant cost variable. This disadvantage can be countered by offering ''F.O.B. origin—freight allowed,'' which means that the buyer can subtract transportation charges from the seller's invoice. However, in this case, the amount the seller receives from each buyer varies with the amount of the freight bill.

Delivered Pricing   In F.O.B. *delivered* pricing, the seller maintains title to the product until delivery is made at the customer's location. The seller arranges transportation and pays the transportation charges. In uniform delivered pricing, all buyers pay the same price for the product, including transportation, regardless of their location. The net effect of this policy is that buyers located close to the seller are subsiding the freight cost of those located further away.

Zone pricing is simply a modification of the uniform delivered pricing method. The market is divided into geographic zones and a delivered price is established for each zone. This practice reduces, but does not eliminate, some of the inequities of subsidization that occur under uniform delivered pricing.

Customer Pickup Allowance   Because some form of delivered pricing is the norm in most industries, sellers most frequently are responsible for transportation arrangements and charges. However, in today's distribution environment many national or large regional wholesalers and retailers have their own transportation equipment that is used to deliver products from their warehouses to store locations. Thus, as buyers, these firms have transportation equipment available that would not be utilized after those deliveries are made. To use this equipment more efficiently, many wholesalers and retailers prefer to use their own trucks to pick up their purchases at the supplier's location and transport them to their own distribution centers or warehouse. To accommodate such situations, many manufacturers today offer a ''customer pickup allowance,'' which reimburses the customer for transportation cost that was built into the delivered product price. The size of this allowance has become an issue of negotiation (and a serious issue of conflict) between distribution channel members.

Price Changes

Price changes are inevitable in any economy, and as long as they are not substantial and have relatively equal effects across all competitors, they do not represent major channel issues. There may, however, be short-term impacts of permanent price changes which need to be addressed by channel members. In addition, frequent changes in prices or allowances may have substantial implications for marketing channel design.

Permanent Increases   Inflationary changes in cost of labor, material, and supplies ultimately are passed on by suppliers to their customers. When a supplier changes prices, it is clear that distribution channel members should reevaluate their own practices in terms of whether to continue to stock that supplier's products, what prices they might establish, and what margins they earn. Frequently, suppliers announce price changes in advance to give channel members an opportunity to make additional purchases at the existing lower level. The potential negative impact of such a practice is that channel members may place large orders just as the price increase is about to take effect, thus straining the supplier's ability to meet the short-term increase in demand efficiently.

Short-Term Price Changes   A particularly vexing problem for all distribution channel members is the impact of short-term price changes such as frequent changes in discounts and promotional allowances. Some retailers, for example, have attempted to establish an image as "Everyday low price" stores. They do not have frequent "sales" to consumers, and they attempt to compete with other retailers by assuring consumers that their store will have consistently low prices. Wal-Mart has used this approach for many years, and the strategy has more recently been adopted by other retailers such as Sears.

Frequent price changes by suppliers, however, make it difficult for these outlets to maintain their strategies. Because of the frequency of new allowance programs and discounts offered by manufacturers for short-time periods, and the reluctance of most suppliers to announce those price changes in advance, Wal-Mart and Sears may have difficulty in determining their actual product cost in advance so that a consistently low price can be established in their store. It is likely that such retailers in the future will pressure their suppliers to establish greater consistency in their pricing or may even refuse to participate in channel arrangements with suppliers who are unable or unwilling to do so.

SUMMARY

This chapter has dealt with critical issues in marketing channel design and the interaction of other marketing strategy variables with marketing channel design. The beginning point in design is customer analysis and the identification of target market segments. Customer analysis also includes analysis of buyers' behavior with particular emphasis on how, when, and where buyers prefer to obtain products to satisfy their needs. In industrial as well as consumer-goods markets, the buying behavior of organizations is particularly critical. Some organizations, termed ''always-a-share'' buyers, prefer to deal with multiple suppliers of a product while others, termed ''lost-for-good,'' desire a longer-term relationship with a single supplier of that product.

Marketing channel design is significantly impacted by the product component of the marketing mix. Product characteristics such as value, handling characteristics, perishability, and technical complexity affect channel design. New-product development and brand decisions also are reflected in marketing channels. Channel design generally must be modified as a product moves through its life cycle.

Promotional strategies also have an important interrelationship with marketing channels. Manufacturer's pull or push strategies set the framework within which other channel promotional decisions of trade advertising, cooperative advertising, trade promotions, and personal-selling efforts must be made.

Pricing is initiated by manufacturers and must allow sufficient margins to motivate and stimulate participation by wholesalers and retailers in the channel. While list prices must reflect normal margins, considerable flexibility may arise in negotiation of quantity, functional, cash, and seasonal discounts. Transportation charges also have an impact on channel design and strategy and must be carefully considered when pricing decisions are made. Finally, the impact of both permanent as well as short-term price changes on marketing channel design and relationships must be considered.

QUESTIONS

1 For each of the following products, give an example of an industrial and a consumer target market. How do the distribution channels differ?
   a Toothpaste
   b Tractors
   c Microcomputers
   d Cake mix
2 Provide an example for each store–product combination depicted in Table 6-2. Are some of the combinations more common than others?
3 Differentiate between ''always-a-share'' and ''lost-for-good'' buying behavior. Why is there a trend in the industrial market for customers to reduce their number of suppliers?
4 Considering the attributes of the following products, what type of distribution channel structure would you predict?
   a Lettuce
   b Soft drinks
   c Candy bars
   d FAX machines
5 How does a product's life-cycle stage impact its distribution channel structure? To support your conclusions, give examples of products in each stage.
6 Why would a manufacturer be reluctant to provide private-brand merchandise to a major retailer such as K mart?
7 Describe the differences between manufacturers' push strategies and pull strategies. Do all manufacturers in an industry typically adopt the same strategy?
8 What are the advantages and disadvantages of cooperative advertising programs for manufacturers? for retailers?

9 How would you explain the explosive growth of consumer couponing by manufacturers? How has this growth impacted distribution channels?

10 Describe the practice of forward buying.

11 Since many manufacturers of consumer products actually sell very little of their output at "list" price, what is the purpose of list price? Why does a large percentage of their sales occur at a price lower than list?

12 Michigan Food Company utilizes a distribution structure that consists of wholesalers that sell to retailers. The company is in the process of introducing a new line of cake mix with a list price of $100 per case. The functional discount structure is list less 25 less 10. The company also offers a quantity discount of $2 per case for orders of fifty cases or more. How much would a wholesaler pay per case for an order of 100 cases?

CHAPTER 7

LOGISTICS DESIGN

CHAPTER OUTLINE

THE LOGISTICS MANAGEMENT PROCESS
  Value-Adding Process
  Boundary Spanning
ESTABLISHING SERVICE GOALS
  Basic Customer-Service Measurements
  Zero Defects
  Selective Service Segmentation
INTEGRATED LOGISTICS PERFORMANCE
  Total Cost Analysis
  Cost-Service Sensitivity Analysis
SUMMARY

The primary purpose of the logistics channel is timely delivery of inventory and supportive administration. The logistics channel provides the physical aspects of customer satisfaction. Whereas the marketing channel serves to facilitate transactions by coordination of product, price, and promotional initiatives, the logistics channel provides time and place availability for products and services. As such, the logistics channel is the major customer-service delivery system.

In Chapter 4 the concept of structural separation within the overall channel was introduced and illustrated. Structural complexity results from designing and operating separate channels. The basic motive for introducing separation is the potential it offers to increase functional specialization. Because of the wide variety of businesses that provide specialized logistics services, it is possible to design delivery systems capable of providing significantly superior customer service while simultaneously reducing total cost. The achievement of high levels of logistics competency does not necessarily require operation of separate transaction and logistics channels. However, design separation offers two potential benefits. First, functional separation allows the overall marketing effort to focus on unique customer-market segments. This is achieved through the deployment of highly focused transaction strategies. The second reason for channel separation is to position logistics as a strategic resource. Superior logistics performance can be the prime reason why a firm is selected from among the competitive pack as a preferred supplier. Specialized channel design facilitates the integration of logistics into a customer's business. Thus, design separation increases the likelihood of a firm simultaneously being positioned as both a low-cost supplier and a provider of superior customer service.

The purpose of this chapter is to examine design of the logistics support channel. The first section introduces the logistics process that is essential to the overall support of a firm's operational requirements. As such, logistics is initially positioned as an integral part of the value-added process—from procurement to internal operation to final-product customer delivery. Next, attention is directed to establishment of service goals that are integral to implementation of marketing strategy. In terms of service performance requirements, key differentials may exist in the design of consumer-goods channels, industrial channels, and direct-marketing situations. Other situational differentials may be critical in terms of "made to order" versus "deliver from stock" to support customers' requirements. The primary purpose of the second section is to identify service performance requirements as the primary determinants of logistics channel design. The third section introduces distribution costing by reviewing total-cost trade-off analysis. The identification of an operational system capable of achieving customer-service targets at lowest associated total-cost expenditure is the goal of logistics channel design. The chapter concludes with an examination of logistics operational designs widely employed in highly competitive situations. In total, the chapter serves to introduce and position logistics design considerations into channel strategy planning.

THE LOGISTICS MANAGEMENT PROCESS

In 1990, firms in the United States expended over $600 billion to support business operations logistically. Table 7-1 provides a breakdown of 1990 logistics expenditures by cost category.[1] Transportation, that aspect of logistics concerned with the actual movement of products and commodities from one place to another, accounted for an overall expenditure of $352 billion, or more than one-half the total logistics cost. In terms of relative level of expenditure in the economy, logistics consumed approximately 11 percent of the $5.45 trillion 1990 United States gross national product (GNP). Inventory holdings during 1990 represented $756 billion of raw material, work-in process, and finished products. In an aggregate sense, average inventory held

[1] The data presented concerning aggregate logistics cost is extracted from Robert V. Delaney, "State of Logistics Annual Report," Cass Logistics, Inc., 1991.

TABLE 7-1 ESTIMATED LOGISTICS EXPENDITURES UNITED STATES, 1990

Cost component	$ Billions	Percentage of Total
Inventory carrying costs		
Interest	66	
Taxes, obsolescence, depreciation	84	
Warehousing	61	
Subtotal	221	36.8%
Transportation costs		
Motor Carriers:		
Public and for-hire	77	
Private and for own account	87	
Local freight services	113	
Subtotal	277	42.2%
Other carriers:		
Railroads	32	
Water carriers	21	
Oil pipelines	9	
Air carriers	13	
Subtotal	75	12.5%
Shipper-related costs	4	.6%
Distribution administration	23	3.9%
TOTAL LOGISTICS COST	600	100%

Source: Robert V. Delaney, "State of Logistics Annual Report," Cass Logistics, Inc., 1991.

in the overall United States logistics structure was equal to approximately 14 percent of GNP. This ratio means that firms that collectively constitute the total United States economy turned inventory approximately 7.1 times. Naturally, inventory turns experienced by individual firms varied extensively, based on the industry's class, position in the distribution channel, and degree of logistics management operational competency.

Table 7-2 provides a compilation of statistics that provide greater insight into the way that inventories are typically structured by position in the distribution channel. Inventory profiles are presented for five publicly held manufacturers, wholesalers, and retailers engaged in consumer-goods industries. Total fiscal year-end 1989 inventories for the fifteen firms are presented in dollars and as a percentage of annual sales and year-end total assets. The relationships provide some isolated but interesting comparisons when viewed in terms of channel position. For at least these select firms, the closer one operates to the point of consumer sale the greater the ratio of total assets committed to inventory. Retailers as a group reported 43.37 percent of total assets committed to inventory at the year's end. Wholesalers as a group reported

TABLE 7–2 INVENTORY COMPARISONS BY CHANNEL POSITION RANKED
BY TOTAL INVENTORY, 1989

	Total inventory, millions	Sales, %	Inventory to assets
Manufacturers			
IBM	9463.0	22.75	12.17
Texaco Inc.	1353.0	4.17	5.28
Merck and Co.	779.7	11.90	11.54
Arco Chemical Co.	710.0	4.43	3.19
Warner Lambert	374.3	8.92	13.09
Group Average		10.43	9.05
Wholesalers			
AVNET	479.5	24.99	42.58
Sysco	436.8	6.38	23.37
Bergen Brunswig	413.5	10.54	41.95
Fisher Foods	56.2	5.90	32.13
Getty Petroleum Corporation	41.5	4.11	14.08
Group Average		10.38	30.82
Retailers			
Wal-Mart	3351.4	16.23	52.70
GAP	193.3	15.44	40.18
Pier 1 Imports	130.2	31.40	43.41
Fretter Inc.	60.4	26.12	50.29
Gantos	26.2	15.39	30.25
Group Average		20.92	43.37

Source: Annual Reports.

30.82 percent and manufacturers had 9.05 percent of total assets committed to year-end inventory. As a general rule, the greater the percentage of overall assets committed to inventory, the more risk associated with inventory management. Such evidence suggests that retail firms may have the greatest inventory exposure in the distribution channel whereas manufacturers may generally have a less-risky inventory position. The primary purpose of the data presented in Table 7–2 is to dislodge any predisposition that may exist in a reader's mind that logistics is primarily a manufacturer's concern and not a major consideration for the management of wholesale and retail firms. To the contrary, the fundamental business of a wholesaler is to provide logistics support for retailers. The same generalization is also true of industrial distributors that provide material, operating supplies, and repair (MRO) support for industrial or business use. Retailers, the firms that provide consumers broad product assortments, may at the peak of some seasonal selling seasons have total inventory exposure and payment liabilities that exceed 100 percent of net worth. In fact, a soft selling season such as Christmas 1989, in which sales volumes for some retailers were insufficient to generate cash flow required to meet trade debt, can lead to financial insolvency.

The critical points concerning logistics are: (1) the total expenditure for logistics in firms that operate in highly developed economies such as the United States is a matter for significant managerial concern (United States logistics expenditures in 1990 were approximately equivalent to 11 percent of GNP); (2) the total cost of logistics is much greater than the highly visible expenditures for transportation (indeed, approximately 37 percent of the total cost is related to the maintenance and administration of inventories throughout all stages of the material-logistics process); and (3) the burdens and risks associated with material-logistics management impact all primary participants independent of the level at which they operate in the distribution channel (thereby fully dispelling any notion that logistics is primarily a manufacturing concern). To better understand managerial concerns related to logistics channel design it is useful to examine the overall materials-logistics process within a typical firm in terms of value-adding and boundary-spanning considerations.

Value-Adding Process

One way to view the overall logistics channel is as a chain of value-adding events.[2] Building upon the basic mission to achieving time and place positioning of products and services, one can view the logistics channel as a pipeline, chain, or process. The central idea is that "real" value is not realized until a product assortment is physically and temporally positioned and configured to facilitate the transfer of ownership.

To illustrate, a consumer product such as a window air conditioner has little value to a potential buyer when stored in a wholesaler's or manufacturer's warehouse. The potential for adding value for a consumer is significantly greater if the air conditioner is available at a retail store when and where the consumer wants. However, if the consumer has to wait two or three days for delivery, a great deal of the motivation to buy an air conditioner may be diluted. In fact, if the heat wave ends before the air conditioner can be delivered, the potential buyer may decide to postpone purchase altogether in order to acquire some more timely product or service.

The reality of any channel arrangement is that a firm's ability to make a product or service available to its customers on a dependable basis is essential to success. While many transactions take place within a logistics channel among participating firms, the only fundamentally important transaction is the purchase by an industrial or a consumer buyer for consumption. In a demand-driven economy, product and service consumption both fuel and guide what constitutes value-added performance. Unless the stream of business transactions performed within a channel ultimately achieve buyer appeal, acceptance, and satisfaction, no substantive value is added by the costly process.

The fact of the matter is that most logistics activity in highly developed economies

---

[2] Donald J. Bowersox, Phillip L. Carter, and Robert M. Monczka, "Computer Aided Purchasing, Manufacturing and Physical Distribution," *Proceedings National Council of Physical Distribution Management Annual Meeting,* Oak Brook, IL: September 16–19, 1984, pp. 142–146.

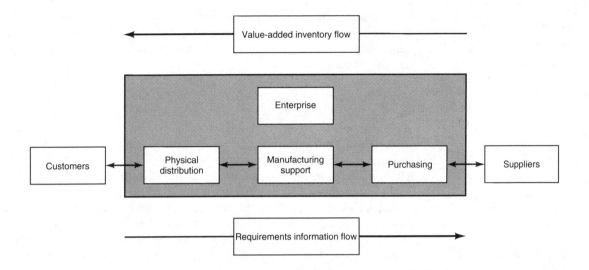

FIGURE 7-1 Value-added pipeline or chain. (*Source:* Modified with permission of Macmillan Publishing Company from Donald J. Bowersox, David J. Closs, and Omar K. Helferich, *Logistical Management,* 3d ed., New York: Macmillan, 1986, p. 16. Copyright © 1986 by Macmillan Publishing Company.)

is performed in *anticipation* that the value added will be wanted. In other words, a great deal of the logistics process is anticipatory and performed in advance of any binding purchase commitment on the part of a consumer or industrial buyer. A retailer, for example, plans merchandise assortments for an upcoming selling season many months in advance of actual need and must anticipate the specific products that will be required to satisfy consumers' purchase requirements. All other channel members, transaction as well as logistics, assume risk and perform essential functions in anticipation of an ultimate result: that the selected activities performed will add value in the eyes of buyers. Purchase action, and only purchase action, on the part of end users signals that the value-adding planning and execution process was successful.

If a channel arrangement is assumed to be able to accomplish the value-adding sequence of events on a repetitive and predictable basis, overall logistics performance is effective. In other words, while the structural configuration of the logistics channel may not be as efficiently designed as possible, successful performance of the value-added process achieves the essential end result. Unless a channel is effective in value-added performance, operating efficiency is a nonissue. In situations in which more than one way or alternative exists to meet and sustain value-added goals, efficiency becomes a key managerial concern. In an overall sense, the managerial focus in logistics design is to identify and implement a channel arrangement that will achieve value-added performance as efficiently as possible.

Figure 7-1 illustrates the value-added chain or pipeline concept. The central idea is to view all activities that are essential to the process as an interrelated sequence of events or actions. The logistics value-added chain simultaneously links a firm to its supply base and customers. In the center of the flow diagram are the enterprise's internal arrangements or operations that facilitate inventory movement into, throughout, and out of the firm.

Inbound flow is facilitated by procurement or materials management activity that links the firm to a supply base network. For a manufacturer, the procurement network may consist of a wide variety of material sources and linkages with firms that supply essential component parts or key ingredients. In a wholesale operation, procurement, sometimes called ''buying'' or ''purchasing,'' is concerned with the establishment and maintenance of business relationships with manufacturers that supply key items; these items are then resold in combinations to other businesses. If a wholesaler takes title to the goods and sells them primarily to retail establishments, then it is classified as a merchant wholesaler. When the primary customer is a manufacturer or another wholesaler, the specific type of business is referred to as an industrial distributor.[3]

A significant portion of the value-added chain is devoted to logistics operations. Logistics operations are a series of specific steps or activities that a firm undertakes to facilitate the value-added process. The exact operational details vary, depending upon requirements unique to each specific type of business. In retailing and wholesaling, essential logistics operations involve material handling, storage, and transportation of inventory; in manufacturing, logistics operations involve scheduling timing and sequencing of materials and arrival of component parts. When the plant structure of a firm encompasses several different types of specialized production and assembly operations, the logistics coordination of the overall manufacturing process can become very complex.

The final area of logistics deals with outbound movement of products to customers. While all firms require physical distribution services, once again the configuration of how they go to market varies significantly. For a manufacturer, finished-product distribution can range from shipments of one or a few cartons to unit trains of double-stacked containers. For a wholesaler or an industrial distributor, physical distribution consists of creating assortments of products produced by different manufacturers for orders that can range from a few cartons up to full-truckload shipments. Retail physical distribution typically involves many movements of a large volume of assorted merchandise from central warehouses to specific retail stores. For example, it is common practice for retailers such as Kroger, Jewell, or Shaws to operate distribution centers to facilitate retail-store inventory replenishment. However, a significant part of a retailer's merchandise may be transported directly from wholesale or manufacturing sources to individual retail stores. Such *direct store delivery* (DSD) has the advantage of reducing the retailer's need for warehousing and multiple-inventory handling prior to the merchandise's arrival at individual retail stores. In addition to reduced handling, DSD has the potential to improve inventory turnover. The trade-off is between these improvements and the increased complexity associated with shipping smaller lot sizes of merchandise directly to retail outlets. While the vast majority of retailing is currently conducted on a self-service basis, several products, such as appliances, larger

---

[3] See Chapter 2, pp. 41.

televisions sets, and furniture, require home delivery and installation. For retailers that provide home-delivery services, the scope of physical distribution operations is larger than for a supermarket that is essentially a self-service business.

Of particular interest in logistics channel design are situations necessitating reverse or backward movement of products. Environmental issues have increased awareness and need for effective recovery of products and packaging materials. In many states it is required by law that empty beverage containers be reclaimed by manufacturers for recycling. As the list of products designated for recycling expands, the burden placed upon the logistics system to help reduce the cost of solid-waste disposal also increases. A critical concern of retailers is how to effectively participate in recycling without turning high-cost retail locations and facilities into reclamation centers.

Totally independent of waste disposal is the secure recovery of damaged, defective, and date-expired merchandise. A significant reverse-operational burden is the cleansing of logistics channel merchandise no longer suitable for sale. Some defective merchandise is suitable for consumption in the sense that it can perform as originally planned despite minor defects. Other merchandise may not be functional or safe for consumption and must be either recovered or destroyed as part of warranty or sales-satisfaction guarantee. In all reverse-logistics situations, participants must resolve a host of validation, financial, and control issues as part of the value-adding process in the overall channel. More than one manufacturer has donated defective merchandise to a charity only to later find the same inventory selling through nonauthorized distribution channels. Effective management of reverse logistics is an essential overall aspect of the value-added process.

In summary, adding value in terms of physically positioning inventory in the time and at the place needed is the essential purpose of a logistics channel. By the yardsticks by which logistics performance is measured, first and foremost is how effective the channel is in support of procurement, operational, and physical-distribution operations. To the extent that alternatives exist regarding ways to meet customer-service performance goals, then operating efficiency becomes a vital managerial concern. The nature of logistics is somewhat different for manufacturers, wholesalers, and retailers. While the specifics of logistics practices and concerns vary by channel position, the basic ingredients of the value-added process are similar. To further complicate the design of a logistics arrangement, it is often necessary to accommodate reverse movement in the channel. The accommodation of reverse movement can be both complex and costly. Whereas economy of scale can guide the design of forward movement in a channel arrangement, the irregular volume and ever-changing configuration of service requirements make reverse logistics complex and costly to perform. Essential to the overall planning of logistics channels is the need to integrate information flow among channel members.

Boundary Spanning

A unique characteristic of logistics is that it constitutes a series of functions and activities that are *boundary spanning*. The term ''boundary spanning'' is used to describe activities that extend beyond the typical limits of a job or managerial area of responsibility. For example, transportation as a service crosses the normal work domain of both the shipping and receiving firms, thereby linking two or more separate businesses. One of the complications of designing a logistics channel is that most essential functions are, to some degree, boundary spanning. From the perspective of logistics channel design, boundary spanning is viewed in terms of internal or external relationships.

Internal Boundary Spanning Logistics within an enterprise serves to coordinate the activities of marketing, manufacturing, and finance. At a high level of abstraction, all organization units seek attainment of common goals such as increased sales, improved profits, and continuous growth of shareholder value. However, the day-to-day actions of these major organizational units may, in fact, be highly contradictory.

Manufacturing, by the very nature of its preoccupation with the form-changing process, must have economic production carefully planned in lot sizes that achieve cost and quality objectives. New production strategies may emphasize flexibility and rapid changeover of plant facilities to produce a wide variety of different products, but such flexibility must be tempered to assure retention of manufacturing scale and scope efficiency. In the final analysis, manufacturing is evaluated on the cost per unit and product quality.

A major focus of marketing is sales volume and market share. In many industries, the promotional thrust of marketing is geared to sales increases that must be accomplished within very well defined time spans such as calendar months or quarters. The marketer's world is further complicated by the need to generate a continuous stream of novel promotions and new products to retain or improve relative market position. Therefore, despite a generally clear understanding that, in the short run, volume and profits may not react identically, a marketing executive is constantly under pressure to maintain or improve market share. Such singular focus can result in significant discontinuities or breakdowns between marketing and manufacturing operations. Trade promotion practices can also create significant irregularities in logistics support requirements.

The financial managers of an enterprise need to reconcile the overall goals of growth and financial success. However, their frame of reference is focused on investor-based operating results. The fact that most organizations of any size are publicly held corporations and many are highly leveraged places continuous pressure to maintain earnings and positive cash spin-off. For example, following the leveraged buyout, RJR-Nabisco's daily interest on its debt exceeded $6 million per day. In situations characterized by an extreme need to generate positive cash flow the deployment of assets can be highly restricted and even rationed. When capital is invested in such situations, expectations regarding return on investment and hurdle-rate requirements will be high. This type of financial constraint can place significant pressure on logistics operations to be fluid and to hold investment in areas such as inventory to an absolute minimum.

The inherent conflicts that exist between operating areas of a manufacturing firm are also apparent in wholesale and retail businesses. The inherent framework of conflict that exists among basic internal organizational units of a typical enterprise has been one of the main motivations behind the rapid expansion of integrated logistics.

Integrated logistics serves to mediate and reconcile differences among internal organizations of an enterprise. As a boundary-spanning activity, logistics serves to facilitate the integration of manufacturing and marketing. For example, strategic storage of semifinished products in the logistics system serves to postpone speculative forward allocation of overly specialized or customized inventories. To reconcile such differences between manufacturing and marketing, the logistics organization must develop exacting time and form-postponement strategies.[4] By spanning the boundaries of essential operational areas of an enterprise, logistics serves to reconcile and rationalize an overall strategic thrust.

External Boundary Spanning   Spanning boundaries among firms in a channel is far more complex than within an individual firm. Contradictions within individual firms are magnified and intensified when viewed across the full channel. In essence, the channel becomes the arena within which participating firms resolve differences. Firms that join together in channel arrangements most often have different structures, traditions, and values. To the extent that the logistics channel is a behavioral arrangement the need to resolve and reconcile individual differences becomes very important.[5]

The critical mission of the channel in reconciling key differences between trading partners results from the fact that most boundary-spanning activities are logistics-based. To illustrate, consider the working relationship between a vertically integrated retailer and a consumer-products manufacturer. While sales and transfer prices are key marketing negotiations, the day-in and day-out working relationship between the two organizations must be executed and maintained by the firms' respective logistics operations.

In summary, the logistics channel structure and behavioral framework worked out among participating firms will be at the core of continuous operations. Each participant can be expected to routinely undertake specified roles and exchange essential information concerning countless operational details in an effort to make the overall logistics channel function as planned. The orchestration of such interorganizational performance is from meshing the internal and external boundary-spanning performance of all channel members. At the vortex of channel management is the belief that the collective boundary spanning of member firms can be strategically planned and administered.

ESTABLISHING SERVICE GOALS

The primary logistics mission is to service customers. Customer-service competency positions logistics to function as an integral part of a firm's overall marketing strategy. The purpose of this section is to identify the aspects of logistics operations that create superior customer-service performance.

---

[4] See Chapter 4, pp. 99–102, for a discussion of postponement strategies.
[5] See Chapter 4, pp. 102–107, for classification of alternative channel structural arrangements.

From a logistics viewpoint, a firm needs to service both external and internal customers. External customers typically get the most visibility in channel-planning situations because they represent the sales-revenue stream that is essential for profitability. Thus, how well a firm services customers and how that service enables those customers to service their customers is critical to planning logistics performance. For example, how well a pharmaceutical manufacturer services a drug wholesaler is significant, but it is secondary in importance to how well the drug wholesaler services the retail drugstore. However, none of the upstream performance is relevant unless the final consumers are provided with the product choices and availability they require. Customer-service performance at any one stage in the overall logistics process is only important when viewed from the perspective of the value added for the channel's ultimate customer.

A second aspect of logistics service in a typical firm is related to internal operations. Internal logistics customers are the facilities and manufacturing process for which inventory and other value-added services are performed. The logistics of internal operations is essential for the maintenance of efficient and flexible operations. For a manufacturing firm, internal logistics includes sequencing inbound vendor shipments to efficiently utilize production capacity. Manufacturing logistics may also be concerned with coordination of inventory to integrate production of several different plants into full-line availability.

Overall, customer-service performance is viewed from three perspectives. First, traditional measures of customer service are reviewed. Second, the notion of zero defects is discussed as it relates to logistics performance and customer satisfaction. Finally, the relationship of segmentation and selectivity is developed in terms of structured logistics performance. In total, this section develops the ways by which logistics performance can contribute to competitive superiority or differential advantage.

Basic Customer-Service Measurements

Traditional customer service can be measured in three ways: (1) inventory availability, (2) service capability, and (3) service quality. Each represents a way to put quantitative measurement on day-to-day logistics performance. Actual performance is typically measured and compared to predetermined standards or operational goals. Each area of basic customer-service performance is discussed.

Inventory Availability   The most focused measure of customer service is how well a firm's inventory is capable of meeting customers' demands. Firms that service customers from stock have a continuous need to replenish shipping location inventories from manufacturing and supply sources. Inventory availability at ship-from facilities offers a measure of how well customers' expectations are satisfied over an operating period. Availability can be measured in three ways; in each, performance is viewed from a different vantage point.

The most basic measure of availability is *in-stock or out-of-stock percentage*. Typically measured at a point in time, the stock percentage represents how many products or stock-keeping units (SKUs), planned to be in stock at a facility, are actually available for shipment to customers. Thus, if a firm plans to stock 100 items in a warehouse and a review at the start of a business day indicates that 93 are available to ship, then the in-stock situation would be 93 percent. Conversely, the out-of-stock measure would be 7 percent. Of course, the fallacy of looking only at a percentage in stock as a measure of customer service is the likelihood that fast movers or SKUs critical to a customer may be out of stock. If a few items support the majority of sales, then availability of those items is critical to customer-service performance. Thus, simply tabulating the percentage of items in or out of stock does not capture the dynamics of customer service. To better understand how inventory matches customers' requirements, most firms also measure order-fill rate.

Order-fill rate measures the SKUs shipped as a percentage of all SKUs ordered by a customer. For example, if a customer orders a total of 100 cases and is shipped 97, then the order-fill rate would be 97 percent. The benefit of tracking order-fill rate is that it measures customer-service performance on a weighted basis. To maintain a high order-fill rate, a firm must plan inventory to properly cover SKUs that have significantly different sales. Only if total inventory investment is balanced in terms of customers' requirements is it possible to maintain a high order-fill rate. To measure order-fill rate, performance should be tracked on the basis of a customer's original unit and quantity requests prior to any substitution, deletion, or other order modification. While many firms negotiate satisfactory order modifications or product substitutions with customers to reduce out-of-stock situations, fill-rate measurement should be based on a firm's ability to satisfy a customer's original order.

The most stringent customer-service measure of inventory availability is the percentage of *orders shipped complete.* As the measure implies, orders shipped complete is a measure of the frequency or number of times that a firm provides 100 percent of all items ordered by a customer. Orders shipped complete is a zero-defect measure that allows no latitude for being anything other than perfect. While extremely difficult to achieve in day-to-day operations, shipping a high percentage of orders complete means that a firm is providing the SKU assortment and quantity that customers desire.

A combination of the three availability measures offers an assessment of how well the inventory management of a firm is meeting customers' expectations. The triad of availability measures helps a firm decide upon the level of performance to be maintained over time. The relationship of inventory investment to product availability is direct. As a general rule, the greater the overall performance in terms of availability, the greater the required inventory investment. This relationship as well as alternatives will be more fully developed in the zero-defect discussion.

Service Capability   Service capability involves the speed, consistency, and flexibility of a firm's order-fulfillment operations. The focus of customer-service capability is the planned order cycle. Figure 7-2 illustrates the activities that constitute a typical order cycle. They are: (1) customer order transmittal, (2) credit approval and processing, (3) inventory availability, (4) transportation, and (5) invoicing and delivery. Speed, consistency, and flexibility of customer service are directly related to the overall order-cycle structure.

Speed of service is the total performance time a customer expects from a firm from

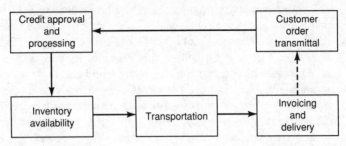

FIGURE 7-2 Order-cycle activities.

which they purchase. In situations where inventory is consigned to customers, the speed of service would be instantaneous. In all other situations, the five interrelated order-cycle activities require performance time. Such times can range from a few hours (when a vendor is located relatively close geographically to a customer) to many weeks (in some multinational trading situations). Naturally, most customers want delivery as fast as possible. Such speed is the essential ingredient in just-in-time and quick-response inventory replenishment arrangements.[6] The counterbalance is that speed of service typically is costly. The justification for rapid replenishment must be found in the positive trade-offs that can result from such arrangements. For example, stocking a high-value medical instrument at a central warehouse with delivery via air may be justified in terms of customer's requirements and may also be less costly than maintaining numerous decentralized inventories throughout the market. The important aspect of speed of service is that the customer's perception of the total performance time required to receive inventory from a vendor is the only relevant framework for calibrating speed of service. Speed of service is a measure of planned to actual time required to complete all essential order-cycle activities.

Order-cycle consistency is typically a more critical measure of customer-service capability than performance time. Consistency, measured over a larger number of order cycles, compares actual performance with planned performance. A great many potential disruptions can cause the actual time for performance of any of the planned order-cycle activities to exceed standard or expected time. In fact, expected time for any of the five activities can be greater or less than expected during the same order cycle. Thus, in actual practice specific disruptions can be additive or offsetting. For example, a delay in order selection and preparation for shipment could be offset by expedited transportation that results in delivery to customers as planned. However, failure to take corrective action could further dissipate service performance, if expected transportation times are not achieved. The delay in transportation would be added to the delay in order selection and preparation, resulting in a significant extension of overall performance time. Figure 7-3 illustrates the essence of order-cycle consistency. Because each activity included in the planned order cycle has its own statistical dis-

[6] For detailed discussion of these time-based strategies see Chapter 13, pp. 413–414.

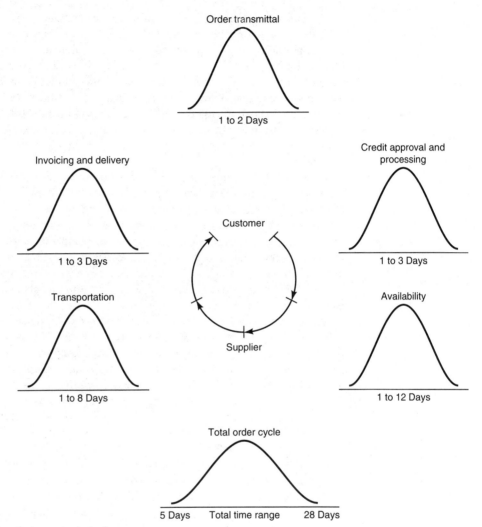

FIGURE 7-3   Order-cycle dynamics.

tribution of actual performance times, the consistency of the overall cycle will be the combined or aggregate time required to perform all individual activities. The potential time duration for completion of the total order cycle is from four to twenty-eight days. From the customer's viewpoint, the expected time for a vendor to complete the overall order cycle in comparison to the actual or average time over a number of order cycles is the measure of consistency. Because customers plan manufacturing or inventory replenishment operations upon expected performance by suppliers, it is widely acknowledged that consistency of service is considerably more important than potential speed of service.

Flexibility involves a firm's ability to accommodate special customer-service requests. In actual operations, flexibility can be in response to a service breakdown or may be the planned or preferred way to accommodate a special customer-service request. For example, if a stock-out of a critical item occurs at a distribution facility that services a key customer, a firm may obtain the part from an alternative facility using high-speed transportation. In fact, it may be possible for a firm to obtain a short-supply item from an alternative service facility and include it in the regularly planned delivery to customers. In such situations, the attributes of flexibility will be transparent to the customer. With such flexible operational capability, service breakdowns can be prevented.

A planned flexible operation to meet customers' requests represents a different form of service capability. Depending upon the customer's request, a supplier may decide to utilize a different planned method of providing the requested service. For example, the typical pattern of servicing a customer may be to ship directly in full-trailer quantities from manufacturing plants to customers' warehouses. However, from time to time when customers request direct store delivery (DSD), the planned method of distribution may be to ship mixed assortments from a public warehouse that specializes in providing such services. Thus, the supplying firm has planned flexible distribution capability to accommodate a key customer's request for alternative DSD service.

The combination of the three capability measures provides a way to assess how well a firm's operations meet customers' requirements. Speed of service is important, but it is of secondary concern compared to consistency over time. Firms depend upon suppliers to help hold down inventories while maintaining high levels of product availability to customers, which means that operational consistency is critical. To get the maximum performance out of logistics operations, most sophisticated systems rely upon flexible capability to supplement normal operations. Such flexible or alternative logistics arrangements may be implemented to offset an unexpected breakdown or to accommodate a customer's special request.

Service Quality *Service quality* concerns a firm's ability to perform all order-related activities error-free. The overall customer-service process is involved with several aspects of quality. With inventory availability and service capability, quality considerations must be made, since both attributes are essential so that customers' expectations can be met. Beyond availability and capability, quality of service means that shipments arrive damage-free; invoices are correct, or error-free; returns are handled in an effortless manner and unexpected problems are rapidly resolved. These and other aspects of overall quality are hard to measure or quantify. However, simply stated: Customers expect a wide variety of business detail to be routinely handled by suppliers in a manner readily apparent to everyone. A process such as logistics has what could be called an *everytime expectation*. Regardless of the string of consecutive times customers receive excellent service, they still expect the highest quality service performance on all current and future orders. Average performance figures do not measure quality of logistics performance.

Firms that excel in service quality have at least three distinctive characteristics. First, they have implemented mechanisms that facilitate customers' access to accurate and timely information about open orders and other service-related inquiries. Such information, and a response, is often available from a single call as a result of sales-service access to computer supported on-line order-status data. Second, firms committed to providing quality performance have developed ways to resolve customers' requests and special requirements without extensive delays for management approval or for other corrective action. The empowerment of front-line employees to use their best judgment to make on-the-spot decisions greatly facilitates high-quality performance. Finally, customer-service leaders, when confronted with breakdowns or unexpected situations, typically exhibit what has been referred to as an ability to make brilliant recoveries.[7] A *brilliant recovery* is a resolution to a service breakdown in which the service provider takes extraordinary efforts to meet customers' requirement. A brilliant, or ''immaculate,'' recovery involves a management culture that recognizes that service breakdowns will occur and that fast resolution can, in the final analysis, cement customers' loyalty.[8]

Some firms place a premium on developing and maintaining quality relations with customers while others only give it lip service with no consistent follow-through or organizational commitment. This fact is reflected by survey results in the grocery-products industry. Due to the large number of promotional allowances, special prices, pickup allowances, and other nonroutine events, the average number of disputed invoices or unsubstantiated invoice deductions was reported by several manufacturers to be in the 45 to 60 percent range.[9] For many of these manufacturers, the trouble of resolving these discrepancies is viewed as being routine to the business. However, a few manufacturers interviewed had reduced the level of disputed invoices to 10 percent or less and were seeking ways to further improve performance. The performance differential appeared to be based primarily on the attitude of employees and the relationship with customers. Whereas the firms having the large percentage of discrepancies placed emphasis on resolving problems, the high-quality performers tended to emphasize prevention and quick resolution of problems. For example, they allowed drivers and other front-line personnel to resolve differences within very liberal dollar limits. The result was the placing of a value on the customer's satisfaction as contrasted to being only concerned with the cost of resolving the discrepancy.

Zero Defects

It is clear that customers have a set of expectations regarding service. Perhaps the most difficult expectation to satisfy is the simplest to state: ''Give me what you said you wanted to sell when you said you would deliver it—that's all I expect.'' The simplicity of the above statement is elusive. Because firms have traditionally been unable to provide 100 percent service without resorting to prohibitively high inventory

---

[7] Christopher W. L. Hart, James L. Heskett, and W. Earl Sasser, Jr., ''The Profitable Art of Service Recovery,'' *Harvard Business Review,* **90**:4, July–August 1990, pp. 148–156.

[8] Ron Zemke, *The Service Edge,* New York: Penguin Books, 1989; and James L. Heskett, W. Earl Sasser, Jr., and Christopher W. L. Hart, *Service Breakthroughs,* New York: Free Press, 1990.

[9] A. T. Kearnery, *Customer Service Issues and Trends in the Grocery Industry,* a special report for the Grocery Manufacturers of America, 1989.

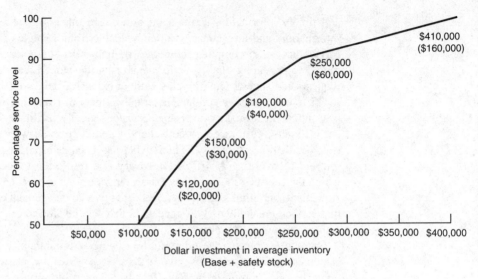

FIGURE 7-4   Relationship of inventory and service availability.

levels and have been unable to eliminate inconsistent delivery, they have developed what they feel are acceptable standards of service. For example, a fill rate of 97 percent coupled with delivery plus or minus one day in 95 percent of the situations represents what traditional firms might consider an acceptance *service window*. The problem with service programs aimed at operating within an acceptable window, when viewed by a service-sensitive customer, is that they guarantee at least a 3 percent inventory-availability deficiency that can occur anytime within a seventy-two-hour period. In other words, such service programs guarantee partial failure as part of day-to-day operations.

The notion of *zero defects* is that a supplier strives to provide customers what they ordered, delivered when and where it was wanted. However, such complete service cannot be based totally on inventory availability. The relationship between inventory and service is well documented. The general relationship is that as inventory increases, the incremental degree of customer service gained decreases. In other words, availability as an attribute of overall customer service increases at a decreasing rate as inventory is increased. The basic relationship is illustrated in Figure 7–4.

One way of elevating logistics performance to near-zero defects is to utilize a combination of customer alliances, information technology, inventory-stocking strategies, premium transportation, and selectivity programs to match available resources to key customer requirements. Firms that achieve superior customer service place overall attention on achieving zero defects. By having a low tolerance for errors, coupled with a commitment to rapidly resolve whatever discrepancies occur, these high-performance firms exceed standards of acceptable service within an industry.

Selective Service Segmentation

A careful examination of alternative-service programs clearly suggests that a firm can elect to use customer-service competency as a means of gaining differential advantage. To be a serious and effective competitor, a firm in an industry must be able to complete product delivery within the *accepted industry service window*. As noted above, what constitutes *acceptable time* may range from hours to weeks or even months. For every marketing situation, a maximum elapsed time from order receipt to product delivery establishes the limit of acceptable service. Similar limits exist concerning inventory availability. The degree to which a firm consistently responds faster and with higher inventory availability than the accepted limit or industry standard determines its potential to become a superior performer in the eyes of service-sensitive customers. Hence, differential advantage can be built around the competency of a firm's logistics system.

The high-performance firm will develop customer-service strategies around two basic commitments. First, service will be viewed in terms of reliable delivery of the customer's order, with all requirements met, at a specified time. In other words, the concept of an acceptable window is replaced by a very specific point-in-time service commitment.

The second commitment that enables high performance is selectivity concerning which customers are offered specified levels of service. The notions of segmentation and selectivity are fundamental to marketing strategy.[10] Service competency needs to be focused on key customers that offer significant market-share potential and that are willing to buy more product as a result of outstanding service. Likewise, customers must be receptive to working closely with suppliers to develop operational arrangements that benefit both parties. Just as all customers do not offer similar potential, receptiveness, and willingness to cooperate, not all SKUs in a product assortment are equally popular or profitable. It is a well-established paradigm in marketing that 20 percent of all products typically account for 80 percent of all sales. The same 20-80 ratio also can be applied to potential customers. The key to selective matching is to link high-volume profitable products and high-potential customers. This matching or linking can only be based on a careful assessment of relative cost-benefits. Such service-sensitivity analysis builds upon a careful examination of total cost and the establishment of a basic service program.

The fundamental element of a high-performance strategy is to focus on key market segments or customers that will respond to superior service with increased share and loyalty. The balance of the market can be serviced consistent with the acceptable performance standards of the industry. This strategic perspective of structured customer service is further developed later on.

In summary, the level and intensity of service that a firm selects to offer specific customers can become a major element of marketing strategy. Traditional customer service is measured in terms of availability, capability, and quality. Until recently, most customer-service strategies were based on an average or acceptable level of

---

[10] See Chapter 6, pp. 170–171.

performance that was less than 100 percent of each attribute. Recently, selected firms have begun to elevate service expectations in an effort to achieve zero-defect performance. At the root of such zero-defect strategies is a careful delineation of a potential customer's receptivity or sensitivity to high-service performance. The segments of an industry that will respond to superior service with increased market share and loyalty become the target segments for the high-performance suppliers.

The customer-service competency of a firm is the direct reflection of its logistics system design. The logistics system can be designed to provide whatever level of basic service that is strategically desirable. The key is to develop a logistics delivery system capable of meeting desired customer-service expectations at the lowest possible total cost. Because of the complexity of forging together the human, systems, and design elements of integrated logistics, such competency, once achieved, is difficult to duplicate.

INTEGRATED LOGISTICS PERFORMANCE

The design of a firm's logistics system requires the creation of an integrated operational structure capable of achieving customer-service goals at the lowest associated total cost. For every level of customer-service performance there is a least-total-cost logistics solution. The design objective is twofold: (1) identify the least-total-cost design, and (2) establish the basis for conducting cost-service sensitivity analysis. Each aspect of integrated design is discussed.

Total-Cost Analysis

The concept of total-cost analysis is elusively simple. The basic idea is that a firm should identify and evaluate all costs that will be impacted by any logistics system design. For discussion purpose, logistics costs can be grouped into two categories: (1) transportation-based, and (2) inventory-based.[11] In a logistics system design, these two cost categories typically interact, creating the opportunity for cost-to-cost trade-offs. In other words, selected increased expenditures for transportation services may significantly reduce inventory expenditures. A trade-off is positive if inventory-associated costs are reduced by a greater amount than transportation cost was increased. Table 7-3 provides a numeric illustration of the basic idea behind total-cost analysis. In the simple example of Table 7-3, an air-direct system of transportation results in lower total cost than the alternative of using a field warehouse system. With use of an air-direct system, the total cost of transportation is greater but all costs associated with inventory and warehousing are significantly reduced. This type of cost-to-cost trade-off is the typical reason why a firm may select to consolidate previously decentralized inventory into fewer warehouses. Inventory cost declines as a result of substantial reduction in safety stock when inventory is stocked at fewer locations. Because transportation dependency is increased, the associated freight cost of the centralized inven-

---

[11] This discussion is based on materials presented in Donald J. Bowersox, David J. Closs, and Omar K. Helferich, *Logistical Management,* 3d ed., New York: Macmillan, 1986, Chapter 9.

TABLE 7-3 TOTAL-COST ANALYSIS BASIC EXAMPLE

Cost account	Motor/warehouse	Air-direct
Production plant		
Land and building	$ 25,000	$ 75,000
Wages and salary	75,000	225,000
Taxes	10,000	25,000
Insurance	20,000	50,000
Inventory	200,000	500,000
Equipment	10,000	25,000
Packaging	5,000	30,000
Utilities	15,000	45,000
Supplies	1,000	3,000
Total	$ 361,000	$ 978,000
Plant to warehouse or customer		
Insurance	$ 20,000	$ 10,000
Inventory	400, 000	200,000
Transport local	—	450,000
Transport intercity	1,000,000	3,000,000
TOTAL	$1,420,000	$3,660,000
Warehouse		
Land and building	$ 225,000	—
Wages and salaries	625,000	—
Taxes	70,000	—
Inventory	1,500,000	—
Equipment	35,000	—
Packaging	18,000	—
Utilities	75,000	—
Supplies	6,000	—
TOTAL	$2,554,000	—
Warehouse to customer		
Insurance	$ 15,000	—
Inventory	250,000	—
Transport	$ 300,000	—
TOTAL	$ 565,000	—
SYSTEM TOTAL COST	$4,900,000	$4,638,000

tory system is greater than the decentralized logistics structure. However, the balance of the trade-off is favorable because overall, or total, cost is reduced.[12]

While the concept of total cost is simple, it is often difficult to implement in actual practice. Because of well-established accounting practices based on time-formatted, natural account classification, it is often difficult to identify and quantify activity-based costs (ABCs). In many situations, the control centers that must interact to implement total-cost solutions report to separate and distinct managerial units. Problematic

---

[12] While a relatively simple concept, total-cost logistics analysis is generally accepted to have originated in Howard T. Lewis, James W. Culleton, and Jack D. Steel, *The Role of Air Freight In Physical Distribution,* Cambridge, MA: Harvard University Graduate School of Business Administration, 1956.

cross-functional and boundary-spanning total-cost analysis becomes even more diffi-cult to quantify and implement when the managerial responsibilities span more than one business or firm. Thus, while simple in concept, the implementation of a total-cost-based logistics system design solution may be difficult when it requires substantial boundary spanning. The following discussion takes a closer look at transportation and inventory costs, respectively.

Transportation Cost Transportation costs result from the need to bridge geo-graphic distance. Specialization of manufacturing and geographic dispersion of demand means that firms and customers conduct business at different locations. The actual cost associated with the transportation depends upon physical characteristics and value of a product. Different products affect basic transportation cost as a result of their densities, values, perishability, and susceptibility to damage. The greater the density of a given product, the lower the associated cost, because larger quantities can be loaded into a transport vehicle. For example, heavy raw materials typically have a lower transportation cost per unit of weight than lighter, more valuable manufactured products. Railroad and trucking companies have developed elaborate classification schemes to group products on a relative basis for the purpose of pricing.[13] Given similar classification, two products of identical size being shipped between the same origin and destination by truck or train could have substantially different freight rates.

Two basic economic considerations influence the cost of transport: (1) the size of a shipment, and (2) the length of haul. Each of these basic considerations are briefly discussed.[14]

The first aspect of transport economics is related to economy of scale. As a general rule, the larger a shipment, the lower the cost-per-hundredweight (CWT) per unit of distance. A shipment of 10,000 pounds between two locations would have a lower actual cost per pound than one of 500 pounds. The economy of scale reflects the sharing of cost associated with essential functions such as pickups, delivery, and the benefits of improved equipment utilization. The impact of shipment size on transpor-tation cost is often referred to as the *quantity discount*. Freight rates are typically described as being quantity or less than quantity. For example, truck rates are typically classified as truckload (TL) or less than truckload (LTL). Truckload shipments are normally larger than 10,000 to 15,000 pounds. LTL shipments may be any size up to TL. A minimum charge is a flat amount that a shipper must pay, regardless of the weight of a shipment, to use the service. Thus, transportation of very small shipments is typically priced at the minimum charge. As LTL shipment size increases, the cost per hundredweight decreases. The rate of decrease becomes greater as a shipment qualifies for TL rates. Similar quantity discounts exist in transportation rates for rail, water, and air services. The basic economic principle at work is the economy of scale

---

[13] The truck scheme is the ''National Motor Freight Classification.'' The rail system is the ''Uniform Freight Classification.'' Following passage of the Staggers Act in 1980, freight classification procedures were discontinued by administrative and judicial decisions for most forms of rail transport. This topic was discussed in greater detail in Chapter 3, pp. 67–68.

[14] Bowersox et al., op. cit, pp. 287–288.

in operation of the transportation equipment. Such economy of scale exists in both for-hire and private transportation.

The second fundamental aspect of transport economics is the length of shipment distance. As a general rule, the longer the haul, the lower the cost per unit of distance. Thus, a shipment of 1000 miles would have a lower cost per mile than the same-size shipment being transported 500 miles. Once again, the basic principle at work is economy of scale related to the miles traveled. The impact of distance on transport cost is traditionally referred to as the *tapering principle.*

The combined impact of the quantity discount and the tapering principle is that the larger and the longer the transportation movement, the lower the cost-per-hundred-weight mile. These principles, combined, encourage logistics system designs that facilitate long-haul consolidation of transportation shipments supported by corresponding short-haul small-shipment distribution. These objectives are generally achieved by a decentralized logistics network. The logistics system designed to minimize transportation cost would maximize the distance that large shipments are transported while minimizing the distance of smaller shipments. As a general rule, maximum transportation consolidation will result in minimum movement cost. However, as indicated earlier, transportation commitments need to be viewed in terms of impact of inventory cost so that one can arrive at the least-total-cost logistics solution.

Inventory Cost   Inventory costs are time-based. Inventory represents an essential asset for a firm engaged in manufacturing and in most types of marketing. Naturally, to reduce the cost and risk of doing business, firms desire to maintain as little inventory as possible. The objective is to maintain the lowest possible inventory that will support customer-service and manufacturing objectives. The overall appraisal of inventory requires: (1) cost identification, (2) establishment of service policies, and (3) determination of geographic dispersion. Each is discussed.

Table 7-4 lists aspects of cost typically associated with inventory. In a broad sense, the total cost of maintaining inventory is considerably more than the capital cost of the asset. Inventory must be maintained in distribution facilities, and the cost associated with insurance, obsolescence, order processing, and maintenance of inventory-control records all must be factored into the total cost of maintaining inventory. The key to achieving low inventory cost is turnover or velocity. During the past decade,

TABLE 7-4   COSTS TYPICALLY ASSOCIATED WITH INVENTORY

Maintenance	Ordering
Capital	Communication
Storage and handling	Processing
Tax	Record update
Insurance	Administration
Obsolescence	

considerable attention has been focused on ways to support greater sales on lower inventories. The phrase *turn and earn* has gained popularity as firms seek logistics solutions that encourage maximum velocity and reduce overall inventory exposure.

As noted earlier, service policies supported by inventory directly impact the quantity of assets held throughout the logistics channel. Figure 7-4 illustrated the traditional incremental relationship of customer-service availability and the size of inventory holdings. If high-service performance is the goal of an enterprise, considerable attention must be directed to the innovative use of information technology and transportation creativity to meet customers' expectations. To the extent that service policies are supported by inventory, higher average investment will be required at each stocking location.[15]

The final factor that impacts the total inventory required to support business operations is the geographic dispersion that results from logistics system design. The basic questions are: (1) How many stocking locations should a firm utilize to service customers? and (2) Which items or SKUs should be maintained at each facility? Once again, strategic decisions can be guided by principles concerning trade-offs involved. If the level of planned availability of items is held constant, average inventory in a logistics system will increase as the number of stocking locations is increased. The inventory increase is a direct reflection of expanded safety stock required to maintain business operations with a larger network of stocking locations. Conversely, as safety stocks are centralized, a desired fill rate and the capability of shipping customers' orders complete can be maintained on lower total or aggregate systemwide inventory investment. Naturally, the option also exists for improving service performance or yield of a given level of inventory by consolidating existing stocks in fewer facilities.

The combined economic impact of availability and stock location tend to push inventory-stocking policies toward centralization in which there are fewer facilities, all strategically located. With a base of consolidated inventory from which to work, a high level of service availability can be maintained or supported on a lower level of asset deployment. Of course, such centralization directly impacts the service-capability aspects of customer service, since speed, consistency, and flexibility are all affected by network design. Thus, the major economic benefit or motivation concerning inventory appears to draw a firm's logistics system design in the opposite direction to those forces impacting transportation economics.

Integrated Cost   Total-cost analysis is based on a reconciliation of the principles of transportation and inventory economics. Such reconciliation is achieved by having the primary relationship of transportation and inventory be the least-total-cost logistics structure capable of satisfying the desired service goals. Experience dictates that the least-total-cost solution to logistics system design will typically not be at the point of either minimum transportation or minimum inventory cost.

Figure 7-5 frames the essence of total-cost analysis. Assume for illustration purposes that a firm's logistics requirements are such that a network of potential inventory-stocking locations is acceptable. The design question then becomes, How many

[15] See Chapter 7, p. 218.

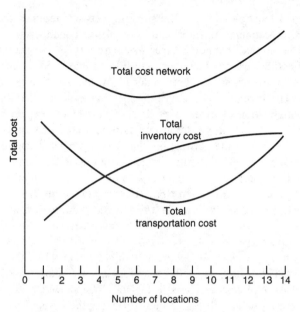

FIGURE 7-5 Total-cost integration logistics system design. (*Source:* Reproduced with permission of Macmillan Publishing Company from Donald J. Bowersox, David J. Closs, and Omar K. Helferich, *Logistical Management,* 3d ed., New York: Macmillan, 1986, p. 289. Copyright © 1986 by Macmillan Publishing Company.)

and which warehouses should be incorporated in the logistics system design? To simplify the illustration, assume that for initial planning all inventory-stocking facilities are full-line. This restriction is relaxed later when service sensitivity is discussed.

The vertical axis of Figure 7-5 measures total logistics cost. The horizontal axis indicates the number of stocking locations. Three cost curves are illustrated: (1) transportation, (2) inventory, and (3) total cost.

The shape of the transportation curve is often described as a "bathtub" configuration because costs initially decline as locations are added and then increase as stocking locations are further expanded. The shape of the curve is a direct reflection of the size of shipment and the length of haul of transport services required to support inventory movements. At the low-cost point, consolidated long-haul movement is maximized and short-haul movement is minimized, resulting in the lowest total transportation expenditure. In other words, the quantity discount and tapering principles that lead to lowest possible transportation cost are being fully reconciled within the requirements of the logistics mission.

The shape of the curve for inventory cost is significantly different than that for transportation. The inventory cost for a single-location system is pegged at a level reflective of the cost of providing the customer with service to meet the demands of availability, capability, and quality. As the network of stocking locations is expanded, average inventory and its associated cost increase at smaller rates with each addition.

The second location added to the stocking network requires the greatest incremental inventory investment. As additional locations are added, each requires a smaller increment of additional inventory. Near the extremity of the inventory cost curve, once most potential locations have been considered, the curve is nearly flat. However, the total cost of inventory is never reduced by the addition of an additional stocking location. The inventory cost curve is reflecting the consolidation of assets that results from centralization of inventories. It is important to keep in mind that the level of inventory availability is held constant as the number of locations is expanded.

The total cost of the network is illustrated by what is commonly referred to as an *envelop curve*. An envelop curve reflects nothing more than the sum of the transportation and inventory cost associated with any particular number of stocking facilities. A quick glance at the total-cost presentation points out the significance of integrated costing. *The lowest total cost for the logistics system is at neither the point of low transportation nor the point of minimum inventory cost.* Thus, the trade-offs inherent in total-cost analysis are clearly illustrated. The essence of integrated costing is to get a fix on how inventory and transportation interact when the cost-to-cost trade-offs associated with a firm's logistics requirements are being sought.

The least-total-cost design of a logistics system will be significantly different for firms operating within the same industry. How the costs play out will depend upon a firm's product assortment and customer configuration. The width and depth of product assortment will be significantly different for a full-line supplier than for a niche supplier. Firms will also experience significant differences in logistics requirements, depending upon the basic nature of products being distributed. For example, degree of seasonality and perishability will directly impact design requirements. In a general sense, logistics design requirements will depend upon the marketing channel decisions a firm seeks to implement. The key is to identify the least-cost logistics arrangement that satisfies customer-service requirements while containing as much risk as possible. The development of a logistics channel design strategy opens the door to potential proactive use of operational competency to gain competitive advantage.

Cost-Service Sensitivity Analysis

To undertake total-cost integration it is necessary to initiate the analysis with an initial inventory availability policy. The objective of a cost-to-cost trade-off is to seek the logistics configuration that will satisfy desired service requirements at the least total cost. Cost-service sensitivity analysis seeks to explore the relationship between incremental service benefits and associated logistics cost. The idea of such cost-benefit sensitivity analysis is to more fully understand the relationship of service and cost. Service sensitivity analysis can be viewed in terms of basic design considerations and selective allocations.

Basic Design Modification In a basic sense, service can be increased (or decreased) by placing greater (lesser) emphasis on one or a combination of the variables contained in the least-cost equation. In Figure 7-5 basic service can be increased by adjustments in the transportation, inventory, or location structure. Each adjustment will have an impact upon corresponding total cost. Each is briefly examined.

Transportation performance can be affected by a change in the method of movement to a mode or carrier that can provide the desired service faster or more reliably. A particular carrier may be equipped with in-truck satellite tracking capability that will provide positive identification of where and when inventory will be delivered. While such a service may cost more, thereby increasing total transportation expenditure, the result could be a reduction in uncertainty leading to lower safety stock requirements. Thus, the decision to select a higher-performance carrier will reconfigure the transportation cost curve and may also impact the level of the inventory cost curve. Independent of inventory, the substitute of faster and more reliable transportation services will typically improve overall performance related to customer-service capability. Each such adjustment in transportation will modify the cost curve. Such transport cost reconfiguration will directly impact total cost for the total system.

The inventory cost curve is a direct reflection of the level of desired availability. What in fact exists is a family of inventory cost curves, each associated with a different level of availability. Thus, the decision to improve availability simply means that the appropriate cost representation shifts to a higher curve. The shape of the inventory cost curve will not change as the level of service is modified. The primary determination of the shape of the inventory cost curve is the geographic dispersion of external or internal customers being serviced by the logistics system. Thus, adjustments in inventory strategy will shift the inventory curve up or down but will not change its shape.

The most direct way to impact service is to increase or decrease the number of stocking locations. A movement away from the initial least-cost solution in either direction will increase total costs. In essence, since transportation and inventory strategies are being held constant, what results from a location modification is movement along the total-cost curve. However, from a customer-service perspective, the direction of movement is critical. Movement to a greater number of stocking locations will increase total cost but will also position inventories closer to customers, thereby increasing potential speed of service. Movement to fewer locations will be dysfunctional in that cost will be increased while potential service is simultaneously jeopardized.

The essence of cost-service sensitivity analysis is to test ways that service can be improved and to provide an estimate of associated cost. In terms of traditional economic analysis, service should be increased to the level that it is capable of generating revenue sufficient to offset corresponding cost. From a theoretical perspective, profits will be maximized at the point where marginal cost of performing the service is equal to the marginal revenue generated by the service enhancement. While clear in theory, such finely balanced cost-service solutions are difficult to realize in day-to-day logistics operations. In part, the key to using logistics competency to impact key customers is based on selective resource allocation.

Selective Resource Allocation   A host of strategies exists for the selective deployment of logistics resources. The basic nature of selectivity and segmentation have been discussed earlier. Most firms have a substantial differential in the profitability of specific items within the overall line. Likewise, the range of customers' responsiveness to high-level service offerings will vary significantly. Selective allocation strategies can be focused to impact these unique opportunities.

From a strategic viewpoint, a logistics system should be designed so that all of a firm's customers can be serviced within the acceptable limits of the competitive situation. Selective allocation offers a way to leverage operations to a higher level of support for customers willing to reciprocate with incremental business. In essence, what is designed is a selective logistics competency within the framework of the broad-based logistics strategy. Selective allocation is best illustrated by two specific examples.

The widely publicized business relationship between Wal-Mart and Procter & Gamble (P&G) represents a highly leveraged logistics arrangement. P&G in cooperation with Wal-Mart has designed a unique way to provide selective value-added service. Based on information sharing, P&G has assumed responsibility for maintaining inventory in Wal-Mart warehouses and is directly responsible for the level of performance that each stocking location provides to retail stores. This shared responsibility results in a unique logistics competency that P&G has designed and operates to accommodate the Wal-Mart opportunity. From the perspective of P&G's product-supply organization, the Wal-Mart solution is a system within an overall logistics structure that is focused on a specific account.[16] The Wal-Mart solution represents an economically justified value-added service designed by P&G specifically to exploit the market opportunity. While P&G can and does accommodate several other marketing opportunities wherein logistics performance can be leveraged, each represents a unique modification to the company's basic logistics service program.

Similar situations in terms of exploiting a unique opportunity are alliances in place between Toys "R" Us and selected suppliers of baby-related products. In an effort to attract mothers (and grandmothers) of young children to their stores, Toys "R" Us has worked out agreements to stock Enfamil, a baby formula distributed by Bristol Myers; Huggies, which are disposable diapers produced by Kimberly-Clark; and Gerber baby foods. The arrangement calls for specific products to be sold often in configurations unique to Toys "R" Us. The logistics arrangement is selective in that products are shipped directly to an individual retail store or to combinations of retail stores by the suppliers. In all situations, the suppliers have modified basic logistics services typically offered to customers so that business could be gained and maintained for Toys "R" Us. Because of the volume involved, each supplier has been able to justify selective allocation of logistics services. The solution implemented by all three suppliers represents a customized system within their overall framework of logistics operations.

The only limit to the creation of such selective distribution arrangements is managerial imagination. A wide variety of accommodations in basic performance are possible. These can be highly profitable for all parties to a logistics arrangement. So that

[16] "P&G Rewrites the Marketing Rules," *Fortune,* November 6, 1989, pp. 34–48. Courtesy of Fortune Magazine. For a detailed discussion of strategic alliances in distribution see Chapter 10, pp. 313–323.

resources can be focused on specific opportunities, a close working arrangement between channel members must be built. In essence, channel members become trading partners. Such engineered logistics solutions typically depend upon the synergism of the channel; members work together to leverage performance to a higher level than possible with a single enterprise working alone. In a great many situations the focused logistics solution is only attainable between a supplier and customer because of the intervention of specialized channel participants. Such specialized participants may be transportation, warehouse, or information service providers that are able to help fuse together a customized logistics competency that exploits the potential of the unique situation.

SUMMARY

The overall material logistics management process spans the entire global business community. It is a costly process, which in the United States alone consumes 11 percent of the total gross national product. While cost reduction and containment are vital aspects of logistics, the provision of customer service is the element that transcends the channel of distribution.

Logistics provides inventory time and location positioning, which is essential to successful marketing. Regardless of a firm's position in the channel of distribution, successful logistics performance is a prerequisite to profitability and long-term achievement of strategic goals. The logistics system of a channel adds value in terms of both basic and specialized services. Finally, a logistics system must span boundaries to effectively accomplish broad-based operating goals. Such boundary-spanning challenges exist both within and without a specific organization. The internal boundary-spanning challenges are the basis of logistics management; external boundary spanning is a vital aspect of channel management. Both boundary-spanning tasks are essential for the development and maintenance of maximum logistics impact.

The design of a logistics channel originates with the establishment of service goals. The logistics competency of a firm is linked to its ability to provide three areas of traditional customer service: (1) *inventory availability,* which deals with strategies related to inventory; (2) *service capability,* which is concerned with speed of performance consistency over a large number of engagements, and flexibility to meet and satisfy special requests; and (3) *service quality,* which is concerned with both a firm's overall ability to perform services without errors and its recovery capacity when service initiatives fail. Many firms are seeking to improve service performance to a level of *zero defects.* Such initiatives are typically based on selective service allocations to specific segments of the market. To use customer service in a proactive manner, a firm needs to identify ways to leverage or elevate performance above industry-accepted standards. Such selective matching requires a penetrating insight into the cost of providing integrated logistics service.

Total-cost analysis provides a basic framework for planning a firm's logistics strategy. The overall process starts with delineation of basic service goals and identification of the logistics system design that will achieve the performance objectives at the lowest total cost. Total-cost analysis is often difficult to conduct because it requires configuration of financial data that do not directly flow from the typical accounting system. The key is to develop activity-based costs so that the key factors that impact transportation and inventory costs can be identified. The combination of two primary-cost centers serves to capture cost-to-cost trade-offs. The general rule is that the lowest total cost for obtaining a specific level of basic service will not be the least cost for either transportation or inventory. Several basic economic principles exist to guide the formation of activity-based costs for logistics.

Service sensitivity analysis, which is the essence of logistics system design, allows original assumptions about customer service to be reconsidered. Such cost-service sensitivity analysis can explore both basic design modification and selective allocation. The initial form of sensitivity analysis is to refine a firm's basic service program by evaluating cost-service trade-offs. As a general rule—one that is all but impossible to measure and implement in actual practice—a firm should offer incrementally higher levels of service as long as the marginal revenue generated is equal to or greater than the marginal cost of providing the service. Once developed, the basic service platform becomes the logistics mission of the enterprise and serves as the broad-based program upon which business is transacted.

The essence of channel management is the selection of service allocations that are forged out over and above the basic logistics offering. These specialized arrangements are selective in that they are focused on specific trading arrangements that evolve from strategic alliances. In these situations, logistics competency is being jointly exploited by trading partners so that performance of the overall channel can be elevated. Such selective logistics arrangements are cooperatively based, link trading partners together in arrangements typically having substantial longevity, and generate a synergism that leverages logistics performance to a higher level while joint performance is used to reduce costs. Many such selective arrangements among trading partners involve the in-depth participation of service specialists that facilitate and energize the basic trading relationship.

QUESTIONS

1 How does inventory risk and exposure vary with a firm's channel position?
2 Why is trucking often referred to as the backbone of the nation's transportation system?
3 Why is the total cost of logistics much greater than the highly visible expenditure for transportation?
4 What is the fundamental meaning of "value-added process"?
5 Why are most logistics activities performed in an anticipatory mode? What are the other alternatives?
6 Why does direct store delivery (DSD) have the potential to improve inventory turnover?
7 Why are logistics operations typically boundary spanning? Does this boundary-spanning tendency impact both internal and external operations?
8 Explain the difference between speed of service and consistency of service. Why do most logistics managers feel that consistency of service is more important than speed of service?
9 What is the concept of zero defects? How does zero defects relate to traditional customer-service measures such as fill rate and orders shipped complete?

10 What constitutes a ''brilliant recovery''? How does the ability to recover brilliantly influence a firm's customer-service image?

11 Why does inventory increase as a firm seeks to offer customers higher levels of product availability by having more items in stock? Can high levels of availability be supported by use of logistics resources other than inventory?

12 Why can a firm provide a specific level of inventory availability with less total inventory as warehouses are consolidated into fewer locations?

CHAPTER 8

PLANNING AND ANALYSIS FRAMEWORK

TRANSACTION COST ANALYSIS
Human Factors
Environmental Factors
Conclusion: Transaction Cost Analysis

ANALYTIC TOOLS FOR EVALUATING ALTERNATIVE STRUCTURES
Key-Factor Scoring
Profitability Analysis
Mathematical and Simulation Techniques

EVALUATION OF CHANNEL MEMBERS
Manufacturer's Evaluation of Intermediaries
Supplier Evaluation by Intermediaries

CHANNEL MODIFICATION
Stimulus for Modification
Modification Strategies

MULTIPLE CHANNELS

SUMMARY

The previous two chapters have dealt with major issues related to the design of both the marketing and logistics channels of distribution. An erroneous conclusion that might be drawn from these discussions is that the design process results in one alternative distribution channel that is optimal for achieving a firm's channel objectives. In fact, the channel design process normally reveals multiple channel design alternatives that must be subjected to further analysis so that the most appropriate distribution structure can be chosen.

This chapter presents methodologies that can be used in making this evaluation. Channel objectives derived from the firm's corporate strategy have been discussed in Chapter 5. The objectives should include economic dimensions of profitability and return on investment as well as market coverage, channel control, and flexibility considerations. These objectives become the criteria by which alternative channel structures are judged. The chapter begins with a discussion of transaction cost analysis. This provides a perspective on whether distribution functions are best performed by an organization internally or through the formation of relationships with independent channel members. The chapter then discusses techniques for analyzing alternative channel structures in terms of their ability to meet the firm's channel objectives. Once the most appropriate structure is identified, attention is devoted to the problems of identifying and selecting specific firms to include as partners in the distribution process.

It should be noted that the perspective taken in this chapter is that a firm's management designs and evaluates distribution alternatives independent of existing methods of distribution. The final portion of the chapter is devoted to a discussion of channel modification decisions and strategies for modification, which require analysis of the impact of change on existing channel relationships. This perspective is somewhat different from the analysis of performance of existing channels and channel partners. As will be seen in Chapter 11, many of the concepts and methods are similar, but their implementation differs in view of the fact that management has information available regarding past distribution capabilities and performance.

TRANSACTION COST ANALYSIS

As discussed in Chapter 4, there are several basic types of organizational arrangements for distribution, ranging from total vertical integration (corporate vertical marketing systems) at one extreme to loosely aligned conventional channels on the other. The first basic structural decision any firm must make is the extent to which it will attempt to perform distribution functions: Will those functions be done internally or by other firms with whom the firm has distribution relationships?

Vertical integration offers the advantage of channel control. Distribution activities can be coordinated and integrated, resulting in efficient functioning of distribution activities with minimal overlap or duplication of effort. Integration provides continuous performance and control over marketing functions. Thus, when Sherwin Williams chose to manufacture, distribute, and sell paint through its own retail outlets, it gained substantial control over the destiny of its products.[1] However, vertical integration typically requires substantial financial investment so that a functional capability for distribution is developed. This may involve inventory, facilities, equipment, and human resources required to perform the full range of activity. Such investments may also severely restrict the flexibility of the organization in a dynamic environment.

---

[1] F. Robert Dwyer and Sejo Oh, "A Transaction Cost Perspective on Vertical Contractual Structure and Interchannel Competitive Strategies," *Journal of Marketing,* **52**:2, April 1988, p. 21.

The polar alternative to full-scale vertical integration is the loose alignment of independent firms called "conventional distribution channels." The benefits derived from such arrangements come from the increased specialization of labor which, theoretically, results in more efficient, and therefore lower-cost, functional performance. The limitations of conventional channels are loss of control and the existence of differing and potentially conflicting objectives among trading partners. These differences may lead to conflict within the channel, which can disrupt the effective functioning of the system.

Frequently the choice between vertical integration and a more traditional distribution channel is posed as a classic economic "make versus buy" decision. Channels are, ultimately, economic arrangements intended to yield profits for their members. If the firm can "make" (perform for itself) the distribution functions more cheaply than they can be "bought" (from other firms), the decision will be to vertically integrate. On the other hand, a firm may opt to functionally "spin off" those activities so that other firms can perform them more efficiently.[2]

Given the multitude of functional specialists in an advanced economy, make-or-buy analysis can be performed for each marketing and distribution function. Thus, a firm may choose to accomplish personal-selling activities through its own sales force or by hiring independent selling agents. Transportation can be accomplished by private trucking fleets or by third-party carriers. Public warehouses may be contracted rather than private warehouses being built. Or, full-function wholesalers may be used by a manufacturer to accomplish all of these activities. The major problem encountered in classical make-or-buy analysis is to account for all of the costs and the variance in revenue associated with each alternative.[3]

The decision between accomplishing distribution functions internally or externally is actually somewhat more complex than can be accommodated in the normal "make versus buy" framework. *Transaction-cost analysis* (TCA) provides both an economic and behavioral perspective on this critical decision.

Originally introduced by Williamson, TCA has been discussed extensively in recent marketing literature.[4] The fundamental thesis of TCA is the same as any economically rational decision: The lowest-cost structure is the most appropriate form of distribution organization. The key is to identify the impact of channel structure on transaction costs.

Transaction costs are defined as those costs associated with assembling information, bargaining, and monitoring performance of distribution activities. TCA proposes that, *under ideal conditions,* transaction costs are always minimized by contracting with an

[2] Bruce C. Mallen, "Functional Spin-Off: A Key to Anticipating Change in Distribution Structure," *Journal of Marketing,* **37,** July 1973, pp. 18–25.

[3] See Joseph Cavinato, "How to Calculate the Cost of Outsourcing," *Distribution,* January 1988, pp. 72–76.

[4] Oliver E. Williamson, *Markets and Hierarchies: Analysis and Antitrust Implications,* New York: Free Press, 1975; Dwyer and Oh, op. cit, pp. 21–34; Robert W. Ruekert, Orville C. Walker, and Kenneth J. Roering, "The Organization of Marketing Activities: A Contingency Theory of Structure and Performance," *Journal of Marketing,* **49:**1 Winter 1985, pp. 13–25; George John, "An Empirical Investigation of Some Antecedents of Opportunism in a Marketing Channel," *Journal of Marketing Research,* **21:3,** August 1984, pp. 278–289.

external firm, because of competition between firms.[5] Therefore, both economic and flexibility objectives are best met through conventional channels. Why, then, do firms choose to vertically integrate and absorb distribution activities? Williamson has suggested two sets of factors that prohibit, or at least, inhibit the existence of ideal conditions in the marketplace. These factors are described as *human* and *environmental.*

Human Factors

The human factors that lead to imperfect market conditions are characterized by Williamson as "bounded rationality" and "opportunistic behavior." While the majority of the research involving TCA has focused on opportunistic behavior, the notion of bounded rationality deserves some attention.

Bounded rationality refers to the limited abilities of human decision makers to process extensive amounts of information and solve very complex problems. This limited capacity may result in decisions that are not objectively "rational" since the decision maker is not able to absorb and process all available information. Since ideal market conditions would normally include characteristics such as a large number of firms from which to choose and perfect availability of information about each of those firms, human decision makers may be unable to cope with these conditions. In addition, it is difficult to assess performance of externally contracted firms and determine how well distribution functions are actually being performed. Vertical integration minimizes these problems by enabling a firm to more closely monitor performance.[6]

Opportunism is a second human factor that influences the nature of transaction costs. Opportunism is defined as *self-interest seeking with guile.* A somewhat pessimistic assumption by Williamson concerning human behavior asserts that human beings will behave opportunistically whenever such behavior is possible and profitable. Consequently, firms may distort information or withhold information from channel partners, shirk their obligations and responsibilities in the channel relationship, or even fail to fulfill commitments to channel partners if they view these actions to be in their own long-term best interest. To protect oneself from such actions by a channel partner, a firm must invest in capability to administer and monitor performance, thus raising transaction costs considerably. The alternative is to organize the distribution effort internally through vertical integration.

Environmental Factors

The key environmental factors of importance in transaction-cost analysis are uncertainty or complexity of the environment and the number of alternative channel partners available.

There are numerous sources of uncertainty and complexity in the exchange envi-

[5] Erin Anderson, "The Salesperson as Outside Agent or Employee: A Transaction Cost Analysis," *Marketing Science,* **4**:3 Summer 1985, p. 238.

[6] Erin Anderson and Barton A. Weitz, "Make or Buy Decisions: Vertical Integration and Marketing Productivity," *Sloan Management Review,* Spring 1986, p. 11.

ronment. Every channel of distribution is structured with explicit and implicit assumptions about the environment in which it will operate.[7] If that environment is unstable — that is, highly variable—uncertainty increases. Environmental heterogeneity also increases the complexity of the environment. Thus, firms dealing across multiple cultures or political boundaries face increasingly complex environmental demands. Rapid change or variations in any of the environmental forces discussed in Chapter 5 leads to increasing uncertainty in the overall environment for distribution performance.

The availability of (potential) channel partners is a second critical environmental characteristic that further relaxes the conditions of the ideal marketplace. When large numbers of competitors are not available, transaction costs may be significantly higher due to the tendency of those firms to behave opportunistically. Thus, when the alternatives available to channel partners are limited, the potential for such behavior is increased substantially.

A key determinant of this *small-numbers* situation is the existence or even the necessity of *transaction-specific assets*. If a particular distribution channel requires specific assets tailored to that structure, few companies are likely to risk the necessary investment, particularly if the asset is not transferable to other situations. Coors Brewing Company, for example, requires that its products be distributed in refrigerated trucks and stored in refrigerated warehouses, a requirement not imposed by other breweries. Thus, distributors that make this investment cannot easily transfer the assets to a relationship with other suppliers. Simultaneously, Coors cannot easily find alternative distributors because other distributors do not possess the necessary capability. The existence of these transaction-specific capabilities means that each firm may be willing to tolerate some opportunistic behavior on the part of the others because of the difficulty of replacement. If, however, the potential for this behavior is raised beyond a tolerable level, vertical integration may represent the best alternative.

According to Williamson, distribution channel structures are designed so as to "economize on bounded rationality while simultaneously safeguarding against the hazards of opportunism."[8] Essentially, this statement can be interpreted as follows: Traditional market organization (conventional channels) are more efficient when the level of environmental uncertainty is low, there is little specificity in assets required (alleviating the small-numbers conditions), and performance assessment is straightforward and simple (reducing the potential for opportunistic behavior).[9] When these conditions are not met, vertical integration, or administered vertical marketing systems governed by clear obligations and control mechanisms, are more efficient.

An important variable in transaction cost analysis is described by Williamson and others as "information impactedness." This condition exists when one party has information that is not available to others or is difficult for others to obtain. The existence of impacted information allows extreme forms of opportunistic behavior; for example, one firm could refuse to divulge its knowledge or could seriously mislead other firms

---

[7] Ravi Singh Achrol, Torger Reve, and Louis Sten, "The Environment of Marketing Channel Dyads: A Framework for Comparative Analysis," *Journal of Marketing,* **47**:4, Fall 1983, p. 63.

[8] Oliver E. Williamson, "Transaction Cost Economics: The Governance of Contractual Relations," *Journal of Law and Economics,* **22,** 1979, pp. 223–260.

[9] Reukert, Walker, and Roering, op. cit., p. 16.

to enter into agreements that would be detrimental to their own situation. The more uncertain or complex the environment, the more likely information impactedness is to occur.

As discussed in other sections of this book, information has become a highly valued asset as firms attempt to develop new approaches to marketing channel performance. Just-in-time, quick-response systems, inventory reduction strategies, and many other approaches require free access to accurate, timely information. The potential for information impactedness and resulting opportunistic behavior may be a prime explanation for the emergence of close strategic alliances among channel members with clear-cut roles and requirements in the form of long-term contracts, as opposed to the more flexible free-flow conventional channels that dominated earlier decades. The potential for opportunism is high in *informal* long-term relationships because termination of such relationships cannot be achieved easily or cheaply.[10] In addition, these informal relationships typically lack the necessary explicit specification of role definition and performance measurement to provide adequate safeguards. In such circumstances, opportunism can be reduced by the formation of vertically integrated structures or contractual obligations that provide greater ability to monitor performance and establish sanctions for performance failure.

Conclusion: Transaction Cost Analysis

As discussed in Chapter 3, many firms in recent years have attempted to refocus their attention on the core functions of their business and rely more on outside firms to provide specialist services. While this trend may seem to contradict the logic of transaction cost analysis, a closer examination of the emerging relationships shows that it is, in fact, quite consistent.

TCA argues that the economically rational decision is to undertake only those channel functions that can be performed and administered internally at a cost lower than the cost of having them performed by others in an openly competitive marketplace. The decision to vertically integrate is rational when transaction costs are high, that is, when marketplace competition is reduced (small numbers) and/or opportunism is probable. To both gain the advantages of economic specialization and simultaneously reduce the risks of opportunistic behavior, vertical strategic alliances are chosen as a preferred channel structure for many firms. These alliances maintain many of the administrative benefits of integration through pooling of interest and sharing of operational efficiencies (for example, see Chapter 3 for a discussion of upside/downside contracts). However, attempts are made to protect each party from opportunistic behavior through explicit performance requirements. The dramatic increase in contract warehousing and contract transportation services (as opposed to traditional public warehousing and common carriage) provides strong support for this view in logistics channels. "Preferred supplier" and "preferred customer" agreements among manufacturers, wholesalers, and retailers demonstrate similar characteristics in marketing channels.

[10] John, op. cit., p. 279.

TABLE 8-1   IMPACT OF TRANSACTION-COST-ANALYSIS VARIABLES ON MAKE-OR-BUY DECISIONS

Variable	Buy	Make
Difficulty in monitoring performance of partners	Low	High
Complex/uncertain environment	Low	High
Need for transaction specific assets	Low	High
Availability of alternative channel partners	High	Low

Table 8-1 summarizes some of the key variables in transaction cost analysis and their impact on the make (use of a vertically integrated system) or buy (use of external partners) decision. It should be noted, however, that there are several limitations to the TCA framework. First, it is extremely difficult to measure transaction costs. Most such costs result in overhead for a firm because of the establishment of bureaucracies to gather information and monitor performance. Second, even though TCA may reveal the desirability of vertical integration, the investment required for integration may be beyond the firm's financial capability. Finally, transaction costs must be weighed against other channel objectives. For example, TCA analysis may reveal that vertical integration is the better alternative, but such integration may reduce the firm's flexibility, especially in an uncertain or complex environment.

ANALYTIC TOOLS FOR EVALUATING ALTERNATIVE STRUCTURES

Once alternative channel structures have been identified, a means for comparing the advantages and disadvantages of each option is required. While the focus of the decision clearly must be on the ability of each channel to meet the firm's objectives in terms of market coverage, control, and flexibility, the decision-making tools for making such comparisons are relatively limited. Perhaps the "bounded rationality" notion in transaction cost analysis helps explain the difficulty managers have in formally analyzing the trade-offs inherent in each viable channel option. In this section, three methodologies that may be used in channel evaluation are discussed. Beginning with relatively simple methods of *key-factor scoring,* the discussion proceeds through the increasingly sophisticated technique of *profitability analysis* and *direct product profitability,* to *mathematical* and *simulation* techniques.

Key-Factor Scoring

Key-factor scoring requires that the decision maker first clearly identify the viable channel alternatives. The second step is to specify the objectives and constraints that will be utilized to compare each alternative. Third, the relative importance of each objective and/or constraint must be determined. Finally, the performance of each alternative with respect to each objective and/or constraint must be estimated. Relative importance and performance estimates are normally subjective judgments made by a firm's management. With this information at hand, the "best" channel can be chosen in a variety of ways.

As an illustration of these steps, suppose a manufacturer of restaurant equipment and supplies has identified three distribution channel alternatives for its product line:

1 Using its own sales force and distribution centers to sell and distribute to national chains and independent outlets
2 Using a network of brokers and independent food-service distributors
3 Using its own sales force and independent food-service distributors

The firm has also specified the following set of objectives and constraints that will be considered in the comparison of the three alternatives:

A: Sales volume
B: Profitability
C: Flexibility
D: Control
E: Investment
F: Risk

The third and fourth steps are accomplished by establishment of a matrix, indicating the relative importance of each objective and/or constraint to the firm, and estimation of the performance of each channel with respect to each objective. Table 8-2 illustrates the process for this example. Note in the table that the performance of alternative channels is rated on a scale of 1 to 10. A high score on the objectives of sales volume, profitability, flexibility, and control indicate that the channel scores high in achieving that objective. The constraints of investment required and risk are scored in the opposite manner, with a low score indicating that higher levels of investment and risk are necessary and therefore less desirable.

TABLE 8-2   KEY-FACTOR SCORING MATRIX FOR CHANNEL EVALUATION

Objective/Constraint	Relative Importance	Channel Alternative Rating		
		A	B	C
Sales volume	.1	10	4	7
Profitability	.15	8	4	7
Flexibility	.1	3	8	6
Control	.1	10	2	6
Investment	.25	3	10	8
Risk	.3	2	10	10
	1.0			

With the establishment of this decision matrix, the alternatives can be compared on the basis of weighted averaging, preference ordering, or minimum requirements.

Weighted Averaging   The weighted averaging method of evaluating the decision matrix involves multiplying the relative importance scores for each objective and/or constraint by the performance score of each channel alternative and summing the results. In this example, the scores are as follows:

$$\text{Channel A} = .1(10) + .15(8) + .1(3) + .1(10) + .25(3)\ \ + .3(2)\ \ = 4.85$$
$$\text{Channel B} = .1(4)\ \ + .15(4) + .1(8) + .1(2)\ \ + .25(10) + .3(10) = 7.5$$
$$\text{Channel C} = .1(7)\ \ + .15(7) + .1(6) + .1(6)\ \ + .25(8)\ \ + .3(10) = 7.95$$

Channel C, using its own sales force and a network of independent food-service distributors has the highest weighted average and would be the alternative selected if this decision rule were used to evaluate the alternatives.

It is important to note that this decision rule allows high scores on some factors to compensate for low scores on other factors. Thus, the importance scores for each factor are critical and directly affect the choice of the most desirable channel. A change in the weighing of relative importance of the factors will change the evaluation and, therefore, the most desirable alternative.

Preference Ordering   Preference ordering utilizes the same information as the weighted average approach, but it requires the decision maker to compare the alternatives on an objective-by-objective basis, beginning with the objective that has the highest relative importance. The alternative chosen is the channel that has the highest score on the most important objective or constraint. In this example, both alternatives B and C have the same score with respect to the most important factor (risk), so the decision maker must next look at the second most important factor (investment required). Alternative B, brokers and independent food-service distributors, scores highest on this characteristic (requires less investment) and, therefore, represents the best choice under this decision rule. The flaw in this decision rule is that the decision is based on the most important factor. Other factors are ignored.

Minimum Requirements   This decision rule requires that an extra step be taken. The decision maker may feel that there are minimum levels of achievement for each objective which any channel must achieve for it to be considered as a viable alternative. For simplicity, assume that in our example the minimum level of attainment for each objective and/or constraint has been established as 5. In this situation, both alternatives A and B would be eliminated because they fail to meet minimum requirements on these factors. Only alternative C meets the minimum on every objective and/or constraint.

This situation is not unrealistic. It is quite plausible that a particular distribution channel may appear to be ideal on the basis of one, or several, attributes. In the example, the use of brokers and food-service distributors scores the maximum in terms of reducing risk and requiring little investment. However, it does not meet even minimum requirements for sales volume, profitability, or channel control and should, therefore, be eliminated. This decision rule can be viewed as a fail-safe strategy in which the chosen alternative may not be ideal, but it at least will not be disastrous.

Key-factor scoring, regardless of the particular decision rule chosen, represents a simple, straightforward method of comparing distribution channel alternatives. The method suffers from two limitations, however. First, the data used is subjective in nature. It is extremely difficult to objectively assess the relative importance of various objectives and constraints. In fact, it is quite likely that different individuals within a firm would provide different estimates of these parameters. Even if a consensus in terms of importance existed, it is likely that the actual ratings given to the various alternatives would differ significantly among managers. Second, the method does not result in, or even require, a careful assessment of actual volumes or profitability of each alternative. All that is required is a relative comparison of channels with respect to these factors.

Despite these limitations, key-factor scoring probably represents a realistic view of how distribution channel alternatives are compared with one another. While the techniques discussed below (profitability analysis, direct product profitability, and simulation) provide more objective estimates of critical data, the difficulty in obtaining the required information renders them extremely difficult to apply in practice.

Profitability Analysis

Profitability analysis is a powerful analytic tool for comparing alternative distribution channels. It can add considerable precision to the key-factor rating scheme discussed above when management is capable of estimating actual sales and costs incurred under different channel structures. Such estimates are, of course, extremely difficult to develop when actual operating experience in a specific channel is lacking. Nevertheless, in-depth marketing research and analysis of company and industry cost structures can be used to project profitability for each alternative. While these projections should be treated with the same caution as any forecast, it is likely that the level of accuracy will be sufficient to allow cross-channel comparisons.

A suggested format for computing the profitability of alternative channels is illustrated in Table 8-3. The data in the table are hypothetical data relative to the choice of the three alternative distribution channels under consideration by the manufacturer of restaurant equipment and supplies discussed earlier. It is important to note that the appropriate costs charged to the channels do not include general overhead and other expenses or assets, which remain constant regardless of the channel alternative chosen. Only those expenses and assets directly related to the channel alternative under consideration should be included.

A specific application of profitability analysis, *direct product profitability* (DPP), has been developed in the grocery products industry. DPP promises to have numerous uses for distribution channel analysis and decision making. One of these uses discussed below is in the evaluation of distribution channel alternatives.

TABLE 8-3   CHANNEL PROFITABILITY ANALYSIS: AN ILLUSTRATION
(Revenue in Thousands of Dollars)

	Channel		
	A	B	C
Revenue	$10000	$8000	$9000
Less: Variable production and marketing costs incurred specifically for the channel	7000	6000	6500
Channel contribution margin	3000	2000	2500
Less: Nonvariable costs incurred specifically for the channel	2000	1400	1750
Channel controllable margin	1000	600	750
Less: Deduction for assets specific to the channel	400	300	350
Net channel margin	$ 600	$ 300	$ 400

Source: Adapted from Frank H. Mossman, Paul M. Fischer, and W. J. E. Crissy, "New Approaches to Analyzing Marketing Profitability," *Journal of Marketing,* **38**:2, April 1974, p. 45.

Direct Product Profitability   The basic concept underlying DPP is that all factors that contribute to a product's cost in a distribution channel should be accounted for in judging a product's profitability. Basically, it takes cost accounting to the specific product level. While the concept of DPP is widely accepted in a number of industries, applying the concept has been extremely difficult due to problems associated with gathering and processing the required information.

In 1985 the *Food Marketing Institute* (FMI) began an industrywide effort to develop a methodology for DPP analysis that could be applied by wholesalers and retailers. The result, known in the industry as the *unified DPP method,* is described in this section.[11]

Figure 8-1 illustrates the overall steps in the unified DPP method. Direct product profit is calculated by subtracting cost of goods sold from the selling price, yielding the traditional measure of gross margin. Gross margin, however, must be adjusted to reflect other revenues that may be forthcoming. For example, if a supplier offers early payment discounts, advertising or promotional allowances, forward-buying opportunities, or backhaul allowances, gross margin for the product should be adjusted accordingly.

Three primary cost centers must be evaluated in the model. The first is warehouse costs. The direct-labor cost of receiving, storing, and handling products in the warehouse as well as associated space and inventory carrying costs must be computed. The second cost center is transportation, the cost of moving product from the warehouse to individual store locations. Finally, store direct costs include labor for receiving and stocking as well as cost for space and checkout. After the costs from these three centers are summed, they are subtracted from adjusted gross margin to yield direct product profit.

[11] This discussion is based on the *Direct Product Profit Manual,* 1986, Food Marketing Institute, Introduction and Chapters 1 to 3.

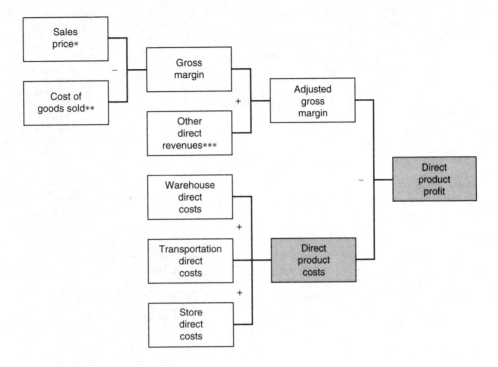

* Retailer: the price consumers pay for the product
   Wholesaler: the price retailers pay for the product

** Retailer: the price paid for a product, either to a wholesaler or to another supplier
    Wholesaler: the price paid to the supplier for the product

*** Deals, allowances, net forward-buy income, prompt-payment discounts, and so on. (When earning these revenues involves extra costs, the user must also enter these costs into the model.)

FIGURE 8-1   Direct product profitability. (*Source: Direct Product Profit Manual,* Food Marketing Institute, 1986, p. I-2.)

In the unified DPP method, the costs at each center are computed in the following manner. First, ''cost-component factors'' are determined. Some of these factors measure the time a specific activity takes to perform (such as unloading a truck, picking an item in a warehouse, etc.), while others measure operating expenses (such as warehouse rent, wage rates, etc.). Next, specific ''product inputs'' are measured. This information includes such data as the cubic volume of the product, the number of units in a case, handling procedures, and so on. ''Product assignment factors'' are attributes of a product that can be used to determine the appropriate cost in each cost center for each specific product. These factors include the product's cube, weight, cost, delivery, case pack, and turnover rate. A series of formulas have been developed which relate the cost components to product inputs. Figure 8-2 illustrates the general methodology for the unified DPP method.

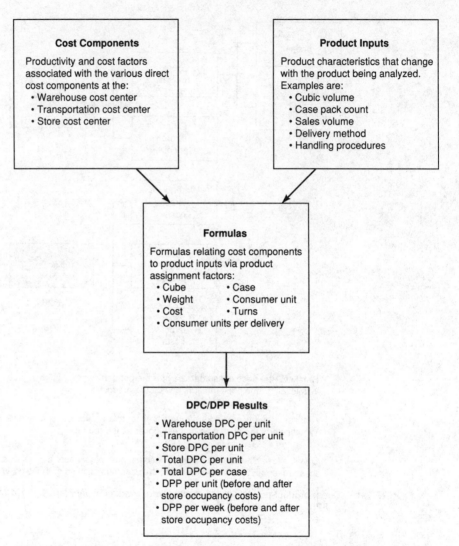

Cost Components

Productivity and cost factors associated with the various direct cost components at the:
• Warehouse cost center
• Transportation cost center
• Store cost center

Product Inputs

Product characteristics that change with the product being analyzed. Examples are:
• Cubic volume
• Case pack count
• Sales volume
• Delivery method
• Handling procedures

Formulas

Formulas relating cost components to product inputs via product assignment factors:
• Cube   • Case
• Weight   • Consumer unit
• Cost   • Turns
• Consumer units per delivery

DPC/DPP Results

• Warehouse DPC per unit
• Transportation DPC per unit
• Store DPC per unit
• Total DPC per unit
• Total DPC per case
• DPP per unit (before and after store occupancy costs)
• DPP per week (before and after store occupancy costs)

FIGURE 8-2 United DP model: general methodology. (*Source: Direct Product Profit Manual,* Food Marketing Institute, 1986, p. I-5.)

One of the primary applications of DPP has been in the choice of distribution channels. Specifically, should a wholesaler or retailer move products through a warehouse or distribution center, or should the channel be direct delivery from the supplier to individual store locations? Table 8-4 illustrates data from such an analysis. On the basis of gross margin and adjusted gross margin, moving the product through the warehouse appears to be the best alternative. It is assumed in this example that the supplier would charge a lower price for the one delivery required to a warehouse

TABLE 8-4 DIRECT PRODUCT PROFIT EVALUATION OF TWO ALTERNATIVE DISTRIBUTION METHODS

	Through warehouse	Direct store delivery
Selling price	$1.00	$1.00
Cost of goods sold	.60	.65
Gross margin	$ .40	$ .35
Plus: Cash discount	.01	.01
Promotional allowances	.01	.01
Forward buy	.02	.00
Backhaul allowances	.01	.00
Adjusted gross margin	$ .45	$ .37
Direct product cost		
Warehouse cost	.10	.00
Transportation cost	.02	.00
Store cost	.10	.12
Total direct product cost	.22	.12
Direct product profit	$ .23	$ .25

rather than multiple LTL deliveries to numerous store locations. It is also assumed that the buyer would not be able to take advantage of forward-buy opportunities or backhaul unless product was to be moved to and stored at the warehouse. In this example, however, the costs at the warehouse and of transportation from the warehouse to the store locations is high enough to offset the increased adjusted gross margin earned under the warehouse alternative. This makes direct store delivery the most profitable alternative.

This example should not be interpreted to indicate that direct delivery is always the best alternative. As stated by Hugh Smith of Hannaford Brothers supermarkets:

> In some cases, you have a choice as to how you want to receive a product—DSD from a distributor or directly through your own warehouse. In that case, it's obvious that you want to do a DPP analysis of the costs that are being offered to you through the various distribution methods, and then you make a decision that fits your situation best.[12]

Mathematical and Simulation Techniques

While profitability analysis provides an estimate of revenues and costs for alternative channels of distribution, it has the drawback of aggregating data into a fixed time perspective. It also does not provide for testing of different environmental conditions or of assumptions about each alternative. In recent years, mathematical and simulation modeling have been proposed as techniques for distribution channel analysis that can provide these capabilities.

Both mathematical and simulation models of distribution channel design have been

---

[12] "How Does DPP Cut Warehouse and Transportation Costs?," *Supermarket News,* September 21, 1987, p. 30.

developed. The mathematical models involve precise equations for the analysis and evaluation of channel relationships. These types of models offer the potential of determining improved channel designs as well as suggesting the impact of any channel design modifications, but mathematical sophistication and elegance are required for their development. Simulation models, or so-called input-output models, require a mathematical description of channel functions and relationships. While simulations are beneficial in evaluating different channel alternatives through direct experiments with a model of a real system, they do not identify the optimal channel design.

Corstjens and Doyle developed a mathematical model to solve three significant channel decisions in a multiple-channel system: the manufacturer's choice of channels, the number of outlets to operate within each channel, and the pricing structure between channels. Their model assumes constant demand and cost functions, expressed in terms of elasticities, and its goal was to maximize manufacturers' profits. Then, a number of operational constraints were considered for optimizing the above decisions. The model is subject to several weaknesses, including the rare availability of data to estimate the parameters in the demand and cost functions and the limitations of sophisticated nonlinear programming.[13]

Few actual simulation models have been developed for distribution channels due to the complexity involved. However, Forrester has simulated various parts of a firm's marketing channels, stressing the interrelationships in the channels of distribution.[14]

Balderston and Hoggart developed a large-scale simulation of channel structure in the West Coast lumber industrial market without specifically dealing with the problem of distribution strategy.[15] Amstutz developed a simulation model of a distribution channel system which includes internal and external factors to assess the effects of changes in marketing strategy. This model considers consumer behavior as the input to the channel decision, but requires an extensive database for operation.[16]

Simulation has been used more extensively in the area of logistics channel design. Among the most advanced examples is the *simulated product sales forecasting* (SPSF) model, which not only simulates channel operations but also provides the capability to evaluate the performance of different logistics structures under varying conditions of demand.[17]

Mathematical and simulation models hold considerable promise for evaluation of channels. However, they require precise formulation of mathematical relationships between channel variables and are, therefore, quite difficult to operationalize. As information processing technology and systems design techniques improve, further developments in these tools can be expected.

[13] Marcel Corstjens and Peter Doyle, "Channel Optimization in Complex Marketing Systems," *Management Science,* **25**:10, October 1979, pp. 1014–1025.

[14] J. W. Forrester, "Industrial Dynamics," *Harvard Business Review,* **36**:4, July–August 1958, pp. 37–66.

[15] F. E. Balderston and A. C. Hoggart, *Simulation of Market Processes,* Berkeley: University of California, Institute of Business and Economic Research, 1962.

[16] A. E. Amstutz, *Computer Simulation of Competitive Market Response,* Cambridge, MA: M.I.T. Press, 1967.

[17] Donald J. Bowersox et al., *Simulated Product Sales Forecasting,* East Lansing: Michigan State University, 1979.

EVALUATION OF CHANNEL MEMBERS

Channel design does not end with the specification of an appropriate channel structure. Regardless of the technique(s) used, the previous step in the process results in an "idealized" structure which specifies the types of channel members necessary to accomplish the firm's objectives. The problem still remains of identifying and selecting specific channel partners to accomplish the distribution function. It cannot be assumed that any firm of a given type is capable of joining or willing to join in a distribution channel with any other firm. Identifying, evaluating, and recruiting those potential channel members represents a critical, and difficult, decision.

Manufacturer's Evaluation of Intermediaries

Selecting intermediaries is not as simple a task as it may appear. Wholesalers and retailers of a specific type vary considerably in their ability to perform the functions associated with their position in the channel. A specific procedure and set of criteria are needed to evaluate the desirability of one channel member over another. Table 8-5 lists a set of criteria suppliers can use in selecting channel partners. From this list, four primary areas of investigation are discussed.

Financial Strength   The financial strength of prospective intermediaries is particularly important. This key indicator provides evidence of the firm's overall abilities as well as information concerning the firm's ability to perform specific channel functions. For example, a financially weak firm may not be able to extend credit to its customers, maintain adequate inventory, or finance sales growth as desired by the manufacturer. At the very least, a financially weak wholesaler or retailer represents a substantial risk to the manufacturer in terms of its ability to compensate the firm for the merchandise as it moves through the distribution channel.

Market Coverage and Sales Performance   Geographic coverage provided by the firm in terms of the number of outlets and sales performance is another critical factor. This may also include consideration of the firm's sales-force size and abilities.

TABLE 8-5   CRITERIA FOR SELECTING CHANNEL MEMBERS: THE SUPPLIER'S VIEWPOINT

1. Financial strength
2. Market coverage and sales performance
3. Trade standing
4. Management strength
5. Product lines
6. Advertising and sales promotion
7. Training programs
8. Plant, equipment, and facilities
9. Ordering and payment history
10. Services offered
11. Willingness to cooperate in joint programs
12. Willingness to share data

It should also include analysis of the product lines currently carried, including potential complementary or competitive overlaps.

Trade Standing   What the intermediaries' competitors and customers think of them is an important factor in the selection process. A firm's reputation within an industry and among its customers may be an important measure of the overall quality of its abilities.

Management Strength   In the long run, success is a function of the intermediary's management. Although management strength is extremely difficult to judge, the structure, depth, background, training, and adequacy of strategies employed indicate the desirability of including the firm in the distribution channel.

Alternative Evaluation   Much of the information required for the selection process is subjective and difficult to use in reaching an objective choice of middlemen. To provide a more objective basis, a format similar to the key-factor rating methodology, discussed earlier, is often employed. When managers can identify the most important criteria, provide estimates of the importance of each criterion, and estimate each intermediary's score, a decision framework as illustrated in Table 8-6 can be used. In this particular example using the weighted average decision rule, intermediary A scores 8, B scores 6.9, and C scores 6.8, resulting in the manufacturer's choice of A as the most desirable channel partner.

Supplier Evaluation by Intermediaries

There is a common misconception that channel intermediaries are simply agents who are "hired" by manufacturers and who are available at the will of the manufacturer. In fact, this is rarely the situation. It is far from a foregone conclusion that simply because a supplier believes Wal-Mart, Price Club, Super Valu, or Marshall Field's are excellent outlets for distribution that those firms will be willing to purchase and resell that manufacturer's product line. Intermediaries carefully consider which products to stock and which brands to carry, and they are not simple conduits for any product a manufacturer may wish to sell. As discussed elsewhere in this text, retailers and whole-

TABLE 8-6   EVALUATION OF INDIVIDUAL INTERMEDIARIES

Key criteria	Weight	Intermediary score		
		A	B	C
Financial strength	.3	8	5	7
Sales performance	.2	7	9	8
Reputation	.2	9	6	5
Management quality	.3	8	8	7

TABLE 8-7   SUPPLIER EVALUATION CRITERIA IN CONVENIENCE GOODS CHANNELS

Unsold return merchandise accepted	Well-trained salespeople
Return of damaged merchandise accepted	Stable sales force
Complaints handled promptly	Sales-force empathy
Honest	Availability of new products
Good reputation	Variety of products
List prices allow adequate margin	Displays provided
No minimum order size	Promotional advice
Convenient delivery time	Promotional allowances
Convenient delivery quantity	Credit terms
Ease of ordering	Quantity discounts
Cooperative advertising	Overall promotional support

Reprinted from: James R. Brown and Prem C. Purwar, "A Cross-Channel Comparison of Retail Supplier Selection Factors,"in Richard P. Bagozzi et al. (eds.), *Marketing in the 80s: Changes and Challenges,* Chicago: American Marketing Association, 1980, pp. 217–220.

salers have undertaken major efforts to reduce the number of suppliers with whom they deal. Too many brands may lead to a slowdown in inventory turnover, poorly trained personnel with inadequate product knowledge to service and sell to customers, as well as lack of interest from key manufacturers in the industry.

Evaluation and selection criteria used by intermediaries vary from industry to industry. Table 8-7 provides a listing of key supplier evaluation criteria frequently used by wholesalers and retailers in the distribution channels for convenience goods. Table 8-8 contains a similar list of criteria used by department store buyers to evaluate suppliers of fashion goods.

Direct product profit, discussed earlier in this chapter, can also be used as methodology for formally analyzing the profit potential of a supplier's product or product line, in addition to evaluation of distribution methods. Hugh Smith of Hannaford

TABLE 8-8   SUPPLIER EVALUATION CRITERIA IN DEPART-MENT STORES

Reputation/cooperation
Brand names/image
Price/markup
Quality/fit
Manufacturer's size/history
Newness/creativity
Marketability

Source: Elizabeth Hirschman, "An Exploratory Comparison of Decision Criteria Used By Retail Buyers," in *Retail Patronage Theory,* Ed. Robert F. Lusch and William R. Darden, New York: Elsevier-North Holland Publishing, 1983, p. 5.

Brother Supermarkets has said, "To improve product mix, you'd use a measure of DPP to help you decide which items gave you the best profit picture. We do a DPP analysis of every new item and compare it against the DPP of items in the same category. . . .[18]

The final structure of a distribution channel and the participants in that structure are typically the results of mutual evaluation and selection by all channel members. When the potential for a relationship from all parties overlaps, the basis for forming a distribution channel is established. This chapter has dealt with the planning and analysis framework for determining these potentially desirable relationships. Channel design is not done, however, until the participants initiate and complete the negotiation process in which performance roles and expectations are established. The negotiation process is the subject of the next chapter.

CHANNEL MODIFICATION

One of the most vexing situations a firm faces is the decision to modify its existing distribution channels. As should be evident by this point, establishment of a distribution channel is an expensive and time-consuming process. Frequently, major investments are made in facilities, equipment, and operating policies and procedures that are necessary to achieve a firm's strategic objectives. Distribution channels typically entail long-term commitments to these investments as well as to the channel partners. For these reasons, major overhauls in distribution strategies and structures are less frequent than changes in product, pricing, and promotional strategies. This does not imply, however, that distribution structures are static. In fact, one of the major channel objectives mentioned in this chapter is flexibility and the ability to adapt to a dynamic environment.

Stimulus for Modification

Distribution structure may have to be modified for many reasons. Changes in customers' buying patterns may signal this need. For example, in the early 1980s, most businesses purchased personal computers (PCs) directly from manufacturers. As the buyers of these computers became more sophisticated, price became less of a factor in their choice and the ability of a system to solve unique, company-specific problems took on more importance. As a result, businesses turned to retail outlets that carried multiple product lines and demonstration-oriented showrooms. Some firms also looked to value-added resellers that purchase components and software from several manufacturers and construct systems that have specialized capabilities. These changes in buying behavior required that some PC manufacturers completely redesign their distribution structures.

As discussed in detail in Chapter 6, the movement of a product through its life cycle may also be a stimulus for channel modification. As the market for a product expands and new buyers enter the marketplace, different methods of distribution are

---

[18] *Supermarket News,* September 27, 1987, p. 22.

likely to emerge. Consider, for example, developments in distribution for facsimile (FAX) machines. Originally these machines were available directly from office equipment manufacturers or dealers, but the market quickly grew. Today FAX machines are distributed through numerous channels, including computer stores, electronics stores, department stores, mass merchandisers, and mail-order firms. One author has described channel modification throughout a product's life cycle as follows:

Introduction: New products tend to enter the market through specialty channels that spot trends and attract early adopters.

Growth: As buyers' interest expands, higher-volume channels emerge that offer service, but less than the specialist channels.

Maturity: As growth slows, lower-cost channels develop.

Declining: As decline begins, very low value–added channels emerge.[19]

Channel modification may be necessitated by environmental change. Deregulation of the transportation industry in the early 1980s brought about numerous changes in logistics channels and relationships as firms reacted to the new legal environment. Multimodal carriers and expanded backhaul programs represent just two of many examples of these changes. Changes in economic conditions, such as rapid inflation, frequently result in channel modification. Changes in industry and competitive conditions, such as the numerous mergers, acquisitions, and buyouts that characterized the mid-1980s, frequently result in altered channel arrangements. When RJR purchased Nabisco, for example, the decision was made to distribute Planters nuts and snacks through tobacco wholesalers as well as through traditional distribution channels.

Modification Strategies

There are two forms of channel modification that a firm may consider at any given time. The first of these is the deletion or addition of specific channel partners. Deletion of a specific firm in a distribution channel typically results from inadequate performance by that firm. Methods of evaluating channel members' performance are the subject of Chapter 11. Addition of a channel partner may occur for other reasons. A manufacturer, for example, may decide to add a wholesaler or retailer so that it can enter a new geographic region, provide more intensive coverage in an existing region, or reach a different type of customer in an existing market.

A second and more complex channel modification is the decision to delete or add an entire marketing channel. Deletion may result from an analysis that reveals inadequate channel performance. Addition of a channel or creation of a new channel in parallel with an existing channel involves reassessment of the entire distribution strategy and requires a plan for implementation. Channel modifications of this type frequently require reassessment of the entire marketing mix as well as evaluation of the impact on existing distribution channels. For example, General Motors decided that

---

[19] Miland M. Lele, ''Matching Your Channels to Your Product's Life Cycle,'' *Business Marketing,* **71**:12, December 1986, p. 64.

its newest automobile line, the Saturn, would not be sold through any existing GM dealership even though many dealers believed that they had the ability to effectively market the line. This decision might be partially related to GM's desire to position the Saturn directly against imported automobiles and avoid cannibalization of its existing brands. In another situation, Jhirmack Enterprises decided to market its line of hair-care products through mass-market retailers. Its historic channel partners, professional hair-care salons, discontinued the product line as this strategy became evident to them. The challenge in channel modification is to maintain the loyalty and motivation of existing channels as the change is implemented.

In implementation of major channel modifications, some manufacturers may choose to overhaul several aspects of the marketing mix simultaneously. Support from traditional channels may be maintained if different models of the product or different brand names are introduced through the new channel structure. For example, most manufacturers of golf equipment that typically marketed their top-of-line clubs through golf pro shops made major changes to their product lines and prices when they added mass merchandisers as a distribution channel. Most of these firms developed lower-cost, standardized clubs for the new channel, reserving the custom-fit lines for pro shops.

MULTIPLE CHANNELS

The implications of this chapter thus far are that a firm must plan, analyze, and select *one* distribution channel. In fact, it is a rare situation in which a firm selects only one channel. More commonly, several channel structures are selected to ensure broader market coverage, to appeal to different market segments, or to gain deeper penetration of target markets. Frequently, the overall channel structure of a firm includes a mixture of direct channels using few or no channel partners and indirect channels involving the use of several partners. For example, in some geographic regions, a manufacturer may use its own sales force and private warehouses while relying on merchant wholesalers in other areas.

The use of direct channels may be greater than is typically thought. For example, in 1989 expenditures for direct-response advertising alone totaled over $62 billion.[20] Many manufacturers whose well-known products are available on retail store shelves also market through direct channels. Pepperidge Farm bakery products are available through Pepperidge Farm Mail Order Company; Aluminum Company of America sells Wearever cookware through direct marketing efforts; and IBM markets software through retail stores and through direct-response channels. These three examples illustrate the fact that channel structures can, in fact, be much more complex than is apparent at first glance.

SUMMARY

Planning and analysis of channel alternatives begins with an evaluation of the desirability of vertical integration. Transaction cost analysis suggests that, under ideal market conditions, conventional distribution channels provide the lowest-cost alternatives

---

[20] *Direct Marketing,* **53**:10, February 1991, p.4.

and maximum flexibility. However, ideal conditions may not exist due to the human factors of bounded rationality and opportunism due to environmental complexity and the existence of small numbers of competing firms. Transaction-specific assets and impacted information both contribute to a less-than-ideal market condition. These characteristics generally increase transaction costs and may render vertical marketing systems more desirable than conventional channels.

Key-factor scoring is one technique for evaluating channel alternatives. The technique requires that the relative importance of key objectives and related constraints be specified and that the peformance of each alternative be evaluated. Channel-profitability analysis requires a more detailed estimation of actual revenues and direct costs for each alternative. Direct product profitability has been developed in the grocery industry as an approach to this analysis. Mathematical and simulation techniques offer considerable promise for channel analysis, but their use requires considerable sophistication.

Channel analysis also requires evaluation of specific channel partners. Both manufacturers and intermediaries must develop criteria to guide the choice and selection of channel partners.

Channel modification may be required due to changes in customers, products' life cycles, markets, or environmental conditions. Modification may involve adding or deleting specific partners or entire distribution channels. A major difficulty in such situations is maintaining motivation of existing channel members as modification is implemented.

QUESTIONS

1 Do you believe that "bounded rationality" and "opportunism" are realistic descriptions of human behavior? Give examples of each to support your position.
2 The text uses as an example of a transaction-specific asset refrigerated trucks utilized by Coors for beer. What other examples can you offer?
3 Using transaction cost analysis as the framework, describe the rationale for the contractual vertical marketing system that characterizes the distribution of automobiles. What, in your opinion, are some of the limitations of transaction cost analysis?
4 What are the relative advantages and disadvantages of key-factor scoring, profitability analysis, and mathematical techniques for channel evaluation?
5 Evaluate the following matrix using each of the decision rules discussed in the text.

Objective	Relative importance	Channel alternative rating				Minimum acceptable
		A	B	C	D	
Sales volume	.2	4	7	9	8	5
Profitability	.2	8	5	5	5	4
Flexibility	.3	6	3	6	5	4
Risk	.1	2	8	4	5	3
Control	.2	5	4	4	5	3

Which decision rule do you believe is the most realistic?

6 Suppose a DPP analysis reveals that paper napkins and paper towels should be delivered from the supplier directly to a retail chain's fifty individual store outlets. Are there reasons that the retailer might still choose to have those products delivered to a central warehouse?

7 Does a manufacturer whose primary objective is intensive distribution still face the necessity of evaluating and selecting specific intermediaries? Why or why not?

8 Taking the viewpoint of a retailer, how would you rate the importance of the criteria listed in Table 8-7 in evaluating potential suppliers?

9 Suppose a manufacturer of cosmetics has determined that the most appropriate distribution channel includes both department stores and drugstores. Discuss the difficulties that the firm may encounter in implementing this distribution structure.

10 What specific factors may indicate the need to reevaluate distribution channels and modify the existing structure?

11 Suppose a manufacturer of television sets has decided to change its distribution strategy from an approach using exclusive dealerships to one relying on mass merchandisers. How would you suggest this decision be implemented? Would you recommend other strategic changes as well?

12 Investigate the actual distribution channels for a local manufacturer. What direct channels does the firm use? What indirect channels does it use?

CASES FOR PART TWO

CASE 2-1: W-G-P Chemical Company

John White, Vice President of Distribution for W-G-P Chemical Company, was preparing for the annual strategy session conducted by the firm's executive committee. He was charged with the task of evaluating his firm's physical distribution costs and customer-service capability for his firm's packaged dry and liquid agricultural chemicals.

W-G-P DISTRIBUTION SYSTEMS

Exhibit 1 outlines the existing physical distribution system for W-G-P Chemical Company. Four types of facilities comprise the system: (1) two continuous, company-owned manufacturing plants; (2) nine seasonal contracted manufacturing plants; (3) numerous in-transit distribution centers; and (4) twenty-eight full-time distribution centers. Growing environmental activism has influenced management to reject any relocation of the manufacturing plants. W-G-P distributes 129 different products or stock-keeping units (SKUs), on a national basis. For distribution considerations, the products may be grouped into two different categories. Category A consists of thirteen SKUs of a product called Prevention. The sales of Prevention are highly seasonal and account for 85 percent of W-G-P's total revenue. The 116 Category B products (called Support) sell throughout the year but also have a seasonal pattern similar to that of Prevention's sales. Although the sales volume of Category B is only 15 percent of W-G-P's total revenue, this group of products contributes approximately 30 percent of total before-tax profits. The typical end user of W-G-P's products purchases a variety of both A and B products. In many cases, the products are used jointly in agricultural applications. W-G-P's total product line is marketed through a network of agricultural dealers. The company sells to the dealers, who then resell the products to farmers. The typical dealer provides farmers with a broad line of products, including those that are directly competitive with W-G-P products. Historically, farmers tend to purchase both A and B products one to two weeks before field application. Application occurs at different times in different parts of the country and is directly related to the intensity of rainfall. Thus, W-G-P's products must be available precisely when the farmers need them. Likewise, the quantity needed per acre varies, depending on the rainfall received in an area. Therefore, although W-G-P produces Prevention and Sup-

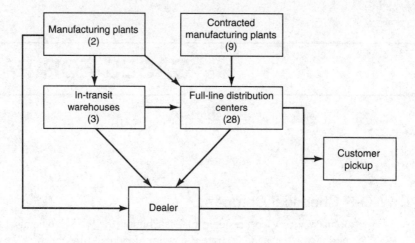

EXHIBIT 1

port all year, sales to farmers take place during a very short time period. Farmers' requirements vary in time and duration of use throughout the country.

To even out physical distribution to dealers across the year, W-G-P offers discount incentives and warehouse allowances to dealers that purchase at least ninety days in advance of estimated application dates. This early-order program accounts for 30 to 40 percent of the total annual sales of Prevention and Support. For the dealer, placing an early order means taking an inventory position on Prevention in advance of farmers' purchases. However, since both Prevention and Support products are available, in effect, the early-order warehouse allowance means a special discount on the Support products, which sell all year. To avoid abuse of the program, W-G-P requires that a proportional amount of Prevention products accompany each order. W-G-P also agrees to accept returns up to 15 percent of the total quantity of early-ordered Prevention products. The return policy requires a refund of the full purchase price, provided dealers repay the return freight to W-G-P's warehouse.

The advantages afforded W-G-P through the early-order program are twofold.

1. W-G-P can schedule shipments at its convenience to achieve the lowest possible transportation cost.
2. Dealers are given an additional discount if their own transportation equipment is issued to pick up early orders, provided the cost is less than transportation paid for by W-G-P.

Seasonal sales, those sales that dealers buy within ninety days of estimated application dates, account for 60 to 70 percent of sales. Thus, to a significant degree, seasonal sales volume depends on W-G-P's ability to deliver products rapidly. During the seasonal period, dealers expect Prevention and Support to be available for pickup at distribution centers within a few hours of order placement. During this period,

TABLE 1   ANNUAL SALES, 1987

Dollars	525,146,747
Weight (pounds)	242,717,768
Cubic feet	26,887,513
Cases	2,912,753
Product lines per order	25,392
Orders	19,139

approximately 50 percent of the dealers pick up products. When transportation is arranged by W-G-P, dealers expect overnight delivery. Although the service level required during the seasonal period is high, these sales are very profitable for dealers because the farmers who purchase the products are willing to pay the full retail price. The capability to provide products during the application period is one of the most important criteria dealers use when selecting a chemical firm. Historically, sales have been concentrated in eight midwestern states, which account for 80 percent of annual revenue. A summary of 1987 sales data is presented in Table 1.

The distribution pattern for W-G-P products is relatively simple. Two company-owned manufacturing plants are located in Alabama and Louisiana. The Alabama plant produces Support, while the Louisiana plant produces both Prevention and Support. Both facilities are continuous-process plants, and their location at deep-water ports facilitates economical inbound raw-material movement. The nine contracted seasonal manufacturing plants have passed the environmental audits and are strategically located at key transportation gateways.

The three in-transit warehouses are utilized because the manufacturing plants have only enough storage space for two or three days' production. Table 2 lists the in-transit facility locations.

In terms of total system, the in-transit warehouses have three functions: (1) storage is provided until forward shipments are required; (2) the close proximity of the in-transit warehouses to manufacturing plants postpones the risk of advance shipments; and (3) the use of in-transit warehouses provides a combination of transportation rates that are lower to field distribution centers than the sum of published rates into and out of the in-transit warehouse. In a sense, the in-transit warehouses are economically supported by special transportation rates. All warehouses and distribution centers in the W-G-P system are public facilities. Therefore, W-G-P's costs are based on volume throughput and duration of storage. The twenty-eight full-line distribution centers are primary facilities from which dealers are served. Although some early orders are shipped directly from plants and in-transit warehouses to dealers, they represent less

TABLE 2   IN-TRANSIT WAREHOUSES

Birmingham, Alabama
Memphis, Tennessee
Alexandria, Louisiana

TABLE 3   WAREHOUSE LOCATIONS
(City and State)

Indianapolis, Indiana
Memphis, Tennessee
Ennis, Texas
Alexandria, Louisiana
Fresno, California
Baton Rouge, Louisiana
West Helena, Arkansas
West Sacramento, California
Greenville, Mississippi
Weslaco, Texas
Omaha, Nebraska
Evansville, Indiana
Albany, Georgia
Montgomery, Alabama
Birmingham, Alabama
Kansas City, Missouri
Brooklyn Center, Minnesota
Rockford, Illinois
Memphis, Tennessee
Phoenix, Arizona
Orlando, Florida
Milwaukee, Oregon
Goldsboro, North Carolina
Des Moines, Iowa
Decatur, Illinois
Columbia, South Carolina
Pennsauken, New Jersey
Houston, Texas
Lubbock, Texas
Charlotte, Michigan
Lima, Ohio

---

than 10 percent of the annual tonnage shipped to dealers. Ninety percent of all tonnage is either shipped from or picked up by dealers at the full-line distribution centers. Table 3 provides a list of distribution center locations. Replenishment of distribution center inventories is primarily on an allocation basis and is controlled by central inventory planning. All orders are processed in an online basis at the central office after they are received over a telecommunications network. The elapsed time from order entry to shipment release from the distribution center is less than twenty-four hours. The primary method of shipment from plants to in-transit warehouses and distribution centers is motor carrier.

THE SYSTEM REVIEW

A primary objective of the physical-distribution system review is to evaluate the cost and service levels of the existing program in comparison with alternative methods of

TABLE 4   DISTRIBUTION COST, 1987

Storage	$ 3.1 million
Handling	$ 1.3 million
Ordering	$ 3.5 million
Average inventory level	$90.0 million
Transportation to warehouse	$ 2.3 million
Transportation transfer between distribution centers	$ 1.2 million
Transportation to customers	$ 5.6 million

operation. Despite relatively smooth operations, the fact remains that at the end of each application season, many dealers' requirements have not been satisfied, while other dealers have returned inventory. Thus, sales are lost that could have been enjoyed if products had been available to the dealers in need. A critical element of customer service is forward-inventory availability to accommodate customers' pick-ups. In preparing the study, John White asked the Accounting Department to provide standard costs. The following standards were developed:

1. Order processing at a standard fixed cost per month with a variable cost per order.
2. Inventory at before-tax cost of 18 percent per annum of average inventory per field warehouse location.
3. Handling and storage at actual local cost for each existing and potential facility. Appropriate storage rate applicable at in-transit warehouses.
4. In-bound transportation from plants and in-transit warehouses to field warehouses based on point-to-point rates.

The costs for the reference year 1987 are contained in Table 4.

QUESTIONS

1 What is the total distribution cost for W-G-P Chemical Company? What is the cost per pound, cubic foot, case, line, and order? How can these measures contribute to the distribution review process?
2 On a map, plot the distribution facilities and network for W-G-P Chemical Company. What product and market characteristics can help explain this distribution structure?
3 What alternative methods of distribution should W-G-P consider for Prevention and Support?
4 Discuss the rationale for:
  a the early order program
  b customer pickup policies
  c use of public versus private warehouse facilities

CASE 2-2: Sears: A Giant in Transition*

INTRODUCTION

In September 1989, Edward A. Brennan, Chairman of Sears, Roebuck and Company, was confronted with a difficult situation. Faced with mediocre profits over a period of years in the merchandising segment and the threat of a hostile corporate takeover, Brennan had championed numerous changes in the late 1980s. Sears introduced brand-name products to compete with existing private-label brands, streamlined its sales and distribution system to reduce expenses, slashed overhead by reorganizing its head-quarters and store staff into six autonomous business units, and examined alternative specialty retailing formats to recover lost customers. Perhaps the most heralded of all Brennan's moves culminated on March 1, 1989, when Sears reopened its 827 stores after having permanently reduced prices on 75 percent of the merchandise. This new "everyday low pricing" strategy was designed to make Sears more competitive in its traditional retail segments. However, analysts were skeptical. Lauren Lambert of Drexel Burnham Lambert stated that Sears has "changed more since the beginning of this year than they have in a long time. It's not going to turn on a dime. I think the company's agility could be improved."[1]

COMPANY BACKGROUND

In 1886, Richard W. Sears began his career in the retailing business while working as a railroad agent in Minnesota. Through a consignment agreement, he managed to sell an entire shipment of watches that had been refused by a local merchant. After experimenting with other products, he eventually quit his job and founded the R.W. Sears Watch Company. The business grew quickly and in 1887 he moved his company to Chicago.

In an effort to expand profits, Sears decided to buy component parts and assemble the watches himself. He advertised for a watchmaker in the *Chicago Daily News,* and Alvah C. Roebuck joined the firm. Sears sold the business to Roebuck in March of 1889 for $72,000 and later formed another watch and jewelry company that he eventually sold to Roebuck in 1891. Within a few weeks, Sears sought to rejoin the company and became an equal partner with Roebuck. Soon thereafter, the company published its first catalog, which included thirty-two pages of watches and an eight-page insert of jewelry and sewing machines. By the following year, the catalog included 140 pages and a wider selection of products, most of which were less expensive than other stores could offer.

Sears' early success relied almost entirely on ever-increasing sales that were often the result of exaggerated claims. Roebuck, unsure of the business's future potential, sold his portion of the company to Sears in 1895 for $25,000. Julius Rosenwald joined the firm that same year and provided stringent financial controls as the business

---

* *Sears: A Giant in Transition* was written by David J. Frayer.
[1] *USA Today,* September 7, 1989, p. B2.

expanded. In 1906, the company issued its first preferred stock to help finance growth. By 1908, the business climate had changed and Sears was forced to adjust its marketing tactics by providing more accurate, highly detailed descriptions of products. Sears became chairman of the board in 1908, but rarely took an active part in business operations. He resigned in 1913.

While not the first catalog company, Sears, by 1917, was publishing two large general-merchandise editions and several hundred specialty catalogs. General Robert E. Wood joined Sears in 1924 after leaving rival Montgomery Ward and immediately decided to expand the business into retail outlets. While the catalogs had successfully penetrated the rural markets, the retail stores sought to capitalize on the growing metropolitan areas. The first retail merchandise store opened in 1925 in the Chicago Catalog Merchandise Distribution Center. By 1929, Sears had opened 324 stores, and in 1931, retail sales surpassed catalog sales for the first time.

By 1931, Sears realized the growing importance of the automobile in shaping American lifestyles and began to offer low-cost auto insurance through the mail. The Allstate Insurance Company, named after a popular line of Sears' tires, was founded to handle these transactions which were solicited through the general catalog. In 1933, Sears introduced over-the-counter insurance sales by expanding Allstate operations into Sears' retail outlets. This move broke with prevailing customs and provided another avenue for Sears' continued growth. In 1945, Sears' yearly sales exceeded $1 billion for the first time.

Following World War II, Sears embarked on a second period of retail expansion. While other retailers hesitated in fear of a postwar recession, Sears anticipated growth in the suburbs and moved quickly to capitalize on delayed consumer spending. In 1953, Sears introduced the revolving charge account, which expanded the purchasing power of consumers. Beyond merchandise sales, Allstate added life insurance to its growing portfolio of products in 1957, and the company was soon setting growth records.

As Sears continued to support its corporate growth strategy through additional retail outlets and an expanded product and service offering, profits continued to soar. Management began to search for attractive uses for the firm's financial resources. In 1961, Allstate purchased a California Savings and Loan Institution to further diversify its insurance operations. Sears continued to develop retail shopping centers and embarked on a plan to consolidate its operations in a single location. During the 1960s, Sears passed A&P to become the world's largest general-merchandise retailer. Sears' corporate stature reached a pinnacle with completion of the Sears Tower in 1973. The leading retail and insurance firm had constructed a corporate headquarters that dwarfed other buildings in the Chicago skyline, much like Sears towered over its nearest competitors.

By 1980, Sears recognized that the traditional financial services system was not providing adequate service to its customers. Already an established presence in insurance and personal banking, Sears in 1981 acquired Coldwell Banker for real estate and Dean Witter for investments to create a new kind of broad-based, consumer-oriented financial services institution. Allstate, Coldwell Banker, Dean Witter, and Sears Savings Bank (formed in 1984) were assembled as members of the Sears Financial Network, a partnership of leading firms working in collaboration to develop and distribute unique financial services. Sears Financial Network Centers were established in retail outlets and many services were introduced, including the Discover card in 1985.

While Sears developed into a major participant in the financial services arena, retail operations relied on outdated merchandising strategies to extend corporate growth. Following a series of merchandising mistakes in the late 1970s, Sears reported a $7 million retailing loss in the first quarter of 1980. Sears had lost much of its market to K mart and other retailers, as merchandising operations slipped further behind the highly profitable insurance segment. By 1982, it became apparent that major changes were necessary. The "Store of the Future" debuted in 1983 as an attempt to minimize the adverse effects of competition from national discounters and specialty retailers. To stimulate sales, Sears renovated its stores and introduced new product lines. However, as Sears entered its second century in 1986, it remained under attack from all sides. The strategic advantages that had transformed this small mail-order watch operation into the world's largest retailer appeared to have become liabilities.

INDUSTRY DEVELOPMENTS AS OF JANUARY 1988

Despite the initial success of Sears' "Store of the Future" campaign, sales remained relatively flat. Selling expenses as a percentage of sales continued to lead the industry. In 1988, Sears' selling and administrative costs were 32 percent of sales, compared with 24 percent at K mart, 23 percent at Wal-Mart, and 17 percent at The Limited. "You don't get an expense structure until you're 100 years old," joked Joseph Batogowski, an executive vice president of merchandising for Sears, Roebuck and Company.[2] In reality, the company had trailed far behind industry competitors in most measures of retail productivity for quite some time. Despite belt-tightening efforts, Sears' costs had continued to grow faster than sales every year since 1985 and Sears' market share had declined almost 33 percent since 1980. Only about 55 percent of Sears' floor space in its largest stores was devoted to sales, while K mart and many other department stores approached 80 percent.

Retail merchandising, though, was not the only area that suffered. Sears' catalog sales had declined as a percentage of total company sales and had shown only marginal gains during a period when the consumer mail-order industry grew over 44 percent. Exhibit 1 contains selected financial data for the years 1979 through 1988.

Sears traditionally used its size to derive scale economies through mass purchasing and combined staff organizations. For several years, a centralized approach to marketing resulted in advertising and product decisions originating exclusively in Chicago. Power struggles between headquarters staff groups and store managers often slowed and distorted implementation of even the simplest ideas. Sears' giant bureaucracy had even failed to recognize regional weather patterns, attempting to sell space heaters in Hawaii and distributing catalogs in Miami with heavy winter parkas on the cover. Despite a strong brand franchise, Sears continued to lose customers to discounters and

---

[2] *Chain Store Age*, General Merchandise Trends, December 1985, p. 12.

EXHIBIT I SELECTED FINANCIAL DATA FOR SEARS, ROEBUCK AND COMPANY

Reported in millions of dollars, except for common-share data

Operating results	1988	1987	1986	1985	1984	1983	1982	1981	1980	1979
Revenues	$50,251	$45,904	$42,303	$39,349	$37,898	$35,257	$29,559	$27,243	$25,082	$24,301
Costs and expenses	$45,617	$41,222	$38,139	$35,384	$33,766	$31,751	$26,866	$25,182	$23,170	$22,323
Nonrecurring expenses	$ 751	$ 105	—	—	—	—	—	—	—	—
Interest	$ 2,937	$ 2,721	$ 2,653	$ 2,629	$ 2,528	$ 1,703	$ 1,628	$ 1,520	$ 1,133	$ 918
Operating income	$ 946	$ 1,856	$ 1,511	$ 1,336	$ 1,604	$ 1,803	$ 1,065	$ 541	$ 693	$ 1,060
Other income	$ 157	$ 239	$ 282	$ 277	$ 246	$ 66	$ 28	$ 101	($11)	$ 43
Income from continuing operations before income taxes, minority interest, and equity in net income of unconsolidated companies	$ 1,103	$ 2,095	$ 1,793	$ 1,613	$ 1,850	$ 1,869	$ 1,093	$ 642	$ 682	$ 1,103
Income taxes										
Current operations	$ 54	$ 521	$ 444	$ 306	$ 498	$ 565	$ 238	$ 10	$ 98	$ 317
Fresh start and deferred tax benefits		($172)			($60)					
Income from continuing operations	$ 1,032	$ 1,726	$ 1,336	$ 1,280	$ 1,422	$ 1,326	$ 866	$ 646	$ 604	$ 820
Income (loss) from discontinued operations	($122)	($93)	$ 3	$ 14	$ 30	$ 11	($5)	$ 4	$ 6	$ 10
Cumulative effect of change in accounting for income taxes	$ 544									
Net income	$ 1,454	$ 1,633	$ 1,339	$ 1,294	$ 1,452	$ 1,337	$ 861	$ 650	$ 610	$ 830
Percent return on average equity	$10.5	$12.3	$10.8	$11.4	$14.0	$14.4	$10.1	$8.2	$8.1	$11.4

Financial position

	1988	1987	1986	1985	1984	1983	1982	1981	1980	1979
Investments	$29,136	$25,120	$22,183	$19,249	$17,203	$15,434	$13,497	$12,229	$11,336	$ 9,985
Receivables	$28,685	$26,026	$21,417	$18,942	$17,565	$15,511	$11,532	$10,827	$ 8,956	$ 8,967
Property and equipment, net	$ 5,179	$ 4,790	$ 4,593	$ 4,541	$ 4,361	$ 3,938	$ 3,396	$ 3,312	$ 3,153	$ 3,061
Merchandise inventories	$ 3,716	$ 4,115	$ 4,013	$ 4,115	$ 4,530	$ 3,621	$ 3,146	$ 3,103	$ 2,715	$ 2,680
Total assets	$77,952	$75,014	$66,009	$66,426	$57,073	$46,177	$36,541	$34,406	$28,218	$26,904
Insurance reserves	$17,329	$13,169	$10,014	$ 8,090	$ 6,919	$ 6,262	$ 5,667	$ 5,161	$ 4,407	$ 4,075
Short-term borrowings	$ 8,978	$ 7,055	$ 4,306	$ 3,996	$ 3,887	$ 4,596	$ 2,820	$ 3,233	$ 4,436	$ 4,293
Long-term debt	$ 9,736	$ 9,562	$10,067	$ 9,907	$ 9,531	$ 7,405	$ 5,816	$ 5,324	$ 2,965	$ 2,966
Total debt	$18,714	$16,617	$14,373	$13,903	$13,418	$12,001	$ 8,636	$ 8,557	$ 7,401	$ 7,259
Percent of debt to equity	$ 133	$ 123	$ 110	$ 118	$ 123	$ 123	$ 98	$ 103	$ 97	$ 97
Shareholder's equity	$14,055	$13,541	$13,017	$11,776	$10,903	$ 9,782	$ 8,812	$ 8,269	$ 7,665	$ 7,446

Shareholder's common-stock investment

	1988	1987	1986	1985	1984	1983	1982	1981	1980	1979
Book value per share (year end)	$37.75	$35.77	$33.90	$31.66	$29.46	$27.59	$25.08	$23.77	$24.32	$23.44
Shareholders	351,999	328,446	319,686	326,201	340,831	339,644	350,292	354,050	349,725	339,459
Average shares outstanding (millions)	379	378	369	363	358	353	350	316	316	320
Net income per share										
Income from continuing operations	$2.72	$4.55	$3.57	$3.47	$3.92	$3.76	$2.47	$2.05	$1.91	$2.57
Income (loss) from discontinued operations	($0.32)	($0.25)	$0.01	$0.04	$0.08	$0.03	($0.01)	$0.01	$0.02	$0.03
Cumulative effect of change in accounting for income taxes	$1.44									
Net income	$3.84	$4.30	$3.58	$3.51	$4.00	$3.79	$2.46	$2.06	$1.93	$2.60
Dividends per share	$2.00	$2.00	$1.76	$1.76	$1.76	$1.52	$1.36	$1.36	$1.36	$1.28
Dividend payout percent	52.1%	46.5%	49.2%	50.1%	44.0%	40.1%	55.3%	66.0%	70.5%	49.2%
Market price (high–low)	46–32.3	59.5–29.8	50.4–35.9	41.1–30.9	40.4–29.5	45.1–27	32–15.8	20.8–14.9	19.5–14.5	21.6–17.9
Closing market price at year end	40.9	33.5	39.8	39	31.8	37.1	30.1	16.1	15.4	18
Price earnings ratio (high–low)	12–8	14–7	14–10	12–9	10–7	12–7	13–6	10–7	10–8	8–7

Source: 1988 Sears, Roebuck and Company Annual Report.

EXHIBIT II   COMPARISON OF TOP RETAILERS

	Revenue (in billion $)	Share of top five retailers, %
1971		
Sears, Roebuck	10.1	44
J.C. Penney	4.8	21
Kresge (now K mart)	3.1	13
Woolworth	2.8	12
Montgomery Ward	2.3	10
	Revenue (in billion $)	Share of top five retailers, %
1988		
Sears, Roebuck	30.2	29
K mart	27.3	26
Wal-Mart	20.6	20
J.C. Penney	15.2	14
Dayton-Hudson	12.2	11

Source: Business Week, July 10, 1989.

specialty stores (see Exhibit 2). However, in 1987, Sears established a network of twenty-five consolidated retail regions which brought merchandising strategy to the local level.

In a 1985 interview with *Chain Store Age,* Joseph Batogowski confirmed the retailer's historic commitment to private-label merchandise. In reference to Kenmore, Sears' highly successful line of home appliances, Batogowski commented, "I doubt you'll ever see another [brand of] washing machine on our floor."[3] Such confidence in Sears' traditional approach to consumer marketing was prevalent among corporate executives even as Sears faced critical challenges from a number of new sources. Specialty retailers like The Limited and Toys 'R' Us made Sears' private-label merchandise appear shabby and neglected, while low-overhead discounters such as K mart and Wal-Mart utilized efficient networks to attack Sears' prices. Sears' position as the nation's leading retailer was clearly in jeopardy, but other external threats provided a more dangerous and complex challenge for the firm's management.

Continued poor performance by Sears' merchandising group had focused the attention of Wall Street investors on the value of Sears' diversified portfolio. Despite its size, $48.4 billion in 1987 corporate sales, Sears was not invulnerable to a hostile takeover. The recent buyout of RJR Nabisco had proven that even corporate giants could become suitable targets. By summer of 1988, investors were preparing breakup analyses, indicating that Sears' stock was undervalued by as much as 50 percent. Sears' chairman, Edward A. Brennan, insisted that the value of Sears was greater than

[3] *Chain Store Age,* General Merchandise Trends, December 1987, p. 11.

the sum of its parts (Sears' Merchandise Group, Dean Witter, Coldwell Banker, and Allstate Insurance). However, to reestablish a 15 percent corporate return on equity, Brennan needed to improve the merchandising group's 12.2 percent return on equity.

The extent of Sears' logistics requirements also became an operational issue. In 1984, Sears purchased products from over 6000 domestic sources whose accounts were handled through a computerized billing system. Sears, a leading advocate of transportation deregulation, was able to reduce the number of carriers from 4200 to about 180 by 1984. More efficient transportation also permitted Sears to reduce the number of distribution centers from a high of 110. Joseph Batogowski conceded that the company still needed to improve distribution and inventory controls by approaching a just-in-time delivery system. On average during 1986, merchandise required eighteen weeks to reach the stores once a buyer had ordered it. By cutting the average delivery time by a single day, Sears could save an estimated $43 million per year. Overall, Sears' distribution costs remained a shocking 8 percent of sales in 1987, compared with approximately 2 percent for both K mart and Wal-Mart. To help reduce some of these costs, Sears planned to close five more of its twelve remaining distribution centers by 1989, idling 5700 of the company's 18,500 distribution center employees.

In the fall of 1987, Sears finally organized perhaps its best marketing tool, the Sears Household File. This computerized database contains information on the buying habits of every household in America that does business with Sears. Approximately three-quarters of all United States households are involved, a healthy 68.3 million total. According to Allan Stewart, senior vice president for planning, "The key . . . is to increase multiple relationships."[4] This means persuading Die-Hard battery buyers, Craftsman tool customers, and Kenmore washing-machine families to trust Sears with their investment money as well. Sears must recapture a generation of children who began to shop elsewhere for more modern merchandise. As these children establish their own families, Sears must provide them with goods and services that meet their criteria of value and style.

When Sears celebrated its diamond jubilee year in 1961, management felt: "The ultimate test of value is not Sears' judgment, but the customer's response. It is the customer who renders the final verdict."[5]

By January 1988, Sears' customers were responding by shopping elsewhere. If Sears was to remain competitive in the retail segment, comprehensive changes were needed to revitalize the company's merchandising operations. Sears' entire cost structure required dramatic reductions, while logistics operations needed to be more carefully integrated. Poor managment of Sears' sales and distribution channels had resulted in an inefficient corporate structure. A strong performance by the companies of Sears' Financial Network made strategic decisions even more critical in light of the firm's breakup value. Now, more than ever, Sears needed to capitalize on the firm's internal synergies.

[4] *Forbes,* March 7, 1988, p. 61.
[5] *1961 Annual Report,* Sears, Roebuck and Company, p. 12.

ESTABLISHING SYNERGIES THROUGH NETWORKS

In January 1988, Sears reorganized its principle businesses into two distinct operating units, the Sears Financial Network and the Sears Retail Network (see Exhibit III). The restructured company was the culmination of an intensive, organizationwide evaluation of the various business units and was designed to implement the firm's refocused strategy. The overriding objective was to insure that Sears would achieve increased shareholder value through distinct competitive advantages lasting well into the 1990s. As outlined in the 1988 annual report:

> Among the key elements of the consumer focused direction are the revitalization of the Merchandise Group, broadening it into the Sears Retail Network, and the focusing of our financial services on the consumer.
>
> The 'network' concept that has existed among our financial services companies for several years includes a wide range of distribution channels—from traditional branch offices to locations in Sears stores. Research developed during our strategic evaluation shows that while Coldwell Banker, Dean Witter and Allstate each have strong identities as individual companies, consumers say their strength is enhanced through their collective membership in the Sears Financial Network.
>
> Employing the same network concept, the Merchandise Group has established several distinct businesses, creating the Sears Retail Network which capitalizes on the trust, integrity and financial strength of Sears.
>
> The end result is two powerful, interrelated organizations—the Sears Retail Network and the Sears Financial Network. They are the vehicles through which the company will implement the revitalization of the Merchandise Group and the refocusing of financial services on the consumer.[6]

SEARS FINANCIAL NETWORK

The Sears Financial Network includes several businesses that operate in three primary areas: insurance, financial services, and real estate. Through the Allstate Insurance Group, Sears offers policies covering life, auto, home, and business. Financial services are the primary focus of the Dean Witter Group whose operations include retail brokerage, investment banking, consumer lending, and the Discover Card. The Coldwell Banker Group provides real estate services, products, and financing through its three primary business units: Coldwell Banker Residential Group, Sears Mortgage Group, and Homart Development Co.

The corporate reorganization that took place in January 1988 focused the attention and resources of the Sears Financial Network companies on the consumer. Commercial businesses were divested or restructured to better support consumer businesses. A number of key changes are outlined in the 1988 annual report:

• Allstate's group life and health business has been sold. The Allstate Life Insurance Company will concentrate on individual life products, annuities, pensions and direct response marketing products.

---

[6] *1988 Annual Report,* Sears, Roebuck and Company, p. 5.

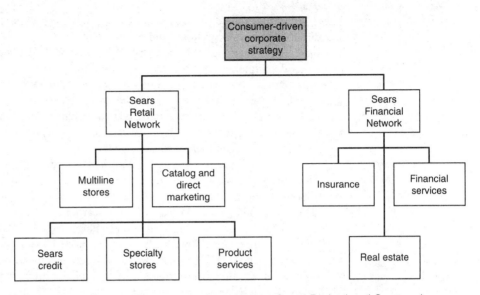

CASE 2-2 Sears' organization chart. (*Source: 1988 Annual Report*. Sears, Roebuck and Company.)

- Allstate's business insurance division has been refocused to direct its attention to the small to midsize market, and its national accounts business is being de-emphasized.
- Coldwell Banker's commercial division is being divested. Homart will continue to create value for shareholders by developing and managing quality real estate projects.
- Sears Mortgage Company's business has been transferred from Dean Witter to Coldwell Banker, which will permit more efficient offering of mortgages to residential clients.
- Dean Witter has restructured its securities-related organization. Dean Witter Financial will concentrate on sales and marketing and Dean Witter Capital will focus on investment banking and product development.
- Discover Card has been aligned as a stand-alone unit reporting directly to the chairman of Dean Witter.[7]

The companies of the Sears Financial Network have strong market positions individually and through powerful affiliations with one another. The linking of programs, such as selling Allstate investment products through Dean Witter account executives, helped provide critical business synergies to strengthen the entire Financial Network.

SEARS RETAIL NETWORK

While the Sears Financial Network was created as an alliance of separate but interrelated companies, the Sears Retail Network attempted to distinguish among several distinct businesses that were formerly integrated within the Sears Merchandise Group.

---

[7] *1988 Annual Report*, Sears, Roebuck and Company, pp. 7–8.

These businesses include multiline stores, specialty stores, product services, catalog and direct-marketing operations, and Sears credit.

Conventional Sears retail outlets that carry a broad assortment of product lines in numerous departments were identified as multiline stores. The selected merchandise categories build upon Sears' established market strengths: home appliances, home improvement, automotive goods, home fashions, men's and children's apparel, and women's apparel. When coupled with updated merchandising strategies, this structure increased accountability by product line, streamlined decision making, and improved competitiveness in each merchandise category.

Specialty stores were the newest enterprises in the Sears Retail Network. These outlets were developed both internally and externally and included McKids stores, sleep shops, paint and hardware stores, eye-care centers, and free-standing auto centers. This segment was designed to increase Sears total market share in selected merchandise categories through acquisition and management of growing companies.

The provision of selected product services permitted Sears to capitalize on a nationwide organization of 850 service facilities, 19,000 technicians, and 14,000 service vehicles. Sears' reputation in product repair coupled with expansion of service capabilities to include brand-name merchandise provided significant marketing opportunities within this segment.

The final two business segments included in the Sears Retail Network can be easily distinguished as independent operations. The catalog and direct-marketing organization was established as a business independent of the retail structure. Such a format allowed Sears to leverage its historic strength in catalog sales to provide improved performance across the segment. Sears' credit operation was the first Merchandise Group business to be separately organized. This distinction permitted clear performance measures to be established and monitored more effectively.

The network structure, which had been so effective in the financial services organization, was intended to improve performance among the merchandise businesses. By providing customers with the right goods at the right price and at convenient locations, management expected to raise corporate returns through increased profitability in each market segment. However, structural change alone was not sufficient to achieve these objectives.

STRATEGIC RESPONSE

In order to support the extensive structural changes that created the Sears Retail Network, the Merchandise Group simultaneously developed its retail, catalog, and service strategies for the 1990s. Four primary strategic responses emerged—power formats, everyday low pricing, vertical business accountability, and corresponding logistics support—which operated within the framework of intense cost containment necessary for success in a highly competitive environment. Michael Bozic, chairman and chief executive office of Sears Merchandise Group, insisted that each of these new strategies was "aimed at delivering quality, value, trust and integrity to the consumer."[8] However, the success of these strategic responses depended on two key assumptions:

[8] *1988 Annual Report,* Sears, Roebuck and Company, p. 10.

1 Sears can properly implement and control these programs.

2 These responses address the fundamental problems that have resulted in the Merchandising Group's declining market share and reduced return on investment.

A careful examination of each strategic response highlights key areas of concern.

Power formats were designed to convert Sears' retail outlets into "stores of superstores." They were developed in key areas, including: automotive, lawn and garden, home improvement, home fashions, men's clothing, and women's apparel. The concept debuted in 1988 with the introduction of Brand Central. This area featured home appliances and home entertainment equipment in a dramatic new setting surrounded by improved signs and an expanded product assortment. To enhance Sears' appeal and strengthen the store's competitive position, over fifty national brands including Whirlpool, General Electric, Sony, RCA, and Zenith were added, while the Kenmore franchise remained in place. Since Kenmore commanded gross margins in excess of 30 percent, Sears' primary source of profit appeared threatened. To protect this revenue, Sears planned to heavily advertise Kenmore appliances and provide sales staff incentives to push high-margin products.

Results from initial market tests in eighteen Indiana and Kentucky stores reinforced the decision to expand Brand Central into 400 additional stores during 1989. Carpet departments were also converted to a power format during early 1989. After several months of testing in three markets, well-known national brands replaced the house label in 726 Sears' stores. Exclusive marketing agreements with McDonald's and Walt Disney Studios turned Sears into a formidable competitor for Kids "R" Us. By providing a greater selection and improved service, Sears hoped to attract consumers from both national and local discount chains.

In conjunction with these power formats, Sears adopted an everyday low pricing strategy. After being tested in three Wichita stores during the fall of 1988, the plan was implemented nationwide on March 1, 1989. It was hoped that lower prices everyday would encourage customers to shop more often and more widely rather than wait for promotions. This resulted in more consistent shopping patterns, which permitted better control of inventories, reduced operating costs, and lighter work loads at all levels in the organization. A new advertising campaign was developed to support the pricing program. "Your Money's Worth and a Whole Lot More" expressed Sears' desire to create power formats that delivered quality, value, trust, and integrity. The campaign emphasized the price/quality relationship between Sears' merchandise and various value-enhancing programs such as dedicated customer service, credit options, delivery, merchandise installation, and product repair. The combination of reduced prices and after-sale service created a value-based mix that Sears believed few discounters could match completely.

With the third strategic element introduced by the Merchandise Group Sears recognized the need to carefully manage each business segment according to the merchandise, services, and other characteristics of that business. Through vertical business accountability, headquarters and field organizations were aligned to become more responsive to market changes and were evaluated based on specific performance measures. This concept is critically linked with the structural reorganization of the Merchandise Group into the Sears Retail Network. The future success of power formats and catalog operations was closely tied to vertical accountability, which has been tested within the credit organization.

Effective integration of merchandise planning, inventory management, and physical distribution was a primary concern of Sears' Merchandise Group, which sought improved logistics efficiency and support for merchandising operations. One major consideration for this fourth strategic response was development of systems to serve the newly separated retail and catalog businesses. Inventories, which had previously been consolidated, were handled separately after mid-1989. This focused on reduced overhead through elimination of seven catalog distribution centers by mid-1990. Simultaneously, Sears' distribution facilities were divided based on the desired product flow. Major appliances purchased in a retail outlet were sent directly to the consumer's home from a distribution facility, while smaller "take-with" items were distributed to stores. This improved product flow reduced inventories while providing better customer service. Central to improved logistics was Sears' commitment to convert to a standardized electronic language for communication with suppliers and a state-of-the-art system for processing customer orders, managing inventory, and operating distribution facilities. Through creation of a distribution system that grew with the business, Sears hoped to avoid frequent stockouts on popular items. Such channel management systems were critical in providing adequate support for Sears' merchandising activities.

Two additional strategies designed to enhance Sears' logistics system included expanded distribution and further development of specialty merchandising formats. In 1988, Sears opened thirteen new multiline stores and relocated eighteen others. By 1994, the Merchandise Group plans to increase the number of multiline stores to 1050 from the 1988 year-end total of 824, including 226 new locations and 87 relocations. A portion of this expansion is designed to improve market penetration in underserved suburban and urban areas through creation of Sears Ltd., with complete power formats selected for local market demographics. Expansion of specialty merchandising formats occurred primarily through acquisition of Western Auto Supply, Eye Care Centers of America, and Pinstripes Petites. In addition, the focus of Sears Business Systems Centers was adjusted to emphasize small and medium-sized businesses, while improving service to the consumer market.

PRELIMINARY RESULTS THROUGH AUGUST 1989

When Sears, Roebuck and Company slashed prices permanently on 75 percent of the items sold in its 827 stores March 1, 1989, management had hoped to reverse five years of dismal sales. As expected, the preliminary results did not indicate the plan was an immediate success. Same-store sales in March were up 9.6 percent over March 1988, and April gained 6.8 percent over April 1988. Revenues then dropped a shocking 2.4 percent in July and 1.1 percent in August across stores that had been open at least one year (see Exhibit 4). Industry observers expected Sears' aggressive new pricing policies to primarily impact sales in discount stores. While K mart registered a 1 percent drop in same-store sales in April, Wal-Mart, Hills, and Target posted solid

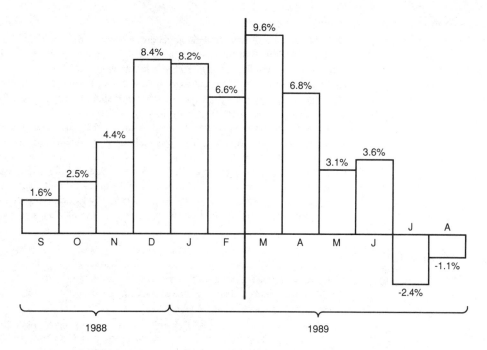

CASE 2-3   Percentage change in same-store revenue (from the previous year). (*Source:* "Slow start for pricing strategy," *USA TODAY,* September 7, 1989. Copyright 1989, USA TODAY. Reprinted with permission.)

gains. According to analyst Wayne Hood of Prudential Bache Securities, "They still have a long way to go to convince the consumer that day in and day out you can find lower prices at Sears."[9]

Despite advertising claims, Sears' prices were not always the lowest in town. In one market, a Magnavox 13-inch color television cost $269 at Sears, while the same television sold for $249 at K mart across town. In fact, some of Sears' old sale merchandise was actually priced lower than the new permanent price points.

In May 1989, a series of surveys conducted by Impact Resources of Columbus, Ohio, indicated that in many markets Sears had failed to convince consumers that it was indeed a price leader. In Cleveland, Chicago, and Buffalo more shoppers cited price as a reason for picking Sears, while the percentage of shoppers who rated price as their primary motivator in selecting Sears declined in Milwaukee, Kansas City, and Denver.

Still, optimism remained high at Sears Tower in Chicago. When an angry shareholder scolded management for squandering its hold over the American consumer, Edward Brennan, chairman and chief executive officer, replied; "Give us a try. We want you back."[10]

[9] *Lansing State Journal,* September 11, 1989, p. B5.
[10] *Business Week,* July 10, 1989, p. 55.

QUESTIONS

1 Describe the primary strategic advantages Sears used to support corporate growth from 1886 through 1979. Will these strategic advantages remain viable tools for Sears to support merchandising activities in the 1990s? Why or why not?

2 Explain the network concept as applied at Sears, Roebuck and Company. Why are networks important? Can Sears develop true operating synergies alone, or will it require participation by other channel members? Why or why not?

3 How do channel management issues relate to the crisis facing Sears in 1988? How have these changed by August 1989? What additional problems do you foresee? Provide solutions where possible.

4 How have the changes instituted at Sears between 1985 and 1989 changed the strategic positioning of the firm? What are the implications of these changes for Sears' channel strategy, logistics channels, supplier evaluation and selection, and relationships with suppliers? In particular, consider the impact on channel relations of closing five distribution facilities.

REFERENCES

1961 Annual Report, Sears, Roebuck and Co., pp. 9–13.

1984 Annual Report, Sears, Roebuck and Co., pp. 5–14.

1988 Annual Report, Sears, Roebuck and Co., pp. 1–41.

"The Big Store's Big Trauma," *Business Week,* July 10, 1989, pp. 50–55.

"Brands to Join Kenmore in Test," *Chain Store Age,* December 1987, p. 11.

"Master Plan to Revitalize Sears Still under Scrutiny," *Chain Store Age Executive,* January 1989, pp. 38–40.

"Minding the Store," *Forbes,* April 7, 1986, pp. 31–32.

"On the Rebound," *Forbes,* June 20, 1983, p. 12.

"Sears' Big Book: Dinosaur of Phoenix?" *Direct Marketing,* July 1986, pp. 71–74.

"Sears Faces a Tall Task," *Business Week,* November 14, 1988, pp. 54–55.

"Sears' Family Stores Leap into New Century." *Chain Store Age,* December 1985, pp. 11–91.

Sears Pricing Strategy Still in Doubt," *Chain Store Age Executive,* October 1989, p. 124.

"Sears: Trimming the Worst of the Corporate Fat," *Business Week,* March 16, 1987, p. 39.

"Sears Works on Appeal to Make Up for Five Bad Years," *Lansing State Journal,* September 11, 1989, p. B5.

Shaking Sears Right Down to Its Work Boots," *Business Week,* October 17, 1988, pp. 84–87.

Slow Start for Sears' Price Strategy," *USA Today,* September 7, 1989, pp. B1–B2.

"They Buy Their Stocks Where They Buy Their Socks," *Forbes,* March 7, 1988, pp. 60–67.

"Today, Each of the Big Three Travels along a Different Path," *Stores,* July 1987, pp. 23–24.

"Too Early to Gauge 'New' Sears Impact," *Chain Store Age Executive,* June 1989, p. 85.

"Transportation: Making It Work," *Stores,* February 1984, p. 38.

"Will the Big Markdown Get the Big Store Moving Again?" *Business Week,* March 13, 1989, pp. 110–114.

CASE 2-3: Baskin-Robbins' 31 Flavors: Managing "Cooperative" Advertising*

Don Wilson, owner of two Baskin-Robbins franchises in a medium-sized midwestern metropolitan area, was concerned about the results of the recent year's cooperative advertising program. The program had been greeted with great enthusiasm by most franchisees at the previous year's national franchisee meeting, and Don strongly supported the concept. He had been chosen "market captain" for his area and worked hard to develop a successful program. As he reflected over the past several months, however, he was disappointed with the results and wondered what changes might be necessary.

BACKGROUND

Don's two Baskin-Robbins ice cream stores were located about 8 miles apart, in a metropolitan area of about 250,000 people. It was a good, healthy market for franchised food operations. The local economy was diverse, including state government, automobile manufacturing, and a major state university.

Don's first store was located across from a university campus, in a free-standing building. There was excellent access from a major highway and considerable walk-by traffic from off-campus students. The closeness of a Burger King, Pizza Hut, and local restaurants helped the in-store traffic for his store. As long as he had sufficient supply of chocolate flavors, Wilson's campus store was a big hit with the students.

Don acquired his second store a year after he bought the first. This store was located in a neighborhood strip center. The neighborhood was largely residential, and contained a good mix of government workers and employees of the nearby auto assembly plant. Family groups made up the principal customer base—birthday parties to be catered and walk-in traffic from the strip-center business.

While the first store had been profitable from the day it became a Baskin-Robbins franchisee, the second store had a troubled past. Two prior owners in the past three years had given poor customer service, which led to a bad reputation. Don bought the store at a good price—and had managed a turnaround to profitability in two years of consistent management. Don was considered to be an excellent franchisee: young and aggressive, with excellent store results.

BASKIN-ROBBINS' ADVERTISING PROGRAM

Each Baskin-Robbins store was responsible for all local-market-area advertising. The company provided advertising materials in the form of ad slicks, preprinted billboard posters, television spots on videotape, radio copy, and other promotional items. Most of these materials were available free or at very low cost to the franchisees. Media costs and placement were the responsibility of the individual franchisee, who designed promotional campaigns that seemed desirable for the local market.

---

* *Baskin-Robbins 31 Flavors: Managing Cooperative Advertising,* was prepared by Daniel Wardlow.

The company also provided a national-spot television campaign each year. The campaign was paid for entirely by Baskin-Robbins, and for over twenty-five years had been handled by a major advertising agency in Los Angeles, near the company's headquarters in Glendale. The television campaign focused on six major ice cream "holidays"—Valentine's Day, Easter, Mother's Day, Father's Day, Thanksgiving, and Christmas. The advertisements promoted the extensive line of custom-made desserts—festive ice cream pies, cakes, and novelty items—made by the franchisees for consumers to take home for special occasions. While franchisees were informed of the items to be promoted on television, they had no input into the selection of the items nor into any other aspect of the campaign decisions.

Baskin-Robbins has over 3000 franchised stores in the United States. Placement of the company-paid advertising was based on the number of stores in each television market area. Each market area received an allocation of gross rating points (GRPs) based on the number of stores in the market. Allocations were not based on dollars, with the idea being to maximize the impact of high-store-density markets through more GRPs. This decision had been made by the company and its advertising agency.

The national advertising program had always been administered by the company, with no formal input from the franchisees. Many franchisees were unhappy with previous campaigns and media placement, so the company proposed to open up the process to franchisees.

THE COOPERATIVE ADVERTISING PROGRAM

At the national franchisee convention, Jerry Salters, regional vice president of operations for Baskin-Robbins, presented a new proposal for television advertising. Jerry opened the discussion by introducing Barbara Sutton from the Olander and Mays advertising agency located in Los Angeles. Ms. Sutton's presentation is summarized below.

As all of you know, we've always done national television advertising from Los Angeles. We have an exciting new campaign prepared for next year, and I wanted to be here in person to tell you about it and answer your questions. The new campaign will effectively double our GRPs in each market, and we are very pleased to involve you as franchisees in our national television campaign for the first time. Before I get to the details, I want to share with you some of the creative executions already prepared for the Valentine's Day and Easter promotions, and show you the proposed storyboards for the remaining four holiday pushes.

The agency had created a thirty-second and a fifteen-second advertisement for each of the holidays. A videotape showed each of the commercials three times. The ads had a unique style, catchy theme, and cute humorous touches:

Roses are red
Violets for lovers;
Baskin-Robbins has hearts
In 31 Fluvvers

When the tape ended, the franchisees broke into applause. Obviously, there was support for these new spots. Barbara also narrated storyboards that were projected from slides, and the additional advertisements to be produced appeared that they would be a good follow-up to the early advertisements in the campaign. Barbara explained the new advertising program.

> We have worked hard to make your limited advertising budget pay off. We have always encouraged your company to spend more on television nationally. In the past years, the company has always given us slight increases in funds for media placement. But as media prices have risen, it has been difficult to maintain our share of media voice around the holidays. We considered moving our advertising to less competitive periods, but decided that we'd be shooting ourselves in the foot. If there's one thing the franchisees seem to agree on is the importance of dessert advertising around the holidays.

Most franchisees agreed. Store sales of desserts were very important in countering weather cycles in the northern climate of the midwest. Four of the holidays occurred during slack walk-in periods, when the extra sales meant the difference between profit and loss for a month. Ice cream desserts also paid the highest profit margins of any product sold in a Baskin-Robbins store.

Barbara continued:

> "We've brainstormed on how to increase our GRP's without additional funds from the company. We've developed the first National Cooperative Campaign ever placed by your company. The company has committed itself to spending dramatically more than in past years on television advertising. The amount they actually spend will depend on you, the franchisees. Beginning with the Valentine's Day campaign, the company will match dollar for dollar the advertising contributions of the franchisees in each market area. This program is entirely voluntary for franchisees. We are suggesting that each franchisee contribute 1 percent of each month's gross store sales to the National Cooperative Advertising Campaign. The company will match the money raised in each market area, effectively doubling what had been done before. The great thing about this plan is that there is no limit to the company's contribution. If you'd like to contribute 2 percent or 3 percent to the fund, the company will match you dollar for dollar.
>
> Under the terms of the existing franchise agreements, the company cannot compel you to participate. If advertising is placed in a market area, all franchisees in that area will benefit from it. We are counting on your cooperative spirit as fellow franchisees to make this Cooperative Campaign a success.

The program was to be administered by having the franchisees from each market area elect a market captain to collect and disburse the advertising funds. The arrangements for collection were entirely up to the franchisees in the market area. Two months before the beginning of each campaign, the market captain would contact the agency and report how much money the market franchisees wished to spend on that holiday push. The agency arranged for matching funds from the company and for the media placement. Two weeks before the push was to begin, funds were due at the agency. When funds are received, the agency notified the television stations involved, and the campaign began.

The discussion at the meeting became quite lively, with numerous questions which Jerry and Barbara attempted to answer.

"What happens if we decide not to participate?"

Jerry explained, "If one store declines, it becomes a free-rider. It will benefit from the contributions made by other area franchisees. Its absence will hurt the campaign because there will be less funding available locally, and obviously less for matching from the company. If an entire market area declines, the company will place no television advertising in that market area. You'd have to count on spillover effects through cable TV, but that would be sketchy at best."

"Is this program a foregone conclusion?"

Jerry answered, "Yes, the company believes this is the only fiscally sound approach it can take in the short term. We've talked about rewriting franchise agreements to include a mandatory fee for national advertising, similar to that used by McDonald's and Burger King. But we don't want to renegotiate everyone's franchise agreement before its due date. We're confident that a cooperative spirit among franchisees will carry this program, and that no mandatory advertising contribution clauses will have to be included in your franchise renewal when your five-year term rolls along."

"What kinds of input do we have into designing the advertising?"

Barbara answered, "Some—quite a bit, actually. The film you saw today is locked in. But the storyboards are still subject to change. We appreciate your input, and would consider any changes that make life easier for you, and still keep us within the campaign objectives."

"What about placement? Last year in our market, we had Mother's Day ads placed on the *David Letterman Show*. I don't like that show. I don't think any viewers would order a Mother's Day cake from my store."

Barbara continued, "Well, rather than talk about specific placements, let me just say that we examine each television program for the type of demographics it delivers. We attempt to match the delivered demographics with our targets for that holiday push, and place ads to generate maximum GRPs. For Mother's Day, a targeted group was young adults, who may be thinking of a treat for mother on her day. Without checking my records, I'd have to say the *David Letterman Show* must have fit our program profile. But, if we argue over each placement, we'll have a very difficult time buying your advertising. At the agency, we have very expert people who select our advertising buys. I'm not an expert in this area, and I trust our pros. I hope you will trust them, too."

"What happens to me if I don't participate?"

"Well, nothing at first. But I certainly hope that peer pressure will help you see the light on this one. The company can't do anything to you directly. But we hope everyone will get into the spirit of this and pitch in their fair share."

PROGRAM IMPLEMENTATION

Don was chosen market captain for his area. There were three other owners in the market, each of whom he knew well. Each owned one Baskin-Robbins store. Two of Don's fellow franchisees were within the same city; one was located in an adjacent urban area some 35 miles from Don's stores. This urban area was small and considered a part of Don's television market.

Adam Sleight owned the oldest store in the market. It was located in an older regional strip center that had been converted into a covered mall. While two major regional malls had been built in recent years, Adam's center retained a high traffic count due to its major anchor, Sears. Adam's store was estimated to have over $250,000 a year in gross sales.

Sal Bodoni owned the store that was out of town. Sal felt isolated from the other three owners, simply because he didn't meet for coffee as often as the others. Sal owned the only Baskin-Robbins store in his town, which was generally regarded as a well-run store. He'd been talking about selling his franchise because his wife Jean was in poor health and he wanted to retire.

Mara Orlowski owned a store on the west side of town. It was the newest Baskin-Robbins store in the market, having been open just a little over a year. Mara and her family were recent immigrants from Poland, who pooled family money to make a start in business. Mara and her husband Arkady had two daughters in high school, and the family ran the store with no outside employees.

Don proposed that the store owners in his market go along with the 1 percent contribution rate. Mara and Sal agreed, but Adam wanted each store owner to contribute whatever they felt they could afford each month. After considerable discussion and other proposals, they finally settled on the 1 percent rate. Most other market areas agreed to similar proposals, although the contribution levels varied from .5 percent to 1.5 percent.

Over the course of the next several months, a number of problems arose in managing funds for the program. The following summaries of several phone calls between Don and the other franchisees provide evidence of these problems.

Month One

"Adam, Don here. I didn't get your check for advertising yet. Oh, no, not postmarked by the tenth; in the bank by the tenth. Okay, what was your contribution?"

Month Two

"Sal! Heard you put the store up for sale! Well, it's probably for the better. I didn't get your check this month, yet. Oh, well I understand you have to do some remodeling before you sell, but remember we all agreed to participate. Okay. Next month, you'll make it up?"

Month Three

"Adam? Don. I got your check this month, but it's only for 50 dollars. Did you send me the wrong check? Hmmmm, well, no I didn't think they did a bad job of placing the last holiday push. Well, we can't penalize them by placing less advertising in our market. That's just hurting ourselves. If you don't like it, you should call Barbara. No, it's not just me who can talk to her—call her yourself!''

Month Four

''Mara? Don. I didn't get your check yet this month. Well, yes, I realize it's getting into spring and we all need to build up our inventory levels. But advertising is what helps us to move that inventory. Please, send what you can this month and make it up next month.''

''Sal? Don. About that back amount you owe to the advertising fund. Of course I understand it's voluntary, but it's also cooperative. No, I'm not accusing you of being uncooperative. Hmmmm . . . well, okay, I mean, if that's how you feel, contribute what you want.

Month Five

''Jerry? Don from store 181. This cooperative advertising fund is a pain in the rear! I'm the captain, and no one is 'cooperating!' Everyone has got an excuse each month. I feel like I'm carrying the ball here, and if I stopped hassling them, I'd be the only contributor. No, it's more than Adam this time. Mara's short on cash this year, and Sal's remodeling seems more important to him than promotion. I know there's nothing you can do to enforce it, but could you use some gentle persuasion?''

Month Six

''Hello? Adam! How's it going? You're what? You can't pull out just because the Mother's Day ads didn't say 'order early!' You have to plan ahead for the demand. It was a good spot. I had enough stock on hand, and you should have too! Won't you rethink this? I'll have to let Sal and Mara know about it if you pull out. What? You already talked with them?''

Month Seven

''Mara? Don. Will you contribute while it's busy this summer so we can have some TV in our market for Christmas? Anything would help. Thanks.''

''Sal? Don. Mara says she'll kick in some advertising money during the busy months so we can buy some Christmas time on TV. Yeah, I know Adam's getting a free ride on this, but not contributing to the fund is like cutting off your nose to spite your face! C'mon, help us all out. Yes, I know you won't benefit if your store is sold by then, but think of the new owner.''

CURRENT SITUATION

Don felt he'd been a failure as a market captain. Other markets didn't seem to be having problems. Jerry and the company had not offered any help. Their hands were tied, it was a voluntary program. Don wondered how he could salvage the remainder of the television advertising campaign. He hoped the company would come up with something different for the next year.

QUESTIONS

1 Is the Baskin-Robbins channel strategy with its franchisees consistent with the advertising strategy it has employed?
2 What are the advantages and disadvantages of a voluntary program such as the one structured by Baskin-Robbins?
3 What could the franchisees in each market area have done in structuring their local agreements to avoid Don's problems?
4 How would you structure a national advertising program that mandates participation by franchises?

CASE 2-4: Happy Grove Dairy

INTRODUCTION

Reflecting on the call he received last Friday from Joe Martin, president of Good's Supermarket, Jack Rowland, president of Happy Grove Dairy, realized he should not have been surprised. But he was.

His secretary informed him that Joe was on the line just as Jack was starting his daily inspection trip through the milk processing plant. Jack picked up the phone and had the following conversation:

Joe: Good morning, Jack—hope you've been well.

Jack: Can't complain too much, Joe. What's happening?

Joe: Well, Jack, all our retailers were together for the monthly meeting yesterday. Our new member from Stockville once again got on the subject of milk cost. Seems he was buying milk from Farmer's Cooperative Dairy at a price much less than ours from Happy Grove. He's sure putting pressure on our gang to shift to Farmer's.

Jack: Joe, we've been over this before. . . .

Joe: I know, Jack, but it looks like I can't keep the troops happy with talk. Despite the fact that we can only get gallons and half-gallons and not the rest of the line from Farmer's, some of our store owners feel we should go for the lower price. I can't . . .

Jack: I'm sorry to interrupt, Joe, but you know we sell to you now for $1.49 a gallon and our costs are almost $1.48. You can't squeeze blood out of a turnip. What the hell is Farmer's offering now?

Joe: Well, I'll tell you because we've been together a long time. Farmer's is offering $1.45 per gallon as well as a price $.03 lower than yours on half-gallons. Looks like they've got you coming and going on price. The only difference is that they plan to deliver by semivan twice a week to each store.

Jack: Well, Joe, even if you can live with twice-a-week delivery, how about special and weekend deliveries? We've been over all this before. Full-distribution service is worth something.

Joe: Jack, I hope we can work it out, but I need facts and a presentation for our store owners. They're ready to switch to Farmer's if Happy Grove can't improve over our present deal. We would like you to come over next Thursday and let us know what you can do. As much as I hate to say it, Jack, things don't look too good. You had better take a good look at every angle and get close to Farmer's offer or it will be out of my hands.

Jack: I'll do the best I can. What time Thursday?

Joe: How's 9 A.M. at our board room?

Jack: Fine. See you then, Joe.

BACKGROUND

Happy Grove Dairy was founded in 1936 by the combining of three smaller dairy operations. Two retail store groups split off their farms and milk processing plants and merged with a local milk wholesaler and home-delivery operator who also operated farms and dairy herds. The new organization became known as Happy Grove Dairy and was operated by Allen Rowland, Jack's father. The operation of Happy Grove consisted of the dairy farms plus a retail home-delivery distribution system that serviced a medium-sized metropolitan area in northeastern Michigan. In addition to home delivery, Happy Grove operated a wholesale delivery route to a small number of retail stores. The two retail groups that were partial owners of Happy Grove operated thirty stores. In addition, approximately seventy-five other retailers were served on a daily basis. The typical wholesale delivery consisted of stocking the milk cooler each day with a full line of dairy products. During the early years, wholesale delivery was on a daily basis, six days a week, while home delivery was on an every-other-day basis.

Business was good for Happy Grove from its inception. Despite the constraints of World War II, Happy Grove continued to grow and was profitable every year of its operation until 1950 when Allen Rowland retired and turned the operation over to his son, Jack. By 1950, several major changes had taken place in Happy Grove. The most significant are listed below:

● *In 1946 the dairy farms were sold to raise cash to buy out the two retail groups that helped form Happy Grove.* This action was justified by two events. First, dairy ingredients could be purchased on the open market as cheaply as or more cheaply than produced on Happy Grove's own farms. Second, the fact that Happy Grove was partially owned by two retailers created some conflict with other retail stores that felt they were helping their competition if they purchased from Happy Grove. After the farm sale and repurchase of the original stock of the two retailers that participated in founding Happy Grove, the dairy became wholly owned by the Rowland family.

● *By 1948 it became clear that the trend in shopping was toward supermarkets.* Beginning in 1946, home-delivery customers rapidly began to discontinue Happy Grove in favor of retail stores from whom they could obtain lower prices for milk products. Thus, the nature of Happy Grove's volume was rapidly shifting from retail to wholesale. In 1950, Happy Grove's business was 80 percent wholesale and 20

TABLE 1   HAPPY GROVE DAIRY 1975 SALES DISTRIBUTION

Customer	Stores	Percent of total business
Smudt's Supermarkets	22	16
Kroger Supermarkets	10	12
Good's Supermarket	15	10
Jones Markets	12	8
Ready Convenience Stores	31	7
All others	547	47
Totals	637	100

percent retail. In 1940, the split had been 70 percent retail and 30 percent wholesale.
• *By 1950 the concentration of Happy Grove's wholesale business had shifted from a number of individual stores to several different groups of supermarkets.* This change of customer pattern reflected the normal growth of supermarket chains throughout the United States.

Happy Grove's business continued to grow at a profitable rate for over two decades, until the mid-1970s. In 1975, the dairy had both record sales and profits. The management was very proud of the 1975 figures, since sales topped $10 million for the first time and profits just exceeded $1 million.

By 1975 the retail portion of Happy Grove's business had been completely phased out. The dairy became fully wholesale, serving 637 individual retail stores. Although Happy Grove had 637 retail delivery stops, the customer count was somewhat lower because of chains and cooperative groups. Table 1 shows the distribution of Happy Grove's 1975 business. Jack Rowland was not happy at that time with the fact that 14 percent of his customer's stores accounted for 53 percent of his total milk volume.

From 1976 to 1990, Happy Grove Dairy began to feel the pressure of "bigness" in both retail and dairy operations. At the wholesale level, the dairy business became more and more concentrated as national dairies such as Sealtest and Borden's purchased a great many local dairies. In addition, farmer cooperatives became a major force in the wholesale dairy business. These cooperatives had the main objective of supporting farm-level prices. As such, they were difficult to compete with on a price basis.

At the retail level, a great many changes occurred during the period from 1976 to 1990. Most large regional supermarket chains went extensively into private-label milk. More and more small stores were forced out of business or, if their size was sufficient, they became affiliated with cooperative buying groups. In addition, small stores were being replaced by the rapidly growing number of convenience stores. The convenience-store concept consisted of limited-line multiple outlets owned and operated like a minisupermarket chain.

The combined changes over the fourteen-year period had a significant impact on Happy Grove's operations. Although volume was maintained at around the $10 to

TABLE 2   HAPPY GROVE DAIRY 1990 SALES DISTRIBUTION

Customer	Stores	Percent of total business
Good's Supermarkets	38	28
Jones Markets	20	18
Ready Convenience Stores	50	16
ABC Convenience Stores	16	15
All others	307	23
Totals	431	100

$12 million range, after-tax profits dropped to an average of $300,000 per year. The period was characterized by constant changes in business as customers were either gained from or lost to competition. During this period, Happy Grove lost its two largest customers, Smudt's Supermarkets and Kroger. Both instituted private-label milk programs. The distribution of Happy Grove's business on January 1, 1990, is illustrated in Table 2.

As Table 2 shows, Happy Grove's total retail count had dropped by over 200 stores. In terms of distribution, 28 percent of the large customer stores accounted for 77 percent of total milk volume. What is perhaps even more significant is the fact that one customer, Good's Supermarket, provided 28 percent of Happy Grove's total dairy volume.

In 1989, dairy operations had a gross volume of $11.2 million and profits of $265,000, or 2.4 percent of sales. The nature of operation was, for the most part, to deliver directly to retail stores on an every-other-day basis. With few exceptions, dairy products were delivered to a back-room storage area. Retail stocking was the responsibility of retail store personnel. However, Happy Grove did maintain a detail sales force to ensure that retail store managers in larger stores displayed their product properly in the dairy cases. A significant problem that Happy Grove experienced in the late 1980s was a sharp increase in accounts receivable. On January 1, 1990, overall accounts receivable amounted to $589,916, compared to a total of $319,400 on January 1, 1989. For the most part, the increase of $270,516 was concentrated in large accounts of customers who generally paid on the first and fifteenth of each month regardless of volume purchases.

THE GOOD'S SUPERMARKETS NEGOTIATION

In review of the Good's situation, Jack Rowland was well aware that 28 percent of Happy Grove's total milk volume was sold to the thirty-eight member stores of the retail cooperative. Happy Grove's specific volume to Good's stores in 1989 was $3.136 million. The total sales consisted of a full line of dairy products. However, the majority of the volume was in 1-gallon and half-gallon cartons of various milk products.

As a standard practice, Happy Grove delivered milk to thirty stores on an every-

TABLE 3   HAPPY GROVE DAIRY COST AND SELLING PRICE TO GOOD'S SUPERMARKET

	Total processing	Ingredients	Total dock	Delivery	Sales	Total	Price
Gallons	$.361	$.913	$1.274	$.163	$.036	$1.473	$1.49
Half-gallons	$.175	$.456	$ .631	$.081	$.018	$ .730	$ .75

other-day basis. The remaining stores were larger, and delivery was required on a daily basis. While Happy Grove felt that such frequent delivery constituted outstanding customer service, the managers of Good's Supermarkets felt that the frequency of delivery created unnecessary work for the stores' personnel. However, Happy Grove trucks were not sufficiently large to handle larger shipment sizes. Despite the difference of opinion regarding desired frequency and size of shipment, all agreed that Happy Grove's current practice resulted in a consistently fresh supply of all dairy products.

In terms of Happy Grove's accounts receivable balance, Good's account represented 50 percent of all accounts outstanding, or just under $300,000. This year-end balance was close to Good's average outstanding accounts receivable total over the year. However, the balance had not changed out of proportion to Good's purchases over the past few years. Jack figured it cost Happy Grove approximately $30,000 per year to finance Good's accounts receivable.

Because of purchase volume, Good's stores were buying at the lowest delivered price offered by Happy Grove Dairies. Table 3 provides Happy Grove's cost and selling price to Good's.

As Jack reviewed the figures, it was clear that Happy Grove had little if any margin to offer Good's in the form of a straight price reduction. Based upon Joe's call, he was aware that Farmer's Cooperative was offering Good's a price of $1.45 per gallon and $.72 per half-gallon. Jack was sure that Joe was not bluffing about Farmer's offer. Jack and Joe had done business for a number of years without a formal contract. The relationship had always been on a good and fair basis.

As Jack planned for the Thursday meeting, he was well aware he couldn't meet Farmer's prices if Happy Grove continued to perform all services in the current manner. He reviewed the deal being offered by Farmer's Cooperative Dairy and tried to appraise his alternatives and the relative power of Happy Grove's negotiating position.

QUESTIONS

1 How have changes in the consumer and retail market over time forced Jack Rowland to reevaluate the strategic position of Happy Grove Dairy?

2 How has Happy Grove modified its marketing and logistics channels to accommodate these changes?

3 What alternatives can Jack formulate for distributing milk to Good's Supermarkets?

4 What would you recommend to Jack?

CASE 2-5: Williams Institutional Food Company

In July 1990, Jack Jones and Bill Williams were discussing the latest computer print-out of sales results for Williams Institutional Food Company. After some time, Jack said:

> Bill, the Vacation Motel restaurants are still keeping our total gross margin too low. Even though we need an average gross margin of about 15 percent to break even, we get only about 10 percent on our sales to their restaurants. If you look at the sales of products under the Vacation brand name, we are in even worse shape. We get only about 8 percent margin on those items. Now that they are pressuring us to expand our territory and service more of their restaurants, I think it's time we seriously evaluate the entire Vacation Motel program.

COMPANY BACKGROUND

Although Williams was founded in the 1930s as a meat processor catering to the retail grocery trade, many changes had occurred by 1990. Williams no longer processed any meat items, having phased out this aspect of the business of operation in the 1960s. In addition, the retail grocery trade in its market area had become so dominated by national and regional chains and local cooperatives that the firm shifted its customer focus to institutional and industrial markets. Recognition of this shift in customers was formalized in 1965 when the name of the firm was officially changed from Williams Sausage Company to Williams Institutional Food Company (WIFCO). By 1986, WIFCO was the second largest independent institutional food distributor in its market, with a sales volume of approximately $35 million in that year.

As an institutional food distributor, WIFCO's customer base included such outlets as restaurants, cafeterias, hospitals, schools, colleges, and industrial plants with in-house feeding facilities. The company carried a complete product line of dry, canned, refrigerated, and frozen food items to meet the needs of these customers. The product line consisted of approximately 2500 items. The only items WIFCO did not carry that customers normally needed were fresh produce and paper products. These items were not sold by most other institutional distributors but were available to customers from several special-line wholesalers.

WIFCO management felt that the company had an excellent reputation among the institutional trade, based on its quality products, honesty and fairness in dealing with customers and competitors, and emphasis on customer service. WIFCO sales personnel were expected to be more than simply order-takers. They were expected to acquire sufficient knowledge about products to advise their customers on which particular product would be best for use in a particular situation. They were also expected to learn each customer's business to be able to make suggestions concerning changes in the menu and new items that might be appropriate for use. Sales personnel were expected to handle any problems in serving the customer and any complaints that arose.

WIFCO also undertook other methods to increase its customer service. The company made every effort to avoid stock-outs of any item in inventory. Whenever stock-outs did occur, employees who loaded the trucks were instructed to substitute, whenever possible, an item that could best serve the customer's needs. If the substituted product was higher in price, the customer was charged only for the product originally ordered. Efforts had also been made to upgrade service by improving the efficiency of truck drivers. For a short period of time, drivers had been offered an incentive plan by which the customer was allowed to judge the quality of the driver's service and conduct. Sales personnel distributed cards to selected customers (whose identify was unknown to the drivers), and when the customer felt the driver had performed adequately and demonstrated a desire to serve the customer, the card would be given to the driver. The driver returned this card to the company and received $20. In addition, a list was kept showing how many cards each driver had received, and this became a matter of great pride to the drivers.

COMPETITIVE SITUATION

There were several institutional distributors in the area, two of which were members of controlled-label cooperatives. Most of their products were purchased through a cooperative which was responsible for having the products manufactured under the appropriate label. These two distributors handled the Nugget and Pleezing brand products. Several other distributors in the area were, like WIFCO, independent distributors. These independent distributors sold products packed under their own brand names. All distributors, both independent and controlled-label, also sold national brand items. WIFCO, for example, carried a complete line of Hunt-Wesson and Pillsbury products. WIFCO was the second largest distributor in the area; another independent distributor was the largest. However, WIFCO executives felt that their recent growth rate had considerably closed the gap between the two, and they hoped to be the largest soon. They felt that their reputation developed in recent years would be instrumental to this growth.

Competition was also entering from another source. Amalgamated Grocers of Alabama had recently established an institutional division. Within a few months this firm had been able to establish a strong position in the institutional market. Amalgamated Grocers had not made an attempt to compete in service with other distributors, but its strong financial position in the retail market had allowed the company to compete by selling at very low prices.

The 1960s and 1970s saw the failure of several small food distributors in the area. As these companies went out of business, the other distributors had taken the customers from the failed companies and increased their own sales. It looked as if this trend would continue until there would be only two or three major distributors left in the area. In the summer of 1983, the Vacation Motel Food Sales Division of the Vacation Motel Corporation (VM) had been looking for a new food distributor in central Alabama. Under its proposal, Vacation Motel would grant exclusive rights to distribute merchandise under the VM label to all restaurants owned by Vacation Motel in the distributor's area. Approximately half of all Vacation Motel restaurants were company-owned, while the rest were franchised to independent operators. The managers of the company-owned restaurants were required to buy all merchandise available under the VM label from the VM distributor in the area. For example, the managers had to purchase VM catsup only; they could not purchase other brands. It was estimated that merchandise under the VM label would account for 60 percent of a restaurant's food purchases. The distributor, on the other hand, was expected to maintain a complete inventory of VM merchandise that was purchased through the Vacation Motel Food Sales Division. Vacation Motel Food Sales issued a price list each month for all products. This price list showed the distributor's cost and the price at which to sell to the restaurants. The distributor had no discretion in this area. Products under the VM label included many meats, frozen and canned fruits and vegetables, seafood, poultry, desserts, prepared entrees, and portion-packed dry products. If restaurant managers desired items that were not included on the price list, they were free to deal with any distributor.

WIFCO decided to accept this program for distribution to the five company-owned inns in Birmingham. It was estimated that sales to these inns would be approximately $100,000 per month in VM products. Vacation Motel also asked that WIFCO take over distribution to inns located in Hattiesburg, Mississippi; Dauphin Island, Alabama; and Destin, Florida. These represented sales of $125,000 to $150,000 per month in VM products. Although WIFCO did not operate in those areas at that time, there had previously been much discussion about the feasibility of hiring sales personnel to develop those territories. It was decided that WIFCO could use the Vacation Motels as a sales base to justify hiring a new person to further develop the territories. The management therefore decided to serve these inns.

Adoption of the VM program also created some problems for WIFCO. First of all, Bill Williams wondered about the inventory that would be necessary to fully serve the inns. Although there was enough space at that time to accommodate the inventory, it was expected that within a few years normal growth of the company would utilize this space. Especially critical was room in the 10,000-square-foot freezer. The program necessitated that the company duplicate many products under the VM label that were already available under the WIFCO label or some other label. The initial inventory required to begin deliveries to the restaurants required an investment of approximately $750,000, which was about one-half the company's present inventory.

During the next two years the VM program was revised many times, with most changes involving minor additions and deletions from the product line. In April 1985, however, the program underwent an extensive modification. Vacation Motel Food Services decided to eliminate almost one-half of the products under the VM label. These products were primarily the canned and frozen fruits and vegetables that accounted for a great deal of the physical space used. However, the products accounting for the largest dollar volume, the meat items, were retained.

MARGIN ON THE SALES

Table 1 shows a breakdown of margins allowed on VM products by product group versus the margins obtained by WIFCO on similar items with other brand names. Although the VM program guaranteed the distributor a large volume of sales, the gross margin allowed was very low. When the management of WIFCO accepted the program, it had hoped that the company would also be able to distribute noncompeting

TABLE 1   AVERAGE MARGINS ALLOWED ON VACATION MOTEL
PRODUCTS VERSUS NORMAL DISTRIBUTOR MARGINS

Product category	Margin allowed (percent)	Normal distributor margins (percent)
Processed meats	6	18
Red meats	5	20
Frozen foods	12	18
Seafood	12	18
Desserts	12	16
Frozen entrees	10	18
Nonfrozen foods	10	14
Coffee and tea	6	14

products to these inns. The margin on these products varied considerably, but it averaged from 16 to 18 percent. Thus, Williams believed that the overall margin on total sales to the inns could be raised to approximately 14 percent. However, competitive pressures had not allowed this. Competitors were cutting their prices to get a share of the VM business. Also, restaurant managers who were required to purchase over half their merchandise from WIFCO were reluctant to concentrate the remainder of their business with this one supplier. There was some resentment on the managers' part that they had no discretion in purchasing many of their items. Thus, although WIFCO's total sales to Vacation Motels were $350,000 to $400,000 per month, over 80 percent of these sales were in VM products, which had a very low margin (see Table 2).

SALES COSTS

WIFCO sales personnel were compensated on the basis of their gross margin on sales. Although they had a guaranteed salary per month, they were expected, and usually were able, to earn more by their commissions. Sales personnel were guaranteed $2000 per month. Each month the company received a computer report showing each salesperson's gross margin for the month. The company took 25 percent of this gross margin and deducted $10 for each delivery the salesperson had accounted for during that month. The purpose of this deduction was to encourage sales representatives to seek larger orders rather than numerous small orders. If the result was greater than $2000, sales personnel received the difference as additional pay to their guaranteed salary. Otherwise, they received the $2000.

DELIVERY EXPENSE

WIFCO leased all its delivery trucks from one company. The leasing firm charged a flat fee of $1110 per week, plus $5 per hour on the refrigeration unit for each hour it was running, plus $.40 per mile. The drivers and other hourly personnel were paid an average of $8 per hour.

TABLE 2   SAMPLE OF VACATION MOTEL INVOICES DURING A TYPICAL WEEK

Invoice number	VM amount	Other	Total	Percent VM
10765	$3,206.80	$ 707.00	$ 3,913.80	81.9
10766	4,178.90	551.40	4,730.30	88.3
10875	2,367.60	433.10	2,800.70	84.5
10901	2,970.00	582.00	3,552.00	83.6
10922	3,442.00	761.10	4,203.10	81.9
10934	1,526.70	176.00	1,702.70	89.7
10956	3,735.30	756.50	4,491.80	83.2
10974	4,982.00	5,661.80	10,643.80	46.8
11002	4,071.80	579.10	4,650.90	87.5
11015	7,097.30	1,971.90	9,069.20	78.3
11036	8,429.50	2,583.80	11,013.30	76.5
11051	5,574.50	449.00	6,023.50	92.6
11078	3,652.20	—	3,652.20	100.0
11079	5,466.30	—	5,466.30	100.0
11091	7,769.00	1,318.70	9,087.70	85.5
11094	4,070.20	950.60	5,020.80	81.1

DISTRIBUTION TO VACATION MOTELS

After the acceptance of the VM program, WIFCO decided to hire a salesperson to work in the northeastern Florida and southern Mississippi areas. By June 1985, this territory developed to the point that sales were approximately $400,000 per month. About half these sales were to Vacation Motels in the area. Deliveries were made to this territory three times per week, and total mileage required for the trucks was approximately 1900 miles. Deliveries to Mississippi covered 700 miles and the driver was expected to make the trip in one day. The trip usually required that the driver be paid for twenty-four hours. The delivery into the Mobile area required 550 miles and took about twenty hours. The trucks were usually empty on the return trip, which accounted for 40 percent of the time involved, and the refrigeration units were shut off.

Between 1983 and 1990, Vacation Motel Food Sales had added several inns to WIFCO's area of coverage. Although these inns could be covered with existing drivers and sales personnel, they did add to the inventory problem. By June 1990, WIFCO had an inventory of about $1 million tied up in VM products, in spite of the fact that the number of products had been reduced considerably. The program had thus far necessitated the addition of one new truck to serve the new territories. The plant manager estimated that the increased workload had accounted for the hiring of two hourly workers—one to unload shipments from manufacturers during the day and one to load WIFCO trucks on the night shift.

PROPOSAL TO SERVE GEORGIA

In July 1990, the Vacation Motel Food Service requested that WIFCO take over deliveries to four restaurants in Georgia. At the time, WIFCO was not operating in that territory. The four inns represented a combined sales potential of approximately $70,000 per month on VM products. It would be necessary to make deliveries to these inns once each week. The estimated round-trip distance on the route was 650 miles and would be twenty-four hours' time for the driver. It was believed that WIFCO's sales supervisor could call on these accounts periodically but that, in most cases, the orders would be taken by telephone. The divisional vice president of Vacation Motel's Food Sales Division indicated that if WIFCO refused to deliver to the restaurants in Georgia, VM might look for another distributor to undertake the entire program for its restaurants in Alabama, Florida, Mississippi, and Georgia.

Since the adoption of the VM program, WIFCO executives had questioned the profitability of delivering to the inns. However, no one had ever undertaken an in-depth analysis of the program. The proposal to take the four inns in Georgia caused them to seriously reconsider the entire Vacation Motel program. They knew that the program had provided several benefits to WIFCO. In addition to providing increased sales to Vacation Motels, the fact that the firm was a distributor for Vacation Motel had been a successful selling tool in approaching other customers. The sales base provided by Vacation Motels had also been very useful in opening new territories, especially in the case of the Florida–Mississippi route. However, the low margins, increased inventory, and other operating expenses caused WIFCO executives to question the desirability of the program. They had considered alternatives such as pressuring Vacation Motel Food Sales to increase distributor margins or to require that restaurant managers purchase non-VM items from WIFCO. Finally, WIFCO management wondered how to respond to the threat by Vacation Motels to terminate its program if WIFCO refused to open the Georgia territory.

QUESTIONS

1 Diagram the distribution channel for VM food products. What elements of this channel make it different from distribution channels for other institutional food products?
2 Perform a profitability analysis of the proposal to serve the VM restaurants in Georgia.
3 What criteria would you suggest be used in the evaluation of this alternative?
4 What would you recommend to Bill Williams?

PART **THREE**

CHANNEL DEVELOPMENT
AND MANAGEMENT

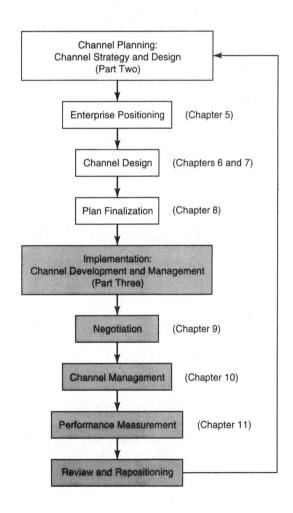

The final three steps involved in developing an effective channel strategy relate to various aspects of implementation. They are: (1) Negotiation; (2) Channel Management; and (3) Performance Measurement. Implementation is the topic of Part III.

NEGOTIATION

The establishment of a channel is typically the product of negotiation between potential participants. In many situations the parties to a negotiation are a combination of primary and specialized participants. Channel negotiation is a unique form or subset of the broad spectrum of bargaining. A basic feature of marketing negotiation is that it tends to focus on problem solving as contrasted to share bargaining. The more relational the proposed channel arrangement the greater the attention devoted to problem solving during the negotiation process. Channel negotiation is the topic of Chapter Nine.

CHANNEL MANAGEMENT

Channels, similar to firms, require continuous management. The extent to which a channel is, in fact, managed will be directly related to how clear cut the member's perceptions are concerning interorganizational dependency and leadership.

Similar to all forms of organized behavior problems can be expected to arise in even the most stable channel situations. Understanding the most common causes of conflict and developing methods of resolution are critical aspects of channel management. Extended enterprise management is the topic of Chapter Ten.

PERFORMANCE MEASUREMENT

A final aspect of distribution strategy is accurate channel performance measurement. The anticipated result of performance assessment is the identification of ways to improve existing distribution arrangements. The need to change structure from time to time renders channel planning and implementing a dynamic change management process. Performance assessment is the topic of Chapter Eleven.

CHAPTER **9**

CHAPTER

NEGOTIATION

CHAPTER OUTLINE

NEGOTIATION IN MARKETING
   Negotiation Process
   Negotiation Framework
   Conclusion: Negotiation in Marketing

NEGOTIATION STRATEGY
   Scope of Channel Negotiation
   Prerequisites for Negotiation

POWER IN NEGOTIATION
   Power-Dependence Relationships
   Sources of Power
   Conclusion: Channel Power

CHANNEL NEGOTIATION PROCESS
   Transaction Negotiation
   Operational Negotiation
   Conclusion: Negotiation Process

SUMMARY

Previous chapters developed the economic, behavioral, and legal settings within which channel arrangements are formulated. Although all firms may desire to be totally self-sufficient, none can achieve this goal. Even the largest industrial and marketing organizations require extensive working arrangements with customers, suppliers, and vendors. The management process by which distribution channels are created and, over time, dissolved is *interorganizational negotiation.*

Interorganizational negotiation is defined as *the management process of reaching*

285

agreement about which activities a firm will perform and how it will benefit from a marketing channel arrangement. Negotiation is a form of cooperative behavior in which participants agree to specified duties and rewards prior to actual performance. For example, when a retailer agrees to stock a specific manufacturer's product line, interorganizational negotiation will usually precede a final commitment. Important matters to be negotiated will usually include price, discounts, delivery terms, promotional allowances, cooperative advertising, and other aspects of the marketing mix.

Negotiation of marketing arrangements is a key managerial process. In this chapter, a comprehensive review of the negotiation process serves as a bridge from strategy and design issues to the process of channel management. The first section introduces the importance of negotiation in the formation of channel arrangements. To set the stage, the process and framework of marketing-based negotiation is reviewed. Next, attention is directed to selected aspects of negotiation strategy. The third section provides in-depth coverage of power and dependence relationships. Commonly accepted sources of power are reviewed and positioned with respect to applicability in marketing channel negotiation. The final section discusses specific negotiation objectives related to transactional and operational considerations.

NEGOTIATION IN MARKETING

Alderson discussed the origin of the term *negotiation* and its essential application to business:

> The word "negotiation" has an interesting history in relation to business. The term for business in the Latin language is *negocio.* This word is related in its original significance to the word "negation." In classical times anyone who was in government or the army, in philosophy or the arts, had a recognized occupation. Businessmen were not engaged in any of these recognized occupations, so they were regarded as occupied with negotiating—in other words, doing nothing.[1]

Negotiation—once thought of as the occupation of doing nothing—is now viewed as the main process by which the resources of two or more organizations are aligned in a business arrangement. It is the process by which economic values and the activities that each business will perform are specified. Through the negotiation process a firm positions itself in one or more channel arrangements. Thus, negotiation is viewed as the key process in formulation of channel strategy.

Within limits, each firm in the overall marketing system is free to choose the specific channel arrangements it seeks to develop and perpetuate. The prerogative to initiate negotiation can be exercised by any firm in the marketing channel independently of relative size or power. Likewise, all firms have the right *not* to negotiate. Over the course of a year, thousands of business organizations may seek to establish marketing arrangements with a large retailer such as Dayton-Hudson. Even without examining specifics, Dayton-Hudson's management may reject offers to initiate negotiation with a majority of those firms. Similarly, a relatively small firm may reject an

---

[1] Wroe Alderson, *Marketing Behavior and Executive Action,* Homewood, IL: Irwin, 1957, p. 130.

offer from Dayton-Hudson to negotiate contract manufacturing because of fear of overcommitment to one organization and potential loss of autonomy. With interorganizational negotiation, it is important to realize from the outset that participation is a form of *self-resolution* on the part of all involved firms. Once the negotiation process begins, it becomes dynamic and develops a track record. Following initial negotiation, future self-resolution is clouded by the history of commitments and performance.

Negotiation Process

The fundamental need to negotiate results from the high degree of mutual dependence that develops among channel members as they each pursue their independent business objectives. A marketing channel negotiation is properly classified as a value-based process. Firms engaged in negotiation are not obligated to make a deal. If the negotiation ends in deadlock, then the potential channel arrangement will not materialize. While power is an important aspect of marketing negotiations, the goals of the participating organizations must be such that they will benefit from the synergism of the jointly conducting business. In other words, the ideal negotiation process is driven by a problem-solving synergy. Perhaps more than any other feature, problem-solving negotiation serves to differentiate marketing from labor bargaining.

The marketing negotiation process requires leadership. While the overall process of channel leadership is fully developed in Chapter 10, it is of particular importance in marketing negotiations. During the negotiation process, prospective channel members must gain a common vision or perception of reality, the context in which joint operations are being structured, and expectations concerning their participation. The role of leaders during negotiation is to guide prospective participants to a mutually satisfactory solution.

Despite the cooperative nature of marketing negotiation, the process of reaching agreement requires that all parties try to ''negotiate'' the best possible arrangement for their own organizations. Thus, deadlocks can be expected to occur along the road to agreement. A negotiation leader's role can be considered to be the process managing of a series of issue-based deadlocks to a mutually satisfactory conclusion.

The discussion that follows tends to focus on the unique features of marketing negotiation as opposed to specific negotiation tactics; however, keep in mind that the process is among people—computers do not negotiate. The ultimate success of the marketing arrangement may well rest on the feelings and relationships that emerge among participants during the negotiation process. The personal relationships over time may prove to be the lifeblood of the arrangement.

Negotiation Framework

Negotiations are typically classified as either new or mature.

New Channel Negotiation   New channel negotiation is characterized by lack of experience—that is, no business track record exists between the negotiating organizations. The objective of the negotiation may be a one-time transaction or the formation of an ongoing channel relationship. In either case, parties to a new negotiation have limited or no history of commitments or performance to draw upon in evaluating the business agreement.

In totally new channels, initial negotiation is typically driven by the need to establish selling and buying transactions. Such negotiations must stipulate conditions for ownership transfer. In many situations, the ownership-transfer price may be the least difficult aspect to negotiate. The unprecedented wheat deal between the U.S.S.R. and the United States in 1976 was a prime example of a one-time-only new channel negotiation. As a deal materializes, issues that become difficult to resolve tend to involve operations—for example, the timing of ownership transfer and how transportation will be performed.

In contrast, when two firms negotiate a franchise agreement, the process may be simple, involving limited variations to the standard agreement. If an individual wishes to franchise and operate a McDonald's restaurant, terms and conditions under which the agreement will be structured will be specified far in advance of the actual negotiation. McDonald's, like most organizations offering a strong franchise, insists upon standardization concerning almost every phase of the proposed operation. The primary subject of negotiation in such situations is the financial and managerial qualification of the potential franchisee.

In these two illustrations, commitments resulting from the negotiation range from a one-time deal to a long-term relationship. New negotiations typically involve several stages of agreement and commitment prior to finalization of a deal. If the new negotiation results in repeat transactions, the business arrangement will soon evolve into a mature negotiation. If the negotiation covers a single transaction, the business arrangement ends once all terms and conditions are satisfied. Of course, future negotiations between the involved parties will be framed in terms of previous experience. The significant advantage of a new channel negotiation is that an interruption or time gap between deals provides the involved parties with the opportunity to frame a new structure without obligation to previous arrangements. In essence, the firm is once again in the position of self-resolution with respect to future deals.

Mature Channel Negotiation   Mature channel negotiation takes place between organizations that have ongoing relationships that require modification. In certain situations, contracts will require routine renegotiation prior to expiration. For example, a tool and die shop may have a contract with Chysler for the 1991 model year. Both Chrysler and the tool shop may expect to extend for future years, but each renewal requires renegotiation. Beyond routine renewal negotiations, the most common types of mature negotiation are necessitated by: (1) changing balance of relative power, (2) conflict resolution, and (3) termination. Each is discussed and illustrated.

It can be expected that members of a channel of distribution will, over time, experience a relative change in power. Thus, one form of mature negotiation may reflect repositioning of an ongoing business arrangement. A prime example of changing balance of power has been the restructuring of channels to reflect the rapid growth of large retailers. Because of size and market power, suppliers dealing with retailing giants such as K mart are often required to make substantial modifications in their traditional methods of operation. At one time a supplier may have shipped products directly to individual K mart stores. However, due to increased volume, K mart may prefer larger shipments of select merchandise items to be distributed through distribution warehouses. For other items, they may desire to retain direct store delivery. The switch back and forth from direct store delivery to warehouse redistribution typically requires negotiation of items such as price, delivery schedule, freight payment terms, discounts, and other important aspects of the total transaction. Accommodation of a changing relative power position within an existing channel is a common form of mature negotiation. Both parties to the negotiation plan to continue the channel relationship unless the desired day-to-day adjustments become matters of substantial conflict.

Another form of mature channel negotiation can result from the development of conflict.[2] Conflict resolution is only a matter of degree of emphasis when viewed in comparison to routine power adjustments. When conflict erupts, continuation of the channel may be in jeopardy. The actual event creating the conflict may or may not be the real issue. For example, one member may seek realignment of channel structure or functional relationship without full cooperation of the other. Depending upon the propensity of the parties to negotiate and compromise their traditional positions, the original channel arrangement may ultimately be either modified or terminated.[3]

The final form of mature channel negotiation is termination of an agreement. In most terminations, the conflict between channel members has become dysfunctional. The typical termination requires that many issues be resolved. The degree to which a termination can be administered on a mutually satisfactory basis depends upon each firm's perception of how fairly it has been treated by the other party during the time the channel arrangement was operative. To whatever extent possible, it is desirable to resolve business arrangements in a way that permits possible reconstruction of the relationship in the future if and when deemed desirable. An example of such reconciliation is Apple Computer and Computerland's recent agreement to restructure their channel arrangement.[4] In the early stages of PC industry growth, Apple and Computerland combined to develop one of the most effective distribution channels in the industry. Conflict that developed over Computerland's decision to also distribute IBM PCs eventually became dysfunctional. The result of considerable negotiation was that Computerland dissolved the channel agreement. From the viewpoint of some of the individual franchises of Computerland, not having Apple products was a serious marketing impediment. To resolve their competitive dilemma, some retailers obtained Apple products, without authorization from Computerland. The situation developed to the point that Computerland decided to reverse its previous termination decision, and it negotiated a new channel agreement with Apple. When terminations occur, it is wise to keep the door open for possible reconciliation.

---

[2] Conflict development and resolution is developed in greater detail in Chapter 10, pp. 323–336.

[3] Howard Raiffa, *The Art and Science of Negotiation,* Cambridge, MA: Harvard University Press, Belknap Division, 1982.

[4] Kenneth G. Hardy and Allan J. Magrath, *Marketing Channel Management,* Glenview, IL: Scott, Foresman, 1988, pp. 531–534.

Termination negotiation can range from a relatively peaceful settlement to an extensive legal battle, depending upon each party's perception of the other party's obligation. The negotiability of a termination varies with each situation. Most termination negotiations require extended time before a full settlement can be reached. An increasingly popular feature of strategic alliances is to negotiate a termination framework as a feature of the original agreement. The idea is not to doom the agreement to eventual failure by preoccupation with dissolution. Rather, at the time that commitments are being made and risks that each party is agreeing to assume are being negotiated, the timing is ideal to position the procedure and "what if" issues of potential termination.

Conclusion: Negotiation in Marketing

It should be clear from the above discussion that many different types of negotiation are a regular part of marketing channel management. The fact that most business agreements are performed in a channel context makes negotiation critical in the formulation of distribution arrangement. From a strategic viewpoint, a clear distinction can be made between new and mature channel negotiation. The actual negotiation may focus on environmental, structural or functional concerns. Negotiation can be expected to proceed differently, depending on whether it is new or mature. The stake involved in each situation is substantially different. The next section deals with the strategy of channel negotiation.

NEGOTIATION STRATEGY

When approaching a channel negotiation, each party has at least a vague idea of what they feel would constitute an ideal arrangement. The fundamental objective of negotiation is to stimulate joint opportunity. In situations other than single-transaction negotiations, the expectation is that the agreement will result in a form of routinized or expected behavior beneficial for all parties.[5] Thus, the uncertainty inherent in an initial marketing situation is to a degree replaced by articulation and negotiation of each party's expectations. Strategic negotiation is a form of cooperative behavior wherein participants first prescribe each individual's share in the output of the economic activity and then decide what action is required from each.[6] Thus, negotiation leads to agreement, which serves to reduce the anticipatory nature and related risk of the distribution process. In this section attention is directed to the scope of negotiable actions and the prerequisites to successful negotiation.

Scope of Channel Negotiation

There are five types of actions that describe the range of bargaining activities.

Share bargaining. The process by which opponents share or ration the settlement range. If one gets more, the other gets less.

[5] See Chapter 10, pp. 309–311.
[6] John L. Graham, "A Theory of Interorganizational Negotiations," in *Research In Marketing,* Greenwich, CT: JAI Press, 1987, pp. 163–183.

Problem solving. The process by which both parties work together to solve joint problems. In this process both parties gain.

Attitudinal bargaining. The process by which a mutually workable attitudinal relationship is developed to facilitate negotiation.

In-group bargaining. The process by which a negotiator bargains with members of his or her own team and decision-making group to derive attainable organizational objectives.

Personal bargaining. The process by which a negotiator makes a behavioral choice involving conflicting personal needs and goals.[7]

All the above types of bargaining are important in the formulation of channel relationships. The most common are negotiations directed toward share bargaining and problem solving. As will be illustrated, many negotiated channel arrangements do in fact result in synergism. As a general rule, new channel negotiation is characterized by a significant degree of share bargaining. The more mature the negotiation situation, the greater likelihood it will be characterized by joint problem solving.

While reviewing the scope of channel negotiations, remember that the process has the primary objective of identifying and establishing the way that business will be conducted. Unlike labor bargaining, the parties in marketing negotiation are not typically cast in adversarial roles.

Prerequisites for Negotiation

Four characteristics are necessary for successful channel negotiation to occur. Unless the following characteristics are present during the negotiation process, a satisfactory compromise is unlikely.

First, parties to the negotiation must have alternative courses of action. Availability of alternatives is important in both new and mature channel negotiations. Unless alternatives exist, no effective balance of power will be available to guide the negotiating process. Second, to arrive at an effective agreement, the involved parties must establish credible rules or procedures to guide negotiation. In essence, this form of prenegotiation agreement constitutes a form of attitudinal bargaining. Unless each party fully understands the ground rules, successful negotiation will be difficult. Third, to engage in effective negotiation the parties must be in a position to exchange benefits or rewards. If a retailer wants a drug wholesaler to preprice selected merchandise, the retailer must be willing to offer some form of incentive. The incentive offered by the retailer in such a situation could range from direct payment for the value-added service to an agreement to feature and promote the wholesaler's product line. The capability of both parties to grant rewards is essential to the negotiation process. Finally, each party to a negotiation must be willing to commit. The entire process of marketing negotiation is based upon a willingness of the negotiating parties to assume roles or positions in a distribution relationship.

[7] Chester L. Karrass, *The Negotiating Game,* New York: World Publishing Company/Times Mirror, 1970, Chapter 11; Richard E. Walton and Robert B. McKersie, *A Behavioral Theory of Labor Negotiations,* New York: McGraw-Hill, 1965.

The four prerequisites—alternatives, rules and procedures, reward capability, and commitment—are essential to good-faith marketing negotiation. In single-transaction or free-flow negotiations, many of the prerequisites are tested by the parties involved. If each party is satisfied, the free-flow arrangement may evolve into an extended behavioral relationship in which each party has expectations and confidence that the other will perform. Mature channel negotiation initiates from the foundation of expectation and confidence based upon past experience. Regardless of whether negotiation is centered on a new or mature situation, each party must formulate a negotiation strategy.

POWER IN NEGOTIATION

From a strategic viewpoint, power assessment is a critical aspect of negotiation. The objective of this section is to expand development of interorganizational negotiation strategy by examining the impact of relative power. Attention is focused upon the concept of power—how it is obtained and how it is utilized in a marketing negotiation. In Chapter 10, the complex and interrelated nature of power and conflict are examined in terms of leadership and channel management.

Many definitions of power exist. In the social sciences, power is usually defined as the ability to get someone to do something that would not otherwise be done.[8] An alternative is to view power as the ability to induce change.[9] Power in a distribution channel is the ability of one channel member to influence or alter the decisions of other channel members.[10] For example, a manufacturer has power over wholesalers and retailers to the extent that marketing decisions of those firms can be influenced. If the retailer changes a product's shelf position in response to a manufacturer's request, power has been exercised. It is important to understand the factors that cause a specific firm to have power.

Power-Dependence Relationships

Power in channel negotiation depends upon the degree of perceived dependence that exists among participants. The concept of mutual dependence implies that, to some degree, each channel member is in a position to facilitate or to hinder the goal attainment of one or more members.[11] Emerson described mutual dependence as:

> The dependence of actor A upon actor B is (1) directly related to A's motivational investment in goals mediated by B, and (2) inversely proportional to the availability of those goals to A outside of the A-B relation.

---

[8] James G. March, "An Introduction to the Theory and Measurement of Influence," *American Political Science Review,* 1955, p. 434.

[9] Michael Levey and Dwight Grant, "Financial Terms of Sale and Control of Marketing Channel Conflict," *Journal of Marketing Research,* **17**:4 November 1980, pp. 524–530.

[10] Punam Anand and Louis W. Stern, "A Sociopsychological Explanation for Why Marketing Channel Members Relinquish Control," *Journal of Marketing Research,* **22**:4 November 1985, pp. 365–376. For practical applications, see Roger A. Dickerson and Anthony Herbst, "What Retailers Should Know about Discount Rates," *Retail Control,* September 1983, pp. 43–50.

[11] Richard Emerson, "Power-Dependence Relations," *American Sociological Review,* February 1962, p. 32.

A very broad meaning can be attached to the term "goal." Goals may be either tangible gratifications consciously sought or unconscious psychological satisfactions that are obtained from a relationship. By "mediation," Emerson is referring to one party's ability to influence another party's capability to satisfy goals. "Motivational investment" refers to the strength of the desire to achieve a goal.

These definitions help explain how a marketing channel functions. Channel members enter into an arrangement because they are unable to efficiently perform all the functions necessary to achieve their goals. To the extent that a firm has established its goals and can only identify limited alternatives, it will be extremely dependent upon other firms. As a result, other channel members will be able to influence and perhaps change the decisions and behavior of the dependent firm. For example, in the retail industry it is common for each geographic market area to contain a few large brokers who have well-established ties with discount and department store buyers in the area. A new manufacturer desiring market penetration would be well advised to arrange representation by one of these established brokers. For the manufacturer, the alternatives are few and the goal is clear. Because of the manufacturer's dependence, brokers may be able to exert considerable influence upon the relationship. Conversely, a well-known manufacturer may be able to exert considerable influence over brokers due to brand acceptance by consumers.

A number of important concepts emerge from viewing channel power as a function of dependence. The first is the idea of power advantage. Each channel member possesses some degree of relative power. Rarely, if ever, does one channel member have complete power. When channel negotiations are being planned, it is important to focus upon the relative degree of power and the extent to which one participant holds an advantage.

The second important concept concerns power perceptions. Power is not necessarily observable in all interactions among channel members. It often exists only as a potential force to be utilized when and where needed. The effectiveness of potential power depends upon how it is perceived by others. A wholesaler may not perceive the power advantage held by the manufacturer and therefore may not cooperate with a manufacturer's program. The result could be serious conflict. On the other hand, it is quite possible to perceive that a firm holds more power than it actually does. In such situations, the firm perceived to hold power will be able to influence the decisions of the others. The perceptions, in a sense, become self-fulfilling prophecies. If a retailer *thinks* a manufacturer is powerful, the retailer will act as if the manufacturer *does* have that power. The importance of perceptions is critical in negotiation.

The third important concept is that power is limited both in scope and in domain. *Limited scope* means that the issues or decisions a channel member can influence are limited. A manufacturer may be able to exert considerable influence over a retailer's advertising but will have little influence on store location or layout. The scope of power depends upon the relative advantage or power balance between channel members and circumstances of a particular situation. A retailer may be susceptible to a manufacturer's attempts to regulate pricing, but government regulations may prevent any direct effort on the part of the manufacturer. Recently, General Electric (GE) tried to encourage dealers to offer $50 off on specific appliances. In national television advertising, GE stated that the discount would be offered only by "participating dealers." In this case, GE could not force dealer participation but, as the manufacturer, it clearly used power when publicly announcing the discount.

The concept of limited domain refers to the fact that power is limited with respect to the number of parties over whom it may be exercised. In a distribution channel, the manufacturer may exert control over retailers but not over wholesalers. Or, some retailers in the system may be influenced by the manufacturer while others may not. Domain, then, may be considered to include only those firms over which a power advantage is enjoyed.

Sources of Power

The primary foundation for channel power is mutual dependence. Firms in a distribution channel can influence each others' goal attainment in many ways. Each gives rise to a source of power that may be utilized to influence channel members' behavior. Five types of power particularly applicable to distribution channels have been identified by sociologists: reward power, coercive power, legitimate power, referent power, and expert power.[12] Each type of power is based on source or origin.

Reward   Reward power lies in a channel member's ability to give other members something of value that will facilitate their goal attainment. Thus, all channel members have some degree of reward power. Retailers can provide rewards such as preferred shelf space, feature space in advertising, and point-of-sale support. All these actions may be desired by manufacturers to help promote sales. In such situations, retailers may be able to influence a manufacturers' support by promising such rewards. Similarly, manufacturers can provide rewards desired by other channel members. These rewards include cooperative advertising money, expedited shipments, discounts, allowances, extended payment terms, and lower prices. Retailers may be inclined to change their behavior if such rewards are offered. In all cases, the strength of reward as a source of power depends upon the perceived probability that benefits will be received in return for the desired behavior. A firm's ability to use rewards as a source of power may increase after a successful experience, because the perceived impact has materialized. In other words, if a channel member promises and fulfills a reward, future promises will be more credible. On the other hand, failure to fulfill a promise will reduce the future potential of rewards as a source of power.

An excellent example of reward power was the development of the *Universal Product Code* (UPC) in the food industry. Retailers desired UPC because of the perceived benefits of faster checkouts of customers, fewer transactional errors, less labor, and improved inventory control information. Food suppliers were influenced to proceed with the development of product-symbol marking (the thick and thin vertical lines on product packages) by the promise of retail executives that they would be allowed to share in the benefits of the system. Specifically, manufacturers were led to

[12] For baseline work, see John R. P. French and Bertram Raven, "Bases of Social Power," in *Studies in Social Power,* ed. Durwin Cartwright, Ann Arbor: University of Michigan, 1959, pp. 154–155.

believe that retailers would make available to them the vast market data provided by the retail scanning devices. These data include market-share information, product preferences, and product trends on almost a real-time basis. Manufacturers proceeded to develop the symbols, labels, and packaging needed to implement the scanning concept. In some special cases where UPC was implemented, certain retailers decided that the information provided was so valuable that manufacturers should pay for it. In this instance, failure to deliver the promised reward seriously hindered future attempts by these retailers to use the promise of reward.

Coercive Coercive power is similar to reward power in that it is based on a channel member's control of resources or ability to influence other channel members' goal achievement. Coercion, however, is based on a channel members' belief that punishment will be forthcoming unless that member cooperates. Although punishment may only consist of the withholding of a reward that was previously offered, any threat to restrict cooperation is coercive. As with reward, actual exercise of punishment may condition future use of coercive power.

Because of the similarities in reward and coercive power, it is tempting to group them under the heading of "sanctions." However, the implications of reward and punishment on the cooperative nature of channel relationships differ considerably. Consistent use of punishments or threats may encourage members to change or terminate the channel relationship entirely, whereas exercise of reward power may strengthen the relationship.[13] A dealer that is consistently threatened with the loss of a product or distribution rights may decide to seek out an alternative source of supply. Because of the negative aspect of coercive power, it is normally employed only when the advantage is clear and the member being influenced has limited alternatives. Even then, coercive power can be expected to lead ultimately to channel conflict because of the natural tendency of a channel member to resist force.

Legitimate Legitimate power is the most complex source of power. Essentially, it is based on the belief by one party that another has the "right" to prescribe behavior.[14] In marketing channels, legitimate power arises from a channel member's reputation, position, and role. For example, manufacturers may be considered to have the right to make certain decisions simply because they design and produce products. In reality, there is little reason for such "rights" to be accepted as inviolable. Legitimate power results from a channel member's value system, which more or less grants power automatically. In other words, legitimate power exists in a firm or channel position because of traditional values of other channel members. Legitimate power may, of course, be enhanced and given formal recognition through legal actions such as brand-name registration, patent rights, or franchising arrangements. On the other hand, repeal

---

[13] For a discussion of this general concept, see John F. Gaski, "Interrelations among a Channel Entity's Power Sources: Impact of the Exercise of Power and Coercion on Expert, Referent and Legitimate Power Sources," *Journal of Marketing Research,* **23**:1 February 1986, pp. 62–77; and related comments by Howell, **24**:1 February 1987, pp. 119–126.

[14] For the baseline stream of research, see John R. P. French, "A Formal Theory of Social Power," *Psychological Review,* 1956, p. 184.

of fair-trade laws gave formal recognition to the retailer's legitimate right to determine selling prices.

Referent   Referent power results from one channel member's identification with, or attraction to, another channel member. Thus, the roots of referent power are psychological. The following two situations illustrate referent power.

The first example is a situation in which channel members believe that it is consistent with the desired image to identify with certain other firms or organizations. For example, motel owners who want their motels to be identified as high-quality establishments may join a well-known national chain.

Referent power is exhibited when a channel member in a long-term relationship responds to influence because it desires to preserve the stability of the channel.[15] Thus, a distributor that has been associated with a manufacturer for a long period of time may respond to change because of a desire to maintain harmony and cooperation. The distributor may feel that resistance could lead to disruption. In this instance, the manufacturer would be drawing upon a base of referent power to induce the desired changes in the distributor's actions.

Expert   Expert power is based on a channel member's superior knowledge or information that is perceived to be important to other members. Although knowledge or information can sometimes be used to supplement a channel reward system, it differs in that it is potentially self-defeating.[16] Knowledge or information, once provided, may lose its validity as a source of power. It is a resource that, if shared as a reward, cannot be withdrawn. As a result, the recipient of the information gains expert status.

Expert power in distribution channels is common. In many industries the primary role of the manufacturer's sales force is to provide information and advice to dealers or retailers in order to assist them in merchandising. Distributors may turn to a manufacturer's sales force as a source of information, not only about products, but also about such diverse topics as market trends, inventory control, promotional techniques, and store planning. In such situations, the manufacturer has a strong power position based on superior knowledge of that industry. This form of expert power is common in the computer industry.

The preceding discussion of power sources presents a topology that is widely accepted in marketing literature. It would be rare for any particular attempt to influence behavior to be limited to one basic power source. In most instances, a power position results from a combination of several bases, including marketing success. In marketing situations, most power flows from high brand or store acceptance by consumers. A manufacturer attempting to influence a retailer to order larger quantities may use information concerning inefficiencies of sporadic buying and the total cost savings

[15] John F. Gaski and John R. Nevin, "The Differential Effects of Exercised and Unexercised Power Sources in a Marketing Channel," *Journal of Marketing Research,* **22:**2 May 1985, pp. 130–142.

[16] Frederick J. Beier and Louis W. Stern, "Power in the Channel of Distribution," in *Distribution Channels: Behavioral Dimensions,* ed. Louis W. Stern, Boston: Houghton Mifflin, 1969, p. 101.

possible from improved ordering techniques. If this approach fails, quantity discounts may be offered as a reward for appropriate-size orders. If the reward fails, the manufacturer may threaten to refuse small orders or introduce a special handling charge. In such instances, reliance upon several power sources may be effective, since each reinforces the other in an effort to obtain compliance.

Power in a channel situation is primarily applied to shape the outcome of negotiation. Not all agreements are the result of power solutions, however. On the contrary, the best application of power may simply be realization by both parties that it exists. For example, if a manufacturer is aware that a given retailer has sufficient consumer loyalty to get by without stocking a specific assortment of brand products, attitudes and willingness to compromise will be considerably different during negotiation. In such situations, the retailer need not demonstrate power to realize associated benefits. Thus, any negotiation is influenced by a combination of real and perceived power.

An interesting paradox is that in selected channel situations power exists simply from the fact that one party to the negotiation has no power. In a vertically administered channel situation, some members may be at the mercy of the dominant organization. A large organization such as General Motors can and does dominate a vast number of organizations by virtue of its power to ensure survival by granting contracts. In these unique situations, prerequisites to successful negotiation exist, but the balance is so much in favor of the dominant firm that a protective atmosphere surrounds the negotiation process.

Conclusion: Channel Power

In summary, four characteristics of power are of particular interest in formulating a negotiation strategy. First, all power involved in channel negotiation is relative and is thus limited. New negotiations are particularly vulnerable to power violations. One party may perceive its power as being greater than the other party is willing to concede. The result can be termination of negotiations simply because one party went too far or demanded too much. Although channel negotiations are not usually balanced or countervailing in the sense that both parties have equal power, the relative power differential between two parties may be slim. In most channel situations, a power advantage exists and the art of framing a negotiation consists of a proper assessment of relative balance.

A second characteristic of negotiation power is that it need not be exercised to be effective. In mature channel situations, the most cohesive force preventing dysfunctional conflict is often a realization on the part of all concerned that a balance of power exists. The mere recognition that one firm enjoys more relative power than another can expedite negotiation.

Third, negotiation power must be real. In many other bargaining situations, brinkmanship may be important in achieving the best settlement. In channel negotiations that are expected to continue, bluffing can be a costly tactic. Parties to channel negotiations have every reason to believe their counterparts are acting in good faith since all will be engaged in the resulting arrangement for a indefinite time period.

Finally, negotiation power will change over time. This shifting power base is one of the prime reasons that mature channel negotiation is a continual process. To maintain a viable channel relationship over time, all parties must acknowledge and adapt to power shifts inherent in a competitive system.

From the above discussion it can be concluded that relative power assessment is an important aspect of channel strategy and that the foundation of negotiation strategy is power. Therefore a careful assessment of relative power is essential to developing negotiation objectives.

CHANNEL NEGOTIATION PROCESS

The basic objective of negotiation is to establish, maintain, or alter a channel arrangement. Specific channel negotiations are classified as either transactional or operational. Although this delineation is convenient for presentation purposes, it should be remembered that in practice both types of negotiations combine to structure a firm's overall marketing channel arrangement.

Transaction Negotiation

The most fundamental negotiation involves terms and conditions related to ownership transfer of goods and related services. Transaction negotiation incorporates all aspects of the marketing mix. The marketing mix of each channel member represents the way a firm differentiates its competitive activities. The overall marketing mix of manufacturers, wholesalers, and retailers is composed of four subcombinations: the product mix, the distribution mix, the communication mix, and the price mix. Each is briefly discussed to illustrate typical negotiation interactions among firms engaged in channel arrangements.[17]

Product Mix   A primary focus of all marketing activity is the assortment of products and related services offered to consumers and customers as a result of the combined efforts of all channel members. At the individual firm level, selection of the product-market target is one of the firm's primary strategic commitments. Similarly, the established product strategy is one of the fundamental forces leading to establishment of specific channel arrangements.

The primary negotiation among channel members about product mix is the decision to stock or not to stock a product line. In many industries, specific negotiations may have as a goal the design and production of customized or private-label products to ease marketing or to reduce costs. Examples range from minor packaging adjustments to the complete design of a product assortment.

For many years Johnson & Johnson (J&J) followed the practice of applying customer stock-keeping numbers to its products for major retailers at the manufacturing level of the channel. Applying the retailers's unique stock identification number facilitated identification and handling of J&J's products throughout the marketing channel and improved overall inventory control. The practice was a convenience for the

[17] The marketing mix concept was fully developed in Chapter 6.

retailer. Like most negotiations, however, this particular practice represented both a cost and a benefit to J&J. The benefit was a close and repetitive purchasing arrangement with key distributors. The cost was the labor required to place each involved retailer's stock number on cases and anticipatory commitment of specific inventory to a specific account.

A second form of product negotiation is contract preparation of private-label or generic-label merchandise by manufacturers and processors for specific retailers. As a result of negotiated agreements, a manufacturer may produce an inventory under the label of a particular retailer. For example, Weight Watcher–brand food products are packed under contract by a number of different manufacturers. Likewise, many retailers contract for "house- or private-label merchandise." Once produced, such private labels are only valuable to the retailer that negotiated for their manufacture. In such situations, both the retailer and the manufacturer are committed and must assume a share of the related risk.

Distribution Mix   One of the primary functions performed through collective effort by marketing channel members is logistics. Terms and conditions of delivery are an important aspect of the overall transaction process. In many cases, specialists such as public warehouses and transportation companies are used by one or more members of the channel to facilitate the logistics process. Each logistics arrangement performed within the marketing channel requires negotiation.[18]

In recent years, many innovations have been introduced to the channel in an effort to improve logistics efficiency. Many public-warehouse firms provide value-added services during the logistics process. For example, Dry Storage operates a special facility to build point-of-sale displays for manufacturers. Such displays are designed to facilitate the space and merchandising requirements of specific retailers. This form of negotiated value-added service increases efficiency, which works to the benefit of all concerned.

Another example of distribution negotiation among channel members is the practice of using joint inventories to satisfy market demand. For appliances or television sets the most effective logistics channel may be one in which consolidated inventories are maintained at a public warehouse rather than by individual dealers or retailers. This cooperative behavior allows all dealers to draw upon the centralized inventory with two direct benefits. First, dealers do not have to assume the risk of in-depth inventory stocking of all items in the product line since they can obtain rapid delivery of products when required. Second, the overall effectiveness of the channel is improved because inventory is not shipped to dealers in anticipation of sales that may never materialize. Inventory is strategically available from the public warehouse when needed.

Beyond negotiation of specific or customized logistics arrangements, agreements must be reached regarding such matters as point of shipment, size of order, elapsed time for delivery, freight-payment responsibility, transportation consolidation arrangement, and a host of other details essential to efficient marketing channel operations.

---

[18] For a discussion of logistics functionality, see Chapter 7, pp. 212–221.

At some point during transactional negotiation such details must be identified and negotiated.

Communication Mix   The communication mix consists of the advertising, promotion, and personal selling activities of firms engaged in a channel arrangement. The communication mix is unique in that a great deal of an individual channel member's promotional effort is directed toward influencing the behavior of other channel members. For example, a substantial portion of a manufacturer's communications may be aimed at encouraging retailers or wholesalers to participate fully in a marketing program.

In addition to the persuasive aspect, a great deal of marketing communication consists of a joint effort by retailers, wholesalers, and manufacturers to stimulate purchases by consumers. The details related to all such programs must be negotiated. A significant form of interorganizational joint communication is cooperative advertising. A cooperative advertising program may be offered wherein retailer expenditures will be matched or partially reimbursed by the manufacturer, provided specific products are featured in the ads.

One of the most common forms of interorganizational communication effort is the manufacturer's cents-off coupon. The manufacturer provides consumers with coupons entitling them to discounts on specific products purchased at retail. The coupons are usually distributed in newspaper advertisements or by direct mail. However, it is also common for coupons to be distributed by the retailers as part of their weekly promotional effort. When the consumer purchases the product, the retailer applies the discount off the market price. The retailer is then reimbursed for the discount plus an agreed-to handling charge by the sponsoring manufacturer.

Some of the most complex transactional negotiations involve coordination of communication aimed at consumers. In many situations, such programs involve special product or label modifications that must be specially handled through the distribution channel. For example, special promotional packages marketed for a limited period of time must be stocked and distributed to the point of sale prior to the promotion launch. Following the promotion, unsold special packages must be liquidated or removed from the channel.

The process of negotiating channel communication is complicated by the fact that not all promotions are limited to vertical arrangements. In certain cases two manufacturers may jointly promote their products at the retail level. Such joint promotions usually develop around products with complementary demand, such as soft drinks and snacks during a holiday period.

The variety of potential communication negotiations is never-ending. Such promotion is at the heart of creative marketing. The significant point is that all channel members have a stake in how products are sold to consumers. In industrial marketing, the communication negotiation may center on combined personal-selling efforts by manufacturers and their agents in cooperation with dealers and distributors. In consumer marketing, the selling effort must center on the coordination of joint advertising and promotional programs. Details of all such joint efforts must be agreed to beforehand as an integral part of the communication transaction negotiation.

Price Mix   Negotiation of price is critical in arriving at a final transactional agreement. Price is properly viewed as the placement of a monetary value on the combination of product, distribution and communication performed by each firm in a channel arrangement. As noted earlier, negotiation is a form of cooperative behavior in which participants identify what they will do and who will get what *prior to* performance of specified marketing functions. Agreed-to transfer price places performance of marketing roles into a cost-revenue perspective.

Negotiation of price involves more than identification of transfer value. Important aspects of price negotiation are discount structure, credit limit, return allowances, and terms of payment that will prevail in the channel arrangement. A closely related matter is the negotiation of who is responsible for payment of freight and associated claims.

Price negotiations focus the overall channel arrangement. All other aspects of transactional negotiation become meaningful only within the perspective of a price agreement.

Operational Negotiation

Whereas transactional negotiation is aimed at arriving at an agreement regarding how to do business, operational negotiation is the process through which mature channel arrangements are maintained or modified. For purposes of discussion, operational negotiation is divided into functional, performance, and performance postponement categories.

Functional   In effect, establishment of a channel arrangement means that agreement has been reached regarding which members will perform which functions. Following initiation of operations, a continuous modification of functional performance agreements will be required. Individual firms are engaged in a constant process of functional spin-off or absorption, depending upon the relative economics and power balance of the channel.[19]

Functional spin-off occurs when one firm transfers a function to another firm. The spin-off may or may not be desired by the receiving firm. Functional spin-off is usually chosen when a firm finds it economically advantageous to subcontract or delegate specific functions to specialized firms. Two common forms of spin-off are the use of for-hire transportation or public warehousing in logistics operations, and manufacturers subcontracting packaging of specific products to a processor. In both cases, the assumption is that the firm accepting the spun-off function will benefit from having a lower-average-cost curve. In reality, however, often the firm receiving the spun-off function takes on the added work only because it fears repercussions if it does not cooperate. Thus, a manufacturer may agree to extend credit terms or perform a specific packaging function if noncompliance could result in loss of the retailer's business.

In many ways, functional absorption is the opposite of spin-off. It is true that one firm must absorb a function for another firm to be able to spin it off. However, situations may develop wherein a firm desires to absorb performance of a function

---

[19] For a more detailed discussion, see Chapter 1, pp. 17–18.

that another firm does not want to give up. The firm wishing to absorb the function may have lower cost or may be seeking greater control over the channel arrangement. A prime example of functional absorption is a manufacturer's decision to ship products directly to dealers from manufacturers' warehouses and bypass distributors. As a result, the distributor no longer performs product logistics. While distributors may participate in selling and promoting activities, the manufacturer absorbs the logistics responsibility. The incentive for establishing such programs is reduced total per-unit logistics cost for the channel. However, the scope of the distributor's involvement and control is reduced despite the fact that the total channel is rendered more efficient by the elimination of duplicate handling and shipment.

Functional negotiation is critical to mature channel situations. Channel structure must be reviewed and, if appropriate, functional assignment must be modified in order to remain effective. The prime justification for functional realignment is improved efficiency. However, both functional spin-off and absorption can also result from a shift in basic power.

Performance Performance negotiation deals with day-to-day operations in a mature channel arrangement. Once a channel has been established and functional assignments agreed to, many situations will arise that require clarification or modification of established operational performance. An area of constant operational adjustment is service and warranty of products. In the automobile industry, for example, terms of reimbursement for dealer warranty service have changed several times in recent years. In certain situations, such as in some franchise operations, performance agreements exist regarding purchase of supplies and materials. However, from time to time such agreements may need to be renegotiated due to shortages or local price fluctuations.

The range of potential performance negotiations within a mature channel is unlimited. For the most part, adjustments are minor and are not viewed by participants as negotiations. However, the importance of a channel mechanism in the accomplishment of performance negotiation cannot be overemphasized. Most legal disputes within mature channels originate from situations that were initially minor operational adjustments.

Postponement The concept of postponement was introduced and discussed in Chapter 4.[20] Over the past few years, the negotiating of postponement into channel arrangements has received increased attention. With traditional marketing, emphasis has been placed on movement of products in anticipation of future transactions. Anticipatory action is a common characteristic of manufacturing, wholesaling, and retailing. Generally, products are produced, transported, stored, handled, bought, and sold several times before arriving at a location where they are finally sold to end users.

Postponement is a risk-reducing practice that requires extensive cooperation. To the extent that agreements can be negotiated that postpone final manufacturing or

[20] See Chapter 4, pp. 99–102.

logistics of a product until final commitment by the customer, anticipatory action is reduced, resulting in reduced risk or potential error.

The attributes of postponement may be incorporated into a logistics system design on the basis of *form* and/or *time*. Form postponement consists of not performing final manufacturing, assembly, or packaging until a customer's order is received. The classic example is mixing paint to customer's specifications at retail stores. Time postponement consists of delaying movement of products until customers' orders are received. Introduction of postponement into a marketing channel involves a special type of negotiation. Postponement negotiation may or may not involve functional realignment among channel members.

Conclusion: Negotiation Process

The process of ''agreeing to do business'' means that channel members must negotiate all aspects of a transaction before performing as an interorganizational unit. The nature and subject of negotiation varies among new and mature channel situations. Despite this fact, the focus of negotiation will be on those activities that constitute combined marketing efforts to be performed by channel members. Specific aspects of transactional negotiations have been presented in reference to marketing mix decisions. Although examples have not been exhaustive or comprehensive, they are typical of the many facets of transactional negotiation.

Operational negotiation is concerned with maintaining or modifying existing channel arrangements. Three types of operational negotiation have been discussed: functional, performance, and postponement. Although the categories may overlap, each is unique and may be critical to the maintainence of channel efficiency and effectiveness.

SUMMARY

This chapter has dealt with the scope and strategy of interorganizational negotiation. Negotiation in a channel context has been defined as *the management process of reaching agreement* about which activities a firm will perform and how it will benefit from a marketing channel arrangement. Negotiation has been identified as a form of cooperative behavior in which participants agree in advance to roles and rewards.

Negotiation is the process by which channel structure and function are identified. All firms have the right to initiate negotiations as well as the right not to participate. Thus, it is important to keep in mind that participation in initial negotiation is a form of *self-resolution*. Once agreement has been reached, future negotiations are clouded by performance track record.

From a managerial perspective, channel negotiations can be viewed as new or mature. The reason for new negotiations is to seek effective channel arrangements. Mature channel negotiations result from (1) a changing balance of power, (2) conflict resolution, and/or (3) termination settlements.

Considerable attention has been directed to the strategy of negotiation. Prerequisites for negotiation are (1) alternatives, (2) procedures, (3) reward potential, and (4) willingness to commit.

The capability to direct negotiation strategy is related to a firm's relative power position. Power has been defined as *the ability of one party to influence the behavior of other channel members.* Power arises from mutual dependence in a channel system and exists as a potentially disruptive or cohesive force. Specifically, power arises from five sources: reward, coercion, legitimacy, reference, and expertness. Leadership potential results from a firm's power position relative to other members of a channel system. Cooperation, which stems from the desire to work together to achieve mutual goals, is the most common behavior in distribution channels. Cooperation exists on a voluntary basis and is intensified as a result of conflict resolution by a channel leader.

The overall goal of channel negotiation is to establish, maintain, or alter a channel arrangement. Depending upon the situation, negotiations may focus on transactional or operational matters. In total, negotiations establish a firm's domain and participation in a specified marketing channel strategy.

QUESTIONS

1 What are the significant differences between new and mature negotiation?

2 In your words, describe the role negotiation plays in the planning of channel structure.

3 What role does relative power play in the establishment of the negotiation process? Illustrate by using a practical example.

4 How do you resolve the fact that in negotiations each firm is trying to act in its own best interest with the fact that there is an overall need to develop a channel synergism?

5 What is meant by the statement ''computers don't negotiate''?

6 What are some common events that necessitate mature channel negotiation?

7 Discuss the idea of perceived power and its importance to the negotiation process. Illustrate by using a practical example.

8 What type of bargaining is most representative of channel negotiation?

9 Does personal bargaining exist in a channel negotiation?

10 List the prerequisites for successful negotiation. Which one do you feel is most important, and why?

11 What source of power is most important in channel negotiation? How does market share work into the typical assessment of channel power? Illustrate by using practical examples.

12 Contrast transactional negotiation with operational negotiation. What are the key differences in the two types of negotiation and how do they relate to each other?

CHAPTER 10

CHANNEL MANAGEMENT

CHAPTER OUTLINE

LEADERSHIP
Tolerance to Follow
The Leadership Process
Example of Channel Leadership
VERTICAL MARKETING SYSTEMS
The Business Rationale for a VMS
VMS Principles
Creating a Successful VMS
Reasons Why VMS Arrangements Fail
Integrating a VMS Arrangement: Electronic Linkage
CONFLICT
Types of Conflict
Conflict Defined
Causes of Conflict
Results of Conflict
Conflict Resolution
SUMMARY

In channel arrangements characterized by acknowledged dependence among participants, it can be assumed that one of the participating firms is providing some degree of leadership. If one of the member firms is acknowledged as the most powerful, other participants typically look to that dominant firm for leadership. Thus, relative power serves as the cohesive force that enables channel management. In Chapter 9, relative power was discussed as a basis for advantage in interorganizational negotiation. To the extent that a firm has a power advantage, it can influence channel design. Other members, both primary and support, will participate in the proposed channel arrangement when they perceive it to be to their advantage.

This chapter presents an in-depth look at the channel management process. First, the leadership process is reviewed, with particular attention being given to the interorganizational dynamics that enable channel management. Second, attention is directed to the nature of *vertical marketing systems* (VMS). The VMS concept describes a broad range of interorganizational arrangements, from administered to contractual.[1] All VMS arrangements have the common attribute of acknowledged dependence. Acknowledged dependence is not as typical in a free-flow or conventional channel. The final section of this chapter focuses on the inevitable occurrence of channel member conflict. Both the origin and resolution of conflict is discussed in terms of the impact upon channel solidarity.

LEADERSHIP

As noted in Chapter 9, channel power is limited in scope and only applies to specific issues. All members of a channel possess a degree of power as a result of acknowledged dependence. However, power is not equal among all channel members, and those with a relative advantage often assume a position of channel leadership. Firms seek to lead so that they can influence the decisions and behavior of other channel members. The goal of leadership is to contribute to a better level of performance for either the leader or the overall channel.[2] Although the leadership position typically is based on power advantage, it also depends upon the tolerance of other channel members.

Tolerance to Follow

A firm's tolerance for being controlled is based on a number of factors in regards to its relationship with other channel members. Tolerance is directly related to the firm's dependence upon other channel members and the degree to which performance can be improved by submitting to control.[3] If a firm is highly dependent upon others, by definition it is in an extremely poor relative power position. Such a firm may have no choice but to tolerate leadership. A rural retail grocery store may have only one wholesaler willing to make deliveries. As a result of the strong dependence and lack of available alternatives, the retailer would tolerate a wide range of behavior on the part of the wholesaler.

The second factor encouraging a firm to tolerate leadership is the expectation of enjoying higher-level performance. This perception might exist even when two firms

---

[1] See Chapter 4, pp. 102–107, for a review of alternative channel structure arrangements.

[2] Gary L. Frazier and Jagdish N. Sheth, "An Attitude-Behavior Framework for Distribution Channel Management," *Journal of Marketing,* **43**:3 Summer 1985, pp. 38–48.

[3] Louis P. Bucklin, "A Theory of Channel Control," *Journal of Marketing,* **37**:1 January 1973, pp. 39–47.

enjoy relatively equal power. If a firm perceives that total channel performance will be improved or, more specifically, its own performance will be enhanced by submitting to leadership, it is likely to be tolerant. Although tolerance is related to reward power, a difference between the two terms exists. Tolerance based on the expectation of improved performance does not necessarily have to result from a leader's reward. A retailer may decide to follow a manufacturer's dictates because it expects to realize higher profits. Many retailers cooperate with manufacturers' suggested resale price policies and coupon promoting for no other reason than their belief that higher profits will result. Of course, this perception may differ among retail firms. Others may follow the suggested-price policy because they fear if they do not, the manufacturer may discontinue distribution.

Like power, tolerance is issue-specific.[4] It can be expected to change over time and with circumstances. When a firm realizes a level of profit that management considers sufficient, it may suddenly become less tolerant of being controlled, even though the potential for higher profits exists. This situation is similar to the traditional conflict between big and small business. A small business that achieves satisfactory income may reject a larger firm's attempt to exercise control simply because the small-business management resents intrusion upon their independence. Many people who are engaged in small business have chosen to do so primarily because of their desire for self-control. In such instances, tolerance for control from others will be very low unless perceived performance improvements are significant.

The Leadership Process

Channel leadership results from power advantage and tolerance on the part of other firms to accept direction or follow. By exercising leadership and coordinating decisions, the channel leader is better able to predict and direct overall performance. This ability to lead permits the overall channel to undertake activities that will maintain or enhance overall performance. The fundamental purpose of leadership is to use power in improving not only the system's but also individual performance. A strong case may be constructed to support almost any type of institution in its effort to achieve the leadership position.[5] Circumstances coupled with different environmental influences make it impossible to generalize concerning what type of intermediary will be apt to lead a channel system most effectively. The firm elevated to a leadership role will be the one best able to utilize power effectively to stimulate the channel toward more efficient performance. Those managers who desire to elevate their firm into the leadership role must examine the applicable sources of available power, the relative power position of channel members, and the tolerance level each member will have for leadership initiatives. As a result of leadership, a channel will begin to some measurable degree to function on an interorganizational basis.

[4] Gary L. Frazier, "On The Measurement of Interfirm Power in Channels of Distribution," *Journal of Marketing Reseach,* **20**:2 May 1983, pp. 158–166.

[5] Patrick L. Schul, William M. Pride, and Tayor L. Little, "The Impact of Channel Leadership Behavior on Intrachannel Conflict," *Journal of Marketing,* **47**:3 Summer 1983, pp. 21–34.

Example of Channel Leadership[6]

Kraft General Foods has actively been involved in developing a channel leadership process they refer to as the "extended enterprise." The purpose of the extended enterprise is to leverage overall performance through development of strategic alliances that span the total trading channel. The rationale for development of the extended enterprise is to coordinate the overall value-added process in an effort to improve product and service quality while achieving superior financial performance for that industry.

Figure 10-1 illustrates the Kraft General Food concept of the extended enterprise. So that maximum impact is achieved, the trading channel structure is defined to incorporate customers, service suppliers, and material suppliers. The relationship of these primary and support channel participants is far-reaching. Figure 10-2 provides a more detailed breakdown of each set of business relationships facilitated by the leadership process. The customer relationships illustrate the broad range of customer segments that the total channel must service in the domestic food industry. The service-supplier relationships span the full range of support participants. In the material supplier category, all ingredients required for successful marketing and manufacturing are included.

The basic idea of the extended-enterprise concept is to combine and coordinate the activities of all parties involved in the value-added process. This coordination is facilitated through Kraft General Food performing the channel leadership process. Attention is now directed to various aspects of vertical marketing systems (VMS) to further examine the scope and working dimensions of interorganizational arrangements.

VERTICAL MARKETING SYSTEM

The term *vertical marketing system* (VMS) is adopted to encompass all cooperative relationships designed to facilitate either selling or delivery of products in a timely manner. There are a variety of different VMS arrangements. Figure 4-6 provided illustrations of four common formats of such interorganizational alliances.[7]

A distinguishing feature of a VMS is that combined performance of the participants typically exceeds or is broader than each would achieve on an individual basis. For example, when a retailer shares detailed cash-register sales information with a manufacturer, the data may substantially reduce the need to forecast. Likewise, two firms working together may be able to eliminate the need for intermediate warehousing. The synergistic potential of a VMS builds upon effective boundary spanning.[8] While degrees of leadership occur in all forms of channel organization, the alternative VMS arrangements represent structures in which a need for coordinated performance is openly acknowledged.

---

[6] The following example is based on Donald J. Bowersox and Jack Brown, "The Extended Enterprise," unpublished presentation at the 1990 Council of Logistics Management Conference.

[7] See Figure 4-6, p. 102.

[8] For a more detailed dicussion of boundary spanning, see Chapter 7, pp. 201–203.

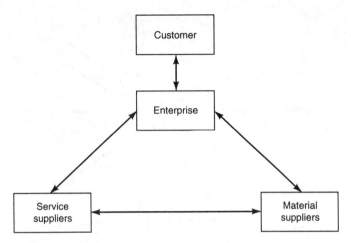

FIGURE 10-1   The extended enterprise.

The Business Rationale for a VMS

The driving force behind development of a VMS is elusively simple—increased competitiveness and capability to accommodate market change. The business environment is becoming increasingly conducive for marketers to exploit joint competence to gain and maintain competitive advantage. Firms that aggressively establish VMS arrangements are seeking to leverage their joint competencies.

The anatomy of a channel system builds upon three interrelated propositions. First, the business arrangement must constitute a relationship far more formalized and comprehensive than is usual when products or services are bought or sold. In the traditional purchasing situation, outsourcing is a make-versus-buy decision guided primarily by cost considerations. In contrast, the VMS is positioned as a business arrangement wherein involved parties seek to benefit from the synergism of working together. In such synergism, typically described as a win-win situation, two organizations work out the complexity of meshing operations to enhance joint capability. It is important to understand that a VMS is in fact a super- or extended organization that develops clearly specified roles, rules, values, and expectations. Long-standing VMS arrangements possess a unique culture.

Second, firms that enter into a VMS arrangement appropriately focus on developing long-term relationships as contrasted to single transactions. Parties engaged in a VMS are expected to view their channel involvement as a relationship focused on long-term benefits. Many VMS arrangements are long-term, running from five to ten years.[9] The involved parties perform their specialized roles in a highly integrated manner as they

---

[9] Russell Johnson and Paul R. Lawrence, "Beyond Vertical Integration: The Rise of the Value-Adding Partnership," *Harvard Business Review,* **66**:4 July–August, 1988, pp. 94–101; Jordan D. Lewis, *Partnerships for Profit: Structuring and Managing Strategic Alliances,* New York: The Free Press, 1990.

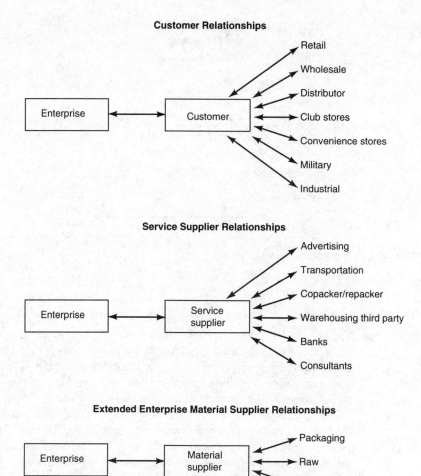

Customer Relationships

Enterprise → Customer → Retail, Wholesale, Distributor, Club stores, Convenience stores, Military, Industrial

Service Supplier Relationships

Enterprise → Service supplier → Advertising, Transportation, Copacker/repacker, Warehousing third party, Banks, Consultants

Extended Enterprise Material Supplier Relationships

Enterprise → Material supplier → Packaging, Raw, Promotional

FIGURE 10-2   The extended enterprise: a detailed relationship.

seek to achieve mutually identified objectives. In some situations, the VMS is formed by a formal contract. In a surprising number of arrangements, the working relationship is one of convenience. This is particularly true in alliances and administered channel arrangements. Firms in these less formal arrangements often work out complex relationships that guide performance over extended time without the benefit of contracts. A common characteristic of a VMS is its behavioral context. The traditional adversarial mode of doing business is replaced with a cooperative mode, one based on gaining competitive advantage by virtue of allying with other organizations.

Finally, a high degree of perceived dependence in the relationship should stimulate cooperation. Firms participating in a VMS typically feel a dependence and responsibility toward one another that intensifies with time. They are, in reality, partners that benefit from one another's prosperity. Rosabeth Moss Kanter has described the relationship of parties in an alliance as falling short of marriage—more like living together.[10] A philosophy of trust in a highly dependent situation has no room for adversarial actions or tactics. Leaders of the combined effort must focus on end-user or final-customer satisfaction and loyalty. Few areas of business operations require the level of cooperation typical of a VMS. Although the theory of cooperation is less developed than other theories of behavior, an understanding of the basic nature of cooperation is important so that VMS arrangements and the way they work can be understood.

Two fundamental human drives exert opposite forces on a channel arrangement. The first is *monostasy,* the desire to be independent, and the second is *systasy,* the drive to stand together.[11] The urge to stand together normally arises from the realization that more can be accomplished by working together than individually. When systasy predominates, cooperation results. When monostasy predominates, conflict may be expected. In channels of distribution, the drive for systasy typically outweighs monostasy due to recognition that the welfare of all parties is enhanced and superordinate goals can be accomplished. During periods of little or no stress, channel members will cooperate to achieve the system goals that will also result in attainment of their individual objectives. In such a situation, channel members voluntarily cooperate with one another to achieve mutual objectives. Nevertheless, stress may arise for any of the reasons discussed previously. When it does, the system may develop conflict, during which time the drive to be independent will temporarily overtake the urge to cooperate. Usually, however, channel members desire to reestablish harmonious relations. The processes of conflict resolution may emerge to eliminate or subordinate the cause of stress. It is interesting to note that most methods of conflict resolution involve utilization of power or leadership to return the system to equilibrium. Channel members draw on their arsenal of power resources to solve problems, persuade, bargain, or campaign in order to resolve a conflict episode and continue normal functioning of the system. In fact, the means by which channel members attempt to dominate or lead the system's activities are nothing more than methods by which cooperation is enforced. The last section of this chapter deals with conflict resolution in greater detail.

VMS Principles

The benefits of a VMS evolve from at least four interrelated principles: (1) specialization; (2) joint risk, (3) revenue leverage, and (4) shared creativity. If each is not present to some significant degree, potential benefits of a VMS may be jeopardized.

Specialization The basic fact that specialization generates economy of scale is the economic cornerstone of VMS arrangements. As noted previously, a firm that

---

[10] Rosabeth Moss Kanter, "Becoming Pals: Pooling, Allying, and Linking across Companies," *The Academy of Management Executives,* **111**:3, 1989, pp. 183–193.
[11] Wroe Alderson, "Cooperation and Conflict in Marketing Channels," in *Distribution Channels: Behavioral Dimensions,* ed. Louis W. Stern, Boston: Houghton Mifflin, 1969, pp. 195–196.

TABLE 10-1   MAJOR CORNING GLASS JOINT VENTURES

Venture	Partner	Year
Pittsburgh Corning	PPG Industries	1937
Owens-Corning*	Owens-Illinois	1938
Dow Corning	Dow Chemical	1943
Iwaki Glass	Asahi Glass	1965
Samsung-Corning	Samsung	1974
Seicor	Siemens	1977
Genencor	Genentech and Eastman Kodak	1982
Ciba Corning Diagnostics	Ciba-Geigy	1985
Corning Asahi Video Prod.	Asahi Glass	1988

* Corning sold last of its interest in 1986.
Source: "Partnerships Have Become a Way of Life for Corning," *Wall Street Journal*, July 12, 1988, p. 6. Reprinted by permission of *Wall Street Journal*. © 1990 Dow Jones & Company, Inc. All rights reserved worldwide.

specializes in the performance of a specific task can generate both learning and low-cost performance as a result of a critical mass and dedicated resource base.[12]

Joint Risk   The risk involved in a channelwide operation is sufficiently broad to cause firms to seek relief. An appealing attribute of a VMS is that meshed operations offer what amounts to risk insurance. As a result of specialized organizations, each doing what it does best in a coordinated and focused manner, the chance of error is dramatically reduced. When the relationship involves interfirm performance guarantees, consequences of failure are shared. The idea of sharing risk between two or more companies is not new. Table 10-1 provides a summary of major joint ventures that Corning Glass has been involved in since 1937. While the Corning formula typically builds upon joint ownership, contracting and alliances offer an alternative way of sharing risk. For example, Trammell Crow Distribution Services (TCDC) operates state-of-the-art facilities for warehousing and processing chemicals. TCDC's Plastics and Chemicals Group provide flexible blending, packaging, warehousing, and specialized services for handling both normal and hazardous chemicals for such companies as BASF and Mobile.

Risk avoidance assumes a wide variety of different formats in VMS arrangements in which primary and support channel members participate. The reduction of risk is a primary force behind the motivation to establish a VMS.

Revenue Leverage   One common aspect of a VMS is that parties involved typically end up conducting business with fewer suppliers and customers. The typical relationship is a tight business situation wherein the stronger each party, the greater the overall strength of the VMS. The natural extension or outreach is that parties to a VMS begin automatically to seek growth opportunities for one another. Proven performance or truck record of the VMS works to everyone's advantage. For a service supplier, the potential benefit is referral of business opportunities both internal and

[12] See Chapter 1, pp. 20–22.

external to the product marketer's organization. For the marketer, the benefits of working hand-in-hand with customers or suppliers is a state-of-the-art resource base capable of being applied to other opportunities.

Shared Creativity   No firm has a monopoly on creativity. When firms jointly seek creative applications and improvements in a basic process, the chance for significant productivity breakthrough is greatly increased. The uniqueness of a VMS relationship that consists of marketers, customers, and suppliers is that each views the value-added process from a radically different vantage point.

Creating a Successful VMS

Assuming that potential benefits appear worthwhile, what specific actions and agreements are necessary to establish and maintain a successful VMS? At least six concerns are critical: (1) channelwide perspective, (2) selective matching, (3) information sharing, (4) role specification, (5) ground rules, and (6) exit provisions.

Channelwide Perspective   To perform effectively in a VMS arrangement, the leader and all involved parties should view their participation in terms of the overall trading channel. The key vision is to understand the overall purpose of the VMS as contrasted to specific assignments or roles. This is not to suggest that each member can neglect the basics or detail of its specific assignments. Rather, individual assignments should be viewed in terms of their overall contribution to the entire VMS structure. Retaining a perspective of the "big picture" protects against becoming role-myopic. With complex distribution arrangements, participants must understand that the tangible benefits that result from a specific task may impact a different level in the marketing channel. VMS arrangements in which reverse channel movement of products is coordinated normally offer retailers a significant value-added service. From a manufacturer's viewpoint, such reverse operations are costly and difficult to manage. Radical changes in traditional practice that enable significant productivity improvements are best initiated throughout the total channel. More often than managers would like to admit, the idea to improve a process comes from an individual who didn't know it could be done a different way. Understanding the total process offers a safeguard against "continuing to do something well that shouldn't be done at all."

Selective Matching   Not all channel situations justify or are capable of supporting the extensive commitment necessary to make a VMS work. From a marketer's perspective, an ideal VMS is one that generates unique services focused on key customers or niche markets. Thus, focused services should be concentrated on the strong links of any distribution system.[13] In order to justify using customized services to gain competitive superiority, effort must be concentrated on high-yield opportunities and coordinated with overall strategic planning.

[13] Randy Myer, "Suppliers: Manage Your Customers," *Harvard Business Review,* **67**:6 November–December 1989, pp. 160–168.

For example, Wal-Mart's formula for establishing alliances with key suppliers is guided by the volume of potential business at stake and the participating vendor's sophistication in information technology. Unless the supplier is capable of direct electronic linkage via the Wal-Mart satellite communication network, it is not practical or economical to share the assortment of information required to function as a VMS. The players in a VMS must be economically and managerially strong. A VMS is typically a long-term arrangement in which ups and downs characteristic of most business situations are expected to be confronted. To support a strong VMS, all parties must have staying power. Thus, equally important to significant high-side volume that causes a VMS arrangement to flourish is the capability of involved parties to cope with the realities of downside business.

Information Sharing Information sharing is the "glue" that holds a VMS together. Information-sharing needs range from planning strategies to operating details. Joint performance requires open disclosure of information. Complete information exchange is essential so that the synchronization of VMS member operations can be ensured.

Some service providers involved in VMS arrangements are establishing a full-disclosure information system capability. Systems are supported that provide real-time tracking of shipments at case level or stock-keeping unit detail throughout the logistics process. In selected situations, such as one in which Skyway Freight Systems, Inc., is involved, VMS participants can track in-transit status of shipments in terms of projected arrival time. Projections of estimated time of arrival provide the information for the evaluation of the cost-benefit of expediting a shipment to meet a desired delivery. Such positive control is a key feature of the American Presidential Lines/Union Pacific Railroad double-stack container service that links Pacific Rim manufacturers directly to retailers in North America. The service provides containerized delivery on hangers of garments that are size- and color-sequenced to retailers' specifications prior to their being loaded in Asia.

Nabisco Foods is pioneering a unique information-sharing arrangement with key transportation supplies. By linking with Nabisco's Distribution Requirements Program (DRP), participating carriers are provided daily shipment plans three weeks in advance of an actual shipment. This information sharing permits carriers to plan equipment requirements and line-haul operations. Delivery appointments can be arranged with destination customers so that rapid unloading when the shipment arrives can be guaranteed. Facilitating documentation is exchanged between Nabisco and the participating carriers with use of EDI. For the carriers, the arrangement provides critical information for the stabilization of operations. Nabisco is ensured a regular supply of quality transportation equipment and consistent delivery. This arrangement is effectively working across a variety of transportation modes—Hub City Terminals–Piggyback (TOFC), Schneider National (truck), and American President Lines (double-stack container).

Adequate information technology currently exists for the creation and control of unique and far-reaching VMS arrangements. Direct electronic linkage of computer resources is essential so the power inherent in such technology can be fully exploited.

To make a VMS work, all parties involved need to trust their operating partners. The development of mutual trust is the most essential aspect, as well as one of the most difficult, of a VMS. Full disclosure does not come easy to generations of managers who were schooled in the belief that information is power and should only be shared on a need-to-know basis. Overcoming information hoarding is a key step toward eliminating adversarial relationships.

Role Specification As in all team efforts, in a VMS participants must perform specified roles. These roles are typically identified and scoped during negotiations that establish the arrangement. Performance to specific goals requires each participant to have a clear operating domain plus an understanding of the big picture. The involvement of multiple parties in the distribution process creates the opportunity for details to be overlooked and functions to be duplicated. The marketing channel value-added process occurs across a vast geographic area in what amounts to a twenty-four-hour, seven-day-a-week, fifty-two-week-a-year engagement. No room exists for ambiguity regarding who is responsible for performing specific functions during the value-added process. A primary benefit of a VMS, once established, is that some of the traditional roles of participants can be modified.[14] Because the concerned parties develop interdependence and well-defined working relationships, such behavior as prenegotiation positioning can be reduced to a minimum. Likewise, joint applications of technology can be implemented faster, often with new and unique procedures being worked out that eliminate checks and balances typical of an adversarial or transaction-based business relationship. The familiarity of the working relationship permits early identification and resolution of potential problems at the operational level.

Ground Rules To effectively function day in and day out, a VMS requires clear and comprehensive rules. It is essential that parties fully understand and absorb the VMS arrangement commitment into their organizational culture. Cultural absorption can be difficult when a firm is simultaneously engaged in multiple VMS arrangements. Even when VMS member firms are not direct competitors, they must learn, acknowledge, and accommodate unique cultural differences.

The prevailing state of affairs in any VMS arrangement is cooperation. Nevertheless, problems develop and they must be resolved. When ground rules are well established, they facilitate conflict resolution. The prime objective is to adjudicate inevitable conflict before it becomes dysfunctional. Prenegotiated roles and clear ground rules serve to perpetuate alliance longevity.

Tables 10-2 and 10-3 provide a summary of the basic rules that are followed by two firms that are actively involved in VMS arrangements. Table 10-2 is a statement of principles followed by Kraft General Foods, a broad-based manufacturer of consumer food products. The basic guidelines of Schneider National, Inc., a major trucking firm, are listed in Table 10-3.

Freedom to Exit The voluntary and cooperative nature of a VMS makes it essential that all parties fully understand that even good relationships sometimes must end.

---

[14] "Getting Cozy with Customers," *Business Week,* January 8, 1989, p. 86.

TABLE 10-2   PRINCIPLES TO GUIDE CHANNEL ALLIANCE

- Share all relevant nonproprietary information.
- Clearly define common-interest boundaries.
- Share forecasts.
- Develop common performance measures for continuous improvement.
- Establish guidelines for the resolution of issues; empower local resolution whenever possible.
- Share risk.
- Discourage adversarial relationships by eliminating short-term quid-pro-quo mentality.
- Share benefits.

Source: Reproduced with permission of Kraft General Foods, Inc.

In fact, the basic business incentive leading to the arrangement is likely to change over time and may necessitate termination of a long-standing relationship. Over the years, the relationship of Signal Freight, a division of Leaseway Transportation, and Sears-Whirlpool, for whom Signal Freight provides logistics support, has shifted significantly to accommodate operational changes. Sears recent merchandising decision to stock a wide variety of national brand appliances was a basic change that directly impacted the alliance.

While one objective underlying formation of a VMS is to establish the foundation for a long-term and stable arrangement, provisions must be made for the accommodation of change. Termination or modification rules can be difficult, because the power balance of a typical VMS favors one member organization. Therefore, significant changes or termination issues are always sensitive. VMS arrangements introduce long-term commitment into the equation. Achievement of long-term stability must be tempered by acknowledgment of each party's potential future need to exit if such a move becomes in that party's best long-term interest. Success will encourage continuation of the VMS; however, no barriers should prohibit dissolution of the arrangement. Across a broad range of different types of alliances, the abandonment rate has been estimated to exceed 70 percent of all attempts launched.[15] VMS arrangements fail for a variety of reasons and therefore must be dissolved. Because of the importance of failure, the next part of this section provides a detailed discussion of typical causes. The significant point is that termination options need to be negotiated up front at the time optimism about the arrangement is high. Freedom to exit is delicate, but it should not be ignored.

Reasons Why VMS Arrangements Fail

Six common causes of VMS failure can be identified: (1) fuzzy goals, (2) inadequate trust, (3) lip-service commitment, (4) human incompatibility, (5) inadequate operating framework, and (6) inadequate measurement.

[15] "Corporate Odd Couples," *Business Week,* July 21, 1986, pp. 100–105.

TABLE 10-3   BASIC INGREDIENTS FOR A SUCCESSFUL ALLIANCE

Thorough assessment of participant strengths	Build a relationship based on those identified strengths that provide necessary elements for successful operation of the partnership.
Value consistency	Identify a partner with similar corporate values to insure that both firms are able to commingle human and financial resources without substantial debate.
Clear understanding of objectives	Ensure that clearly defined goals and objectives are discussed in preliminary negotiations for the facilitation of further coordination of activities.
Agreement of measurement standards	Establish measurement criteria that clarify the initial partnership vision at the activity level for employees of both participants.
Long-term focus	Create a long-term perspective on the relationship that does not endanger the initial investment through expectation of immediate results.
Multiple-level commitment	Provide continuity and depth of commitment through approval and reinforcement of the partnership across several management levels (including the CEO)
Working relationship at interface level	Foster coordination of the partners at the interface level to ensure that daily activities are successfully accomplished once the task forces have clearly established the goals and objectives.
Limited number of relationships	Limit the number of legitimate partnerships in which either firm is actively engaged to acknowledge the extensive time requirements at key levels in the company.
Elimination of "quid pro quo" mentality	Maintain an attitude that allows for changes in the original agreement which benefit the entire product supply chain, regardless of the timing of individual costs or returns (i.e., permit suboptimization).
Prices are negotiated, not bid and subject to change	Remain committed to ultimate resolution of conflict through negotiation in the interest of continuing the relationship over the long term.

Source: Reproduced with permission of Schneider National, Inc.

Fuzzy Goals   The interaction between VMS members is complex and, in terms of traditional business practice, unorthodox. Because of this complexity, organizations involved in a VMS run the risk of not fully understanding all the ramifications and implications of the arrangement. A typical complaint among executives is that other channel members do not fully understand their requirements.

In some cases, firms are not clear as to what they fully expect to gain from the arrangement. One sentiment is: "VMS arrangements are fashionable, so we should get involved." Executives who have closely studied the pros and cons of such arrangements are quick to point out that if the real objective is limited to cutting cost, then the most expeditious arrangement may be a traditional and proven channel. If the objective of a VMS is to improve the competitiveness of the overall value-added process, then the clarification of objectives and the development of realistic expectations becomes essential.

The understanding of interrelationships and the development of a clear vision regarding mutual expectations in a VMS is further complicated by the difficulty in testing such arrangements. Because of the complexity and the high visibility of an interorganizational arrangement, tests are highly vulnerable to the "halo" or so called "Hawthorne" effect. Given close scrutiny by the senior management of participating organizations, the results of a test may generate false or unrealistic expectations. While simulation of new structural arrangements is possible, actual operations must often be launched on a conviction of faith and trust.[16] It is important to remember that the excitement of closing the deal can potentially result in the creation of hasty and unrealistic expectations and the introduction of seeds of dysfunctional conflict when the alliance fails to match vague expectations.

Inadequate Trust   As noted earlier, mutual trust must be in evidence for a VMS to prosper. The development of a trust level necessary to make a VMS excel requires an "open door" attitude. This is not easy for executives schooled in adversarial traditions.

In traditional adversarial-based negotiation, a host of competitive checks and balances exists to assure buyers that they are getting the best possible deal. In a VMS, trust must substitute for many of the perceived benefits of competitive bidding. If traditional bidding practices are implemented, a VMS can get aborted by the reluctance of prospective partners to share innovative ideas up front and to disclose confidential information. The dilemma is how to build trust in situations in which no track records exist.

As a VMS matures, trust level and operational success become inseparable. Failure to build initial trust will ultimately result in difficult times. Building trust is not simple. Full disclosure and in-depth understanding appear to be the only ways to overcome this potentially fatal barrier.

Lip-Service Commitment   The reality of a VMS is that one of the involved parties typically has more at stake or risk than others. This imbalance in risk, and most often power, potentially can create uneven commitment. A party to a potential VMS may be willing to dabble with the new arrangement, but no real commitment may be present to change operations.

---

[16] See Chapter 8 for a discussion of channel design techniques.

When the United States–based automotive industry first faced foreign management practices, the response was a quick adoption of just-in-time (JIT) procurement concepts with little or no real commitment to comingle and modify operations to facilitate efficiency of key suppliers.[17] In many situations, JIT in practice translated to a reduction in the number of suppliers. Those who survived were forced to assume greater inventory and operating responsibility in a basic production system that was unchanged. Pushing inventory "back on suppliers" by virtue of sheer power was highly resented by many key vendors. After some very disappointing results and an increase in adversarial sentiments, several redesigned arrangements began to flourish on trust and cooperation. The disciplined approach of a working relationship based on mutual trust and concern began to generate some real benefits for *all* involved. Assets were reduced, productivity was improved, and creativity was increased.

Human Incompatibility   In developing a VMS, remember that people, not technologies, make the unique business solutions work. In some situations, the managers involved in a VMS simply are not capable of overcoming the realities of their different business cultures. For example, Genencor, a joint venture between Corning Glass and Genentech, Inc., was seen as a near-perfect pairing of two research-based companies that could dominate the industrial enzymes market by pooling their resources. The arrangement initially failed to meet expectations because of human incompatibility and split loyalty.[18] Successful firms in an industry may have wide differences in basic values. Given the fact that people have a natural resistance to change, it appears reasonable to expect culture and style clashes when employees from two or more firms comingle. In many situations, employees of VMS member firms must work side by side, often sharing the same physical facilities.

When the arrangement is driven top-down, the problem may be as basic as middle managers simply not understanding the big picture. However, in some situations, the establishment of a VMS may be viewed as a way of putting one's career in jeopardy. Middle-level managers play a key role in successful performance. These executives often see their areas of competence becoming the prime consideration for outsourcing. If their perception is that the primary objective of a VMS is to cut cost, they may have difficulty in understanding why the old and proven techniques are not better. If these managers become the "keepers of the VMS," a satisfactory conclusion to the problem would not be likely.

To overcome the myriad of potential human-resource pitfalls, many firms use expert-systems capabilities to forge out cross-cultural relationships. Digital Equipment Corporation (DEC) has developed a proprietary top-mapping technology to isolate organizational differences and identify potential synergisms among alliance hopefuls.[19] As a neutral third party, DEC has helped to isolate and resolve potentially destructive issues, or "show stoppers" early in the process of building an integrative VMS.

---

[17] For a general discussion of overcommitment, see Christopher W. L. Hart, "The Power of Unconditional Service Guarantees," *Harvard Business Review,* **66**:4 July–August 1988, pp. 54–62.

[18] "Partnerships Are a Way of Life for Corning," *Wall Street Journal,* July 12, 1988, p. 6.

[19] Top mapping is a proprietary product of the Digital Equipment Corporation.

Inadequate Operating Framework Business cannot be conducted as usual under the umbrella of a VMS. Parties to the arrangement need to share authority over aspects of the combined venture that exceed their rightful ownership boundaries. Such cross-organizational empowerment runs contrary to traditional management paradigms. In traditional day-to-day operations, it is difficult to separate ownership from control. In a VMS, it is an essential daily practice.

As illustrated in Tables 10-3 and 10-4, what is required is a framework of interorganizational operating principles related to what the VMS is going to do and how it is going to get done. The procedures are mutually acceptable to all and are used as a guide to corrective action when things go wrong, as they invariably will. All managers and employees involved in the alliance need to fully understand the "commitment." In other words, ownership of the joint process must exist at all levels of the involved organizations.[20]

The importance of an operative framework is an everyday necessity in a working VMS. A well-orchestrated channel can be permanently ruptured by adversarial practice. In one situation, a carefully planned quick-response inventory replenishment system was brought to an abrupt halt by the receiving practices at a retailer's warehouse. Management at the local warehouse followed a practice of only granting delivery appointments twenty-four hours in advance and on a first come, first unload basis. The result was that dedicated equipment loaded with time-sensitive merchandise was delayed at the retailer's warehouse. Given a lack of a total-operations framework, VMS goals were placed in serious jeopardy. It is a natural tendency to revert to adversarial tactics when simple links in an operation bog down.

Inadequate Performance Measurement A final source of potential VMS failure can result from failure to adequately measure performance. The appropriate accounting for total-cost and asset-driven management decisions is difficult to achieve, even within a single enterprise. The task becomes increasingly more complex on an interorganizational basis.[21]

From the viewpoint of a VMS member, the key to effective measurement is an in-depth understanding of the other businesses' critical success factors. For example, standards based on average cost have little or no usefulness for measuring specialized services. In a true VMS, trading margins might be substantially lower than in a conventional channel, but utilization of assets might be significantly higher. Bergen-Brunswig has recently reported significant improvement in *earnings before income tax* (EBIT), despite substantial gross margins reductions.[22] These earnings result from the disciplined approach to distribution and improved *return on net assets* (RONA) from retail alliances with druggists.

Establishment of a successful interorganizational alliance requires creative perfor-

---

[20] Jay L. Johnson, "Internal Communication: A Key to Wal-Mart's Success," *Direct Marketing,* **52**:7 November 1989, p. 68.

[21] See Chapter 11 for a detailed discussion of performance measurement.

[22] *Bergen-Brunswig Annual Reports,* 1988 and 1989.

mance measurements that have been mutually agreed to. Each participant in a VMS needs to operate within the agreement. Firms joined together in a VMS arrangement are not responsible for one another's earnings. Price negotiations do and should take place. Competitive bidding is usually replaced with joint evaluation of alternative ways to complete the channel process. Over the long run, the VMS can only prosper if all key performers gain from the relationship. Measurement techniques and procedures to develop and maintain a vigorous VMS are not typically found in accounting textbooks. Failure to negotiate mutually accepted performance measurements could ultimately place the VMS arrangement in jeopardy.

Integrating a VMS Arrangement: Electronic Linkage

The growth of VMS arrangements has been facilitated by the rapid expansion of information technology. One impact of information has been to create the technical basis for channel alignments. A firm today is more receptive to long-term channel arrangements than in the past in part because of increased control capabilities. Increased receptivity also is a result of internal-organization trends that encourage outsourcing. The combined result is increased interest in the formation of channel alliances.

The "glue" that holds many channel alliances together is information. In Chapter 12 the rapid development of *electronic data interchange* (EDI) is discussed, including the range of specialized services such as *value-added networks* (VANs), interface translators, and Universal Product Code catalogs (UPC catalogs) that have resulted from the rapid proliferation of information technology.[23]

The marketing channel represents the primary arena in which EDI linkages can facilitate coordinated operations between trading partners. It is becoming common practice to integrate information flows to and from specialized service providers who regularly participate in a channel. From customer order entry to product delivery, every aspect of operations can be electronically coordinated to ensure high-quality performance.

In order for a channel to effectively perform in the value-added process, information exchange among participants should become highly routinized. The establishment of advanced or sophisticated communication is referred to as *electronic linkage*. Electronic linkage, which builds a business relationship around information technology, assumes that critical data will freely flow among firms joined in a channel.

Channel leadership and extended-enterprise engagement become far more practical when information is openly shared. The VMS represents an informal span of control that extends beyond the legal boundaries or operating domain traditionally afforded to a single organization by virtue of its channel position. For example, when Owens Corning Fiberglas actively collaborates in the planning and implementation of joint-marketing strategies with its independent contractor-installers, what results is an effective organizational structure that is larger in scope and intensity than any of the indi-

[23] See Chapter 12, p. 390.

vidual firms involved.[24] Such VMS arrangements depend upon advanced information technology adoption and successful coordination.

At the heart of electronic linkage are three essential ingredients: (1) formalization, (2) information sharing, and (3) connectivity.[25] The extended enterprise comes into existence as a result of commitment to all of these attributes. These three dimensions reflect intensive cooperative behavior between two or more firms involved in an extended organization.

Formalization   Formalization refers to the establishment of interorganizational rules and procedures that detail how the VMS will conduct business operations. If firms that participate in a VMS are seeking mutually desirable objectives, then formalization can result in an interorganizational culture. The VMS culture is unique in that it specifies values and requires compliance to the channel that supersedes typical ownership responsibilities or boundaries. Formalization of the ways and means of doing business as an interorganizational entity serves to create the VMS.

Information Sharing   At the heart of electronic linkage is a commitment to share information. For firms to effectively work together, they must be willing to permit access to strategic-planning information. In other words, they need to agree to an open policy regarding the sharing of information so that achievement of mutual goals can be facilitated. Such information sharing may be as simple as communicating planned production schedules to key vendors. In terms of significant downstream working relationships between retailers and wholesalers or manufacturers, information sharing may necessitate the exchange of warehouse inventory, shipouts, and detailed cash-register sales information. The objective of information sharing is to eliminate some uncertainty by providing access to key operational data. Without such information sharing, firms at one level of the channel may try to forecast events that are matters of history at another level. The key to achieving joint productivity gains is trust. Without trust, the extended enterprise cannot be a reality. Without open information sharing, trust is only an interesting concept.

Connectivity   The final attribute of electronic linkage is connectivity. Connectivity in the sense used here means that two or more firms involved in a VMS arrangement are electronically linked so that information exchange can be facilitated. This level of connectivity represents an advanced form of EDI that often requires establishment of propitiatory standards. Being "linked" means that the firms more or less share a common information architecture critical to VMS success.

The Information Integrated VMS   Figure 10-3 provides a three-dimensional illustration of the structural relationship between formalization, information sharing,

---

[24] Donald J. Bowersox, "The Strategic Benefits of Logistics Alliances," *Harvard Business Review,* **68:**4 July–August 1990, pp. 36–45.

[25] The following discussion is based on a presentation by Donald J. Bowersox, Patricia J. Daugherty, and Maurice P. Lundrigan, "Logistics Strategy and Structure Strategic Linkage," at the *1990 Council of Logistics Management Annual Conference.*

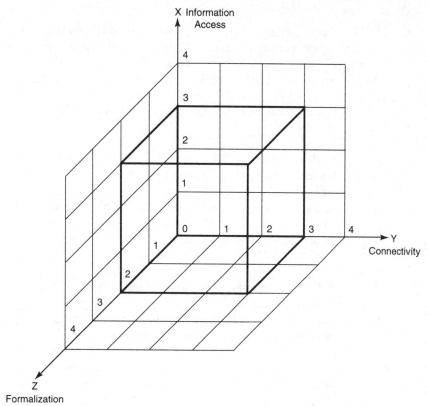

FIGURE 10-3   Measuring electronic linkage in a vertical marketing system. (*Source:* Bowersox et al., "Logistics Strategy and Structure: Strategic Linkage," presented at 1990 Council of Logistics Management Annual Conference.)

and connectivity. Some degree of each attribute exists in all channel arrangements. For a VMS to prevail over an extended period of time channel members must develop their interorganizational relationship based on all three attributes. A high degree of involvement with all three attributes reflects intensive cooperation among trading partners. For example, the relationship of Bergen-Brunswig and McKessen with their cooperating retail pharmacies scores high concerning all three attributes.

CONFLICT

Based upon the preceding discussion of channel management, a more careful examination of the emergence of conflict in VMS arrangements is now possible. While cooperative behavior is most prevalent within the channel, attention must focus on conflict because of its potential ramifications for channel management.

Types of Conflict

Simply stated, potential conflict occurs whenever channel members have distinctly different opinions or perceptions about distribution channel affairs. Conflict in distribution channels occurs in many different forms. In his pioneering work, Joseph C. Palamountain identified three types of distributive conflicts: (1) horizontal, (2) intertype, and (3) vertical.[26] Before examining vertical conflict, which is of primary importance to channel management, an examination of the two other forms provides useful background.

Horizontal Conflict   Horizontal conflict is normally treated in microeconomics because it relates to competition. The term *horizontal conflict* is used because it occurs among firms at the same level in a distribution channel. Retailers such as two hardware stores in competition with each other for the consumer's dollar are involved in horizontal conflict. Similarly, a wholesaler competing against another wholesaler or a manufacturer competing against another manufacturer are other examples of horizontal conflict.

Intertype Conflict   Intertype conflict refers to competition between different intermediaries at the same level in a channel. Intertype conflict differs from horizontal in that it occurs among dissimilar institutions competing for the same customer. The emergence of warehouse furniture outlets has spurred development of new distribution channels that compete with traditional forms of distribution. Intertype competition has significantly intensified since the advent of scrambled merchandising by retailers. *Scrambled merchandising* is the practice among retailers of offering consumers product lines unrelated to the retailers' normal business. Some supermarkets, for example, have added housewares, clothing, and other nonfood items to their merchandising profile in an effort to achieve higher margins. In doing so, they compete with the traditional channels for those products.

Manufacturers may also create intertype competition when they attempt to develop new channels of distribution. An excellent example is the Hanes Hosiery Company and its development of L'eggs pantyhose. Until Hanes introduced L'eggs, most hosiery was sold in department and specialty stores. Hanes pioneered new product packaging and unique supermarket distribution to cultivate retail exposure. Today, about 50 percent of all hosiery sales take place in grocery store and drugstore outlets.

Intertype competition is a significant form of conflict because it stimulates firms to remain efficient and respond to changing market conditions.[27] It is also significant for the ramifications it has on a firm's existing channel relationships and its potential for breeding vertical conflict.

Vertical Conflict   Vertical conflict refers to competition between different levels within a given channel of distribution. When Hanes decided to develop new retail

---

[26] Joseph C. Palamountain, Jr., *The Politics of Distribution,* Cambridge, MA: Harvard University, 1955.
[27] James R. Brown and Ralph L. Day, ''Measures of Conflict in Distribution Channels,'' *Journal of Marketing Research,* **18:**3 August 1981, pp. 263–274.

outlets for hosiery, management expected and received considerable negative reaction from department and specialty store buyers who had traditionally handled their products. Such problems among channel members are potentially devastating to the cooperative relationships existing within a channel. Because of the disruptive nature of aggression among channel members, the remainder of this chapter is devoted to a detailed investigation of the vertical conflict process.

Conflict Defined

Thus far, a formal definition of conflict has not been developed. In fact, there is some lack of agreement among social scientists as to what type of behavior is properly viewed as conflict. One traditional conception of conflict is that of hostile behavior that is designed to injure, thwart, or otherwise harm another party.[28] However, this definition is limited because conflict is only associated with incidents involving hostility. It overlooks the existence of a covert state of disagreement and the importance of subjective perceptions.[29] In terms of channel management, conflict is defined as *a situation in which one member of a distribution channel perceives another member as an adversary engaged in behavior designed to injure, thwart, or gain scarce resources at the expense of the original member.*[30] To gain a deeper understanding, we should review the complex process by which conflict develops, flourishes, and is ultimately resolved. The marketing student will observe, and baseline research indicates, that just as products and institutions follow a distinct life cycle, so does conflict.[31]

Many different events typically lead to the birth and development of hostility among channel members. It is important to understand that rarely does a single event or reason result in conflict.[32] Arising from a range of fundamental situations is often a general feeling of stress among channel members. This stress may exist and conflict may be present in a covert state for an indefinite period of time. In such cases, the frustrated members will take no specific action to voice feelings or change their behavior. However, research has identified the importance that stress plays as a prelude to overt behavior on the part of channel members.[33]

Stress that exists among channel members may ultimately build to a peak and can be expected to surface as conflict during periods of change. Change requires compli-

---

[28] For the traditional perspective, see Raymond Mack and Richard Snyder, "The analysis of Social Conflict: Toward an Overview and Synthesis," *Journal of Conflict Resolution,* **1:**2 June 1957, p. 219.

[29] Gary L. Frazier and John O. Summers, "Perceptions of Interfirm Power and Its Use within a Franchise Channel of Distribution," *Journal of Marketing Research,* **23:**2 May 1986, pp. 169–176.

[30] This definition, which relies on the perceptions of involved channel members, is developed from a generalized definition of social conflict posed in Ralph Goldman, "A theory of Conflict Processes and Organizational Offices," *Journal of Conflict Resolution,* **10:**3 September 1966, p. 335.

[31] Kenneth E. Boulding, *Conflict and Defense,* New York: Harper & Row, 1963, p. 307.

[32] Jehoshua Eliashberg and Donald A. Michie, "Multiple Business Goals Sets as Determinants of Marketing Channel Conflict: An Empirical Study," *Journal of Marketing Research,* **21:**1 February 1984, pp. 75–88.

[33] Louis W. Stern and James L. Heskett, "Conflict Management in Interorganizational Relations: A Conceptual Framework," in *Distribution Channels: Behavioral Dimensions,* ed. Louis W. Stern, Boston: Houghton Mifflin, 1969, p. 292.

ance of the frustrated channel member, which may result in open hostility among channel members. Conflict may be the result of lack of agreement about change issues. Although the distinction between causes and issues of conflict may not be obvious, the difference is important because issues are the *stated* claims or grievances by channel members and are typically quite precise. Causes, however, are generally vague. Channel participants are usually unable or unwilling to express the real causes of conflict. The issues may be considered symptoms of conflict causes. Treating conflict issues may have little effect on the removal of the underlying causes.[34] To distinguish between causes and issues, we can use a medical analogy. Treating a patient's fever does little to remove the serious infection that is causing the fever. Similarly, in distribution channels, dealing with a retailer's specific claim that a manufacturer's minimum order size is too large would do little to remove the conflict that results from the retailer's goal to minimize inventory investment. Although a specific issue may be resolved, it is likely that others will arise unless channel members fully understand the basic conflict.

When hostile behavior erupts among channel members, some mechanism is required for the resolution of the conflict. Different methods of conflict resolution exist, including techniques of problem solving, persuasion, negotiation, and political action.[35] The conflict process may be investigated in two ways. First, and of importance to channel members, is the impact of conflict on VMS roles and the ability to achieve individual goals. Second, from the viewpoint of the total channel, hostility affects overall VMS performance and customer satisfaction.

The conflict process described above is complex. The remainder of this chapter is devoted to a more in-depth examination of this process.

Causes of Conflict

A basic tenet of conflict theory is that if no interdependence exists, there will be no basis for conflict. Thus, mutual dependence creates the basis for conflict. Given the fact that the most common types of VMS behavior are cooperative, it follows that there must be some reason or combination of reasons for the development of disagreement.

Social scientists have carefully studied the basic causes of conflict. From the viewpoint of distribution channels, conflict typically results from: (1) goal incompatibility, (2) position–role–domain incongruency, (3) communication breakdown, (4) differing perceptions of reality, and (5) ideological differences.

Goal Incompatibility   All members of a VMS presumably share the common goal of maximizing their joint effectiveness. It may be assumed that each firm's management anticipates that VMS involvement will facilitate attainment of individual organizational goals. However, each firm remains a separate legal entity. Each has its

---

[34] John F. Gaskin, ''The Theory of Power and Conflict in Channels of Distribution,'' *Journal of Marketing,* **48:**3 Summer 1984, pp. 9–29.

[35] Gary L. Frazier and John O. Summers, ''Interfirm Influence Strategies and their Application within Distribution Channels,'' *Journal of Marketing,* **48:**3 Summer 1984, pp. 43–55.

own employees, stockholders or owners, and interest groups who help shape goals and strategies. Thus, each firm has goals, some of which overlap and may not be totally compatible with those of other channel members. This incompatibility may be the underlying cause of stress, which will ultimately create conflict.

A typical example of goal incompatibility leading to conflict often occurs in disagreements over the appropriate share of channel profits. Naturally, each institution desires the highest possible profit for the channel as a whole. Each individual firm also desires the largest obtainable share of total channel profits. A predictable result is conflict over the allocation process. Disagreement over trading margins represents one such form of conflict. Another form of conflict may result from the financial aid granted for performance of cooperative marketing functions. Some retailers feel that traditional cooperative advertising agreements providing 50 percent support from manufacturers are inadequate due to the high cost of color newspaper advertisements.

Even when goals of firms in a VMS are compatible, disagreement may develop as to methods. All channel members may agree that volume increases are desirable, but they may be in disagreement about how to accomplish them. Manufacturers might desire more shelf space or better positioning of their products. Retailers might feel that more advertising by the manufacturer would better accomplish the objective. Disagreement over which tactic to use in an effort to increase sales could lead to conflict and unexpected actions. For instance, if better shelf position is assigned, the retailer may raise prices to compensate for the improved space and precipitate conflict concerning the objectives of the two firms.

Position, Role, and Domain Incongruency The concepts of position, role, and domain must be recognized and agreed to by channel members. Changes in specification of position or poorly defined roles may precipitate conflict among channel members. A firm can perform or fill a position only if all other channel members agree. Thus incompatibility can develop within channel arrangements as roles and methods of operation change.

In some situations, a position may be clearly specified but the expected behavior of a channel member may not be. There may be considerable ambiguity among channel members concerning the appropriate behavior of each member. Rarely are the roles of channel members static. They can be expected to vary over time and under different circumstances. In cases in which roles change, VMS participants must agree upon the acceptable behavior of involved firms. When consensus is not reached, conflict is likely to result.

Because role definition represents a code of conduct defining a channel member's expected contribution, adequate performance is critical to maintaining harmony. The roles specified for a given channel position permit other members to predict behavior and measure contribution. A wholesaler, for example, expects certain types of behavior and levels of performance from its suppliers. Manufacturers might be expected to ship orders within forty-eight hours after receipt. A well-run wholesaler will plan inventory replenishment based on such performance expectations. If the manufacturer consistently fails to perform as expected or as promised, the wholesaler most likely will consider an alternative supply. At the very least, conflict will exist between the two channel members.[36] Inadequate role performance or failure to behave in the prescribed manner frustrates attempts by one firm to predict what the other will do. This frustration is a major cause of channel conflict. Of course, actual behavior will deviate from the expected since a firm's ability to maintain control results from many situational factors.[37]

Conflict may also arise in distribution channels in which there is a lack of agreement concerning appropriate domain. Domain dissension is a likely precipitator of hostility in at least two situations: (1) when channel members do not know or do not agree on the appropriate operational scope of other firms in the VMS, and (2) when domains overlap and two or more firms lay claim to the same functions, products, or customers. Both of these result in frustration, stress, or tension.

An excellent example of role and domain dissension is the conflict that arose between Quaker State Oil and a group of its distributors and jobbers. Quaker State adopted a policy discouraging its distributors from selling oil to discount stores. This policy was aggressively supported by retail service-station operators who felt that they were losing market share to the discount outlets. Some distributors continued to sell to discounters in violation of the policy. Apparently, these distributors believed that a manufacturer (Quaker State) had no right to limit the customers they service in their geographic area. The distributors that did not conform to policy concerning their roles behaved in a manner that caused dissension with Quaker State. In order to determine which distributors were violating the prescribed behavior, Quaker coded its packages with ink visible only under special lighting. Once the violators were traced, Quaker responded with threats to reduce or terminate deliveries. While there are legal implications to this conflict episode, it should be noted that the basic cause of hostility was dissension concerning organizational domains and role performance.

Communication Breakdown   As highlighted earlier, the importance of communication to smooth functioning of a channel system cannot be overemphasized. Communication breakdown that results in conflict can occur in at least two ways. The first way communication can break down is by a firm failing to exchange vital information with other channel members. A manufacturer wishing to maintain competitive advantage may decide not to announce a new product until a national distribution program is developed. Retailers, on the other hand, want information about new products as soon as possible to prepare their own strategies for the introductory period. Another example is a manufacturer failing to pass along vital information when products are recalled. Such recall notices, which often appear in newspapers, instruct consumers to return the product to retailers for a refund for replacement. A retailer's first awareness of a recall may be when consumers enter the store demanding compliance with the manufacturer's instructions. In such a situation, the retailer can be expected to resent and complain about the manufacturer's failure to communicate.

[36] James C. Anderson and James A. Narus, ''A Model of the Distributor's Perspective of Distribution: Manufacturer Working Relationships,'' *Journal of Marketing,* **48:**4 Fall 1984, pp. 62–74.

[37] Lynn W. Phillips, ''Explaining Control Losses in Corporate Marketing Channels: An Organization Analysis,'' *Journal of Marketing Research,* **19:**4 November 1982, pp. 525–549.

The second way that communication breakdown can occur is through noise and distortion. In a distribution channel, communication noise can arise from incomplete messages or language connotations. When various members of a distribution channel attach different meanings to specific terminology, the potential for stress increases. Such terminology distortion is illustrated by Warren Wittreich's classical example of brewery executives trying to communicate with tavern owners:

> To him (the tavern owner) "profit's a highfalutin' word used by wise guys who think they are better than he is." Being in business to "make money," he is more likely to respond to arguments or appeals which are supposed to lead to "better profits." By the same token, talk about "merchandising" or "promotion" is likely to sail over his head. In order to get him to act you have to speak to him in terms which are familiar and meaningful to him and which promise concrete rewards that he can grasp and understand.[38]

Such communications breakdowns are common in business. Often noise arises because a functional specialist develops terminology that may mean little to anyone except another specialist. Confused meanings that occur when a specialist communicates with a nonspecialist may play a major part in the development of conflict. Recently a major advertising agency realized that many nonadvertising executives did not understand such terms as "weighted target audience" and "pulsing." Consequently, the agency published a twelve-page brochure that defined key advertising terminology and explained methods of computing such measures as "readers per copy." In this manner the agency avoided potential conflict from misunderstood communication with its clients.

Differing Perceptions of Reality   Conflict may occur when VMS members differ in methods of achieving mutual goals or have different solutions to a mutual problem.[39] Even when channel members have a strong desire to cooperate, conflict can result from perceptions of what the real facts are.[40] The problem of varied perceptions occurs because all channel members have different backgrounds, prejudices, and positions in the channel. In any given situation, facts are likely to be interpreted in light of prior experience and access to available information. All members may agree that the channel is not functioning as effectively as desired. However, each member may perceive a different reason for the lack of effectiveness. The manufacturer may feel that the retailer's stock-outs are caused by a failure to maintain adequate safety stock levels. The retailer may feel that inventory policies are realistic and that the problem is caused by the manufacturer's inability to provide reliable inventory replenishment. Each party is interpreting the situation based on past experience and prejudices associated with its VMS position and role.

An interesting example of conflict resulting from different perceptions of channel

---

[38] Warren J. Wittreich, "Misunderstanding the Retailer," *Harvard Business Review,* **40:**3 May–June 1962, pp. 147–150.

[39] Robert W. Ruekert and Gilbert A. Churchill, Jr., "Reliability and Validity of Alternative Measures of Channel Member Satisfaction," *Journal of Marketing Research,* **21:**2 May 1984, pp. 226–233.

[40] George John and Torger Reve, "The Reliability of Key Informant Data from Dyadic Relationships in Marketing Channels," *Journal of Marketing Research,* **19:**4 November 1982, pp. 517–524.

members occurred when Cotton Incorporated, the marketing arm of the cotton industry, became angry with one of the primary users of cotton, Levi Strauss & Company. When Levi began making and promoting a line of denim jeans that contained 35 percent polyester, Cotton Incorporated began an advertising campaign using network television, trade journals, and consumer magazines such as Sports Illustrated and Playboy. Although Levi was not specifically named in the advertisements, the basic theme was that unless denim jeans are 100 percent cotton, they are not in fact denim jeans. Believing that the cotton-polyester blend is easier to care for than pure cotton, Levi countered with: "It's the performance of the fabric and the weave that makes it denim." Thus, conflict was spurred by a very basic difference in perception as to which characteristics constitute denim fabric. The cotton industry felt that denim has to be pure. Levi viewed performance and weave as prime determinants of denim fabric.

Ideological Differences   Ideological or value conflicts are similar to those resulting from differences in perceived roles and expected behaviors. Fundamental ideological conflict can result from big-business and small-business perceptions of the appropriate role of management. A large manufacturer may be so satisfied with the performance of a wholesale distributor that pressure is exerted to expand the business, hire new employees, and move into new territories. The wholesaler, a small individual proprietorship, may be satisfied with the existing business. Expansion may mean loss of personal control because of a need to hire additional managers. Or the expansion may require longer working hours and cause more personal frustration. The small-business owner may indeed value leisure time and fewer headaches and thus may resist expansion pressures. In such a situation, managment of the larger organization may fail to understand the value system of the small business. Conflict can be expected.

In summary, conflict has many origins. Although actual events that precipitate conflict among channel members are limitless, mutual dependence in the channel system carries with it the potential for stress and conflict concerning incompatible goals, position–role–domain incongruence, communications breakdown, differing perceptions of reality, and different ideological values of the involved institutions.

Results of Conflict

Conflict in which channel members exhibit overt hostile behavior needs to be resolved in some way. A number of methods for conflict resolution are available. However, most of the means by which conflict is resolved in a channel rely to a greater or lesser extent upon some form of power or leadership.

Regardless of the method used for conflict resolution, the resulting behavior adjustment made by channel members will depend upon whether the conflict was functional or dysfunctional. Early literature viewed all overt conflict as dysfunctional or disruptive because it forced channel members away from their cooperative relationship. More recently, however, conflict has been considered to have certain beneficial qualities that can enhance the solidarity of a channel.[41] There is no doubt, however, that in some situations dysfunctional conflict may be so pronounced that an effective channel cannot be said to exist. The results of functional and dysfunctional conflict are discussed below.

Functional System Results   The consequences of functional channel conflict can be observed in two distinct situations. The first situation involves unification of the channel system.[42] Channel members may eventually conclude that no alternative relationship exists that could satisfy goals as adequately as the current alignment. A retailer may determine that although the supplier delivers a high percentage of damaged or defective merchandise, no other manufacturer exists that does better. In such a situation, the basic problem still exists but stress is reduced. Cooperation may be fostered in such a situation if the retailer's satisfaction with the manufacturer is increased as a result of the search for alternative supply sources. Increased cooperation may produce more unified efforts to solve other problems in the channel system. In a VMS, two involved firms can work together to improve their joint situation.

The second situation in which channel conflict produces functional consequences is when a change in the system results. If the conflict episode precipitates changes in the system and this improves performance, then the conflict can be judged to be functional. For example, a conflict episode may lead a retailer to integrate operations and reduce dependence on suppliers. If the integrated retailer is able to operate more efficiently, the outcome of the conflict is positive. In essence, contrary to popular belief, *conflict that results in the disintegration of old alliances and relationships is not necessarily dysfunctional.* Rather, such consequences may be positive if the new alliances enable channel members to be serviced better, which results in an improvement in the meeting of customer's needs.

Dysfunctional System Results   Under what circumstances, then, might channel conflict be considered to be dysfunctional or harmful? To answer this question, it is necessary to take perspective similar to that used in judging functional conflict. Two situations represent dysfunctional conflict: (1) when duplication of effort results, and (2) when channel members dissipate their resources in prolonging heightening of conflict rather than seeking constructure solutions.

The duplication of effort that results from channel conflict is illustrated in the following series of relationships:

1 The higher the level of perceived vertical conflict among channel members within any given channel system, the lower the probability of functional cooperation among members.

---

[41] Peter R. Dickson, ''Distribution Portfolio Analysis and the Channel Dependence Matrix: New Techniques for Understanding and Managing the Channel,'' *Journal of Marketing,* **47**:3 Summer 1983, pp. 35–44.

[42] Gary L. Frazier, ''Interorganizational Exchange Behavior in Marketing Channels: A Broadened Perspective,'' *Journal of Marketing,* **47**:4 Fall 1983, pp. 68–78.

2 The lower the probability of functional cooperation, the greater the duplication of effort among channel members.

3 The greater the duplication of effort, the lower the performance of the channel system.[43]

If, for example, the conflicting channel members remain in a VMS relationship but choose not to cooperate in performing marketing functions, it is quite likely that duplication of effort will result. The reduction in efficiency would be dysfunctional. In addition, the increased cost that would result from duplication would probably impair the system's ability to compete effectively.

Conflict that wastes the resources of all channel members and fails to result in formation of a more effective distribution system is dysfunctional. Kenneth Boulding once termed such conflict "pathological" because, in attempting to injure or restrict, a firm's resources are expended and self-desired goals are thwarted.[44] In such situations, the conflicting parties lose sight of the original issues and allow such emotions as revenge, distrust, or insecurity to proliferate and escalate the conflict.

The aim of the marketing manager involved with channel strategy is not necessarily to avoid all conflict; rather, it is to avoid conflict that will have dysfunctional consequences. A level of tension that drives members to seek better solutions to common problems may not only lead to more satisfactory attainment of individual organizational goals but also will improve the competitive posture of the overall VMS. Thus, the major interest of the channel strategist is conflict management rather than conflict avoidance.

Conflict Resolution

It is obvious that power and conflict have close ties. Both result from mutual dependence. A clear statement of the relationship between power and conflict is

> It is apparent that a principal factor differentiating vertical conflict from horizontal and intertype competition is that it is so directly a power conflict. Power relationships among horizontal competitors occasionally are significant, but this power usually is narrowly limited. . . . This later type of competition (intertype) is almost devoid of power relationships. . . . In the plane of vertical conflict, however, power relationships are direct, obvious, and important to the extent that the market is imperfect.[45]

Attempts to utilize power may actually precipitate conflict episodes. If a channel member has a low level of tolerance for control and another system member attempts to exercise leadership, a situation of stress and conflict will develop. It is important to note that the conflict will surface over the issue of attempted leadership, but the underlying cause of conflict may be more difficult to identify. It could stem from such basic causes as goal incompatibility or dissatisfaction over distribution of rewards.

---

[43] Stern and Heskett, op. cit., p. 293.

[44] Kenneth E. Boulding, "The Economics of Human Conflict," in *The Nature of Human Conflict,* ed. Elton B. McNeil, Englewood Cliffs, NJ: Prentice-Hall, 1965, pp. 174–175.

[45] Palamountain, Jr., op. cit., pp. 51–52.

But it is important to understand that when an attempt is made to control a channel member's decisions or behavior and when the level of influence exerted exceeds that firm's tolerance, conflict will result.

Conflict may also develop from a firm's attempt to gain more power.[46] What is not clear is whether the attempt is to gain power or to satisfy the firm's goals. A retailer that undertakes a market study to gain information may simply desire better knowledge so that internal decisions can be made more effectively. However, the information will most likely also serve to increase the retailer's expert power.

The balance of power in itself may create conflict. A relationship in which one party maintains a relative advantage may be considered unstable because it encourages the use of power.[47] The implication is that the more powerful channel member over time will become insensitive to the tolerance level of VMS members.

Although power can precipitate conflict, it is also the means by which conflict or hostility is resolved. Each method of resolution involves, to a greater or lesser extent, a power relationship among conflicting channel members. A marketing manager must be sensitive to the ways in which power is directly or indirectly related to attempts among channel members to maintain cooperative relationships. Once an established channel experiences conflict, a natural tendency exists to seek a satisfactory solution. Four basic processes by which conflict may be resolved have been identified in the field of organizational behavior. These four methods are:

Problem solving. It is assumed in problem solving that conflicting parties share mutual objectives and that the solution is to find a way to satisfy shared goals.

Persuasion. In persuasion, it is assumed that the goals of the conflicting parties differ, but that they are subject to modification. If basic agreement exists regarding objectives, conflict over subgoals can be resolved by reference to common objectives.

Negotiation. In negotiation, disagreement over goals is assumed to be fixed. An end to conflict is sought by the development of new agreements with no attempt to refer to common objectives.

Politics. Politics is similar to bargaining, except participants attempt to increase the number of parties involved in the resolution process.[48]

These four processes for conflict resolution and the ways in which they relate to channel management are explained in greater detail.

Problem Solving A number of problem-solving techniques exist within distribution channels. The two most important are the development and emphasis of superordinate goals, and improvement of the communications process among channel members.

Superordinate Goals Since each VMS member has joined to achieve goals that

---

[46] Gil Butaney and Lawrence H. Wortzell, "Distributor Power versus Manufacturer Power: The Customer Role," *Journal of Marketing*, **52:**1 January 1988, pp. 52–63.

[47] Robert F. Lusch and James R. Brown, "A Modified Model of Power in the Marketing Channel," *Journal of Marketing Research*, **19:**3 August 1982, pp. 312–323.

[48] This long-standing structure is adopted from James G. March and Herbert A. Simon, *Organizations*, New York: John Wiley and Sons, 1958, p. 165.

could not be obtained otherwise, a basis for problem solving exists. Essentially, a superordinate goal is one that all channel members desire but that cannot be achieved by any one firm acting alone. All channel members have a stake in the operating efficiency of the channel system and most likely have as an overriding goal a desire to increase total performance. By increasing total output, all firms may be better off than if they allowed conflict to limit or restrict the system's ability to produce. In such instances, appeals to the superordinate goal may aid in ending a conflict episode.

The establishment of superordinate goals becomes most likely when a channel confronts an external threat. Only a few years ago conflict between gasoline service station operators and oil refineries was common. In recent years, however, this conflict has been reduced as the overall petroleum distribution system has been confronted with numerous threats such as supply shortages and potential congressional actions. Similarly, conflict among members of a channel seems to dissipate when an alternative distribution system arises. The development of superordinate goals and reduction of conflict may be temporary. When the outside threat is removed, internal stress and conflict is likely to occur again.

Communication Processes   A number of methods exist to alleviate communication noise in distribution channels. More efficient flow of information and/or communications in the channel will permit channel members to find solutions to their conflict based on common objectives.

Many industries have established trade organizations that include as members firms from all levels of the distribution channel. The International Foodservice Manufacturers Association (IFMA) is a trade group that deals in distribution of food to the away-from-home market. The membership of the IFMA includes not only food processors, but also equipment manufacturers, food brokers, and hotel and restaurant chains. Through meetings and trade publications, channel members are able to share information and improve communications. In addition, meetings permit member firms to develop solutions to common problems; thus, they reinforce channel relationships.

To some extent, all channel communications are efforts to decrease or avoid conflict. The use of sales representatives by a manufacturer to convey information to and from wholesalers and/or retailers implies that the manufacturer is attempting to encourage attainment of its individual goals as well as common goals. The function of a sales representative for a manufacturer has often been described as that of a problem solver.

Persuasion   Persuasion as a means of resolving conflict implies that the involved institutions draw upon leadership. By its very nature, persuasion involves communication between conflicting parties. The emphasis is upon influencing behavior through persuasion rather than only by the sharing of information. Specifically, the purpose of persuasion in the resolution of conflicts is primarily to avoid or reduce conflict about domain.

Disagreement about or overlap in domains is a primary cause of channel conflict. Since channel members may agree upon superordinate goals, persuasion may be employed to help members resolve differences concerning territories, functions, or customers. The important point is that the persuading member should appeal to the conflicting channel members and remind them of their commitment to superordinate goals of the channel. Agreement that is reached through the process of persuasion alleviates or reduces stress. It also usually results in redefinition among channel members of their domain.

Negotiation[49]   In negotiation, no attempt is made to fully satisfy a channel member. Instead, the objective of negotiation is to halt a conflict. Such compromise may resolve the episode but not necessarily the fundamental stress over which the conflict erupted. If stress continues, it is likely that some issue or another will cause future conflict.

Compromise is one means by which bargains can be reached among channel members. In compromise situations, each party gives up something it desires in order to prevent or to end conflict. Often, compromise is necessary so that consensus about domain can be reached in situations in which persuasion is ineffective.

Both persuasion and negotiation draw upon abilities of the involved parties to communicate. In fact, the resolution of conflicts by the utilization of either of these processes requires that each party develop a strategy to ensure a favorable resolution. Both parties must reach a satisfactory agreement that does not increase hostility. It is extremely important for the marketing manager to understand how effective negotiation strategies are developed.

Politics   Politics refers to the resolution of conflict by the involvement of new organizations or parties in the process of reaching an agreement. Examples of such solutions are coalition formation, arbitration or mediation, and lobbying or judicial appeal.

Coalitions   The formation of coalitions among channel members is, in effect, an attempt to alter the channel power structure. The National Automobile Dealer's Association offers dealers the capability to deal effectively with manufacturers. Voluntary and cooperative retail chains allow smaller retailers to negotiate with food processors on an equal basis with large supermarket chains. The formation of such coalitions represents a political move by channel members. Once a coalition is formed, however, the conflict resolution process may be achieved through problem solving, persuasion, or negotiation. In addition, coalitions may become involved in additional forms of political activity that are discussed below.

Mediation and Arbitration   Both mediation and arbitration involve a third party in the conflict resolution process. In mediation, the third party may suggest a solution to the conflict but channel members are not required to accept that solution. In arbitration, the solution suggested by the intermediary is binding upon the conflicting parties. Although there are many reasons to submit to mediation or arbitration for the resolution of distribution conflicts, actual examples of the use of these mechanisms are rare. Perhaps the major reason for this is that it is difficult to find a neutral third party whose decision would be acceptable to the conflicting channel members.

It is often suggested that trade associations undertake the mediator or arbitrator function. At least two factors usually preclude involvement by trade association. The

---

[49] The role of negotiation in channel planning was the topic of Chapter 9.

first is the fact that trade associations normally have predominant membership from one channel level; thus, members' views will most likely be biased and unacceptable to one or more of the conflicting parties. The second factor concerns the nature of the arbitration or mediation process, which may require that proprietary information be revealed. Neither channel member is likely to want to share this information with other trade members.

Lobbying and Judicial Appeal   Channel members may resort to the governmental process in order to resolve conflicts. Attempts to influence the legislative process through lobbying activities are frequent. Court litigation is also a popular means for the resolution of conflict by the drawing of outside parties into the relationship.

Withdrawal   An additional method for the termination of conflict is the withdrawal of one firm from the relationship so that the hostile behavior existing in the channel can be avoided. Withdrawal is a relatively common method of conflict resolution. A firm that decides to terminate its existing channel relationship should have an alternative available or must be willing to change the nature of its business and goals if such alternatives are not available.

If a firm decides to continue in the same business, channel alternatives must exist. Either the cost of the alternative should be no greater than the cost of the existing system, or the firm should be willing to incur higher costs to avoid the hostility inherent in the existing channel. A retailer may choose to end a relationship with a current supplier because of a specific activity on the part of the supplier. The retailer can easily do so as long as alternative sources of supply exist and can provide essentially the same mix of product and services as the current supplier.

A firm may choose to withdraw from a channel if it decides to alter its mission. In this case, benefits obtained from the existing channel are reduced in importance or at least the goals of the firm have changed so that they are less important. A manufacturer, for example, may terminate relationships with an entire retail chain or group because the profits obtained from a specific line of private-label merchandise are not sufficient to compensate for the effort involved in conflict resolution.

SUMMARY

Businesses differ in their abilities and desires to perform overall marketing functions. Therefore, through the process of specialization, they often align themselves with other firms into organized marketing channels. As a result of this combination, each firm becomes dependent upon others in the channel system for the accomplishment of its objectives. This mutual dependence lays the foundation for three types of behavior that are critical to channel management: cooperation, power, and conflict. A key to channel management is leadership. Most leadership in marketing results from power. In all situations, potential channel members have limited tolerance for following others. The leadership process in a channel can become complex. In advanced situations, what can result is what amounts to an extended enterprise that links a firm with its customers, service suppliers, and materials vendors.

Vertical marketing systems (VMSs) represent channel structures that build upon cooperative behavior. VMS arrangements are characterized by repeat business situations. All VMS arrangements are based upon acknowledged dependence among participants. The chapter looked at basic principles that guide formation of VMS agreements and the attributes of a successful arrangement. Examples of guidelines to build successful alliances were illustrated from the perspective of a manufacturer and a service specialist. Some clear reasons why VMS arrangements fail were also reviewed.

For a VMS to reach the expectations of its participating members, major commitments by those members are required for the sharing of communications in strategic linkage. The information-integrated VMS is becoming a popular form of new business arrangement.

Channel conflict occurs in three forms. The first is horizontal conflict, or competition, which takes place among firms at the same level of distribution. The second is intertype, which takes place between two competing or alternative channel systems. Of particular interest to channel management is the third form of hostility, vertical conflict, which occurs among different levels of a marketing channel.

Although the seeds of vertical conflict lie in mutual dependence, several primary causes of this behavior have been identified. When the goals of individual firms are incompatible with one another or with channel goals, conflict may develop. Poor specification or performance in positions, roles, or domains may lead to hostile behavior. Differing perceptions among firms, communications breakdowns, and differing ideologies may also precipitate conflict.

Vertical conflict can have important ramifications upon channel performance. A low level of tension among firms may lead to better performance but, as conflict escalates, the system may be disrupted. Nevertheless, system disruption is not necessarily dysfunctional. If disruption results in changes or new alignments of firms which then perform marketing functions more effectively or efficiently, the conflict can be considered functional from a macro perspective. Conflict is dysfunctional when resources are wasted or when system adaptations result in new channels that cannot perform marketing functions as efficiently as the original system.

QUESTIONS

1 Discuss the concept of channel leadership. How do potential leaders gain followers?
2 How does the culture of a VMS fit into the typical notion of culture within individual channel member firms?
3 Why do VMS arrangements fail? Give examples of each common reason.
4 Explain the concept of an extended enterprise. What are the benefits for all parties involved?
5 Discuss and illustrate the idea of strategic linkage. What is meant by the concept of a "level playing field"?
6 Why is intertype competition considered a means by which industries remain efficient in their response to changing market conditions?
7 Explain why mutual dependence is considered the basis for channel conflict.
8 Why do you believe the authors feel that conflict that results in disintegration of a channel is not necessarily dysfunctional? Give an example to support this contention.

9 Explain the concepts of position, role, and domain. Draw upon your knowledge of the channels for automobiles to illustrate each concept.

10 How might development of advanced point-of-sale (POS) systems for retail stores help reduce communication breakdowns in channels of distribution? Can you think of circumstances in which conflict might be increased due to these systems?

11 "Since each business firm desires to maximize its own profits, there must necessarily be conflict among channel members about the distribution of total-channel profits." Discuss this statement.

12 Why should a formal definition of conflict rely on the perceptions of the involved parties rather than focus only on overt instances of hostile behavior? How does this impact the use of different conflict resolution mechanisms and their effectiveness? Under what conditions are different mechanisms likely to be effective given the role of perception?

CHAPTER 11

PERFORMANCE MEASUREMENT

CHAPTER OBJECTIVES

A MACRO PERSPECTIVE OF CHANNEL PERFORMANCE
   Macro Objectives
   Macro Efficiency

MEASURING FINANCIAL PERFORMANCE
   Segment Definition
   Revenue and Cost Analysis
   Strategic Profit Model

MEASURING CUSTOMERS' SATISFACTION
   Satisfaction and Service Quality
   Methodology

SUMMARY

A critical aspect of strategic channel management is the measurement of channel performance. Comprehensive performance measurement provides the necessary feedback mechanism that alerts management to problems and opportunities for improvement in channel design and structures, and in individual channel members. This chapter develops a framework for comprehensive performance assessment and provides insight into the managerial process of identifying and correcting performance problems.

The chapter begins with a brief overview of a macroperspective of channel performance. This perspective incorporates a view of how well the distribution system meets society's needs in terms of both efficiency and effectiveness. Efficiency refers to the accomplishment of distribution tasks with the least use of resources, whereas effectiveness is concerned with how well distribution objectives are accomplished. Attention then turns to the key managerial issues of channel performance measurement. Methodologies for measuring channel financial performance, including cost, profitability, and return on investment, are discussed.

Assessment of customer satisfaction and service quality is discussed as a means of evaluating channel performance as well as the performance of channel partners. Satisfaction is presented as a key factor in the maintenance of distribution channel relationships that accomplish channel objectives. The meaning of satisfaction, its relationship to quality, and determinants are discussed. The chapter concludes with a framework for measuring and improving satisfaction levels.

A MACRO PERSPECTIVE OF CHANNEL PERFORMANCE

A recurring question dealing with distribution in society is: Has the consumer been paying too much for goods and services because of the cost of distribution? The answer to this question has been elusive due to many inherent problems associated with two tasks: quantifying the appropriate objectives for distribution in the economic sector and gathering data. To answer the question of whether or not distribution ''costs too much,'' it is first necessary to specify these objectives and then assess current performance relative to those objectives.

Macro Objectives

It has generally been agreed by marketing analysts that the output of distribution is a series of services for consumers. Bucklin suggested that these services can be classified as lot size, waiting time, market decentralization, and product variety.[1] *Lot size* refers to the ability of consumers to purchase products in the quantities they desire. *Waiting time* is the length of time it takes for customers to gain possession of goods after they have purchased them. *Market decentralization* refers to the proximity of goods to buyers and to the customers' convenience in buying. *Product variety* refers to the customers' ability to purchase an assortment of goods and services that matches their unique desires.

Clearly, the measurement of distribution systems on a societal or even an industry level in terms of these service outputs is virtually impossible. In fact, it should not be suggested that society would necessarily benefit from maximization of any one or all of these service outputs. For example, an increase in product variety may lead to an excessive proliferation of products and a trivialization of features in the product assortments. Determination of the optimum performance of an economy's distribution structure in terms of service outputs will, most likely, continue to be difficult.

A related issue concerns how well the distribution system provides equitable access to service for all members of society. For example, in rural areas and urban ghettos

[1] Louis P. Bucklin, ''Marketing Channels and Structures,'' in *AMA Combined Conference Proceedings,* eds. Boris W. Becker and Helmut Becker, Chicago: American Marketing Association, 1973, pp. 32–35.

the assortment of products available, the locational convenience, and the waiting time for service may all be significantly worse than in other markets. Similarly, prices to these consumers are generally higher than in other markets.

Nevertheless, it may be useful in channel management to ask questions about the ability of existing structures within an industry to satisfy customers. Have customers' needs or desires for the four service outputs described by Bucklin been met? Such analysis may reveal a potential for innovation that would otherwise remain undetected. An interesting example is revealed by the changes in the distribution channels for household furniture. For decades, the distribution of furniture required that consumers visit local independent furniture stores. These were, in effect, nothing more than show-rooms that displayed various styles and models of furniture. On visiting a store a consumer could choose, for example, a sofa in a desired style and with a specific pattern of upholstery. The furniture retailer, in turn, would send the customer's order to the manufacturer who would then schedule the item for production. It was not uncommon for the consumer to wait as long as six months for the sofa to be produced and delivered. Due to these long lead times, many customers were dissatisfied. In the 1960s, alternative channels for distribution of furniture emerged. Large furniture retail-ers came into existence that maintained sufficient inventories to allow consumers to take possession of their furniture at the time of purchase. While consumers may have given up some freedom of choice in terms of the product variety available, many are willing to make that trade-off in order to obtain the products immediately. In the 1990s, both channel structures are available to consumers, and one can be selected based on the individual's needs.

Macro Efficiency

A number of studies of distribution efficiency have been conducted in this century that focus on the cost and productivity of distribution performance. As far back as the 1930s, the Twentieth Century Fund concluded that distribution costs, in total, account for 59 percent of the cost of finished goods.[2] These costs include the cost of logistics functions as well as the cost of wholesaling and retailing. Other scholars have focused their attention on specific economic sectors such as the wholesale and retail structure to determine the cost of these activities.[3]

One recent study in the United States compared the cost of selected logistics func-tions prior to the deregulation of transportation in the early 1980s to the cost of those functions after deregulation. Table 11-1 presents the results of that study.

While the costs of performing logistics activities in absolute dollars expended rose consistently throughout the 1970s and 1980s, these costs can be shown to have declined if they are figured as a percentage of total gross national product. There may be several explanations for this more efficient management of logistics functions dur-

[2] "Twentieth Century Fund, Committee on Distribution," *Does Distribution Cost Too Much?,* New York: Twentieth Century Fund, 1939.

[3] See, for example, T. N. Beckman, "Measuring Productivity in Marketing," *Proceedings of the Busi-ness and Economic Section of the American Statistical Association,* Washington, DC: The American Sta-tistical Association, 1960.

TABLE 11-1 UNITED STATES LOGISTICS COSTS (IN BILLIONS), 1972–1988

	Inventory carrying cost	Transportation cost	Logistics administrative cost	Total	Percentage of gross national product
1972	$ 54	$ 97	$ 6	$157	12.6%
1974	83	116	8	207	14.5
1976	80	133	9	222	12.9
1978	107	175	12	294	13.6
1980	153	205	15	373	14.2
1982	161	240	17	418	13.6
1984	159	250	16	425	11.2
1986	172	271	18	461	10.9
1988	196	313	20	529	10.9

Source: Robert V. Delaney, *Cass Logistics, Inc.* Reproduced with permission.

ing the 1980s, including the deregulated transportation environment, more attention to inventory management, and introduction of technologies that brought both analytic and operational efficiencies to logistics functions. Regardless, the implication is clear that as the decade progressed consumers paid less for physical distribution functions as a percentage of their total expenditure.

MEASURING FINANCIAL PERFORMANCE

Costs, revenues, and asset investments made in distribution channels can be used by a firm to determine the relative profitability and financial performance of those channels. As a result of the financial analysis, one or more appropriate managerial actions may be taken. One alternative action may be to seek operational changes that would result in changes in profitability. For example, a change in the product mix sold through a channel might lead to increased profitability. Changes in the frequency of sales calls, the size of minimum orders, or promotional expenses might also lead to changes in profitability. Alternatively, elimination of a distribution channel may be the most viable solution. None of these decisions can be made without a detailed assessment of financial performance.

Comprehensive financial performance measurement requires that management appropriately define proper segments for investigation. Costs, revenues, and investments must be analyzed and charged to the appropriate segments. A format for analysis must be developed. Methodologies for accomplishing these tasks are discussed below. It should be mentioned that a similar form of analysis was discussed in Chapter 8, one related to the evaluation and selection of channel alternatives. In that discussion, the identification of costs, revenues, and assets required forecasts and estimates of activity levels so that the appropriate channel alternative could be selected. In performance measurement, the problem faced by management is somewhat different. It is necessary to determine the performance of existing channel structures so that management can identify appropriate action for improvement.

Segment Definition

A well-accepted principle in business is that a small percentage of a firm's products, channels, territories, or customers normally makes up a large percentage of the firm's sales, costs, and/or profits. This rule of thumb, typically called the 80-20 principle, is a fundamental starting point for segment analysis. The very real problem faced by most firms is that in recent years the number of products, channels, territories, and customers has increased dramatically. The determination of which segments, or combination of segments, are profitable and which are not has become an increasingly complex process. Nevertheless, the decision of how to define segments for analysis represents a critical step in financial performance measurement. Typical segment classifications used by many firms include distribution channels among others.

Distribution Channel Segments Distribution channel segments may be defined in several ways. For example, a firm may wish to investigate the profitability of basic channel structures such as direct sales and delivery versus sales through intermediary institutions. The Eddie Bauer Company, which sells and distributes products through both mail-order catalogs and a network of company-owned retail stores, might find that one of these distribution channels is significantly more profitable than another.

A second type of distribution channel segment can typically be identified in terms of the specific institutional form utilized by a firm within a basic channel structure. For example, a large consumer-goods manufacturer may analyze profitability of sales through traditional supermarkets, wholesale clubs, and mass-merchandise outlets, realizing that the costs of marketing and distribution may vary among the types of outlets due to their differing operational characteristics. Supermarket chains and mass merchandisers typically receive full-truckload shipments at central-warehouse facilities, whereas wholesale clubs require small, frequent shipments to individual store locations. Such varieties in operations may result in dramatically different cost and profitability structures for each type of store.

Other Segment Divisions Segment definition by distribution channel may not provide management with sufficient information to fully assess financial results and determine appropriate corrective action. The above analysis may indicate that financial results are inadequate in a particular channel but not provide insight into the underlying causes of poor performance. A more comprehensive approach to assessment requires that results be segmented in further detail. Recommended approaches to more detailed segmentation are classification within distribution channels of cost and revenue by product, territory, and/or order characteristics.

Product segmentation requires examination of revenues and costs of a specific product or product line. Because most companies produce and distribute multiple products through multiple distribution channels, this type of analysis is useful for two tasks: determining which products return adequate profits through which distribution channels, and making decisions about product addition, deletion, promotions, and pricing strategies. In cases in which product lines are extremely varied, it is useful to group products and conduct an analysis on the basis of such characteristics as product category, the method of packaging (packaged goods versus bulk, for example), or sales volume.[4]

Geographic territory is another commonly used segmentation variable. It is quite likely that certain geographic segments within a distribution channel are profitable while others are not. Geographic territories may be defined by company sales districts, political units such as states or cities, economic units such as metropolitan statistical areas, or even ZIP codes.[5]

Because some orders that a firm receives may be profitable while others may not, many firms analyze profitability of various types of orders. Orders may be segmented according to the dollar value of the order, the number of products on the order, or even the number of units of product on a single order.[6] Other firms may investigate profitability of orders based on the method by which the order was received such as mail, telephone, and electronic transmission.

Financial analysis of segments has been in existence for a number of years. Each firm must develop for itself a method for evaluating performance of various types of channels, products, territories, and orders. Unfortunately, as the number of segment categories increases, so does the complexity and difficulty of performing the actual profitability analysis. As shown in Figure 11-1a and b, even a very simple hypothetical company that utilizes two channels for three products in two territories may find itself with numerous analyses to perform. The addition of a new level of segmentation or an expansion in the segment classifications within a level may increase the complexity of the analysis by a considerable degree. Without segment analysis, however, management is unable to ascertain financial performance in a manner useful for decision making.

Revenue and Cost Analysis

Following segment definition, revenues and costs associated with each segment must be identified. The issue of appropriate segment costing has generated considerable debate in recent years. It is clear that most corporate accounting systems today are inadequate for detailed segment costing. Accounting systems that were originally developed for the purpose of valuing inventory and financial statement preparation do not provide accurate data for measuring operational performance of channels, products, territories, or other critical operating divisions.[7]

Traditional accounting systems tend to collect cost data and aggregate them into so called "natural" categories. Natural expenses include such categories as salaries

---

[4] Donald W. Jackson, Jr., and Lonnie L. Ostrom, "Grouping Products for Profitability Analysis," *MSU Business Topics*, **28**:2 Spring 1980, p. 40.

[5] Ibid., p. 43.

[6] Ibid.

[7] See, for example, Robert S. Kaplan, "One Cost System Isn't Enough," *Harvard Business Review*, **66**:1 January–February 1988, pp. 61–66; Robin Cooper and Robert S. Kaplan, "Measure Costs Right: Make the Right Decisions," *Harvard Business Review*, **66**:5 September–October 1988, pp. 96–103; Robin Cooper and Robert S. Kaplan, "Profit Priorities from Activity-Based Costing," *Harvard Business Review*, **69**:3, May–June 1991, pp. 130–136.

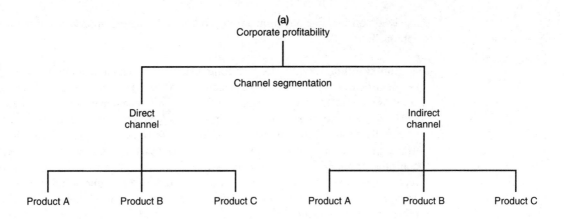

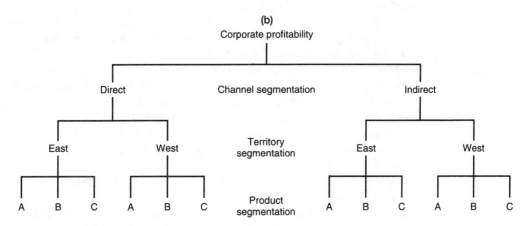

FIGURE 11-1   (a) Segmental analysis by channel and product category; (b) segmental analysis by channel, territory, and product category.

and wages, rent, utilities, supplies, and taxes, which describe the nature of the cost item or the object of the expenditure. It is common for many such natural cost categories to be broken down by business function or responsibility center. For example, management can distinguish between salaries paid to salespeople and wages paid to warehouse employees. One marketing expert suggests seven such functional categories that reflect marketing functions: (1) direct selling costs, (2) indirect selling costs, (3) advertising, (4) sales promotion, (5) transportation, (6) storage and shipping, and (7) order processing.[8] Most companies perform this level of natural or functional cost identification relatively well.[9] The major problem experienced and the subject of considerable controversy concerns the next step: identifying the costs associated with serving specific channels, territories, and/or products. Two approaches that have each

[8] Charles H. Sevin, *Marketing Productivity Analysis,* New York: McGraw-Hill, 1965.
[9] Cooper and Kaplan, op. cit., p. 62.

received considerable attention are the contribution margin approach and the net profit approach.

Contribution Margin   A pure contribution margin approach requires that all costs be identified as fixed or variable according to the behavior of the cost. *Fixed costs* are those costs that do not change in the short run (management salaries, for example). *Variable costs* are those that change in a predictable manner in relation to some level of activity during a time period (sales commissions, for example). Normally (but not necessarily, as discussed later) the level of activity is sales volume. An extended contribution margin approach requires further identification of costs as direct or indirect.[10] A *direct cost* is one that is directly incurred by the segment under consideration. *Indirect costs* (frequently called *joint costs*) are those incurred due to the existence of more than one segment. Stated another way, direct costs are those that would no longer exist if a specific segment were eliminated. Indirect costs would continue to exist even if that segment were eliminated.

Income statements in the contribution margin method of analysis can be prepared that identify profitability for each segment by determination of fixed, variable, direct, and indirect costs. Table 11-2 provides a hypothetical example of such income statements for a firm analyzing profitability of two distribution channel segments. Variable cost of goods sold is directly related to the product mix sold in each channel segment; it includes only direct labor, materials, and supplies. All factory overhead costs are treated as indirect fixed costs in the contribution margin approach. Variable direct costs include such items as sales commissions, discounts, and any other expenses that may vary directly with volume within a channel. (Notice that the percentage of variable direct cost-to-sales may vary in each channel.) Fixed direct costs include any other costs that can be traced directly to a channel segment. Such costs might include sales salaries and expenses (if separate sales forces are utilized), advertising media costs, promotion costs, and other expenses targeted at specific channels. Indirect fixed costs include all expenses that cannot easily be traced to a specific segment.

In Table 11-2, both channels are covering direct costs and making substantial contribution to indirect fixed cost. The health care channel, however has a substantially higher percentage net segment contribution than does the retail channel (37 percent versus 26 percent). A large portion of this difference is attributable to the difference in variable gross profit (58 percent versus 50 percent). This difference suggests that analysis of the product mix for the retail channel should be conducted to determine whether or not emphasis should be placed on a more profitable mix. Elimination of

[10] Terminology in the contribution margin approach can be quite confusing. Various authors classify costs as controllable/noncontrollable, traceable/nontraceable, or relevant/nonrelevant. While minor distinctions may exist among these categories, we have chosen the most common classification scheme of direct/ indirect cost. See Patrick M. Dunne and Harry I. Wolk, "Marketing Cost Analysis: A Modularized Contribution Approach, *Journal of Marketing,* **41:**3 July 1977, pp. 83–94; Leland L. Beik and Stephen L. Busby, "Profitability Analysis by Market Segments," *Journal of Marketing,* **37:**3 July 1973, pp. 48–53; W. F. Christopher, "Marketing Achievement Reporting: A Profitability Approach," *Marketing Effectiveness: Insights from Accounting and Finance,* eds. J. Shapiro and V. H. Kirpalani, Boston: Allyn and Bacon, 1978, pp. 79–100.

TABLE 11-2   CONTRIBUTION MARGIN INCOME STATEMENT BY CHANNEL SEGMENT

	Health care channel	Retail channel	Total company
Revenue	$100,000	$150,000	$250,000
Less: Variable cost of goods sold	42,000	75,000	117,000
Variable gross profit	58,000	75,000	133,000
Less: Variable direct cost	6,000	15,000	21,000
Gross segment contribution	52,000	60,000	112,000
Less: Fixed direct cost	15,000	21,000	36,000
Net segment contribution	37,000	39,000	76,000
Less: Indirect fixed cost			41,000
Net profit			25,000
Net segment contribution ratio	37%	26%	30.4%

the retail channel should be placed on a more profitable mix. Elimination of the retail channel would be a clear mistake, however; the health care channel would then have to bear all of the indirect fixed cost, resulting in a net loss for the total company of $4000.

Net Profit Approach   The net profit approach to financial assessment of segments requires that all operating costs be charged or allocated to one operating segment. Proponents of this approach argue that all of a company's activities exist to support the production and delivery of goods and services to customers. Furthermore, most of the costs that exist in a firm are, in fact, joint or shared costs. In order for the true profitability of a channel, territory, or product to be determined, each segment must be charged with its fair share of these costs.

Significant problems arise in determining how to allocate these costs on a fair and equitable basis. Proponents of the contribution margin approach justify it by contending that such allocations are necessarily arbitrary and result in misleading financial assessment. They point to the use of sales volume as a typical basis for proration of expense and the inherent bias in such an approach. For example, a channel that accounts for 50 percent of total sales volume does not necessarily account for 50 percent of the expense of advertising, warehousing, order processing, or any other shared activity.

Net profit proponents argue, however, that the traditional notions of fixed and variable costs and direct and indirect costs are too simplistic. Many of the so-called indirect fixed costs are not, in fact, indirect or fixed at all. These expenses rise and fall, depending upon demands placed upon the business by the various operating segments.[11]

For example, most firms typically treat a financial services department, which handles such duties as general accounting, accounts payable, accounts receivable, invoic-

[11] B. Charles Ames and James D. Hlavacek, "Vital Truths about Managing Your Costs," *Harvard Business Review,* **68:**1 January–February 1990, p. 144.

TABLE 11-3(a)   PROFITS BY COMMERCIAL DISTRIBUTION CHANNEL (OLD SYSTEM)

	Contract	Industrial suppliers	Government	OEM	Total commercial
Annual sales					
(in thousands of dollars)	$79,434	$25,110	$422	$9,200	$114,166
Gross margin	34%	41%	23%	27%	35%
Gross profit	$27,375	$10,284	$136	$2,461	$ 40,256
SG&A allowance*					
(in thousands of dollars)	$19,746	$ 6,242	$105	$2,287	$ 31,814
Operating profit					
(in thousand of dollars)	$ 7,629	$ 4,042	$ 31	$ 174	$ 11,876
Operating margin	10%	16%	7%	2%	10%

SG&A allowance for each channel is 25% of that channel's revenue.

ing, and database administration, as a fixed indirect cost. One company conducted an in-depth analysis to determine what factors in the firm placed demands on the activities of the department. It found that a division in the firm that dealt with a small number of high-volume customers made very different demands on its activities than did a division that had numerous small-volume customers. Whereas previously the firm charged each division for financial services based on its percentage of sales, it now has instituted a system that allocates costs based on which division and products generate the costs.[12]

The concept implied above is that costs of operation can be traced to the performance and volume of activity, not just the sales volume, generated by a segment. The critical problem lies in determining what activities are the real source of the costs and then tracing the activities to the appropriate segments. This approach is known as *activity-based costing*. The strategic benefits of doing so may be considerable.

Robin Cooper and Robert S. Kaplan report a study of a building-supply company that had distributed products through four commercial channels of distribution. In its original accounting system, the company charged selling, general, and administrative expenses to each channel at 25 percent of sales volume. The result, as seen in Table 11-3*a* was that the original equipment manufacturer (OEM) channel showed low profitability and was a candidate for elimination. A more detailed activity-based analysis showed, however, that the OEM channel used no resources in advertising, sales promotion, and warranty administration and used far fewer resources, proportionately, of other expenses. Table 11-3*b* shows a revised income statement for segments developed from this activity-based analysis of expenses. The analysis demonstrated that the OEM channel segment was, in fact, a good performer.

According to proponents of this activity-based costing method, only two types of costs should be excluded from allocation to segments. First, any cost of excess capac-

[12] Cooper and Kaplan, op. cit., p. 101.

TABLE 11-3(b) PROFITS BY COMMERCIAL DISTRIBUTION CHANNEL (NEW SYSTEM)

	Contract	Industrial suppliers	Government	OEM	Total commercial
Gross profit (from previous table)	$27,375	$10,284	$136	$2,461	$40,256
Selling expenses (all in thousands of dollars)					
Commission	$ 4,682	$ 1,344	$ 12	$ 372	$ 6,410
Advertising	132	38	0	2	172
Catalog	504	160	0	0	664
Co-op advertising	416	120	0	0	536
Sales promotion	394	114	0	2	510
Warranty	64	22	0	4	90
Sales administration	5,696	1,714	20	351	7,781
Cash Discount	892	252	12	114	1,270
Total	$12,780	$ 3,764	$ 44	$ 845	$17,433
General and administrative expense (in thousands of dollars)	$ 6,740	$ 2,131	$ 36	$ 781	$ 9,688
Operating profit (in thousands of dollars)	$ 7,855	$ 4,389	$ 56	835	13,135
Operating margin	10%	17%	13%	9%	12%

Source: Adapted from Cooper and Kaplan, *op. cit.,* "Measure Costs Right: Make the Right Decisions," *Harvard Business Review,* 66:5, pp. 103–104. Reprinted by permission of *Harvard Business Review.* Copyright 1988 by the President and Fellows of Harvard College; all rights reserved.

ity in a firm should not be charged to a segment. Thus, if an order-processing system could process 5 million orders per year but is only utilized for 4 million orders, the excess capacity should not be charged to any segment. Similarly, if a warehouse and its employees could handle 100,000 shipments but are only used for 80,000, the excess capacity is a cost of the time period rather than a cost attributable to an operating segment. In addition, R&D is an expense that should not be allocated to existing operating segments. All other costs, however, can and should be traced through an activity-based system.

Conclusion: Revenue and Cost Analysis Much of the distinction between the contribution margin and net profit approaches to segment cost analysis is apparently disappearing as analysts are developing better approaches to identifying expense behavior. Advocates of direct costing and contribution margin probably go along with the tracing of costs to segments based on activities performed, as long as the basis for tracing reflects the "real" cost of that activity. Historically, their argument has been based on the fairness and appropriateness of the allocation method. Even the most avid proponent of full costing, on the other hand, would not argue in favor of such an arbitrary allocation of cost as that shown in Table 11-3*a*. The development of better activity-based costing systems has the potential for ultimately resolving this controversy which has existed in marketing and distribution for a number of years.

Strategic Profit Model

While profitability is an important measure of financial performance, the most critical measure of strategic success is in terms of *return on investment* (ROI). There are two ways of viewing ROI. The first is *return on net worth* (RONW), which measures the profitability of the funds that the owners of the firm have invested in the firm. The second is *return on assets* (ROA), which measures the profitability of the assets that the firm uses in its operations. While owners and investors are most likely interested in RONW, ROA is a better measure of how well management has utilized the assets of the company to earn profits.

Figure 11-2 presents the *strategic profit model* (SPM), which is an analytic tool frequently used to determine ROI in a business firm. Actually, the SPM is a tool that incorporates both income and balance sheet data and demonstrates how these data relate to each other to result in RONW and ROA.

One of the primary benefits of the SPM is that it shows very clearly that the strategic objective of a firm is ROI. Too often, managers focus on more limited objectives. For example, sales management may focus on sales as the primary objective of the business and therefore, will base their analysis on sales volume. Other managers may focus on cost minimization as the primary objective. Still others may focus on turnover and feel that decisions must be based on increasing the firm's efficient utilization of assets. All three of these approaches neglect the fact that the company must earn an adequate rate of return. Otherwise, investments may be withdrawn from the company and placed where higher returns can be earned.

Another advantage of the SPM is that it demonstrates that there are three ways in which a firm can increase return on net worth. The three prime components of RONW are leverage, asset turnover, and net profit margin. Table 11-4 presents the actual SPM ratios for a group of selected retail firms. It is importance to note that the RONW for all of these firms is considerably higher than the RONW for an average retail store. What is particularly interesting about this data is that although all the firms have achieved a high RONW, their performance with respect to the various components of the SPM varies considerably. Even firms that operate in the same industry elect strategies that emphasize different aspects of the SPM. For example, consider the difference in the variables for Zayre Corporation and Sears. The data Table 11-4 show the differences between Zayre's strategy (which relies on low profit margins with high asset turnover and high leverage) and Sears' strategy (which relies on higher profit margins, low turnover, and little usage of leverage). The conclusion to be drawn from these data is that there are several different paths that may be followed by a particular firm in attempting to achieve a high overall RONW. While no company can totally ignore one of the basic components of return, different firms choose strategies that emphasize different components of the return model. In the sections that follow, the meaning of each of these components of the total SPM is explained.[13]

---

[13] For an excellent discussion, see Jagdish N. Sheth and Gary L. Frazier, ''A Margin-Return Model for Strategic Market Planning,'' *Journal of Marketing,* **47:**2 Spring 1983, pp. 100–109.

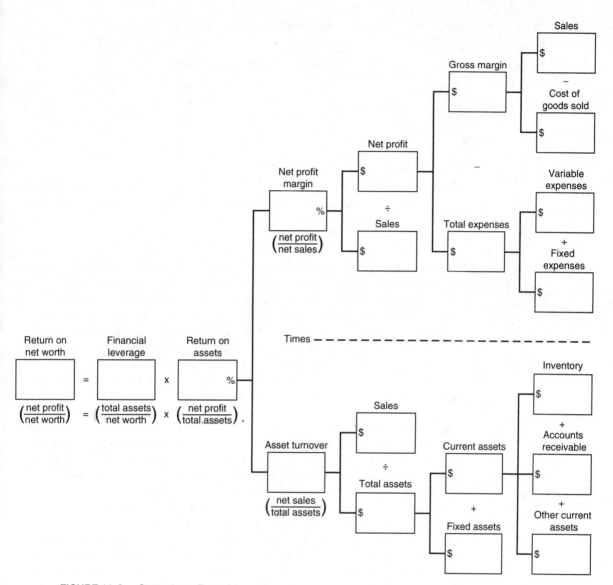

FIGURE 11-2 Strategic profit model.

Net Profit Margin   Defined as a percentage, net profit margin is net profit divided by net sales. Going beyond this simple expression, however, net profit margin actually measures the proportion of each sales dollar that is kept by the firm as net profit. For example, if a firm has a net profit margin of 4 percent, this simply means that $.04

TABLE 11-4   1988 STRATEGIC PROFIT MODEL (SPM) RATIOS FOR SELECTED RETAILERS

	Return on net worth	Leverage	Return on assets	Asset turnover	Net profit margin
Dayton Hudson	14.9%	3.24	4.6%	1.92	2.4%
K mart	17.1	2.48	6.9	2.38	2.9
Limited, Inc.	29.4	2.24	13.1	2.18	6.0
Nordstream, Inc.	21.0	2.33	9.0	1.70	5.3
Rite Aid	15.8	2.19	7.2	2.18	3.3
Sears Roebuck	7.5	5.36	1.4	.67	2.1
Service Merchandise	22.3	4.74	4.7	1.88	2.5
Wal-Mart	31.8	2.18	14.6	3.56	4.1

Source: Standard and Poor's Industry Surveys, *Retailing: Basic Analysis,* April 1990, and author's calculations.

out of every $1 represents net profit to the company. It is important to note that net profit margin can also be divided into a number of specific components. These components are sales volume, cost of goods sold, and operating expenses. For a full evaluation of whether or not a firm's net profit margin is adequate, and whether or not it might be improved, it is necessary to investigate each of these three aspects of net profit margin. For example, net profit margin might be improved by increasing sales volume, decreasing cost of goods sold, or by managing operating expenses more carefully. Any one or a combination of these actions might lead to improved net profit margin performance.

Asset Turnover   Asset turnover is the ratio of total sales divided by total assets. Asset turnover actually measures the efficiency of management in utilizing assets. It shows how many dollars in total sales volume are being generated by each dollar that the firm has invested in assets. For example, a company with an asset turnover ratio of 2.5 to 1 is generating $2.50 in sales volume for each dollar it has invested in assets. As Figure 11-2 indicates, there are a number of assets that the firm has at its disposal and that it uses in order to generate sales. The most important of these are inventories, accounts receivable, and fixed facilities. Inventory is a particularly important asset to most firms because it is typically the largest asset in which investment has been made. Thus, it is common to focus specifically on the management of the inventory turnover ratio. The reason for this emphasis on inventory turnover should be very clear. Since inventory is a major asset investment, the firm that does a good job of managing it and achieves an acceptable rate of inventory turnover should, normally, have an acceptable rate of asset turnover.

Leverage   The result obtained by multiplying net profit margin percentage times asset turnover ratio is return on assets (ROA). For operations management, ROA is the critical measure of performance because it essentially tells how well they have used all of the resources at their disposal to achieve profits for the firm. From an ownership perspective and from a more general strategic perspective, however, it is necessary to realize that not all of the assets that management has at its disposal are necessarily being provided or financed by the owners of the firm. Financial leverage, the third component of the SPM, may be utilized to increase ROA so that an acceptable level of return on net worth is achieved. Mathematically, financial leverage is determined by dividing total assets by net worth. Net worth represents the total amount of dollars that the owners have invested in the firm.

To briefly review the meaning of the SPM and each of its components, consider the example of a firm that has an overall RONW of 15 percent, a leverage ratio of 2 to 1, an asset turnover ratio of 2.5 to 1, and a net profit margin of 3 percent. RONW is 15 percent, and ROA is 7.5 percent.

If these returns are inadequate, there are three routes that might be pursued so that they could be increased: (1) more efficient management of costs in relation to sales volume (margin management) would result in an increase of net profit margins to 4 percent, of ROA to 10 percent, and of RONW to 20 percent; (2) more aggressive utilization of assets (asset management) that would increase asset turnover to three times would increase ROA to 9 percent and RONW to 18 percent; or, (3) an increase in financial leverage (leverage management) to three times would result in no change in ROA but an increase in RONW to 22.5 percent. A combination of all three managerial approaches might also be employed.

Use of the Strategic Profit Model   The SPM is frequently used to review and evaluate performance of the firm. With tracing of a company's performance over time, or with comparison of the company's performance with competitors, an excellent framework for evaluation can be provided. Also, key trends in various components of the model may be spotted that give indications as to which actions should be taken. For example, if a company's RONW has been declining over time or if it is inadequate compared with the competitors' RONW, the source of the decline can be traced to a number of reasons: inadequate profit margins, inefficient use of assets, or failure to keep the business leveraged properly. Management then knows where to devote its attention in trying to improve future performance.

Another important application of the SPM in performance assessment is in segmental analysis of ROI. Two suggested applications are segmental analysis of product lines and of customers.

Product Analysis   With segment analysis of products in which the SPM framework is used, both "return" and "investment" should be carefully considered. Due to problems with allocation of expenses to individual products, return on products is commonly measured as gross margin. Similar problems exist in the determination of the level of investment in a product. The simplest measure of investment is the average level of inventory carried.

The combination of gross margin and inventory investment results in a measure called *gross margin return on inventory* (GMROI), which is measured:

$$\text{GMROI} = \frac{\text{gross margin}}{\text{inventory investment}}$$

TABLE 11-5   GMROI AND DPPROI FOR TWO PRODUCTS

	Product A	Product B
Sales	$100,000	$50,000
Cost of goods	60,000	35,000
Gross margin	40,000 (40%)	15,000 (30%)
Direct expense	25,000	12,000
Direct product profit	$ 15,000 (15%)	$ 3,000 (6%)
Average inventory	$ 40,000	$ 10,000
GMROI	100%	150%
DPPROI	37.5%	30%

However, this ratio can be divided into two separate components:

$$\text{GMROI} = \frac{\text{gross margin}}{\text{net sales}} \times \frac{\text{net sales}}{\text{average inventory investment}}$$

GMROI is a more comprehensive measure of product performance than any single measure such as sales volume, gross margin dollars or percent, or inventory turnover. Calculation of GMROI for products, or product lines, adds considerably to management's understanding of which segments of the business are truly contributing to the firm's overall ROI.

GMROI analysis can be further extended by subtracting direct expenses associated with specific products to calculate direct product profit (DPP, as discussed in Chapter 8). DPPROI can then be calculated as:

$$\text{DPPROI} = \frac{\text{direct product profit}}{\text{average inventory investment}}$$

$$= \frac{\text{DPP}}{\text{net sales}} \times \frac{\text{net sales}}{\text{average inventory investment}}$$

Table 11-5 provides hypothetical data for two products. Notice that DPPROI provides a more exact measurement of product performance and results in quite a different relative evaluation of the two products than does GMROI alone.

An approach that accomplishes an objective similar to DPPROI relies on analysis of residual income. In analysis of residual income, the *cost* of capital employed (inventory and other capital investments) can be subtracted from DPP to determine a product's net earnings.[14]

Customer Analysis   Similar to segment analysis of products the SPM concept can be applied to analysis of specific customers or customer segments. It is clear that profitability among customers differs due to their different purchasing volume, product mix purchased, and cost of servicing. Additionally, net investment differs among cat-

[14] See Michael Levy and Charles A. Ingene, "Residual Income Analysis: A Method of Inventory Investment Allocation and Evaluation," *Journal of Marketing,* **48:**3 Summer 1984, pp. 93–104.

egories of customers. Some customer groups require that suppliers maintain higher inventory levels than others. In addition, terms of sale may differ among customers (or may require more prompt payment than others), so that investments in accounts receivable differ.[15] Profitability of customers is calculated and the investments in inventory, accounts receivable, and any other specifically designed assets are identified so that *customer return on investment* (CRI) can be calculated. The resulting calculation is:

$$CRI = \frac{margin}{net\ sales} \times \frac{net\ sales}{average\ asset\ investment}$$

In combination with detailed profitability analysis, CRI is a measure of which customers and customer segments are truly contributing to the firm's overall financial well-being.

MEASURING CUSTOMER SATISFACTION

Comprehensive channel performance measurement requires assessment of not only financial results. Financial results are primarily oriented toward past performance, although, as discussed previously, insight can be gained into areas of needed improvement. It is equally important to assess channel members' satisfaction with service performance of their channel partners. Channel members who are satisfied with their channel partners are likely to maintain the distribution relationship and cooperate in the marketing and distribution strategies of those partners. Dissatisfied channel members are more likely to terminate their participation in a distribution channel, or at least they are more likely to devote less effort and cooperation with the strategies of those who cause their dissatisfaction.

A recent study of wholesalers and retailers in the food industry supports the notion that satisfaction with suppliers' service performance is a critical factor in channel relationships. Suppliers that have well-established brand franchises among final consumers are not likely to be dropped by wholesalers or retailers. However, if the suppliers' product line has marginal financial performance, dissatisfaction with distribution service may be the final determinant in the decision to eliminate that supplier.[16]

Even suppliers of products whose financial performance is strong must be concerned with channel members' satisfaction. In the study cited above, many wholesalers and retailers indicated that they are more likely to participate in the promotional efforts of manufacturers whose service performance is satisfactory or excellent. They are also much more likely to advertise and feature those suppliers' product lines and to give preferred shelf space to those manufacturers.

---

[15] Randy Myer, "Suppliers: Manage Your Customers," *Harvard Business Review*, **67**:6 November–December 1989, pp. 160–168.

[16] M. Bixby Cooper, Cornelia Droge, and Patricia J. Daugherty, "How Buyers and Operations Personnel Evaluate Service," *Industrial Marketing Management*, **20**:1 January 1991, p. 84.

Clearly, then, customer satisfaction is a critical factor in channel performance measurement. Suppliers must understand channel customers' satisfaction to ensure continued proper functioning of the system. Likewise, the process of satisfaction assessment provides insight into how channel members evaluate the performance of their partners. In the sections that follow, emphasis is placed on satisfaction with service performance. Clearly, as indicated earlier, channel members must also be satisfied with financial performance, including sales volume, profitability, and ROI.

Satisfaction and Service Quality

Customer satisfaction is a fundamental concept in marketing, since marketing strategy is built on the foundation of satisfying the customers' needs and wants. Surprisingly, however, the definition and measurement of satisfaction has been a subject of considerable debate in marketing literature.

Originally, satisfaction was defined simply as an attitude. It was thought that a simple, overall measurement of satisfaction would be sufficient.[17] However, the way in which customers form their judgment of satisfaction is now most widely explained by the "expectancy/disconfirmation" process. Simply stated, if a customer's expectations regarding a supplier's performance are met or exceeded, the customer is satisfied. Conversely, if perceived performance falls short of expectations, dissatisfaction results.[18] Stated another way:

> If perceived performance is equal to or greater than expectations, the customer is satisfied.
>
> If perceived performance is less than expectations, the customer is dissatisfied.

For example, if a wholesaler expects delivery from a supplier within two days but the actual delivery takes three days, the wholesaler is likely to be dissatisfied with that supplier's performance. Interestingly enough, in this example, delivery in one day (which normally would be considered as exceeding the customer's expectation) might also cause dissatisfaction because the wholesaler might not be prepared to accept delivery at that time.

Given this example, it is clear that understanding the exact nature of customers' expectations is a critical step in the assessment of satisfaction. In fact, there are at least three types of expectations that a customer might have about a supplier's performance.[19]

[17] John A. Howard and Jagdish N. Sheth, *The Theory of Buyer Behavior,* New York: Wiley, 1969.

[18] For a full discussion of the expectancy/disconfirmation paradigm, see Richard L. Oliver, "Measurement and Evaluation of Satisfaction Processes in Retail Settings," *Journal of Retailing,* **57**:3 Fall 1981, pp. 25–48; and John E. Swan, "Consumer Satisfaction Related to Disconfirmation of Expectations and Product Performance," *Journal of Consumer Satisfaction, Dissatisfaction, and Complaining Behavior,* **1**:1 1988, pp. 40–47.

[19] Claire F. Bolfing and Robert B. Woodruff, "Effects of Situational Involvement on Consumer's Use of Standards in Satisfaction/Dissatisfaction Processes," *Journal of Consumer Satisfaction, Dissatisfaction and Complaining Behavior,* **1**:1 1988, pp. 16–24.

The first type of expectation concerns what the customer believes actually will occur. For example, based on a supplier's past performance, a supplier's promises of performance, or word of mouth, a customer may believe that the supplier will deliver the product in two days.

Another type of expectation is the customer's belief about what the supplier should be able to provide. For example, even in the absence of any information about performance, a customer may believe and therefore expect that a supplier should be able to provide two-day delivery service.

A third type of performance expectation that customers have is a minimum standard of performance that must be achieved by a supplier. Thus, a customer may have expectations that a supplier should provide delivery in two days, that delivery will actually occur in three days, and that it must occur within four days.

Closely related to customer satisfaction is the concept of quality. In fact, quality has been defined in terms of customer satisfaction. One of the leading experts in quality processes defines quality as "performance which results in customer satisfaction, and freedom from deficiency which avoids customer dissatisfaction."[20] Service quality has been examined with precisely the same framework of expectations, perceived performance, and disconfirmation as used in the determination of levels of customer satisfaction. As has been observed, what is thought of as a marketing issue when termed "customer satisfaction" becomes an operational issue when termed "service quality assurance."[21] While some authors draw a distinction between customer satisfaction and quality, it is clear that the two concepts are sufficiently similar to warrant their being treated simultaneously.

Determinants of Satisfaction and Quality Understanding that customers' satisfaction and quality perceptions depend upon their expectations and perception of the supplier's performance, the question remains concerning what criteria are applied by customers to judge performance. Table 11-6 contains performance criteria frequently used to assess logistics service.

Product availability involves the ability of the supplier to provide a product when it is desired by customers. This is frequently measured in terms of the percentage of items or lines that can be filled from existing inventory, or as the percentage of orders that are shipped complete. Capability refers to the length of time required to fill orders, the ability of the logistics system to adapt to special requirements, and the avoidance of errors such as damage or misshipments. Information support is the assistance of the logistics system in the provision of accurate, up-to-date information concerning customer orders. Life-cycle support is the support by a logistics system of a product throughout its life cycle, including the handling of such situations as product recall.

Customers form expectations of a supplier's abilities in each of these critical logistics performance areas. Frequently they monitor and analyze a supplier's performance with respect to some, if not all, of these criteria. Their satisfaction and perception of

---

[20] Joseph M. Juran, *Juran on Leadership for Quality: An Executive Handbook,* New York: Free Press.
[21] John A. Czepiel, "Managing Customer Service in Consumer Service Businesses," Report No. 80-109, Cambridge, MA: Marketing Science Institute, 1980.

TABLE 11-6   DETERMINANTS OF LOGISTICS SERVICE

Product availability

Stockout percentage
Fill rate
Orders shipped complete

System capability

Order cycle time
Cycle time consistency
System flexibility
Shipment presentation
Damage
Errors/error correction

Information Support

Inventory status
Order status
Shipment tracing
Order document

Life-cycle support

Repair parts and service
Technical service
Installation
Reverse distribution

the logistics quality of that supplier is directly related to how closely the actual performance matches their expectations and their needs.

In a pioneering study of marketing and service quality, three researchers identified a set of ten dimensions used by consumers in assessing overall service quality.[22] While these dimensions, as shown in Table 11-7, are stated in general terms, suppliers must be concerned that customers form specific expectations within each dimension. A comprehensive assessment of perceived quality requires that suppliers translate these general dimensions into specific performance expectations that can be monitored and measured.

Organizational Complexity   In a distribution channel context, customer satisfaction and perceived quality assessment is particularly complex because distribution channel partners are usually business organizations made up of numerous individuals. Some individuals within the firm may be satisfied with performance while others may

[22] A. Parasuraman, Valarie Zeithaml, and Leonard L. Berry, "SERVQUAL: A Multiple Item Scale for Measuring Customer Perceptions of Service Quality," Report No. 86-108, Cambridge, MA: Marketing Science Institute, 1986.

TABLE 11-7   DETERMINANTS OF SERVICE QUALITY

Reliability:	Performance as promised. Service is performed correctly the first time.
Responsiveness:	Willingness and ability to provide prompt service
Credibility:	Believability, trustworthiness
Security:	Confidentiality; freedom from risk
Competence:	Knowledge and skill of personnel
Courtesy:	Friendliness of personnel
Access:	Ease of contact, of obtaining service
Communication:	Explanation and provision of information
Tangibles:	Appearance of facilities and personnel
Understanding/knowing customers:	Adaption to customers' specific requirements

Source: Adapted from A. Parasuraman, Valarie Zeithaml, and Leonard L. Berry, "A Conceptual Model of Service Quality and Its Implications for Future Research," Report No. 84–106, Cambridge, MA: Marketing Science Institute, 1984.

not. This discrepancy can exist because of differences in the level of expectation or the perception of actual performance, or because differing criteria may be used by the individuals. For example, merchandise buyers in a retail organization may be particularly concerned with the suppliers' product availability and on-time delivery. Operations personnel in the same firms may be more concerned with other attributes of the supplier's service. Table 11-8 presents results of a study of buyers and operations personnel that demonstrate these differences.

Methodology

Clearly, the assessment of customer satisfaction is a difficult process. Figure 11-3 provides a model framework to guide this process. The framework suggests a number of "gaps" that must be monitored and measured so that customer satisfaction can be fully understood and quality performance improved.

Gap 1: This gap represents the difference between the channel partners' real expectations and the supplier's perception of those expectations. Buyers' expectations should be measured in terms of all three types of expectations: What they perceive to be ideal, what they perceive actual performance will be, and their minimum requirements. Additionally, the expectations of multiple individuals in the buying organization should be measured so that the complete range of expectations can be understood. Unless this step is completed, there is likely to be a substantial difference between the channel partners' real expectations and the supplier's perceptions of those expectations.

Gap 2: The second gap is the difference between the perception of buyers' expectations and the internal performance standards. For example, the supplier may believe that a buyer expects 100 percent product availability but will still establish an internal performance standard of 98 percent fill rate.

Gap 3: This gap refers to the difference between the standard and actual perfor-

TABLE 11-8 DIFFERENCES BETWEEN BUYERS AND OPERATIONS PERSONNEL IN THEIR IMPORTANCE RATINGS OF SERVICE CRITERIA

	Means ratings[a]	
	Buyers	Operations
Pretransaction phase		
Ease of placing orders	4.01	3.71
Willingness to customize service	3.89	4.11
Advance information concerning orders	4.33	4.20
Transaction phase		
Product availability		
Line-item availability	4.55	4.31
Case fill rate	4.30	4.16
Orders shipped complete	4.76	4.65
Communication		
Ability to provide order status	4.13	4.22
Notification of late delivery	4.13	4.26
Packages clearly identified	4.46	4.82
Delivery capability		
Meets appointments	4.46	4.73
Delivers when requested	4.87	4.70
Frequency of delivery	4.07	3.95
Delivery quality		
Delivered sorted and segregated	4.36	4.75
Palletizing/unitizing capability	3.72	4.37
Master carton packaging quality	3.81	4.48
Shelf unit packaging quality	3.97	4.29
Posttransaction phase		
Complete/accurate documentation	4.54	4.81
Well-documented deal/style codes	4.36	4.60
Invoice accuracy	4.69	4.61
Returned merchandise processing	4.01	3.92
Damage adjustment	3.98	4.22
Throughout the cycle		
Length of order cycle	4.14	3.61
Consistency of order cycle	4.38	3.88
Follows special instructions	4.14	4.39

[a] Five-point scale, 5 indicating high importance.
Source: M. Bixby Cooper, Cornelia Droge, and Patricia J. Daugherty, "How Buyers and Operations Personnel Evaluate Service," *Industrial Marketing Management,* **20:**1 January 1991, pp. 81–85.

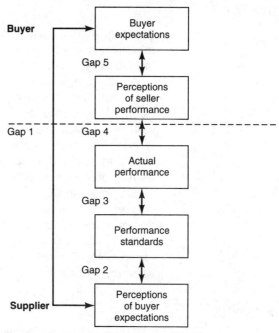

FIGURE 11-3   Model for quality assessment and improvement. (*Source:* Adapted from A. Parasuraman, Valerie Zeithaml, and Leonard L. Berry, "A Conceptual Model of Service Quality and Its Implications for Future Research," Report No. 84-106, Cambridge, MA: Marketing Science Institute, 1984.)

mance. From the above example, if actual fill rates are 95 percent, there exists a gap of 3 percent between standard and actual performance.

Gap 4: Frequently, channel partners perceive performance to be either better or worse than it actually is. The adage that "you're only as good as your last performance" often prevails. Thus, although product availability may average 95 percent over the course of a channel relationship, a few specific instances of poorer-than-average performance may result in an overall perception of poor performance.

Gap 5: This gap is the actual measure of the customer satisfaction and the service quality. As discussed previously, when performance is perceived to be equal to or greater than expected, channel partners are satisfied. When performance is perceived to be less than expected, dissatisfaction results.

Business firms that are truly concerned with customer satisfaction, product and service quality, and the maintenance of effective and efficient distribution channel relationships focus their assessment on each of the gaps suggested by the model in Figure 11-3. When channel members are dissatisfied, whether due to inadequate financial or service performance, relationships within the channel are likely to deteriorate. The impetus exists for dissatisfied channel members to seek alternative channel partners or to realign channel structures. Satisfaction is, then, the ultimate test of the long-term prospects for distribution channel performance.

SUMMARY

A critical step in channel strategy is the measurement of performance. Performance measurement at the macro level addresses the questions of how well distribution structures meet the needs of consumers and whether or not distribution "costs too much."

At the strategic management, or micro, level it is necessary to measure both financial results and customer satisfaction. Financial performance assessment requires a careful delineation of the segments for analysis, the identification of revenues and costs within each segment, and the analysis of ROI. Decisions must be made about contribution margin or net profit approaches to financial assessment. The SPM provides a framework for the analysis of return for a firm and can also be applied to the analysis of a segment's ROI.

Customer satisfaction is closely related to the quality of service provided within a channel. The understanding of how channel members form judgments about satisfaction provides insight into how they evaluate one another. It also provides direction for a firm when it is making strategic or operational changes to meet channel members' expectations. Channel member satisfaction is a crucial element in performance measurement because it affects the continuity of the channel relationship in many ways.

QUESTIONS

1 Do you believe that distribution "costs too much"? Use examples of specific channels of distribution that you feel unnecessarily increase the cost of products to consumers.

2 How would you suggest that the effectiveness of distribution be assessed from a macro perspective? For example, can market decentralization and product variety be measured?

3 Jones Company manufactures two product lines—cosmetics and razor blades—that are each distributed through two types of stores (grocery stores and drugstores). Variable manufacturing cost for cosmetics is 40 percent of selling price and for razor blades is 35 percent. Selling commissions are 5 percent for sales to drugstores and 6 percent for sales to grocery stores. Other costs are

Direct fixed manufacturing cost for cosmetics: $1,000,000
Direct fixed manufacturing cost for razor blades: 750,000
Indirect manufacturing cost: 500,000

SELLING AND DISTRIBUTION COSTS

	Grocery stores	Drugstores	Cosmetics	Razors
Cosmetics	450,000	400,000		
Razors	320,000	280,000		
Indirect to product	330,000	280,000		
Indirect to channel			$220,000	$190,000
Sales of 1990 were:				
Cosmetics	$5,000,000	$3,000,000		
Razors	2,000,000	2,500,000		

Using a contribution margin format, prepare a segment income statement by product line, with a secondary breakdown by channel.

4 Using the same data in Question 3, prepare a segment income statement by channel, with a secondary breakdown by product.

5 Suppose the management of Jones Company approached you for advice about their desire to use a net profit approach to determine segment profitability. What advice would you give? What approach would you take to analyze the indirect costs?

6 Jones Company has determined that it has the following investments in assets:

	Inventory	Accounts Receivable
Grocery store		$1,500,000
Drugstores		1,000,000
Cosmetics	$800,000	
Razors	750,000	

Compute GMROI, DPPROI, and CRI for each segment.

7 Choose two firms that compete in the same industry. In the library, find information to complete the SPM for each firm at two different time periods (preferably five years apart). What does the analysis tell you about the strategies of each firm? Are there indications, based on changes in financial performance over time, that one firm is employing more successful strategies than the other?

8 What are the most significant problems in the conducting of a financial assessment of channel performance?

9 Why is the assessment of customer satisfaction an important component of total-performance analysis?

10 From the listing of ten dimensions of service quality in Table 11-7, develop specific measures that you think would be applicable to most firms.

11 Explain the relationship between customer satisfaction and service quality.

12 Which of the "gaps" in Figure 11-3 do you believe represent the most difficult measurement problem for a firm? Which do you believe are most significant in the process of developing service quality?

CASES

CASE 3-1: P&G Meets Wal-Mart*

After reviewing the most recent financial performance figures, many senior managers wondered whether the new strategic posture of Procter & Gamble (P&G) was in the best interest of the firm's stockholders. In recent years, drastic changes had occurred in the traditional P&G marketing philosophy. While the company once considered retailers tough, penny-pinching adversaries, P&G established special teams to help large customers such as Wal-Mart and Kroger improve inventory, distribution, and sales promotion. To respond more rapidly to changing markets, P&G added category managers with increased spending power and decision-making authority. Product supply managers were added to cut new-product development time through coordination of manufacturing, engineering, distribution, and purchasing. These sweeping changes were designed to better meet the needs of a dynamic channel environment, while P&G's control over key product decisions was still maintained. This new perspective on marketing channel management differed considerably from the one that created sales leaders in twenty-two different grocery categories. In an environment rich with success, internal and external skepticism was to be expected. However, it remained unclear whether such concerns were justified.

PROCTER & GAMBLE: THE TRADITIONAL APPROACH TO MARKETING

More than 150 years ago, James Gamble developed Ivory Soap and established a business based on provision of an excellent product at a reasonable price. Around the same time, William Procter began to sell candles, known for their exceptional quality and value. These two men, who shared a common vision, combined forces during the 1800s to create the Procter & Gamble Company. While a strong customer focus has been associated with the firm since its inception, formal consumer research operations began in 1924. P&G initially examined issues such as which laundry soap was preferred by customers and which perfume used in their Camay soap was liked best. As research sophistication increased, P&G began to study consumers' habits and practices, as well as their wants and expectations. Through telephone interviews, mail

* *P&G Meets Wal-Mart* was written by David J. Frayer.

questionnaires, and focus-group discussions, P&G collected detailed information on consumers. It was this intimate knowledge of the final consumer that guided P&G's marketing strategy through most of the twentieth century.

P&G adopted a hard-line approach to marketing channel management. Extensive research-based knowledge of final consumers allowed P&G to control the retail trade in certain categories. P&G showed retailers empirical evidence of consumers' desires and then provided solutions that invariably increased shelf space for a P&G product. Since retailers had no means for disputing P&G's research, the company was able to effectively dictate pricing policies, promotion allowances, shipment size, delivery terms, and shelf facings. Hercules Segelas, head of the consumer products group at PaineWebber, effectively summarized the industry situation: "Retailers hated P&G, but they needed it. It dominated the trade."[1] An extremely rigid and powerful organization was created that controlled world markets in dozens of categories through the early 1980s. As one of P&G's major customers, Leslie Dietzman, an executive vice president at Ames Department Stores, expressed her understanding of the P&G philosophy: "It was do it P&G's way or hit the highway."[2]

As information-processing capabilities were increased through development of faster microcomputers, the environment that had sustained P&G's phenomenal growth began to change. The ability of retailers to adopt inexpensive technologies for product tracking coupled with the sheer number of grocery products competing for shelf space made it more difficult for P&G to push products through the channel. Power in traditional grocery channels began to shift away from manufacturers and toward retailers. As a result of industry mergers, 100 chains accounted for 80 percent of P&G's United States grocery sales in 1989, versus 15 percent in 1969. Electronic bar coding helped retailers gather their own sales data. P&G could no longer bully its way into stores, waving figures a retailer could not dispute that showed that Tide was outselling All and was therefore entitled to more shelf space. For the first time, P&G had to consider the needs and wants of *its* customers, the retailers. On many issues, P&G was forced to acquiesce to the demands of its primary accounts. The first and most successful challenge to P&G's traditional marketing practices came from an Arkansas-based discounter, Wal-Mart.

WAL-MART: THE RETAIL PHENOMENON

It is widely speculated that by the early 1990s, Wal-Mart stores will become the largest retailer in the United States. Only K mart and Sears are now larger, and the gap between them and Wal-Mart is closing rapidly. Wal-Mart's 1300 discount stores sell over $20 billion worth of goods per year, including clothes, shoes, small appliances, cosmetics, and 50,000 other items. According to Margaret Gilliam of First Boston:

> Wal-Mart is the finest-managed company we have ever followed. We think it is quite likely the finest-managed company in America, and we know of at least one investor . . . who

---

[1] *Fortune,* November 6, 1989, p. 40.
[2] Ibid.

thinks it is the finest-managed company in the world. We do not expect to find another Wal-Mart in our lifetime.[3]

The company's average annual return to investors from 1977 through 1987 was 46 percent, far ahead of the next closest company among Fortune's ten most admired. A $1000 investment in Wal-Mart's 1970 initial public offering would be worth over half a million dollars today.

In 1945, Samuel M. Walton opened his first Ben Franklin store in Newport, Arkansas, after serving with Army Intelligence during World War II. His brother Bud opened a second Ben Franklin store in Missouri, where both had attended high school and the University of Missouri. By the late 1950s, the Waltons had the largest group of independent variety stores in the United States, with sixteen units. Through their experience with Ben Franklin, the Walton brothers discovered that large stores (25,000 square feet) could succeed in small communities (3000 people). Sam Walton attempted to convince the Ben Franklin chain that larger discount stores with margins even smaller than Walton's existing stores could be successful. In a recent interview, Walton recalled:

> Ben Franklin didn't want to give in to the degree that it took for prices to be as low as I felt they should be. [Ben Franklin was charging Walton a 20 to 25 percent margin on gross operating cost.] I knew that I could not sell the merchandise as cheaply as I needed in order to be an honest-to-goodness discounter and give the value needed. If they had been able to sell to me on a 12 percent range, I probably would not have put together the organization that I did. As luck had it, it didn't fit into their program. They may have been like Sears is today, unable to cut their costs to the extent necessary to sell as cheaply as we wanted to buy.[4]

As a result, Sam and Bud Walton opened the first Wal-Mart Discount City in Rogers, Arkansas, in 1963. Founded on the principle that the customer is the boss, Wal-Mart has aggressively maintained this commitment despite remarkable growth. The company's pricing philosophy is based on the premise that the customer prefers to pay the same low price "every day" for brand-name merchandise rather than wait for sale prices. The success of this philosophy can be measured by the phenomenal growth the company has enjoyed and the overwhelming customer acceptance.

As Wal-Mart began to expand, distributors ignored the chain, focusing instead on competitors in larger towns. This forced the company to construct its own warehouses to accommodate low-price volume buying. Wal-Mart needed facilities in which to store merchandise until requested by individual stores. Wal-Mart developed a "saturation policy" that called for clustering stores throughout a 200-square-mile area around the distribution points. This permitted daily delivery of goods. Wal-Mart stores receive 77 percent of their merchandise from the company's sixteen distribution centers, while many smaller chains' stores are forced to secure most of their goods from higher-priced intermediaries. Keeping its stores close to one another and the distri-

---

[3] *Fortune,* January 30, 1989, p. 53.
[4] *Financial World,* April 4, 1989, pp. 60–61.

bution centers also helps Wal-Mart keep advertising costs to .6 percent of sales, compared with 2 to 3 percent for other discount chains.

A combination of high employee productivity, the latest technology, an experienced corporate traffic department, and an efficient private truck fleet makes the distribution system an effective tool for improving Wal-Mart's customer-service performance. In 1988, the firm operated ten regional distribution centers, three specialty facilities, three support facilities, and ten dispatch offices. Incorporated in these centers were over 11.5 million square feet of space. These facilities were vital in maintaining high in-stock levels of merchandise for customers on a continuing basis. Wal-Mart's 10,000 distribution associates processed and delivered over 300 million cases of merchandise in 1988. The private truck fleet delivered merchandise a minimum of five times per week to each Wal-Mart store and in fiscal 1989 made over 300,000 store deliveries. An on-time delivery record of over 99 percent was maintained and order filling accuracy on those same shipments also exceeded 99 percent. Wal-Mart utilizes reward-based incentives as a tool for motivating employees. For example, if a store holds shrinkage below the corporate goal, every associate in that store receives up to $200. Wal-Mart's shrinkage is estimated to be just above 1 percent, compared to an industry average of 2 percent.

In an effort to insure the success of marketing and logistics operations into the future, Wal-Mart has chosen to redefine relationships with its suppliers. Wal-Mart is not particularly interested in preferred-supplier arrangements or supply-chain concepts. Instead, by extracting concessions and dictating terms, Wal-Mart determines how suppliers will service its stores. With scanning in over 81 percent of its stores, Wal-Mart refuses to form long-term relationships with vendors whose goods are not marked with bar codes. Wal-Mart is even reluctant to complete a purchase order on goods without bar codes. Manufacturers' representatives have been eliminated from the buying process at Wal-Mart. Some vendors find the company extremely difficult to do business with, and a high-ranking marketer for a big consumer-goods firm calls Wal-Mart "the rudest account in America."[5]

While this merchandising strategy has been used by other retailers, Wal-Mart is more relentless in both the execution of that strategy and in the operating side of its business. As a result, many of Wal-Mart's suppliers have begun to assess their position by determining the precise services provided, the cost of customers, and whether the business is worth the cost.

THE RELATIONSHIP REDEFINED

Wal-Mart's attempt to redefine supplier relationships had a direct impact on the marketing philosophy at P&G. As Wal-Mart continued to expand, a significant portion of P&G's sales staff relied on a successful relationship with the giant discounter. P&G initially tried to forge preferred-supplier arrangements with Wal-Mart, but diminishing leverage within the channel limited P&G's success. It appeared that P&G's hard-line

---

[5] *Fortune*, January 30, 1989, p. 58.

approach was no longer appropriate with a powerful retailer the size of Wal-Mart. Hence, P&G began the long and arduous process of revising its traditional marketing channel philosophy.

In order to work more closely with key accounts, P&G initiated a team approach to problem solving. Each large retailer was assigned a team consisting of people from Finance, Distribution, Manufacturing, and other departments. These managers were empowered to make immediate decisions based on the requirements of the situation. As one executive at a large supermarket chain commented: "We can call the shots now. If we want to run a Duncan Hines ad, P&G has given its local sales managers the autonomy to say, 'We'll give you $20,000 for it.' "[6]

P&G worked closely with carriers to establish an EDI system for transmission of freight bills. Future applications of EDI also under consideration by P&G included claims processing, electronic payments, and rate transmission. Many of these developments, which resulted in a substantial financial commitment by P&G, were directly related to the information needs of Wal-Mart. A manager of one grocery chain, who anxiously awaited some sign of the new, improved P&G, commented: "We hear a lot about the focus on Wal-Mart, and we want to know more about it."[7] The reaction of retailers to P&G's proposed marketing channel philosophy was immediate, but no one anticipated results to materialize as quickly. After all, according to John Luther, a consultant for Marketing Corporation of America, "Procter is reinventing the packaged goods industry for the year 2000 and beyond."[8]

While P&G adjusted its marketing philosophy to accommodate Wal-Mart's initial requests, Wal-Mart became even more demanding. With a few major manufacturers (P&G, Rubbermaid, and General Electric) Wal-Mart has tried a nonadversarial approach in which it shares sales projection data through computer links, hoping the vendor can anticipate its needs. Wal-Mart has relinquished control of the entire order process to permit some manufacturers to manage product quantities within stores. The manufacturer determines the appropriate number of shelf facings based on anticipated sales. Wal-Mart measures performance by comparing current inventory turnover and stock-out ratios to previous levels. Those firms that improve performance over time may renegotiate prices with Wal-Mart, while those that do not are eventually eliminated from consideration as suppliers. This has required major adjustments by a number of manufacturers. For example, at P&G twelve different individuals have been assembled to address the needs of Wal-Mart. Working with the crew from P&G, the discount giant has set up a just-in-time ordering and delivery system for Pampers and Luvs disposable diapers. When the diapers run low in a store, a computer sends an order by satellite to a P&G factory, which in turn automatically ships more diapers directly to the outlet. As a result, Wal-Mart can maintain smaller inventories and cut the number of times it runs out of Pampers. Through such win-win situations, the objectives of individual firms are replaced by mutually beneficial objectives and costs are reduced for both companies.

[6] *Fortune,* November 6, 1989, p. 42.
[7] *Fortune,* November 6, 1989, p. 38.
[8] Ibid., p. 35.

A LOOK TO THE FUTURE

As management reviewed P&G's performance figures, the future of the consumer-products industry and the role P&G was expected to assume were critical concerns. While the agreement with Wal-Mart was heralded by many as a view of the future, many managers were privately concerned that P&G had not received sufficient immediate returns. Perhaps P&G was giving too much in the attempt to meet demands for an efficient and effective channel. Before committing additional resources, it was necessary to carefully reassess the business arrangement to determine whether it could succeed in the long term.

QUESTIONS

1 What is P&G's new philosophy about marketing channel management? How does it differ from the firm's traditional practices?
2 What is Wal-Mart's philosophy about marketing channel management? Is this philosophy truly unique or innovative?
3 Carefully reexamine the nature of Wal-Mart's supplier management concept. Which P&G marketing approach is most consistent with Wal-Mart's desired program: the old traditional approach or the new flexible approach? Why?
4 How should P&G managers determine the cost to P&G of servicing the Wal-Mart account? Discuss the relevant variables and techniques which could be utilized.
5 Do you anticipate any problems in the future relationship between P&G and Wal-Mart? If so, what are they? Can they be easily corrected?
6 If environmental influences were to shift power in consumer-products channels back toward manufacturers (e.g., P&G), would the existing relationship change? Justify your answer. Feel free to use examples from other industries.

REFERENCES

1989 Annual Report, Procter & Gamble Company.

1989 Annual Report, Wal-Mart Stores, Inc.

"Bar Codes Becoming Universal," *Advertising Age,* April 18, 1988, p. 36.

"CEO of the Decade: Sam M. Walton," *Financial World,* April 4, 1989, pp. 56–62.

"EDI Invoicing Cuts P&G Error 75%," *Traffic World,* December 14, 1987, p. 62.

"Information Systems in Sales and Marketing: Using Technology to Transform Customer Relationships," presented at the Hammer Forum by Mark Schmidt, Director, Technology Development, Wal-Mart Stores, Inc.

"Internal Communication: A Key to Wal-Mart's Success," *Discount Merchandiser,* 29:11 November 1989, pp. 68–73.

"Is Big Business Heading for Small Town, U.S.A.?" *Journal of Business Strategy,* July–August 1989, pp. 4–9.

Myer, Randy, "Suppliers: Manage Your Customers," *Harvard Business Review,* 67:6 November–December 1989, pp. 160–168.

"Play It Again, Sam," *Forbes,* August 10, 1987, p. 48.

"P&G Rewrites the Marketing Rules," *Fortune,* November 6, 1989, pp. 34–48.

"The Fortune Service 500: More Woes than Winnings," *Fortune,* June 6, 1988, pp. D3–D41, 317.

"Wal-Mart: Will It Take Over the World?" *Fortune,* January 30, 1989, pp. 52–61.
"Walton's Mountain," *Nations Business,* April 1988, pp. 18–26.

CASE 3-2: Oakville Mall

In the fall of 1988, Ms. Roberta Brent, president of E. L. Lint Company, a department store firm with branches in three mid-Michigan cities, was concerned about reports that another major department store chain, well-known in several states, was considering opening branch stores in Lint's market areas. In December, Ms. Brent's fears were confirmed when it was announced that the firm, Deming Stores, planned to open two branches in Lint's major market. One of the branches was to be located in a new mall to be developed and built by Deming's Properties. Brent realized that this new mall would present substantial competition for all area retailers, but there was little that could be done to prevent entry by this source of competition. She was extremely concerned, however, about the announcement that Deming also planned to open a store in Oakville Mall, an existing shopping center in which Lint's maintained a large branch store.

OAKVILLE MALL

Oakville Mall opened in 1974. The developer of this shopping center project was Cal Martin Properties, Inc. Oakville was the first enclosed regional shopping center in its market, a standard metropolitan statistical area (SMSA) with a population of over 250,000. The original development contained a gross leasable area of 300,000 square feet. Besides the Lint's store, which was the largest in the shopping center, there were two other large general-merchandise stores in the mall as well as a number of smaller specialty stores. In the original development, however, Cal Martin had considered Lint the primary traffic generator for the project. Lint was in the center of the mall; the other two major tenants were at opposite ends.

As in most shopping centers, lease arrangements between Cal Martin and the tenants of Oakville Mall varied. Lint's contract contained the most favorable rental rates for any tenant, with the store paying a guaranteed minimum rent of $1.25 per square foot of area occupied. Thus, Lint's minimum rent during a year was $112,500. The contract also called for Lint to pay 3 percent of its sales revenue as rent, if that figure exceeded the $112,500 minimum. The highest rental paid by any of the tenants in Oakville Mall called for a $12 per square foot minimum or 16 percent of net sales. The candy shop that signed this lease had a prime location in the center of the main aisle.

After a poor first-year start, Oakville Mall became quite profitable for Cal Martin Properties. Sales volume for most tenants grew steadily, and very few tenants went out of business because of poor performance in the shopping center. However, one of the large general-merchandise stores closed in early 1988. Although this store was paying rent above its minimum, indicating a satisfactory sales volume, the national chain of which it was only one unit filed for bankruptcy in 1988 and closed all its

TABLE 1   OAKVILLE MALL: SELECTED OPERATING ANALYSES

	1986	1980	1975
Income:			
Minimum rents collected	$1,081,000	$1,050,000	$951,000
Miscellaneous income			
(rides, public telephone, etc.)	10,000	8,000	3,000
Percentage rentals collected	321,000	157,000	21,000
Total income	$1,412,000	$1,216,00	$975,000
Expenses:			
Taxes	$ 165,000	$ 125,000	$105,000
Insurance	54,000	46,000	30,000
Promotion (does not include promotional efforts of			
the merchants' association)	35,000	30,000	25,000
Legal and auditing	45,000	42,000	26,000
Miscellaneous	66,000	55,000	48,000
Total expenses	$ 365,000	$ 298,000	$234,000
Cash available for debt service	$1,047,000	$ 918,000	$741,000
Debt service:			
Mortgage (principal and interest)	$ 637,000	$ 637,000	$637,000
Land contract	182,000	182,000	182,000
Total debt service	$ 819,000	$ 819,000	$819,000
Cash throwoff	$ 232,000	$ 99,000	$ 78,000

stores in the United States. The closing of this branch, therefore, was not due to any specific problems with the Oakville Mall unit. Table 1 presents operating analyses from three selected years for Oakville Mall.

Roberta Brent was particularly pleased with the performance of the Lint store in Oakville Mall. Although sales volume in early years had not been great enough to require that the percentage rental clause be in effect, Lint paid a total of $158,600 in rent to Cal Martin in 1986. Ms. Brent considered the Oakville Mall branch of Lint's one of the most successful units operated by the firm.

PROPOSED EXPANSION OF OAKVILLE MALL

The proposal to expand Oakville Mall with the addition of Deming's would also add many new specialty stores. As a result, the total size of Oakville Mall would be increased to 578,000 square feet, with Deming occupying 103,000 square feet. The expansion was to be constructed on vacant land on the westernmost portion of the Oakville Mall site, the only vacant land available. Exhibit 1 contains a site plan of the 1988 Oakville Mall as well as the proposed addition. Brent commented that she was not pleased that Deming's had decided to enter the market. She knew that the competition would be very strong. Deming's was well known as a retailer of fashion-oriented, quality merchandise. With Deming's having tremendous resources at the disposal of the regional firm, Lint would probably have a difficult time maintaining

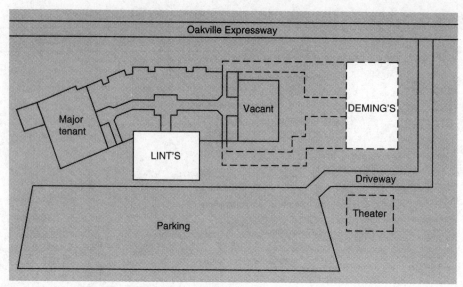

EXHIBIT 1   Oakville Mall site plan, including proposed additions.

its dominant position in the local market. Brent did say, however, that the competition could force Lint's management out of its complacency and into a new era of aggressiveness. The firm had never been challenged in its dominant position.

Although concerned about the new competition, she was also very angry about the proposed changes at Oakville Mall. "I want to make it very clear to everyone that we think competition will be beneficial to area consumers and we therefore welcome Deming's to the market," Ms. Brent said in a newspaper interview. "We even think that their coming to Oakville Mall will be good for all parties concerned. As long as they are going to locate in this area we would rather see them in Oakville than any other shopping center. However, we do not think that there is any need to destroy the present configuration of the mall just to get them into the location. They could move into the recently vacated store which contains 50,000 square feet and begin operations immediately. This would be good for all parties concerned. Cal Martin would have its vacant store leased, Deming's could open its doors sooner, and the present mall configuration would be preserved.

"The major problem with the proposed expansion is that it totally changes the site plan. Whereas our Lint store is presently in the center of the mall, after the expansion we will be at the east end. We contend that this change would greatly inconvenience our customers and would ultimately result in a decline in our sales. Therefore, we must be opposed to this proposal."

In a later conversation, Ms. Brent continued her thoughts: "You know, it is interesting how conditions change. In 1973, when Cal Martin approached us about Oakville Mall, he needed us very badly. Without Lint as a tenant in his project, he could not get mortgage financing to build the mall. Since we were the major retailer in the market, no financial institution would agree to a mortgage unless we were included. We saw it as a worthwhile project, however, and agreed to lease space once the mall was underway. With our promise, he was able to obtain financing, find other tenants, and build Oakville. Now that the mall is a tremendous success, he wants to expand. We are in favor of expansion, but not if it will put us in an inferior position.''

CAL MARTIN'S POSITION

Cal Martin said that he really didn't understand Lint's objections to the mall expansion. He felt that since Deming's entry to the area was inevitable, his efforts to have them locate in Oakville Mall were good not only for him but also for all the Oakville tenants: ''After all, with Deming's located in our mall and the tremendous increase in the number of other stores, we should draw many more customers than ever before. Why, instead of a decline in sales, I expect to see everyone's sales climb after the expansion is completed.''

Martin agreed with Brent's contention that Oakville Mall would not have become a reality in the 1970s without Lint's agreement to locate in the shopping center. He went on to say, however, that the original development had always been considered only the first phase of a major commercial development that was planned ultimately to include office and residential areas as well as the shopping center itself. He said the final project would include 2 million square feet of leased space. Martin claimed that the development was always envisioned as including the area of the proposed expansion and that it should have been obvious to anyone that the acreage west of the mall was intended to be part of the mall someday. ''Why else,'' he asked, ''would I have built the driveway where it is and located the movie theater so far from the mall itself? It was general knowledge that I planned to expand the mall as soon as I became financially able to do so.''

To summarize his position, Martin said: ''I don't know what all the fuss is about. Everyone is going to be better off when I finish this project.''

DEMING'S POSITION

A representative of Deming's commented that Deming's entry to this new market represented the first time the firm had planned to open two stores at one time in a new area. It was felt that such an opening thrust would allow the firm to penetrate the market rapidly. The representative also commented that the firm definitely intended to develop its own mall on the opposite side of town from Oakville Mall, approximately twenty minutes' driving time away.

QUESTIONS

1 What elements of shopping center development can be considered analogous to distribution channels?
2 Do you believe there is any synergy created by having Deming's and Lint in the same mall? Is close proximity to each other critical so that this synergy can be maintained?

3 What principles of negotiation can be observed in the Oakville Mall case?
4 What should Ms. Brent and Mr. Martin do to resolve their disagreement?

CASE 3-3: South Bottling Company

On a warm afternoon in 1978, Sam Stebbins, president of South Bottling Company, was reviewing the consequences of two major strategic decisions he had made in the past five years. As he prepared for the annual meeting with the other 739 Coca-Cola franchisees, he was sure he would be questioned closely about the results of his actions regarding addition of the Dr Pepper product line and adoption of an 8-ounce can for Coke. He knew that other Coke bottlers would be very interested in the profit impact of these two actions as well as any problems that might have occurred in the franchise arrangement.

INDUSTRY BACKGROUND

The channel system in the soft-drink industry is called a "producer-oriented wholesale system." Soft-drink producers sell their syrup to franchise bottlers that operate independently of the parent firm. The group producer, such as Coca-Cola, attempts to minimize risks by shifting functions in the channel to its franchise bottlers. The bottlers provide facilities for actual bottling, relieving the producer from considerable investment in production facilities. In addition, the bottler provides local warehousing and delivery to retail outlets. Thus, the bottler actually provides production, storage, warehousing, and delivery facilities within the channel. Bottlers also handle accounting functions and provide a considerable amount of market information concerning tastes and preferences to their present syrup manufacturers. Thus, the major advantages of this distribution system to the producer are reduced investment in fixed facilities, lower inventory requirements, and economies that result from shipping pure syrup rather than the bottled beverage. The bottlers, who serve as warehousers and "manufacturers" of the final product, ship locally and have a lower total inventory expense than would be the case if syrup producers performed the final distribution function.

The bottler in the soft-drink industry typically is viewed as the lifeblood of the parent company. The functions performed by this channel member are directly related to the success or failure of the syrup producers. In return, the producer supplies syrup (typically developed from a well-protected recipe) and extensive promotional assistance. The assistance includes expenditures for national advertising, cooperative ad allowances granted to bottlers and retailers, and free sampling.

GROWTH OF DR PEPPER

For the years 1965 to 1975 Dr Pepper was the star of the soft-drink industry.[1] The company's cherry-flavored beverage expanded in distribution from the small towns of the South and Midwest into major markets of the United States. In 1974, Dr Pepper completed its national distribution, primarily at the expense of Coca-Cola and PepsiCo, which between them controlled 55 percent of the soft-drink market. During the past decade, Dr Pepper was able to double its sales and profits every four years until it reached a sales level of $227 million and profits of $20 million in 1977.

Dr Pepper's strategy generally called for signing the largest bottler in each local market. In almost every case this meant gaining distribution from the local Coca-Cola bottler. Since Coke bottlers were generally independent of that firm, Dr Pepper was able to sign approximately 25 percent of Coke's franchisees by 1975. In doing so, Dr Pepper achieved distribution through many of the strongest bottlers in the industry and gained 5 percent of the total market with its single-line product mix. This share placed Dr Pepper fifth in the industry behind Royal Crown (6 percent), Seven-Up (7 percent), and the much larger Coca-Cola and PepsiCo firms. The rapid growth rate during the period 1965 to 1975 caused Dr Pepper executives to project that the firm would pass Royal Crown and Seven-Up in a relatively short period of time.

Dr Pepper executives felt that, in order for sales to increase, it was extremely important for consumers to have an opportunity to sample the product. The unique and distinctive taste of the product made the sale of single drinks a very important aspect in building a strong Dr Pepper franchise. (The single-drink market in the soft-drink industry consists of vending machines, fountain sales, and spectator events.) Therefore, Dr Pepper executives planned to put more emphasis on sales promotions such as giveaways at sporting events and shopping center openings. It was felt that this move was necessary before the firm could hope to gain more distribution through supermarkets. It was felt also that the firm should not try to compete directly with Coca-Cola and PepsiCo in advertising since total expenditures for those two firms totaled $130 million—more than Dr Pepper's annual sales. Tables 1 and 2 and Exhibit 1 present financial summaries for Coca-Cola and Dr Pepper.

THE 8-OUNCE CAN

The 8-ounce can of Coca-Cola was introduced by a number of independent bottlers.[2] First brought into the market in Los Angeles, it won quick consumer acceptance there and spread to several other major markets, including New York and Miami. Adoption of this can represented the first time since 1915 that independent bottlers took on a package that the parent firm had not recommended. Since purchase of Coke in 8-ounce cans was more expensive for consumers (2.9 cents per ounce when bought in a six-pack of 8-ounce cans versus 2.3 cents per ounce in a six-pack of 12-ounce cans),

---

[1] The situation for South Bottling Company is totally fictitious. Similarity between the decisions described in this case and any real situation is purely coincidental.

[2] Facts for this part of the case were developed from R. S. Smith, "Dr Pepper: Pitted Against the Soft Drink Giants," *Business Week,* October 6, 1975, pp. 70–73.

TABLE 1   THE COCA-COLA COMPANY AND SUBSIDIARIES FINANCIAL HIGHLIGHTS
(In Million Except per Share Data)

	Year ended December 31		
	1977	1976*	Percent increase
Net sales	$3,559.9	$3,094.5	15.0
Profit before taxes on income	605.3	545.5	11.0
Net profit	326.2	290.7	12.2
Net profit per share	2.67	2.38	12.2
Dividends per share	1.54	1.325	16.2
Shareholders' equity	1,557.2	1,418.5	9.8
Percent net profit to net sales	9.2%	9.4%	
Percent net profit to shareholders' equity	20.9%	20.5%	

* 1976 amounts have been restated to include operations of The Taylor Wine Company, Inc., on a pooling of interests basis and to reflect a two-for-one stock split effective in May 1977.
Source: Coca-Cola Company annual report.

TABLE 2   DR PEPPER FINANCIAL HIGHLIGHTS
(Years Ended December 31, 1977 and 1976)

	1977	1976	Percent change
Net sales	$226,750,000	$187,216,000	+21.1
Earnings			
From continuing operations before income taxes	38,504,000	33,426,000	+15.2
Provision for income taxes	18,182,000	15,834,000	+14.8
From continuing operations	20,322,000	17,592,000	+15.5
From discountinued operations, net of applicable income taxes	—	193,000	−100.0
Net earnings	20,322,000	17,785,000	+14.3
Number of weighted average shares outstanding	20,200,000	20,173,000	—

marketing executives were puzzled at its rapid acceptance. However, some consumers indicated they eventually threw away some of the contents of the 12-ounce cans because they contained more than would normally be consumed at one time. Thus, the 8-ounce can seemed to fit consumers' needs more closely. Still, Coca-Cola did not give this product its backing either through franchise encouragement or through advertising expenditures.

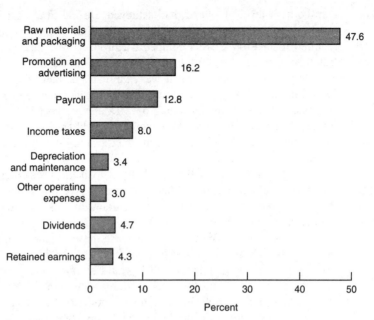

EXHIBIT 1   Dr Pepper: Distribution of revenue.

SOUTH BOTTLING COMPANY

South Bottling Company was located in a major southern metropolitan area with a population of over 700,000.[3] The firm was started as a Coca-Cola bottler by Joshua Stebbins, Sam's father, in 1915. South had enjoyed success commensurate with that of the parent company until Sam took control. Being ambitious, Sam Stebbins added a line of ground coffee to his supermarket distribution network. He also started a packaged sandwich subsidiary that distributed its products through vending machines located in many of the same outlets as his Coke machines.

Stebbins had also added many products intended to make his firm more dominant in the industrial feeding market in his market area. These products included portion-controlled packets of spices and table condiments and a broad base of soft-drink products. By 1977, net sales and profits of South Bottling Company, which by this time had become a corporate entity owned by Stebbins and fifteen other relatives (Sam and his immediate family maintained 25 percent ownership), were $27.8 million and $978,000, respectively.

THE CURRENT SITUATION

South Bottling Company became a Dr Pepper bottler in 1973. Stebbins explained that he had added the product because of Dr Pepper's aggressiveness in the marketplace

---

[3] Facts for this part of the case were developed from "Marketing Observer," *Business Week,* October 3, 1977, p. 64.

and the high level of sales it had achieved. He indicated that Dr Pepper was a very good product and the company did a superb job of promoting it. Since he was not required to take on Coke's competitive product, Mr. Pibb, which had considerably less than 3 percent of the total soft-drink market, he felt that it only made sense to add Dr Pepper. He knew that it was extremely unlikely that Coke would sell a Mr. Pibb franchise to Pepsi or Seven-Up bottlers since the regular Coke bottlers would complain bitterly. Thus, by taking on a Dr Pepper franchise, the Coke bottler could virtually monopolize the cherry-flavored market. This was particularly true since Mr. Pibb suffered from low levels of consumer awareness and received little support from Coke.

South was also one of the first bottlers to begin producing Coke in the 8-ounce can. Stebbins believed that Coke would never give this product a major effort since it had the potential to reduce the total amount of Coke syrup used by local bottlers. On the other hand, he thought bottlers might favor the package since it would reduce their purchases of Coke syrup and increase the per-ounce selling price of their final product. Of course, he realized that this package also increased the number of stock-keeping units required since he felt it would be impossible to eliminate the 12-ounce cans entirely. Thus, although there were some drawbacks, Stebbins' experience showed that profits would increase for the bottler by utilizing the 8-ounce can.

Since he was the only bottler in the United States to add Dr Pepper and begin production of 8-ounce cans of Coke, Stebbins was looking forward to the annual bottlers' meeting. He knew that he would be the center of attention for other bottlers who were considering the same decisions.

QUESTIONS

1 Map the channel network for soft drinks.
2 How does consumers' behavior place the bottler in a dominant channel position? What offsetting buyers' characteristics tend toward producer dominance?
3 What other sources of buyers does South Bottling Company have over Coca-Cola? What about its position relative to Dr Pepper?
4 What can Coca-Cola do to regain its dominance over a firm such as South Bottling Company? What else can South Bottling Company do to maintain its independence from Coca-Cola?

CASE 3-4: Ace Brokerage Company

John Kline is concerned about his recent conversation with Bob Morreaux, vice president of marketing and distribution for the Morreaux Sugar Company. Kline is president of the Ace Brokerage Company, a large food broker located in Steel City, Alabama. During their conversation, Morreaux told Kline that his firm wanted Kline to put more emphasis on developing an institutional trade for sugar. In the past, he had done an excellent job of developing the retail grocery market for Morreaux. As a matter of fact, almost 70 percent of all sugar purchased in Steel City–area supermarkets is Morreaux brand. However, the rapid growth in away-from-home eating had caused Morreaux's sales to level off in the Steel City area. Ace Brokerage had concentrated its efforts on supermarkets in Steel City and had never attempted to obtain institutional distribution for the principals it represented. Kline wondered if he should consider hiring new personal to begin developing the institutional business in response to the request by Morreaux.

BACKGROUND

Steel City is a unique market area for the supermarket industry, particularly food processors and manufacturers, since over 80 percent of all retail grocery sales are made through locally owned chains or local cooperatives. Although the metropolitan area contains over 600,000 people, only one national chain has more than four outlets and that chain captures only about 10 percent of total retail volume. In contrast, Table 1 presents data concerning the major local chains and cooperatives in Steel City. Food processors depend upon Steel City food brokers to present their lines to supermarket buyers since they cannot rely on their contacts with the national supermarket chains to obtain penetration in the market.

There are more than twenty food brokers in the Steel City area. Ace Brokerage is one of the three largest, with brokerage commissions of approximately $500,000 per year. Ace represents twenty-five noncompeting grocery and household supply manufacturers. Although Ace's contracts with its principals (suppliers) specify commission rates varying from 1 to 5 percent, average commissions are slightly less than 3 percent. Thus, Ace accounts for about $18 million in sales for its principals.

To earn the commissions, Ace performs several services for the principals as well as for the supermarket buyers. Ace representatives visit buyers periodically to present new products, take orders, and inform them of possible market changes. In this capacity, the firm acts much as the manufacturer's own sales force might. Ace also employs ten field personnel who visit individual stores to help with counting stock, replenishing shelf stock, delivering manufacturer point-of-purchase displays, and attempting to make sure that Ace principals are receiving adequate support in the stores. Ace also maintains a small warehouse with some inventory (provided on consignment by the principals) to meet any emergency needs of its customers.

Although Ace represents twenty-five principals, Morreaux Sugar Company is one of the largest. Over $80,000 of Ace's brokerage commissions come from Morreaux.

TABLE 1   MAJOR SUPERMARKET OUTLETS IN STEEL CITY

Firm name	Type	Number of stores	Approximate market share (Percent)
Freedom Grocers	Local chain	3	13
Bear Stores	Local chain	18	22
Southern Supermarkets	Cooperative	18	18
Bigg's Super Stores	Cooperative	16	16

The other major account for Ace is a large tuna and canned-fish processor which, like Morreaux, has a 70 percent market share in Steel City and generates about $80,000 per year brokerage fee for Ace. The remainder of Ace's revenues is spread over the other principals, with yearly commissions ranging from less than $1000 to $35,000.

Kline believes that his firm has an excellent reputation with supermarket buyers due to the quality of service offered by his firm as well as the principals represented by Ace. As one example of Kline's emphasis on quality products and service, he had recently withdrawn from a brokerage agreement with a processor of fruits and pie fillings due to some indications of quality-control problems in the processor's plant. Two supermarket buyers had asked Kline to remove a few cases of the product from their shelves and arrange reshipment and credit due to poor quality. Although both buyers indicated that they would reorder from the same manufacturer (specifying different canning dates from those of the off-quality goods), Kline felt that quality problems caused his field personnel too much trouble and might, in the long run, damage the reputation of Ace Brokerage. Even though this principal had paid brokerage commissions of over $30,000 to Ace in the previous year, Kline terminated his relationship with the processor and found another fruit packer desiring representation in the Steel City market. While the lost revenues have not been totally replaced by the new principal, Kline is satisfied that his firm has been able to generate commissions of $12,000 from a principal who is new to the Steel City market.

Kline admits that his lack of concern over the lost commission may be partially due to the fact that Ace Brokerage Company will report a net profit of $85,000 for the year. As owner of 60 percent of the shares in the firm (the remainder is held by three other employees), he seems satisfied with his salary as president and the dividends paid from the firm's earnings.

ACE-MORREAUX RELATIONSHIP

Ace Brokerage Company has represented the Morreaux Sugar Company in the Steel City market for four years. Prior to this arrangement, Morreaux utilized the services of Underwood Brokers, Inc., whereas Ace represented Provincial Sugar. Underwood Brokers is another of the three largest firms in Steel City. Four years ago, Morreaux was unhappy with the performance of Underwood, as their brand had only one-third of the total market at that time. Bob Morreaux felt that stronger effort by the broker would result in higher market share. Underwood was unwilling to devote more effort to Morreaux and expressed the belief that sugar was such a competitive commodity that a market share of more than 30 to 35 percent is unreasonable. At that same time, John Kline and Ace Brokerage had become disenchanted with Provincial Sugar because of that firm's refusal to commit more money to advertising and promotion in Steel City. Kline felt he could increase Provincial's penetration considerably more than its 25 percent market share with more promotional effort by the firm. It was under these conditions that Kline and Morreaux met and decided that the two firms seemed compatible in their goals. In effect, a swap was arranged, with Morreaux being represented by Ace and Provincial handled by Underwood. Morreaux is very pleased that he was correct about the potential to increase market share in the retail grocery business. On the other hand, he knows that Provincial Sugar still has 20 percent of the retail market for sugar and that Underwood Brokers has actively solicited whole-sale distributers in the institutional field to carry the provincial brand. As a result, Provincial controls about 30 percent of the institutional sugar sales. Morreaux, on the other hand, obtains very little of this business since it has no active representation in the field.

PRIMARY CONCERNS OF MORREAUX SUGAR COMPANY

Morreaux is concerned about the failure of Ace Brokerage Company to solicit whole-sale institutional distribution for several reasons. Obviously, the lost sales potential is a major concern. Although the institutional food business is not as large as the retail grocery field in sales volume, it still represents a major opportunity for food processors and manufacturers. The growth of the away-from-home eating market is a particular concern to everyone in the food industry. Morreaux had read reports that estimated that approximately one-third of all meals consumed in the United States during 1985 were consumed away from home. He is particularly interested in projections estimating that, by the mid-1990s, one-half of all meals will be consumed away from home.

The growth of the institutional business may explain Morreaux's second concern, which is the leveling off of sales in the Steel City area. With a 70 percent share of a market and no expectations of substantial real growth, he believes it will be very difficult to increase sales substantially unless alternative forms of distribution are developed. Incremental gains to be realized from capturing further market-share points would, in his opinion, be outweighed by the costs involved.

Morreaux is also concerned because he has recently concluded meetings with several major restaurant, fast-food, and institutional feeding companies, all of which have outlets in the Steel City area. Some of these firms wanted to sign contracts with Morreaux that would specify that Morreaux Sugar be used in their outlets. In return, Morreaux would package the sugar in individual serving envelopes imprinted with messages specified by the customers. Morreaux's major problem lies in promising distribution capability to these companies. While two of the feeding institutions maintain their own distribution centers in Steel City and could be supplied directly, the others utilize Steel City wholesalers and would need to have the product available from at least one of them.

Morreaux believes he could find time himself to call on a distributor in Steel City and find the means to fulfill these contracts. Most distributors would be willing to handle the product, since its sale is essentially guaranteed by the contract and because it would immediately give the distributor a means to develop sales of other products to the outlets. However, Morreaux knows that this action would not solve the basic problem of Ace's failure to cultivate the institutional market.

ALTERNATIVES

Both Ace Brokerage Company and Morreaux Sugar Company have several possible solutions to their problem. Kline may simply refuse to open an institutional sales division and wait to see the reaction of Morreaux to this decision. He knows that if he makes this decision, Morreaux can do one of two things. First, Morreaux may decide to forgo the lost opportunity in the institutional field and be satisfied with the retail grocery trade. Second, Morreaux may cancel its relationship with Ace and look for a broker with capability in both retail and institutional sales. Kline hopes that since the other large brokers already have principals for sugar, Morreaux will be afraid to cancel their agreement since dealing with a small brokerage firm would be somewhat risky for Morreaux. Of course, Morreaux could also find a broker to handle its products for the institutional business only. Kline is afraid that if Morreaux took this course and other principals followed, a fourth large brokerage firm might emerge in the Steel City market. Kline knows that developing an institutional division would require addition of least two new staff members and would create a new set of customers and problems with which he would have to deal. He also knows that Morreaux has to be concerned about Ace's reaction to any of Morreaux Sugar Company's decisions since, after all, Ace has been largely responsible for Morreaux's market dominance in Steel City.

QUESTIONS

1 How would you assess the relative power positions of these two firms? What power bases can each draw upon? Be specific. In your opinion, who has the power advantage?
2 How would you prepare for negotiation, if you were John Kline? if you were Bob Morreaux?
3 If you were John Kline, what would you do? Why?
4 If you were Bob Morreaux, what would you do? Why?

CASE 3-5: The Formation of a Strategic Alliance*

Mr. Smith, president and chief executive officer of Sparrow Transport, was reading a recent edition of the *Harvard Business Review* when he came across an article entitled ''The Strategic Benefits of Logistics Alliances.'' The article described the recent trend away from traditional adversarial business relationships toward more innovative agreements involving complex partnerships. These arrangements establish operating synergies through resource and information sharing. Mr. Smith was particularly interested in a section which proposed that firms exploit their logistical competency to achieve strategic advantage. This requires close coordination of business activities with other channel members. The article identified strategic alliances in a number of industries that have dramatically expanded business opportunities for the firms involved. Mr. Smith began to wonder whether this new business practice could be successfully implemented by his firm as a means for improving business performance in automotive parts distribution.

* *The Formation of a Strategic Alliance* was written by David J. Frayer.

SPARROW TRANSPORT

Sparrow Transport is a medium-sized, privately owned regional motor carrier that offers contract carrier service between locations in Michigan, Ohio, Indiana, and Illinois. A significant portion of the firm's business is accounted for by just-in-time shipping of automotive parts to assembly plants within the region. Unfortunately, as domestic manufacturers have begun relying more heavily on offshore production of automotive parts, regional carrier business has declined. Shipments between suppliers and domestic automobile plants within the Midwest have decreased significantly. While a number of plants remain in the region, part shipments now require long hauls from Pacific coast ports and plants in the Maquiladora region of Mexico. Sparrow Transport previously bid on these long-distance contracts, but they found their cost structure unable to compete with low-cost national motor carrier and rail double-stack container operations. Still, Mr. Smith remained convinced that his firm's experienced drivers and innovative trailer design provided a strategic advantage that could play a significant role in the future delivery of automobile parts.

Sparrow Transport is widely heralded for its modern, well-maintained fleet of tractor-trailers. The company relies heavily on equipment (soft-sided trailers that can be unloaded from all sides) and technological advances (computerized tracking) to provide a competitive advantage within the trucking industry. Most of the firm's managers are young and innovative, which has made the firm more responsive than many of its competitors. The corporate culture at Sparrow Transport is relaxed, and many managers wear blue jeans in the headquarters building. Reporting relationships are flexible and Mr. Smith strongly believes in employee empowerment. Sparrow drivers are encouraged to make on-site decisions to improve customer-service performance. While excellent internal communication has facilitated these efforts, actual lines of communication remain informal.

Sparrow Transport's primary competitors can be classified into two basic groups: motor carriers and railroads. Following deregulation, competition in the motor carrier industry increased dramatically. With increased competition came lower prices, reduced margins, and industry consolidation. Many of the small private carriers were acquired by large national and regional carriers. Sparrow managed to remain independent by maintaining adequate service levels in peripheral businesses while focusing attention on delivery of automotive parts. As domestic manufacturers began to import large quantities of automobile parts, shipments by regional carriers such as Sparrow Transport decreased and low-cost national carriers increased market share. However, few national carriers could offer the customized service of Sparrow Transport. Within the automobile industry, a substantial need remained for a flexible long-haul carrier.

The railroad industry was also able to increase business in automotive parts distribution through emphasis on low-cost scheduled deliveries over long distances. The nature of automobile parts distribution required that railroads utilize local motor carrier service for final delivery. In order to capture additional business, some of the major national railroads established their own local carrier service. However, lack of experience and limited initial business opportunities made these fleets very expensive. Mr. Smith privately delighted in the railroad's lack of success at operating trucking lines, because the railroads' failure now presented a growth opportunity for Sparrow Transport.

AMERICAN-PACIFIC RAILROAD

The Great American and Pacific Railroad Company (APR) was one of the primary beneficiaries of the increased importation of automobile parts by American manufacturers. Through use of double-stack containers trains, automobile parts were sequence-loaded and transported daily from Mexico and Pacific ports to assembly plants in the Midwest. However, final distribution for APR required use of a local carrier to complete intracity movements. Employment of double-stack container trains in the automobile industry increased APR's sales by almost 15 percent. Such a lucrative business opportunity began to attract other railroads, many of whom had access to final-delivery vehicles to complete the job on a single invoice. Some of these railroads attracted significant business away from APR by offering customized service and less complicated procedures. The lack of an inexpensive local-carrier link jeopardized APR's financial position.

APR is a traditional railroad operator, with an extensive network of rail lines crossing the nation. Reporting relationships are formal and the management style has been characterized as quite staid. The firm relies on its traditional strengths, including on-time performance and lack of damage. The adoption of double-stack container trains was viewed as a radical departure from traditional management philosophy and was pioneered solely by Bill Davis, then a vice president. While seen as a tremendous risk to the firm, this decision propelled Davis to the top spot and returned the firm to profitability after nearly a decade of losses.

THE OPPORTUNITY

As Mr. Smith read the article from the *Harvard Business Review,* he recalled the situation currently facing his firm. Market share had been declining steadily for three years, making the firm quite vulnerable to acquisition by one of the large national transportation companies. Based on information obtained from a recent *Wall Street Journal* article, Mr. Smith was aware of the situation facing APR. The railroad's president, Bill Davis, feared that the revenue generated by transcontinental shipments might disappear without a local-carrier link. This could send APR into a financial tailspin, jeopardizing his firm's future. While Mr. Smith realized that neither firm had the available capital to acquire the other, there appeared to be a good match between the firms. Mr. Smith hoped that he could strategically link his firm to APR and provide final delivery of containerized goods. He knew from the *Wall Street Journal* article that this was one of APR's shortcomings that Sparrow Transport could immediately address. Establishment of synergies through single-invoice billing, time-sequenced delivery, better shipment coordination, and joint business operations could benefit both Sparrow Transport and APR. It was hoped that improved service and lower overall transportation costs would make the two firms more competitive in the marketplace.

In order for the strategic alliance to be successful, Mr. Smith needed to identify alternative sources of income for the combined operation. While automotive parts distribution was a significant market, all of the transit was in a single direction. Back-haul agreements would need to be negotiated with companies such as United Parcel Service and Sears, Roebuck, and Company so that return revenue could be ensured.

The firms needed to share more than equipment and routes in order to establish operating synergies. Human and financial resources would need to be committed from both sides. This type of interaction would require management support at the highest levels. Moreover, information linkages were needed to tie the organizations together and permit order tracking at even the most basic level. Mr. Smith believed that his firm had the technological capacity to propel APR into the twenty-first century, but would APR be willing to attempt such an endeavor?

CONCLUSION

Based on his knowledge of the strengths and weaknesses of both Sparrow Transport and APR, Mr. Smith needed to determine whether a strategic alliance was the appropriate response to his business's needs. Armed with the article from the *Harvard Business Review* and a vision of the future, Mr. Smith set out to meet with Bill Davis, president of APR, to discuss the potential for a strategic alliance.

QUESTIONS

1 What are the respective strengths and weaknesses of Sparrow Transport and APR? Are these companies well-suited for a strategic alliance?
2 What should Mr. Smith's primary consideration be in negotiations with APR?
3 What characteristics internal to the firm are necessary for the successful operation of a strategic alliance? Do these firms appear to have similar cultures? Could the differences be successfully minimized?
4 Is it important to provide a means for ending the relationship in the basic agreement? Why or why not?
5 Discuss how strategic alliances between a product marketer and a service provider, two or more vertically aligned product marketers, and two or more horizontally aligned product marketers would differ from the example in this case. Can you identify strategic alliances in any other industries? How have these relationships fared across time?

REFERENCES

Bowersox, Donald J., "The Strategic Benefits of Logistics Alliances," *Harvard Business Review,* **68:**4 July–August 1990, pp. 36–45.

EXPANDED CHANNEL PERSPECTIVES

Part Four discusses the general application of channel structure and strategy concepts in less traditional situations. Chapter 12 develops the increasing importance of information technology on practices of channel management and reviews the process of institutional change and the role of change agents in channel dynamics. Chapter 13 illustrates less traditional applications of channel concepts, techniques, and management practice by illustrating international, third-world, and service channel arrangements. The coverage concludes in Chapter 14 with a speculative look at the future composition of channel systems.

CHAPTER 12

CHANNEL DYNAMICS

CHAPTER OUTLINE

DAWNING OF THE INFORMATION AGE
    Information Technology
    Competing in Time
    Organizational Structure Impact
CHANNEL CHANGE
    The Economics of Differentiation
    Explanations of Channel Change
    Channel Change Model Limitations
MANAGEMENT OF CHANNEL CHANGE
    Institutionalizing Process
    Role of the Change Agent
    Characteristics of Successful Change Agents

One word, "technology," serves to sharply differentiate channel arrangements of the 1990s from the past. In particular, information technology has redefined the scope of channel opportunities and stimulated managerial attention toward reevaluation of traditional arrangements. In the first section of the chapter, the impact of information technology on channel arrangements is reviewed. Information technology is shown to be the major reason why age-old channel practices are being modified. Information technology adoption has ushered in the concepts of time-based competition and has significantly impacted organizational structure. The first section also examines the close relationship between information technology and channel change.

The second section discusses the channel modification process and reviews theories of the causes of change. The final section deals with management of the change.

DAWNING OF THE INFORMATION AGE

One of the most incredible features of the 1980s was the rapid rate of technology expansion and adoption. The basic nature of channel relationships was permanently altered by the steady stream of technological innovation and adoption. In particular, proliferation of information technology created new pressures on and opportunities for distribution channel performance. In this section, information technology and its impact upon marketing channels structure is discussed. Following a brief overview of the scope of information technology, the impact of this new capability in terms of competitive timing, organizational structure, and practical enabling of postponement strategies is reviewed.

Information Technology

Information technology consists of a combination of data-transmission and computational capabilities. Widespread adoption of computer-based technology has established the means by which numerous transactional details can be tracked and formatted as meaningful information. The combination of point-of-sale devices and database structures offers the capability for the rapid formatting of transactional detail into structured business information. Such information enables users to rapidly respond to customers' requirements.

The potential of information is realized by its availability in a timely manner at key decision points throughout the channel. Data transmission involves the collection of information from various locations for presentation when and where needed so that channel management can be facilitated. In the case of distribution channels, information facilitates transfer of product ownership.

The most visible form of information-based technology besides computerization being currently deployed in channel arrangements is electronic data interchange (EDI). EDI is defined as computer-to-computer transfer of information through use of standard formats.[1] With EDI, transactions can be completed between two parties in a standardized manner without negotiation of details. Thus, EDI represents considerable advancement beyond facsimile (FAX) machines because of the computer-to-computer connectivity. EDI also offers a greater degree of sophistication than direct data transmission (modem) because of the availability and use of standard transactional structures or sets by numerous different trading partners.

The range of standard transactional structures for EDI is currently expanding. In the United States, the basic EDI formats use the convention of the American National Standards Institute (ANSI.X12). Numerous industries have formed action groups to

---

[1] Anne E. Skagen, "Nurturing Relationships, Enhancing Quality with Electronic Data Interchange, *Management Review,* **78:**2 February 1989, pp. 28–32; and Benn R. Konsynski and F. Warren McFarlan, "Information Partnerships: Shared Data, Shared Scale," *Harvard Business Review,* **68:**5 September–October 1990, pp. 114–120.

TABLE 12-1 INDUSTRY EDI STANDARD GROUPS

AIAG	Automotive Industry Action Group
CIDX	Chemical Industry Data Exchange
EAGLE	Hardware Industry Standards
EDGAR	Electronic Data Gathering Analysis & Retrieval (Securities & Exchange Commission)
EDX	Electrical Data Exchange
EIDX	Electronics Industry Data Exchange
GMAIC	General Merchandising and Apparel Implementation Committee
HIBCC	Health Industry Group
ICOPS	Industry Committee on Office Products Standards
IGES	International Graphics Exchange Standard
REDI	Retailer Electronic Data Interchange
TAMC	Textile Apparel Manufacturing Communications
TCIF	Telecommunications Industry Forum (Exchange Carriers Standards Association)
TDCC	Transportation Data Coordinating Committee
TDED	Trade Data Elements Directory Standards
TRADACOMS	Trading Data Communications Standards
UCS	Uniform Communication Standard
VICS	Voluntary Interindustry Communications Standards
WINS	Warehouse Information Network Standards

Table reprinted with permission of the Electronic Data Interchange Association (EDIA).

develop transactional structures to accommodate their specific requirements. Such transactional sets typically provide standards for uniform communications such as purchase orders, invoices, correction notices, and transfer of funds. Table 12-1 provides a listing of several industries that have developed standard transactional formats. At the international level, the United Nations has served as a catalyst in developing multinational standards. The coordinated standards of the United Nations are known as EDIFACT (EDI for Administration, Commerce and Transport). While the compatibility of ANSI.X12 and EDIFACT is not completely worked out, most experts agree that, ultimately, transparent conversing will exist.[2]

Attention focused on EDI has resulted in the development of a number of specialized support businesses aimed at the facilitation of data transfer. Three such facilitators are important to channel arrangements: (1) value-added networks, (2) interface translators, and (3) Universal Product Code Catalogs.

Value-Added Networks   Value-added networks (VANs) are satellite-based communication networks for the support of data transmission. VANs serve as an alternative to radio-frequency and land-based telephone lines in the transfer of data. Several businesses operate VANs for their internal proprietary use. Many, such as Wal-Mart, Sears, IBM, General Electric, and Wards, offer paid network access for other businesses. In the case of Wal-Mart and Sears, vendors are required to use their networks

---

[2] *25 Key Issues in EDI: Challenges for Users and Vendors* (Alexandria, VA: TDCC/Gortner Group, 1988), p. 10.

when they engage in EDI transactions. Networks such as GE's and Wards' are available to potential users on the basis of a cost per transaction. For example, when a person uses a Shell credit card, the typical transmission is over a local telephone line to a Wards origin terminal location and then via satellite to the message destination. Many networks, however, are configured for direct computer-to-computer transmission. A common VAN application is to offer methods for interrupted message transfer (Mailbox). Using a mailbox procedure, a firm can transmit a document, such as a purchase order, for collection by a vendor at a future time. The vendor will receive the purchase order when the designated mailbox is electronically accessed.

Interface Translators   The term *interface translators* describes a broad range of business specialists who facilitate communications between two channel participants. The translator offers a protocol that permits two otherwise noncompatible computer systems to communicate. In the trade, the actual product provided by a translator is referred to as an *envelope* because it conveys information between two parties to a transaction.

Universal Product Code Catalog   The Universal Product Code Catalog (UPC-Catalog) is a service that Quick Response Service, Inc., and GE Information Services began to offer the public in 1988.[3] The function of the UPC-Catalog is to provide a dictionary of product specifications. The purpose of the catalog is to reduce the vendor and product detail that must be maintained by a potential buyer of prospective products. Using a catalog service, buyers can access and obtain up-to-date UPC detail in computer-readable format when they need it; thus, the establishment and maintenance of a database is facilitated.

Beyond EDI and associated services, a number of specific information technologies are making significant contributions to distribution channel arrangements. A particularly promising device is *radio-frequency* (RF) technology that is being applied for positive identification of merchandise both while in transit in transport vehicles and during materials handling. Satellite tracking of transportation equipment has advanced to the point that it is capable of enabling two-way communication for the tracking of merchandise locations and delivery capabilities.[4] Electronic scanning of bar codes is a technology capable of facilitating accurate database updating during merchandise delivery. Bar-code scanning also can be used to facilitate electronic ordering of merchandise.

This brief review of information-based technology offers some insight into the variety of ways that traditional channel working relationships are being modified. All of the technologies serve to facilitate rapid and accurate transmission among channel members of transaction-based information. Accurate and timely information is the ingredient that enables time compressed (faster paced) competition.

---

[3] Gary Robins, "Using the UPC Catalog," *Stores,* **71:**2 February 1989, p. 61.

[4] Thomas W. Heard, "Some Observations on Implementing Electronic Data Interchange," *Transport Topics,* April 20, 1987, pp. 20–21; and Ron Schneiderman, "Tracking Trucks by Satellite," *High Technology Business,* May 1989, pp. 24–28.

Competing in Time

During the 1980s, speed became a critical aspect of the competitive process. Firms capable of performing the distribution process fast and error-free offer greater appeal as preferential channel partners. The attribute of speed has little or no value unless quality is maintained. However, when total quality is achieved, the benefits of speed may be the source of competitive advantage.

There are numerous examples of more rapid development of new products from concept to market introduction with use of new concepts of organization and principles of synchronized or parallel development.[5]

Less obvious than the length of the development cycle is the impact of time upon the ownership transfer that occurs throughout the distribution channel. As a result of exacting procurement of component parts, such concepts as *just-in-time* (JIT) and *quick-response* (QR) inventory replenishment have gained widespread popularity. Each concept has broader ramifications than a simple performance of traditional processes quickly.

Just-in-Time Inventory Replenishment *Just in time* (JIT) is a strategy of procurement that embodies three interrelated ideas. First, purchase quantity is limited to the exact quantity of a component required for planned manufacturing or assembly. Care is taken to eliminate any carryover inventory or remnants.

Second, as JIT implies, the exact quantity is planned to arrive at a precise time. The timed-phased arrival at a manufacturing plant of shipments when they are needed eliminates the need for warehousing.

Finally, JIT embodies the benefit of carefully planned utilization of transportation vehicles. In some situations it embodies the use of specialized equipment for the facilitation of efficient materials handling at the delivery destination. For example, use of production-sequenced loaded curtain or soft-sided trailers permits automotive assembly components to be simultaneously unloaded from both sides as well as from the rear doors. The ideal circumstance is to directly move components from the delivery trailer to the assembly location in one materials handling effort.

Quick-Response Inventory Replenishment *Quick response* (QR) represents time-sensitive principles applied to distribution of finished products. The basic idea of QR is to rapidly replenish merchandise sold at retail stores by the electronic transmittal of orders, rapid processing at the warehouse, and expedited delivery. An example of QR that has received considerable publicity is Levi-Link, Levi's computer program for electronic communication with key customers. The idea behind Levi-Link is to reduce the total elapsed time from the initial identification of a retailer's inventory need and delivery of the desired garments. Formalization of Levi-Link is reported to have significantly reduced elapsed time required for replenishment of retailer's

[5] See Chapter 2, p. 36. Also see Peter G. W. Kern, *Competing in Time,* 2d ed., New York: Ballingher, 1988, and George Stalk, Jr., and Thomas M. Hout, *Competing against Time,* New York: Free Press, 1990.

shelves, which has resulted in increased sales and reduced inventory.[6] Perhaps far more important than order cycle speed is the capability to rapidly match retail inventory to customers' color, style, and size preferences.

The above examples illustrate how business solutions are seeking to replace sluggish and erratic business channels with precise, rapid arrangements. The impact upon business practice in a channel of distribution can be revolutionary. Custom-ordered furniture has traditionally required a lead time of from ninety days to six months from custom manufacturing to delivery to customers. One solution for the reduction in order cycle times is to warehouse finished household furniture in anticipation of customer orders. The results of warehousing have been disappointing, since it is almost impossible to forecast exactly when and what consumers will order. Recently, efforts have been made to rapidly transmit consumers' desired orders once manufacturers have efficiently built to order from a predetermined number of fabric and style options. This has reduced custom delivery times to four weeks or less. Firms such as Expressions and Design Concepts have introduced this new service-driven channel structure for custom-built household furniture. Firms specializing in office furniture, such as Steelcase and Herman Miller, have introduced modular design concepts to improve their custom-order response time.

These examples illustrate the emphasis that is placed upon the speeding up of the process of responding to customer orders. To a large extent, the ability to create new and faster ways to compete rests directly upon information technology. Information technology has also significantly impacted traditional organizational structure.

Organizational Structure Impact

The structures of modern organizations are changing to accommodate the impact of information networking. Many people have examined ways that traditional organizations are changing in order to facilitate information-rich decision making. Figure 12-1 highlights the contrast between line and staff command structures and serves to illustrate the concept of networking.[7] Peter Drucker has discussed new practices of management that must evolve for the facilitation of information flow; this could serve to doom traditional hierarchical command and control-organization structures.[8] Christopher Meyer and David Power have predicted that traditional structures of enterprises will undergo the storm of disintegration prior to enjoying the calm of information integration.[9] John Rockart and James Short have determined the challenge of the 1990s as the need to develop techniques for managing interdependence.[10] All of the above

---

[6] Neal E. Boudette, "Electronic Data Interchange: A Leap of Faith," *Industry Week,* August 7, 1989, pp. 52–55.

[7] Charles M. Savage, *Fifth Generation Management,* Boston: Digital Press, 1990.

[8] Peter F. Drucker, "The Coming of the New Organization," *Harvard Business Review,* **88:**1 January–February 1988, pp. 45–53.

[9] Christopher Meyer and David Power, "Enterprise Disintegration: The Storm Before the Calm," *Commentary,* Lexington, MA: Tample, Barker and Sloane, 1989.

[10] John F. Rockart and James E. Short, "IT in the 1990s: Managing Organizational Interdependence," *Sloan Management Review,* **30:**2 Winter 1989, pp. 7–17.

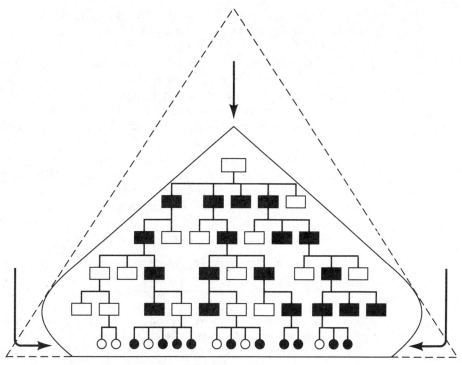

FIGURE 12-1   Impact of information technology on traditional organization structure. (Reprinted with permission from *Fifth Generation Management* by Charles Savage, copyright © 1990 Digital Press/Digital Equipment Corporation, 12 Crosby Drive, Bedford, MA 01730.)

predictions are based on a belief that information technology is to have a far-reaching and permanent impact upon traditional concepts of organizational structure. The question remains: To what extent will the predicted change affect channel relationships?

The potential impact of information technology on organizational structure and the resultant impact on channel alignments seems to involve three related concepts: (1) flatness, (2) empowerment, and (3) outsourcing.

Flatness   Structural flatness refers to the generally accepted span of reportability to or control by executives. The traditional accepted or managerial span of control has been 8 to 1. In other words, no executive is expected to have more than eight subordinates who report directly to him or her. This traditional concept of span of control has been seriously challenged by information technology. The central flatness idea is that superior information can enable an executive to effectively supervise many more direct report subordinates. Span of control extension to as many directly reporting subordinates as twelve or more has the net impact of flatting the organizational pyramid. The more the structure becomes "pancaked," the shorter the organizational distance from the most senior management to customers. From the viewpoint of distribution arrangements, flat organizations should be inherently committed to the building of strong channel alliances. Commitment to a flat organization is in direct contrast to a strategy of vertical integration. The ownership of consecutive stages of distribution works in direct opposition to flatness.

Empowerment Closely related to the notion of flat organizational structure is a readily identifiable trend toward increased empowerment. Empowerment simply means that authority to act is delegated or pushed down the organization to lower levels. In part, such empowerment is a direct reflection of the emphasis that is placed on speed. Empowerment also flows from flat structure since increased span of control means that managers must be free to act in order to avoid unnecessary delays. Flat structures without empowerment could quickly lead to organizational paralysis. Of course, the real enabler of empowerment is information technology which provides the means for senior management to maintain control. Speaking to a group of retailers, Jack Shewmaker, former vice chairman of Wal-Mart, described the company's empowerment strategy as one of "centralized direction and decentralized application." He described the working relationship as follows:

> By withholding information from Wal-Mart employees we were penalizing the very people who needed some way of measuring their contributions to the company. Today Wal-Mart issues monthly operating data, including every cost, every charge for every operating division of the company. It comes out a few days after the end of every month. Every department manager, every sales clerk gets finite data on his or her department compared with everyone else's in that particular store, in the district, in the region, in the industry. Not only do they get information, we expect them to understand it and make use of it.[11]

It is clear that with the information to take initiative comes responsibility. From a channel perspective, organizations that believe in high levels of empowerment are relatively better positioned than traditional command and control structures to enter into distribution alliances.

Outsourcing A final concept related to information technology and organization structure is the sharply increased insistence on outsourcing. The incentive for outsourcing is to capitalize on the benefits of specialization. As noted repeatedly, firms rely upon specialists to improve channel efficiency. Since the rapid expansion of information technology, the practice of outsourcing of functions appears to have accelerated. At least in part, such expanded outsourcing is a reflection of an increased confidence in the ability to maintain control as a result of superior information. The economic incentives for outsourcing were recently highlighted in a *Business Week* feature entitled "The Hollow Corporation."[12] Trends concerning the rapid growth of brokers and the mushrooming of full service logistics firms discussed in Chapter 3 suggest that increased outsourcing is impacting both the sales and logistics dimensions of channels.[13] This trend toward increased outsourcing means that channel relationships gain more prominence in strategic planning.

---

[11] Jay L. Johnson, "Internal Communication: A Key to Wal-Mart's Success," *Discount Merchandiser*, November 1989, p. 68. Reprinted with permission of *Discount Merchandiser*.

[12] "The Hollow Corporation," *Business Week*, March 3, 1986, pp. 56–71.

[13] See Chapter 3, pp. 79–80.

In terms of channel structure, a strong case can be made that acceptable and desirable distribution arrangements are directly influenced by forces that modify firms' internal organizational structure and management practices. Information technology has created a major revolution in organizational structure. Three trends—flatness, empowerment, and outsourcing—all directly affect the way that an organization can be expected to interact with channel partners. The combination of all three trends results in an increase in the degree of commitment and the dependence a firm is likely to seek in a channel arrangement.

CHANNEL CHANGE

The initial section of this chapter discussed the rapidly expanding impact of information technology upon channel managements. The continuous interaction between function and structure causes channels to constantly adjust and realign. Over time, most channel arrangements will change dramatically. Some participants must undergo a significant change in their channel role. Others will be replaced by entirely new members. To understand why channels of distribution are not static, it is necessary to look more closely at some fundamental characteristics of a competitive system.

Channel dynamics are examined with a review of management of the change process. First, the economics of differentiation and the relationship between innovation, neutralization, and economic growth is developed. Alternative models that explain channel change and inherent limitations are then discussed.

The Economics of Differentiation

A major distribution challenge satisfied by channel arrangements is the matching of heterogeneous supply with unique demand for products and services. When matching is successful, suppliers and buyers initialize transactions and, in more advanced situations, negotiate relationships. Suppliers seek to establish loyalty among buyers to ensure that the relationship will endure. The potential rewards are continuous sales and a predictable share of market.

How do sellers establish buyers' loyalty? They seek to differentiate products and services in an effort to create a positive impact. The potential for differentiation is limited only by the creativity of the selling firm's management. The overall process is called *competition for differential advantage.* Every participant in a channel of distribution engages in some form of differentiating behavior. The manufacturer usually engages in (1) product differentiation, (2) communication differentiation, (3) logistics differentiation, (4) differentiation through the ensuring of service, warranties, and guarantees, and (5) differentiation in price and terms of sale. Wholesalers, retailers, and support channel participants also engage in a variety of actions aimed at differentiating their firms. A support participant in a channel, such as a financial institution or a public warehouse, may be very specialized in terms of the services it offers. Nevertheless it will seek to differentiate in terms of competitive alternatives. All channel participants engage in differentiating behavior aimed at capturing a competitive niche.

Innovation, Neutralization, and Economic Growth   The dynamics of competition for differential advantage result in economic growth. At any point in time, the market share of each participant is based on its success in achieving differentiation. Participants not content with relative market share will initiate new competitive activities aimed at improving their attractiveness to potential buyers. The dynamics of change force all participants to continually seek ways to protect and expand their relative positions. Economic growth is the result of the dynamics of change.

The continual process of innovation, neutralization, and innovation that results in economic growth led Schumpeter to describe the competitive system as one of "creative destruction."[14] As soon as an innovation is successful, it is challenged by the next round of innovations.

Not all managers understand the inherent nature of competitive change. In fact, change that cuts at the heart of an industry's market and threatens traditional practice is usually resisted in every way possible, including requests for governmental intervention.[15] Over time, the neutralization will result despite resistance. Society benefits from economic growth. From a channel management perspective, all participating institutions must be viewed as being continuously engaged in change, sometimes as the initiators, and other times as the responders.

Explanations of Channel Change

Change in a specific channel structure occurs in two basic ways. First, existing participants may accommodate change by adopting roles and modifying operations to remain viable channel members. A prime example of a firm that adopted its traditional channel role to accommodate change is Woolworth's. Confronted with the decline in popularity of 5&10-cent-store merchandising, the firm repositioned itself as an important participant in specialty retailing. W. T. Grant was a former retail great that didn't adapt to change and failed. A second form of change is the emergence of new businesses as important channel members. The recent development of broad-based logistics service firms was in direct response to an opportunity to differentiate by offering integrated services.[16] A number of models have been proposed to help understand and manage the change process. Three of these—the core-fringe, the cycle, and the crisis change model—are the most comprehensive. Each is described.

Core-Fringe Model   The core-fringe model was initially presented by Wroe Alderson as an explanation of survival and growth.[17] The model builds on the central notion that all successful businesses must have a core market in which they have deep penetration and one or more fringe markets in which their penetration is relatively weak. Core market strength provides the financial resources and time for the devel-

---

[14] See Joseph Schumpeter, *Capitalism, Socialism, and Democracy,* New York: Harper & Brothers, 1947, Chapter 7.

[15] Michael Beer, Russell A. Eisenstat, and Bert Spector, "Why Change Programs Don't Produce Change," *Harvard Business Review,* **68:**6 November–December 1990, pp. 158–166.

[16] See Chapter 3.

[17] See Wroe Alderson, op. cit., p. 56.

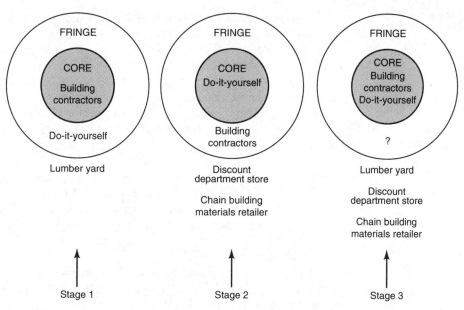

FIGURE 12-2   Core-fringe explanation of channel change in the building materials industry.

opment of strategies to improve competitive position in selected fringe markets or to diversify. Failure of a firm to develop fringe markets may open the door for competition.

Change in the building materials industry can be explained by the core-fringe concept. The traditional lumberyard was positioned at the core of a market and primarily serviced building contractors. A fringe market segment consisting primarily of do-it-yourself consumers began to emerge. This consumer-based niche represented a market segment that the traditional lumberyard was not ideally positioned to service. Initially, the traditional lumberyard did little to accommodate fringe market requirements. As the potential of the fringe market grew, new channel participants such as discount stores and chain building materials retailers emerged to service the segment. Over time, the new channel participants began to penetrate the lumberyard core market by appealing to both do-it-yourself and professional contractors. Some lumberyards modified their merchandising strategies to cater to both markets. Thus, the structure of the building materials channel changed considerably as the result of two new forms of distribution. The change stages are diagramed in Figure 12-2. Over time, the stage 3 fringe market will again be challenged. One possibility is that large builders might eventually bypass all intermediaries in the channel and do business directly with supply firms.

Being positioned in a core market insulates a firm from direct or frontal attacks from selected competitors and may provide the stability to support diversification into growth segments. The lesson learned is that focus on a core market to the neglect of high-growth fringes may render a firm vulnerable to competitors.

Life-Cycle Models Life-cycle models are widely used to illustrate stages that a product passes through from introduction to obsolescence. When used to explain channels of distribution, life-cycle models concentrate on the participants' role changes. If the hypothesis that institutions have a life cycle is accepted, it is conceptually possible to trace the historic change, examine factors that have caused the change, and then predict likely future change.

One long-standing cycle model is the "wheel of retailing" developed by Malcolm P. MacNair.[18] He hypothesized that new retailers with new forms of retailing enter the market as low-status, low-margin, low-price competitors. If consumers respond to low-end merchandising, the core market is threatened by the new fringe. To effectively compete, low-end retailers, over time, will upgrade stores and introduce expanded services. Each effort to upgrade requires a capital investment and increases operating costs. Eventually, low-end merchandisers evolve into high-status, high-margin, and high-price establishments. Over time, they become vulnerable to the reentry of new firms that initially enter the market as low-end merchandisers. The stage is set for the life cycle to repeat.

The typical life cycle consists of four cost-revenue stages: (1) innovation, (2) accelerated development, (3) maturity, and (4) decline.[19] The *innovation stage* is characterized by rapidly increasing sales but low profits as a result of heavy start-up expenditures. In the *accelerated development stage,* sales and profits increase rapidly. During the *maturity stage,* sales increase, but at a slower rate, and profits continue to increase. In the *decline stage,* both sales and profits begin to drop. During the accelerated development and maturity stages, retailers become high-status, high-margin, and high-price operators. The decline stage is accelerated by new competition in the form of low-status, low-margin, low-price merchants.

The life cycle of appliance dealers from 1920 to the 1990s is a history of the growth and decline of different types of dealers. The stages of development are illustrated in Figure 12-3. During the first stage, from 1920 to 1930, appliance sales began to increase. From 1930 to 1950, sales increased further, but by 1950 the market was glutted with a wide assortment of appliances, many dealers were not efficient, and a shakeout and consolidation was occurring among traditional manufacturers. From 1950 until the 1970s, the overall market experienced slow growth with primarily the same traditional structure of distributors and dealers being used. Original appliance dealers, innovators in retailing, never were low-status, low-margin, low-price operators. Rather, the educational tasks required to introduce a new product line made them full-service establishments from their inception with high status, high margins, and high prices. After 1950, the share of the market shifted to mass merchandisers that entered the innovation stage as low-status, low-margin, low-price operators. Traditional specialized appliance dealers began to decline. During the 1980s the innovative life cycle continued with the establishment of highly specialized discount retailers

---

[18] See Malcolm P. MacNair, "Significant Trends and Development in the Postwar Period," in *Competitive Distribution in a Free High-Level Economy and Its Implications for the University,* ed. A. B. Smith, Pittsburgh: University of Pittsburgh, 1958, pp. 17–18.

[19] See William R. Davidson, Albert D. Bates, and Stephen J. Bass, "The Retail Life Cycle," *Harvard Business Review,* November–December 1976, pp. 89–96.

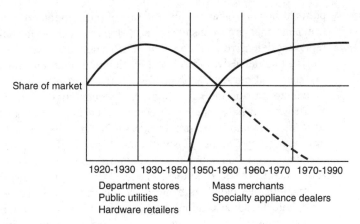

FIGURE 12-3 Institutional cycle theory in the appliance industry.

such as Circuit City, Fretter, and Highland. This, in turn, stimulated significant change in the traditional approach used by full-service retailers. Some retailers such as Wards stopped selling appliances altogether. Others sought to expand their overall product-service offerings in an effort to extend the institutional life cycle. For example, in 1989 Sears adopted a ''Brand Central'' strategy in which the private labels such as Kenmore were expanded to offer consumers national-brand alternatives.

Other examples of a retail institutional life cycle are department stores replacing general stores, followed by discount stores aggressively competing with the department stores in general-merchandise lines, and supermarkets replacing the full-service food retailer. In today's competitive retail market, department stores face serious challenge by competing specialty retailers. The supermarket is undergoing significant structural change to accommodate club stores and wholesale clubs.

Crisis Change Model The crisis change model seeks to identify phases that an organization passes through as it reacts to new forms of competition. Typical phases are shock, defense, acknowledgment, and adaptation.[20]

The *shock phase* occurs when a channel participant recognizes that a threat exists either to its own survival or to the overall channel success. Usually such recognition occurs when a significant new type of competition enters a well-established market. Many actions, ranging from passive to very aggressive, are initiated to combat the intruder. Typical actions might include lobbying for political protection, persuading suppliers not to sell to the new competitors, or engaging in aggressive sales promotion in an effort to influence customers to remain with the traditional channel.

The *defense phase* is characterized by threatened institutions beginning to cooperate to reduce the effectiveness of the intruder. In many states, retail druggist associations faced with the advent of vertically integrated chains collectively have lobbied for

---

[20] See Stephen L. Fink, Joel Beak, and Kenneth Taddeo, ''Organizational Crisis and Change,'' *Journal of Applied Behavioral Science,* **7:**1 January–February 1971, pp. 15–37.

political sanctions that prohibit the sale of prescription drugs at discount prices. Advertisements that urge consumers to "support local businesses" or "buy American" represent defensive measures that directly retaliate against new forms of competition. During this defensive phase, wishful thinking often prevails about an eventual return to "the good old days." Typically, a great deal of money and effort is expended in an attempt to stop the natural competitive evolution of the free-market system.

The *acknowledgment phase* begins when the traditional firms realize that a new form of competition is here to stay. It is typically characterized by a serious self-examination by and a criticism of those firms. In the defense phase, managerial attention was focused on attempts to mold practices of the new competitor into the function and structure of the traditional channel. During the acknowledgment phase, the traditional channel members begin to adopt practices of the new competitive structure. Also, threatened institutions begin to examine their options and their distribution arrangements closely. Because of the channel members' need to counter new forms of competition, the potential of conflict among them is highly probable. Some members of the traditional channel may continue to resist change. In some situations, a new leader will emerge to help reconfigure the traditional distribution arrangement.

The *adaption phase* occurs when threatened channel members develop a strategy to cope with the new competitive situation. Adaption usually involves significant change in the traditional way of doing business and may stimulate a new period of growth. The threat to grocery wholesalers and independent grocers created by the growth of the supermarket chain was eventually minimized by formation of wholesaler-sponsored voluntary groups and retailer cooperatives. Not all channel arrangements and participants are able to adapt. Some that try to cling to traditional practices ultimately lose out if customers prefer the new way of doing business. Institutions that successfully adapt to the new structure remain major competitors.

Channel Change Model Limitations

All three institutional change models offer ways to explain structural dynamics. All three models generally suffer from the fact that they are overly descriptive, excessively aggregative, and unable to explain the underlying causes that stimulate specific types of change. Each limitation is briefly discussed.

Descriptive Limitation Given the benefit of hindsight, it is relatively easy to explain what is happening with any of the constructs. None provide a way to predict or manage change. With the core-fringe concept, the fact that a competitor is developing a strategy for the fringe market is not known until the competitor actually enters the market. The same holds true for the cycle model. It does not explain change until an innovator emerges. The cycle model creates an awareness that change is rhythmic. If the cause of past change is understood, then the next change may be predicted. However, exceptions typically modify life-cycle duration and direction. Attempts to predict change can be faulty. Stanley Hollander points out a number of nonconforming examples, particularly in underdeveloped countries and in automatic merchandising in the United States. The latter entered the cycle as high-cost, high-margin, high-convenience retailers.[21]

The crisis change model is somewhat less descriptive than the two other constructs. It does not predict specific actions by the threatened channel. However, based on historic evidence, it does predict expected behavior. Although the study of past patterns of institutional behavior provides valuable insights, "innovation" should not be construed to be synonymous with "new." Complete repetition is not likely. Each innovation introduces new actions that are likely to require unique responses.

Aggregation Limitation All three change models are aggregative in the sense that they lump a number of causal factors into a single explanation of change. For example, in the case of the building materials channel, the traditional lumberyards were serving their core markets adequately. The fringe market did not exist until the do-it-yourself market was stimulated. A new market segment emerged that discounters and chain lumberyard companies capitalized upon. The traditional lumberyard was not directly threatened until the innovators began to penetrate the building contractors. Such facts are submerged in the aggregation of the usual core-fringe explanation. The cycle explanation is the most aggregative of the models. Hollander points out that statistics that show changes in retail margins and expenses, the core of the "wheel" hypothesis, are scarce. When available, they are usually in the form of averages across lines of business reported in retail census data.[22]

Of the three explanations, the crisis change model is the least aggregative. During the expected phases, not all threatened institutions or channels behave in the described manner. Some move from awareness of new competition to immediate adaptation. Rather than becoming defensive, members in some channels move immediately to develop and implement a retaliatory strategy. When mass merchandisers with lower prices threatened traditional department stores, many prestigious stores advertised that they would not knowingly be undersold. The response was immediate and successful. Some institutions are resilient; they adapt and change rapidly. Others are resistant. The crisis change model best describes institutions that experience all phases of the crisis.

Causation Limitation Descriptive and aggregative features at best offer superficial explanation about the causes of change. For example, the tendency for traditional indirect channels to change to a more direct method of doing business can be described in the context of the models. However, these models do not explain the underlying reasons for the change. For example, for many products the traditional channel structure once consisted of manufacturer to distributor to dealer to customers. As inflation and competitive pressures eroded gross margins, manufacturers began to exercise stringent inventory control measures to maintain the target ROI. This stimulated attempts

[21] See Stanley C. Hollander, "The Wheel of Retailing," *Journal of Marketing,* **25**:1 July 1960, pp. 37–42.
[22] Ibid., p. 144.

to spin off inventory responsibility to other channel members. Faced with similar pressures, distributors refused to accept the financial burden of larger inventories. To remedy the situation and reduce the risk of lost sales, some manufacturers instituted channel separation policies and began to perform the logistics process. Having absorbed the channel risk associated with inventory ownership, manufacturers logically moved next to circumvent distributors and service dealers or deal directly with consumers.

Paradoxically, inflationary and competitive pressures have also stimulated some manufacturers that have traditionally sold directly to consumers to consider establishment of a distributor-dealer structure. This is particularly true for manufacturers that sell products that require significant sales and service support. The causation chain stimulating such structural adaption is not adequately explained by change models.

MANAGEMENT OF CHANNEL CHANGE

Change in distribution channel structure need not be instigated by new forms of competition. The modification of a traditional channel structure can be planned and accomplished by effective leaders. In this section, the process of change management is examined in terms of the institutionalizing process and change agent characteristics.

Institutionalizing Process

If an alternative new structural arrangement is to be introduced rapidly and economically, a comprehensive understanding of the change process is essential. The probability of success in planned channel change can be greatly increased through an understanding of how new ideas and methods are institutionalized.

In channel change two kinds of institutionalization are important. First, changes in basic values and norms that serve to modify channel functions and structure may be planned. The process of this type of institutionalization is based on communication of change ideas by established channel participants. The creation of agencies to disseminate new ideas is typically not effective in an established channel arrangement. This indirect process of institutionalization is referred to as *diffused institutionalization*. It is most commonly used when underdeveloped channels are helped to accommodate change.

A second form of institutionalization involves the impact of specialized participants whose sole objective is to innovate. This second kind of institutionalization is termed *institution building*. In institution building, changes in values and norms are typically focused on a particular channel leader. For example, new relationships were established between customers and suppliers when discounters entered the retail structure. Prior to the entry of discounters, manufacturers dominated the distribution practices. Customers were accustomed to receiving extensive services when they purchased products. Discount houses established new relationships with suppliers which shattered many existing service norms. This basic change was exemplified by the legal breakdown of resale price maintenance. Discount houses offered consumers minimum service in return for their sale of products or services at significantly lower than manufacturer's suggested retail prices. As a change agent, the discounter recognized traditional practice but chose to modify behavior by introducing a new type of operation. The objective of the change agent is to create new behavior on the part of traditional institutions. In many instances, change is achieved by the introduction of institutions whose primary purpose is to promote change.

Role of the Change Agent

Planned change in advanced distribution channels typically involves innovative institution building. The process establishes new norms and values that are translated into a modified structure and functional assignments. The institutionalizing process depends on the attributes of the change agent. In other words, the magnitude of change will depend upon the innovating institution and the environment within which it operates. The environment consists of the traditional institutions with which the change agent interacts. Given the traditional norms, functions, and institutions, the change agent impacts traditional structure by espousing a new set of norms and values. The change agent's effort will likely be met with resistance and hostility from established channels. The primary functional interactions between a change agent and traditional channel participants are transactions and negotiation. The change agent must identify channel participants it seeks to influence, perform functional transactional analysis related to the existing channel arrangement, and prescribe the desired institutional structure it desires to implement. For organizational change to take place, three types of linkages are required: enabling, normative, and diffused.

An *enabling linkage* involves the building of relationships with external organizations that are critical for success. In a channel change situation, substantial support is required from institutions such as merchandise suppliers, financial sources, advertising media, and governmental regulatory agencies. *Normative linkages* involve relationships with traditional channel participants who practice the existing method and structure of doing business; these members, when confronted by change, will often be hostile. A change agent can follow practices that will not intensify such resistance. *Diffused linkages* involve relationships with the public whose opinion is influenced by media. If a change agent is to be successful, the new values and norms proposed must be generally accepted.

In summary, the change agent must identify institutions that can facilitate or inhibit the planned program. Appropriate enabling, normative, and diffused linkages must be established with key institutions.

Characteristics of Successful Change Agents

Successful change agents will have several basic characteristics. These characteristics are leadership, doctrine, program, resources, and internal structure. Each is discussed.[23]

---

[23] The characteristics of the change agent and the change management model described are based on Donald A. Taylor, *Institution Building in Business Administration: The Brazilian Experience,* East Lansing, MI: Graduate School of Business Administration, Michigan State University, 1968.

Leadership   If the change agent is already a powerful channel leader, the process of modification will be relatively easy. Leadership can be acquired in many ways.[24] Association of the change agent and the new idea with recognized business leaders increases the chances of success. Support of the idea by recognized government leaders will help in its acceptance. Backing by prestigious financial institutions also can add an aura of acceptability to the change agent and the idea. To be successful, the change agent will need to gain leadership status.

Doctrine   There must be a compelling reason why a planned change should replace existing systems and methods of operation. Advantages and benefits of the new process must be carefully spelled out. Amway Corporation and Mary Kay cosmetics developed very persuasive support of in-house buying. They appealed to and stimulated the entrepreneurial spirit of independent agents by emphasizing the need to preserve the free-enterprise system. Operational changes introduced by a channel leader in a vertical marketing system are usually given catchy phrases such as TDP ("Total Distribution Plan for America") or FITIC ("'financial improvement through inventory control"). The ideas are then explained in detail to potential participants so that their support can be enlisted.

Program   While the doctrine elaborates reasons for change, the program spells out how change is to be made. Actions or roles must be specified so that the idea can be made a reality. Similar to a marketing plan, the program should detail the time required to implement the new process and the required financial resources. The importance of a sustaining program should not be underestimated. Lack of a creditable program may be the primary reason that change initiatives fail.

Resources   Innovations are costly and require extensive professional management. It is essential to have adequate financial and human resources for the implementation of a change program. Introduction of change requires special skills. Managers of change agents must understand those agents' empowerments and limitations toward implementing the change process.

Structure   Given human and financial resources, successful implementation will depend upon establishment of procedures and systems to enable the change agent to publicize the doctrine and implement the change. Implementation standards are required so that progress can be determined and evaluated.

A situation in which all characteristics are present is ideal. However, in actual practice, each characteristic will only exist to a degree and the balance will vary among change agents. With these characteristics, linkages can be developed with key institutions so that hostility can be countered and the eventual acceptance of the planned change can be facilitated. The change management model is diagrammed in Figure 12-4.

---

[24] See Chapter 10, pp. 306–308.

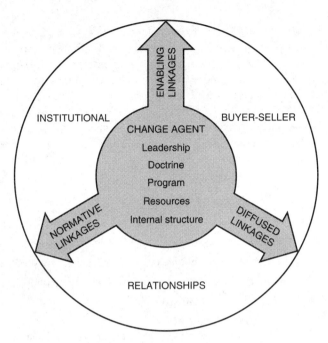

FIGURE 12-4   An institutional change management model.

SUMMARY

There are a number of forces in the competitive system that help explain why channels of distribution are forever changing. The economics of differentiation and relationships among innovation, neutralization, and economic growth are integral parts of a system of competition for differential advantage.

The impact of information technology upon channel structure and strategy is real and significant. New technology has introduced speed as a significant aspect of competitive behavior. Information technology provides the mechanism for the control of new forms of channel arrangements that exploit the potential inherent in various types of postponement. To effectively manage new channel arrangements, firms are modifying organizations so that outsourcing can be facilitated.

Channel change is a situation in which participants are forced to change well-established practices. As a result of such change, original behavior may become barely recognizable. In some situations, entirely new institutions emerge as dominant channel members while traditional firms recede. Change has traditionally been described by three models: the core-fringe, life-cycle, and crisis change models. Although helpful, these models have limitations. First, they are descriptive and have limited predictive value. Second, they are excessively aggregate. Third, all models fail to fully develop forces that cause change. Resistance to change by existing channel institutions can be expected. In spite of inherent resistance, change occurs.

Change agents are typically outsiders to or leaders in an existing channel. The idea of channel design and strategic implementation is based on the premise that change can be managed. A change management model offers one way to view orderly change. The change agent reviews important relationships between primary and secondary participants to identify those in which either conflict or concurrence is expected. The potential resistance centers become primary targets for the change agent. Linkages must be made with support and resistance centers by the establishment of enabling, normative, and diffusion relationships. The change agent must develop certain characteristics to effectively lead the process. These characteristics are leadership, doctrine, program, resource, and structure.

QUESTIONS

1 What is information connectivity? How does it relate to EDI?

2 What role does a Universal Product Code Catalog play in marketing channel operations?

3 Compare and contrast just-in-time (JIT) and quick-response (QR) inventory replenishment.

4 How can information technology impact traditional organizational structure?

5 Discuss the concept of "centralized direction and decentralized application." Is this Wal-Mart philosophy practical for other organizations?

6 What is the importance of "flatness," empowerment and outsourcing to channel organization?

7 How do innovation and neutralization contribute to economic growth?

8 What are the similarities and dissimilarities among the core-fringe, cycle, and crisis change models?

9 In the crisis change model, does experience indicate that all participants go through all phases? Why or why not?

10 Can a change in a distribution channel be managed? Explain the underlying institutionalizing process that permits change management.

11 Explain linkages the change agent must make with the environment.

12 What are the characteristics of a successful change agent? Does every company have these characteristics or must they be developed?

CHAPTER 13

INTERNATIONAL AND SERVICE CHANNELS

CHAPTER OUTLINE

INTERNATIONAL DISTRIBUTION CHANNELS
Export
Export Documentation
Channels of Distribution Within Foreign Countries
International Logistics
Evaluation of International Channel Alternatives
Countertrade
CHANNELS OF DISTRIBUTION FOR SERVICES
Characteristics of Services
Classification of Services
SUMMARY

Two of the most significant economic developments in recent decades are the increased internationalization of business and the growth of the service sector of the economy. The United States alone exports approximately $350 billion goods and services yet still has a net trade deficit because of imports that total almost $500 billion.[1] The percentage of the United States GNP derived from exports has doubled in two decades to over 10 percent. Of course, the figures for export and import drastically underestimate the scale of international business since they do not include the vast

[1] U.S. Department of Commerce, *Statistical Abstract of the United States,* Washington, DC: U.S. Government Printing Office, 1988, p. 768.

overseas operations of United States firms, many of whom (General Motors, Coca-Cola, Johnson & Johnson, and Gillette, for example) earn a higher percentage of their profits from foreign operations than from domestic.

Concurrent with the growth in international trade has been the increasing importance of services in the economy. In 1989, almost 60 percent of all employment in the United States occurred in the service sector. Furthermore, over 70 percent of new jobs created were in services.

This chapter is devoted to discussion of unique aspects of distribution channels for international expansion and for service firms. The channels *between* countries and middlemen involved are explained, followed by consideration of the differences in distribution channels *within* countries. International logistics and countertrade are discussed. Channels of distribution for service firms are then discussed, with a focus placed on the major differences between products and services. The methods of classifying services are explained and a framework for service channel strategy is introduced.

INTERNATIONAL DISTRIBUTION CHANNELS

A comprehensive discussion of the strategic decision to enter international markets is beyond the scope of this text. Additionally, there are numerous decisions that must be made about pricing, product modification, and promotion that are not treated.[2] After the decision to enter international markets *has* been made, there are several potential modes of entry, each of which raises its own unique problems for distribution. The primary modes of entry are exporting, licensing, joint venture, and direct foreign investment. Licensing, joint ventures, and direct foreign investment involve the establishment of production facilities in foreign countries, and channel strategy for these modes of entry is concerned with channel structure within the foreign countries. Attention is first directed to channels *between* countries, and then to distribution channels within foreign countries.

Export

The majority of international business is conducted by firms that sell into foreign markets from their domestic facilities. Most firms begin their international involvement by exporting. Frequently, this activity begins when requests are received from buyers in foreign markets, but the effort is usually sporadic and unorganized. Recognition that profits are available in foreign markets, combined with growing experience, typically leads exporters to seek more permanent distribution channels. Exportation can be accomplished *indirectly* through a variety of specialized middlemen or *directly* to foreign buyers. Figure 13-1 shows the primary indirect- and direct-export channels and the types of intermediaries typically encountered.

---

[2] The interested reader is directed to Subhash C. Jain, *International Marketing Management,* 3d ed., Boston: PWS-Kirt, 1990; or Philip R. Cateora, *International Marketing,* 7th ed. Homewood, IL: Irwin, 1990.

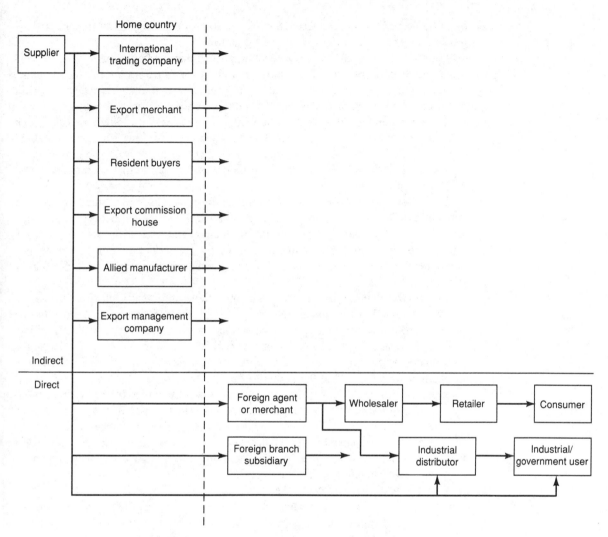

FIGURE 13-1 Major direct and indirect export channels. (*Source:* Adapted from Franklin R. Root, "Export Marketing," in *Handbook of Modern Marketing,* 2d ed., ed. Victor P. Buell, New York: McGraw-Hill, 1986, pp. 105–107.)

Indirect Export Indirect exporting requires the least effort on the part of the supplying firm. It involves dealing with another domestically located firm that serves as an intermediary. The principal advantage of indirect exporting is that it provides a way to penetrate foreign markets without encountering many of the complexities involved in documentation and physical distribution across national boundaries. It also requires little investment for the exporter, but it also leads to a firm's loss of control over the destiny of its products. This loss of control can become an important issue if a firm later decides to move to direct exporting.

As seen in Figure 13-1, there are several types of intermediaries that may be utilized in indirect-export channels. The major types and their functions are discussed below.

International Trading Companies   An international trading company is a firm that specializes in international trade. Although normally associated with Japan, trading companies are actually common in many countries. Major trading companies such as the Japanese Mitsubishi Corporation and C. Itoh and Company are involved in both export and import for their home countries. In fact, the major Japanese trading companies account for over 68 percent of all products imported to that country and about 45 percent of products exported.[3]

General-trading companies perform numerous functions. They purchase and sell commodities, arrange for transportation and physical distribution between and within countries, provide management consulting, finance and absorb the risk of currency fluctuations, and take part in numerous other activities. About the only functions they do not perform are manufacturing and retailing, although they may enter joint ventures for these activities.[4]

Export Merchants   Export merchants are wholesalers that specialize in international markets. They tend to operate as any other wholesale merchant by purchasing products from a large number of manufacturers within a country, and then packing, marking, and shipping the goods to foreign markets under their own control. Although some export merchants have facilities in the foreign market, most commonly they sell to intermediaries located in the country of destination.

Resident Buyers   Many firms and governments maintain facilities in foreign countries for the primary purpose of purchasing goods in those countries. For example, Sears maintains buying offices in several countries so that it can purchase goods to resell through Sears stores in the United States. Similarly, many foreign wholesalers and retailers have buying offices in the United States so that they can locate, purchase, and arrange for shipment to their countries.

Export Commission House   An export commission house is similar to a resident buyer except that it is not a permanent employee of the foreign firm. The commission house (or agent) places orders with manufacturers, negotiates terms of sale, and handles all shipping details. The commission house is paid by the foreign buyer, generally as a percentage of the purchase. Selling through commission houses is a convenient means of exporting since there is little risk to the manufacturer and few details to be completed.

Allied Manufacturer   An interesting mechanism for exporting is to use the facilities and expertise of another manufacturer for export. This arrangement, frequently

---

[3] Bradley K. Martin, "Japan's Trading Giants Look to the Year 2000," *Wall Street Journal,* March 31, 1986, p. 23.

[4] Tom Roehl, "The General Trading Companies: A Transaction Cost Analysis of Their Function in the Japanese Economy," in *Marketing Channels: Domestic and International Perspectives,* eds. Michael G. Harvey and Robert F. Lusch, Norman, OK: University of Oklahoma, Center for Economic Research, 1982, pp. 86–100.

termed "piggybacking," is a long-standing and growing form of exporting. General Electric, for example, has sold the products of other United States companies in Latin America since the 1930s.[5] The arrangements between the two firms vary with each relationship, but the potential for this form of strategic alliance among firms is quite interesting. A company that is already established in foreign countries, for example, may want to handle other companies' products in order to complete its own product lines or to increase utilization of its foreign capacity. Thus, this form of indirect exporting represents an excellent distribution opportunity for small firms or companies that do not want to invest in foreign distribution.

Export Management Company   An export managment company (EMC) is a specialist firm that acts as the export department for one or several manufactures of noncompeting products. The EMC usually becomes so closely aligned with its manufacturers that foreign buyers may not realize they are dealing with an independent firm. Most EMCs solicit business as selling agents in the name of their manufacturers, although a few larger ones actually purchase products for resale.

There are over 2000 EMCs in the United States alone.[6] Most of these are small and tend to specialize either by product line or by foreign market. Given this specialization, they frequently have comprehensive knowledge of foreign markets and well-established relationships with foreign buyers.

Direct Export   In general, the indirect exporting discussed above offers several advantages. It is relatively simple, requires little investment of time, money, or other resources, and is relatively risk-free. Nevertheless, many firms prefer *direct* exporting in which the firm markets directly to a buyer located in a foreign country. The major advantage of direct exporting is that the firm enjoys substantially greater control over the destiny of its products. While direct export involves substantially higher costs, profitability may be greater due to this increased control.

A firm that chooses direct exporting must establish an internal organization to handle the problems associated with marketing and distribution to foreign countries. This organization is responsible for selecting and motivating intermediaries to represent the firm in foreign markets; motivating and controlling those intermediaries; handling international shipping, insurance, and financing; and dealing with export documentation. Once a company has organized itself internally to deal with direct exporting, distribution channels must be established in each foreign market. The three major channels used to reach foreign markets are foreign agents or merchants, foreign sales branches or subsidiaries, and direct sales to end users.[7]

Foreign Wholesale Agents and Merchants   The variety of wholesale agents and merchants available in most countries is relatively similar,[8] although the wholesale and retail structures of various countries differ dramatically (as discussed below).

[5] Gerald Albaum, Jesper Strandskov, Edwin Duerr, and Lawrence Dowd, *International Marketing and Export Management,* Reading, MA: Addison-Wesley, 1989, p. 170.
[6] "Basic Question: To Export Yourself or Hire Someone to Do It for You," *Business America,* **161:**10 April 27, 1987, p. 14.
[7] Albaum et al., p. 173.
[8] Cateora, p. 606.

While there are many different specific types of agents and distributors, some generalizations can be made. A *foreign sales agent* uses the supplier's promotional literature and samples to present the product to potential buyers. The agent generally works on a commission basis, assumes no risk, and works under a contract that defines territory, terms of sale, compensation, and other details. The exporter makes direct shipment to the buyer and receives payment from that buyer. The agent is compensated by a percentage commission on each sale.

Foreign merchant distributors are merchants who purchase goods from the exporter and resell on their own account. The distributor then has control over prices, promotion, and other marketing practices within the country unless contractual restrictions have been established. Normally, the distributor is also responsible for product support and service.

Foreign Sales Branch/Subsidiary Firms with substantial sales volume in a specific country may elect to establish a sales branch or subsidiary (a nonproduction facility) in a foreign country. This type of facility circumvents some of the foreign intermediaries and provides substantially more control over distribution activity within the country. Sales branches and subsidiaries may become essential when foreign agents or distributors are unable or unwilling to provide the skills and services necessary for the effective marketing of the exporter's products. This is particularly true for high-technology products such as computers, office equipment, and machine tools which require installation, instructions for uses, and maintenance. The facility may be fully owned by the exporter or may be operated as a joint venture with a firm located in the foreign market. Wholly owned facilities require greater investment but the exporter gains control in the foreign market. Joint ventures reduce investment requirements and provide local expertise in the country's internal distribution structure and customs. Some governments require that such facilities include a partner from the domestic country.

Direct Sales Direct-to-end-user channels are the least commonly used form of direct exporting. Products that are very expensive and that are sold to a relatively small number of potential users (government units, businesses, or major institutions) may, however, be most effectively distributed with this alternative.

Export Documentation

One of the most complex issues in export marketing is the plethora of documentation required to complete an international transaction. It is precisely due to this complexity (and difficulties associated with financing and payment) that many firms either avoid exporting or seek indirect channels for export. To move products from France to the United States, for example, may require as many as eighteen different documents.[9] Documentation required varies substantially from country to country, but Table 13-1 summarizes the most common documents required to complete export transactions.

---

[9] Albaum et al., p. 374.

TABLE 13-1   COMMONLY REQUIRED EXPORT DOCUMENTATION

Commercial invoice:	A statement of the goods sold that summarizes details of the sales, name, and address of exporter, shipper, and consignee; date; shipping information; delivery and payment terms; product description, quantities, prices, and discounts.
Consular invoice:	Prepared in multiple copies on forms obtained from the importing country's consulate. Must be in the importing country's language. Contains details of of seller, buyer, and destination; description of goods; and statement of their value.
Certificate of origin:	Certifies place of origin of merchandise.
Inspection certificate:	Certifies quality, quantity, and conformance of goods in relation to the order.
Export declaration:	Summarizes shipping information, descriptions, quantities, and values. Filed by exporter, given to shipping company, filed with customs specialists.
Packing list:	Itemizes each package in a shipment (contents, size, and weight).
Insurance certificate:	Specifies type and amount of insurance on the shipment.
Bill of lading:	Most important document. Establishes ownership of products, serves as contract between shipper and carrier, and receipt for goods from carrier.
Licenses:	Both export and import licenses may be required. Because of restrictions on import and/or export of some specific products, licenses must be obtained from the appropriate government agencies.

Channels of Distribution Within Foreign Countries

Although the distribution functions that must be performed are universal, the structure and functional performance of distribution activity varies dramatically from country to country. Distribution structure is so closely intertwined with a country's social, cultural, economic, technological, and political conditions and development that it is impossible to generalize about one specific form or structure throughout the world. A few examples of these environmental influences on distribution illustrate this point:

1. Japanese homes tend to be very small compared to those in the United States due to limited space and very high land values. (Approximately 120 million people—half the population of the United States—live in a country that has a usable land area smaller than New York State.) Japanese homemakers, therefore, have limited storage space and shop several times per week. This necessitates a distribution structure with a large number of small, conveniently located retail shops, supported by a large number of wholesalers to accomplish the sorting function.

2. In many underdeveloped and less developed countries, per capita income is so low that consumers cannot purchase large quantities of merchandise in one transaction. It is quite common in many South American countries for retailers

TABLE 13-2   WHOLESALE AND RETAIL STRUCTURE IN SELECTED COUNTRIES

Country	Population (millions)	Number of retailers	Number of wholesalers	Population per retailer	Population per wholesaler
Austria	7.5	37,524	12,890	200	582
Brazil	129.7	2,817,000	46,000	46	2,820
Egypt	45.2	2,136	1,766	21,161	25,595
Ireland	3.5	32,332	3,073	108	1,139
Israel	3.8	40,000	4,862	95	782
Italy	56.8	937,372	120,366	61	472
Japan	119.3	1,721,000	429,000	69	278
South Korea	40.4	945,800	45,568	42	387
Soviet Union	263.4	659,700	1,000	400	263,400
United States	234.5	1,923,000	416,000	122	564

Source: Adapted from Subhash C. Jain, *International Marketing Management,* 3d ed., Boston: PWS-Kent, 1990, pp. 511 and 514.

to sell cigarettes one cigarette at a time. Likewise, retailers purchase cigarettes from wholesalers only a few packs at a time.

3. Australia's political development led to each of its seven states having regulatory control over its own internal rail system. As a result, there are three different sizes of rail gauge used, making rail transport across the continent virtually impossible. This occurs in a country with land area almost equal to the United States but a population only about one-fifteenth its size.

It was believed at one time that channel structure within a country depended upon the country's level of economic development. Thus, industrialized countries should have similar structures and developing nations would mimic the structures of those nations. The examples above, and the data in Table 13-2 tend to refute this premise. As Table 13-2 shows, there are dramatic differences between the United States and Japan, for example, in terms of the number of consumers served by the average retail store, and the number of wholesalers used to support that retail structure. Brazil and Egypt, two developing countries, demonstrate even more remarkable differences in structure.

As a final example, Figure 13-2 shows typical channels of distribution for industrial materials in Japan. The most common channel for these goods requires the use of two intermediate wholesalers between the manufacturer and the end user. In the United States, industrial goods channels tend to be distributed directly from the manufacturer to the end user, or require only one intermediate industrial distributor.

Clearly, there is a relationship between a country's channel structure and its environment.[10] This relationship, however, is not well understood. Marketing practices are

[10] Susan P. Douglas, "Patterns and Parallels of Marketing Structures in Several Countries," *MSU Business Topics,* **25**:2 Spring 1977, p. 47.

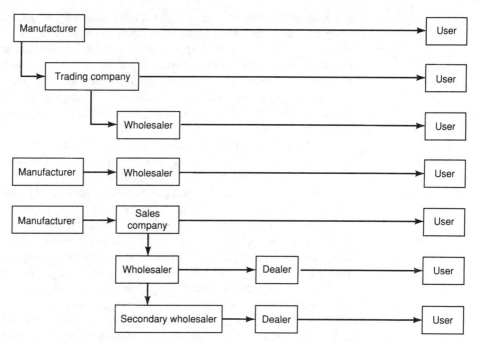

FIGURE 13-2 Domestic distribution channels for industrial materials in Japan. (*Source: Selling in Japan,* Tokyo: Japan External Trade Organization, 1985, p. 114. Reprinted by permission.)

bound by local conditions and must be adapted to the local environment.[11] Firms that pursue international expansion must devote considerable effort to understanding the unique differences in channel structure that impact their ability to accomplish channel objectives.

International Logistics

Discussion thus far has centered on marketing channels for international distribution. Only peripheral attention has been paid to problems of physical movement of goods. Even firms doing business in only one or a small number of foreign countries have substantial logistics problems due to the expansion of geography and time required to support those markets. Inventory holdings are typically larger than those required to support domestic markets, and transportation costs increase substantially with the distance to market.[12]

Several means are used to solve the problems posed by international logistics. Small firms tend to use indirect exporting, thus deferring the problems to an intermediary

---

[11] Suzanne Hosley and Chow How Wee, "Marketing and Economic Development: Focusing on the Less Developed Countries," *Journal of Macromarketing,* **8:**1 Spring 1988, p. 51.

[12] Donald J. Bowersox and Jay U. Sterling, "Multinational Logistics," *Journal of Business Logistics,* **3:**2 1982, p. 15.

that specializes in these arrangements. Direct exporters frequently engage the services of an *international freight forwarder*. The freight forwarder is an agent intermediary that arranges for complete shipping documentation, insurance, information on transportation rates and schedules, export/import restrictions, and licensing requirements. Full-service freight forwarders even provide warehouse storage, packing and containerization of shipments, and ocean cargo or air-freight space.[13] Because the freight forwarder specializes in these arrangements, even many large, experienced exporters utilize their services.

The full complexity of international logistics is realized when a firm develops a global perspective of its business strategy. Such firms produce and distribute their goods in numerous countries to capitalize on long-term growth markets and to achieve economies in procurement, manufacturing, and logistics. A full discussion of such global strategies is beyond the scope of this text, but it is clear that a logistics system perspective as discussed in Chapter 7 has potential to add considerably to those strategies. A unified logistics system can guide the orderly flow of resources from global procurement sourcing, into a multinational manufacturing and assembly complex, and through a variety of domestic distribution systems to customers located throughout the world.[14] Unfortunately most firms have not adopted such a perspective and, instead, view international logistics as a series of individual country-by-country decisions.

Nike, Inc., is one firm that apparently has taken such a global view. Based in Beaverton, Oregon, Nike contracts with manufacturing facilities in Hong Kong, South Korea, Singapore, Taiwan, Thailand, and the People's Republic of China. Crucial components of the athletic footware are sourced in the United States and shipped overseas for manufacture and distribution to over fifty countries. Depending upon the country, Nike may use exclusive distributors responsible for selling to retailers or a combination of its own distribution subsidiaries and independent distributors. Manufactured shoes may be sent from the plants to Nike, its distributors, or directly to the customer if the order is large enough. Throughout this complex process, Nike holds the number-one position in its industry in terms of meeting delivery commitments to its customers.[15]

Evaluation of International Channel Alternatives

The firm's objectives for international channels do not differ significantly from the objectives for domestic channels. These include economic objectives related to sales and profitability as well as market exposure, channel control, and flexibility. In addition to considerations discussed throughout the text, there are several specific factors that influence the evaluation of channel alternatives for international distribution.

To a significant degree, channel choice for international distribution is limited by the sales volume and sales potential for the product. Small markets necessitate indirect

[13]Robert Vidrick, "How to Choose and Use an International Freight Forwarder," *Distribution,* October 1988, pp. 78–84.
[14] Donald J. Bowersox, David J. Closs, and Omar K Helferich, *Logistical Management,* 3d ed., New York: Macmillan, 1986, p. 491.
[15] "Nike Outdoes Competition in Delivery to Customers," *Global Trade,* March 1988, p. 8.

distribution due to limited sales potential. Volumes may not be substantial enough to cover the cost of more expensive direct-distribution alternatives.

Customers' requirements for service are another factor that influences channel evaluation and selection. For products that require a high level of service, the firm frequently must establish its own sales and distribution facilities in numerous countries. This is so that services can be provided that are not available from domestic middlemen.[16]

Government requirements have a significant impact on distribution channel selection. "Local content" laws may require that products be manufactured (fully or partially) in the local country. Government units may pressure international firms to use local agents or distributors rather than establish their own distribution networks. Governments frequently place restrictions on the amount of foreign investment or require that local partners be included in any new facility.

A firm's familiarity with culture, customers, and distribution practices is a critical determinant of channel evaluation. United States firms, for example, are much more likely to vertically integrate distribution channels in Western Europe than in Japan and Southeast Asia, which are culturally dissimilar.[17]

Availability of intermediaries and access to needed distribution capabilities can dictate the choice of channel. For example, finding that many retailers were unavailable, Levi opened a chain of 400 Levi's Only stores in Brazil. These stores account for 65 percent of the firm's $100 million volume in the country.[18] One reason for the limited availability of retailers is that large numbers of international firms compete for the services of a relatively small number of available distribution channels. Associations of middlemen within a country also sometimes restrict the distribution channel alternatives. Druggists in many countries, for example, have effectively prohibited the distribution of a wide variety of goods through any outlets except drugstores.[19]

Countertrade

While most established firms obviously prefer money as the form of payment in international transactions, countertrade is becoming an increasingly important aspect of international distribution. Countertrade occurs in several specific forms, but the essence is that the seller agrees to take or purchase products from the buyer as part of the transaction. Such agreements have financial consequences for the seller, but the major implications for distribution channels relate to the problems associated with the disposal of goods received as payment.

For example, Pepsi supplies syrup to the Soviet government, which bottles and markets the soft drink with practically no control from Pepsi. In return, Pepsi is paid for the syrup by receiving exclusive rights to distribute Stolichnaya, the only Russian

[16] Michael Etgar, "The Effects of Forward Vertical Integration on Service Performance of Distributive Industry," *Journal of Industrial Economics,* **26**:3 March 1978, pp. 249–255.

[17] Erin T. Anderson and Anne T. Coughlan, "International Market Entry and Expansion Via Independent or Integrated Channels of Distribution," *Journal of Marketing,* **51**:1 January 1987, p. 71.

[18] "For Levi's, A Flattering Fit Overseas," *Business Week,* November 5, 1990, p. 77.

[19] Cateora, op. cit., p. 582.

vodka sold in the United States. The amount of syrup purchased by the Russian government depends on the amount of Stolichnaya that Pepsi sells and distributes.[20] The channels of distribution in the United States for alcoholic beverages are quite different from those for soft drinks. This arrangement between Pepsi and the Soviet government required that Pepsi develop entirely new distribution arrangements.

It is estimated that 20 percent of all international transactions involve some form of countertrade and this percentage is predicted to increase in the future.[21] If this prediction is true, many firms will find themselves faced with distribution channel decisions that they had never anticipated.

CHANNELS OF DISTRIBUTION FOR SERVICES

The normal practice in marketing is to define the word "product" as a "good, service, or idea." Thus, the marketing of services is frequently discussed in the same context as the marketing of physical goods. There are many compelling reasons to treat marketing of physical goods and services simultaneously, and many basic concepts related to physcial products are equally applicable to services. However, this practice ignores basic differences between physical goods and services, and these have important implications for the strategy and management of distribution channels. These differences and their implications for channels are discussed in the following paragraphs. Classification of services and a framework for service channel strategy are presented.

Characteristics of Services

There are four distinguishing characteristics of services that have important implications for distribution channels. These characteristics are intangibility, inseparability of production and consumption, perishability, and heterogeneity.[22]

Intangibility of a service relates to its essence. In contrast to a *good,* which is a tangible, physical object that can be seen, held, smelled, tasted, and the like, a *service* is an intangible deed, act, or performance.[23] There may be physical manifestations of the service, such as a new hairstyle, but the service itself can only be experienced by the customer in *intangible* ways. There are also physical objects used in the performance of a service, such as a B-747 for air transportation, but the physical object is typically of secondary importance to the service act.[24]

Inseparability of production and consumption has two important dimensions. First, the production of a service and its consumption frequently occur simultaneously. Plays, concerts, and air travel, for example, are consumed even as they are being produced. The second dimension concerns the customers' participation in the production process of services. Customers often literally enter the service "factory" where

---

[20] Vern Terpstra, *International Dimensions of Marketing,* 2d ed, Boston: PWS-Kent, 1988, p. 58.

[21] Cateora, op cit., p. 557.

[22] Valarie A. Zeithaml, A. Parasuraman, and Leonard L. Berry, "Problems and Strategies in Services Marketing," *Journal of Marketing,* **49:**2 Spring 1985, pp. 33–46.

[23] Leonard L. Berry, "Services Marketing Is Different," *Business,* May–June, 1980, p. 24.

[24] Donald H. Light, "A Guide For New Distribution Channel Strategies for Service Firms," *Journal of Business Strategy,* **7:**1 Summer 1986, p. 57.

the service is performed. Hairstylists or doctors, for example, cannot perform their services without the physical presence of customers who are actually involved in the production process.

Perishability is related to inseparability in that once a service is produced, it is no longer available for sale until production occurs a second time. After a play is completed or an airline flight has left the gate, the unused seating capacity represents a lost sales opportunity. Service firms face a serious dilemma with capacity because of perishability and the fact that demand tends to be highly variable. Consider the problem of the airline that faces heavy demand between December 20 to 25, only to see that demand fall dramatically shortly after the Christmas vacation period. If capacity is built to meet peak period demand, substantial underutilization of resources exists during long slack periods.

Heterogeneity in service production and delivery occurs due to the labor intensiveness of the service industries and the fact that production occurs under "real time" conditions. Different employees within the same service firm, or even the same employee at different times of the day, may vary in the ability or willingness to perform the service. Standardization and quality control, therefore, are extremely difficult to maintain in service firms. Some service providers have built their marketing programs around their ability to deliver a consistent, standardized service level. Holiday Inn, H&R Block and McDonald's represent three examples of such firms.

Channel Implications   The above characteristics have two important implications for service channels. First, because services are intangible and production occurs simultaneously with consumption, there is little need for logistics functions for many services. The service factory cannot build inventories of intangible acts that remain in a warehouse or on retail shelves awaiting customers' demand. Inventory, storage, and transportation are, therefore, typically ignored in the design of service channels. This lack of attention to logistics may lead to a lack of creativity in service channels, as will be discussed in a later section.

Lack of logistics functions in service channels leads to the second major implication: lack of merchant middlemen in service channels. To the extent that middlemen exist in service channels, they are typically sales agents or brokers since there are no inventories to be purchased and distributed. Thus, service channels tend to be relatively direct from service providers to users; some of the complexities of distribution channels for physical products are avoided.

Classification of Services

Christopher Lovelock has developed several methods of service classification that provide considerable insight into a new framework for service channel strategy and management.[25] Two of these classification formats require consideration of the nature of the service act and the method of service delivery.

---

[25] This section draws heavily on Christopher H. Lovelock, "Classifying Services to Gain Strategic Marketing Insights," *Journal of Marketing,* **47**:3 Summer 1983, pp. 9–20; and Lovelock, "Marketing of Services," in *Handbook of Modern Marketing,* ed. Victor P. Buell, 2nd Edition, New York: McGraw-Hill, 1986, pp. 5-1 through 5-13.

TABLE 13-3   UNDERSTANDING THE NATURE OF THE SERVICE ACT: WHO OR WHAT IS THE DIRECT RECIPIENT OF THE SERVICE?

	People	Things
What is the nature of the service act? Tangible actions	Services directed at people's bodies: • Health care • Passenger transportation • Beauty salons • Exercise clinics • Restaurants • Haircutters	Services directed at goods and other physical possessions: • Freight transportation • Industrial equipment repair and maintenance • Janitorial services • Laundry and dry cleaning • Landscaping/lawn care • Veterinary care
Intangible actions	Services directed at people's minds: • Education • Broadcasting • Information services • Theaters • Museums	Services directed at intangible assets: • Banking • Legal services • Accounting • Securities • Insurance

Source: Christopher H. Lovelock, "Classifying Services to Gain Strategic Marketing Insights," *Journal of Marketing,* **47:**3 Summer 1983, p. 18. Reprinted with permission of American Marketing Association.

Table 13-3 contains a classification scheme based on the nature of the service act. As shown in the table, some services are physical acts, some are intangible. Additionally, a service can be performed on a person or it can be performed on an object. The resulting four-way classification offers a better understanding of the core benefit produced by the service provider. It also helps in the determination of whether or not the service provider actually requires a high level of contact with the customer. Services performed on people obviously require a higher degree of direct customer contact.

Table 13-4 contains a second classification format for services. The table shows

TABLE 13-4   METHOD OF SERVICE DELIVERY

Nature of interaction between customer and service organization	Availability of service outlets	
	Single site	Multiple set site
Customer goes to the service organization	Theater Barbershop	Bus service Fast-food chain
Service organization comes to the customer	Lawn care service Pest-control service Taxi	Mail delivery AAA emergency repair
Customer and service organization transact at arm's length (mail or electronic communication)	Credit card company Local TV station	Broadcast network Telephone company

Source: Christopher H. Lovelock, "Classifying Services to Gain Strategic Marketing Insights," *Journal of Marketing,* **47:**3 Summer 1983, p. 18. Reprinted with permission of American Marketing Association.

that there are three distinct methods in which the service provider may have contact with customer: (1) requiring the customer to come to the firm, (2) the firm going to the customer, and (3) conducting transactions at "arm's length" via mail, telephone, or electronics. Also, service outlets may be available in single locations or in multiple sets.

Careful thought concerning these two classification schemes may reveal innovative approaches to service channel strategy management. Three guidelines are suggested as an approach to creative strategy development: seek physical manifestation of services, develop alternative contact methods, and develop logistics channels where none existed previously.

Physical Manifestation of Services   Although services themselves are intangible, many services have physical objects associated with them, or may even be transformed into physical objects. The implications for channel strategy are enormous.

Consider, for example, passenger transportation. Although the actual service is intangible and requires direct contact between provider and customer, there is a physical object involved with the purchase of the service. This physical object, the ticket, does not *require* contact between the provider and customer. Tickets can, therefore be sold and distributed through a number of distinct distribution channels. Development of distribution channels for airline tickets provides an excellent example of the distinction between the service and its physical manifestation.

Figure 13-3 diagrams the major distribution channels for airline tickets. Consumers can purchase the tickets by directly visiting the airline's facilities at airports or distribution outlets located in major cities. Alternatively, tickets for airline service can be purchased by telephone, picked up at an airline ticket counter, or mailed to the customer. Consumers may purchase tickets through travel agents, in person, or by telephone. Some travel agents have extended the notion of customer contact by providing delivery of tickets to the purchaser's home or office in their own delivery vehicles.

Distribution channels for airline transportation can actually be quite complex, involving multiple levels of intermediaries. Consider, for example, a consumer purchasing a cruise that requires travel from home to the cruise line's port city. Most cruise lines purchase blocks of space from the airlines, the cost of which is included in a packaged price for the cruise. The cruise line, in turn, markets and distributes the packaged service through a network of independent travel agents. Thus, two levels of intermediaries are involved in what might have been a direct channel between the consumer and the airline itself. The consumer benefits, however, from the convenience of one-stop shopping and the cruise line's ability to negotiate favorable air transportation rates.

The physical manifestation of services may result in even more innovative channels when the entire service can be transformed into a physical object. Education provides an interesting example. Where once direct contact was usually required between customer and provider in a classroom setting (where the customer comes to the service provider, or vice-versa), education can now be delivered in arm's-length transactions via television. Educational service can be provided on videotape, a physical object,

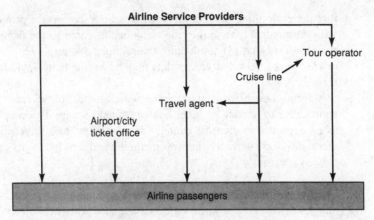

FIGURE 13-3   Selected distribution channels for passenger airline service.

which then can be mass-produced, inventoried, transported, and distributed through a multitude of channels, from video-rental stores to bookstores to numerous college and university campuses. Tom Peters, noted authority and lecturer on customer service, is one service provider who has successfully developed such multiple-distribution channels.

Development of Alternative Contact Methods   While a few services may *require* only one method of contact, the extent of such situations is actually limited. Unfortunately, many service providers fail to recognize that alternative delivery methods exist. Library services represent an example of alternative delivery methods.

Figure 13-4 shows that library services can, in fact, be delivered in multiple channels. Originally, most cities had one "main" library location, which meant that the customer had to visit the service provider to obtain a book or information desired.[26] Library service channels were later extended to include multiple-site locations for branch library facilities. Real innovation in distribution of library service came with the development of traveling facilities such as the "bookmobile" which moves to customer locations such as community centers and nursing homes. Perhaps further innovation is possible whereby consumers can call the library to request a book which can then be mailed to the borrower.

Numerous firms have developed innovative, and profitable, strategies for service channels simply by developing alternative methods of customer contact. USAA is a major insurance service firm that relies exclusively on the telephone and mail to transact with its customers. There are no company-employed independent agents in the field for sales or claims processing. Nevertheless, USAA consistently receives among the highest ratings of any insurance company in terms of the quality of service provided to its customers.

[26] Charles W. Lamb and John L. Crompton, "Distribution Decisions for Public Services," *Jounal of the Academy of Marketing Science,* **13:**2 1985, pp. 107–123.

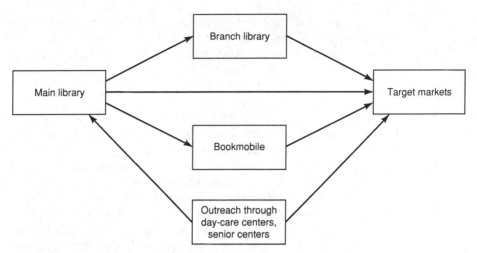

FIGURE 13-4   Distribution channels for library services. (*Source:* Charles W. Lamb and John L. Crompton, "Distribution Decisions for Public Services," *Journal of the Academy of Marketing Science,* **13**:2 Summer 1985, p. 117. Reprinted with permission.)

Development of Logistics Channels Where None Existed Previously   Several of the above examples suggest that logistics functions do, in fact, exist for services. Bookmobiles and physical manifestations of services (airline tickets) both require logistics activities. This logic can be extended when considering distribution channels for services directed at products. The point to remember is that the goods requiring logistics functions belong to the customer rather than to the service provider. Equipment repair and dry cleaning offer excellent examples.

Repair of a broken television set can be accomplished by having a technician visit the consumer's home and attempt repair, or by sending someone to pick up the set and return it to the repair shop. Alternatively, the consumer may transport the broken set to the repair facility. Frequently, however, extensive repair may require that the product be transported to a central facility where greater expertise is available.

In dry-cleaning service channels consumers are required to take laundry to the dry cleaner's location. The cleaner may then pick up laundry at several branch locations, transport it to a central facility, perform the service, and then redistribute the laundry to the appropriate branch locations. Alternatively, the dry cleaner may contract with mass merchants or supermarket retailers to have those firms collect laundry from consumers. The dry cleaner picks up and delivers to those stores, never having contact with its actual consumers. Some dry cleaners even have vans that go directly to consumers' homes or offices to pick up and deliver clothing (a distribution channel that was more prevalent in the past than it is today).

The above examples demonstrate that creative strategies can be developed for service channels of distribution. Much of the lack of creativity can be traced to over-emphasis on the differences between goods and services and the failure to clearly distinguish conceptually between service production and distribution.[27] As the service economy grows and competitive activity within service industries increases, more creative solutions to distribution problems will be necessary.

SUMMARY

Two significant economic developments are the increasing internationalization of business and the explosive growth of the service sector. Each of these developments has implications for distribution channel strategy and management.

International distribution raises issues about channels *between* countries as well as differences in distribution structure *within* countries. The majority of international business is conducted by firms that export, either indirectly or directly, to foreign countries. A large number of specialized middlemen have arisen to avoid or facilitate the performance of complex export sales, documentation, shipping, and financing.

Channels within foreign countries differ dramatically in terms of the number, types, sizes, and utilization of middlemen. Differences in geographic characteristics, economies, cultures, and political development require careful study on a country-by-country basis so that the unique characteristics of distribution within each country can be understood.

International logistics involves the physical movement of goods between two countries. The international freight forwarder is an intermediary that specializes in providing logistics services for exporters. A global perspective of logistics may be a critical component of strategy for firms that procure, manufacture, and distribute goods in numerous countries. International distribution frequently requires countertrade transactions which involve receipt of products rather than money as payment. Channels must be developed to dispose of the goods received.

Services account for about 60 percent of all United States GNP, but distribution of services is a neglected area of study and research. Service distribution channels demonstrate unique characteristics because of service intangibility, inseparability, perishability, and heterogeneity. Two classification schemes for services were introduced and three guidelines for creative service channel strategy were introduced.

QUESTIONS

1 Describe the major types of intermediaries for export channels. What are the differences in functions performed by each?
2 What are the differences between indirect export and direct export? What are the advantages of each?
3 Suppose a small manufacturer of industrial fasteners (nuts, bolts, rivets, etc.) that produces entirely for domestic sales approached you for advice about international sales and distribution. What advice would you give?
4 Find a firm in your local community that markets its products in other countries. What

---

[27] James H. Donnelly and Joseph P. Guiltinan, "Selecting Channels of Distribution For Services," in *Handbook of Modern Marketing,* ed. Victor P. Buell, New York: McGraw-Hill, 1986, p. 24–7.

means does the firm use to distribute to those countries? What channels are used within each country? Why has the firm utilized these distribution channels?

5 In the library, find material that describes distribution channels in two foreign countries. What environmental factors cause the differences in channels in those two countries?

6 What is countertrade? Give three examples, not discussed in the book, of countertrade transactions and the distribution problems associated with each.

7 What is meant by service intangibility? inseparability? perishability? heterogeneity?

8 What are the major implications of the unique characteristics of services for distribution channel strategy?

9 In the library, research the distribution channels for health care services. Develop a diagram of the various channels. How do these channels reflect the framework discussed in this chapter?

10 How does understanding the "nature of the service act" (Table 13-3) aid in the design of distribution channels for services? Provide three additional examples of services for each of the four categories in Table 13-3.

11 How does consideration of the "method of service delivery" (Table 13-4) aid in design of distribution channels for services? Provide three additional examples of services for each of the six categories in Table 13-4.

12 Beyond those discussed in the chapter, provide examples of services that can be distinguished from physical manifestations of the service. What new distribution channels might be developed as a result of this separation?

CHAPTER 14

FUTURE DISTRIBUTION ARRANGEMENTS

CHAPTER OVERVIEW

CHANNEL MANAGEMENT: A SYNTHESIS
   Universal Foundation of Channel Systems
THE NEED FOR DISTRIBUTION INNOVATION
   Invention versus Innovation
   The Productivity Gap
INNOVATIVE DISTRIBUTION IDEAS: FACT OR FICTION?
   Speeding Autos To Market
   Home Delivery Of Food
   Applianceless Dealers
   Purchasing Corporations
CONCLUDING STATEMENT

When he was a senior General Motors executive, Boss Kettering often criticized his contemporaries for their preoccupation with day-to-day manufacturing and marketing operations at the expense of future planning. Kettering's perspective was simple and fundamental: ''Executives must be concerned with the future because that's where they will spend the rest of their lives.'' In this final chapter, speculation is made about future distribution channel arrangements.

To set the stage, the first section provides a brief synthesis of the basic ideas around which this book has been structured. Next, the general challenge of continuous productivity and quality improvement is positioned in terms of the need for increased distribution innovation. In the next section, four innovative distribution arrangements are described. While far different than today's business practice, each of the arrangements presented is feasible within the capabilities of today's technology. These innovative arrangements are shown to be ways that productivity could be enhanced. However, the arrangements do not appear to be gaining wide support. The reader is left to speculate why they are not.

CHANNEL MANAGEMENT: A SYNTHESIS

The marketing channel has been described and discussed as an ever-changing system of relationships that exists among institutions involved in the process of buying and selling. Because channels are dynamic, it is difficult to crystallize institutional relationships that exist at any point in time into a neat classification. For purposes of differentiation, three basic channel arrangements have been identified: (1) the vertical marketing system (VMS), which may be structured legally on a corporate, contractual, or administered basis; (2) free-flow marketing channels; and (3) single-transaction channels. Each can be easily observed in contemporary marketing. This classification scheme builds upon the degree of direct acknowledgment of mutual dependence between some or all of the channel members.

Universal Foundation of Channel Systems

Although marketing channels are significantly different from one another, observations have shown that they all have some degree of six fundamental environmental and behavioral features: legal-social setting, complexity, specialization, routinization, dependence, and disproportionate risk.

Legal-Social Setting The most common features among distribution arrangements are those that reflect the legal-social setting within which channels function. All enterprises, regardless of size, are subject to the judicial, legislative, and administrative laws of all the political jurisdictions within which they operate. Although enforcement policies vary, the basic legality of a specific act generally does not. With increasing frequency, executives are being held responsible for their managerial actions and the subsequent impact upon society. The past few years have seen direct prosecution of corporate executives for activity by their firms judged to be in violation of antitrust laws. An example of the extent to which the doctrine of public trust has expanded is reflected in a 1975 Supreme Court ruling. The Court held a firm's chief executive officer responsible for the failure of employees to comply with federal food laws.[1] This doctrine of executive responsibility was further institutionalized in the United States by passage of the Foreign Corrupt Practices Act on December 19, 1977 (Public Law 95–213).

The impact of culture upon channel relationships is clearly less direct than law.

---

[1] "Justice Department Charges General Electric with Sherman Antitrust Violation" and "U.S. Charges Reciprocity on Purchasing," *Wall Street Journal,* May 19, 1972, p. 2; and "Turbine Makers Get Sued Again: Antitrust Suit against General Electric and Westinghouse," *Business Week,* January 8, 1972, p. 24.

Many traditions of a society are reflected in the ways and means of accepted business practice. These traditions extend from simple practices such as selling in specific units of measurement like dozens and quarts, to very complex but, in many situations, unwritten rules about the responsibility of merchants to their customers. For example, beer is typically sold in units of six (a six-pack) in the United States. In most Latin American countries, it is commonly sold by the individual container. Likewise, the responsibility of retailers to stand behind products they sell varies among nations. The very manner by which an ownership transaction takes place is culturally based. Shopping is one of the most visible forms of human interaction and is learned behavior. The culture-based pattern of acceptable shopping behavior serves as a constraint as to which marketing methods society will accept.

The important point about legal and social settings within which channels function is that they are universal. While the acceptable and legal practices vary substantially from one setting to the next, they exist in all settings. Firms that conduct business in a multinational channel must be sensitive to individual countries' legal and social constraints. Distribution strategies must be structured to accommodate contradictory behavior patterns.

Complexity A second common feature of marketing channels is their complexity. In a society as large as the United States, wholesale sales far exceed those of retailers. For every retail ownership transfer, a product may be bought and sold multiple times between channel participants.

The complex nature of marketing channels is a reflection of modern marketing practice. The prevailing practice of growth through new-product development and proliferation of retail merchandise lines has resulted in similar items being sold at many different and competitive locations within the same market area. Managers throughout the world concerned with developing a marketing channel strategy can be expected to confront significant structural complexity.

Specialization Specialization is at the essence of an industrial society. The economic benefits of specialization and their impact upon channel development was discussed in Chapter 1.[2] Specialized services create economic opportunity. The result is a sufficiently large and varied assortment of institutions that perform unique channel services. Such specialization is common throughout nations that conduct business based on a free-market mechanism.

Routine Searching The routinization of searching is a primary reason why marketing channels emerge. The basic contribution of routinization to efficiency was developed in Chapter 1.[3] Routinization eliminates the need to search for suppliers and negotiate new arrangements each time a product or service is required. To the extent that a channel is routinized, there is a potential for participating firms to jointly improve their overall performance. For example, if sufficient business volume exists, technology such as *electronic data interchange* (EDI) can be introduced to reduce

---

[2] See Chapter 1, pp. 20–21.
[3] See Chapter 1, p. 19.

overall transaction cost. Indeed, routinization between buyer and seller has enabled a cohesive bond to be formed that reduces uncertainty and creates dependence.

Dependence   A logical extension of specialization and routinization between business firms is dependence. Dependence emerges when managers formally acknowledge that it is in their self-interest to maintain a business relationship. Dependence is often informal as a result of repetitive practice or may be formalized in a legal contract. Acknowledgment of mutual dependence is a key indicator of the emergence of a marketing channel. At the most basic level, managers develop expectations about one another's roles in the channel arrangement. Such roles may involve performance of specific functions or may be specific to products or territories. Establishment of role dependence creates both the incentive to cooperate and the source of potential conflict.

Disproportionate Risk   Coexistent with dependence is the realization that seldom will two organizations have the same risk in a channel arrangement. The fact that one enterprise has more at stake than another is common. Among participants in a channel, variance typically exists in perceived and actual risk. Two points in regard to relative risk are important.

First, if the channel relationship has not evolved to a relatively high level of acknowledged dependence, then one or more of the channel participants can be expected not to feel commitment to the arrangement. For example, a trucker may provide specialized services for channel members but may not perceive any dependence, risk, or commitment beyond the performance of the specified transportation. Such a carrier would, at best, be a weak channel member in terms of willingness to compromise individual goals for the good of the overall channel. However, if the carrier were contracted to haul freight exclusively for the channel, both perceived and actual risk would be greater as a result of increased dependence.

Second, disproportionate risk creates the opportunity for leadership. Acknowledgment of disproportionate risk coupled with a desire to develop joint operations creates a need for leadership. Most firms that perform contract manufacturing for large retailers participate in joint planning of product design, packaging, and quantities to be produced in advance of a selling season. Agreements related to such issues are typically discussed on an open basis. Little, if any, question exists that the retailer who has the most at risk is the formal channel leader. Unless some level of disproportionate risk exists, the channel will typically not be managed as a vertical marketing system.

In summary, the six universal foundations—legal-social setting, complexity, specialization, routinization, dependence, and disproportionate risk—can be readily observed in all types of channel arrangements. These foundations form the nucleus around which channels emerge or are strategically planned. The result may be an informal or a highly formal channel arrangement. The degree to which the foundations are formalized reflects the maturity of a specific distribution arrangement.

Formulation of a channel strategy by enterprise management represents a significant part of an overall marketing strategy. A channel planning and management change process to guide implementation of a channel strategy was introduced. It consists of the following six steps: (1) enterprise positioning, (2) design of marketing and logistics performance structure, (3) planning and analysis, (4) negotiation, (5) channel management, and (6) accurate measurement of channel performance.

In the final analysis, the ability to plan the direction and tempo of future channel arrangements rests upon the capability of management to eliminate resistance to change and assume a leadership role. To a large degree, the change process starts with acknowledgment of a basic need for increased distribution innovation.

THE NEED FOR DISTRIBUTION INNOVATION

A great deal of change has taken place in the structure of marketing channels. The most significant change has taken place in the nature of agreements between participants rather than in the basic distribution processes. In other words, a significant degree of planning and functional transfer has occurred between institutions. The net result has been that channel participants and their relative roles have changed substantially. However, with few exceptions, the overall value-added distribution process has remained relatively unchanged.

The grocery products industry provides a good example. The primary method of processed food distribution during the first half of the twentieth century consisted of manufacturers selling to wholesalers who, in turn, supplied retailers. In a sense, the distribution arrangement was typical of the classic M to W to R channel model that has dominated marketing literature (see Chapter 1, Figure 1-1). Over the years, the food distribution system has evolved from a free-flow marketing structure characterized by small retailers to a combination of contractual and administered vertical marketing arrangements dominated by large integrated supermarket organizations. In terms of participants' roles and functional responsibility, the channel structure has experienced radical change.

At least four major evolutions, or planned changes, can be identified in the food industry. First, supermarkets emerged as a replacement for small food retailers. Second, the vertical integration of supermarket chains for the incorporation of the wholesale function led to establishment of retail-owned distribution centers supplied directly by manufacturers. This stage of development resulted in a significant decline and consolidation of independent wholesalers. The third stage of the evolution was characterized by integrated chains pressuring food manufacturers to provide mixed truckload shipments of products to their distribution centers. This pressure caused many manufacturers to establish mixing distribution centers for provision of the required product assortments. Thus, a new activity was introduced into the marketing channel. The final phase continues to unfold today. Integrated retailers are trying to push inventory holding responsibility "up to the channel" toward manufacturers. This pressure is reflected in such practices as store-sequenced trailer loading, which permits the chain to cross-dock products for store delivery without warehousing. Other examples are trailer trip leasing, just-in-time (JIT), quick response (QR), pickup and backhaul allowances, and direct store delivery (DSD). All of these modifications in traditional practice represent ways to shift inventory responsibility and to increase velocity or turnover at the retail level.

The significant point of this food industry example is that logistics channel structure has experienced substantial changes; however, the process of selling food has remained relatively the same.

Invention versus Innovation

A case can be made that major changes in marketing channels at least since World War II have resulted from a shift in relative power between institutions coupled with a steady influx of new technology. Returning to the food distribution example, we can see that the relative balance of power has shifted from manufacturers to large retailers. A significant portion of the change in distribution practices can be traced to invention and development of transportation, warehousing, and order-processing technology. In a general sense, new technology has been deployed so that traditional steps in the distribution process can be performed better. Power and technology have been deployed to shift responsibility for performing traditional distribution functions more efficiently as contrasted to seeking new and better ways to satisfy customers. Innovation, on the other hand, is directed toward seeking totally new ways or processes for accomplishing necessary marketing functions.

The Productivity Gap

The need for innovative distribution arrangements has never been greater. A steady stream of new technology can be expected to emerge during the remainder of the twentieth century. The track record of the past decades suggests that technology alone cannot achieve the desired productivity growth.

Figure 14-1 illustrates the United States productivity trend in comparison to other major industrial nations that have a free-market environment. Productivity is defined as the ratio of real output produced to real resources consumed. The graph clearly shows that the United States has only begun to keep pace with other industrialized nations. Although many different approaches can be utilized to improve productivity, one sure method is to reduce duplication and waste in the distributive process.

INNOVATIVE DISTRIBUTION IDEAS: FACT OR FICTION?

In this final section, four innovative ideas that can introduce radical change in distribution practice are highlighted. These ideas can be used as potential ways to improve productivity. Most of the ideas described are or have been studied by firms within the related industry. The reader is encouraged to identify and isolate changes that would make the new arrangement work and to evaluate the economic validity of the idea. Keep in mind that most innovative system changes have traditionally originated from outside the involved industry and have been implemented by people who ''didn't know it couldn't be done.''

Speeding Autos to Market

It has long been a dream of the automobile industry to transport automobiles by air from assembly plants to airports close to dealer showrooms. Given modern commu-

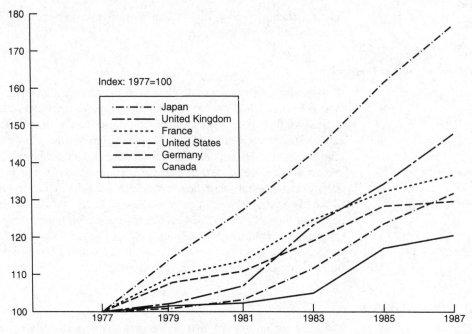

FIGURE 14-1 Increase in output per labor hour, 1957–1987. (*Source: Bureau of Labor Statistics.*)

nication and air transportation capability, such air-auto distribution has increasingly become technologically possible. Among benefits for the automobile industry would be a reduction in the average time the finished-vehicle inventory is in the distribution pipeline, from 30 to 50 days from assembly plants to dealers. All of these automobiles in the pipeline are typically completely assembled, thereby representing anticipatory commitment to what production schedulers forecast customers will desire to purchase. In recent years, factory and dealer rebates have been introduced to give consumers an incentive to buy products that were produced in anticipation of future demand.

Naturally, if air distribution is used, the cost of freight will be several times higher than current per-vehicle cost for using rail tri-level and truck distribution. It would seem that an air-distribution program could only be afforded if inventory savings and reduced rebates across the distribution channel would offset the increased transportation costs.

From a technology innovation viewpoint, the issue should be approached from a much broader perspective. First, what would faster delivery of cars mean, if anything, to retail customers? In 1991, over 600 different distinct models of cars were available in the United States. Customers might benefit if a rapid-delivery system afforded the opportunity to place custom orders. Manufacturers in such rapid-response systems would benefit from fewer canceled orders. Thus, to make the concept work, it might be necessary to introduce telecommunications capability that would allow customers to, in effect, design their own car. Such an innovative method of marketing would have far-reaching implications in terms of expertise needed at the dealership level. It would also redefine the traditional role of dealers in the distribution channel. In fact, Toyota completely reorganized its selling and manufacturing organizations to achieve faster response.

Second, to gain full benefits of flexible rapid delivery of automobiles it would be necessary to introduce postponement into the manufacturing process. For example, automobiles might be mutually produced in a few engine and body styles, painted in a primer coat, and inventoried with no interiors or accessories. Building a smaller assortment of models would facilitate automation of some aspects of assembly. Upon receipt of a customer order, customized assembly could be completed in a secondary process within a few hours. With such an integrated system, a car ordered by a customer on Monday could be customized on the secondary assembly line on Tuesday and flown to the dealer market on Wednesday or Thursday.

Third, to make such a concept work, major changes will be required in the traditional relationship between automobile manufacturers and their dealers. Such a program could exist only if given substantial financial support and training by the manufacturing organization.

Although the aforementioned concept is highly speculative, its appeal rests in multiple trade-offs among manufacturing, distribution, and finance, and in coordinated manufacturer-dealer relationships. It is obvious that neither a firm nor its customers can afford the transportation cost unless other cost-reducing changes are introduced. Is the concept valid? It was sufficiently exciting to stimulate extensive study by General Motors Corporation as early as the 1960s. While not utilizing air distribution, Toyota has modified its process of ordering and manufacturing so that a custom-designed automobile can be delivered in an average of eight days across Japan. The company has a goal of performing to-order manufacturing in two days in Tokyo and Osaka, two cities that account for roughly two-thirds of Japan's population.[4]

Among distribution personnel in the automotive industry, concepts dealing with order-cycle compression are viewed as having potential but not here-today applications. The question is: Will management ever make the changes necessary to exploit technology and make such a system a reality? If so, what would be required for the reconfiguration of traditional manufacturing and distribution channel arrangements? Are there any parallels in the approach General Motors took with Saturn?

Home Delivery of Food

One customer service offered by retail grocery stores before the widespread growth in supermarkets was home delivery. This practice was not generally adopted by large chains. However, some retailers kept their foot in the door by operating specialized home delivery routes. An example is the *Jewel Company's* home delivery system. Evidence suggests that home delivery of such items as food may have lost its appeal to both consumers and retailers. Total food delivered to the home dropped from 8.6 percent of total sales in 1960 to 1.2 percent in 1977 and less than 1 percent in 1990.

[4] George Stalk, Jr., "Time: The Next Source of Competitive Advantage," *Harvard Business Review,* **66:**4 July–August 1988, p. 49.

Most home delivery is in specialized areas such as frozen-food plans. Is the concept dead forever, or is the reestablishment of home delivery just not timely?

The potential of interactive video-text-based ordering from the home directly to warehouselike supermarkets has long been discussed. The following is typical of how this subject has been examined:

> The future of retailing, and in particular the prospect of telecommunication systems for shopping, has enormous consequences for manufacturers, suppliers, and equipment manufacturers as well as, of course, retail stores. . . . [V]isions of automation . . . were described by Edward Bellamy in 1888 and have been issuing ever since from various experts. . . . [L]ikely developments during the next few decades are closely connected with past trends[:] the evolution of retail institutions, the shortening of retail life cycles, the influence of consumers and their lifestyles on retailing, the rise of specialty stores, and other happenings. . . . [L]ooking ahead, [we] see these trends combining and mixing with other developments, such as new technologies, to produce a vastly different retail scene. While [we] believe that specialty stores will continue to thrive, the retailing of routinely ordered staples will be transformed. Telecommunication shopping, or "teleshopping," is definitely in prospect for this great area of marketing.[5]

Retail food store operators do not appear to be enthusiastic abut teleshopping systems. However, the concept has made inroads in the form of television shopping channels. Direct marketing of general merchandise, clothing, and gift items is growing at a rate greater than overall retailing. From a total-cost perspective it may be possible to provide consumers with better service than they receive at a typical retail store at a lower total cost. Such a radical innovation would require significant institutional changes and greatly modified consumer shopping habits. Will such a concept of food retailing ever become a reality? Kroger instituted a test of home delivery in Detroit in early fall 1992. Some industry experts think home delivery will grow in the future. Most do not. Meanwhile, manufacturers dream.

Applianceless Dealers

A different form of direct home delivery that offers productivity improvement potential is a system wherein appliance dealers do not stock inventory. The dealers under this distribution arrangement only stock display models for consumer inspection and purchase evaluation. A consumer sale by a dealer is communicated to a distribution center strategically located to service the geographic area. Upon receipt of an order, the appropriate appliance is selected from the distribution center inventory and arrangements are made for direct delivery to the consumer's home. Such direct logistics systems have the potential to eliminate duplicate handling and transportation to and from dealers. The direct-delivery arrangement would virtually eliminate inventory from the channel. In addition, consolidation of multiple dealers' inventories into one strategically located warehouse would provide significantly better product availability with lower average channel inventories.

---

[5] Malcolm P. McNair and Eleanor G. May, "The Next Revolution of the Retailing Wheel," *Harvard Business Review,* 56:5 September–October 1978, p. 81. Copyright © 1978 by the President and Fellows of Harvard College; all rights reserved.

Such direct-to-customer distribution has been tested for a number of years. In particular, Whirlpool and General Electric have tested the direct-delivery concept. There are situations in which an appliance sold on Monday was delivered to a customer on Wednesday. In some situations, the appliance delivered on Wednesday had not been manufactured when it was purchased. The appliance was selected directly from the assembly line, loaded on a truck, and transported to the local facility where it was assigned to a delivery route. When appliance products are warehoused, the trend is toward manufacture of a generic product without selected accessories and color attachments. The appliance can then be customized to a customer's request by adding such accessories as timers or front color panels after that customer's order has been received. Thus, a single basic stock item can be customized into a variety of different products at the distribution center. As indicated, the system has been tested, and many people in the industry are convinced it will become the accepted method of appliance marketing and distribution in the future. This innovation faces substantial obstacles, but it offers the benefit of significant economies. Will this arrangement become tomorrow's dominant channel for consumer durables?

Purchasing Corporations

Large-scale manufacturing often requires many different production and processing stages so that a product can be completed. In many situations, the total process requires multiple specialized-component manufacturing and final-product assembly plants. An understandable concern in such situations is the maintenance of a continuous supply of materials and labor for conversion into finished products. One persistent problem in such organizations is the high relative cost of obtaining maintenance, repair, and operating (MRO) supplies. While secondary to the primary mission, MRO can consume critical time and represent significant expenditure. The ideal logistics solution would be a system that facilitated purchasing in small quantities at an economic price and with timely delivery so that on-site stock piling could be reduced. A new concept is emerging wherein third-party organizations are assuming the role of MRO supply specialists for manufacturing organizations. A master purchase order is negotiated by the manufacturer with vendors. The vendors, in turn, transport products to third-party warehouses when requested. The third party maintains inventory for the support of manufacturing requirements. The individual manufacturing plants draw upon the MRO warehouse in much the same way that supermarkets place replenishment orders to their supporting distribution centers. Delivery of critical supplies could be expedited in a few hours. The normal order cycle would consist of next-day delivery to the location of the user. Ordering can be paperless, with direct electronic billing to appropriate authorized accounts.

The economic advantage of MRO outsourcing is the capability to aggregate economy-of-scale purchases geographically close to a group of manufacturing plants. The establishment of a central inventory provides the capability to rapidly distribute exact quantities of MRO items to the location where they are needed in a manufacturing plant. From the manufacturer's viewpoint, many small shipments are consolidated into a single supply order. In addition, it is not necessary to manage inbound movement associated with many purchases and in-plant storage. Finally, broader assortments and low-bid purchasing are additional economies of specialization.

The concept of centralized purchasing corporations offers many interesting possibilities. If a single firm can enjoy significant economies of scale with this type of centralized operation, wouldn't it be feasible for a single supply corporation to perform customized purchasing for multiple manufacturing concerns? The essential difference between the purchasing corporation and the traditional industrial supplier is an extended commitment, specialized operations, and dependence between user organizations and the MRO supply business corporation. In certain circumstances, the purchasing corporations could expand activities to include joint use of specialized equipment and light manufacturing, fabrication, and the performance of value-added services to accompany MRO operations. Such corporations exist today. Those with the highest visibility now serve *IBM, Hughes Aircraft, Union Pacific Railroad, Gulf Oil,* and *Dow Chemical.* To what extent does this innovative concept have widespread practicality, and will it become the preferred way of doing business in the 1990s?

CONCLUDING STATEMENT

This book has attempted to explain and illustrate the reality of management in marketing channels. In this final chapter, description has given way to problem assessment and speculation. The plea is for critical examination of traditional practices in pursuit of increased productivity. The goal is change, but not purely for the sake of change. It appears clear that the challenge to continue profitable growth rests with management's ability to innovatively apply available technology. The challenge for the future is to fix the process by negotiating greater productivity through cooperative synergism among channel participants as contrasted to simple ownership transfer between firms.[6] It remains to be seen how fast managers can implement such coordinated behavior in a profit-oriented free-market system.

[6] Harold Sirkin and George Stalk, Jr., "Fix the Process, not the Problem," *Harvard Business Review,* **68:**4 July–August 1990, pp. 26–33.

CASES FOR PART FOUR

CASE 4-1: IKEA North America: The Vikings Rediscover America

INTRODUCTION

It was early 1990 and Bjorn Boyle, president of IKEA North America, was remembering that exciting day in July 1985—the opening, which had gone off with extraordinary success, of the first American IKEA store at Plymouth Meeting, 20 miles from Philadelphia. The roads had been jammed with traffic for miles around. The event had been covered on television and had drawn 100,000 people in the first four days. Customers had lined up around the building, waiting their turn to shop. IKEA, a lifestyle furniture retailer from Sweden, specialized in ready-to-assemble furniture. Now, three more stores later with plans to have ten stores in the United States by 1992, was a time to reflect on the entry strategy for the United States and to assess the planned expansion strategy.

FROM FISH TO FURNITURE

In 1947, at the age of 22, an entrepreneurial Ingvar Kamprad quit his home deliveries of fish and milk to start selling flower seeds and ballpoint pens by mail order to customers in his native Sweden. Fired by the success of this venture, he turned his attention to the local furniture industry. He saw opportunities to improve the distribution methods and to sell the products at lower prices. He began to sell the furniture output of the local carpenters through his catalog at prices 30 to 50 percent lower than his competitors'. He achieved the low prices by having the furniture manufactured in a knockdown form for his customers to assemble at home.

His strong competition earned him the boycott of the local industry and he was forced to seek suppliers beyond his native Sweden. This was the start of a supply strategy that eventually led to a broad base of 1500 suppliers in fifty countries. To maintain low manufacturing costs, a piece of furniture could be assembled from components sourced from a number of different suppliers. For example, the cover, frame, and metal fittings of a chair could come from three different suppliers. Kamprad

IKEA North America: The Vikings Rediscover America was written by G. Peter Dapiran.

emphasized low cost, not only in product design, but also in all facets of operations, as the basis for success.

Six years later, he opened the first IKEA showroom in the small southern Swedish town of Almhult.

IKEA, a name coined by the founder from the initial letters of his name, together with the names of the farm, Elmtaryd, and the parish, Agunnaryd, in which he grew up, prospered.

He opened his second store outside Stockholm, Sweden. This site was to become the flagship and the largest IKEA store in the world at 463,000 square feet.

Stores in Norway and Denmark followed. It was not until 1973 that IKEA ventured beyond Scandinavia, with a store near Zurich in Switzerland.

European expansion, restrained to ensure it was always within the financial capability of the organization, continued into Germany, Austria, France, and Belgium. By the mid-1980s, IKEA had 85 stores in nineteen countries in Europe and as far afield as Australia, Kuwait, and Hong Kong. By 1984, 14 percent of sales were derived outside Europe and Scandinavia. With growth opportunities declining in the European and home markets, and with the experience gained in a variety of foreign locations, it was time to tackle the larger American market.

THE UNITED STATES FURNITURE MARKET

The total American retail furniture market was considered to be about $35 billion, as depicted in Table 1.

Expenditure on furniture was closely tied to the well-being of the housing sector and the real growth in disposable income. Cost of credit also had an impact, as furniture was more likely to be financed than nondurable consumer goods. The forecast into the middle 1990s was for a slight growth in domestic furniture shipments.

TABLE 1   THE FURNITURE MARKET

SIC*	Value of product shipments for house furniture (in millions of dollars)			
	1987	1988	1989	1990†
2511 Wood furniture	7,421	7,421	7,310	7,164
2512 Upholstered	4,895	4,944	4,894	4,796
2514 Metal furniture	1,893	1,912	1,874	1,846
2515 Mattresses	2,706	2,773	2,801	2,801

	Total new supply of house furniture (in millions of dollars)		
	1987	1988	1989
Domestic	17,765	18,610	19,063
Imports	2,889	2,910	2,765

Notes: * SIC = Standard industrial classification   † Forecast
Source: Adapted from U.S. Industrial Outlook 1990, U.S. Department of Commerce, January 1990.

TABLE 2   THE FURNITURE BUYERS

Annual expenditures on furniture by age of householder (in millions of dollars)			
	1985	1990	1995	2000
Under 25	1017	872	807	831
25 to 34	7286	7711	7253	6553
35 to 44	6503	7903	8897	9426
45 to 54	4761	5440	6799	8144
55 to 64	2954	2782	2765	3142
65 to 74	1997	2148	2209	2119
75 and older	431	515	583	656

Percentage of college-educated adults by age by type of store where they would expect to find furnishings that would appeal to them

	Age			
Store type	Total	Less than 30	30 to 49	50+
Furniture store	47%	46%	46%	52%
Specialty store	29	37	31	18
Department store	16	14	15	20
All about equal	3	1	3	3
Other	3	1	3	3
Not sure	2	1	2	3

Source: Adapted from "Sitting Pretty," by J. Schlossberg, *American Demographics,* May 1988, pp. 24–28. Reprinted with permission © *American Demographics,* May 1988.

Another set of factors of significance in the American economy into the 1990s was the aging of the baby boomers, those born between 1945 and 1965. As the decade progressed, these people would move into the thirty to forty-nine age bracket. This shift would bring with it peak earnings, higher disposable incomes, a propensity to buy more expensive furniture, and a lifestyle that emphasized quality of life, family values, and a focus on the home, as shown in Table 2.

One of the challenges facing the furniture industry was how to convert these demographic changes into actual higher spending on furniture.

THE NORTH AMERICAN ASSAULT

The mode of entry into a market is a crucial decision that faces any potential exporter. The possibilities are numerous, and nearly all had been used by European companies entering the United States market. (See Table 3.)

IKEA was aware of the factors deemed by former successful entrants from Europe to be important for success in the United States. (See Table 4.)

In the mid-1970s, IKEA established itself in the Canadian market through a franchising arrangement as it had done in some of the other more remote locations such as Australia. Canada was considered important not only for its own sake but also because it was seen as a test market for the much larger United States market.

TABLE 3   SELECTED EUROPEAN COMPANIES WITH UNITED STATES INVOLVEMENT

Company (Origin): Core retail business—Main United States interest.

Ahold (Netherlands): Food—Owns three supermarket chains (Bi-Lo, Giant Food Stores, First National Supermarkets).

Asko (West Germany): Food—Minority stake in Furr's Supermarkets.

Austin Reed (U.K.): Men's apparel—Licensing agreement with Hartmax Corporation of Chicago to make and sell Austin Reed.

Benetton (Italy): Fashion knitwear—Approximately 700 franchised stores.

BAT (U.K.): Department stores, catalog showrooms—Owns Saks Fifth Avenue and Marshall Field's.

Dixons (U.K.): Home electrical—Owns Silo.

Dunhill (U.K.): Menswear—Chain of company-owned stores.

Fastframe (U.K.): Picture framing—Twenty-eight franchised stores.

GIB Group (Belgium): Department stores, food, DIY—Owns Scotty's DIY 164-store chain.

Printemps (France): Department stores—One store trading as a joint venture in Denver.

Tie Rack (U.K.): Neckties—Thirty-one company-owned stores; further expansion through franchising.

Vendex International (Netherlands): Department stores, home furnishings, apparel, food—50% stake in Barnes & Noble bookstores, minority stake in Dillards department stores.

Source: Adapted from "Global Links in U.S. Retailing," *Discount Merchandiser,* September 1989, pp. 26–31. Reprinted with permission.

TABLE 4   SOME OPINIONS OF SUCCESS FACTORS FOR EUROPEAN RETAILERS IN THE UNITED STATES

Americans have already shown that they like a total-concept store. You can't always transplant a store as it existed in Europe. Any European retailer is in danger the first three years. There is the product risk, the location risk, and the management risk if the company franchises.

J-M. Loubier, Director, International Division, Descamps (Home textiles).

"Americans like big shopping areas."

S. Fischer, Director, Public Relations, Benetton (Fashion casual wear).

"Here [in the United States], advertising is a very big deal. Names are important in America but not in Europe. You have to sell a look and an image. Any European company that does not hire an American to run its U.S. operation deserves to fail. You can't understand a country unless you're of that country. Business today is in the mass market. . . . Lower price points attract a bigger market. A lot of Europeans who come here make big mistakes and have trouble adapting. . . . With proper adjustments, you can build a success."

P. Dora, President, Conran's (Home furnishings).

"The diversity of consumers and the extensive amount of advertising required to achieve market penetration were hurdles that (British based BAT, French Agache-Willot, German Hugo Mann—all retailers) failed to overcome."

Source: Adapted from N. M. Miller, "The New Immigrants," *Chain Store Age Executive,* February 1986, pp. 16–18.

The franchises were not successful, partly because, it was thought, the franchisees chose to sell a limited number of lines. This prevented the store from conveying the IKEA concept effectively. IKEA bought out the Canadian franchisees.

IKEA's strategy for success was to make shopping an easy and pleasurable experience, and to offer well-designed, functional, quality furniture at low prices.

The target segment was considered to be the active urban adults of twenty-five to thirty-five years with an annual household income of more than $50,000.

The American plan was to open two to three stores a year grouped in five to six stores per region, each region serviced by a separate distribution center, management team, and maybe even a marketing staff. IKEA planned to have ten stores in the United States by 1992.

The first American store was opened with great fanfare in June 1985. The opening was promoted heavily through a mailing based on household income. Local promotion through television, radio, newspapers, and even the backs of buses, was extensive. One million catalogs were distributed for the event.

The 165,000-square-foot store was located at Plymouth Meeting just outside Philadelphia, away from the crowded city center. The location was consistent with IKEA's idea of the ideal site—a low-cost real estate suburban site away from city traffic congestion, allowing large parking lots and easy access to and from the motorways.

A second store of 156,000 square feet was opened in Washington in the fall of 1986, followed by the 200,000-square-foot Baltimore store at the end of summer 1988.

Pittsburgh was the site of the fourth store, which opened in the summer of 1989.

IKEA established two large distribution centers in Montreal, Canada, and Philadelphia to service the East Coast of America and was looking for suitable sites to establish its West Coast attack.

THE IKEA SHOPPING EXPERIENCE

A key IKEA philosophy was that shopping had to be made a relaxed and pleasant event. Its large accessible parking lots at sites away from crowded city centers initiated this experience for the potential IKEA customer.

Supervised child minding and indoor play areas, together with a restaurant offering Swedish food, were all elements of IKEA's philosophy of pleasurable shopping undisturbed by the demands of otherwise bored children.

Pencils, paper, tape measures, and a product catalog inside the front entrance were designed to make shopping easy. Unobtrusive staff, located in a central service area, could be called upon for assistance if necessary, but otherwise customers were left to consider the merchandise in their own time.

The spacious stores decorated with colorful banners had a carnival atmosphere. Furniture was laid out in room settings where customers could see and try the products in a simulated home environment. Swing tags on each piece of furniture clearly indicated the style and model names, product dimensions, and price.

The furniture, 90 percent of which was designed in-house, was upscale modern Scandinavian—functional with simple lines and forms. It was available exclusively in knockdown form in flat packs and was ready to be assembled at home by the customer with only a simple tool, which came with each pack. IKEA had a commitment to product quality. To this end, furniture was tested and appropriately labeled with the Swedish testing authority tag.

Although furniture was the main product category, it was complemented with merchandise that included housewares, home textiles (bed and bath, fabric, rugs), lighting, bedding, floor tiles, china, cutlery, glassware, and wallpaper. A total of 14,000 product lines helped the customer create the IKEA home.

All products were described in a catalog that IKEA considered to be a key marketing tool. Half of the marketing budget of an estimated $10 million was devoted to the lavishly produced catalog. It clearly displayed the products, indicated module sizes, provided instructions for calculating needs, and listed price information. The catalog was designed not simply to communicate IKEA's products and prices but also to serve as the principal communication device in conveying the difference between IKEA and its competitors. It conveyed the IKEA concept.

Prices were fixed for twelve months. This allowed customers to plan their interior design at home by using the catalog and then space their purchases over the year. Price credibility was maintained by having a single sale of selected lines just before introduction of the new catalog each September. IKEA offered unconditional return of goods within fourteen days if the customer was dissatisfied.

After the customers made their selection in the showroom, information on the swing ticket directed them to a location in the well-signed warehouse where they picked up their own orders and placed them on trollies. This transfer of warehouse labor to the customer contributed to IKEA's low-cost operation and eliminated a typical warehouse problem and its associated costs—that of errors in picking out merchandise. The customers then wheeled their purchases out through checkout points to their car. Home delivery could be arranged with an independent carrier at the store exits. IKEA made no money from this arrangement; it simply provided space for an external carrier organization as an added service to its customers. Alternatively, car roof-racks were available for purchase at the checkout. Point-of-sale cash registers captured sales movement to aid in the electronic reordering of stock.

THE COMPETITION

IKEA saw as its competition not simply the furniture store down the road, but, more broadly, as all those big expenditures that made a claim on a household's disposable income, such as vacations, a videocassette recorder, even a night out on the town.

More prosaically, a range of furniture sellers competed for the same customers as IKEA. The leading American furniture specialist, Levitz, had annual sales of over $879 million (Table 5). Furniture sales of each of the top three department stores, leading with Sears, with annual furniture sales of more than $780 million (Table 6), dwarfed even the second largest furniture specialist, Seaman's.

The department stores found that they could achieve better sales per square foot from other products in the same high-cost space taken up by the furniture sections of their stores. This created a trend toward free-standing furniture outlets, which also served to enhance the department store presence in the furniture market. At the same time, these free-standing specialist stores could be seen to be more readily in direct competition with IKEA.

TABLE 5   SALES OF SELECTED FURNITURE STORES

Company and Rank	1986 Sales, millions of dollars	1987 Sales, millions of dollars	Stores*	Per square foot
1. Levitz	840	879	105	413
2. Seaman's	230	254	30	406
3. W.S. Badcock	210	247	251	96
4. Rhodes	235	240	89	109
5. Haverty's	189	218	79	N/A
6. Breuners	215	198	19	107
7. Wickes	135	177	16	221
8. Value City	101	150	32	213
9. Heilig-Meyers	141	142	259	90
10. Nebraska Furniture Mart	132	142	1	676
12. Pier One	182	117	350	12
13. Art Van	110	113	15	N/A
16 Scandinavian Design	108	101	68	345
21. IKEA	50	77	2	N/A
27. Conran's	47	65	15	14
33. Jordan's	30	55	3	570

* Number of stores in 1987.
† Sales per square foot in dollars
Source: Adapted from "Balancing the Retail Equation," *HFD—The Weekly Home Furnishings Newspaper,*
June 20, 1988.

Ready-to-assemble (RTA) furniture, distributed through a variety of channels, was starting to come into its own with annual sales of over $2 billion in 1988, as depicted in Table 7.

TABLE 6   FURNITURE SALES OF SELECTED DEPARTMENT STORES
(in millions of dollars)

Rank	Company	1986 Sales	1987 Sales	Branches
1	Sears	750	788	480
2	Montgomery Ward	530	543	302
3	J.C. Penny	400	401	300
4	Macy's New York/New Jersey	154	162	24
5	Bloomingdale's	70	81	13
6	Dayton Hudson	68	71	16
7	Macy's California	65	67	15
8	The Broadway	56	57	10
9	Abraham & Straus	54	56	13
10	Burdines	50	55	17
11	Marshall Field's	40	44	16
46	Dillard's	8	10	67

Source: Adapted from "Balancing The Retail Equation," *HFD—The Weekly Home Furnishings Newspaper,*
June 20, 1988.

TABLE 7   SALES OF SELECTED READY-TO-ASSEMBLY (RTA) FURNITURE RETAILERS
(in Millions of Dollars)

Rank	Company	1988	Category
1	K mart	110	Discounter
2	Wal-Mart	95	Discounter
3	IKEA	90	Lifestyle
4	Target	85	Discounter
5	Aymes/Zayre	80	Department store
6	Sears	80	National retailer
7	Bombay Company	60	Lifestyle
8	Service Merchandise	45	Catalog show-room
9	Best	40	Catalog show-room
10	Venture	35	Discounter
12	Conran's	32	Lifestyle
14	STOR	30	Lifestyle
16	J.C. Penney	27	National retailer
19	Levitz	23	Furniture retailer
20	Pier One	21	Lifestyle
21	Meijer	20	Discounter
22	Price Club	19	Wholesale Club
25	Montgomery Ward	17	Department store
26	Pergament	16	Home center
36	Radio Shack	11	Electronics
42	Heilig-Meyers	10	Furniture retailer
43	Office Depot	10	Office furniture
67	Macy's New York	4	National retailer
Top 80 RTA retailers	1500		
Total RTA market	2000		

Source: Adapted from "Top 80 RTA Retailers," *HFD–The Weekly Home Furnishings Newspaper,* July 10, 1989.

Besides the traditional department stores and furniture stores, discounters, specialty stores, home centers (which saw themselves as natural outlets for RTA furniture), and wholesale clubs also sold RTA furniture, often in combination with a self-service warehouse environment.

Heilig-Meyers, which offered a range of home furnishings, including electronics, appliances, and lawn and garden implements, saw RTA furniture as an avenue to their expansion and upscaling strategy.

The nature of RTA furniture also made it a natural for sale through mail-order catalogs. The products were ideal for shipment by United Parcel Service and hence, rapidly available for home assembly and use. The whole range of J.C. Penney RTA furniture was sold through their catalog.

One of the biggest challenges facing the industry was overcoming the negative attitude of the American consumer toward RTA furniture. This was being tackled to some extent by application of manufacturing techniques that did not make the furniture look knockdown. An additional problem was that of missing parts. IKEA was not immune from this, with a return rate of 1.6 percent of sales in the latest 1987 survey— a decline from 3 percent in the early 1980s.

IKEA, however, saw itself as being unique in the RTA field in two respects: it presented a complete range of furniture and not just the limited number of pieces offered by most of the other retailers, and it was marketing a concept, not simply selling a collection of knockdown furniture.

Specialty stores, such as Pier One, and more especially Conran's, and the large department stores were seen as IKEA's key competitors. Conran's, however, felt that it catered for the more upscale customer.

THE FUTURE

IKEA was considered to be the world's largest multinational furniture chain. This status was attributed to the logistics savings made possible by its flatpack furniture and the innovative channel possibilities that this had opened up, and the low costs achieved through its sourcing policies and the transfer to the customer of assembly and warehouse costs. Only Conran's, of the UK, could also be considered a multi-national furniture store operation.

The flatpack design concept also provided a number of customer benefits: the ability to carry home and enjoy the purchase immediately, considered a particular advantage by the target market that was thought to be in constant search of instant gratification; and the low prices that flowed from the low costs. A continuing commitment to product quality also helped to alleviate the concerns about RTA furniture as a concept.

A Newark, New Jersey, store opened in the spring of 1990; one opened in Los Angeles, California, in October 1990; and one in Long Island, New York, in 1991.

At this stage, IKEA did not offer a mail-order service like its competitors.

Also, other furniture makers had adapted their merchandise to fit different regional needs. IKEA resisted this line of approach, preferring to push its so-far-successful formula.

Recently, IKEA decided to establish a United States buying office to boost the volume of product sourced from the United States. Its current level is 20 percent of the line.

A new and rapidly growing segment that appeared in the marketplace was that of home office furniture. IKEA was not strong in this area.

There were a number of issues to be resolved about the future. Bjorn Boyle sat there and thought.

QUESTIONS

1 What are the success factors that help in making IKEA the largest multinational furniture specialist?

2 Discuss the international distribution channel for furniture.

3 Discuss the options available to IKEA for its expansion in the United States market.

REFERENCES

Arbose, J., "The Folksy Theories that Inspire Lifestyle Merchant IKEA," *International Management,* November 1985, pp. 51–59.

Moore, S. D., "IKEA Bucks Home-Furnishings Trends," *Wall Street Journal,* February 23, 1990, p. A7D.

Reynolds, J., "IKEA: A Competitive Company with Style," *Retail & Distribution Management,* May-June 1988.

"Why Competitors Shop for Ideas at IKEA," *Business Week,* October 9, 1989.

CASE 4-2: 1-800-PIRATES

INTRODUCTION

Peter Martocci, president and owner of Ornate Wallcoverings in Arlington Heights, Illinois, is facing severe competition. The retail wallpaper company, founded by his father in 1952, sells wallpaper and small home furnishings. The store is situated in a small strip mall in suburban Chicago and specializes in multicolored and fabriclike textured wallcoverings. Wallpaper sales comprise 80 percent of his business. The company grosses $5 million a year and provides wallpaper for many small-scale interior designers in the area. Martocci sells wallpaper from twelve different manufacturers, using sixty different books to display the various patterns and colors.

Until recently, Martocci's business was doing quite well. Historically, his greatest competitors were the local retail stores. This never worried Martocci very much, since his father taught him years ago how to run a successful business and beat the competition. However, Martocci was totally unprepared for the type of competition he would experience in the 1980s and 1990s. Martocci and other retailers in the wallpaper industry are dealing with mail-order companies that survive by using retail personnel, books, and store-related overhead to attract customers. These companies then sell wallpaper to consumers through the mail at 30 to 50 percent off retail prices. Quite simply, the wallpaper industry does not know how to address this competitive threat.

WALLPAPER INDUSTRY

Even without this new-found competition, the wallpaper industry has been on a somewhat rocky road. In 1940, the industry peaked at a record 400 million rolls sold. However, by 1970, sales decreased to 90 million rolls. Mike Landau, vice president of the wallcovering division at F. Schumacher & Company, blames this incredible decline on the introduction of latex paint and the paint roller. "The paint industry, which we consider to be our main competitor, introduced a real do-it-yourself orien-

1-800-PIRATES was written by Robert S. Bradley, based on an original paper by David O'Leary.

tation complete with advertising,'' Landau said. ''I think that had much to do with the decline.''[1] Furthermore, Landau said that the wallcovering products were difficult to install and remove and they were not durable.

During the mid-1980s, wallpaper sales increased to a total of 200 million rolls sold and retailers moved about $1 billion worth of goods. This recovery was largely attributed to the availability of improved merchandise. In recent years, manufacturers have pooled their resources and created manufacturing associations that are helpful with technological advancements and better consumer understanding. Since 80 percent of the residential market of wallpaper users are ''do-it-yourselfers,'' it is extremely important to find ways to make the wallpaper easier to clean, hang, and remove. Dick Paul, an executive at the Columbus Coated Fabrics division of Borden Chemicals, believes this has been accomplished. ''There have been vast improvements, evidenced by the fact that old-fashioned wallpaper which had to be pasted and had to be steamed and scrubbed off has virtually dropped out of the market,'' Paul said.[2]

Landau attributes the sales increase to changes in consumer interests, and to new style and color selections. Consumers may now purchase multicolored patterns, including tweeds, silk, stipple, grasses, and other vinyl-textured patterns. Furthermore, the development of new markets has emerged through the promotion and advertising done by K mart and Target stores.

While these new markets help, the most important stores are the paint and wallpaper outlets or home decorating centers. They account for 42 percent of the transactions and 40 percent of the rollage. They are mainly rivaled by the Wallpaper Specialty Store.

It is interesting that department stores play a minor role in the selling of wallcoverings. This is because there are limitations to what the traditional stores can do with the product. Department stores generally do not have a trained and experienced sales staff; salespersons lack the necessary knowledge of the product to inspire customers' confidence and thus close a sale. Furthermore, department stores lack the amount of service, floor space, and inventory investment needed to become a threat to home decorating stores. However, as an add-on to departments selling domestics or curtain and draperies, wallpaper can be merchandised successfully in the traditional department store. The most successful way wallcoverings have been sold in a department store is with a shop concept. This involves a whole lifestyle being shown to a customer by a designer, such as at Laura Ashley stores. In this type of retailing, wallcoverings are an easy add-on.

SAMPLE BOOKS

One serious problem for all these markets is that there are too many sample books. Sample books are provided to consumers to assist them in their selections. The problem arises with the cost of these books. Wallpaper manufacturers sell these books to the retail outfits at a charge of roughly $100. Each manufacturer has several books,

[1] Jules Abend, ''Strategies for Wallcoverings,'' *Stores,* August 1986, p. 15.
[2] Ibid.

and most retailers want to provide a diversity in selection, but this becomes quite expensive. The typical retailer may have up to 300 books, which leads to another problem. As a customer, where do you start when you have 300 books to choose from? Market studies have shown that consumers want more retail how-to clinics and information to make it easier for them when they go to a store.

DISCOUNTING

Ease of shopping is not the only goal of wallpaper buyers; ease on the pocketbook is another main goal. Consequently, discounting of merchandise may be an alternative for channel constituents. Manufacturers, distributors, and retailers all find that discounting is imperative so that they can stay alive. Here arises Paul Martocci's problem—the discount mail-order companies that specialize in discounted wallpaper. The service these mail-order companies provide is exceptional if consumers know what paper to order, the brands, the colors, and so on. These companies usually operate through toll-free 1-800 numbers that customers call to order the brands, patterns, colors, and yardage needed. Companies in the wallcovering industry refer to these outfits that specialize in discounted wallpaper as 1-800-Pirates. This is because they feel they are unjustly losing sales to these companies.

1-800-PIRATES

Mail-order companies usually advertise in magazines oriented toward home decorating. They offer outlandish discounts with advertisements which usually read, "Shop at your local wallpaper retailer and phone us with the pattern number for an order."[3] Martin Silver Wallpaper is one of these companies. Martin Silver, of Philadelphia, offers discounts from 30 to 60 percent off retail. Delivery is free, orders are shipped within five business days, and there is no sales tax (unless you live in Pennsylvania). Another firm is Post Wallcovering Distributors in Bloomfield Hills, Michigan. Post offers a flat rate of 27 percent off the retail price of any brand or pattern. No deposit is required, and merchandise is shipped free. No returns are allowed, except on defective paper, so it is important that the customer order the correct style, color, and so on.

These companies use the service of retail wallpaper stores to run their business. These businesses benefit directly from their competition because they do not need to purchase the books from the manufacturers. Furthermore, they do not need experienced salespeople to sell the product nor a store from which to work. The retail stores provide these services for them; therefore, the mail-order companies' overhead is extremely low and they can offer deep discounts. In addition, the 1-800-Pirate is not obligated to charge sales tax when shipping out of state. It is easy to see why retailers are so distraught with these businesses. To make things worse, point-of-purchase computers are showing higher traffic counts, more books being checked out, and yet far

[3] David O'Leary, *The Shakedown in the Wallcovering Industry,* unpublished paper, Michigan State University.

fewer orders being placed. This means that these mail-order companies are getting more and more of the retail business.

COMPETING WITH THE "PIRATES"

How do these home decorating stores, such as Mr. Martocci's, compete? Most retailers are saying "If you can't beat 'em, join 'em." Their answer is do the same, and discount. However, all this discounting leads to one thing—smaller margins.

Firms cannot compete at all levels, and discounting is killing many of the small retailers, such as Mr. Martocci's. Furthermore, these 1-800-Pirates often increase the manufacturer's suggested list artificially in order to advertise larger discounts. It is hoped that retailers can make customers aware that mail-order discounters may not be comparing the prices fairly; thereby, Martocci can once again begin to focus on fair competition with other retailers.

To cope with these mail-order pirates many retailers and distributors are forming buying groups. By joining resources, these groups can successfully fight the mail-order onslaught. They have been responsible for a multitude of changes, including the creation of private labels, the passing of federal legislation against the "pirates" for lost state sales taxes, and the introduction of bar coding and scanners to prevent the use of books by unwarranted businesses. Other companies are resolving matters on their own. Some companies are using bogus pattern numbers. These companies recode each pattern number in their books so that if a customer orders through an 800 number, the order will go through, but the wrong paper will be ordered. Also, retailers are using the 1-800 number to their benefit. Companies have been known to use a computer dialer that automatically dials the 800 number and hangs up. This makes for a very expensive phone bill. Other retailers actually order precut wallpaper themselves but have it sent to a bogus address. When returned to the "pirate," it cannot be sold back to the manufacturer or resold because it is already cut.

A PROBLEM

How are Martocci and others like him to deal with these pirates? Should they resort to the aforementioned actions as others have done? Is this the proper response? Mr. Martocci was never taught by his father to stab competition in the back, but these tactics may be the only way to spurn the advances of the "pirates."

QUESTIONS

1 Do you feel that these 1-800-Pirates are unethically taking business away from retailers? What do you suggest Mr. Martocci do in this situation?
2 What ways do you think that these 1-800-Pirates actually help Mr. Martocci's business? Are these long-term or short-term outcomes?
3 What should be the role of wallpaper manufacturers in the competition between traditional retailers and the 1-800-Pirates?
4 How does the emergence of the 1-800-Pirates fit with the theories of channel evolution discussed in the text? What future changes do you anticipate?

REFERENCES

Abend, Jules, "Strategies for Wallcoverings," *Stores,* August 1986, pp. 15–25.

Kollman, Richard, "Selecting Wallcoverings: Know Your Area," *Lodging Hospitality,* April 1986, pp. 80–84.

O'Leary, David, *The Shakedown in the Wallcovering Industry,* unpublished paper, Michigan State University.

"One-Source Programs Spur Chains' Wallpaper Growth," *Discount Store News,* March 18, 1985, p. 17.

"Rollbacks," *Money,* September 1984, p. 42.

CASE 4-3: The Recall of Perrier Brand Bottled Water

INTRODUCTION

In the 1980s, Perrier brand bottled water had become a preferred substitute to soda and alcoholic beverages among many adult Americans. During that time, health-conscious Americans had thirsted for this bottled water as an alternative to highly caloric and alcoholic beverages. Furthermore, the increasing concern about water pollution and purity helped to spawn the successful launch of Perrier in the United States in the late 1970s and helped to make bottled water the fastest-growing industry in the United States.

Since the introduction of Perrier brand sparkling water in the United States, Perrier's earnings have skyrocketed. In 1989, Perrier brand bottled water took in $119 million in sales from the United States alone. But this remarkable success turned into a disaster.

On February 9, 1990, the Perrier Group of America announced that thirteen bottles of Perrier brand bottled water had been found to be contaminated with traces of benzene. Benzene, a clear solvent linked to cancer in laboratory animals, was found in excessive amounts in bottles distributed to the United States. As a preventive measure, the company recalled 72 million bottles from 250,000 North American outlets. Further findings showed high benzene concentrations in bottles distributed elsewhere and on February 14, 1990, Source Perrier recalled the bottled water worldwide, a total of 160 million bottles. The world recall caused many problems for Perrier: lost market share, legal problems, loss of shelf space, consumer distrust, and shareholder distrust, among others. Can Perrier jump back on its feet and regain lost market share? Can it ever win back consumers' trust? How Perrier deals with these problems is critical to the future success of its infamous bottled water and to the success of the company.

BOTTLED WATER INDUSTRY

The bottled water industry is growing rapidly worldwide. Some of the reasons for this increased growth are (1) the high profile of brand leaders, Perrier and Evian, (2) the use of bottled water as a mixer, (3) the search for a sophisticated alternative to alcohol,

The Recall of Perrier Brand Bottled Water was written by Robert S. Bradley.

(4) consumer health consciousness, and (5) recent reports of increasing water pollution from high levels of nitrates and erosion of many sewage systems.

In general, there are two kinds of water producers, still-water producers (water similar to tap water) and sparkling or seltzer water producers (water with fizz). The majority of bottled still-water companies sell spring water as well as less expensive drinking water that comes from filtered municipal water.

In the United States, bottled water producers of both kinds rely upon the baby boomers' obsession with health—a huge factor related to industry prosperity. Therefore, many bottled water companies are placing their interest in the United States where the health obsession is burgeoning and the market for imported bottled water is booming. In 1989, Americans drank less than a quarter of a gallon of bottled water per person compared with more than 48 gallons for soft drinks. Bottled water's share is expected to increase dramatically. Bottled water is the fastest growing segment of the United States beverage industry. Table 1 shows the average annual growth rates of U.S. beverages for the years 1985–1989. Sales are moving more than three times the growth rate of soft drinks.

Internationally, bottled water is booming as well. Bottled water is also the fastest-growing drink in the United Kingdom, although adult soft drinks (as they are called in the United Kingdom) are a small market at present. Analysts expect that adult soft drinks will grow due to a range of trends relating to lifestyles, gender, affluence, and consumption.

INDUSTRY DEVELOPMENTS IN THE UNITED STATES

In America's huge and growing bottled water market, more than 400 brands divided up $2.17 billion in sales in 1988, according to the Beverage Marketing Corporation, an industry research group. About 95 percent of the nearly 2 billion gallons of water is domestic and sells for less than $1 a gallon, mainly in supermarkets and convenience stores. There is an uneven demand for bottled water in the United States. For example, of the total United States consumption, 19.9 percent is in California. See Table 2 for a complete breakdown. The cost of water in the United States from the small foreign market is considerably more. This is primarily due to the expense of shipping and distribution. Perrier, for example, costs $.99 to $1.09 for a 23-ounce bottle in super-

TABLE 1   AVERAGE ANNUAL GROWTH, 1985–1989

Bottled water	11.1%
Soft drinks	3.2
Milk	1.5
Tea	1.2
Beer	0.4
Coffee	− 0.4
Wine	− 0.2
Distilled spirits	− 2.6

Source: Beverage Marketing Corporation.

TABLE 2 WHERE UNITED STATES BOTTLED WATER CONSUMERS LIVE
figures do not include Club Soda or Seltzer

	Gallons of sparkling and still water consumed per capita in 1988
California	19.9
Arizona	17.1
Louisiana	11.1
Massachusetts	9.9
Maryland/Washington, D.C.	8.4
Florida	7.5
Texas	6.3
New York	6.2
Pennsylvania	3.6

Source: Beverage Marketing Corporation, Impact Databank

markets, but $2.50 or more for an 11-ounce bottle in restaurants. San Pellegrino, a bottled water from Italy, costs more than $5.40 a gallon retail.

Of the 400 brands in the United States market, only a few dominate nationwide. This is because bottled water brands are regional by nature. The expense of shipping and distributing water keeps the brands and the businesses regional and, therefore, near their water sources. Of the large national leaders, Perrier bottled waters have a commanding lead, at 18.2 percent of the United States bottled water market. McKesson is second largest with its Sparkletts, Alhambra, and Crystal brands, most of which are sold in supermarkets or delivered to homes or offices. Clorox is fifth largest, with its Deer Park and Deep Rock brands giving it 1.9 percent. Evian ranks only seventh, with a market share of 1.7 percent. See Table 3 for a more complete listing. According to Beverage Marketing Corporation, the leading brands in the United States market, based on 1988 market share, is as follows:

Arrowhead	7.7%
Sparkletts	5.9%
Perrier	5.7%
Poland Spring	3.5%

TABLE 3 1988 UNITED STATES BOTTLED WATER MARKET

Perrier-owned Brands	18.2
Anjou International	5.2
McKesson Corporation	5.2
Suntory International	4.2
Clorox	1.9
Culligan	1.8
Evian	1.7
Sammons	1.4
Belmont Springs	1.0
Black Mountain	0.8

Source: Beverage Marketing Corporation.

COMPANY BACKGROUND

Perrier is the largest bottled water company in the United States. Besides Perrier brand bottled water, nine other American brands help the company to dominate the United States market. Among them is the best-selling Arrowhead, a still water similar to tap water. Perrier acquired the Arrowhead division from Beatrice Foods of Monterey, California. The business, with 1988 sales of $200 million, consists largely of delivering 5-gallon jugs of Arrowhead in California and Arizona, Great Bear in Mid-Atlantic states, and Ozarka in Texas to homes and businesses.

Volume sales for Perrier have jumped remarkably in the past few years. Impact International, a beverage industry research publication, estimates that Perrier sold 32 million gallons, or more than half of the 56 million gallons sold in 1989. This compares with only 10 million gallons for Evian, more than 2 million for San Pellegrino, and less than 2 million for Vittel, a French water bottled by a unit of Nestlé. In the imported-water segment (48 million gallons), Perrier was the market leader in 1989 with a 57 percent share. In 1989, Perrier Group's United States sales were $640 million, up 16 percent from the previous year. Of the total United States sales, $119 million came from the Perrier brand.

PERRIER BRAND BOTTLED WATER

Perrier brand bottled water became so popular in the 1980s that it won a unique niche in the psyche and vocabulary of the time. According to Dan Rose, a bartender at a Manhattan restaurant, Perrier had come to mean mineral water. "People ask for Perrier when they want mineral water," Rose said, "the same way they ask for a Kleenex when they want a tissue."[1] In seven years, sales have jumped 190 percent. Perrier entered the American market in 1976 with fanfare and uncanny timing, benefitting from the switch of hard liquor and the attendant fitness craze.

In the world market, Perrier is doing extremely well. The most recent figures show that while the Perrier brand had a 5.7 percent share of the total market in 1988, its other brands accounted for another 18 percent, according to Beverage Marketing. More than one-fifth of Perrier Group's revenues come from the Perrier brand. But Perrier is not only producing high revenues, it is also producing high profits, especially at the retail level. One Perrier distributor said Perrier brand is among the most profitable items in grocery sales, with a standard 18 to 20 percent profit margin at retail.

PERRIER RECALL

In February 1990, Perrier voluntarily recalled 72 million bottles of the brand in the United States because traces of benzene had been found in some of its products. After first pulling off only bottles exported to the United States and Canada, the French company extended the recall to every bottle of Perrier in the world. Government officials in North Carolina, who once used Perrier as their standard dilutant in labo-

---

[1] Nancy Gibbs, "Let Them Drink Seltzer," *Time,* February 26, 1990, p. 43.

ratory tests, found traces of the cancer-causing solvent benzene in some of the bottles. The amounts of the hydrocarbon found were about 15 parts per billion. These were relatively low levels, but they far exceeded the U.S. Food and Drug Administration's (FDA) limit of 5 parts per billion. Source Perrier, the Paris-based parent company, said world stocks of the mineral water totaled 160 million bottles and were worth $70 million.

At first, company officials in France said the benzene had come from a cleanser used by a careless worker to remove grease from machinery. The cleaned machinery was on the bottling lines for Perrier for North America. But when traces of benzene were found in Perrier selling in the Netherlands and Denmark, company officials offered a different explanation. They said that benzene is naturally present in carbon dioxide, the gas that makes Perrier bubbly. Some scientists were baffled by this disclosure. Although benzene is naturally found in certain foods, it is more commonly known as a petroleum-based distillate used in many manufacturing processes. "I think it's probably man-made pollution if you have benzene in the water in certain concentrations," Clifford Morelli, an engineer and consultant to the beverage industry, said. "But however it got there—if by nature or by man—it's contaminated.[2] Perrier managing director said the substance is usually filtered out, but workers failed to change the filters and the benzene had seeped into the water, thereby affecting all bottling lines, not just those in North America.

As a result of the contamination, the company hired a hydrologist and environmental consultant, Duncan M. Finlayson, a director for the Robertson Group P.L.C. Finlayson analyzed and investigated the source of the problem. Finlayson said later that the charcoal filters that screen out impurities in carbon dioxide gas were now being monitored every two hours at the Vergeze plant, instead of weekly. Based on his company's records and procedures, Mr. Finlayson said there was a "supposition" that the plant had produced benzene-contaminated water since last June. He also noted that the amounts of benzene found in contaminated bottles were less than the dose of benzene a person would get from breathing fumes while filling the gas tank of a car. Other producers have since checked their waters' purity to prevent any similar dilemmas.

French mineral water producer, Vittel, withdrew its Hepar brand from stores for pollution checks. Vittel recalled 500,000 bottles of Hepar, which sells almost exclusively in France, after some supplies were polluted by a coal filter. "The contaminated supplies have all already been destroyed but since a lot of consumers seemed confused about whether the bottles they had bought were safe we decided to withdraw all stocks," said managing director Alan Dorfner.[3]

COMPETITOR ACTIONS

While Perrier was generating confusion, rivals hoped to generate profits. Just as Perrier was busy with its worldwide recall, Evian Waters of France was launching its biggest

---

[2] E. S. Browning and Alix M. Freedman, "Perrier Expands North American Recall to Rest of Globe," *Wall Street Journal,* February 15, 1990, p. B1.

[3] "Mineral Water Withdrawn by a Second Bottling Firm," *Wall Street Journal,* February 22, 1990, p. C18.

advertising campaign ever. "It's coincidence," said Evian CEO David Daniel. "We just happened to be ready to kick off our 1990 advertising. . . . We have no intention of trying to capitalize on their misfortune."[4] In 1990, Evian has increased advertising more than 50 percent to an estimated $6 million. These plans included tripling the spending on the brand Saratoga, Evian's sparkling water that directly competes with Perrier. Evian Waters, unlike Perrier, emphasized that Evian brand bottled water (a still water) is appropriate for drinking at any time of the day. As a carbonated mineral water marketed mainly as a nonalcoholic aperitif, Perrier tends to be taken at meal times. Thus, more than one-third of its bottles are shipped to restaurants, hotels, and bars, compared to 5 to 10 percent for Evian.

PepsiCo also entered the market by test marketing their H₂Oh! bottled water in Denver but took a "wait and see" attitude about expanding their market area. G. Heilman Brewing Co. took advantage of Perrier's predicament with a campaign that stressed the purity of its LaCroix sparkling water sold in the Midwest. Other competitors, partly fearing that a Perrier attack would hurt the entire 2.2 billion market, still hoped to increase sales. Quibell Springs increased its bottling capacity by 50 percent to meet customer orders from distributors in twenty-six states. Quibell Corp. took orders for 4.5 million bottles of sparkling water in just one day. They normally sell that amount in about six months.

CONSEQUENCES OF THE CONTAMINATION AND RECALL

As a result of the contamination and recall, Perrier established a toll-free number for consumers to call with questions. However, they did not intend to publicize the number, leaving that decision up to individual supermarket chains. Furthermore, Perrier did not mount a campaign to inform the public of what actually occurred. Instead, Perrier used media reports to communicate with consumers. Many experts feel that this "somewhat passive" approach could prove detrimental to future success. Frank Blod, a partner at the New England Consulting Group, states that if the proper information is not communicated to consumers in a proactive manner, one of the risks could be the potential for misinformation and, ultimately, rumors. Nevertheless, the company believed it would be more effective to unleash a media blitz when it re-enters the market.

Company executives say they would not pay any retailer fees or slotting allowances to get back on the shelves. They believe that many retailers have saved their space by stocking shelves with other Perrier brands such as Poland Spring, Arrowhead, and Calistoga sparkling waters.

Can Perrier regain lost market share? Ronald Davis, Perrier Group president and CEO, thinks so. Davis said that in research commissioned by Burson-Marsteller, the marketer's crisis managment team, 85 percent of Perrier's consumers said they would buy the product again and 90 percent said they believed the company acted responsibly. These numbers led Mr. Davis to predict Perrier will regain 85 percent of its sales by the end of 1991. Tom Pirco, president of BevMark, a beverage consulting

---

[4] Winters, Patricia, "Evian Readies Push as Perrier Pulls Out," *Advertising Age,* February 19, 1990, p. 2.

firm, had first expected Perrier to lose 15 percent of its gross sales. Now, he believes that if the relaunch goes smoothly, sales should fall no more than 5 percent and may eventually surpass previous performances.

THE RELAUNCH

Perrier sparkling water returned on the shelves of Paris in March and started in mid-April to return to America. Because Perrier brand water is bottled at one source, the spring in Vergeze, France, it took several months to refill the worldwide pipeline due to time allotted for bottling, loading, shipping, clearing customs, distribution, and delivery by trucks. The expected date of return to some of the larger United States cities was as follows:

New York	April 26
Miami	May 2
Baltimore/Washington	May 4
Los Angeles	May 8
Philadelphia	May 10
Boston	May 15
Chicago	May 22
San Francisco	May 24

The bottles returning to the United States were to be accompanied by a $25 million marketing campaign. On the day each market is reentered, the company will start a two-week television and newspaper campaign with the theme ''We're back'' and will declare that ''the problem has been fixed.'' The tagline says, ''Perrier. Worth waiting for.'' In promotions, Perrier will conduct sampling in fifteen top markets via portable ''Perrier cafes,'' complete with staffers in ''We're back'' apparel. Advertisements will appear in *USA Today,* the *Wall Street Journal,* and other newspapers in fifteen large metropolitan markets. Radio advertisements will follow print ones. The advertisements will run through the summer, when Perrier is expected to be fully restocked. Then a more traditional campaign is expected.

QUESTIONS

1 Develop a map of the distribution channels for bottled water. What are the major retail outlets? Who are the channel intermediaries?
2 Should Perrier have handled the recall differently?
3 Evaluate Perrier's strategy for reintroduction. Is it likely that Perrier will reach the same level of distribution intensity it had prior to the recall?
4 What additions or changes would you suggest to Perrier's strategy for reintroduction?

BIBLIOGRAPHY

Baker, Russell, ''The Joy of Daring,'' *New York Times,* February 21, 1990, p. A17.
Browning, E. S., ''Perrier's Recall Drives Down Its Stock Price,'' *Wall Street Journal,* February 13, 1990, p. A16.

Browning, E. S., "Perrier Sets U.S. Relaunch of Its Water; Analysts Become Cautiously Optimistic," *Wall Street Journal,* April 23, 1990, p. B5.

Browning, E. S., and Ali M. Freedman, "Perrier Expands North American Recall to Rest of Globe," *Wall Street Journal,* February 15, 1990, pp. B1, B6.

Freedman, M. Alix, and Thomas R. King, "Perrier's Strategy in the Wake of Recall: Will It Leave Brand in Rough Waters?," *Wall Street Journal,* February 12, 1990, p. B1.

Gibbs, Nancy, "Let Them Drink Seltzer," *Time,* February 26, 1990, p. 43.

King, Thomas R., "For Perrier, New Woes Spring Up," *Wall Street Journal,* April 26, 1990, p. B1, B12.

Kreitzman, Leon, "Food and Drink: Going Soft," *Marketing,* January 12, 1989, pp. 33, 36.

Magiera, March, "Bottled Waters Spring Up: National Marketers Plunge into Market," *Advertising Age,* September 21, 1987, p. 24, 83.

Miller, Annetta, and Elizabeth Bradburn, "Perrier Loses Its Fizz," *Newsweek,* February 26, 1990, p. 53.

"Mineral Water Withdrawn by a Second Bottling Firm," *Wall Street Journal,* February 22, 1990, p. C18.

"Perrier Drops Hal Riney, Picks Waring & LaRosa," *Wall Street Journal,* March 29, 1990, p. B6.

"Perrier Water's Relaunch Is Behind Schedule in U.S.," *Wall Street Journal,* April 12, 1990, p. A11.

Pouschine, Tatiana, "Perrier, Your Bubbles Are Too Big," *Forbes,* May 1, 1990, p. 106, 107, 112.

Ramirez, Anthony, "Perrier Recall: How Damaging Is It?" *New York Times,* February 13, 1990, pp. C1, C5.

Ramirez, Anthony, "Perrier Rival Talks of 'Serendipity'," *New York Times,* February 24, 1990, pp. 33, 37.

Ramirez, Anthony, "Perrier to Return to U.S. Early Next Month," *New York Times,* February 13, 1990, pp. C1, C4.

Rothenberg, Randall, "Perrier Plans Return with a New Voice," *New York Times,* March 29, 1990, p. C16.

"Sacre bleu! Bubble Trouble," *Time,* February 19, 1990, p. 67.

Schnorbus, Paula, "Water, Water Everywhere," *Marketing & Media Decisions,* September 1987, pp. 97–112.

Seligman, Daniel, "Perrier Speaks," *Fortune,* March 12, 1990, p. 139.

Sellers, Patricia, "Perrier Plots Its Comeback." *Fortune,* April 23, 1990, pp. 277–278.

Winters, Patricia, "Evian Readies Push as Perrier Pulls Out," *Advertising Age,* February 19, 1990, pp. 2, 74.

Winters, Patricia, "Perrier Rivals Refuse to Make Waves," *Advertising Age,* March 12, 1990, p. 74.

Winters, Patricia, "Perrier's Back," *Advertising Age,* April 23, 1990, pp. 1, 34.

CASE 4-4: Third World Institution Building: The Cali Experiment

INTRODUCTION

In the mid-1970s, officers in the Inter-American Development Bank were reviewing a joint loan application for $18 million requested by the government of Columbia, the municipality of Cali, and the state government of Valle.[1] The requested funds were to be used for the construction and implementation of a new central marketplace in Cali.

GEOGRAPHIC AREA

Cali, at the time of the planned central market establishment, was a city with about 1 million inhabitants located in the southwest area of Colombia. Cali served as the principal commercial center for the 125-mile-long Cauca Valley. Most of the agricultural land in the valley was concentrated in large farms. The major exceptions were fruits and vegetables, which were produced by small growers. The valley provided the principal food source for Cali.

A wide distribution of income existed in Cali. Table 1 illustrates dispersion of monthly income per household and per capita. Given the fact that the exchange rate at that time equaled 16.90 pesos per United States dollar, the relational income level was low.

CALI URBAN FOOD DISTRIBUTION SYSTEM

Food for Cali inhabitants represented a significant proportion of disposable family income. The average family spent 42 percent of its disposable income on food. The lowest quarter of the population spent 80 percent, with the second lowest quarter spending about 66 percent of total disposable income on food.

The traditional distribution system, which evolved to supply food to the city, originally consisted of a central market (the Galeria Central), five satellite public markets, a network of free-standing retail stores, and numerous wholesalers. The characteristics of each set of institutions are described below.

THE CENTRAL AND SATELLITE MARKETS

The central market, the Galeria Central, operated by the municipality, was located in the center of the business district. Constructed in 1897, the Galeria Central was the trading hub of Cali. The facility housed 2410 retailers involved in selling most food products. The five satellite public markets located around the city served to house

---

[1] This case was originally written by Donald A. Taylor and is based on the facts presented in *Market Coordination in the Development of the Cauca Valley Region, Colombia,* Marketing in Developing Communities Series, Research Report No. 5, Latin American Studies Center, Michigan State University, East Lansing, Michigan, 1970. However, the situation illustrated concerning the construction of a new central market is fictitious.

TABLE 1   PER CAPITA AND PER HOUSEHOLD INCOME (IN PESOS) AND THE POPULATION DISTRI-
BUTION CLASSIFIED BY LEVEL OF DISPOSABLE CASE INCOME, CALI*

Range of per capita income	Percent of households	Percent of people	Income per capital		Income per household	
			Mean	Median	Mean	Median
1 Less than 125	20.3	25.5	86	92	686	600
2 126–240	27.8	29.1	176	167	1,167	1,000
3 241–500	28.7	25.3	352	333	1,962	2,000
4 More than 500	23.2	20.1	1,157	893	6,340	5,000
All families	100.0	100.0	395	214	2,500	1,500

* Based upon reports of the 520 out of 625 households who provided income information on the Proyecto Integrado de Mercadeo Urbano y Rural General Consumer Survey in Cali.

1345 additional retail operators. In combination, the central and five satellite markets constituted the traditional retail structure of the public market system. In addition, a large number of specialized wagon vendors, particularly in fruits and vegetables, operated from sidewalks near the various public markets. The public market retailers constituted 42 percent of total foot outlets in Cali and handled 20 percent of all retail food sales.

In anticipation of the 1970 Pan-American games, the city politicans decided to close the Galeria Central and reassigned resident retail operators to the five satellite public markets. The Galeria, in continuous operation for over seventy years, had become increasingly undesirable for handling food. Consumer shopping patterns were forced to shift to satellite public markets and to higher-cost neighborhood stores. Unfortunately, the satellite markets were not well-served by public transportation and inconveniently located for a large number of purchasers. In general, the food distribution system was inadequate. It was felt that a need existed for an institution similar to the old central market; however, it was necessary to consider a new location. A proposal was developed to establish a new central market structure at the outskirts of Cali. An architectural plan was completed, incorporating distribution innovations at a total expenditure of $36 million. The loan request was for local funding from the Inter-American Development Bank.

STRUCTURE OF PRIVATE RETAIL OUTLETS

In addition to the public market retail structure, a wide variety of private neighborhood retail food stores existed in Cali. These stores varied significantly in their size and method of operation. The private retail outlets were classified as personal-service, self-service, or specialty stores.

Personal-Service Stores

There were 4241 personal-service stores scattered throughout Cali, with the largest concentrated around the old Galeria Central location. These stores, the most common form of retailing, sold about 50 percent of all food. They offered different assortments of food products with the exception of fruits and vegetables. The personal-service stores could be subclassified on the basis of the produce assortment sold. *Tiendas* offered a narrow line of processed foods and grains plus limited household cleaning and personal-care products. Small and large *graneros* offered a broader product assortment than did *tiendas*. The final subclassification was retailers who only sold meat.

Self-Service Stores

Self-service, at the time of the loan activity, had not come of age. Only fifty-four self-service stores existed in Cali. In combination they sold about 13 percent of the total food to a segment consisting primarily of high-income families. Nineteen supermarkets offered full-line assortments in a self-service shopping environment. There were also seventeen cooperative food stores. In addition, four supermarkets were operated by the government and fourteen general-merchandise stores were owned by five chains. The high-volume stores did sell at lower margins, using some items as price leaders.

Specialty Stores

As in most developing countries, a high degree of retail specialization existed in Cali. A total of 864 stores specialized in poultry, eggs, dairy products, and meats. Specialty stores, along with twenty-four retail-wholesale combination outlets, represented 17 percent of total consumer food sales.

In total, there were 8914 retailers in Cali. About 42 percent, primarily those operating in the public markets were, in part, subsidized by the municipal government.

THE WHOLESALE STRUCTURE

The area immediately around the old Galeria Central was the food wholesaling center. Seventy percent of the total city food supply was handled by this wholesale structure. Only fresh milk, poultry, eggs, soft drinks, and selected processed foods that were distributed directly to retail stores bypassed this wholesale structure. Ninety percent of fruits and vegetables, 80 percent of meat, and 90 percent of all grains and basic processed goods were handled by specialized wholesalers and wholesaler-retailers in the area. A wide variety of related businesses, such as hardware stores, drugstores, packaging materials outlets, restaurants, bars, and transportation companies, were also attracted to the area.

Of 868 wholesalers in Cali, 103 specialized in grains and processed foods, 231 in meats, 450 in fruits and vegetables, and 84 in poultry and eggs. Similar to the retailers, each wholesaler was small and highly specialized. The size of its physical facilities afforded limited storage space. The typical wholesaler carried two days' supply or less.

TABLE 2   AVERAGE NUMBER OF PURCHASES PER MONTH PER ITEM WITHIN PRODUCT GROUP
BY TYPE OF RETAILER, CALI

	Self-service	Personal service	Public market
Grains	3.0	3.2	4.0
Processed staples	2.5	3.2	3.0
Fruits and vegetables	15.0	25.0	20.0
Meat	20.0	25.0	30.0
Poultry and eggs	7.0	6.0	9.0
Milk	30.0	30.0	—

Source: Proyecto Integrado de Mercadeo Urbano y Rural, retailer survey.

RETAILER-WHOLESALER RELATIONSHIPS

The restricted scope and scale of food wholesaling made it very difficult to supply retailers with value-added services such as consistent availability, quality, credit, delivery, and price stability. Because the wholesale structure was too fragmented, retailers needed to purchase from a number of different establishments to accomplish a full assortment of desired products. Table 2 shows the average number of purchases per month, per item by different types of retailers. It is estimated that a *tienda* operator handling five fruits and vegetables would have to conduct 125 transactions per month in order to procure desired products. Only four out of all the wholesalers had sales personnel to facilitate transactions. The typical purchase pattern was for retail representatives to make buying trips to wholesalers to collect an assortment. The fragmented wholesale structure created a serious logistics challenge. Faced with numerous small-quantity purchases, the actual physical collection and transportation of products was a serious barrier. The retailer owner-operator, a class that included most retailers, spent about 75 percent of the time supplying the store.

Continuous product availability was another ever-present problem. The small scale of both retail and wholesale establishments rendered storage almost impossible. Most of the facilities were old homes that were inadequate for conducting wholesale operations. If rains prevailed for two days, roads from the Cauca Valley became impassable, resulting in disruption of food supply to wholesalers. Within four days all stocks would be depleted. The flow of essential agricultural inputs from Cali to the Cauca Valley, such as equipment, feed, seed, and fertilizers, was equally vulnerable to the inadequacies of the transport sector.

WHOLESALER-SUPPLIER RELATIONSHIPS

Exhibits 1, 2, and 3 map channel structure for tomatoes, rice, and fertilizers. These channel structures are representative of those typical for fruits, vegetables, processed grains, and agricultural inputs. In many respects, the primary supply channels match the mini-retailing and wholesaling structure of the urban distribution system. Table 3 illustrates supplier relationships for fruit and vegetable wholesalers. The number of purchases was significant, and the associated transport requirements were an important

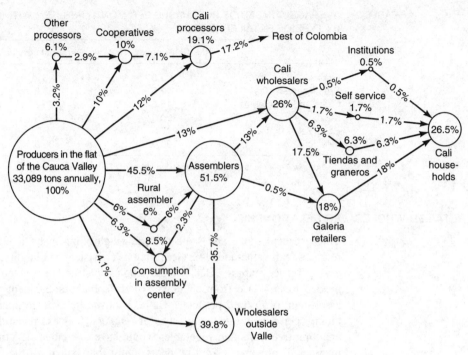

EXHIBIT 1   Market channel for tomatoes, California.

problem. Sixty-two percent of the wholesalers were forced to purchase products FOB the valley. Thus, wholesalers were forced to absorb the risk and cost of transportation.

Products were typically moved from the Cauca Valley to Cali by truck. Most truck operators were independents. In selected situations, they actually purchased products outright for future sale in Cali, which more or less made them primary channel participants. Products delivered to the wholesale area typically passed numerous retail stores that eventually would be supplied by the wholesalers. Local culture and custom, plus a lack of adequate information technology, prohibited direct store delivery. Even though most product distribution from the valley to Cali occurred at night, about 330 trucks still entered the wholesale area daily. Gridlock from trucks, pushcarts, and taxis was overwhelming.

Cali, to say the least, faced serious food distribution problems as officers of the Inter-American Development Bank considered the loan request. Cali represents a classical case of the accumulation of individual decisions into a combined distribution infrastructure that was inadequate to support food logistics and transactional requirements. All agreed that corrective action was necessary. However, would the proposed new Galeria Central work? Was a location on the fringe of the city really suitable, given the location of the wholesale structure? In fact, was the real problem the deficiencies of the wholesale and the freight transportation systems as contrasted to the

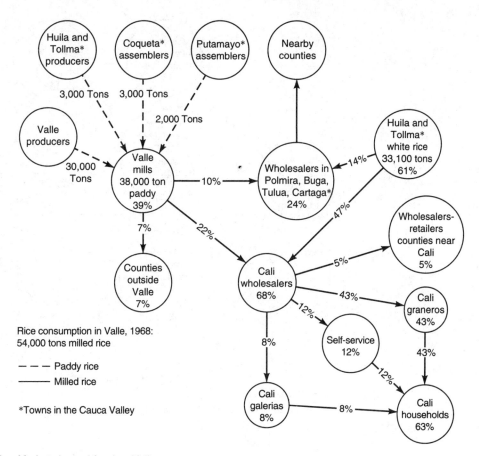

EXHIBIT 2   Market channel for rice, Valle.

lack of a central market? How would the large number of retailers who operated on a free-market basis react to the plan to recreate a "new and improved" Galeria that would be subsidized by the government loan? If the idea to proceed was funded, how should the new Galeria be institutionalized? What procedures should be followed to assure that the desired changes would result from reestablishing the Galeria?

The Cali experience illustrates how some basic and essential functions can be neglected as a result of poor planning and lack of a full understanding of the universal relationships upon which channel arrangements build. If a plan were derived that would result in the proper infrastructure and business alignments, how would or could it be implemented? Even if a fail-safe plan were devised, the road to full implementation would be a difficult transition to manage.

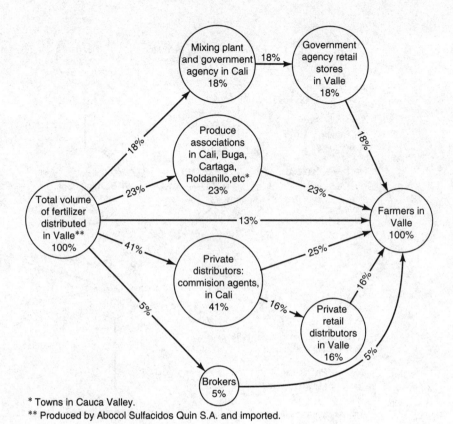

* Towns in Cauca Valley.
** Produced by Abocol Sulfacidos Quin S.A. and imported.

EXHIBIT 3   Market channel for fertilizers, Valle.

TABLE 3   SUPPLIER RELATIONSHIP OF FRUIT AND VEGETABLE WHOLESALERS, CALI

	Potatoes	Tomatoes	Platanos	Other
Major supply sources:				
Direct from farmers	10%	30%	38%	32%
Negociantes outside Cali	83	31	37	43
Negociantes in Cali	7	—	—	7
Truckers in Cali	—	21	15	9
Other	—	18	10	9
Percentage buying from one supplier	8	28	39	22
Average number of suppliers talked to before buying	3.2	3.0	3.0	3.6
Percentage of purchases on which credit is obtained	76	83	82	89
Average number of days credit received	9.6	3.5	4.6	5.2

Source: Proyecto Integrado de Mercadeo Urbano y Rural, wholesaler study.

QUESTIONS

1 What were the major problems associated with the old system when Galeria Central was in operation?

2 What solutions to these problems do you suggest? Would you have recommended closing Galeria Central?

3 Will construction of a new central market on the outskirts of the city solve some of the distribution problems?

4 If the new central market is constructed, what activities would you recommend be conducted in it?

CASE 4-5: Hershey Goes Home

It was mid-1989 in Hershey, Pennsylvania, and Mr. Roger Clarke, Vice President of International Sales for Hershey International, a division of Hershey Foods Corporation, was reviewing the Australian experience. He had a board meeting to attend in a week's time and had to present his assessment of what the cause of failure had been in Australia. Was it a strategic mistake or had implementation been the problem, and what strategy would be appropriate for reentry?

COMPANY BACKGROUND

In 1913, Milton Snavely Hershey sold his caramel confectionery business to establish a chocolate-making factory in what is now Hershey, Pennsylvania. His interest in chocolate making had been sparked by the new chocolate-making equipment he had first seen at the Chicago exposition of 1893. His innovations in the mass production of chocolate confectionery and his emphasis on product quality ensured his success.

Milton Hershey's focus on quality remained a key emphasis for the corporation, together with a strong focus on customers' needs. Consumer value, new-product development, a commitment to quality, and strong trade relations remained high priorities for the firm. Its financial growth and success rested on a two-pronged strategy: high promotional/advertising expenditure (which in 1970 was 3.6 percent of consolidated net sales and in 1981 was 8.5 percent) and lowered manufacturing costs through improved productivity, plant modernizations, and more efficient use of facilities, as Table 1 shows.

The corporation's objective was to become a major diversified food company. In trying to meet this objective, it has rarely been tempted to stray from its core chocolate business. Its sharp focus has ensured that, for the American consumer at least, Hershey and chocolate have become synonymous.

To ease the uncertainty caused by fluctuating prices and the vagaries of the world sugar and cocoa bean markets, Hershey was tempted to diversify through the purchase of the Friendly Ice Cream Corporation in 1979. Friendly was a chain of over 700 family restaurants and ice cream shops. This change of strategic direction proved

Hershey Goes Home was written by G. Peter Dapiran.

TABLE 1   SELECTED FINANCIAL RESULTS OF HERSHEY FOODS CORPORATION (Millions of United States Dollars)

	1984	1985	1986	1987	1988
Net sales	1423	1527	1635	1864	2168
Cost of sales	935	982	1032	1150	1326
Selling/marketing/administration	310	345	387	468	576
Income–continuing operations	88	97	107	124	145
Net income	109	112	133	148	214
Depreciation	23	28	31	35	44
Advertising	71	77	84	97	99
Promotion	95	105	123	171	230
Payroll	208	222	239	264	298
Working capital	188	225	174	190	274
Total assets	1052	1116	1262	1544	1765
Long-term debt	103	87	186	281	233
Stockholders' equity	661	728	728	832	1006

Source: Adapted from *Hershey Inc. Annual Report, 1989.*

unsuccessful; the chain did not perform to expectations, and in 1988 Friendly was sold to allow Hershey to concentrate on its expertise—the manufacture, marketing, and distribution of packaged consumer foods, mainly chocolate, confectionery, and pasta products. It pursued these tasks through its main operating divisions—Hershey Chocolate USA, Hershey International, Hershey Pasta Group, and Hershey Canada.

The costs of its other major chocolate-making raw materials—milk, almonds, and peanuts—were all unaffected by international market fluctuations.

To pursue its diversification and growth objectives, Hershey embarked on a string of significant acquisitions in North America.

In late 1986 it purchased for $102 million The Dietrich Corporation, thereby acquiring the Luden's and Queen Anne confectionery product lines. In mid-1988 the United States confectionery operations of Cadbury Schweppes were bought for $285 million. This purchase included the operating assets of the confectionery business and the license to manufacture, market, and distribute Cadbury brands in the United States. Integration of the Cadbury operations into the Hershey operations brought with it significant cost savings while catapulting Hershey into the position of market leader with 20.5 percent share of the United States confectionery market. Archrival Mars, Inc., trailed with an 18.5 percent share.

The mid-1987 $162 million purchase of the Canadian confectionery and snack nut operations of Nabisco Brands Limited allowed Hershey Canada, Inc., to increase its market presence significantly. This acquisition was part of Hershey's strategy to become the low-cost producer in Canada and to rationalize the excess chocolate production capacity there.

The acquisition was followed by a year of consolidation and rationalization. Hershey closed its acquired Toronto plant, expanded the Smith Falls, Ontario, facilities, and introduced just-in-time philosophies in the plant. The closure of Sherbrooke, Quebec, was also planned. This would allow construction of a 110,000-square-foot distribution center at Smiths Falls, which would lead to reduced distribution costs and an increased concentration on customer service.

In late 1989, Hershey entered the refrigerated foods market with the introduction of chocolate bar–flavored puddings. Research showed that the majority of dry and refrigerated puddings sold were chocolate flavored. Entry was reliant on the strong consumer association between Hershey and chocolate.

THE UNITED STATES CONFECTIONERY MARKET

The United States market was dominated by the two giants, Hershey and Mars, Inc., who between them had the top ten selling chocolate bars and 39 percent of the confectionery market, as shown in Table 2. Jacobs Suchard and Nestlé, the Swiss multinational confectioners, both came in a poor third, each with 6.7 percent of the market. Fourth place, with 5.6 percent, was filled by Leaf, Inc., owned by the Finnish company Huhtamaki Oy.

The all-important per capita consumption of confectionery had shown little growth over a number of years and seemed a long way short of the industry target of 25 pounds by 1995 (Table 3). Forecast demographic changes alone were not likely to help in achieving this ambitious target.

Expansion of the market hinged on strategies aimed at increasing per capita consumption, especially through products developed for the adult market. Research showed that consumers over eighteen years consumed 55 percent of all confectionery and that most consumption took place in the home. New products developed in response to customer health concerns would also help to increase consumption. Strategies to promote consumption of existing lines included increasing shelf space, having

TABLE 2   TOP 10 CHOCOLATE BARS IN THE UNITED STATES OF AMERICA SALES BY CANDY AND TOBACCO DISTRIBUTORS

Product	Manufacturer	Rank	
		1988	1987
Snickers bar	Mars	1	1
Reese's Peanut Butter Cups	Hershey	2	2
M&M's peanut chocolate candies	Mars	3	3
Kit Kat	Hershey	4	5
M&M's plain chocolate candies	Mars	5	4
Hershey's milk chocolate with almonds	Hershey	6	6
Milky Way bar	Mars	7	7
Twix caramel cookie bars	Mars	8	12
Snickers bar, king size	Mars	9	13
3 Musketeers bars	Mars	10	9

Source: Adapted from J. Echeandia, and J. Kitt, "State of the Industry," *Candy Industry,* July 1989, pp. H2–H18. Reprinted with permission of Edgell Communications. Copyright © July 1989, Candy Industry Magazine.

TABLE 3   UNITED STATES CONFECTIONERY MARKET CONSUMPTION

	1980	1982	1984	1985	1986	1987	1988
Annual (million pounds)							
Chocolate type	1845	2069	2317	2328	2333	2380	2400
Nonchocolate type	1576	1642	1945	2044	1909	1891	1900
Total*	3561	3886	4458	4570	4441	4472	4600
Per capita (pounds)							
Chocolate type	8.1	8.9	9.8	9.7	9.7	9.8	9.9
Nonchocolate type	6.9	7.1	8.2	8.5	7.9	7.8	7.8
Total	15.7	16.7	18.9	19.1	18.4	18.3	18.5

* Totals do not equal the sum of the two components because some confectionery consumption is not classified as either.
   Source: Adapted from *U.S. Industrial Outlook 1989,* U.S. Department of Commerce, January 1989, pp. 39-17–39-21.

multiple-store locations for confectionery sales points, manufacturing larger packs for take-home enjoyment, and making more stock available on the retail shelf.

Another effective strategy had been to position confectionery as a snack food, a market significantly larger than confectionery, alongside the traditional potato chips, cookies, and pretzels. Mars scored a coup when it purchased the right to name Snickers and M&M's the official snack foods of the 1984 Olympic Games.

HERSHEY INTERNATIONAL

Although the North American market was of extreme importance to Hershey, the company recognized the strategic importance of expanding into international markets and actively looked at international growth opportunities.

That an interest in the global market place was an integral part of its thinking was revealed in its mission statement, which read:

Hershey Foods Corporation's mission is to become a major diversified food company and a leading company in every aspect of our business as:

The number-one confectionery company in North America, moving toward worldwide confectionery market share leadership.

A respected and valued supplier of high quality, branded consumer food products in North America and selected international markets.

Hershey's desire to participate in international growth was strongly motivated by the likelihood that any further high-growth opportunities in its own domestic market were severely limited following its purchase of Cadbury.

The purchase in 1988, for $4.5 billion, of the British Rowntree by the Swiss Nestlé made Nestlé the second largest confectionery maker in the world, trailing Mars, Inc. This was followed by the purchase of Perugina (Italy) in 1988 and of the remaining

TABLE 4   WORLD PER CAPITA CONSUMPTION OF CONFECTIONERY

	Kilograms per person per year
Switzerland	13.2
United Kingdom	12.7
Germany	12.6
Belgium	10.6
Netherlands	10.4
United States	8.5
Australia	8.1
Canada	5.7

Source: Adapted from *Retail World,* March 12, 1986, p. 31. Reprinted with permission, *Retail World,* Sydney, Australia.

50 percent of Allen Life Savers (Australia) in 1989. It was important that Hershey participate in this international activity.

In 1988, the value and volume of United States confectionery exports grew significantly, aided by the weakened United States dollar, tariff cuts (Japan, Taiwan, Korea), liberalized import policies of some Far Eastern countries, and aggressive promotion by the confectionery industry assisted by funding from the Department of Agriculture's Targeted Export Assistance (TEA) program. Japan, Canada, Taiwan, Hong Kong, and the Philippines accounted for 71 percent of export sales for the first six months of 1988. The European Community represented only 4 percent of total United States confectionery exports in spite of that area's representing the world's largest confectionery-consuming population, as illustrated in Table 4.

Hershey participated in this growth, experiencing record export sales in 1988. Major markets existed in Japan, South Korea, and other Far East locations.

Hershey had used a range of strategies to penetrate the international area. It had always relied heavily on direct exports to smaller markets but had also participated in acquisitions, joint ventures, licensing agreements, and strategic alliances of various sorts.

A licensing agreement operated in South Korea for chocolate products. Joint-venture operations existed in Mexico and the Philippines.

In December 1986, a full-ownership arrangement in Brazil was converted to a joint venture with the Bunge Born Group. Hershey retained 45 percent ownership of the jointly held pasta-making operations. This gave Hershey access to a finished-goods distribution network and also to flour and fat raw materials for pasta-making operations of the two venture partners.

In 1987, a leading Swedish sugar and chocolate confectioner, AB Marabou, was licensed to manufacture and market Hershey's Kisses chocolates with a distinctive European blend of chocolate. In 1988, this company purchased companies in Sweden and Denmark to strengthen access to the European market. In 1989, Hershey took out an equity interest in this company.

In July 1989, a licensing agreement was converted to a joint-venture arrangement with Fujiya Company, Limited, to form Hershey Japan Company. Under the licensing arrangements, Hershey chocolate had been positioned as an exclusive imported product and sold through department stores and imported-goods shops. The joint venture was established to broaden the market base by appealing to a larger consumer segment. Establishment of the joint venture was prompted by the results of a market search undertaken at the end of 1988 to determine the most suitable products for the Japanese market.

THE AUSTRALIAN CHOCOLATE MARKET

In 1987, Hershey began exporting to Australia. Generations of Australians had been raised on Cadbury's chocolate with "a glass and a half of fresh dairy milk in every block." To Australians, Cadbury was chocolate, and only those relatively few attuned to American culture could associate chocolate with Hershey.

In 1987, the A$1.1 billion Australian confectionery market for a population of under 17 million was dominated, as it had always been, by Cadbury Schweppes, which held a market share of 46 percent. Nestlé held a 36 percent share, with Mars at a low 10 percent. Such combined muscle provided a tight grip on distribution channels in Australia. New arrivals found it costly to access supermarket shelf space where the key success factor was to maximize the amount of space available to a company's products. This was especially important in such a high-impulse-buying segment as confectionery. The dominance of these companies was reflected in the lucrative A$400 million chocolate bars segment of the market, as depicted in Table 5. In 1987, Mars' Mars Bar was the undisputed leader, followed by Kit Kat, manufactured by Nestlé since that company's purchase of Rowntree, as shown in Table 6. Ironically, Kit Kat, a product that had dominated sales since the late 1950s in Australia and had held its market position consistently with continued sales growth, was owned by Hershey in the United States.

Restructuring of the world confectionery market, with its resultant significant concentration of ownership in Australia, had created strong competitive pressures in the Australian market.

Mars Confectionery, the wholly owned subsidiary of Mars, Inc., established a manufacturing plant in Victoria, Australia, in 1979. Mars had been active in Australia

TABLE 5 THE AUSTRALIAN CONFECTIONERY MARKET
(Million A$)

	1986	1987	1988
Chocolate bars	293	336	378
Block chocolate	179	199	229
Total chocolate	720	821	914
Total sugar	297	317	358
Total confectionery	1017	1138	1272

Source: Adapted from *Retail World,* March 1, 1989, p. 10.
Reprinted with permission, *Retail World,* Sydney, Australia.

TABLE 6   TOP TEN CHOCOLATE BARS IN AUSTRALIA, 1988

Rank	Product	Manufacturer	Market share (percent)
1	Mars Bar	Mars	12.7
2	Cherry Ripe	Cadbury	8.1
3	Kit Kat	Nestlé	7.8
4	Crunchie	Cadbury	7.2
5	Flake	Cadbury	6.9
6	Aero	Nestlé	6.7
7	Picnic	Cadbury	5.3
8	Snickers	Mars	5.2
9	Violet Crumble	Nestlé	4.9
10	Milky Way	Mars	4.8

Total annual Australian chocolate bar market is A$378 million, which represents 26 percent of the total confectionery market.

Source: Adapted from N. Shoebridge, "Mars Wants Us to Eat More Bars a Day," *Business Review Weekly,* May 26, 1989, pp. 111–113. Reprinted with permission from BRW—Australia's leading business magazine.

since the 1960s. At that time, the products were made and sold by MacRobertsons, a long-established Australian confectioner. In 1967, Cadbury beat Mars to a takeover of MacRobertsons. Cadbury continued to manufacture Mars products under license until Mars established its own facilities. Mars concentrated on six brands of chocolate-enrobed bars, allowing it to minimize production costs through high-volume outputs.

Jacobs Suchard's move into Australia had been part of the company's global strategy to minimize reliance on its European markets. It had been beaten by Nestlé in its attempt to purchase the Rowntree group. In 1988, Jacobs Suchard set up an Australian subsidiary to handle its range of block-chocolate products led by the well-accepted Toblerone line. The Toblerone range had been previously manufactured under license by Red Tulip, a chocolate confectioner owned by Beatrice Confectionery. Red Tulip was sold to Cadbury in 1987. The license agreement was cut short with the entry into Australia of the Jacobs Suchard subsidiary. The Toblerone range was subsequently imported from European manufacturing locations.

Jacobs Suchard's strategy for development of the Australian market was to provide a limited range of high-margin products supported by high advertising expenditures. It also offered to the retail trade an alternative confectionery supplier to the two giants of the Australian trade—Cadbury and Nestlé. A factory to supply the Asian-Pacific region was being planned for the 1990s.

HERSHEY COMES . . . AND GOES

In 1985, Hershey signed an agreement with an Australian marketing company, American Foods Proprietary Limited, for distribution in 1986 of a limited range of Hershey chocolate products, including Hershey Bar, Mr. Goodbar, Krackel, Reese's Peanut Butter Cups, and Reese's Pieces. American Hershey chocolate bars were to be introduced to the Australian market without a change in formulation. American Foods was planning to import the products from the United States with the result that retail prices were expected to be 30 to 40 percent higher than the competing products. Because of the premium pricing, the target market was to be the adult population segment.

Test marketing of Hershey products was limited to a trial through Grace Brothers, a department store chain in Sydney, the largest city in Australia with a population of around 3.8 million. Although sales were not as successful as anticipated, the products were considered to be well-accepted. A separate study was carried out to determine the awareness of the Hershey brand in Australia. A surprisingly high 37 percent of respondents was found to recognize the Hershey name and associate it with chocolate.

Following financial problems at American Foods, an arrangement that included a purchase of equity in American Foods by Hershey was finalized and the launch of the Hershey range was delayed until late 1987. The product was distributed to the grocery chains in August. A large television advertising campaign was launched in September and October with the advertising message, ''You can't hide a Hershey smile.''

Distribution was to be through Streets Ice Cream, a company owned by the Dutch multinational Unilever, which allowed access to refrigerated logistics facilities, including warehouses and delivery vehicles. Initial retail trade acceptance had been good.

At that time, the main competitors in the Australian confectionary market were Rowntree Hoadley (with a market share of 12 percent), Cadbury Schweppes (25.9 percent), Mars Confectionery (7.6 percent), Allen's Life Savers (10 percent), and Beatrice (2.5 percent), all with long experience in the Australian confectionery market.

An advertising budget of at least A$3 million was expected to be necessary in the first year so that product awareness could be gained in the face of such strong competition. This compared with an estimated annual advertising budget of A$5 million for Mars and A$6 million for Cadbury.

By early 1988, it became obvious to many in the retail trade that Hershey's sales expectations were not being met. Difficulties were being experienced in achieving distribution to Brisbane and Perth (two of the states' capitals) and to some key supermarket chains in the states of New South Wales and Victoria—the two most densely populated states.

Retail chains suggested that the two main problems were the high retail prices and insufficient promotion by Hershey. Two large supermarket chains were considering dropping the Hershey line. The New South Wales supermarket chain of Coles Myer, the nation's largest retail organization, decided to distribute only five of the sixteen product lines. The prices of Hershey products had an immediate demotivating effect at the supermarket shelves where the impulse-buying decisions were made. Hershey cut its prices to bring them to within $.03 or $.04 of the main Cadbury and Nestlé lines and reduced the number of lines from sixteen to ten.

In February 1989, Hershey went home. However, it seemed that Australia was too lucrative a market to abandon. What had gone wrong? If the Australian market was valuable, what was the best way to successfully reenter it? Roger Clarke had to find the answers for the forthcoming board meeting.

QUESTIONS

1 Do you believe Hershey should reenter the Australian market?

2 What major mistakes did Hershey commit in its initial efforts in the Australian market?

3 What channel alternatives might Hershey consider if it chooses to reenter the Australian market?

4 What recommendations would you make to the board if you were Mr. Clarke?

REFERENCES

Annual Reports for 1987, 1988, 1989, Hershey Foods Corporation.

Flanagan, Barry "Hershey Prices Cut across the Board," *Retail World,* March 9, 1988.

Shoebridge, Neil, "A Middle-Aged Name with Sweet Appeal," *Business Review Weekly,* April 24, 1987, pp. 98–101.

Shoebridge, Neil, "America's Hershey Aims at Australian Sweet-Tooths," *Business Review Weekly,* May 29, 1987, pp. 77, 81 and 84.

Shoebridge, Neil, "Sweet Dream Fails in Australia," *Business Review Weekly,* January 15, 1988, pp. 54.

Weber, Joseph, "Why Hershey Is Smacking Its Lips," *Business Week,* October 30, 1989, pp. 140.

INDEX

A&P (Great Atlantic and Pacific Tea Company), 18
Absorption, functional, 18, 301–302
Acceptable service window (acceptable time), 210–211
Acceptance, 13–14
Accumulation, 91–92
Ace Brokerage Company (case study), 378–382
Adjustment, 19
Advertising, 76, 182–186
consumer promotions, 184–185
cooperative, 183–184
effect on marketing channels, 182–184
sales promotion, 184–185
trade, 182–183
trade promotion, 185–186
Advertising agencies, 76
Advisory and research firms, 76–77
Agents:
change, 405–406
merchandise, 42–43
specialized, 78
wholesale, 413–414

Airline transportation, 423–424
Alderson, Wroe, 398
Alignment of channels, 8
Alliances, 105–106
Allocation, 91–92
Allowances, legality of, 163
"Always-a-Share," 172
AMOCO (Standard Oil Company of America), 81
American National Standards Institute (ANSI.X12) conventions for EDI, 390–391
American President Companies (APC), 62, 71
Amway Corp., 406
Analysis and evaluation of alternative structures, 224–245
analytic tools for, 230–239
channel modification in, 242–244
evaluation of channel partners in, 239–242
key-factor scoring in, 230–233
make-or-buy analysis and, 226
manufacturer's evaluation of intermediaries and, 239–240

Analysis and evaluation of alternative structures (Cont.):
mathematical and simulation techniques in, 237–238
multiple channels, use of, 244
profitability analysis in, 233–237
supplier evaluation by intermediaries, 240–242
transaction cost analysis (TCA), 225–230
ANSI conventions for EDI, 390–391
APC, 62, 71
Apple Computer, 289
Appliance dealers, 436–437
ARCO (Atlantic Richfield Oil Company), 81
Arrangers, 77–78
diverters, 78
liquidators, 78
specialized agents and brokers, 78
Assembly, 69–70
Assortment, 91
Attitudinal bargaining, 291

Auto industry, distribution innovation in, 433–436

Bargaining, 290–291
(*See also* Negotiation, interorganizational)
Baskin-Robbins (case study), 265–271
Behavioral channel system, 104
Belknap Hardware and Manufacturing Company (case study), 118, 121–124
Benneton, 101
Bergen Brunswig, 175, 320
Bergen Drug Company (case study), 118–121
BIC Co., 178
BLS, 101
Bonus packs and tie-ins, 185
Boundary spanning, logistics support of, 201–203
Bounded rationality, 227
Brands
loyalty to, 175–176
private distributor, 181
proprietary, 45
Brand strategies:
brand-central strategy, 11
impact on marketing channel design of, 180–181
Bright cans, 101
Bucklin, Louis, store classification of, 172–173
Buffa and Miller classification of product inventory systems, 30–32
Business-to-business sales, 87
Business volume concentration, 12
Buyer behavior (*see* Consumer behavior)
Buying, as marketing function, 15

Cali, Colombia, central marketplace (case study), 460–467
Case studies:
Ace Brokerage Company, 378–382

Case studies (*Cont.*):
Baskin-Robbins, 265–271
Belknap Hardware and Manufacturing Company, 118, 121–124
Bergen Drug Company, 118–121
Cali, Colombia, central marketplace, 460–467
CSX Transportation, 129–135
Davis Manufacturing Company, 127–129
Gillette Sensor, 110–118, 179
Happy Grove Dairy, 271–275
Hershey International, 467–475
IKEA North America, 439–448
Oakville Mall, 370–374
1-800-Pirates, 448–452
Perrier brand bottled water recall, 452–459
Procter & Gamble and Wal-Mart, 364–370
Rundel's Department Store, 124–129
Sears, Roebuck and Company, 252–264
Simplesse, 135–140
South Bottling Company, 374–378
Sparrow Transport, 382–385
W-G-P Chemical Company, 247–251
Williams Institutional Food Company, 276–281
Cash-and-carry wholesalers, 42
Cash discounts, 189
Celler-Kefauver Act (1950), 158–159, 161, 164
Census, U.S. Bureau of the, store classification system and, 46–47
Central market system, 87–89
Change agents, 405–406
Channel change, 397–404
economics of differentiation, 397–398
limitations of models, 402–404, 407
management of, 404–407
models of process, 398–402

Channel classification, 102–107
conventional, 103–104
free-flow, 103
single-transaction, 102–103
vertical marketing systems and, 104–107
Channel decisions, model of, 238
Channel dynamics, 389–408
change, 397–407
management of, 404–407
information technology and, 390–397
Channel leadership, 104, 306–308
definition of, 17
example of, 308
logistic service providers and, 61–62
specialized service providers' increase in, 60–62
tolerance to follow, 306–307
Channel management process, 305–337
conflict and, 323–336
definition of, 17
leadership and, 306–308
overview of, 25
synthesis of, 429–432
vertical marketing system and, 308–323
(*See also specific topics*)
Channel modification, 242–244
Channel performance, 26, 340–342
Channel planning, 23–25
Channel specialists, 16
Channel strategy, 431–432
implementation of, 25–26
(*See also specific channels*)
Channel structure, 85–108
complex distribution arrangements in, 96–102
distribution channels, 87–90
distribution processes and, 90–96
structural classification, 102–107
Channels:
alignment of, 8
business volume concentration and, 12
defined, 4–6
conventional, 103–104, 226

Channels (*Cont.*):
design of, 24
features of, 429–432
complexity, 430
dependence, 431
disproportionate risk, 431–432
routine searching, 430–431
specialization, 430
involvement with specific trading partners, 11–13
members of, 4, 239–242
primary and specialized members, 4
reasons for seeking channel arrangements, 14–22
functional performance, 15–18
reduced complexity, 18–20
specialization, 20–22
separation of, 96–99
(*See also specific channels*)
C. H. Robinson, 61
Clayton Antitrust Act (1914), 156–157, 160, 162, 164
Codes of conduct, 13
Coercive power, 295
Colgate Doctrine, 164
Collusion and price maintenance, 164
Colombia, Cali central marketplace (case study), 460–467
Combination stores, 50
Communication:
breakdown of, 328–329
improvement of, 334
industrial standards for uniform, 391
mix, 300
in retailing, 48
(*See also* Information technology)
Competition (competitive process):
competitive analysis and, 150–152
crisis change model of reaction to, 401–402
for differential advantage, 397–398
identification and assessment of competitors in, 152

Competition (*Cont.*):
industry structure and, 150–152
speed as an aspect of, 393–397
Complexity of channel systems, 430
Computerland, 289
Conflict, 14
causes of, 325–330
communication breakdown, 328–329
differing perceptions of reality, 329–330
goal incompatibility, 326–327
ideological differences between channel members, 330
position, role, and domain incongruency of channel members, 327–328
definition of, 325
horizontal, 324
intertype, 324
mutual dependence in, 326
relation to power and, 332–333
resolution of, 332–336
coalition formation in, 335
developing superordinate goals in, 333–334
improving communication processes in, 334
interorganizational negotiation for, 289
lobbying and judicial appeal in, 336
mediation and arbitration in, 335–336
negotiation in, 335
persuasion in, 334–335
withdrawal from the relationship and, 336
results of, 330–332
types of, 324
vertical, 324
Consultants, 76–77
Consumer behavior:
industrial buyers and, 172–176
model of, 172–173
Consumer cooperatives, 81
Consumer promotion, 184–185

Consumers:
as channel participants, 80–82
(*See also entries beginning with* Customer)
Consumption of a service, separability of production and, 420–421
Continental Freezers, 71
Continuous manufacturing, 30–31
Conventional channels, 103–104, 226
Cooperation, 14
Cooperative advertising, 183–184
Coors Brewery Co., 228
Core-fringe model of channel change, 398–399
Corning Glass joint ventures, 312
Corporate strategy, enterprise positioning and, 145–148
mission statement and, 147–148
objectives of, 148
strategic alternatives and, 146–150
Corstjens and Doyle, mathematical model of channel decisions of, 238
Cost-leadership strategy, 145
Cost-service sensitivity analysis, 218–222
Costs:
activity-based (ABCs), 213, 348
fixed, 346
haul length and, 214–215
indirect (joint), 346
integrated, 216–218
of inventory, 215–217
of logistics support in the United States, 195–198
organization of data on, 344–349
shipment size and, 214–215
total-cost analysis, 212–218, 221–222
transaction-cost analysis, 225–230
transport, tapering principle of, 215
transportation and, 214–217
variable, 346

Costs (*Cont.*):
  (*See also* Financial performance, assessing)
Cost-to-cost trade-offs, 218
Cotton Incorporated, 330
Countertrade, in international distribution, 419–420
Coupons, 73, 184–185
Creative Artists Agency, Inc., 78
Crisis model of channel change, 401–402
CSX Transportation (case study), 129–135
Cultural issues, international distribution channels and, 419
Curtis Mathes, 146
Customer analysis:
  consumer behavior model and, 172
  of customers' buying behavior in different segments, 172–175
  determinants of industrial buyers' behavior and, 174
  industrial buyer's behavior model and, 172–176
  marketing channel design and, 170–175
  of market segment, 148–150
Customer pickup allowance, 190
Customer return on investment (CRI), 355
Customer satisfaction, 355–361
  capability and, 357
  information support and, 357
  life-cycle support and, 357
  model framework for assessing, 359, 361
  product availability and, 357
  rating criteria of, 359–360
  service quality and, 356–359
Customer service (*see* Logistics channel)
Customer service measurements, 204–209
  flexibility, 208
  inventory availability, 204
  order-cycle consistency, 206–207
  order-fill rate, 205
  orders shipped complete, 205

Customer service measurements (*Cont.*):
  service capability, 205–208
  service quality, 208
  speed of service, 205–206
  zero-defects concept, 209–210

Dauphin Distribution Services, 71
Davis Manufacturing Company (case study), 127–129
Dayton-Hudson, 286–287
DEC top mapping technology, 319
Delivery of a service, 421–423
Dependence, as feature of channel systems, 431
Design:
  of channels, 24
  of products, 36–37
  (*See also specific channels*)
Detailers, 73
Differentiation:
  economics of, 397–398
  strategy for, 145–146
Diffused institutionalization, 404
Digital Equipment Corp. (DEC) top mapping technology, 319
Dillard department stores, 52
Direct distribution, 87–88
Direct product profit (DPP), 233–237, 354
Direct product profit return on inventory (DPPROI), 354
Direct-response channels, 244
Direct sales, in exporting, 414
Direct store delivery (DSD), 200–201
Discounts, 188–189
  everyday low price approach, 51
  legality of, 163
Distribution channels, 4
  for airline transportation, 423–424
  central market system, 87–89
  complex arrangements and, 96–102
  control and, 166

Distribution channels (*Cont.*):
  costs of various systems and, 93–95
  direct, 87–88
  DPP use in, 236–237
  dual, 11
  emergence of, 87–90
  exclusive, 166
  flexibility and, 166–167
  future of arrangements, 428–438
  innovation in, 432–438
    by appliance dealers, 436–437
    by auto industry, 433–435
    home delivery by supermarkets, 435–436
    invention versus, 433
    MRO outsourcing and, 437–438
    productivity gap and, 433
    purchasing corporations, 437–438
  intensive distribution and, 165
  invention versus innovation in, 433
  legal issues affecting, 161–165
  multistage distribution and, 89–90, 93–95
  objectives of, 165–167
  postponement and, 99–102
  selective, 165
  service outputs and, 95
  structural separation and, 96–99
  theory of, 90–96
    sorting, 90–92
    spatial closure, 92–95
    temporal closure, 95–96
  (*See also* Marketing)
Distribution mix, 299
Distributors, industrial, 200
Diverters, function of, 78
DPP, 233–237, 354
DPPROI, 354
Drop shippers, 42
Drugstores, foreign, 419
Dry Storage Co., 299
DSD, 200–201
Dual distribution, 11

Economic environment, enterprise positioning and, 155–156
Eddie Bauer Company, 343
EDI (*see* Electronic data interchange)
Effectiveness, definition of, 340
Efficiency, definition of, 339
80–20 principle for segment analysis, 343
Electronic data interchange (EDI):
  conventions for transmission in, 390–391
  facilitators of, 391–392
  mandate for, 75
  multinational standards developed by United Nations, 391
  standards for uniform communications in industries, 391
  in VMS, 321–323
EMC, 413
Emerson, Richard, 292–293
Empowerment, increased, as result of information technology, 396
Enterprise positioning, 143–167
  competitive analysis in, 150–152
  corporate strategy in, 144–148
  customer analysis of market segment in, 148–150
  distribution channel objectives in, 165–167
  environmental analysis in, 153–165
  internal analysis in, 152–154
  legal environment's effect on, 156–165
  market coverage and distribution intensity and, 165
  overview of, 23–24
  sociocultural environment in, 154–155
  strategic alternatives in, 144–146
  technological environment's effect on, 255
Envelop curve, total costs and, 218
Environment:
  analysis of, in enterprise positioning, 153–165

Environment (*Cont.*):
  economic, 155–156
  sociocultural, 429–430
  technological, 255
  transaction-cost analysis and, 227–229
  (*See also* Legal issues)
European retailers in the United States, 442
  IKEA North America (case study), 439–448
Evaluation (*see* Analysis and evaluation of alternative structures)
Everytime expectation, definition of, 208
Exclusive distribution, 166
Exclusive territorial agreements, legality of, 161–162
Exel Logistics, 60
Expectancy/disconfirmation process of customer satisfaction, 356–357
Expert power, 296
Export, 410–415
  direct, 413–414
  documentation of, 414–415
  indirect, 411–413
Export commission house, 412
Export management company (EMC), 413
Export merchants, 412
Extended enterprise, 308–310

Facilitating, definition of, 15
Facilitators (*see* Specialized service providers)
Farmers' markets, 89
  Cali, Colombia, central marketplace (case study), 460–467
Federal agencies, regulation of business by, 159
Federal Air Express, 67
Federal Express, 71
  Business Logistics Services (BLS), 101
Federal Trade Commission Act (1914), 160, 167

Financial performance, assessing, 342–355
  definition of segment for investigation, 343–345
  return on assets (ROA), 350
  return on investment (ROI), 350
  return on net worth (RONW), 350
  revenue and cost analysis, 344–349
    contribution margin approach, 346–347
    net profit approach, 347–349
  strategic profit model and, 350–355
    asset turnover, 352
    customer analysis, 354–355
    leverage, 352–353
    net profit margin, 351–352
    product analysis, 353
Financial services, 74–75
Financing, as marketing function, 15
First World Cheese, 44
Flexible manufacturing, 37–38
FOB origin and delivered pricing, 190
Focus strategy, 146
Food industry, distribution innovation in, 432–433, 435–436
Ford, Henry, 18
Foreign countries, distribution channels in, 415–417
Foreign retailers
  access to, 419
  in the United States, 439–448
Form postponement, 100–101
Forward-buying of merchandise, 78–79
Free-flow channels, 103–104
Freight forwarders, international, 418
Fulfillment, 70–71
Full-function merchants, 40–42
Full-line forcing, 163
Functional absorption, 18, 301–302
Functional discounts, 189
Functional services providers, 62–74

Functional services providers
(*Cont.*):
  assembly and, 69–70
  fulfillment and, 70–71
  merchandising and, 72–73
  sequencing and, 71–72
  specialists, 62–63
  transportation and, 63–68
  warehousing and, 68–69
  (*See also specific topics*)
Functional spin-off, 301
Functions of exchange, 15

GE, 75, 146, 293–294, 413, 437
GE Information Services, 392
General Electric (GE), 75, 146,
  293–294, 413, 437
GM, 243–244, 428, 435
General Mills, 170
General Motors (GM), 243–244,
  428, 435
Gillette Sensor (case study), 110–
  118, 179
Global Logistics Venture, 61
GMROI, 353–354
Godiva Chocolates, 166
Government requirements, interna-
  tional distribution channels
  and, 419
Gross margin return on inventory
  (GMROI), 353–354
Group technology in manufactur-
  ing, 35

Halo (Hawthorne) effect, 318
Handling characteristics, 17
Hannaford Brother Supermarkets,
  242
Happy Grove Dairy (case study),
  271–275
"Hawthorne effect" (halo effect),
  318
Hershey International (case study),
  467–475
Heterogeneity in service production
  and delivery, 421
High-performance strategy, 211–
  212

Hollander, Stanley, 402–403
Home Depot, 50–51
Human factors, transaction-cost
  analysis and, 227
Human resources, in manufactur-
  ing, 35
Hypermarkets, 50

IFMA, 334
IKEA North America (case study),
  439–448
Industrial buyer's behavior model,
  172–176
  "Always-a-Share" category,
  172–176
  determinants of behavior, 174
  "Lost-for-Good" category, 174–
  176
  marketing implications of, 174–
  176
Industrial distributors, definition of,
  200
Industry structure, model of, 150–
  152
Information, market, 16
Information impactedness, 228–229
Information services, 75
Information technology, 390–397
  bar codes, 392
  channel arrangements and, 390–
  392
  form postponement and, 100–
  101
  organizational structure and,
  394–397
    empowerment, 396
    flattening of organizational
    pyramid, 395–396
    outsourcing, 396–397
  outsourcing and, 396–397
  radio-frequency technology, 392
  satellite tracking of transportation equipment, 392
  in vertical marketing systems,
  314
  (*See also* Electronic Data Interchange)

In-group bargaining, in negotiation,
  291
Innovation versus invention, 433
Institutionalization, in channel
  change, 404–405
Insurance:
  marketing, 78
  risk and, 76
  USAA's alternative contact
  methods and, 424
Intangibility of a service, 420
Integrated service providers, 63,
  79–80
Intensive distribution, 165
Interface translators, 392
Intermittent manufacturing, 31–32
Internal analysis, in enterprise positioning, 152–154
International distribution channels,
  409–420
  countertrade in, 419
  cultural issues and, 419
  customers' requirements and,
  419
  distribution channels in foreign
  countries, 415–417
  evaluation of channel alternatives, 418–419
  export, direct and indirect, 410–
  415
  government requirements and,
  419
  intermediaries and, 419
  international logistics, 417–418
International Foodservice Manufacturers Association (IFMA),
  334
International trading companies,
  412
Interorganizational negotiation (*See*
  Negotiation, interorganizational)
Invention, innovation versus, 433
Inventory:
  costs of, 215–217
  customer service and, 204, 216
  DPPROI, 354
  GMROI, 353–354
  inventory cost curve, 219

Inventory (*Cont.*):
joint, use of, 299
just-in-time inventory replenishment, 393
order-fill rate, 205
orders shipped complete, 205
production inventory systems, 30–32
profiles of, and channel position, 196–197
quick-response inventory replenishment, 393
stock-keeping units, 204–205
stock percentage, 204–205
Itel Distribution Systems, 59–60

Jackson, Barbara Bund, buyer's behavior model of, 172–176
J.C. Penney, 52
Jewel Company, 435–436
Jhirmack Enterprises, 244
J.I. Case Company, 162
JIT inventory replenishment, 393
JIT sequencing, 71–72
Johnson & Johnson, 78, 298
Hospital Supply Company, 11
Joint risk in vertical marketing systems, 312
Just-in-time (JIT) inventory replenishment, 393
Just-in-time (JIT) sequencing, 71–72

Kentucky Fried Chicken, 163
Key-factor scoring, 230–233
K mart stores, 289
Kraft-General Foods, 308
Kravis, Kohlberg and Roberts, 61, 74

Leadership, channel (*see* Channel leadership)
Legal issues:
distribution and, 161–165
enterprise positioning and, 156–165

Legal issues (*Cont.*):
judicial law in, 159, 161
legal-social setting and, 429–430
legislation affecting channels, 156–161
L'eggs, 146
Legitimate power, 295–296
Less-than-truckload (LTL) carriers, 67
Lever Brothers, 164
Levi Strauss & Company, 330, 419
Levi-Link, 393–394
Life-cycle models of channel change, 400–401
Liquidators, definition of, 78
List price, 187–188
L.L. Bean, 51–52
Lloyds of London, 76
Logistics channel (logistics support), 15, 194–222
anticipatory nature of, 199
boundary spanning quality of, 201–203
customer service measurements and goals and, 204–209, 212–221
definition of, 24–25
described, 97–98
design of, channel separation and, 194–196
expenditures, in United States, 195–198
external boundary spanning of, 203
financial pressure on, 202
geographic dispersion, affect on, 216
internal boundary spanning of, 202–203
international, 417–418
inventory, effect on, 216
logistics management process in, 195–203
negotiation of, 299
outbound movement of products in, 200
performance, 199, 212–221
cost-service sensitivity analysis, 218–221

Logistics channel (*Cont.*):
total cost analysis, 212–218
postponement in, 303
reverse movement of products in, 201
selective resource allocation in, 219–221
service channel and, 421, 425–426
value-adding process in, 198–201
(*See also specific topics*)
Logistic service providers, 61–62
"Lost-for-Good" buyer behavior, 174–176
Lovelock, Christopher, 421
Loyalty, brand, 175–176
LTL carriers, 67

McDonald's, 9–10, 288
McGuire Act, 164
MacNair, Malcolm P., 400
Mail-order wholesalers, 42
Maintenance, repair, and operating (MRO) outsourcing, 437–438
Make-or-buy analysis, 226
Management process, channel (*see* Channel management process)
Manufacturers, defined, 4
Manufacturers' coupons, 73
Manufacture to forecast, 32–33
Manufacturing, 29–40
allied (piggybacking), 412–413
continuous, 30–31
continuous improvement in, 36
definition of, 29
flexible, 37–38
focused, 38–39
group technology in, 35
human resources in, 35
intermittent, 31–32
management issues in, 33–37
manufacturer's evaluation of intermediaries, 239–240
philosophy of, 39–40
processes, 35–36

Manufacturing (*Cont.*):
  sales branch and sales office, 43–44
  SPC in, 35
  structure of, 30–33
  traditional versus modern, 39–40
  zero-defects concept in, 36, 209–210
Manufacturing design, 36–37
Market definition, 148–150
Market information, 16
Marketing:
  channel design, 169–192
    customer analysis and, 170–175
    market segmentation in, 170–172
    product impact on, 176–181
    price impact on, 187–191
    promotion impact on, 181–187
  channel separation in, 97–98
  functions, 15–18
  insurance, 78
  market segmentation and, 150, 170–172
  mix, negotiating, 298–301
  (*See also* Distribution channels)
Market-paced manufacturing, 37–38
Mary Kay cosmetics, 406
Massed reserves, principle of, 96
Mature channel negotiation, 288–289, 291
Merchandise agents, 42–43
Merchandising, 72–73
  mass, 51
  private label, 299
  scrambled, 10–11
Merchant wholesalers, 40–42, 200
Merchants:
  export, 412
  foreign, 413–414
Mergers, legality of, 164
Miller-Tydings, 164
Minimum total transactions, principle of, 95
Missionary selling, 187

Mission statement, 147–148
Monostasy, 311
Motor-Carrier Regulatory Reform and Modernization Act of 1980, 66
MRO outsourcing, 437–438
Multiple-channel arrangements, 10–11, 244
Multistage distribution, 89–90, 93–95
Mutual dependence, channel negotiation and, 292–294

Nabisco Foods, 314
Negotiation, interorganizational, 25, 285–304
  accommodation in, 289
  channel, process of, 298–303
    operational negotiation, 301–303
    transaction negotiation, 298–301
  channel leadership in, 287
  of communication mix, 300
  for conflict resolution, 289
  definition of, 285–286
  distribution mix and, 299
  of functional performance agreements, 301–302
  of joint inventory use, 299
  of logistics, 299
  in marketing, 286–290
  mature channel, 288–289
  new channel, 287–288, 291
  operational, 301–303
  of performance, 302
  of postponement, 302–303
  power in, 292–298
    power-dependence relationships, 292–294
    sources of power, 294–297
  prerequisites for, 291–292
  of price mix, 301
  as problem-solving, 287
  of product mix, 298
  for repositioning of an ongoing business arrangement, 288–289

Negotiation (*Cont.*):
  scope of, 290–291
  strategy in, 290–292
  termination of an agreement as, 289–290
  transaction, and marketing mix, 298–301
Niche marketing, wholesalers' use of, 45
Nike, Inc., 418
Nintendo, 164
Nordstrom's, 51
NutraSweet Company (case study), 135–140

Oakville Mall (case study), 370–374
1-800-PIRATES (case study), 448–452
Operational negotiation, 301–303
Opportunistic behavior, 227
Order-cycle consistency and dynamics, 206–207
Organizational structure, impact of information technology on, 394–397
  empowerment of, 396
  flattening of organizational pyramid in, 395–396
  outsourcing of, 396
Outside expert, role of, 77
Outsourcing, 21
  effect on channel relations, 396
  MRO, 437–438
Ownership of goods
  transfer of, 16
  service channel and, 425

Pepsi, Soviet Union countertrade of Stolichnaya and, 419–420
Performance measurement, 339–362
  of channel, 26, 340–342
  of customer satisfaction, 355–361

Performance measurement (*Cont.*):
  financial, 342–355
    revenue and cost analysis,
      344–349
    segment definition, 342–344
    strategic profit model, 350–
      355
  functional, 15–18, 301–302
  logistics of, 212–221
    total-cost analysis, 212–218
    cost-service sensitivity analy-
      sis, 218–221
  negotiation of, 302
  (*See also specific topics*)
Perishability:
  marketing channel design and,
    17
  of a service, 421
Perrier brand bottled water recall
  (case study), 452–459
Personal bargaining, in negotiation,
  291
Personal selling, 186–187
Physical distribution, 15
Piggybacking, 413
Pillsbury, 170
Plan finalization, overview of, 25
Porter, Michael:
  five-factor model of industry
    structure developed by,
    150–152
  strategies for industry position
    developed by, 145–146
Postponement, 99–102, 302–303
  form, 100–101
  time, 101–102
Power, 292–298
  channel leadership and, 307
  characteristics of, 297–298
  coercive, 295
  conflict and, 332–333
  conflict-resolution and, 332–333
  definition of, 292
  expert, 296
  legitimate, 295–296
  limited scope and domain of,
    293–294
  negotiation and, 292–298

Power (*Cont.*):
  power-dependence relation-
    ships, 292–294
  sources of power, 294–297
  perception of, and effectiveness,
    293
  referent, 296–297
  reward, 294–295
  types of, 294–297
Price:
  changes in, channel design and,
    191
  customer pickup allowance's
    effect on, 190
  discounts, 51, 163, 188–189
  FOB origin and delivered pric-
    ing, 190
  list, 187–188
  marketing channel design and,
    187–191
  mix, 301
  permanent increases in, 191
  in retailing, 47–48
  short-term price changes' effect,
    191
  transportation charge's impact
    on, 190
  zone pricing, 190
  (*See also specific topics*)
Price Club, 81, 170
Primary channel participants, 4
  (*See also* Manufacturing; Retail-
    ing; Wholesaling)
Private-distributor brands, 181
Problem solving, in negotiation,
  291
Procter & Gamble, 70, 164, 182,
  183, 220
  and Wal-Mart (case study), 364–
    370
Product design, 36–37
Product:
  analysis of, 353
  life cycle of:
    channel modification during,
      243
    marketing design and, 179–
      180

Product (*Cont.*):
  models and stages of, 400–
    401
  marketing channel design and,
    176–181
    brand strategies' effect on,
      180–181
    life cycle and, 179–180
    new-product development,
      178–179
    product attributes, 177–178
    standardization and, 178
  mix, 298–299
  proliferation, 33–34
Production:
  of a service, 420–421
  inventory systems, 30–32
Productivity gap, U.S., 433
Profitability analysis, 233–237
Promotion, marketing channel
    design and, 181–187
  advertising, 182–184
  personal selling, 186–187
  push versus pull strategy, 182
  sales promotions, 184–186
  (*See also specific topics*)
Proprietary brands, wholesale use
  of, 45
Public warehousing, 58–59, 68–69
Punishments, channel relations and,
  295
Purchasing corporations, distribution innovation and, 437–
  438
Push versus pull strategy of manufacturers, 182

QR inventory replenishment, 393–
  394
Quality, total, 34–37
Quantity discounts, 189
Quick Response Service, Inc., 392
Quick-response (QR) inventory
  replenishment, 393–394

Rack merchandisers, 42
Rail transport, 65–68

Ralston-Purina, 185
Recovery, brilliant, as resolution to
    a service breakdown, 209
Recycling, in logistics support
    channel, 201
Referent power, 296
Resident buyers, in foreign coun-
    tries, 412
Resource allocation, selective, 219–
    221
Retailing, 46–52
    communication in, 48
    customer-service emphasis in,
        51–52
    direct, 52
    discounting as a strategy in, 51
    foreign:
        access to, 419
        in the United States, 439–448
    functioning of, 5–6
    high-end strategy in, 49
    location's effect on, 48–49
    logistics in, 48
    low-end strategy in, 49
    management issues in, 46–49
    mass merchandising in, 51
    merchandise variety in, 47
    price decisions in, 47–48
    retail mix, components of, 46–49
    service choices in, 48
    special packs and, 72–73
    store atmosphere in, 48
    strategies in, 49–52
    structure of, 46
    superspeciality strategy in, 50–
        51
    supplier relationships in, 52
    wheel of, model in, 400
    (See also specific topics)
Return on assets (ROA), 352–353
Revenue leverage in vertical mar-
    keting systems, 312–313
Reward power, 294–295
Risk taking:
    disproportionate, as feature of
        channel systems, 431–432
    insurance and, 76
    as marketing function, 16
RJR-Nabisco, 202

ROA, 350, 352–353
Robinson-Patman Act (1936), 157–
    158, 160, 163
ROI, 350
RONW, 350
Routinization:
    in channel design, 19
    of searching, as feature of chan-
        nel systems, 430–431
Rundel's Department Store (case
    study), 124–129

Sales, retail (see Retailing)
Sales branches, foreign, 413
Sales promotion (see Promotion)
Sam's Club, 9, 81, 170
Schneider National, 13
Schumpeter, Joseph, 398
Schwinn decision, 161
Scrambled merchandising, 10–11
Searching:
    definition of, 92
    routinization of, 430–431
Sears, Roebuck and Company,
    147–148, 350, 401
    case study, 252–264
Seasonal discounts, 189
Selective distribution, 165
Self-resolution, 13
Selling, as marketing function, 15
Sequencing, 71–72
Service breakdown, brilliant recov-
    ery as resolution to, 209
Service distribution channels, 420–
    426
    alternative contact methods and,
        424
    characteristics of services in,
        420–421
    classification of, 340–341, 421–
        423
    goods ownership in, 425
    logistics functions in, 421, 425–
        426
    physical manifestation of ser-
        vices and, 423
Service outputs, 95

Share bargaining, in negotiation,
    290
Sherman Antitrust Act (1890), 156,
    160, 161, 164
Sherwin Williams, 225
Shewmaker, Jack, 396
SIC, 30–31
Simplesse (case study), 135–140
Single-transaction channels, 102–
    103
SKUs, 204–205
Skyway Freight Systems, Inc., 314
Small-numbers conditions, costs
    and, 228
Snap-on Tools, 146
Sociocultural environment, in
    enterprise positioning, 154–
    155
Sock Shop, 50–51
Sony, 146
Sorting, 19, 90–92
South Bottling Company (case
    study), 374–378
Southern Bonded Warehousing, 69
Soviet Union:
    Pepsi countertrade of Stolich-
        naya and, 419–420
    wheat deal with (1976), 288
Span of control, information tech-
    nology and, 395–396
Sparrow Transport (case study),
    382–385
Spatial closure of distribution sys-
    tems, 92–95
SPC, 35
Specialization, 311–312
    of channel systems, 430
Specialized service providers, 4,
    55–83
    changing nature of, 56–62
    channel leadership of, 60–62
    classification of, 62–64
    concentration and alliances of,
        59–60
    economic justification for using,
        57–58
    information technology's effect
        on, 58

Specialized service providers (*Cont.*):
 leveraged buyouts' effects on, 61
 risk involvement of, 58–59
 (*See also* Functional services providers; Support services providers)
Special pack, 72
Specific point-in-time service commitment, 211
Speed, as aspect of competitive process, 393–397
 JIT inventory replenishment and, 393
 QR inventory replenishment and, 393–394
Spin-off, functional, 301
Staggers Rail Act, 66
Standard Fashion Company, 162
Standard Industrial Classification (SIC), 30–31
Standardization, 90
 as marketing function, 15–16
 of product, marketing channel design and, 178
Statistical process control (SPC), 35
Stock-keeping units (SKUs), 204–205
Stock percentage, 204–205
Storage, 15
 warehousing, 58–59, 68–69
Store classification:
 by consumer behavior, 172–173
 U.S. Bureau of the Census system, 46–47
Structure, channel (*see* Channel structure)
Subsidiaries, foreign, 413
Supermarkets, 49
Superstore, 50
Super Value stores, 44
Superwarehouse, 50
Support services providers, 63, 74–79
 advertising and, 76
 advisory research and, 76–77
 arrangers of, 77–79
 financial, 74–75

Support services providers (*Cont.*):
 information on, 75
 insurance and, 76
 (*See also specific topics*)
Systasy, 311

Tapering principle of transport costs, 215
TCA (*see* Transaction cost analysis)
Teachers' Insurance and Annuity Association (TIAA), 76
Technical complexity, marketing channel design and, 177–178
Technological environment, enterprise positioning and, 255
Temporal closure, 95–96
Terminal grain elevators, 42
Termination, negotiation of, 289–290
TIAA, 76
Tie-ins, 185
Time postponement, 101–102
Total-cost analysis, 212–218, 221–222
Total quality, initiatives in, 34–37
Toyota, 435
Toys 'R' Us, 220
Trade advertising, 182–183
Trade promotion, 185–186
Trading companies, international, 412
Training programs, for personal selling, 186
Transaction-cost analysis (TCA), 225–230
 bounded rationality and, 227
 environmental factors and, 227–229
 human factors and, 227
 key variables in, 230
 opportunism and, 227
 vertical integration and, 227
Transaction negotiation, 298–301
Transaction-specific capabilities, 228

Transportation, 63–68
 as marketing function, 15
 costs of, 63–68, 214–217, 219
 deregulation and, 66–68
 distribution channel structure and, 190
 DSD, 200–201
 for-hire revenues in, 67
 multimodal transportation companies, 67–68
 pricing and, 190
 truck, 63–68
 (*See also* Logistics; *specific types of transportation*)
Truck distributors, 42
Truck transport, 63–68
 LTL carriers, 67
Turn and earn, 216
Tying arrangements, legality of, 162–163

Union Pacific, 77
United Nations, multinational EDI standards developed by, 391
United Parcel Service, 67
United States, productivity gap and, 433
Unit value, marketing channel design and, 177
Universal Product Code (UPC), 294–295
 Catalog, 392
UPC, 294–295
 Catalog, 392
USAA insurance company, 424

Value-added networks (VANs), 391–392
Value-added services, wholesalers' use of, 45
Value-adding process, in logistics support channel, 198–201
VANs, 391–392
Vertical integration:
 advantages of, 225–230
 definition of, 18
 disadvantages of, 225–230

Vertical integration (*Cont.*):
  transaction-cost analysis and, 227
Vertical marketing system (VMS), 104–107, 308–323
  administered, 106–107
  alliances, 105–106
  business rationale for, 309
  contractual, 105
  cooperation in, 310–311
  corporate, 104–105
  electronic linkage of, 321–323
  failure of, 316–321
    fuzzy goals and, 317–318
    human incompatibility and, 319
    inadequate operating framework and, 320
    inadequate performance measurement and, 320
    inadequate trust and, 318
    lip-service commitment and, 318–319
  human drives in, 311
  long-term relationships in, 309–310
  principles of, 311–313

Vertical marketing system (*Cont.*):
  successful, creation of, 313–317
    channelwide perspective and, 313
    freedom to exit and, 315
    ground rules and, 315
    information sharing and, 314
    role specification and, 315
    selective matching and, 313–314
  synergism in, 309
  top-mapping technology to aid, 319
  trading margins in, 320
Visibility, of participant in channels, 9–10
VMS (*see* Vertical marketing system)

Wagon (truck) distributors, 42
Wal-Mart, 49, 51, 314, 396
Warehouse stores, 50
Warehousing, 68–69
  public, 58–59, 68–69
  super-, 50

Weighted averaging, in key-factor scoring, 232
Weight Watchers, 299
W-G-P Chemical Company (case study), 247–251
Wheat deal, U.S.–U.S.S.R. (1976), 288
Wheel of retailing model, 400
Whirlpool, 437
Wholesale agents, foreign, 413–414
Wholesaling, 40–46
  emerging strategies in, 44–45
  management issues in, 44
  role of, 6
  structure, 40–43
Williams Institutional Food Company (case study), 276–281
Williamson, Oliver E., 226, 228
Woolworth's, 398
Work Wear Corporation, 165
W.T. Grant, 398

Zayre Corporation, 350
Zero-defects concept, 36, 209–210
Zone pricing, 190